THE BARBOUR COLLECTION
OF CONNECTICUT TOWN
VITAL RECORDS

THE BARBOUR COLLECTION OF CONNECTICUT TOWN VITAL RECORDS

GOSHEN 1739–1854

GRANBY 1786–1850

GREENWICH 1640–1848

Compiled by
Christina Bailey
and
Lorraine Cook White

General Editor
Lorraine Cook White

Copyright © 1999
Genealogical Publishing Co., Inc.
Baltimore, Maryland
All Rights Reserved
Library of Congress Catalogue Card Number 94-76197
International Standard Book Number 0-8063-1591-1
Made in the United States of America

INTRODUCTION

As early as 1640 the Connecticut Court of Election ordered all magistrates to keep a record of the marriages they performed. In 1644 the registration of births and marriages became the official responsibility of town clerks and registrars, with deaths added to their duties in 1650. From 1660 until the close of the Revolutionary War these vital records of birth, marriage, and death were generally well kept, but then for a period of about two generations until the mid-nineteenth century, the faithful recording of vital records declined in some towns.

General Lucius Barnes Barbour was the Connecticut Examiner of Public Records from 1911 to 1934 and in that capacity directed a project in which the vital records kept by the towns up to about 1850 were copied and abstracted. Barbour previously had directed the publication of the Bolton and Vernon vital records for the Connecticut Historical Society. For this new project he hired several individuals who were experienced in copying old records and familiar with the old script.

Barbour presented the completed transcriptions of town vital records to the Connecticut State Library where the information was typed onto printed forms. The form sheets were then cut, producing twelve small slips from each sheet. The slips for most towns were then alphabetized and the information was then typed a second time on large sheets of rag paper, which were subsequently bound into separate volumes for each town. The slips for all towns were then interfiled, forming a statewide alphabetized slip index for most surviving town vital records.

The dates of coverage vary from town to town, and of course the records of some towns are more complete than others. There are many cases in which an entry may appear two or three times, apparently because that entry was entered by one or more persons. Altogether the entire Barbour Collection--one of the great genealogical manuscript collections and one of the last to be published--covers 137 towns and comprises 14,333 typed pages.

TABLE OF CONTENTS

GOSHEN 1

GRANBY 73

GREENWICH 157

ABBREVIATIONS

ae.------------age
b. ------------born, both
bd.------------buried
B. G.---------Burying Ground
d. ------------died, day, or daughter
decd.---------deceased
f.--------------father
h.--------------hour
J. P.-----------Justice of Peace
m.-------------married or month
res.------------resident
s.---------------son
st.--------------stillborn
w. ------------wife
wid.-----------widow
wk.-----------week
y. ------------year
* ------ Please note in the town of Kent in the 3rd column where * is used, in the original manuscript it means page # and 1/2.

THE BARBOUR COLLECTION OF CONNECTICUT TOWN VITAL RECORDS

GOSHEN VITAL RECORDS
1739 - 1854

	Vol.	Page
ABBOT, Elizabeth, m. Lucas* **BEECH**, Jr., June 1, 1775 *("Linus" in Hibbard's Hist. of Goshen	1	240
ABERNETHY, ABERNETHA, Cyrus, s. Jared, b. June 11, 1767	1	236
Jared, m. Lois **THOMPSON**, May 26, 1766	1	233
ACKAMAN, James, m. Betty **ROWE**, b. of Goshen, Mar. 20, 1831, by Rev. Grant Power	M	33
ADAMS, ADDAMS, Lydia, of Goshen, m. Benjamin **BULLARD**, of New Marlborough, Mass., May 1, 1834, by Rev. Grant Powers	M	44
Sophia E., m. Carlton N. **NICHOLS**, Sept. 3, 1854, at the house of Asa G. **ADAMS**, by Lavalette Perrin	M	83
Susannah, d. Jona[than], b. Dec. 28, 1762	1	224
Susannah, m. Samuell **BALDWIN**, Jan. 11, 1769	1	233
ADKINS, ADKIN, Adna, s. Hezekiah, b. Feb. 27, 1772	1	239
Hezekiah, m. Rachel **BARNS**, Apr. 5, 1771, in Middletown	1	233
Rachel, d. Hezekiah, b. May 28, 1773	1	239
ALEXANDER, Samuel, m. Mary E. **BARTRUM**, b. of Goshen, Nov. 23, 1845, by Rev. David L. Marks	M	70
ALLEN, [see also **ALLYN**], Adaline L., of Goshen , m. Ezra H. **MINER**, of Cornwall, Apr. 25, 1838, by Rev. John Lucky	M	54
Althia, m. Morris **TUTTLE**, b. of Goshen, Feb. 3, 1831, by Rev. Grant Powers. Int. Pub.	M	32
Benjamin, his child, d. Jan. 10, 1817, ae 3	2	397
Mary L., of Goshen, m. William E. **DENISON**, of Stonington, [Mar.] 4, 1827, by Theren Towner, J. P.	M	19
ALLYN, [see also **ALLEN**], Anna, of Goshen, m. Horace J. **THOMSON**, of Humphreyville, Mar. 2, 1834, by Rev. Grant Powers	M	43
Austin, m. Hannah Elizabeth **IVES**, Nov. 16, 1847, at the house of Cephas **IVES**, by Rev. Lavalette Perrin	M	74
Emily, of Goshen, m. Henry D. **DENISON**, of Groton, Apr. 4, 1830, by Rev. Harmon Ellis	M	29
Fanny, of Goshen, m. John J. **ROOT**, of Farmington, Mar. 10, 1839, by Rev. Grant Powers	M	55
Lucy E., of Goshen, m. Samuel **DEAN**, of Sharon, Feb. 20, 1850, at the house of Austin **ALLYN**, by Lavalette Perrin	M	76
Paithena, m. Birdsey T. **HOWE**, Sept. 7, 1835, by Rev. Albert G. Wickmore	M	46

	Vol.	Page
ALLYN, (cont.),		
Rebecca A., m. Austin **WOOSTER**, b. of Goshen, Mar. 2, 1845, by Rev. J. D. Marshall	M	67
Temperance A., m. Amos **DAVIDSON**, b. of Goshen, June 25, 1845, by Rev. D. L. Marks	M	68
ALVORD, Catharine, m. Chauncey **BEECH**, Dec. 24, 1772	1	240
Chauncey, of Middletown, m. Harriet **LOBDILL**, of Goshen, Aug. 1, 1827, by Rev. E. Washburn	M	20
John, m. Phebe **BROWN**, b. of Goshen, Jan. 4, 1832, by Rev. Luther Mead	M	36
AMIS, -----, Mr. his child d. Feb. 27, 1817, ae 1	2	397
ANTHONY, George, m. Lucina **PRINCE**, Feb. 10, 1828, by Samuel Chapin, J. P.	M	22
APLEY, Alanson D., m. Mary **NORTHROP**, b. of Goshen, Jan. 1, 1838, by Rev. Asahel Gaylord	M	53
Alfred, m. Abigail **TIBBALS**, b. of Goshen, Jan. 15, 1851, by Frederick Marsh	M	78
Amanda, m. Hiram **CURTIS**, b. of Goshen, Oct. 31, 1835, by Rev. Thomas Sparks	M	46
Clarina, m. Nelson **AUSTIN**, b. of Goshen, [Mar.] 29, 1832, by Rev. George Carrington	M	37
Mary, m. Jabez **GIBBS**, b. of Goshen, Apr. 4, 1833, by Rev. George Carrington	M	40
Philo, of Winchester, m. Emily **CLARK**, of Goshen, Aug. 8, 1830, by Birdsey Baldwin, J. P.	M	30
Sarah Anne, m. William F. **STRONG**, b. of Goshen, Jan. 1, 1834, by Rev. G. Powers	M	42
ARNOLD, Ruth, m. Westal **WILLOBY**, June 5, 1764	1	233
ASHMAN, Eben, s. Lieut. Elnathan, b. Sept. 26, 1773	1	239
Eben, s. Lieut. Elnathan, d. Oct. 2, 1773	1	235
Eben, 2nd, s. Elnathan, b. Nov. 18, 1774	1	239
AUSTIN, Archibald, his w. [ ], d. Aug. 20, 1821, ae 33	2	298
Bushnell, of Goshen, m. Charlotte L. **SKINNER**, of Harwinton, Feb. 6, 1831, by Rev. George Carrington	M	33
Caroline, m. Rufus **WEISLEY**, b. of Goshen, Nov. 24, 1831, by Rev. George Carrington	M	36
Catharine, m. William **JOHNSON**, b. of Goshen, Nov. 24, 1831, by Rev. George Carrington	M	35
Joseph, s. Nov. 10, 1815, ae 57	2	396
Julia A., m. Edwin **BAILEY**, b. of Goshen, Dec. 1, 1847, by Rev. Lavalette Perrin	M	74
Nelson, m. Clarina **APLEY**, b. of Goshen, [Mar.] 29, 1832, by Rev. George Carrington	M	37
AVERY, Abel, of Goshen, m. Eunice L. **BARNES**, of Canaan, Jan. 12, 1834, by Rev. Aaron S. Hill	M	44
AVIATT, Samuel, [d.] Jan. 25, 1804, ae 74	2	392
BAILEY, BAILY, BALY, Abraham, s. Thomas, b. Jan. 11, 1757	1	273
Abram Louis, s. Tho[ma]s, b. Oct. 28, 1760	1	263
Andrew, s. Jos., b. Dec. 2, 1750	1	271
Andrew, s. [Andrew], b. Apr. 12, 1776	1	244

	Page	Vol.
BAILEY, BAILY, BALY, (cont.),		
Andrew, his w. [ ], d. May 10, 1805, ae 53	2	392
Andrew, m. Mary **WILSON**, b. of Goshen, Oct. 16, 1845, by Rev. Chester Colton	M	69
Ann M., m. Dudley F. **HALLOCK**, b. of Goshen, Dec. 15, 1830, by Rev. George Carrington	M	31
Anne Maria, of Goshen, m. Charles Lyman **NORTON**, of Norfolk, Nov. 24, 1825, by Ralph Emerson	M	15
Asahel, s. [Andrew], b. Mar. 21, 1779	1	244
Asahel, m. Mary M. **HUMPHREY**, b. of Goshen, Sept. 7, 1828, by Rev. George Carrington	M	23
Byron, m. Cornelia **SMITH**, Nov. 9, 1820, by Benjamin Sedgwick, J. P.	M	4
Charlotte, d. [Andrew], b. Jan. 17, 1774	1	244
Charlotte, m. Schuyler **BAILEY**, b. of Goshen, Sept. 8, 1841, by Rev. Chester Colton	M	60
Clarissa B., of Goshen, m. Horace **HUMPHREY**, of Goshen, Sept. 18, 1832, by Rev. George Carrington	M	38
Edwin, m. Julia A. **AUSTIN**, b. of Goshen, Dec. 1, 1847, by Rev. Lavalette Perrin	M	74
Eleanor, d. [Jos.], b. Oct. 6, 1754	1	271
Eleanor, m. Justus **SQUIRE**, Dec. 13, 1782	1	240
Eleanor, m. Theron D. **LUDDINGTON**, b. of North Goshen, Sept. 18, 1845, by Rev. Chester Colton	M	69
Eunice, d. Joseph, d. Dec. 20, [1807], ae 18	2	393
Harriet, m. George A. **HILL**, b. of Goshen, Apr. 6, 1830, by Rev. Bradley Selleck	M	29
Jerusha, w. Thomas, d. Jan. 15, 1757	1	272
Jerusha, d. Thomas, b. July 23, 1758	1	273
Joseph, m. Lois **STANLEY**, Mar. 29, 1749	1	261
Lois, d. [Jos.], b. Oct. 9, 1752	1	271
Lucinda, m. Stephen **ROBERTS**, b. of Goshen, Nov. 6, 1833, by Rev. Aaron Hill	M	42
Martha, m. W[illia]m **HURD**, Mar. 6, 1787	1	240
Mary, m. Timothy **STANLEY**, June 18, 1750	1	261
Mary C., m. Silas **HUMPHREY**, b. of Goshen, Dec. 20, 1822, by Rev. Joseph Harvey	M	8
Philo, s. [Andrew], b. Nov. 29, 1781	1	244
Putnam, m. Sarah A. **GRISWOLD**, b. of Goshen, Mar. 12, 1829, by Stephen Mason	M	24
Ruth, d. Andrew, b. May 6, 1777	1	244
Salmon, s. Tho[ma]s, b. Feb. 11, 1763	1	234
Salmon, s. Tho[ma]s, b. Feb. 22, 1763	1	225
Samantha, m. Cicero B. **BEACH**, b. of Goshen, Dec. 7, 1842, by Rev. Chester Colton	M	63
Schuyler, m. Charlotte **BAILEY**, b. of Goshen, Sept. 8, 1841, by Rev. Chester Colton	M	60
Theodore, his d. [ ], d. Jan. 14, 1808, ae 6	2	394
-----, wid., d. Apr. 8, 1812, ae 80	2	395
BAKER, Albert, m. Caroline **IVES**, b. of Goshen, [Jan. 1, 1839], by Rev. Grant Powers	M	55

	Vol.	Page
BALCOMB, -----, d. Jan. 10, 1818, ae 35	2	397
BALDWIN, Abigail, m. Stiles C. PECK, Jan. 26, 1837, by Rev. William Andrews, of South Cornwall	M	50
Amey, m. W[illia]m STANLEY, Mar. 31, 1856* *(Probably "1756")	1	225
Asael, s. Samuel, b. Oct. 5, 1745	1	257
Augustus, s. Step[hen], b. Aug. 27, 1764	1	234
Betsey, [d. Anir], b. Mar. 17, 1810	1	193
Betsey, [d. Aner], b. Mar. 17, 1810	1	249
Birdsey, his child d. Nov. 10, 1822, ae 2	2	399
Boewin*, s. [Samuell & Mary], b. June 17, 1752 *("Brewen")	1	270
Bruin, s. Dea. Nath[anie]ll, d. Nov. 4, 1751	1	272
Brewin, his w. [ ], d. June 10, 1823, ae 60	2	399
Caroline, m. William McDONALD, Apr. 17, 1825, by Rev. Joseph Harvey	M	14
Daniel, his w. [ ], d. May 10, 1808, ae 52	2	394
Dothy, [d. Anir], b. Aug. 23, 1807	1	193
Dothy, [d. Aner], b. Aug. 23, 1807	1	249
Dotha, of Goshen, m. Howell COWELS, of Plymouth, Oct. 26, 1831, by Rev. Grant Powers	M	35
Elisha, his child d. Dec. 8, [1806], ae 10 d	2	393
Elisha, his w. [ ], d. Sept. 6, 1814, ae 45	2	396
Elizabeth, m. Ebenezer HILL, Jr., May 27, 1741	1	254
Enos Stanley, s. [Samuell], b. Nov. 22, 1767	1	237
Freelove L., of Goshen, m. Galpin P. BRONSON, of Winchester, Sept. 3, 1829, by Rev. George Carrington	M	26
Hannah, d. Nath[anie]ll, Jr., b. Nov. 19, 1755	1	271
Hannah, d. Nath[anie]ll, Jr., d. Feb. 1, 1758	1	272
Hannah, w. Nath[anie]ll, d. Apr. 9, 1762	1	272
Hannah F., m. Edward P. BARNUM, Apr. 22, 1846, at the house of Birdsey BALDWIN, by Lavalette Perren	M	71
Harvey, M. D., m. Esther STARR, b. of Goshen, Mar. 30, 1842, by Cornelius B. Everist	M	62
Huldah, d. Sam[ue]l, b. July 1, 1763	1	224
Isaac, s. Nathaniell, b. Mar. 12, 1759	1	262
Jedidah, d. Nathaniel, b. May 9, 1765	1	234
John H., [s. Anir], b. Nov. 4, 1803	1	193
John H., s. Aner, b. Nov. 4, 1803	1	249
Junius, m. Julia HALLOCK, b. of Goshen, Sept. 14, 1828, by Frederick Marsh	M	26
Laura M., of Goshen, m. Jesse MALTBY, of Norfolk, Feb. 11, 1823, by Rev. Joseph Harvey	M	8
Levi, m. Eliza M. POOLER, Feb. 3, 1847, at the house of Hiram SAGE, by Lavalette Perrin	M	71
Lucy, d. Dr. Nathaniel & Elizabeth, b. Jan. 7, 1740/1	1	254
Luice*, d. Samuell, b. Dec. 22, 1765 *("Lucia"?)	1	237
Martha, d. [Samuell & Mary], b. Jan. 22, 1748/9	1	270
Martha, m. Jabez WRIGHT, Feb. 11 or 12, 1767	1	233

	Vol.	Page
BALDWIN, (cont.), Martha, m. Halsey **BIGELOW**, b. of Goshen, Oct. 24, 1820, by Rev. Joseph Harvey	M	2
Mary, d. Samuell, b. July 19, 1760	1	263
Nathaniell, Jr., m. Hannah **IVES**, Mar. 23, 1752	1	269
Nath[anie]ll, Capt., d. Oct. 18, 1760	1	272
Nathaniell, s. Nathaniell, b. July 20, 1761	1	263
Nathaniell, m. Jedidah **BRONSON**, Nov. 30, 1763	1	225
Nathaniel, d. Mar. 25, 1805, ae 85	2	392
Norman C., of Hudson, O., m. Mary **PALMER**, of Goshen, Dec. 17, 1829, by Rev. Grant Powers	M	28
Rachel, m. Benjamin **IVES**, Dec. 6, 1753	1	269
Ruth, d. Nathaniell, Jr., b. Oct. 25, 1752	1	270
Ruth, m. Daniel **MILES**, Dec. 4, 1771	1	233
Ruth, m. Daniell **MILES**, Dec. 4, 1771	1	240
Sam[ue]ll, m. Mercy **STANLEY**, Nov. 28, 1744	1	257
Samuell, s. Samuell, b. May 25, 1755	1	271
Samuell, m. Susannah **ADAMS**, Jan. 11, 1769	1	233
Samuel, [d.] Oct. 22, [1804], ae 79	2	392
Sarrah, m. Nathaniel **STANLEY**, Jr., Nov. 6, 1746	1	257
Stephen, d. May 22, 1810, ae 52	2	394
Stephen, d. Jan. 25, 1811, ae 41	2	395
Sebbil, d. Sam[ue]l, b. Nov. 30, 1757	1	262
Timothy, s. Samuell & Mary, b. Nov. 20, 1747	1	270
Timothy, s. Sam[ue]ll, d. Jan. 20, 1747/8	1	272
Timothy, 2nd, s. [Samuell & Mary], b. June 5, 1751	1	270
Timothy, 2nd, s. [Samuell], d. July 25, 1751	1	272
-----, wid., d. Sept. 10, [1807], ae 83	2	393
BALLARD, Jeffrey, m. Clarissa **THOMSON**, May 10, 1825, by Rev. Joseph Harvey	M	15
BARKER, Lucy, of Goshen, m. Hiram **BUNNEL**, of Cornwall, Sept. 10, 1826, by John Lovejoy	M	17
BARNES, BARNS, Eli, m. Harriet A. **HARRISON**, Oct. 3, 1841, by Nelson Brewster, J. P.	M	60
Eunice L., of Canaan, m. Abel **AVERY**, of Goshen, Jan. 12, 1834, by Rev. Aaron S. Hill	M	44
Rachel, m. Hezekiah **ADKINS**, Apr. 5, 1771, in Middletown	1	233
BARNEY, Jane, m. William **ROBINS**, June 24, 1846, by Rev. William Dixon	M	72
BARNUM, Edward P., m. Hannah F. **BALDWIN**, Apr. 22, 1846, at the house of Birdsey **BALDWIN**, by Lavalette Perren	M	71
Experience, of Goshen, m. Amos **WEBSTER**, of Harwinton, May 13, 1840, by Rev. Grant Powers	M	57
Oby, Mrs., of Cornwall, m. Archibald **SMITH**, of Goshen, Feb. 7, 1841, by Rev. David Osborn	M	59
BARTCH, [see under **BURTCH**]		
BARTHOLOMEW, BARTHOL, Ann, m. Lyman **RICHARDS**, Sept. 14, 1848, at the house of Thomas **BARTHOLOMEW**, by Lavalette Perrin	M	75
Anne, d. [Sam[ue]ll], b. Oct. 23, 1781	1	242
Anne, d. June 23, 1806, ae 25	2	393

	Vol.	Page
BARTHOLOMEW, BARTHOL, (cont.),		
Emily, of Goshen, m. Philo **NORTON**, of Vernon, N. Y., Nov. 14, 1836, by Rev. Grant Powers	M	50
Esther, d. Sam[ue]ll, b. June 13, 1779	1	242
Isaac, m. Thankfull **MALBEE***, Feb. 20, 1775 *("**MALTBY**")	1	240
Jehiel, s. [Isaac & Thankfull], b. Apr. 8, 1777	1	244
Josiah, m. Martha **MALBEC***, Feb. 9, 1775 *("**MALBEE**")	1	240
Josiah, s. Josiah, Jr., b. Nov. 11, 1775	1	241
Josiah, d. Feb. 12, 1777	1	235
Lydia, d. Sam[ue]ll, b. Jan. 8, 1769	1	238
Lydia, m. Ashbel **NORTON**, June 25, 1788	1	240
Mary, d. Samuell, b. Feb. last day, 1771	1	241
Miles, s. Sam[ue]ll, b. Sept. 27, 1774	1	241
Phebe, d. Isaac & Thankfull, b. Mar. 17, 1776	1	244
Sabra, d. [Isaac & Thankfull], b. Aug. 5, 1786	1	244
Samuel, his w. [ ], d. Feb. 4, 1811, ae 63	2	395
Thomas, s. [Samuell], b. Sept. 5, 1776	1	241
Velena E., of Goshen, m. William C. **JOHNSON**, of Bristol, Mar. 27, 1837, by Rev. Grant Powers	M	51
-----, Mr., his child d. Sept. 8, 1813, ae 1	2	396
BARTON, John D., m. Eliza **GARNER**, Apr. 3, 1851, at the house of Erastus **LYMAN**, by Lavalette Perrin	M	78
BARTRUM, Mary E., m. Samuel **ALEXANDER**, b. of Goshen, Nov. 23, 1845, by Rev. David L. Marks	M	70
BASSETT, BASSET, Ezra, s. Lemuel, b. Mar. 23, 1774	1	239
Lemuel, m. Patience **WALTER**, Oct. 23, 1773	1	233
Ruth, m. James **GLASS**, Aug. 29, 1771	1	233
BATES, Mary, m. Zenas **WARD**, May 24, 1743	1	256
-----, Mrs., d. Oct. 4, 1810, ae 50	2	395
-----, his child d. June 6, 1815, ae 2	2	396
BEACH, BEECH, Abel, s. Amos, b. Dec. 25, 1758	1	262
Abi, d. Jno, 3rd, b. Jan. 28, 1757	1	273
Abner*, s. Edmund, b. Jan. 29, 1755 *(Arnold Copy has "Abner **BEECHER**")	1	271
Abraham, s. Amos, b. Jan. 25, 1755	1	271
Abraham, s. Amos, d. June 5, 1777, at Milford	1	235
Adna, m. Hannah **MIELS***, June 9, 1741 *("**MILES**")	1	254
Adna, twin with Ebenezer, s. Adna, b. Aug. 4, 1740	1	260
Adna, s. Adna, d. June 20, 1751	1	261
Adna, 2nd, s. Adna, b. June 16, 1754	1	270
Adna, s. Adna, d. Aug. 1, 1754	1	272
Adna, s. Adna, b. Nov. 10, 1757	1	273
Almeran, of Litchfield, m. Emily **PHELPS**, of Hector, N. Y., Jan. 22, 1832, by Rev. Grant Powers	M	37
Amanda*, d. Edmond, b. Apr. 7, 1764 *(Arnold Copy has "Guida")	1	224
Amanda, d. Luman, b. Apr. 7, 1764	1	236
Ambrose, s. Amos, b. Jan. 14, 1749/50	1	260
Ambrose, s. Amos, d. July 8, 1776, at Crown Point	1	235
Amos, m. Sarah **RICE**, Dec. 24, 1746, by Rev. Mr. Hall	1	258

	Vol.	Page
BEACH, BEECH, (cont.),		
Amos, s. Amos, b. Aug. 27, 1751	1	261
Amzi, [child of Daniel, Jr.], b. Feb. 18, 1820	2	3
Anne, d. Adna, b. Oct. 2, 1752	1	268
Anne, d. Anda, d. July 30, 1753	1	272
Anne, d. Anda, b. May 18, 1755	1	271
Azenah, s. John, 2nd, b. July 12, 1750	1	268
Bethiah, d. Jacob, b. Feb. 10, 1763	1	224
Bruin, s. Amos, b. Mar. 21, 1753	1	270
Caleb, Jr., m. Lois **PRESTON**, Nov. 19, 1756	1	269
Caleb, d. Jan. 13, 1761	1	272
Caleb, of Winchester, m. Ann **RATHBURN**, of Hartland, [ ], by Rev. Grant Powers. Recorded Jan. 23, 1832	M	36
Chauncey, s. Amos, b. Oct. 31, 1748	1	259
Chauncey, m. Catharine **ALVORD**, Dec. 24, 1772	1	240
C[h]loe, d. Amos, b. Sept. 24, 1747	1	258
C[h]loe, m. Lazarus **IVES**, Oct. 29, 1772	1	240
Cicero B., m. Samantha **BAILEY**, b. of Goshen, Dec. 7, 1842, by Rev. Chester Colton	M	63
Clarinda Thomson, d. Hunn, late of Johnstown, N. Y., b. May 26, 1791; d. [ ]	1	193
Clarissa*, d. Hunn, d. Aug. 30, 1805, ae 14 *("Clarinda"?)	2	392
David*, m. Susannah **BEECH**, Feb. 1, 1781 *("Daniel" in Hibbard's Hist. of Goshen)	1	240
Delia, m. Henry **NORTON**, b. of Goshen, May 12, 1842, by C. B. Everist	M	62
Dinah, d. Linus, b. Apr. 20, 1754	1	270
Dinah, m. Step[hen] **MIX**, Dec. 24, 1778	1	240
Ebenezer, twin with Adna, s. Adna, b. Aug. 4, 1750	1	260
Eben[eze]r, s. Adna, d. June 23, 1751	1	261
Ebenezer, s. Adna, b. May 30, 1766	1	236
Edmund, s. Edmund, b. Apr. 27, 1753	1	270
Edmund, s. Edmund, d. Sept. 15, 1755	1	272
Edmund, s. Edmund, b. July 24, 1758	1	262
Elizabeth, of Goshen, m. Joseph **PETERS**, of Warren, June 5, 1821, by Rev. Ananias Dathick, of Warren	M	3
Esther, d. Amos, b. Jan. 7, 1757	1	273
Eunice, d. David, b. June 6, 1762	1	224
Eveline, of Goshen, m. Munson **CARTER**, of Virginnes, Vt., Jan. 14, 1834, by Rev. George Carrington	M	43
Fisk, s. Adna, b. May 15, 1742	1	255
Fisk, m. Martha **CARRINGTON**, Oct. 26, 1763	1	225
Francis, s. Jacob, b. Oct. 13, 1755	1	271
Francis, Jr., m. Maria **HURD**, Dec. 25, 1823, by Rev. Joseph Harvey	M	11
George, m. Caroline **RICHARDS**, b. of Goshen, Nov. 25, 1830, by Rev. Bradley Selleck	M	31
Guida*, s. Edmond, b. Apr. 7, 1764 *("Amanda" in Hibbard's Hist. Of Goshen)	1	224
Hannah, d. Adna, b. Feb. 28, 1745	1	257

BEACH, BEECH, (cont.),

	Vol.	Page
Hannah, m. Uri **HILL**, Oct. 20, 1764	1	225
Hannah, w. Adna, d. Dec. 6, 1775	1	235
Henn* Carrington, s. Henn*, b. Sept. 18, 1794 *("Hunn" in Hist. of Goshen)	1	193
Henry H., m. Mary L. **SAGE**, b. of Goshen, Oct. 8, 1832, by Rev. Grant Powers	1	38
Horace Foot, s. Henn, b. Oct. 20, 1796	1	193
Horatio N., m. Mary **LUCAS**, b. of Goshen, Jan. 28, 1830, by Rev. Grant Powers	M	28
Huldah, d. Lines*, b. Feb. 10, 1769 *("Linus" overwritten)	1	237
Huldah, d. [Daniel], b. Mar. 18, 1784	1	245
Hunn*, s. Fisk, b. July 7, 1764 *("Uri" in Arnold Copy)	1	234
Ira, s. Roger, b. Aug. 28, 1757	1	262
Isaac, s. Jonathan, d. Sept. 5, 1755	1	272
Isaac, s. Amos, b. June 23, 1762	1	234
Israel, s. [Judah], b. July 6, 1759	1	262
Jacob, m. Bethiah **VALSON***, Sept. 19, 1753 *("**WATSON**") in Hibbard's Hist. of Goshen)	1	269
Jeloma*, d. Adna, b. June 14, 1763 *("Salome" in Hibbard's Hist.)	1	224
Job Smith Nathan Benedict, of Cornwall, m. Lucia **BEACH**, of Goshen, Nov. 1, 1832, by Rev. Aaron S. Hill	M	38
John, 2nd, m. Lois **IVES**, Mar. 12, 1755	1	269
John, s. Jacob, b. Apr. 28, 1759	1	262
John, d. May 9, 1773, in the 83rd y. of his age	1	235
John, his w. [ ], d. Mar. 14, 1820, ae 35	2	298
John, m. Lucy **WADHAMS**, b. of Goshen, Nov. 9, 1820, by Rev. J. Harvey	M	2
Jonathan, s. Edmund, b. Oct. 2, 1761	1	263
Julian*, s. Jacob, b. Jan. 19, 1765. Bp. "Julian" but changed by father to "Julius". *(Arnold Copy has "Julian **BEECHER**")	1	234
Julius, see under Julian **BEACH**		
Keziah, d. John, 2nd, b. Aug. 18, 1755	1	271
Lynus, m. Dinah **RICE**, Oct. 21, 1747	1	258
Linus, s. William, b. May 17, 1751	1	261
Linus, s. Linus, b. Nov. 22, 1752	1	270
Linus*, Jr., m. Elizabeth **ABBOT**, June 1, 1775 *(Arnold Copy has "Lucas")	1	240
Loes, d. Edmund, b. Aug. 4, 17[51*] *(Supplied from "Hibbard's Hist. of Goshen")	1	261
Lois, m. Earl **STANLEY**, July 8, 1773	1	240
Lois, [d. Daniel, Jr.], b. Sept. 10, 1817	2	3
Lois, m. Erastus L. **RICHARDS**, b. of Goshen, Nov. 8, 1840, by Rev. David Osborn	M	58
Lorenzo, [s. Daniel, Jr.], b. Dec. 3, 1826	2	3
Lucas*, Jr., m. Elizabeth **ABBOT**, June 1, 1775 *("Linus" in Hibbard's Hist.)	1	240
Lucia, m. Ambrose **HILL**, Oct. 10, 1764	1	225
Lucia, [d. Daniel, Jr.], b. Sept. 19, 1813	2	3

BEACH, BEECH, (cont.),

	Vol.	Page
Lucia, of Goshen, m. Job Smith Nathan Benedict **BEACH**, of Cornwall, Nov. 1, 1832, by Rev. Aaron S. Hill	M	38
Lucy, d. Edmond, b. Jan. 27, 1746	1	257
Luman, m. Anne **HILL**, Feb. 2, 1764	1	225
Luman, m. Anne **HILL**, Feb. 2, 1764	1	233
Lura, d. Linas*, b. Aug. 12, 1764 *("Linus" overwritten)	1	234
Lydia, d. Edmund, b. Oct. 28, 1749	1	259
Mabel, d. Adna, b. Apr. 22, 1748	1	259
Mable, m. John **CARRINGTON**, Jan. 26, 1766	1	233
Margaret, m. Jabez **NORTON**, Nov. 21, 1765	1	233
Martha, [d. Daniel, Jr.], b. Mar. 24, 1828	2	3
Martin, s. Linus, b. Feb. 23, 1758	1	262
Martin, s. Linas, d. Nov. 8, 1776, at New York	1	235
Mary, d. John & Mary, b. Oct. 27, 1739	1	254
Mary, w. Jno, 2nd, d. July 29, 1755	1	272
Mary, d. Jno, 2nd, b. Aug. 12, 1755	1	271
Mary, d. Edmund, b. Aug. 14, 1756	1	273
Mary, d. Lines, b. Aug. 2, 1766	1	236
Mary, d. Lines*, d. Nov. 6, 1771 *(Linus" overwritten)	1	235
Mary, [d. Daniel, Jr.], b. Jan. 28, 1812	2	3
Mary, of Goshen, m. William **LANDING**, of Litchfield, Nov. 22, 1830, by Rev. Bradley Selleck	M	32
Medad, s. Lyman, b. Sept. 9, 1760	1	262
Mencis*, m. Aseneth **IVES**, May 23, 1776 *("Mineas" in Hist. of Goshen)	1	240
Michael, s. Linas, b. Feb. 3, 1756	1	271
Michael, m. [E]unice **HERTER***, Aug. 7, 1773 *("**HESTER**" in Hist. of Goshen)	1	240
Miles, s. Adna, b. Nov. 14, 1743	1	256
Miles, m. Abigail **HOPKINS**, Jan. 3, 1771	1	233
Noah W., of Litchfield, m. Angeline **BIERCE**, of Goshen, Apr. 7, 1840, by Rev. Grant Powers	M	57
Ollive, d. Daniel, b. Aug. 3, 1772	1	245
Ollive, d. Chauncey, b. May 2, 1777	1	241
Oliver, s. Linus, b. Sept. 13, 1748	1	259
Roger*, m. Phebe **SOPER**, June 9, 1756 *("Royce"?)	1	269
Roger*, s. Lines*, b. June 15, 1762 *("Linus" overwritten) *("Royce" in Hibbard's Hist.)	1	224
Roswell, s. Amos, b. July 14, 1764	1	234
Rufus, s. [William], b. Feb. 21, 1785	1	242
Ruth, d. Linas, b. Dec. 8, 1749	1	260
Sabra, d. Jacob, b. Aug. 24, 1761	1	224
Salome*, d. Adna, b. June 14, 1763 *("Jeloma" in Arnold Copy)	1	224
Sarah, d. Jno, 2nd, b. Aug. 4, 1755	1	271
Sarah, d. Amos, b. Oct. 20, 1760	1	263
Sarah, m. Elisha **BLIN**, July 7, 1763	1	225
Sarah, d. Amos, b. Mar. 3, 1766	1	236
Sarah, d. June 2, [1804], ae 81	2	392
Seth, s. Lucas, Jr., b. Feb. 22, 1776	1	239

BEACH, BEECH, (cont.),

	Vol.	Page
Seth, s. W[illia]m, b. Mar. 25, 1780	1	242
Shelton, s. Michael, b. Oct. 2, 1784	1	242
Stella, m. Van Rensalaer **HUMPHREY**, b. of Goshen, Apr. 12, 1821, by Rev. Joseph Harvey	M	3
Susannah, d. Adna, b. Oct. 31, 1760	1	262
Susannah, m. David* **BEECH**, Feb. 1, 1781 *("Daniel" in Hibbard's Hist. of Goshen)	1	240
Susannah, d. [Daniel], b. Feb. 7, 1787	1	245
Truman, m. Eliza **HOSMER**, b. of Goshen, Dec. 30, 1832, by Rev. George Carrington	M	39
Uri*, s. Fisk, b. July 7, 1764 *("Hunn" in Hist. of Goshen)	1	234
Waite, s. Edmund, b. Oct. 25, 1747	1	258
William, s. Caleb, b. Aug. 26, 1757	1	271
W[illia]m, m. Mary **PARMELEE**, June 22, 1779	1	240
-----, wid., d. Feb. 20, [1806], ae 81	2	393

BEARDSLEY, Eliza A., of Goshen, m. Alvin **BUEL**, of Litchfield, Jan. 10, 1841, by Rev. Grant Powers — M 63

Horatio, of Goshen, m. Almira **CHEFELLE** (?), of Canaan, Nov. 10, 1823, by Rev. Joseph Harvey — M 11

Lucia*, m. Abel **PHELPS**, Jr., Nov. 20, 1770
   *(Arnold Copy has "Lucia **BRADLEY**")   1 233

Lyman, m. Margaret **LOCKWOOD**, b. of Litchfield, [Jan. 1, 1839], by Rev. Grant Powers — M 55

-----, Mr. his child d. May 20, 1816, ae 6   2 397

BECKLY*, Mary, m. Isaac **PRATT**, July 21, 1755   *(Arnold Copy has "**BEEKLY**")   1 225

BECKWITH, Mary, m. Nathaniell **NORVEL**, Jan. 29, 1761   1 225

Silena Lamb, m. Elijah **WILLCOX**, Mar. 8, 1765   1 233

-----, wid., d. Mar. [ ], 1819, ae 87   2 298

BEECHER, Abner*, s. Edmund, b. Jan. 29, 1755   *("Abner **BEACH**" in Hibbard's Hist.)   1 271

Abraham*, s. Amos, b. Jan. 25, 1755   *("Abraham **BEACH**" in Hibbard's Hist.)   1 271

Amaret Mariah, d. [David & Prudence S.], b. Aug. 5, 1822	1	194
Amelia Platt, d. [David & Prudence S.], b. Jan. 19, 1802	1	194
Caroline Esther, d. [David & Prudence S.], b. Aug. 19, 1811	1	194
Charles, s. [David & Prudence S.], b. Mar. 25, 1798	1	194
Chauncey, his child, b. June 3, 1774; d. same day	1	239
David, b. Aug. 14, 1773; m. Prudence S. **CHARD**, June 10, 1797	1	194
David, his d. [ ], d. Mar. 1, 1820, ae 9 m.	2	298
David Lyman, s. [David & Prudence S.], b. Feb. 2, 1806	1	194
Emily Morse, d. [David & Prudence S.], b. Feb. 26, 1808	1	194
John Fabian, s. [David & Prudence S.], b. Aug. 19, 1800	1	194
Julian, s. Jacob, b. Jan. 19, 1765. Bp. "Julian" but changed by father to "Julius". (Probably "**BEACH**")	1	234
Julius, see Julian **BEECHER**	1	234
Luther Fitch, s. [David & Prudence S.], b. Feb. 25, 1813	1	194
Mary Eliza, d. [David & Prudence S.], b. Feb. 18, 1804	1	194

	Vol.	Page
BEECHER, (cont.), Sarah A., of Goshen, m. Warren L. **BROWN**, of Norfolk, May 9, 1838, by Rev. Grant Powers	M	54
Susan Allethea, d. [David & Prudence S.], b. May 26, 1819; d. Mar. 1, 1826	1	194
Theodore Collins, s. [David & Prudence S.], b. Aug. 15, 1816	1	194
William Augustus, s. [David & Prudence S.], b. July 24, 1799	1	194
BEEKLEY*, Mary, m. Isaac **PRATT**, July 21, 1755 *(**BECKLY**" in Hibbard's Hist.)	1	225
BELCHER, Jeremiah, m. wid. Phebe **WILCOX**, Oct. 25, 1763	1	225
Rhoda, d. Jeremiah, b. July 26, 1764	1	234
BELL, Julius, of Cornwall, m. Elizabeth **COLLINS**, of Goshen, Jan. 6, 1824, by Rev. Joseph Harvey	M	12
BENEDICT, Lyman, of Winchester, m. Jane P. **SIMONS**, of Sandisfield, Mass., Oct. 25, 1849, by Frederick Marsh	M	75
BENTON, Edwin, s. Jesse, b. July 1, 1796	1	193
Elvina, d. Josiah, b. Oct. 24, 1770	1	238
Erastus, s. Jesse, b. July 25, 1798	1	193
Habia, d. Josiah, b. [ ]	1	237
Jesse, s. Josiah, b. Nov. 25, 1766	1	236
Lucinda, d. Josiah, b. Feb. 28, 1768	1	237
Pamelia, d. Jesse, b. Nov. 25, 1794	1	193
Philo, s. Josiah, b. June 24, 1772	1	238
Philo, s. Jesse, b. Sept. [ ], 1801	1	193
Ruth, m. James **THOMSON**, June 2, 1767	1	233
Steetyn (?), d. Josiah, b. Apr. 19, 1769	1	238
-----, his w. [ ], d. Mar. 10, 1810, ae 55	2	394
BIERCE, [see under **PIERCE**]		
BIGELOW, Elizabeth, m. Charles **CLEMMONS**, b. of Goshen, Mar. 5, 1824, by Rev. Joseph Harvey	M	12
Halsey, m. Martha **BALDWIN**, b. of Goshen, Oct. 24, 1820, by Rev. Joseph Harvey	M	2
Halsey T., of Goshen, m. Maria **BOUNDS**, of Torrington, Dec. 13, 1830, by Birdsey Baldwin, J. P.	M	31
Washington, of Ohio, m. Harriet **OVIATT**, of Goshen, Dec. 21, 1837, by Rev. Grant Powers	M	53
BIRCH, [see under **BURTCH**]		
BIRGE, BURGE, Abijah, s. Elijah, b. Sept. 6, 1762	1	224
Lydia, m. Billious **HILL**, Aug. 9, 1758	1	269
BISHOP, Lois, d. Sam[ue]ll, b. May 10, 1776	1	241
Samuel, m. Lois **GUILERD***, Dec. 13, 1770 (**GAYLORD**")	1	233
Sam[ue]l, s. Sam[ue]l, b. Aug. 24, 1773	1	238
Timothy, s. Sam[uel], b. Sept. 15, 1771	1	238
BLAKE, James, of Cornwall, m. Jane L. **SEELEY**, of Goshen, May 4, 1847, by Rev. D. L. Marks	M	72
BLANCHARD, Mary, m. Gideon **WILLCOX**, Nov. 8, 1751	1	261
[**BLINN**], **BLIN**, Ebenezer, s. Elisha, b. Jan. 24, 1772	1	238
Elisha, m. Huldah **NASH**, Mar. 3, 1755	1	269
Elisha, his child b. June 5, 1755; d. in a few hours; his 2nd child b. June 10, 1756; d. in a few hours	1	273
Elisha, his infant, b. July 15, 1758; d. 19 days after	1	262

[BLINN], BLIN, (cont.),   Vol.   Page
    Elisha, his child, b. Oct. 6, 1759; d. 8th day of same month   1   262
    Elisha, m. Sarah BEECH, July 7, 1763   1   225
    Elisha, s. Elisha, b. Mar. 19, 1770   1   238
    Erastus, s. Elisha, b. Feb. 5, 1765   1   234
    Huldah, w. Elisha & d. of Sam[ue]ll NASH, d. Oct. [ ], 1761   1   272
    Huldah, d. Elisher, b. July 11, 1764   1   234
    Huldah, d. Elisher, d. Aug. 1, 1765   1   235
BOARDMAN, Sylvester, d. Apr. 1, 1822, ae 10   ("He was living with
    Isaac CRANDALL, Jr.")   2   399
BONNEY, Asa, s. [Peris & Ruth], b. Sept. 6, 1751   1   242
    Celia, d.[Peris & Ruth], b. Apr. 16, 1746   1   242
    Giles, s. [Peris & Ruth], b. June 18, 1744   1   242
    Jarvis, s. [Peris & Ruth], b. Feb. 14, 1747   1   242
    Joel, s. Peris & Ruth, b. Aug. 14, 1740   1   242
    Peris, s. John & Elizabeth, b. Mar. 10, 1708/9, in that part of
      Duxboro called Matteketts, and is now called
      Pembroke in the county of Plymouth, New England;
      m. Ruth SNOW, Apr. 20, 1739, by Rev. Daniel
      Perkins   1   242
    Peres, s. [Peris & Ruth], b. July 13, 1742   1   242
    Phebe, of Cornwall, m. John B. SAUNDERS, of Goshen, Jan.
      1, 1833, by Rev. Aaron S. Hill   M   39
BOONE, Anne, m. Nathaniell ROYCE, Jr., July 10, 1755   1   269
BOOTH, George, m. Fanny PERKINS, b. of Goshen, Feb. 23, 1823, by
    Rev. Joseph Harvey   M   8
BOTSFORD, Abner C., m. Laura RUGG, Oct. 13, 1850, at the house of
    Uri MARVIN, by Lavalette Perrin   M   77
BOUNDS, Maria, of Torrington, m. Halsey T. BIGELOW, of Goshen,
    Dec. 13, 1830, by Birdsey Baldwin, J. P.   M   31
BOWHAM, Melinda, m. Alphonso PRINCE (colored), Oct. 27, 1822, by
    Julius Beach, J. P., at his house   M   6
BRADLEY, Caleb, his child d. June 1, 1809, ae 1   2   394
    Caleb, his child d. Dec. 25, [1815] ae 6 m.   2   397
    James, m. Ellen WADHAMS, b. of Goshen, Aug. 30, 1836, by
      Rev. Grant Powers   M   48
    Lucia*, m. Abel PHELPS, Jr., Nov. 20, 1770
      *("BEARDSLEY" in Hibbard's Hist.)   1   233
    -----, Miss, d. Apr. 3, 1809, ae 11   2   394
BRADY, [see also BRIODY], Joseph, m. Nancy McKENNIE*, Apr. 4,
    1853, by Lavalette Perrin
    *("McKEEMIN" in Hibbard's Hist.)   M   82
BREWSTER, Ephraim Starr, [s. Nelson & Lucretia H.], b. July 11, 1835   2   3
    Nelson, m. Lucretia H. ROOT, Dec. 19, 1827, by Rev. Francis
      H. Case   M   21
    William Root, s. Nelson & Lucretia H., b. July 29, 1828   1   195
    William Root, [s. Nelson & Lucretia H.], b. July 29, 1828   2   3
BRICE, -----, see Lanes [   ]   1   246
BRIODY, [see also BRADY], Irena, m. Thomas VESPER, b. of Goshen,
    Oct. 27, 1831, by Rev. Grant Powers   M   35

	Vol.	Page
BRONSON, Anna, m. David **NORTON**, Jan. 29, 1752	1	268
Galpin P., of Winchester, m. Freelove L. **BALDWIN**, of Goshen, Sept. 3, 1829, by Rev. George Carrington	M	26
Jedidah, m. Nathaniell **BALDWIN**, Nov. 30, 1763	1	225
BROOKS, Birdsey, s. [Joseph & Amanda], b. Jan. 3, 1783	1	65
Clarissa, d. [Joseph & Amanda], b. Aug. 15, 1796	1	65
Collins, s. [Joseph & Amanda], b. Feb. 8, 1791	1	65
Fabius, s. [Joseph & Amanda], b. Aug. 23, 1802	1	65
George, m. Jane C. **DOLBY**, b. of Goshen, Jan. 1, 1843, by Rev. Chester Colton	M	63
Herucy*, s. Joseph & Amanda, b. Oct. 26, 1779 *("Harvey" in Hibbard's book)	1	65
Hiram, s. [Joseph & Amanda], b. Nov. 4, 1788	1	65
Homer, s. [Joseph & Amanda], b. Sept. 11, 1799	1	65
Ira, s. [Joseph & Amanda], b. Feb. 21, 1795	1	65
John, s. [Joseph & Amanda], b. Aug. 31, 1784	1	65
Joseph, d. Aug. 18, [1808], ae 55	2	394
Leman, s. [Joseph & Amanda], b. Mar. 1, 1781	1	65
Nancy, d. [Joseph & Amanda], b. Aug. 4, 1786	1	65
Philo, s. [Joseph & Amanda], b. Apr. 15, 1793	1	65
Watts H., m. Mary **WADHAMS**, b. of Goshen, Apr. 3, 1834, by Rev. Grant Powers	M	44
BROWN, Dudley, his d. [ ], d. Mar. 26, 1823, ae 14	2	399
Esther, of Goshen, m. Milo **DICKENSON**, of Cornwall, Apr. 15, 1821, by Nathan Emery, Elder	M	3
Harriet, of Kent, m. Augustus **HAYDEN**, of Plymouth, Jan. 1, 1828, by Rev. E. Washburn	M	22
Jane, of Goshen, m. John **SACKETT**, of Stanford, Dutchess Co., N. Y., Feb. 16, 1834, by Rev. Aaron S. Hill	M	43
Lavina, of Goshen, m. Newton **WOOSTER**, of Oxford, Oct. 1, 1820, by Nathan Emery, Elder	M	1
Lucrecia, d. Sam[ue]ll, b. Feb. 27, 1768	1	241
Mary, m. Samuell **RICHARDS**, Feb. 14, 1754	1	269
Mary, d. [Samuell], b. Aug. 27, 1776	1	241
Mary, of Goshen, m. Cyrus **MASON**, of Salisbury, Aug. 19, 1829, by Grant Powers. Int. Pub.	M	26
Mary M., of Goshen, m. Lewis **BUELL**, of Litchfield, Nov. 11, 1829, by Rev. Bradley Selleck	M	27
Palmer, of Goshen, m. Sarah **COGSWELL**, of Southington, Nov. 22, 1827, by Rev. Ebenezer Washburn	M	21
Phebe, m. John **ALVORD**, b. of Goshen, Jan. 4, 1832, by Rev. Luther Mead	M	36
Rebecca, d. [Sam[ue]ll], b. Apr. 3, 1770	1	241
Samuel, m. Mary **MALTBIE**, Feb. 16, 1765	1	233
Samuell, had s. [ ], b. Jan. 2, 1766	1	236
Sam[ue]ll, s. [Samuell], b. Mar. 3, 1773	1	241
Seth G., m. Lydia Ann **CLARK**, Nov. 23, 1846, by Rev. D. L. Marks	M	71
Warren, m. Esther **TUTTLE**, b. of Goshen, Jan. 5, 1840, by Rev. David Osborn	M	57

BROWN, (cont.), Vol. Page
Warren L., of Norfolk, m. Sarah A. **BEECHER**, of Goshen,
    May 9, 1838, by Rev. Grant Powers   M   54
BRYAN, Hannah, m. Wait **DEMING**, Dec. 25, 1755   1   269
BRYANT, Sally, d. Clark, b. June 23, 1806   1   247
BUELL, BUEL, Alvin, of Litchfield, m. Eliza A. **BEARDSLEY**, of
    Goshen, Jan. 10, 1841, by Rev. Grant Powers   M   63
Asahel, his w. [   ], d. June 20, 1813, ae 52   2   396
Caroline M., of Goshen, m. William P. **ROBINSON**, of New
    Haven, Ill., Aug. 21, 1820, by Rev. Joseph Harvey   M   1
Elias, of Litchfield, m. Cynthia **WEBSTER**, of Goshen, May
    7, 1828, by Rev. Francis H. Case   M   22
Elisha Lewis, [s. Elisha], b. Sept. 29, 1825   1   194
Eunice, d. [Timothy], b. Aug. 11, 1780   1   245
Frederick, s. Pitt, d. Sept. 20, 1819, at Indiana, ae 26   2   298
Giles P., [s. Elisha L. & Julia], b. Nov. 2, 1831   2   3
Harlow, m. Caroline M. **SANFORD**, b. of Goshen, Jan. 28,
    1836, by Rev. Grant Powers   M   47
Isaac, s. Jonathan, b. Sept. 2, 1755   1   271
Jesse, s. Jonathan, b. Apr. 10, 1748   1   259
Jonathan, m. Lydia **LANDON**, Dec. 10, 1741   1   256
Jonathan, s. Jonathan, b. May 29, 1753   1   270
Jonathan, s. [Timothy], b. Oct. 11, 1784   1   245
Jonathan, 2nd, m. Mary* **HOLMES**, Jan. 14, 1845, by
    Lavalette Perrin   *(Overwritten to read "Jane")   M   66
Julia Eliza, [d. Elisha], b. Jan. 15, 1822   1   194
Lewis, of Litchfield, m. Mary M. **BROWN**, of Goshen, Nov.
    11, 1829, by Rev. Bradley Selleck   M   27
Louice, d. Timothy, b. Apr. 7, 1778   1   245
Lucretia, d. Lieut. Josiah, b. June 3, 1763   1   234
Lydia, d. Jonathan, b. Nov. 11, 174[ ]   1   256
Mary, d. Jonathan, b. Nov. 1, 1745   1   257
Nancy, d. Jonathan, b. Aug. 16, 1750   1   260
Oliver, of New Canaan, N. Y., m. Esther **NORTON**, of
    Goshen, Oct. 29, 1823, by Rev. Joseph Harvey   M   10
Pitt, s. Capt. Jonathan, b. Jan. 3, 1767   1   236
Sarah, m. Jabez **NORTON**, Nov. 12, 1767   1   233
Thomas, s. [Timothy], b. May 22, 1787   1   245
Timothy, m. Ollive **NORTON**, Nov. 13, 1777   1   240
-----, wid. d. June 12, 1812, ae 90   2   395
BULLARD, Benjamin, of New Marlborough, Mass., m. Lydia **ADAMS**,
    of Goshen, May 1, 1834, by Rev. Grant Powers   M   44
BUNNELL, BUNNEL, Hiram, of Cornwall, m. Lucy **BARKER**, of
    Goshen, Sept. 10, 1826, by John Lovejoy   M   17
Joseph, of Cornwall, m. Maria **PRICE**, of Goshen, Mar. 29,
    1830, by Rev. Grant Powers   M   29
BURGE, [see under **BIRGE**]
BURR, James, of Norfolk, m. Sarah Ann **TUTTLE**, of Goshen, Oct. 15,
    1837, by Rev. John Lucky   M   52

	Vol.	Page
BURTCH, BARTCH, BIRCH, Eliza Ann, [d. Henry], b. Oct. 30, 1817	1	193
Henry, d. Apr. 5, 1813, ae 59	2	396
Henry, [s. Henry], b. Sept. 25, 1821	1	193
John Daboll, [s. Henry], b. June 6, 1826	1	193
Phebe, [d. Henry], b. Aug. 30, 1819	1	193
Rhoda, m. Asa **LUCAS**, Jan. 6, 1824, by Daniel Brayton, Elder	M	11
BUTLER, Abel, his w. [ ], d. Aug. 10, [1804], ae 69	2	392
Abel, d. Jan. 23, 1816, ae 83	2	397
Elizabeth, w. Abel, d. Sept. 3, 1776	1	235
Experience, d. Abel, b. Aug. 8, 1770	1	239
Irene, d. [Jos.], Oct. 22, 1779	1	243
Israel, s. [Abel], b. Jan. 26, 1773	1	239
Joseph, s. [Jos.], b. Apr. 3, 1784	1	243
Lucretia, d. [Jos.], b. Oct. 31, 1771	1	243
Martin, s. [Jos.], b. Apr. 10, 1778	1	243
Rhoda, d. Jos., b. Apr. 26, 1776	1	243
Salle, d. [Jos.], b. Sept. 13, 1773	1	243
Solomon, s. [Jos.], b. June 10, 1775	1	243
BUTTON, Emily, of Goshen, m. Chester **SPAULDING**, of Sheffield, Mass., Jan. 25, 1831, by Rev. Grant Powers. Int. Pub.	M	32
Lydia, m. Henry W. **THOMSON**, Jan. 1, 1826, by Rev. Walter Smith	M	15
CABLES, William, m. Almira **MAIN**, Sept. 16, 1824, by Samuel Chapin, J. P.	M	13
CADY, Armenia A., of Norfolk, m. Elias **SCOVILLE**, of Goshen, Sept. 13, 1836, by Rev. Grant Powers	M	48
Julia, of Goshen, m. Alden **MINER**, of Norfolk, Feb. 20, 1823, by Rev. Joseph Harvey	M	8
CARLISLE, Elihu, of Marion, Ala., m. Lucretia **NORTON**, of Goshen, July 28, 1840, by Rev. Grant Powers	M	58
Lucretia C. N., of Goshen, m. Samuel B. **TUTTLE**, of Hartford, Oct. 2, 1854, by Lavalette Perrin, at the house of Mrs. Myron **NORTON**	M	84
CARR, Jesse, his child d. Nov. 27, 1805, ae 3 m.	2	392
Rhoda Ann, of Goshen, m. Leman **PECK**, of Watertown, Mar. 11, 1847, by Lavalette Perrin	M	72
William T., m. Elizabeth A. **PALMER**, Sept. 6, 1846, at the house of Samuel **PALMER**, by Lavalette Perrin	M	72
CARRIER, Rufus, of Kent, m. Betsey **WEEKS**, of Goshen, Sept. 24, 1828, by Rev. Silas Ambler	M	23
Triphena, Mrs., d. Feb. 3, 1813, ae 38	2	395
CARRINGTON, Hassey, d. John, b. Aug. 28, 1768	1	236
John, m. Mable **BEECH**, Jan. 26, 1766	1	233
Martha, m. Fisk **BEECH**, Oct. 26, 1763	1	225
CARTER, Almeran M., of Paris, N. Y., m. Dolly E. **WADHAMS**, of Goshen, Sept. 26, 1836, by Rev. E. Washburn	M	49
Elizabeth, m. Benj[amin] **OVIATT**, Dec. 8, 1774	1	240

	Vol.	Page
CARTER, (cont.),		
Munson, of Virginnes, Vt., m. Eveline **BEACH**, of Goshen, Jan. 14, 1834, by Rev. George Carrington	M	43
Nath[an], s. Nathan, d. June 12, 1775	1	235
Roswell, of Buffalo, N. Y., m. Phebe **WADHAMS**, of Goshen, [Mar.] 15, 1838, by Rev. Grant Powers	M	53
Sarah, d. Dec. 1, 1823, ae 73	2	399
CASE, Bissel, s. Jonah, b. May 30, 1764	1	234
Jonah, m. Ruth **PHELPS**, June 23, 1763	1	233
[Josiah], had d. [ ], b. Apr. 22, 1770	1	238
Juliana, of Goshen, m. George A. **VARNEY**, of New York, Sept. 26, 1830, by Rev. Grant Powers. Int. Pub.	M	30
Lucia, m. John **RILEY**, Mar. 20, 1762	1	233
Martha, d. Josiah, b. Oct. 22, 1765	1	238
Mary, d. [Josiah], b. Jan. 12, 1767	1	238
CATLIN, CATLING, Anne, m. Seth **WADHAMS**, June 11, 1767	1	233
John, of Cornwall, m. Clarissa A. **MARTIN**, of Goshen, Jan. 1, 1846, by L. A. McKinstry	M	70
CAU[L]KINS, Henry H., m. Mary C. **WOOSTER**, Dec. 27, 1846, by Rev. D. L. Marks	M	72
CENTER, Nathan, m. Mary **SQUIRE**, June 22, 1774	1	240
CHAPIN, Amasa N., m. Freelove **COLLINS**, b. of Goshen, Nov. 2, 1826, by Rev. Francis H. Case	M	18
Caroline S., m. Horace **NORTON**, b. of Goshen, May 23, 1831, by Rev. Grant Powers	M	34
Joseph N., m. Harriet C. **COBB**, Apr. 27, 1837, by Rev. Aaron Hunt	M	51
Marana, m. Horatio N. **LYMAN**, b. of Goshen, May 9, 1836, by Rev. Grant Powers	M	48
Rachel E., d. Sept. 13, 1817, ae 13	2	397
Sarah C., of Goshen, m. Edwin R. **DAWLEY**, of Pleasant Valley, N. Y., Mar. 18, 1852, by Rev. David Miller	M	80
Virginia Eliza, d. Amasa N. & Freelove, b. Oct. 26, 1827	1	195
CHARD, Prudence S., b. Nov. 14, 1778; m. David **BEECHER**, June 10, 1797	1	194
CHAVALIER, SHEVALEAR, Experience, m. Henry H. **PALMER**, Nov. 15, 1846, by Lavalette Perrin	M	71
Hannah, m. Christopher **CRANDALL**, b. of Goshen, Feb. 6, 1830, by Rev. Harmon Ellis	M	28
CHEFELLE, Almira, of Canaan, m. Horatio **BEARDSLEY**, of Goshen, Nov. 10, 1823, by Rev. Joseph Harvey	M	11
CHOPIN, CHOPINS, Augustus, his child d. Feb. 27, 1820, ae 1	2	298
Samuel, his child d. Mar. 4, 1809, ae 7 d.	2	394
CHURCH, Sarah Ann, m. Zebe B. **MOORE**, b. of Goshen, Jan. 24, 1826, by David L. Parmelee, J. P.	M	16
Timothy, of Waterbury, m. Maria **ROBERTS**, of Goshen, May 4, 1836, by Rev. A. G. Wickmore	M	47
CLARK, Cornwall, of Hartland, m. Harriet **SPELMAN**, of Goshen, Oct. 9, 1836, by Albert G. Wickmore	M	49
Elijah, of Hartland, m. Sarah **ROBERTS**, of Goshen, Dec. 28, 1831, by Rev. Luther Mead	M	36

	Vol.	Page
CLARK, (cont.),		
Emily, of Goshen, m. Philo **APLEY**, of Winchester, Aug. 8, 1830, by Birdsey Baldwin, J. P.	M	30
John T., of Wethersfield, m. Jerusha L. **STODDARD**, of Goshen, Sept. 17, 1854, by John F. Norton. Int. Pub.	M	83
Lydia Ann, m. Seth G. **BROWN**, Nov. 23, 1846, by Rev. D. L. Marks	M	71
Mary Esther, [d. Sheldon & Melissa], b. Dec. 6, 1845	2	4
Sarah Alzira, [d. Sheldon & Melissa], b. Jan. 19, 1850	2	4
Truman P., m. Mary Jane **TIBBALS**, b. of Goshen, Mar. 5, 1849, by Frederick Marsh	M	75
William Lyman, [s. Sheldon & Melissa], b. Aug. 7, 1848	2	4
William T., of new Hartford, m. Chloe E. **LOBDELL**, of Brookfield, July 4, 1827, by Rev. Ebenezer Washburn	M	20
-----, Rev. his child d. Apr. 6, 1810, ae 1	2	394
CLEMMONS, Charles, m. Elizabeth **BIGELOW**, b. of Goshen, Mar. 5, 1824, by Rev. Joseph Harvey	M	12
CLEVELAND, Albert B., now of Harwinton, made affidavit Nov. 11, 1807, before Bernard E. Higgins, Notary Public, that the copy of births and marriage from the family bible of George O. **CLEVELAND**, now in possession of Philo **CLEVELAND**, of Harwinton, a son of George O. **CLEVELAND**, is correct	2	7
Albert Benjamin, [s. George O. & Jane], b. Sept. 16, 1843	2	7
George O., b. Sept. 28, 1810; m. Jane **LAMPHIE**, Feb. 9, 1832	2	7
Mary Elizabeth, [d. George O. & Jane], b. Oct. 2, 1845	2	7
CLUMMINGS, [see under **CUMMINGS**]		
COBB, Harriet C., m. Joseph N. **CHAPIN**, Apr. 27, 1837, by Rev. Aaron Hunt	M	51
COGSWELL, Sarah, of Southington, m. Palmer **BROWN**, of Goshen, Nov. 22, 1827, by Rev. Ebenezer Washburn	M	21
COLBY, COLEBY, John, his s.[ ], d. Dec. 18, 1816, ae 8	2	397
Julia A., of Goshen, m. Charles L. **PERKINS**, of Litchfield, Mar. 11, [probably 1841], by David Osborn	M	59
Lucy C., of Goshen, m. Charles L. **MUNGER**, of Litchfield, Nov. 21, 1841, by Rev. Thomas Ellis	M	61
Phebe, of Goshen, m. Philo **LOPER**, of Sharon, Jan. 24, 1841, by Rev. David Osborn	M	59
COLLINS, Amanda, d. [Cypriam], b. Mar. 27, 1759	1	262
Ambrose, his w. [ ], d. Mar. 4, 1821, ae 61	2	298
Anne, d. [Cyprian], b. Nov. 21, 1762	1	236
Anne, d. [Cyprain], b. Nov. 22, 1762	1	224
Anne, m. Moses **WADHAM**, Jan. 9, 1783	1	240
Cyprian, s. [Cyprian], b. Nov. 6, 1770	1	238
Cyprian, d. Jan. 8, 1809, ae 76	2	394
Cyprian, his child d. Dec. 10, 1818, ae 3	2	298
Cyprian, his wid.[ ], d. Aug. 23, 1823, ae 89	2	399

	Vol.	Page
COLLINS, (cont.),		
Elizabeth, of Goshen, m. Julius **BELL**, of Cornwall, Jan. 6, 1824, by Rev. Joseph Harvey	M	12
Emily, of Goshen, m. Oakley M. **HOAGLAND**, of Rushville, Ill., Oct. 30, 1837, by Rev. Grant Powers	M	52
Freelove, m. Amasa N. **CHAPIN**, b. of Goshen, Nov. 2, 1826, by Rev. Francis H. Case	M	18
Gertrude Emogene, d. John H. & Eliza C., b. Sept. 27, 1824	1	195
Harriet, m. William **MILES**, b. of Goshen, May 19, 1821, by Rev. Walter Smith, of Cornwall	M	3
Homer, m. Ann **WADHAMS**, b. of Goshen, Feb. 3, 1825, by Rev. Joseph Harvey	M	13
John H., m. Eliza C. **WASHBURN**, May 12, 1822, by Rev. Ebenezer Washburn	M	5
Lucinda, d. [Cyprian], b. Aug. 28, 1764	1	236
Lucretia, m. Haskell Gilbert **SMITH**, May 26, 1851, by Rev. N. S. Wheaton	M	79
Martha, d. [Philo], b. Sept. 1, 1789	1	243
Ollive, d. Philo, b. Sept. 19, 1783	1	243
Philo, s. Cyprain, b. Jan. 5, 1761	1	224
Philo, s. Cyprian, b. Jan. 5, 1761	1	236
Philo, m. Ollive **FOOT**, Nov. 3, 1782	1	240
Rhoda, d. [Cyprian], b. June 30, 1766	1	236
Ruth, m. Moses **LYMAN**, Jr.*, June 2, 1767 *("4th" in Hibbard's Hist.)	1	233
Timothy, s. Cyprian, b. Jan. 11, 1769	1	238
Triphena, d. Cypriam, b. Aug. 21, 1757	1	262
Trephena, m. Abraham **WADHAM**, Jan. 15, 1778	1	240
Virgil, m. Jane **LUCAS**, b. of Goshen, May 25, 1836, by Rev. Grant Powers	M	48
COLT, Anne, m. Sam[ue]l **HINMAN**, Jr., Nov. 24, 1774	1	240
COOK, Abigail, w. Lambert, d. Oct. 8, 1758	1	272
Abigail, d. Lambert, b. Jan. 25, 1761	1	263
Amasa, m. Rachel **NORTON**, Mar. 5, 1772	1	233
Amasa, d. Dec. 4, 1821, ae 72	2	399
Dan[ie]ll, s. Dan[ie]ll, b. Aug. 18, 1761	1	263
Daniel, m. Helen M. **KING**, Sept. 2, 1830, by Rev. L. P. Hichok	M	30
Darius B., of Mich., m. Jane M. **WADHAMS**, of Goshen, Aug. 11, 1841, by Rev. Thomas Ellis	M	60
Eliza, m. Salmon C. **HALL**, May 12, 1833, by Rev. David G. Tomlinson, of Milton	M	40
Hannah, m. Roger **PETTIBONE**, June 25 O. S., 1752	1	225
Hannah, m. Roger **PETTIBONE**, June 28, 1752	1	258
Hannah, d. Lem[uel], b. Dec. 25, 1763	1	224
John, s. Walter, b. Oct. 2, 1767	1	237
Joseph, s. Joseph, b. July 13, 1749	1	260
Joseph, d. Mar. 2, 1750	1	260
Joseph, s. Lem[uel], b. Feb. 25, 1762	1	224
Joseph, d. Nov. 7, 1764, ae 82 y.	1	235
Lambert, m. Mindwell **LO[O]MIS**, Dec. 13, 1757	1	269

COOK, (cont.), Vol. Page
    Lambert, his child b. June 11, 1765; d. June 12, 1765   1   235
    Lois, d. Daniell, b. Feb. 27, 1754   1   271
    Lois, m. Joel **GEULERD***, Feb. 11, 1783
      *("**GAYLORD**" (?))   1   240
    Lidia, d. Dan[ie]l, b. Oct. 29, 1756   1   273
    Mary, d. Lambert, b. July 19, 1757   1   273
    Moses, s. Daniell, b. Apr. 15, 1764   1   234
    Phebe, m. Eli **PETTIBONE**, Feb. 21, 1751   1   260
    Phillip, s. Daniel, b. Feb. 2, 1752   1   268
    Rachel, w. Amasa, d. Dec. 17, 1819, ae 68   2   298
    Salla, d. Amasa, b. Dec. 28, 1772   1   239
    Sena, d. [Walter], b. Oct. 12, 1769   1   237
    Susannah, d. [Walter], b. Feb. 26, 1770   1   237
    Walter, s. Walter, b. Sept. 10, 1764   1   234
COWLES, Howell, of Plymouth, m. Dotha **BALDWIN**, of Goshen, Oct.
    26, 1831, by Rev. Grant Powers   M   35
COY, Thomas, s. Elkanah, b. Sept. 15, 1799   1   247
CRAMER, John, of Woodbury, m. Minerva **CUMMINS**, of Goshen,
    Feb. 4, 1828, by Rev. E. Washburn   M   22
CRANDALL, Christopher, m. Hannah **CHAVALIER**, b. of Goshen,
    Feb. 6, 1830, by Rev. Harmon Ellis   M   28
    Harriet L., of Goshen, m. William L. **GRISWOLD**, of
      Litchfield, Dec. 7, 1843, by Rev. J. D. Marshall   M   64
    Hosea, of Stonington, m. Harriet **GRISWOLD**, of Goshen,
      Nov. 30, 1820, by Rev. Joseph Harvey   M   2
    Isaac, his child d. July 9, 1814, ae 1 d.   2   396
    Isaac, his s.[   ], d. July 6, 1818, ae 1 1/2   2   397
    Sarah C., m. Jonathan B. **THOMSON**, b. of Goshen, Jan. 11,
      1846, by Rev. David L. Marks   M   70
CROCKER, Abiah A., m. Joseph **SEELEY**, Mar. 26, 1837, by Albert G.
    Wickmore   M   50
CROSBY, Edwin T., of Litchfield, m. Pamelia **GARDNER**, of Goshen,
    Sept. 5, 1836, by Rev. Grant Powers   M   49
CUMMINGS, CLUMMINGS, CUMMINS, Abba Ann, of New
    Preston, m. Joshua T. **STUDLEY**, of Sharon, July
    19, 1855, by Rev. Albert G. Wickmore   M   45
    Almira, of Goshen, m. Samuel W. **SQUIRE**, of Wolcottville,
      June 26, 1844, by Rev. J. D. Marshall   M   66
    Minerva, of Goshen, m. John **CRAMER**, of Woodbury, Feb.
      4, 1828, by Rev. E. Washburn   M   22
CURTIS, CURTISS, Dorothy, d. [Joseph], b. Jan. 12, 1745   1   258
    Elias, s. [Zachariah], b. Aug. 10, 1745   1   258
    Emily, of Goshen, m. Albert **LOOMIS**, of Torrington, Nov.
      10, 1841, by Rev. Thomas Ellis   M   61
    Hannah, d. [Joseph], b. Dec. [ ], 1736; d. two days later   1   258
    Hezekiah, s. [Joseph], b. May [ ], 1735   1   258
    Hiram, m. Amanda **APLEY**, b. of Goshen, Oct. 31, 1835, by
      Rev. Thomas Sparks   M   46
    Honour, d. [Joseph], b. Sept. 12, 1740   1   258
    James, s. [Joseph], b. Feb. 10, 1743   1   258

CURTIS, CURTISS, (cont.),   Vol.   Page

	Vol.	Page
Jared, m. Olive **MAHANNAH***, July 14, 1831, by Rev. George Carrington *("**MAKANNAS**" in Hibbard's Hist.)	M	34
John, s. [Joseph], b. May 17, 1738	1	258
Joseph, s. [Joseph], b. Jan. 24, 1747	1	258
Joshua, s. Zachariah, b. Oct. 3, 1742	1	258
Mary, d. Joseph, b. May [ ], 1733	1	258
Prudence, m. Joseph **LEE**, Jan. 8, 1749/50	1	260
Satathiel, s. [Zachariah], b. July 26, 1744; d. same day	1	258
Sylva, m. Henry **KIMBERLEY**, b. of Goshen, Dec. 6, 1824, by Rev. Joseph Harvey	M	13
Worthy, m. Affa **PACKARD**, b. of Goshen, June 25, 1829, by Rev. Grant Powers. Int. Pub.	M	25
DARROW, Asa B., of Farmington, m. Sarah **GAINER**, of Goshen, Oct. 14, 1834, by Rev. Charles F. Potter	M	45
DAVIDSON, Amos, m. Temperance A. **ALLYN**, b. of Goshen, June 25, 1845, by Rev. D. L. Marks	M	68
Sarah A.*, m. Frederick M. **FOSTER**, b. of Goshen, June 11, 1845, by Rev. David L. Marks *(Written over "Sarah A. **DICKENSON**")	M	68
DAVIS, Elias, s. [Eleazer], b. Mar. 19, 1749	1	263
Eunice, m. David **LUCAS**, Jr., Sept. 25, 1850, at the house of William **DAVIS**, by Lavalette Perrin	M	77
Hannah, [d. Eleazer], b. Apr. 15, 1751	1	263
Joseph, s. [Eleazer], b. Feb. 2, 1759	1	263
Louis, s. Roger, b. Sept. 22, 1768	1	237
Margaret, [d. Eleazer], b. Feb. 9, 1757	1	263
Phebe, [d. Eleazer], b. Mar. 20, 1753	1	263
Ruth, [d. Eleazer], b. Jan. 12, 1761	1	263
Samuel, s. [Eleazer], b. Mar. 6, 1755	1	263
Sarah, m. Ebenezer **LEWIS**, June 6, 1779	1	240
DAWLEY, Edwin R., of Pleasant Valley, N. Y., m. Sarah C. **CHAPIN**, of Goshen, Mar. 18, 1852, by Rev. David Miller	M	80
DAY, Caleb, of Catskill, N. Y., m. Lucretia **LYMAN**, Jan. 18, 1826, by Rev. Darius O. Griswold, of Watertown	M	16
DEAN, Samuel, of Sharon, m. Lucy E. **ALLYN**, of Goshen, Feb. 20, 1850, at the house of Austin **ALLYN**, by Lavalette Perrin	M	76
-----, wid., d. Jan. 19, 1814, ae 81	2	396
DeFOREST, Elizabeth M., of Plymouth, m. J. W. **LANE**, of Goshen, July 3, 1842, by Rev. Thomas Ellis	M	63
John, of Watertown, m. Lucy S. **LYMAN**, of Goshen, May 17, 1831, by Rev. Grant Powers	M	34
DEMING, Elias, Dr., m. Eunice **HARRIS**, Apr. 7, 1757	1	269
Jonathan, m. Sarah **RICHMOND**, Dec. 19, 1782	1	240
Mary, d. Thomas, m. Gideon **HURLBUTT**, Dec. 30, 1725, by Daniel Goodrich, J. P.	1	255
Prudence, d. Wait & Prudence, b. Mar. 11, 1754	1	270
Prudence, w. Wait, d. Mar. 29, 1754	1	272
Stephen Harris, s. Dr. [ ], b. July 20, 1759	1	262

GOSHEN VITAL RECORDS   21

	Vol.	Page
DEMING, (cont.),		
Wait, m. Prudence **GAILERD**, Jan. 25, 1753	1	269
Wait, m. Hannah **BRYAN**, Dec. 25, 1755	1	269
Wait, s. Dr. Elias, b. May 9, 1758	1	273
DENISON, Henry D., of Groton, m. Emily **ALLYN**, of Goshen, Apr. 4,		
1830, by Rev. Harmon Ellis	M	29
William, d. Mar. 30, 1812, ae 64	2	395
William, his s. [ ], d. June 10, 1812, ae 7	2	395
William E., of Stonington, m. Mary L. **ALLEN**, of Goshen,		
[Mar.] 4, 1827, by Theren Towner, J. P.	M	19
DENNIS, Daniel, of Stratford, m. Laura **TUTTLE**, of Goshen, Dec. 10,		
1828, by Rev. E. Washburn	M	24
Silas Richmond, s. Jonathan, b. Feb. 28, 1784	1	244
DEVERICK, John, s. Jonathan, b. Aug. 28, 1755	1	273
Jonath[an], s. [Jonathan], b. [ ]	1	273
DIBBLE, DIBELL, DIBAL, David, s. John, b. Aug. 27, 1749	1	260
Harris, s. Jno, b. Apr. 15, 1756	1	273
John, Jr., m. Elizabeth **HOLLAND**, Oct. 6, 1746	1	260
John, m. Sibel **KILLBORN**, June 20, 1751	1	261
John, d. Apr. 7, 1756	1	272
Josiah, m. Sibble **PLUMB**, Mar. 18, 1756	1	269
Martha, m. Eb[enezer] **HILL**, Jan. 3, 1716/17	1	253
Mary*, m. John **WILLOUGHBY**, Oct. 2, 1728		
*(Arnold copy has "Mary **TIBELL**")	1	256
Mary, d. John, b. May 30, 1747	1	260
Rachel, d. John, b. Jan. 30, 1740	1	260
Reuben, s. John, Jr., b. Mar. 6, 1755	1	271
DICKENSON, Anne, d. [Thomas], b. Sept. 26, 1774	1	241
Anne, d. Thomas, d. Oct. 19, 1776	1	242
Charles Frederick, s. [Thomas], b. Sept. 8, 1772	1	241
Daniel, s. Tho[ma]s, b. July 7, 1768	1	241
John, s. [Thomas], b. Sept. 15, 1770	1	241
Lewis Samuell, s. [Thomas], b. May 5, 1766	1	241
Lois, d. [Thomas], b. Apr. 20, 1762	1	241
Lois, m. Sam[ue]l **WADHAM**, Mar. 23, 1780	1	240
Milo, of Cornwall, m. Esther **BROWN**, of Goshen, Apr. 15,		
1821, by Nathan Emery, Elder	M	3
Nath[anie]ll Oliver, s. [Thomas], b. May 22, 1778	1	241
Thomas, his child b. Apr. 19, 1761; d. same day	1	241
Thomas, d. Oct. 6, 1811, ae 74	2	395
Thomas Andrew, s. [Thomas], b. Feb. 16, 1774, at Norfolk	1	241
DODGE, -----, Mr. his s. [ ], d. Nov. 20, 1821, ae 4	2	399
DOLBY, Jane C., m. George **BROOKS**, b. of Goshen, Jan. 1, 1843, by		
Rev. Chester Colton	M	63
DOWD, DOUD, Ashbel, s. Jonathan, b. Aug. 6, 1759	1	262
Content, [child] of Cynthia, b. Dec. 7, [ ]	1	268
Cynthia, had child Content, b. Dec. 7, [ ]	1	268
Diantha, d. Jno, b. Sept. 7, 1764	1	236
Hepsibah, d. [Cornelius], b. Jan. 24, 1746/7	1	259
John, m. Elizabeth **NORTON**, June 4, 1763	1	240
Mabel, d. Cornelius, b. Jan. 20, 1743	1	259
Nathaniel Baley, s. [Cornelius], b. May 15, 1748	1	259

	Vol.	Page
DRAKE, Francis, of Winchester, m. Henrietta J. **HILL**, of Goshen, Dec. 13, 1850, by Frederick Marsh	M	78
DUDLEY, Samuel H., of Litchfield, m. Salome **HOWE**, of Goshen, Aug. 26, 1833, by Lawrens P. Hickok	M	41
DUNN, James, of Newton, N. Y., m. Eliza **THOMSON**, of Goshen, Apr. 18, 1827, by Rev. Francis H. Case	M	19
ELKY, Jeremiah, of Sharon, m. Cordelia **HUBBART**, of Goshen, (colored), July 9, 1829, by Rev. Grant Powers. Int. Pub.	M	25
EMMONS, Harriet, m. Isaac H. **STERLING**, b. of Goshen, Oct. 5, 1823, by Rev. Ashbel Baldwin	M	10
Samuel, m. Amanda E. **MORRIS**, of Goshen, Apr. 24, 1836, by Rev. A. G. Wickmore	M	47
FEMING*, Abigail, m. Daniel **HAYS**, Jr., Feb. 14, 1740 *("**FANING**" in Hibbard's Hist.)	1	254
FIELDS, Julius, Rev., m. Minerva **KELLOGG**, May 4, 1824, by Daniel Brayton, Elder	M	12
FITCH, Maria, of Litchfield, m. Peter **WILLIAMS**, of Goshen, Apr. 6, 1823, by Rev. Joseph Harvey	M	9
FLAGIN, Mintus, his child d. Apr. 11, [1806], ae 4	2	393
FOOG, John, of Goshen, m. Sarah **MORDEN***, of Hartford, Dec. 3, 1829, by Rev. Bradley Selleck *("**MAIDEN**" in Hibbard's Hist.)	M	27
FOOT, Laura, of Canton, b. Jan. 8, 1786; m. Lewis M. **NORTON**, s. Ebenezer, Oct. 10, 1805	1	190
Martha, m. Anson **NORTON**, Mar. 15, 1769	1	240
Ollive, m. Philo **COLLINS**, Nov. 3, 1782	1	240
FORD, Nelson D., m. Mary A. **NORTON**, Sept. 25, 1853, by Lavalette Perrin	M	82
FOSTER, Frederick M., m. Sarah A. **DAVIDSON***, b. of Goshen, June 11, 1845, by Rev. David L. Marks *(Overwritten to read "**DICKENSON**")	M	68
FOX, James L., of Cornwall, m. Emily M. **PALMER**, of Goshen, Dec. 5, 1847, at the house of William **CARR**, by Rev. Lavalette Perrin	M	74
John B., of Cornwall, m. Hannah H. **HALL**, of Goshen, May 15, 1849, at the house of wid. **HALL**, by Rev. Joshua L. Maynard, of Cornwall	M	75
FRANCIS, FRANCES, Abigail, d. Asa, b. May 23, 1762	1	224
Abigail, d. Asa, d. July 4, 1762	1	272
Amos, s. Asa, b. July 7, 1768	1	236
Asa, m. Ruth **SMITH**, July 9, 1761	1	269
Asa, s. [Asa], d. Sept. 7, 1776	1	242
Asa, d. Nov. 8, 1819, ae 83	2	298
Bill Smith, s. Asa, b. May 30, 1763	1	234
Esther, d. Dec. 15, 1812, ae 30	2	395
Joanna, d. Asa, d. Sept. 2, 1776	1	242
Joseph, s. Samuell, 2nd, b. May 1, 1771	1	238
Mary, d. Samuell, b. Oct. 8, 1766	1	236
Oliver, d. May 9, 1817, ae 14	2	397
Rhoda, d. Capt. [ ], b. Dec. 30, 1778	1	241
Ruth, w. Capt. Asa, d. Sept. 4, 1776	1	242

	Vol.	Page
FRANCIS, FRANCES, (cont.),		
Sam[ue]ll, s. Sam[ue]ll, b. Mar. 24, 1773	1	238
Samuel, 2nd, his s. [ ], b. Mar. 31, 1775	1	239
Sam[ue]l, m. Mary **PHELPS**, [ ]	1	269
Sarah, d. Sam[ue]ll, b. Oct. 14, 1760	1	263
FREEMAN, Essex, colored, his d. [ ], d. Feb. 28, [1804], ae 19	2	392
Homer, m. Mary Ann **ROE**, Dec. 3, 1829, by Rev. Grant Powers. Int. Pub.	M	27
FRISBIE, Benjamin, [twin with Joseph, s. Benjamin], b. Feb. 16, 1739	1	256
Elizabeth, d. [Benjamin], b. Nov. 12, 1732	1	256
Elizabeth, d. [Benjamin], d. Aug. 28, 1739	1	256
Hephzibeth, d. Benjamin, b. Oct. 19, 1726	1	256
Jabez, s. [Benjamin], b. Nov. 30, 1730	1	256
James, s. [Benjamin], b. Oct. 29, 1728	1	256
Jerusha, d. [Benjamin], b. Feb. 25, 1735	1	256
Joseph, [twin with Benjamin, s. Benjamin], b. Feb. 16, 1739	1	256
Joseph, s. [Benjamin], d. Aug. 28, 1739	1	256
Joseph, s. [Benjamin], b. Jan. 3, 1741	1	256
Lucinda, d. Jan. 28, 1817, ae 20	2	397
Mary, d. [Benjamin], b. Feb. 23, 1737	1	256
Phebe, d. Aug. 24, 1819, ae 24	2	298
Zebolon, [s. Zebelon], b. May 2, 1751/2	1	268
GAINER, [see also **GARNER**], Abby*, [d. Hiram], b. Apr. 12, 1833 *("Abby **GARNER**"?)	2	3
Sarah, of Goshen, m. Asa B. **DARROW**, of Farmington, Oct. 14, 1843, by Rev. Charles F. Potter	M	45
GALLUP, Dwight, of Ledyard, m. Lydia A. **WADHAMS**, of Goshen, Nov. 19, 1849, at the house of Lewis C. **WADHAMS**, by Lavalette Perrin	M	76
GARDNER, Pamelia, of Goshen, m. Edwin T. **CROSBY**, of Litchfield, Sept. 5, 1836, by Rev. Grant Powers	M	49
GARNER, [see also **GAINER**], Eliza, m. John D. **BARTON**, Apr. 3, 1851, at the house of Erastus **LYMAN**, by Lavalette Perrin	M	78
Hiram, m. Rachel C. **REED**, b. of Cornwall, Jan. 31, 1825, by Rev. Arnold Scholfield	M	14
GAYLORD, GAILERD, GEULERD, GEULORD, Charles Henry, [s. Willard & Amy], b. Mar. 7, 1833	2	1
Frederick, [s. Joseph J. & Clarissa], b. Mar. 17, 1830	2	4
Joel, s. Timothy, b. Nov. 8, 1755	1	271
Joel, m. Lois **COOK**, Feb. 11, 1783	1	240
Joseph, s. Sam[ue]ll, b. Aug. 20, 1738	1	253
Joseph, s. Dan[ie]l, b. Aug. 20, 1738	1	258
Joseph, s. Timothy, b. Apr. 24, 1758	1	273
Joseph J., m. Clarissa **NORTON**, b. of Goshen, Nov. 20, 1821, by Rev. Joseph Harvey	M	4
Lois, d. [Timothy], b. Dec. 22, 1751	1	270
Lois*, m. Samuel **BISHOP**, Dec. 13, 1770 *(Written "Lois **GUILERD**")	1	233
Lois, see Lois **GUILERD**	1	233
Mary L., m. Moses W. **GRAY**, May 22, 1850, at the house of Joseph J. **GAYLORD**, by Lavalette Perrin	M	77

	Vol.	Page
GAYLORD, GAILERD, GEULERD, GEULORD, (cont.),		
Mary Lorain, [d. Joseph J. & Clarissa], b. Aug. 8, 1824	2	4
Myron C., of Norfolk, m. Sarah E. **LUCAS**, of Goshen, Jan. 8, 1843, by Rev. Adam Reed	M	63
Polly, d. [Joel & Lois], b. Aug. 14, 1785	1	242
Prudence, m. Wait **DEMING**, Jan. 25, 1753	1	269
Ruth, d. Timothy, b. Sept. 25, 1753	1	270
Salla, d. Joel & Lois, b. Nov. 16, 1783	1	242
Titus, s. Timothy, b. Dec. 27, 1749	1	270
Willard E., m. Sarah E. **WOOSTER**, May 14, 1851, at the house of Sterling **WOOSTER**, by Lavalette Perrin	M	79
Willard Eleazer, [s. Willard & Amy], b. Mar. 26, 1827	2	1
GAYNOR, see under **GAINER**		
GIBBONS, Larkin Green, s. Lemuel & Vadeia, b. Jan. 3, 1795	1	193
GIBBS, Jabez, m. Mary **APLEY**, b. of Goshen, Apr. 4, 1833, by Rev. George Carrington	M	40
GIBSON, GIPSON, Hanah, d. Jonathan, b. Feb. 1, 1745/6	1	259
Jonathan, twin with Mary, s. Jonathan, b. Mar. 21, 1748; d. Apr. 22, 1748	1	259
Mary, twin with Jonathan, d. Jonathan, b. Mar. 21, 1748; d. Apr. 3, 1748	1	259
Mary, d. Jonathan, b. Aug. 11, 1749	1	261
Samuel, s. Jonathan, b. Apr. 30, 1744	1	256
GILLETT, [E]unice, m. David **IVES**, Mar. 25, 1761	1	225
-----, Mr. his child d. Oct. 10, 1822, ae 1	2	399
GILMER, Elizabeth, m. Jeremiah **McKENERY**, Nov. 7, 1850, at the house of Daniel **McKENERY**, by Lavalette Perrin	M	78
GLASS, Cyrenus, b. James, b. Dec. 8, 1773	1	239
Heman, s. James, b. Apr. 24, 1775	1	241
James, m. Ruth **BASSETT**, Aug. 29, 1771	1	233
Rufus, s. James, b. June 28, 1772	1	239
Sarah, d. James, b. July 27, 1777	1	241
GODDARD, Elizabeth N., of Goshen, m. Samuel **HURLBURT** of Baltimore, Md., July 23, 1845, by Frederick Marsh	M	68
Joseph, of New York, m. Elizabeth Marana **NORTON**, of Goshen, Nov. 23, 1825, by Ralph Emerson	M	15
GOODWIN, Abigail, d. Step[hen], b. Aug. 8, 1752	1	270
Abigail, m. Ezekiel **NORTH**, Mar. 4, 1773	1	240
Karena, m. Seth **HILLS**, July 17, 1783	1	240
GOULD, Dan, s. Jno, d. Aug. 2, 1769	1	235
Daniel, s. Jno, b. June 16 or 20, 1769	1	238
Jno, m. Hannah **RICHMOND**, Dec. 20, 1768	1	233
Lydia, d. [Jno], b. Jan. 7, 1770	1	238
GRANT, Bathsheba, m. Zimri **HILL**, May 28, 1752	1	269
Triphena, m. Abijah **NORTH**, Sept. 6, 1764	1	233
GRAY, Moses W., m. Mary L. **GAYLORD**, May 22, 1850, at the house of Joseph J. **GAYLORD**, by Lavalette Perrin	M	77
GRIFFIN, Nehemiah, of Plymouth, m. Clarissa **TUTTLE**, of Goshen, Jan. 6, 1830, by Rev. Bradley Selleck	M	28
GRIMES, Abraham, s. Christopher, d. July 8, 1739	1	254
Abraham, s. Christopher, b. July 3, 1745	1	257
Comfort, d. [Christopher], b. May 14, 1740	1	254

	Vol.	Page
GRIMES, (cont.),		
Honor, d. [Christopher], d. July 27, 1739, in the 13th y. of her age	1	254
Lucretia, d. [Christopher], d. Sept. 4, 1739, in the 3rd y. of her age	1	254
Sarah, d. [Christopher], b. Aug. 14, 1742	1	257
GRISWOLD, Alexander D., his s. [ ], b. Oct. 18, 1760	1	234
Clarissa, m. Eben **NORTON**, b. of Goshen, Apr. 29, 1834, by Rev. Grant Powers	M	44
Darius D., his s. [ ], b. Jan. 15, 1764	1	234
Elvira, of Milton, m. Nelson **WADHAMS**, of Goshen, June 13, 1837	M	51
Giles, m. Mary **STANLEY**, Oct. 28, 1762	1	233
Giles, s. Lieut. Giles, b. May 18, 1774	1	241
Giles, d. Mar. 7, 1817, ae 82	2	397
Hannah, m. David **THOMSON**, Nov. 26, 1766	1	225
Hannah, d. Giles, b. Apr. 13, 1767	1	237
Harriet, of Goshen, m. Hosea **CRANDALL**, of Stonington, Nov. 30, 1820, by Rev. Joseph Harvey	M	2
John, s. Giles, b. Jan. 10, 1722	1	239
Mary, d. Giles, b. July 7, 1765	1	234
Oliver, s. [Zacheus, Jr.], b. Nov. 16, 1757	1	234
Sarah, m. William **NORTON**, b. of Goshen, Mar. 14, 1839, by Nelson Brewster, J. P.	M	55
Sarah A., m. Putnam **BAILEY**, b. of Goshen, Mar. 12, 1829, by Stephen Mason	M	24
Thomas, s. Giles, b. July 29, 1763	1	234
William L., of Litchfield, m. Harriet L. **CRANDALL**, of Goshen, Dec. 7, 1843, by Rev. J. D. Marshall	M	64
Zacheus, Jr., m. Eunice **STANLEY**, Mar. 13, 1755	1	225
Zacheus, Jr., his 1st s. [ ], b. Mar. 6, 1756; bd. next day	1	234
Zacheus, his w. [ ], d. Dec. 15, [1805], ae 74	2	392
Zacheus, his wid., d. Jan. 10, 1806, ae 99	2	393
GROSS, Harvey H., of Poughkepsie, N. Y., m. Ann S. **PRICE**, of Goshen, Aug. 28, 1836, by Rev. Albert G. Wickmore	M	48
GUNN, Delia A., of Naugatuck, m. Horace T. **LEONARD**, of Goshen, June 16, 1844, by Rev. Chester Colton	M	65
HALE, [see also **HALL**], Adino, s. [Justus], b. Apr. 24, 1754	1	263
Justus, s. [Justus], b. Nov. 11, 1761	1	263
Justus, his wid. [ ], d. July 17, [1812], ae 83	2	395
Nathan, d. Sept. 6, 1813, ae 71	2	396
Nathan, his wid., d. Sept. 16, 1813, ae 59	2	396
Pallos, d. July 27, 1806, ae 15	2	393
Sarah, d. [Justus], b. Jan. 19, 1758	1	263
Timothy, s. Justus, b. Dec. 18, 1755	1	263
HALL, [see also **HALE**], Asaph, m. Hannah G. **PALMER**, b. of Goshen, Jan. 29, 1829, by Stephen Mason	M	24
Curtis, m. Martha **HURD**, May 12, 1851, at the house of Stephen **HURD**, by Lavalette Perrin	M	79
Elisha, s. Titus, b. July 8, 1759	1	262
Eunice, d. John, b. July 12, 1775	1	241

	Vol.	Page
HALL, [see also **HALE**], (cont.), Hannah H., of Goshen, m. John B. **FOX**, of Cornwall, May 15, 1849, at the house of wid. **HALL**, by Rev. Joshua L. Maynard, of Cornwall	M	75
Mindwell, m. Titus **HILL**, Dec. 13, 1750	1	260
Salmon C., m. Eliza **COOK**, May 12, 1833, by Rev. David G. Tomlinson, of Milton	M	40
Simeon, s. [John], b. Oct. 12, 1777	1	241
HALLOCK, Dudley F., m. Ann M. **BAILEY**, b. of Goshen, Dec. 15, 1830, by Rev. George Carrington	M	31
Julia, m. Junius **BALDWIN**, b. of Goshen, Sept. 14, 1828, by Frederick Marsh	M	26
Lydia, m. William **HURD**, Apr. 5, 1827, by Rev. Francis H. Case	M	19
HARD, Abner, of Milton, Soc., m. Catharine **WADHAMS**, of Goshen, Oct. 30, 1833, by Rev. Grant Powers	M	42
HARRIS, Abigail, d. Daniel, b. Jan. 29, 1747/8	1	258
Abigail, w. Daniel, d. Feb. 3, 1747/8	1	258
Daniel, s. Daniel, Jr., b. May 11, 1741	1	254
Eunice, m. Dr. Elias **DEMING**, Apr. 7, 1757	1	269
Hannah, d. Daniel, b. Apr. 24, 1743	1	255
Hopestill, d. Daniel, Jr., b. Apr. 18, 1743	1	257
Moses, m. Dorothy **WEST**, Mar. 20, 1746	1	257
Moses, s. [Moses & Dorothy], b. Nov. 8, 1746	1	257
HARRISON, Harriet, A., m. Eli **BARNES**, Oct. 3, 1841, by Nelson Brewster, J. P.	M	60
Heman, m. Mary E. **JUDD**, Apr. 7, 1844, by Rev. Lavalette Perrin	M	65
HART, Alice, d. [Reuben & Ruth], b. Nov. 28, 1790	1	248
Amanda, d. [Reuben & Ruth], b. Feb. 28, 1793	1	248
Amanda, of Goshen, m. Alva **WIX**, of Warren, May 21, 1823, by Rev. Joseph Harvey	M	9
Betsey, of Goshen, m. Deman **WEEKS**, of Warren, Oct. 17, 1822, by Rev. Joseph Harvey	M	6
Elias, of Goshen, m. Julia Ann **PAGE**, of Warren, Jan. 20, 1830, by Rev. Grant Powers	M	28
Jane, of Goshen, m. William **MARTIN**, of Norfolk, Nov. 1, 1854, by Rev. G. A. McKinstry	M	84
Laura Ann, of Goshen, m. John N. **WHITING**, of Torrington, Nov. 5, 1851, by Rev. L. A. McKinstry	M	80
Levi, d. [sic] Reuben & Ruth, b. July 17, 1788	1	248
Seely, m. Jennette **SEELYE**, b. of Goshen, Sept. 27, 1854, by D. W. Lounsbury	M	84
HAWKINS, Mary M., m. Joseph A. **WOOSTER**, b. of Goshen, Nov. 19, 1840, by Grant Powers	M	58
HAY, [see under **HAYS**]		
HAYDEN, [see also **HEIGHTON**], Augustus, of Plymouth, m. Harriet **BROWN**, of Kent, Jan. 1, 1828, by Rev. E. Washburn	M	22
Emily, of Litchfield, m. John **O'NEILL**, of Goshen, [ ], 1840, in Litchfield	2	5
Sarah*, m. Moses **LYMAN**, Mar. 24, 1742 *(Arnold Copy has "Sarah **HEIGHTON**")	1	256

	Vol.	Page
HAYS, [see also HOY], Daniel, Jr., m. Abigail FEMING*, Feb. 14, 1740 *("FANNING" in Hibbard's Hist.)	1	254
Zopher B., m. Sarah L. HUMPHREY, Mar. 6, 1830, by Rev. George Carrington	M	30
HEATON, Hannah, m. John THOMSON, Jan. 31, 1754	1	269
Mary, d. Rev. Stephen, b. Jan. 3, 1746	1	258
Sarah, of Goshen, m. Harry JOHNSON, of New Haven, Sept. 15, 1828, by Rev. Francis H. Case	M	23
Stephen, Rev. m. Mrs. Mary MARSH, Aug. 11, 1741	1	254
HECOCK, William, his w. [ ], d. Feb. 16, 1805, ae 31	2	392
HEIGHTON*, [see also HAYDEN], Sarah, b. Sept. 17, 1716; m. Capt. Moses LYMAN, Mar. 24, 1742 *(Supplied from Hibbard's Hist.)	1	263
Sarah, m. Moses LYMAN, Mar. 24, 1742 *("HAYDEN" in Hibbard's Hist.)	1	256
HERTER*, [E]unice, m. Michael BEACH, Aug. 7, 1773 *("HESTER" in Hist. of Goshen)	1	240
HILL, HILLS, Abigail, m. Jared JONES, Sept. 20, 1773	1	240
Abigail, of Goshen, m. Nelson S. LOOMIS, of Cornwall, Nov. 7, 1827, by David Parmelee, J. P.	M	21
Ambrose, s. Elenezer, Jr., b. Mar. 21, 1744	1	255
Ambrose, m. Lucia BEECH, Oct. 10, 1764	1	255
Anne, m. Luman BEECH, Feb. 2, 1764	1	255
Anne, m. Luman BEECH, Feb. 2, 1764	1	233
Anne, wid., her s. [ ], d. Dec. 15, 1816, ae 2	2	397
Arunah, s. Titus, b. Apr. 16, 1754	1	270
Asa, s. [Ebenezer & Martha], b. Nov. 22, 1719	1	253
Asa, m. Elizabeth RICHARDS, Mar. 13, 1745	1	257
Augustus, s. Zimri & Bathsheba, b. July [ ], 1752	1	270
Augustus, s. Zimri, b. July 23, 1752	1	270
Augustus, s. Augustus [& Phebe], b. Nov. 4, 1777	1	248
Augustus, d. Apr. 18, 1811, ae 55	2	395
Benjamin, of Torrington, m. Mary PRINCE, of Goshen, Jan. 6, 1831, by Rev. George Carrington	M	32
Billious, m. Lydia BIRGE, Aug. 9, 1758	1	269
Cloe, d. Ebenezer, Jr., b. Feb. 19, 1754	1	270
Cloe, d. Billious, b. Mar. 14, 1759	1	262
Dan., s. [Ebenezer], b. June 14, 1734	1	253
Dan, m. Hannah MATTHEWS, Dec. 20, 1757	1	269
David, s. Asa, b. Oct. 31, 1748	1	260
David, s. Asa, d. Apr. 7, 1749	1	260
Eb[enezer], m. Martha DIBAL, Jan. 3, 1716/17	1	253
Eb[enezer], s. Eb[enezer] & Martha, b. Oct. 24, 1717	1	253
Ebenezer, Jr., m. Elizabeth BALDWIN, May 27, 1741	1	254
Ebenezer, s. Ebenezer, Jr., b. Aug. 27, 1746	1	258
Ebenezer, s. Ebenezer, Jr., d. Mar. 3, 1753	1	272
Ebenezer, s. Eb[enezer], Jr., b. Nov. 4, 1756	1	273
Elizabeth, d. Asa, b. Oct. 28, 1751	1	261
Erastus, s. [Augustus & Phebe], b. May 8, 1785	1	248
George A., m. Harriet BAILEY, b. of Goshen, Apr. 6, 1830, by Rev. Bradley Selleck	M	29

HILL, HILLS, (cont.) Vol. Page
Hannah, m. Ephraim **STEER***, Nov. 13, 1769 *(Written
  over "**STARR**") 1 233
Henrietta J., of Goshen, m. Francis **DRAKE** of Wnchester,
  Dec. 13, 1850, by Frederick Marsh M 78
Henry, s. Zimri, d. Dec. 9, 1819, ae 9 2 298
Huldah, d. [Ebenezer], b. Nov. 15, 1736; d. Sept. 6, 1737 1 253
Hulda, d. Eben[eze]r, b. June 4, 1742 1 255
Huldah, m. Benj[amin]**REVES**, Jan. 31, 1764 1 233
Ira, s. Zenas, b. July 17, 1755 1 271
Jaldiack, s. Zenas, b. Nov. 10, 1753 1 270
Jane, of Goshen, m. Marcus R. **SPRING**, of Derby, July 31,
  1845, by Rev. D. L. Marks M 69
John, m. Mary **RITCHARDS**, Mar. 1, 1747 1 261
John, s. John, b. Apr. 12, 1748 1 259
John, m. Jerusha **LEWIS**, Sept. 10, 1754 1 269
Jonah, s. Asa, b. Jan. 15, 1745/6 1 257
Junis, s. John, b. Oct. 21, 1762 1 234
Keziah, m. Zenas **HILL**, Dec. 21, 1752 1 269
Lamela, d. Augustus & Phebe, b. Nov. 16, 1775 1 248
Lois, d. Titus, b. Apr. [ ], 1766 1 236
Lois, d. Titus, d. July 13, 1766 1 235
Louisa, d. [   ], b. Aug. 5, 1767 1 236
Lucina, d. Ebenezer, b. July 29, 1761 1 224
Luke, s. [Ebenezer], b. Apr. 2, 1732 1 253
Lydia, s. Billin[g]s, b. Sept. 30, 1769 1 238
Martha, d. Ebenezer & Martha, b. Feb. 17, 1724 1 253
Martha, d. Jno, b. June 13, 1753 1 270
Martha, d. Asa, b. Jan. 16, 1759 1 262
Mary, d. John, b. Feb. 25, 1751 1 261
Mary, w. Jno, d. June 22, 1753 1 272
Mary, w. Uri, d. May 15, 1762 1 272
Mary, d. Velus, b. Jan. 8, 1763 1 234
Maryann, d. Uri, b. Feb. 3, 1766 1 241
Mary N., of Goshen, m. Frederick P. **WHITING**, of
  Torrington, Feb. 15, 1826, by Rev. Francis H. Case M 16
Medad, m. Sarah **SMITH**, Dec. 5, 1751 1 268
Medad & Sarah, had s. [   ], b. July 19, 1752 1 268
Medad, Col., d. Apr. 9, 1808, ae 78 2 394
Miles, d. Mar. 10, 1815, ae 48 2 396
Nancy, d. Titus, b. Mar. 23, 1757 1 273
Phebe, d. [Augustus & Phebe], b. Feb. 9, 1788 1 248
Rachel, m. Dr. Joel **SOPER**, July 26, 1762 1 225
Rebecca, her child d. Jan. 20, 1814, ae 13 2 396
Reuben, s. Ebenezer, Jr., b. May 26, 1751 1 261
Reuben, s. Medad, b. June 15, 1764 1 234
Reuben, s. Ambrose, b. Jan. 19, 1765 1 234
Reuben, s. Ebenezer, d. Mar. 29, 1765 1 235
Samuel, s. Ebenezer, Jr., b. Oct. 6, 1748 1 259
Sam[ue]l, s. Ebenezer, d. Oct. 7, 1766 1 235
Sarah, d. John & Jerusha, b. Nov. 26, 1755 1 270
Sarah, d. Asa, b. Sept. 6, 1760 1 224
Seth, s. [Uri], b. Aug. 24, 1759 1 273

	Vol.	Page
HILL, HILLS, (cont.),		
Seth, m. Karena **GOODWIN**, July 17, 1783	1	240
Silvy, d. Uri, b. Feb. 9, 1757	1	273
Statira, d. Seth, b. July 6, 1762	1	224
Timothy, s. [Augustus & Phebe], b. Feb. 22, 1780	1	248
Titus, s. [Ebenezer & Martha], b. Mar. 22, 1726	1	253
Titus, m. Mindwell **HALL**, Dec. 13, 1750	1	260
Titus, s. Silas, b. Apr. 1, 1752	1	268
Uri, m. Mary **ROOT**, Mar. 15, 1756	1	269
Uri, s. Zenas, b. Nov. 18, 1757	1	273
Uri, s. [Uri], b. Aug. 19, 1760	1	273
Uri, m. Hannah **BEECH**, Oct. 20, 1764	1	225
William, his infant s. [ ], b. Mar. 31, 1761; d. Apr. 14, next	1	263
Zenas, s. Ebenezer & Martha, b. Jan. 4, 1730	1	253
Zenas, m. Keziah **HILL**, Dec. 21, 1752	1	269
Zimri, m. Bathsheba **GRANT**, May 28, 1752	1	269
Zimri, d. June 4, 1760	1	272
Zimri, d. Sept. 10, 1819, ae 38	2	298
-----, wid. [ ], d. Dec. 1, [1806], ae 70	2	393
HINMAN, Asel, [twin with Asher], s. [Samuel], b. Mar. 13, 1742	1	255
Asher, [twin with Asel], s. [Samuel], b. Mar. 13, 1742	1	255
Grove, his child d. Dec. 5, [1807], ae 4	2	393
Joseph, s. [Samuel], b. Mar. 7, 1738	1	255
Mary, [twin with Samuel], d. [Samuel], b. July 26, 1736	1	255
Miles, s. [Samuel, 2nd], b. Oct. 25, 1776	1	239
Phinehas, s. [Samuel], b. Mar. 31, 1740	1	255
Phineas, his w. [ ], d. Aug. 19, 1819, ae 78	2	298
Sam[ue]l, [twin with Mary], s. [Samuel], b. July 26, 1736	1	255
Sam[ue]l, Jr., m. Anne **COLT**, Nov. 24, 1774	1	240
Sam[ue]l, s. Sam[ue]l, 2nd, b. May 4, 1775	1	239
Sarah, d. Samuel, b. July 5, 1731	1	255
William, s. [Samuel], b. June 8, 1733	1	255
HOAGLAND, Oakley M., of Rushville, Ill., m. Emily **COLLINS**, of Goshen, Oct. 30, 1837, by Rev. Grant Powers	M	52
HOLBERD, [see under **HURLBUTT**]		
HOLBROOK, Huldah, m. Leverett **IVES**, Nov. 26, 1822, by Rev. Joseph Harvey	M	7
Mary, m. Isaac **THOMSON**, b. of Goshen, Jan. 21, 1830, by Rev. Grant Powers	M	28
HOLCOMB, HOLCOM, Luther, s. Mathew **HOLCOM** & Lydia **PORTER**, b. July 26, 1740; d. Mar. 28, 1741	1	254
Sarah, m. Samuell **THOMSON**, Jr., Oct. 29, 1744	1	257
HOLLAND, Elizabeth, m. John **DIBELL**, Jr., Oct. 6, 1746	1	260
HOLLEY, Alexander H., of Salisbury, m. Jane M. **LYMAN**, of Goshen, Oct. 4, 1831, by Rev. Grant Powers	M	35
Mary Ann, d. John M. & Sally Porter, m. Moses **LYMAN**, s. Moses & Elizabeth, May 6, 1834, in Salisbury, by Rev. L. E. Lathrop	2	6
HOLMES, Lebbeus, his w. [ ], d. May 8, [1807], ae 55	2	393
Levi, s. Lebbeus, b. July 24, 1797	1	247
Lucinda Wolmot, d. Lebbeus & Sarah, b. Mar. 17, 1794	1	247

	Vol.	Page
HOLMES, (cont.),		
Mary*, m. Jonathan **BUEL**, 2nd, Jan. 14, 1845, by Lavalette Perrin *(Overwritten to read "Jane")	M	66
HONE*, Philo, m. Lucy C. **WOOSTER**, May 24, 1835, by Rev. Albert G. Wickmore *("**HOWE**"?)	M	46
HOPKINS, Abigail, m. Miles **BEECH**, Jan. 3, 1771	1	233
Mark, s. Lem[ue]ll, b. Mar. 1, 1778	1	241
Mark, his child d. Mar. 5, 1807, ae 7 m.	2	393
Molly, d. Samuell, b. Nov. 16, 1775	1	239
HOSMER, Eliza, m. Truman **BEACH**, b. of Goshen, Dec. 30, 1832, by Rev. George Carrington	M	39
HOTCHKISS, Martha L., m. Lamon* L. **MORRIS**, Nov. 7, 1849, at the house of Jesse **HOTCHKISS**, by Lavalette Perrin *(Overwritten to read "Lyman". Hibbard has "Lauren")	M	75
HOUGH, David, s. Ebenezer, b. Aug. 21, 1752	1	268
Eunice, d. Eben, b. May 4, 1754	1	270
HOWE, HOW, Anna, d. [John], b. Apr. 10, 1762	1	224
Armenia, of Goshen, m. Austin **KELLOGG**, of Smithfield, Pa., July 29, 1821, by Rev. Ebenezer Washburn	M	4
Birdsey T., m. Paithena **ALLYN**, Sept. 7, 1835, by Rev. Albert G. Wickmore	M	46
Deliverance, s. John, b. June 25, 1764	1	234
Elisha, [twin with Joel], s. Ens. Jesse, b. Aug. 8, 1762	1	224
Elizabeth, m. Dan[ie]ll **NORTON**, May 29, 1762	1	225
Esther, m. David **MERRILS**, Nov. 26, 1761	1	233
Experience, d. John, b. Dec. 27, 1759	1	224
Jaazamiah*, July 5, 1816, ae 79 *("Zachariah")	2	397
Jere, m. Martha **NORTH**, Aug. 6, 1761	1	269
Joel, [twin with Elisha], s. Ens. Jesse, b. Aug. 8, 1762	1	224
John, m. Mary **WADDAMS**, Apr. [ ], 1756	1	269
John, m. Lydia **NORTON**, Apr. 15, 1766	1	233
John, s. John, b. Apr. 23, 1767	1	236
Jos., m. Prudence **NORTON**, Oct. 24, 1768	1	233
Joseph, d. Apr. 17, 1807, ae 61	2	393
Judeth, m. Jonathan **WADDAMS**, Aug. 8, 1754	1	269
Lyman, of Canaan, m. Sarah **SMITH**, of Goshen, Jan. 2, 1840, by Benjamin Sedgwick, J. P.	M	56
Mary, w. John, d. Sept. 30, 1765	1	235
Melzer, s. Joseph, b. Oct. 19, 1772	1	239
Philo, d. Apr. 28, 1823, ae 47	2	399
Philo*(?), m. Lucy C. **WOOSTER**, May 24, 1835, by Rev. Albert G. Wickmore *("Arnold Copy has "Philo **HONE**")	M	46
Ruth, d. Jeremiah, b. Oct. 4, 1748	1	259
Ruth, m. Roger **ORVIS**, Feb. 27, 1766	1	233
Salome, of Goshen, m. Samuel H. **DUDLEY**, of Litchfield, Aug. 26, 1833, by Lawrens P. Hickok	M	41
HOY, [see also **ROYCE & HAYS**], Alexander, s. John, b. Mar. 14, 1761	1	224
Ann, Mrs., d. Mar. 4, 1822, ae 84	2	399
Elisha*, s. Jno, b. July 31, 1768 *("Elisha **ROYS**"?)	1	238
John, m. Anne **WADHAM**, Nov. 9, 1760	1	233
-----, Mr., d. Sept. 14, 1805, ae 74	2	392

	Vol.	Page
HUBBART, Cordelia, of Goshen, m. Jeremiah **ELKY**, of Sharon, (colored), July 9, 1829, by Rev. Grant Powers. Int. Pub.	M	25
HUDSON, David, Jr., m. Anne **NORTON**, Dec. 23, 1783	1	240
David Norton, s. [David, Jr. & Anne], b. Feb. 27, 1794; d. Aug. 25, 1796	1	249
Ira, s. David, Jr., b. Sept. 19, 1787	1	245
Laura, d. David, Jr. & Anne, b. June 30, 1798	1	249
Milo, s. [David, Jr. & Anne], b. Oct. 15, 1791	1	248
Milo, s. [David, Jr. & Anne], b. Oct. 15, 1792	1	249
Samuel, s. David, Jr., b. Apr. 4, 1785	1	242
Timothy, s. David, Jr. & Anne, b. May 20, 1726	1	249
William, s. David, Jr. & Anne, b. Nov. 8, 1789	1	248
William, s. [David, Jr. & Anne], b. Nov. 8, 1791	1	249
-----, Mrs., d. Jan. 30, 1805, ae 74	2	392
HUMASON, HUMISTON, Arentia* C., m. Seth T. **NORTON**, Dec. 23, 1845, at the house of Giles **GRISWOLD**, by Lavalette Perrin *("Aurelia" in Hibbard's Hist.)	M	69
Rhoda, of Harwinton, m. Harvey **JOHNSON**, of Sharon, July 15, 1823, by Alfred Walter, J. P.	M	10
HUMPHREY, Abner, s. [Thomas], b. Jan. 10, 1767	1	237
Abraham, s. [Isaac], b. Mar. 1, 1763	1	242
Carloss, s. Thomas, b. Apr. 2, 1733	1	241
Charles, s. Sam[ue]ll, b. Feb. 13, 1742/3	1	257
Charles, his w. [ ], d. Feb. 20, 1810, ae 71	2	394
David, s. David, b. Feb. 16, 1758	1	263
David, d. Mar. 16, 1814, ae 88	2	396
David, his d. [ ], d. Mar. 12, 1823, ae 37	2	399
Deliverance, m. John **SMEDLEY**, Aug. 8, 1753	1	269
Electa, [d. Isaac], b. July 18, 1778	1	242
Elizabeth, d. [Isaac], b. Apr. 7, 1776	1	242
Esther, d. [Isaac], b. Apr. 28, 1769	1	242
Ethan, [s. Isaac], b. Apr. 24, 1765	1	242
Guy, s. [Isaac], b. July 11, 1786	1	242
Horace, of Goshen, m. Clarissa B. **BAILEY**, of Goshen, Sept. 18, 1832, by Rev. George Carrington	M	38
Isaac, s. [Isaac], b. June 26, 1761	1	242
Jonathan, s. [Isaac], b. Mar. 21, 1771	1	242
Lois, d. Sam[ue]ll, b. Aug. 26, 1745	1	257
Lois m. Horatio **NORTON**, Sept. 5, 1822, by Rev. Joseph Hawley	M	6
Lucia, d. David, b. May 23, 1767	1	236
Lucy, d. June 3, 1817, ae 29	2	397
Lydia, d. David, b. Apr. 8, 1774	1	239
Malinda, m. Nelson **OVIATT**, b. of Goshen, Oct. 8, 1820, by Rev. Joseph Harvey	M	1
Mary M., m. Asahel **BAILEY**, b. of Goshen, Sept. 7, 1828, by Rev. George Carrington	M	23
Nancy, d. [Thomas], b. Apr. 30, 1778	1	241
Noah, s. Sam[ue]ll, b. Nov. 21, 1747	1	258
Noah, d. June 10, 1819, ae 71	2	298
Noah, his w. [ ], d. Sept. 8, 1821, ae 40	2	298

	Vol.	Page
HUMPHREY, (cont.),		
Noah, his s. [ ], d. July 28, 1822, ae 7 m.	2	399
Obed M., m. Mary Ann **POOLER**, b. of Goshen, Oct. 29, 1833, by Rev. Grant Powers	M	42
Olliver, s. Simeon, b. Mar. 29, 1786	1	242
Roseannah, d. [Isaac], b. Sept. 14, 1767	1	242
Roswell, [s. Isaac], b. June 22, 1774	1	242
Ruby, d. Isaiah, d. Oct. 14, 1809, ae 18	2	394
Russell, s. Thomas, b. Jan. 23, 1765	1	237
Sam[ue]ll, s. Isaac, b. Aug. 31, 1759	1	242
Samuel, Ens., d. Oct. 16, 1759	1	272
Sarah L., m. Zopher B. **HAYS**, Mar. 6, 1830, by Rev. George Carrington	M	30
Silas, m. Mary C. **BAILEY**, b. of Goshen, Dec. 20, 1822, by Rev. Joseph Harvey	M	80
Simeon, s. [David], b. Dec. 8, 1760	1	263
Thomas, s. [Thomas], b. Oct. 5, 1775	1	241
Uriah, s. David, b. Nov. 1, 1763	1	224
Van Rensalaer, m. Stella **BEACH**, b. of Goshen, Apr. 12, 1821, by Rev. Joseph Harvey	M	3
William, s. [Isaac], b. June 5, 1783	1	242
HUNGERFORD, Philenda, b. Dec. 19, 1785	2	18
Philenda, m. Norman **WADHAMS**, Aug. 18, 1822	2	18
HUNT, Aaron, Rev. of Sharon, m. Nancy **THOMSON**, of Goshen, Apr. 12, 1832, by Rev. Laban Clark	M	37
HUNTER, James, m. Elizabeth **STEWART**, b. of Goshen, Dec. 1, 1843, by Rev. J. D. Marshall	M	64
HUNTLEY, Seth P., m. Lucy **NORVEL**, b. of Goshen, Mar. 4, 1838, by Rev. Asahel Gaylord	2	395
HURD, Benjamin, his child d. Oct. 6, 1812, ae 1	2	395
Jane A., m. William **PLATT**, b. of Goshen, Mar. 20, 1845, by Rev. Chester Colton	M	67
Maria, m. Francis **BEACH**, Jr., Dec. 25, 1823, by Rev. Joseph Harvey	M	11
Martha, m. Curtis **HALL**, May 12, 1851, at the house of Stephen **HURD**, by Lavalette Perrin	M	79
W[illia]m, m. Martha **BAILEY**, Mr. 6, 1787	1	240
William, m. Lydia **HALLOCK**, Apr. 5, 1827, by Rev. Francis H. Case	M	19
-----, wid., d. Apr. 20, 1808, ae 82	2	394
HURLBUTT, HOLBERD, Abigail, d. Gideon & Mary, b. Dec. 9, 1726	1	255
Abigail, m. Nathaniel **WILCOX**, Nov. 24, 1748	1	259
Almira, d. David, b. May 6, 1784	1	245
David, s. Gideon & Mary, b. Dec. 27, 1730	1	255
David, s. Jno, b. Mar. 2, 1757	1	273
David, m. Lonce* **THOMSON**, Mar. 3, 1783 *("Louisa" in Hibbard's Hist.)	1	240
Elisha, s. Gideon & Mary, b. Apr. 14, 1736	1	255
Elisha, d. Feb. 17, 1808, ae 73	2	394
Elisha, his wid. [ ], d. Dec. 24, 1814, ae 72	2	396
Frederick, m. Lucy **THOMSON**, b. of Goshen, May 4, 1826, by Elder Eli Barnett	M	17

	Vol.	Page
HURLBUTT, HOLBERD, (cont.), Gideon, m Mary **DEMING**, d. Thomas, Dec. 30, 1725, by Daniel Goodrich, J. P;	1	255
Gideon, s. Jere, b. Apr. 11, 1754	1	271
Jeremiah, s. Gideon & Mary, b. Nov. 25, 1728	1	255
Jeremiah, m. Esther **THOMAS***, June 23, 1751 *(**"THOMSON"** in Hibbard's book)	1	261
Lucia, d. Jeremiah, b. Mar. 11, 1752	1	270
Lucia, d. [David], b. Nov. 30, 1786	1	245
Mary, w. Lieut., d. June 17, 1778	1	235
Samuel, s. Gideon & Mary, b. Jan. 8, 1732/3	1	255
Samuel, d. July 7, 1817, ae 85	2	397
Samuel, of Baltimore, Md., m. Elizabeth N. **GODDARD**, of Goshen, July 23, 1845, by Frederick Marsh	M	68
INGERSOLL, Alvan, of Lee, Mass., m. Hannah **LYMAN**, of Goshen, Jan. 13, 1825, by Rev. Joseph Harvey	M	13
INGRAHAM, Orange, s. Job., b. Sept. 28, 1776	2	393
-----, wid. [ ], d. Dec. 6, [1807], ae 63	2	393
IVES, Aseneth, m. Mencis*, **BEECH**, May 23, 1776 *("Mineas" in Hist. Of Goshen)	1	240
Benjamin, m. Rachel **BALDWIN**, Dec. 6, 1753	1	269
Benj[amin], his s. [ ], b. Aug. 17, 1754; d. Sept. 6, 1754	1	271
Caroline, m. Albert **BAKER**, b. of Goshen, [Jan. 1, 1839], by Rev. Grant Powers	M	55
David, m. [E]unice **GILLETT**, Mar. 25, 1761	1	225
Edwin, m. Cornelia A. **WARREN**, May 20, 1847, by Rev. William H. Moore	M	72
Elizabeth, d. Benj[amin], b. Nov. 28, 1755	1	271
Esther, d. Lazarus, b. Oct. 10, 1774	1	241
Esther, of Goshen, m. Norman **SPUR**, of Sheffield, Mass., Aug. 23, 1841, by Rev. Thomas Kile	M	60
Hannah, m. Nathaniell **BALDWIN**, Jr., Mar. 23, 1752	1	269
Hannah Elizabeth, m. Austin **ALLYN**, Nov. 16, 1847, at the house of Cephas **IVES**, by Rev. Lavalette Perrin	M	74
Jesse, s. David, b. June 7, 1762; d. Dec. 11, following	1	234
Jesse, s. [Lazarus], b. June 21, 1776	1	241
Lazarus, m. Cloe **BEECH**, Oct. 29, 1772	1	240
Lazarus, his s. [ ], d. June 6, 1818, ae 34 ("He was drowned and body found by Rufus **IVES**")	2	397
Leverett, m. Huldah **HOLBROOK**, Nov. 26, 1822, by Rev. Joseph Harvey	M	7
Levi, s. Benjamin, d. Nov. 11, 1753	1	272
Levi, m. Caroline **PRATT**, Nov. 3, 1784	1	240
Lois, m. John **BEECH**, 2nd, Mar. 12, 1755	1	269
Mary Ann, m. William **LYMAN**, b. of Goshen, Mar. 19, 1834, by Rev. Grant Powers	M	43
Mineas, his child, d. Jan. 16, 1817, ae 6	2	397
Ruth, m. Martin **WILLCOX**, Mar. 2, 1758	1	269
Ruth, s. David, b. Mar. 19, 1764	1	234
Sabin, m. Allice **LANDON**, b. of Goshen, Mar. 4, 1854, by Rev. Daniel W. Loundsbury	M	83

	Vol.	Page
IVES, (cont.),		
Sarah, of Goshen, m. Amos **JOHNSON**, of Cornwall, Oct. 12, 1826, by Rev. Walter Smith, of Cornwall	M	18
Silas, s. Lazarus, b. July 15, 1768	1	241
JEWITT, -----, Mr. his w. [ ], d. Oct. 24, 1819, ae 26	2	298
JOHNSON, Amos, of Cornwall, m. Sarah **IVES**, of Goshen, Oct. 12, 1826, by Rev. Walter Smith, of Cornwall	M	18
Charles, m. Catharine **MORRIS**, Jan. 18, 1852, by William Platt, J. P.	M	81
Earl, m. Lucia Ann **WADHAMS**, Jan. 9, 1833, by Rev. Walter Smith, of Cornwall	M	39
Harry, of New Haven, m. Sarah **HEATON**, of Goshen, Sept. 15, 1828, by Rev. Francis H. Case	M	23
Harvey, of Sharon, m. Rhoda **HUMISTON**, of Harwinton, July 15, 1823, by Alfred Walter, J. P.	M	10
Harvey, of Norfolk, m. Maria E. **NORTON**, of Goshen, May 12, 1852, at the house of C. L. **NORTON**, by Rev. Joshua L. Maynard, of Cornwall	M	81
Peter, m. Deborah **MERRILS**, Jan. 1, 1767	1	233
Salmon, s. Moses, b. Apr. 26, 1767	1	236
William, m. Catharine **AUSTIN**, b. of Goshen, Nov. 24, 1831, by Rev. George Carrington	M	35
William C., of Bristol, m. Velena E. **BARTHOLOMEW**, of Goshen, Mar. 27, 1837, by Rev. Grant Powers	M	51
JONES, Jared, m. Abigail **HILL**, Sept. 20, 1773	1	240
Nancy, of Warren, m. Jacob **PRINCE**, of Goshen, Jan. 18, 1822, by Rev. Grant Powers	M	39
JUDD, Mary E., m. Heman **HARRISON**, Apr. 7, 1844, by Rev. Lavalette Perrin	M	65
KELLOG, Austin, of Smithfield, Pa., m. Armenia **HOWE**, of Goshen, July 29, 1821, by Rev. Ebenezer Washburn	M	4
Minerva, m. Rev. Julius **FIELDS**, May 4, 1824, by Daniel Brayton, Elder	M	12
Sam[ue]l, Jr., m. Sarah **ROGERS**, Dec. 9, 1780	1	240
Samuel, wid., d. June 12, 1813, ae 95	2	396
Thaddeus G., m. Melinda S. **WASHBURN**, b. of Goshen, Sept. 4, 1822, by David Miller	M	6
KELLY, KELLEY, Deborah M., of Goshen, m. Joseph W. **WARNER**, of Dover, Dutchess, Cty., N. Y., Mar. 4, 1839, by Rev. John Lucky	M	55
Elias, m. Deborah **TUTTLE**, b. of Goshen, Sept. 23, 1833, by Rev. Grant Powers	M	41
Harriet L., of Goshen, m. Willard H. **LEACH**, of Norwich, N. Y., Jan. 22, 1845, by Rev. J. D. Marshall	M	67
Sheldon, d. July 22, 1823, ae 24	2	399
KETTEL, Enos, his child b. [ ]; d. [ ]	1	243
Jonathan, s. [Enos], b. May 26, 1779	1	243
KILLBORN, Sibel, m. John **DIBELL**, June 20, 1751	1	261
KIMBERLY, KIMBERLEY, Freelove, m. Adison **SWEET**, Dec. 24, 1821, by Rev. Ebenezer Washburn	M	5
Henry, m. Sylva **CURTISS**, b. of Goshen, Dec. 6, 1824, by Rev. Joseph Harvey, of Goshen	M	13
-----, wid. her s. [ ], d. June 10, 1822, ae 17	2	399

	Vol.	Page
KING, Edward, of Baltimore, Md., m. Mary Ann KING, of Litchfield, Mar. 5, 1835, by Charles F. Pelton	M	45
Helen M., m. Daniel COOK, Sept. 2, 1830, by Rev. L. P. Hichok	M	30
Mary, Mrs., m. Samuel PETTIBONE, Apr. 2, 1766	1	233
Mary Ann, of Litchfield, m. Edward KING, of Baltimore, Md., Mar. 5, 1835, by Charles F. Pelton	M	45
KNAPP, -----, Mr. or Mrs., d. Feb. 1, 1813, ae 60	2	395
-----, wid., d. Feb. 24, 1815, ae 63	2	396
KNIGHT, Benjamin, m. Sarah OSBORN, of Goshen, Apr. 22, 1823, by Rev. Joseph Harvey	M	9
KNOX, Daniel G., m. Virginia M. NORTON, July 31, 1851, by Lavalette Perrin	M	79
LAMPHIE, [see also LANPHER], Jane, m. George O. CLEVELAND, Feb. 9, 1832	2	7
LAMPSON, Amos, of New Milford, m. Sarah WAY, of Goshen, May 7, 1833, by Rev. Grant Powers	M	40
LANDING, [see also LANDON], William, of Litchfield, m. Mary BEACH, of Goshen, Nov. 22, 1830, by Rev. Bradley Selleck	M	32
LANDON, [see also LANDING], Allice, m. Sabin IVES, b. of Goshen, Mar. 4, 1854, by Rev. Daniel W. Lounsbury	M	83
Idia, d. David, b. Jan. 31, 1780	1	244
Lydia, m. Jonathan BUELL, Dec. 10, 1741	1	256
LANE, LANES, J. W., of Goshen, m. Elizabeth DeFOREST, of Plymouth, July 3, 1842, by Rev. Thomas Ellis	M	63
-----, alias Brice, had d. Julia [ ]	1	246
LANPHER, [see also LAMPHIE], George, of Stonington, m. Betsey ROBERTSON, of Goshen, Jan. 12, 1826, by Alfred Walter, J. P.	M	16
LATHROP, John, of New Milford, m. Anna NORTHROP, of Goshen, Oct. 28, 1839, by D. Osborn	M	56
LAWTON, John, of Wolcottville, m. Harriet S. LEONARD, of Goshen, Jan. 11, 1844, by Rev. J. D. Marshall	M	65
Joseph M., of Westfield, Mass., m. Maria WADHAMS, of Goshen, May 19, 1852, by Rev. L. A. McKinstry	M	81
Zebulon C., m. Mary E. WOOSTER, b. of Goshen, Mar. 17, 1845, by Rev. J. D. Marshall	M	67
LEACH, Jonathan, d. June 30, 1810, ae 22	2	394
Willard H. of Norwich, N. Y., m. Harriet L. KELLEY, of Goshen, Jan. 22, 1845, by Rev. J. D. Marshall	M	67
LEAVENWORTH, Ann, m. Benjamin ROBERTS, b. of Goshen, May 19, 1833, by Rev. Grant Powers	M	41
LEE, Andrew, m. Margaret McCLANE, June 4, 1854, by T. Hendricon	M	83
Elizabeth, w. Joseph, d. May 30, 1749	1	260
John, s. [Anson & Elizabeth], b. May 20, 1749; d. May 31, 1749	1	268
John, s. Joseph, b. Dec. 10, 175[ ]	1	261
Joseph, m. Prudence CURTIS, Jan. 8, 1749/50	1	260
Mary, m. Jacob WADHAMS, Jan. 10, 1754	1	269
Mary, m. Caleb MUNSON, Mar. 19, 1767	1	240
Prudence, d. Ensor, b. Aug. 11, 1754	1	271

	Vol.	Page
LEE, (cont.),		
Sarah, d. Joseph, d. Jan. 16, 1748/9	1	260
Sarah, d. Anson & Prudence, b. Aug. 24, 1752	1	268
LEONARD, Harriet S., of Goshen, m. John **LAWTON**, of Wolcottville, Jan. 11, 184, by Rev. J. D. Marshall	M	65
Horace T., of Goshen, m. Delia A. **GUNN**, of Naugatuck, June 16, 1844, by Rev. Chester Colton	M	65
LEWIS, Allyn, had child b. Apr. 3, 1787	1	244
Annie, d. Eben, b. Apr. 9, 1788	1	246
David, s.[Allyn], b. Feb. 24, 1785	1	244
Ebenezer, d. Apr. 16, 1778	1	235
Ebenezer, m. Sarah **DAVIS**, June 6, 1779	1	240
Elihu, s. [Eben], b. Feb. 7, 1786	1	245
Elihu, s. Elihu, d. Dec. 23, [1807], ae 14	2	393
Elisha, s. Nehemiah, b. Jan. 18, 1771	1	238
Elisher, s. Eben, d. Nov. 22, 1788	1	235
Elizabeth, m. Sam[ue]ll **NORTON**, Jr., Jan. 1, 1772	1	240
Emeline, of Hudson, m. Alphonso **PRINCE**, of Goshen, Jan. 3, 1827, by Rev. Francis H. Case	M	19
Enos, s. Nathaniell, b. May 16, 1772	1	238
Ephraim, his child d. May 4, 1820, ae 1 m.	2	298
Eunice, d. Eben, b. Mar. 7, 1780	1	245
Experience, m. Ebenezer **NORTON**, Jr., May 7, 1769	1	240
Ezekiel, his child d. July 4, 1820, ae 10	2	298
Heman, s. [Allyn], b. Dec. 5, 1782	1	244
James S., m. Esther A. **SPENCER**, Oct. 12, 1846, by Rev. D. L. Marks	M	71
Jerusha, m. John **HILLS**, Sept. 10, 1754	1	269
Julia, w. Ephraim, d. Oct. 25, 1817, ae 20	2	397
Julia, m. Charles **WALTER**, b. of Goshen, Aug. 9, 1829, by Rev. Grant Powers, Int. Pub.	M	25
Luice, d. [Eben], b. Sept. 29, 1782	1	245
Miles, s. Nehemiah, Jr., b. Feb. 18, 1769	1	238
Nehemiah, Jr.(?), m. Esther **LYMAN**, Dec. 31, 1767	1	233
Ollive, d. Allyn, [b.] May 2, 1781	1	244
Sarah, d. Ebenezer & Sarah, b. June 5, 1791	1	247
Susannah, d. Abraham, b. July 20, 1782	1	242
William, s. [Eben], b. Dec. 25, 1783	1	245
LOBDELL, LOBDILL, Chloe E., of Brookfield, m. William T. **CLARK**, of New Hartford, July 4, 1827, by Rev. Ebenezer Washburn	M	20
Harriet, of Goshen, m. Chauncey **ALVORD**, of Middletown, Aug. 1, 1827, by Rev. E. Washburn	M	20
LOCKWOOD, Margaret, m. Lyman **BEARDSLEY**, b. of Litchfield, [Jan. 1, 1839], by Rev. Grant Powers	M	55
LOGAN, Ruth, d. Sam[ue]l, b. Apr. 2, 1766	1	236
LOMBARD, Ithiel, of Belchertown, Mass., m. Mary **TUTTLE**, of Goshen, Mar. 1, 1840, by Nelson Brewster, J. P.	M	57
LONG, Abigail, m. John **SEELEY**, May 5, 1777	1	240
LOOMIS, LOMIS, Albert, of Torrington, m. Emily **CURTISS**, of Goshen, Nov. 10, 1841, by Rev. Thomas Ellis	M	61
Mindwell, m. Lambert **COOK**, Dec. 13, 1757	1	269

	Vol.	Page
LOOMIS, LOMIS, (cont.),		
Nelson S., of Cornwall, m. Abigail **HILLS**, of Goshen, Nov. 7, 1827, by David Parmelee, J. P.	M	21
LOPER, Philo, of Sharon, m. Phebe **COLBY**, of Goshen, Jan. 24, 1841, by Rev. David Osborn	M	59
LUCAS, Allen, d. Mar. 11, 1820, ae 67	2	298
Allyn, m. Sarah **THOMSON**, Oct. 8, 1780	1	240
Ann P., m. Jonathan **WADHAMS**, Jr., b. of Goshen, Feb. 2, 1841, by Cornelius B. Everist	M	61
Anna, d. Thomas, b. Apr. 21, 1755	1	271
Anne, m. Joathan **THOMSON**, July 13, 1785	1	240
Asa, m. Rhoda **BURTCH**, Jan. 6, 1824, by Daniel Brayton, Elder	M	11
Augustus, d. June 1, 1811, ae 24	2	395
Daniel N., m. Marilla L. **PRICE**, Sept. 13, 1840, by David Osborn	M	58
David, m. Sarah **STANLEY**, Apr. 9, 1767	1	233
David, s. [Allyn], b. Feb. 24, 1785	1	243
David, his child d. May 16, 1815, ae 2	2	396
David, Jr., m. Eunice **DAVIS**, Sept. 25, 1850, at the house of William **DAVIS**, by Lavalette Perrin	M	77
Hannah, of Goshen, m. Rufus **SMITH**, of Norfolk, Jan. 14, 1824, by Rev. Joseph Harvey	M	12
Heman, s. [Allyn], b. Dec. 5, 1782	1	243
Huldah, d. David, b. Oct. 15, 1767	1	236
Jane, m. Virgil **COLLINS**, b. of Goshen, May 25, 1836, by Rev. Grant Powers	M	48
Mary, m. Samuel **NORTON**, Nov. 27, 1740	1	255
Mary, m. Josiah **NORTH**, Mar. 8, 1771	1	235
Mary, m. Horatio N. **BEACH**, b. of Goshen, Jan. 28, 1830, by Rev. Grant Powers	M	28
Ollive, d. Allyn, b. May 2, 1781	1	243
Sally, d. Allen, d. Nov 23, 1815, ae 21	2	396
Sarah, m. Josiah **NORTH***, Mar. 8, 1770 *("**NASH**" in Hibbard's Hist.)	1	233
Sarah E., of Goshen, m. Myron C. **GAYLORD**, of Norfolk, Jan. 8, 1843, by Rev. Adam Reed	M	63
LUDDINGTON, LUDDENTON, LUDINGTON, Aaron, s. [Moses], b. Apr. 9, 1739	1	256
Abigail B., of Goshen, m. Chauncey **WILCOX**, of Grenwich, Nov. 6, 1828, by Rev. George Carrington	M	24
David, s. [Moses], b. Aug. 28, 1733	1	256
Nathaniel, s. [Moses], b. May 9, 1742	1	256
Theron D., m. Eleanor **BAILEY**, b. of North Goshen, Sept. 18, 1845, by Rev. Chester Colton	M	69
Theron S., d. Aug. 3, 1817, ae 31	2	397
LYMAN, Abigail, [d. Erastus & Abigail], b. Sept. 4, 1814	2	1
Alice, [d. Moses & Mary Ann], b. May 15, 1845	2	6
Anne, d. [Moses], b. Mar. 1, 1746	1	260
Anne, d. [Capt. Moses & Sarah], b. Mar. 1, 1746	1	263
Delight, of Goshen, m. Elisha **YALE**, of Canaan, Nov. 21, 1822, by Rev. Joseph Harvey	M	7
Eliza, [d. Samuel & Sarah], b. Oct. 1, 1800	2	1

LYMAN, (cont.)	Vol.	Page
Eliza, of Goshen, m. James B. **PINNEO**, of New York City, Nov. 7, 1832, by Rev. Grant Powers	M	38
Ephraim, [s. Erastus & Abigail], b. June 3, 1810	2	1
Erastus, Jr., [s. Erastus & Abigail], b. Nov. 29, 1816	2	1
Esther, d. [Capt. Moses & Sarah], b. Sept. 16, 1754	1	263
Esther, m. Nehemiah **LEWIS**, Jr. (?), Dec. 31, 1767	1	233
Frederick, [s. Erastus & Abigail], b. Dec. 7, 1819	2	1
Hannah, d. Moses, b. June 21, 1751	1	261
Hannah, d. [Capt. Moses & Sarah], b. June 25, 1751	1	263
Hannah, of Goshen, m. Alvan **INGERSOLL**, of Lee, Mass., Jan. 13, 1825, by Rev. Joseph Harvey	M	13
Holley*, [s. Moses & Mary Ann], b. Jan. 22, 1855	
*("Holley Porter **LYMAN**" in Hibbard's Hist.)	2	6
Horatio N., [s. Erastus & Abigail], b. May 2, 1804	2	1
Horatio N., m. Marana **CHAPIN**, b. of Goshen, May 9, 1836, by Rev. Grant Powers	M	48
Jane M., [d. Erastus & Abigail], b. Feb. 7, 1808	2	1
Jane M., of Goshen, m. Alexander H. **HOLLEY**, of Salisbury, Oct. 4, 1831, by Rev. Grant Powers	M	35
Lucretia, [d. Moses & Elizabeth], b. Feb. 13, 1801	2	1
Lucretia, m. Caleb **DAY** of Catskill, N. Y., Jan. 18, 1826, by Rev. Darious O. Griswold, of Watertown	M	16
Lucy S., [d. Erastus & Abigail], b. Dec. 19, 1805	2	1
Lucy S., of Goshen, m. John **DeFOREST**, of Watertown, May 17, 1831, by Rev. Grant Powers	M	34
Lydia, m. Step[hen] **TUTTLE**, Mar. 23, 1758	1	269
Mary, [d. Moses & Mary Ann], b. Aug. 15, 1839	2	6
Mary, 2nd w. Col. Moses, d. [ ], 18[ ]	2	19
Moses, Capt., b. Oct. 2, 1713; m. Sarah [**HEIGHTON***], Mar. 24, 1742 *(Supplied from Hibbards's Hist.)	1	263
Moses, m. Sarah **HEIGHTON***, Mar. 24, 1742 *(**'HAYDEN'**)	1	256
Moses, s. Moses [& Sarah], b. Mar. 20, 1743	1	256
Moses, s. [Capt. Moses & Sarah], b. Mar. 20, 1743	1	263
Moses, Jr.*, m. Ruth **COLLINS**, June 2, 1767 *("4th" in Hibbard'd Hist.)	1	233
Moses, d. Jan. 6, 1768, in the 56th y. of his age	2	19
Moses, Dea., d. Jan. 6, 1768	1	235
Moses, s. Moses, b. Apr. 16, 1768	1	237
Moses, Col., his 1st w. [ ], d. June 8, 1775, in the 28th y. of her age	2	19
Moses, Dea., his wid. [ ], d. Aug. 27, [1808], ae 92	2	394
Moses, Jr., [s. Moses & Elizabeth], b. Oct. 1, 1810	2	1
Moses, Col., d. Sept. 29, 1829, in the 87th y. of his age	2	19
Moses, s. Moses & Elizabeth, m. Mary Ann **HOLLEY**, d. John M. & Sally Porter, May 6, 1834, in Salisbury, by Rev. L. E. Lathrop	2	6
Moses, [s. Moses & Mary Ann], b. Aug. 20, 1836	2	6
Phebe, d. [Capt. Moses & Sarah], b. Dec. 29, 1756	1	263
Richard, [s. Moses & Mary Ann], b. June 27, 1848	2	6
Samuel, s. Moses, b. Jan. 25, 1748	1	259
Sam[ue]ll, s. [Capt. Moses & Sarah], b. Jan. 25, 1749	1	263

	Vol.	Page
LYMAN, (cont.)		
Samuel, Jr., [s. Samuel & Sarah], b. May 25, 1803	2	1
Samuel, only s. Samuel, d. Oct. 3, 1815, in the 13th y. of his age	2	19
Samuel, Jr., d. Oct. 3, 1815, ae 13	2	396
Samuel, [s. Erastus & Abigail], b. July 29, 1822	2	1
Sarah, d. Moses, b. Sept. 29, 1744	1	260
Sarah, d. [Capt. Moses & Sarah], b. Sept. 29, 1744	1	263
Sarah, [d. Samuel & Sarah], b. Apr. 18, 1805	2	1
Sarah, wid. Moses, d. Aug. 27, 1808, in the 92nd y. of her age	2	19
Sarah, of Goshen, m. Dr. Elijah **MEAD**, of New York, May 15, 1827, by Rev. Francis H. Case	M	20
William, [s. Erastus & Abigail], b. Oct. 2, 1812	2	1
William, m. Mary Ann **IVES**, b. of Goshen, Mar. 19, 1834, by Rev. Grant Powers	M	43
MACANZEE, Samuel, d. June 4, [1807], ae 16	2	393
McCLANE, Margaret, m. Andrew **LEE**, June 4, 1854, by T. Hendricon	M	83
McDONALD, William, m. Caroline **BALDWIN**, Apr. 17, 1825, by Rev. Joseph Harvey	M	14
McKENERY, Jeremiah, m. Elizabeth **GILMER**, Nov. 7, 1850, at the house of Daniel **McKENERY**, by Lavalett Perrin	M	78
McKENNIE*, Nancy, m. Joseph **BRADY**, Apr. 4, 1853, by Lavalette Perrin *("**McKEEMIN**" in Hibbard's Hist.)	M	82
McNIEL, Isaac H., of Newark, N. J., m. Harriet **WADHAMS**, of Goshen, May 13, 1833, by Rev. Grant Powers	M	40
MAHANNAH*, Olive, m. Jared **CURTIS**, July 14, 1831, by Rev. George Carrington *("**MAKANNAS**" in Hibbard's Hist.)	M	34
-----, Mrs., her s. [ ], d. June 1, 1812, ae 10	2	395
MAIDEN*, Sarah, of Hartford, m. John **FOOG**, of Goshen, Dec. 3, 1829, by Rev. Bradley Selleck *(Arnold Copy has "**MORDEN**")	M	27
MAIN, Almira, m. William **CABLES**, Sept. 16, 1824, by Samuel Chapin, J. P.	M	13
Calvin, m. Lucy **MILLER**, June 13, 1841, by Collins Baldwin, J. P.	M	61
MAKANNAS*, Olive, m. Jared **CURTIS**, July 14, 1831, by Rev. George Carrington *(Arnold Copy has "**MAHANNAH**")	M	34
MALTBY, MALBY, MALTBIE, MALBEE, Anne, d. Daniel, b. Aug. 13, 1755	1	236
Jehiel Merriman, [s. Daniel], b. Sept. 20, 1767	1	236
Jesse, of Norfolk, m. Laura M. **BALDWIN**, of Goshen, Feb. 11, 1823, by Rev. Joseph Harvey	M	8
Martha, m. Josiah **BARTHOLOMEW**, Feb. 9, 1775	1	240
Mary, m. Samuel **BROWN**, Feb. 16, 1765	1	233
Thankfull, m. Isaac **BARTHOLOMEW**, Feb. 20, 1775	1	240
MARKS, -----, wid., d. Dec. 20, 1811, ae 76	2	395
MARSH, Maria, d. Eliphalet, b. Mar. 15, 1767, at Salisbury	1	244
Mary, Mrs., m. Rev. Stephen **HEATON**, Aug. 11, 1741	1	254
Ruth, m. John **WADHAM**, Jan. 3, 1765	1	225
MARSHALL, Asenath, m. Calieb* **SMITH**, Mar. 2, 1758 *("Chileab")	M	269

	Vol.	Page
MARTIN, Amanda, of Goshen, m. Edwin **BIERCE**, of Cornwall, Jan. 1, 1845, by Rev. Chester Colton	M	66
Clarissa A., of Goshen, m. John **CATLIN**, of Cornwall, Jan. 1, 1846, by L. A. McKinstry	M	70
Jesse, m. Mary A. **NEAL**, Apr. 21, 1850, by Rev. R. H. Reynolds	M	76
William, of Norfolk, m. Jane **HART**, of Goshen, Nov. 1, 1854, by Rev. G. A. McKinstry	M	84
MARVIN, MERVIN, [see also **MERWIN**], Fowler*, d. Feb. 9, 1823, ae 83 *("Fowler **MERWIN**" in Hibbard's Hist.)	2	399
Fowler, his w. [ ], d. Mar. 9, 1823, ae 83	2	399
Harvey C.*, m. Charlotte **NORTON**, b. of Goshen, Nov. 10, 1835, by Rev. Grant Powers *("Harvey C. **MERWIN**" in Hibbard's Hist.)	M	46
Harvey P.*, m. Almira **NORTON**, b. of Goshen, Mar. 6, 1838, by Rev. Grant Powers *("Harvey P. **MERWIN**" in Hibbard's Hist.)	M	53
MASON, Cyrus, of Salisbury, m. Mary **BROWN**, of Goshen, Aug. 19, 1829, by Grant Powers. Int. Pub.	M	26
MATTHEWS, Elizabeth, m. Ichabod **TUTTLE**, Feb. 20, 1772	1	240
Hannah, m. Dan **HILL**, Dec. 20, 1757	1	269
MAYO, Elisha, m. Cynthia **RENOLD**, Feb. 27, 1780	1	240
MEAD, Elijah, Dr. of New York, m. Sarah **LYMAN**, of Goshen, May 15, 1827, by Rev. Francis H. Case	M	20
MERRILLS, MERRELL, MERRELLS, MERRILS, MERREL [see also **NORRIL**], Amy, d. David, b. Apr. 16, 1769	1	237
Anna, d. David, b. Apr. 16, 1769	1	237
Bazaleel, s. D[ ], b. Nov. 17, 1765	1	236
David, m. Esther **HOW**, Nov. 26, 1761	1	233
Deborah, m. Peter **JOHNSON**, Jan. 1, 1767	1	233
Eben, d. Feb. 8, 1820, ae 38	2	298
Elizabeth, m. Jacob **WILLIAMS**, Aug. 24, 1773	1	233
Esther, d. D[ ], b. Dec. 22, 1766	1	236
Mary, had s. George Messenger, b. June 5, 1795	1	249
Mede, s. David, b. Aug. 22, 1762	1	236
MERVIN, [see under **MARVIN**]		
MERWIN, [see also **MARVIN**], Erastus, m. Ann **ROBERTS**, b. of Goshen, Apr. 24, 1834, by Rev. Grant Powers	M	44
Fowler*, d. Feb. 9, 1823, ae 83 *(Arnold Copy has Fowler **MARVIN**")	2	399
Harvey C.*, m. Charlotte **NORTON**, b. of Goshen, Nov. 10, 1835, by Rev. Grant Powers *(Arnold Copy has "Harvey C. **MARVIN**")	M	46
Harvey P.*, m. Almira **NORTON**, b. of Goshen, Mar. 6, 1838, by Rev. Grant Powers *(Arnold Copy has "Harvey P. **MARVIN**")	M	53
Harvey P., m. Sarah **PERSONS**, May 28, 1850, by Lavalette Perrin, at his house	M	77
Uri, his w. [ ], d. Oct. 6, 1820, ae 35	2	298
MESSENGER, George, s. Mary Merrells, b. June 5, 1795	1	249

GOSHEN VITAL RECORDS

	Vol.	Page
MILES, MIELS, [see also **MILLS**], Anner L. of Goshen, m. Ovid **PLUMB**, of Millport, N. Y., July 20, 1852, at the house of Augustus **MILES**, by Lavalette Perrin	M	82
Daniel, m. Ruth **BALDWIN**, Dec. 4, 1771	1	233
Daniell, m. Ruth **BALDWIN**, Dec. 4, 1771	1	240
David Baldwin, s. [David], b. Aug. 6, 1788	1	246
Erastus, s. [David], b. July 11, 1779	1	246
Hannah, m. Adna **BEECH**, June 9, 1741	1	254
Hannah*, d. David, b. Nov. 1, 1772 *("Hannah **MILLS**"?)	1	246
Nancy, d. [David], b. Dec. 19, 1781	1	246
Rhoda, m. Charles H. **OAKS**, May 8, 1850, at the house of Augustus **MILES**, by Lavalette Perrin	M	76
Ruth, d. [David], b. Dec. 12, 1783	1	246
William, s. Dan[ie]l, b. May 23, 1775	1	241
William, s. [David], b. May 23, 1775	1	246
William, m. Harriet **COLLINS**, b. of Goshen, May 19, 1821, by Rev. Walter Smith, of Cornwall	M	3
MILLER, Abraham, of Litchfield, m. Marietta A. **REED**, of New Haven, Aug. 17, 1829, by Grant Powers. Int. Pub.	M	25
Hannah, d. Charles, b. Nov. 30, 1748	1	268
Lois, d. Charles, b. Nov. 12, 1747	1	268
Lucy, m. Calvin **MAIN**, June 13, 1841, by Collins Baldwin, J. P.	M	61
Thomas, s. Charles, b. Jan. 9, 1750	1	268
MILLS, [see also **MILES**], Charity, m. Ebenezer **NORTON**, Jr., June 5, 1782	1	240
Hannah*, d. Daniel, b. Nov. 1, 1772 *("Hannah **MILES**"?)	1	238
MINER, Alden, of Norfolk, m. Julia **CADY**, of Goshen, Feb. 20, 1823, by Rev. Joseph Harvey	M	8
Ezra H., of Cornwall, m. Adaline L. **ALLEN**, of Goshen, Apr. 25, 1838, by Rev. John Lucky	M	54
Rhoda S., of Goshen, m. Ithiel B. **TUTTLE**, of Lee, Mass., Oct. 8, 1823, by Daniel Brayton, Elder. Int. Pub.	M	11
MIX, Betsey, m. Philip **ROSE**, Nov. 16, 1826, by Rev. Francis H. Case	M	18
Step[hen], m. Dinah **BEECH**, Dec. 24, 1778	1	240
MOORE, MORE, Sally, m. Hiram **NORVIL**, b. of Goshen, Mar. 10, 1825, by Rev. Joseph Harvey	M	14
Zebe B., m. Sarah Ann **CHURCH**, b. of Goshen, Jan. 24, 1826, by David L. Parmelee, J. P.	M	16
MORDEN*, Sarah, of Hartford, m. John **FOOG**, of Goshen, Dec. 3, 1829, by Rev. Bradley Selleck *("**MAIDEN**" in Hibbard's Hist.)	M	27
MORE, [see under **MOORE**]		
MORGAN, Deborah, m. Erastus **UTLEY**, b. of Goshen, Dec. 28, 1820, by Rev. Joseph Harvey	M	2
Wells B., m. Caroline M. **WHEELER**, Mar. 27, 1852, by Rev. David Miller	M	80
MORRIS, Amanda E., m. Samuel **EMMONS**, Apr. 24, 1836, by Rev. A. G. Wickmore	M	47
Caroline, of Goshen, m. Benjamin M. **SMITH**, of Cornwall, Mar. 6, 1844, by Rev. Chester Colton	M	65

	Vol.	Page
MORRIS, (cont.),		
Catharine, m. Charles **JOHNSON**, Jan. 18, 1852, by William Platt, J. P.	M	81
Lamon* L., m. Martha L. **HOTCHKISS**, Nov. 7, 1849, at the house of Jesse **HOTCHKISS**, by Lavalette Perrin *("Lyman" written above. Hibbard's has "Lauren")	M	75
-----, Mr., his child d. Oct. 27, 1823, ae 3	2	399
MOSS, Betsey, d. [ ], b. Sept. 27, 1791	1	246
David, illeg. child of Mary **MOSS**, b. June 6, 1785; f. David **THRALL**, 2nd, of Torrington	1	244
Mary, had illeg. child, David, b. June 6, 1785; f. David **THRALL**, 2nd, of Torrington	1	244
Mary, twin with Mercy, d. [ ], b. Mar. 26, 1789	1	246
Mercy, twin with Mary, d. [ ], b. Mar. 26, 1789	1	246
MOTT, Chester, d. May 26, 1815, ae 23	2	396
Sam[uel], s. Lent, b. Feb. 21, 1762	1	234
Sophia, d. Jan. 7, 1808, ae 13	2	394
-----, wid. her s. [ ], d. May 27, [1805], ae 16	2	392
MUNGER, Charles L., of Litchfield, m. Lucy C. **COLBY**, of Goshen, Nov. 21, 1841, by Rev. Thomas Ellis	M	61
MUNSON, Anson, s. Thomas Ens., b. Feb. 10, 1774	1	239
Asa, s. John, b. Jan. 26, 1778	1	241
Caleb, m. Mary **LEE**, Mar. 19, 1767	1	240
Caleb, s. [Caleb], b. June 5, 1775	1	239
Caleb Todd, s. John, b. Feb. 5, 1771	1	238
Deodema, d. John, b. Feb. 18, 1775	1	239
Edwin, [s. Benjamin], b. July 13, 1824	2	1
Elizabeth, [d. Benjamin], b. Oct. 17, 1826	2	1
Hannah, d. Thomas **ENSIGN**, b. July 7, 1769	1	237
Jesse, s. [Caleb], b. Jan. 26, 1772	1	239
John, s. [Caleb], b. Nov. 23, 1769	1	239
Loammis Ruhamis, s. Caleb, b. May 17, 1777	1	241
Louice, d. John, b. May 22, 1768	1	237
Mary, d. Tho[ma]s Ens[ign], b. July 6, 1776	1	241
Rachel, d. Thomas E., b. June 22, 1771	1	238
Ruth, of Goshen, m. Roswell **SHELDON**, of Southbury, Aug. 29, 1827, by Rev. E. Washburn	M	20
Seth, s. Caleb, b. Feb. 18, 1768	1	239
Thomas, his s.[ ], d. Nov. 24, [1815], ae 3	2	397
Thomas Ensign, d. Jan. 20, 1820, ae 79	2	298
NASH, Abigail, d. [William], b. Jan. 12, 1778	1	243
Abraham, [s. Samuel], b. Dec. [ ], 1744; d. June 24, 1748	1	270
Abraham, s. Samuell, d. June 24, 1748	1	268
Abraham, 2nd, s. [Samuel], b. June 3, 1751; d. about 6 days old	1	270
Abraham, s. Sam[ue]ll, b. about June 29, 1751; d. about July 5, 1751	1	268
Abraham, 3rd, s.[Samuel], b. June 25, 1753	1	270
Abraham, s. Sam[ue]ll, d. Jan. 13, 1854	1	272
Anna, twin with Clarinda, d. [William], b. Aug. 2, 1789	1	245
Anne, Jr., d. Sept. 25, 1760, at Opsagachi (?)	1	272
Clarinda, twin with Anna, d. [William], b. Aug. 2, 1789	1	245

	Vol.	Page
NASH, (cont.),		
David Phelps, s. [William], b. Sept. 6, 1774	1	243
Huldah, d. Samuel, b. Jan. 2, 1735	1	270
Huldah, m. Elisha **BLIN**, Mar. 3, 1755	1	269
Huldah, d. William, b. June 6, 1768	1	239
Huldah, see Hulda **BLIN**	1	272
Jerusha, [d. Samuel], b. Oct. 3, 1736	1	270
Jerusha, m. Joel **PHELPS**, Sept. 8, 1757	1	269
Jerushee, d. Josiah, b. May 6, 1774	1	239
Jerushee, d. Josiah, d. [ ]	1	235
Josiah, [s. Samuel], b. Mar. [ ], 1741; d. Nov. 9, 1745	1	270
Josiah, 2nd, s..[Samuel], b. July 2, 1746	1	270
Josiah*, m. Sarah **LUCAS**, Mar. 8, 1770 *(Arnold Copy has "Josiah **NORTH**")	1	233
Margaret, d. W[illia]m, b. Aug. 2, 1772	1	233
Margaret, d. [William], b. Aug. 16, 1772	1	243
Martin, s. Sam[ue]ll, b. Jan. 2, 1756	1	271
Samuel, [s. Samuel], b. Aug. [ ], 1738	1	270
Samuel, had infant child, s.b. Oct. [ ], 1746	1	270
Samuell, s. Josiah, b. Jan. [ ], 1771	1	238
Samuell, s. Josiah, b. Jan. 11, 1771	1	238
Sarah, d. [Josiah], b. Apr. 19, 1772	1	238
Susannah, d. William, b. Jan. 22, 1783	1	245
Silvia, d. [William], b. July 23, 1776	1	243
William, [s. Samuel], b. Feb. [ ], 1743	1	270
William, s. [William], b. Aug. 2, 1787	1	245
NEAL, Darius, m. Mary **PRICE**, b. of Goshen, Oct. 22, 1829, by Grant Powers	M	27
Mary A., m. Jesse **MARTIN**, Apr. 21, 1850, by Rev. R. H. Reynolds	M	76
Simeon, his child d. Jan. 9, 1816, ae 3 m.	2	397
[**NEWELL**], **NEWEL**, Abel, s. Rev. Abel, b. Nov. 30, 1767	1	237
Abigail, d. [Rev. Abel], b. Feb. 20, 1770	1	237
Esther, d. Rev. Abel, b. Jan. 26, 1761	1	263
Esther, d. Rev. [ ], b. Nov. 12, 1762	1	224
Esther, d. Rev. [ ], d. Nov. 23, 1763	1	272
John, s. Rev. Abel, b. July 18, 1765	1	234
Nathaniell, s. Abel, b. Feb. 8, 1759	1	262
NEWTON, Sarah, 2nd w. Jabez, d. Jan. 3, 1777	1	235
NICHOLS, Carlton N., m. Sophia E. **ADAMS**, Sept. 3, 1854, at the house of Asa G. **ADAMS**, by Lavalette Perrin	M	83
NORRIL, [see also **MERRILL**], William*, his s. [ ], d. Sept. 22, [1804], ae 5 *("William **NORVIL**"?)	2	392
NORTH, Abijah, m. Triphena **GRANT**, Sept. 6, 1764	1	233
Amos, s. Stephen, b. Sept. 1, 1780	1	242
Elizabeth, d. [John], b. Jan. 1, 1749/50	1	260
Ezekiel, s. [Joseph], b. Aug. 22, 1747	1	258
Ezekiel, m. Abigail **GOODWIN**, Mar. 4, 1773	1	240
Ezekiel, s. Ezekiel, b. Feb. 20, 1775	1	243
Ezekiel, his w. [ ], d. Apr. 11, 1814, ae 62	2	396
John, s. [John], b. Jan. 4, 1747/8	1	260
Joseph, Dr., d. Aug. 7, 1806, ae 70	2	393

	Vol.	Page
NORTH, (cont.),		
Josiah*, m. Sarah **LUCAS**, Mar. 8, 1770 *("Josiah **NASH**"		
in Hibbard's Hist.)	1	233
Josiah, m. Mary **LUCAS**, Mar. 8, 1771	1	235
Lucy, w. Reuben, d. Oct. 16, 1808, ae 27	2	394
Mabel, d. [Ezekiel], b. Jan. 28, 1779	1	243
Mabel, d. Mar. 8, 1814, ae 35	2	396
Martha, m. Jere **HOW**, Aug. 6, 1761	1	269
Martha, b. Sept. 7, 1782	2	18
Martha, m. Norman **WADHAMS**, Dec. 20, 1809	2	18
Martin, s. Lem[ue]ll, d. Nov. 3, 1776, at New York	1	235
Nancy, d. Ezekiel, d. Sept. 1, 1822, ae 32	2	399
Ollive, d. [Ezekiel], b. Feb. 27, 1777	1	243
Rebecca, d. Joseph, b. Apr. 24, 1743	1	258
Rebekah, m. Elisha **YALE**, Sept. 1, 1761	1	225
Sarah, d. John, b. Sept. 30, 1745	1	260
Selindee, d. Abijah, b. June 28, 1765	1	236
Seth, s. Jno, b. Jan. 18, 1751/2	1	268
Seth, his w. [ ], d. Dec. 27, 1822, ae 69	2	399
Stephen, s. John, b. Apr. 26, 1754	1	270
Theodore, his child d. Apr. 4, 1819, ae 1 m.	2	298
NORTHROP, Anna, of Goshen, m. John **LATHROP**, of New Milford,		
Oct. 28, 1839, by D. Osborn	M	56
Mary, m. Alanson D. **APLEY**, b. of Goshen, Jan. 1, 1838, by		
Rev. Asahel Gaylord	M	53
NORTON, Aaron, s. [Ebenezer], b. Mar. 8, 1743	1	268
Aaron, s. Aaron, b. May 12, 1776	1	243
Abell, s. Samuell, Jr., b. July 17, 1772	1	245
Abell, s. Samuell, Jr., d. Nov. 22, 1774	1	235
Abell, 2nd, s. [Samuell, Jr.] b. Apr. 20, 1776	1	245
Abel, 2nd s. [Samuell, Jr.] d. Sept. 6, 1777	1	235
Abijah, s. [Samuell], b. Feb. 26, 1749	1	260
Abraham, b. June 1, 1773; m. Rhoda **THOMSON**, Nov. 27,		
1794	1	194
Abraham, s. [Ebenezer, Jr.], b. June 1, 1773	1	246
Abraham, Jr., [s. Abraham & Rhoda], b. Sept. 29, 1813; d.		
Mar. 20, 1818	1	194
Abraham, his s. [ ], d. Mar. 20, 1818, ae 4	2	397
Alexander, s. David, b. Mar. 10, 1763	1	224
Almira, m. Harvey P. **MERVIN***, b. of Goshen, Mar. 6, 1838,		
by Rev. Grant Powers *("**MARVIN**" in		
Hibbard's Hist.)	M	53
Amanda, d. [Capt. Miles], b. Jan. 22, 1782	1	245
Anna, d. David, b. Oct. 29, 1760	1	262
An[n]er, wid. David, d. Dec. 7, 1767, ae 91	2	397
Anne, m. David **HUDSON**, Jr., Dec. 23, 1783	1	240
Anson, m. Martha **FOOT**, Mar. 15, 1769	1	240
Ashbel, s. Jabez, b. Aug. 6, 1768	1	237
Ashbel, m. Lydia **BARTHOLOMEW**, June 25, 1788	1	240
Ashbel, s. [Ashbel], b. Sept. 20, 1794	1	248
Betsey, d. Aug. 16, [1808], ae 32	2	394
Birdsey, d. Mar. 27, 1812, ae 48	2	395
Carew, s. David, b. May 7, 1765	1	234

	Vol.	Page
NORTON, (cont.),		
Charity, wid., her child d. [Sept.] 15, [1807], ae 12	2	393
Charles, s. [Daniel], b. Mar. 30, 1771	1	238
Charles Lyman, of Norfolk, m. Anne Maria **BAILEY**, of Goshen, Nov. 24, 1825, by Ralph Emerson	M	15
Charlotte, m. Harvey C. **MARVIN***, b. of Goshen, Nov. 10, 1835, by Rev. Grant Powers *("**MERWIN**" in Hibbard's Hist.)	M	46
Charry Maria, [d. Ebenezer], b. May 31, 1790	1	190
Clarissa, m. Joseph J. **GAYLORD**, b. of Goshen, Nov. 20, 1821, by Rev. Joseph Harvey	M	4
Dan[ie]ll, m. Elizabeth **HOW**, May 29, 1762	1	225
Daniel, s. Daniel, b. Apr. 28, 1769	1	238
Daniel, s. Elihu*, b. Apr. 27, 1771 *(Probably "Elisha")	1	238
Daniel, his child d. Mar. 4, 1810, ae 9	2	394
Daniel, Dea., d. May 9, 1820, ae 50	2	298
David, m. Anna **BRONSON**, Jan. 29, 1752	1	268
David, s. David, b. Mar. 16, 1753	1	270
David, had s. [ ], b. [ ], 1763	1	224
David, Lieut., d. Nov. 2, 1769	1	235
Diantha, d. [Samuell, Jr.], b. Apr. 20, 1783	1	245
Eben, [s. Abraham & Rhoda], b. June 25, 1805	1	194
Eben, m. Clarissa **GRISWOLD**, b. of Goshen, Apr. 29, 1834, by Rev. Grant Powers	M	44
Eben Augustus, [s. Ebenezer], b. Jan. 16, 1792; d. June 27, 1793	1	190
Eben Foot, s. [Amos], b. Nov. 7, 1773	1	239
Ebenezer, s. [Ebenezer], b. Aug. 12, 1748	1	268
Ebenezer, Jr., m. Experience **LEWIS**, May 4, 1769	1	240
Ebenezer, Jr., m. Charity **MILLS**, June 5, 1782	1	240
Ebenezer, d. Sept. 24, 1795	1	190
Ebenezer, s. Col. Ebenezer, s. of Samuel, of Durham [See Lewis M. **NORTON**]	1	190
Eber, s. David, b. July 29, 1753	1	271
Edward, [s. Lewis M. & Laura], b. Feb. 20, 1820	1	190
Elisha, s. Elisha, b. June 19, 1761	1	263
Elisha, s. Elisha, b. July 26, 1767	1	238
Eliza, [d. Lewis M. & Laura], b. Sept. 3, 1807	1	190
Eliza Lawrain, [d. Ebenezer], b. Apr. 17, 1795; d. Sept. 15, 1807	1	190
Elizabeth, d. [Ebenezer], b. Dec. [ ], 1745	1	268
Elizabeth, d. Dr. [ ], b. Mar. 26, 1763	1	224
Elizabeth, m. John **DOWD**, June 4, 1763	1	240
Elizabeth, d. [Amos], b. July 12, 1771	1	239
Elizabeth, wid. Col. Ebenezer, d. Apr. 16, 1811, ae 87	2	395
Elizabeth Marana, of Goshen, m. Joseph **GODDARD**, of New York, Nov. 23, 1826, by Ralph Emerson	M	15
Erastus, s. [Capt. Miles], b. Sept. 28, 1785	1	245
Esther, d. [Capt. Miles], b. Jan. 8, 1767; d. Apr. 18, following	1	245
Esther, d. [Capt. Miles], b. Mar. 5, 1768	1	245
Esther, of Goshen, m. Oliver **BUELL**, of New Canaan, N. Y., Oct. 29, 1823, by Rev. Joseph Harvey	M	10
Eunice, d. [Samuell, Jr.], b. Nov. 10, 1781	1	245

NORTON, (cont.), Vol. Page
Experience, w. Ebenezer, Jr., d. Oct. 30, 1781, in the 30th y.
of her age 1 242
Henry, [s. Lewis M. & Laura], b. Nov. 10, 1815 1 190
Henry, m. Delia **BEACH**, b. of Goshen, May 12, 1842, by
C. B. Everist M 62
Hiram, m. Caroline **WADHAMS**, b. of Goshen, Aug. 14,
1822, by Rev. Joseph Harvey M 5
Horace, m. Caroline S. **CHAPIN**, b. of Goshen, May 23,
1831, by Rev. Grant Powers M 34
Horatio, m. Lois **HUMPHREY**, Sept. 5, 1822, by Rev. Joseph
Hawley M 6
Horatio Augustus, [s. Abraham & Rhoda], b. Feb. 13, 1799 1 194
Huldah, d. Amos, b. Jan. 24, 1770 1 239
Ira, s. [Capt. Miles], b. Oct. 6, 1783 1 245
Isaac, his child d. Sept. 30, 1810, ae 1 1/2 2 395
Isaac, d. Oct. 6, 1812, ae 84 2 395
Jabez, s. [Samuel & Mary], b. Oct. 6, 1741 1 255
Jabez, m. Margaret **BEECH**, Nov. 21, 1765 1 233
Jabez, m. Sarah **BUELL**, Nov. 12, 1767 1 233
Jabez, his infant, b. Dec. 30, 1776; d. in a few hours 1 239
Jabez, s. D[   ], d. Jan. 1, 1777 1 235
Jabez, d. Nov. 18, 1777 1 235
James Thomson, [s. Abraham & Rhoda], b. Feb. 3, 1811 1 194
Jesse, s. [Capt. Miles], b. May 17, 1760; d. Feb. [ ], 1767 1 245
Jesse, s. [Capt. Miles], b. June 14, 1770 1 245
John, s. David, b. Nov. [ ], 1758 1 273
John Foot, s. [Lewis M. & Laura], b. Sept. 8, 1809 1 190
Joseph, s. [Elisha], b. July 25, 1759 1 263
Joseph, m. Experience **SMITH**, May 7, 1779 1 240
Laura, [d. Lewis M. & Laura], b. Dec. 15, 1824; d. Nov. 9,
1826 1 190
Laura, [d. Lewis M. & Laura], b. June 25, 1827; d. Aug. 18,
1828 1 190
Laura Clarinda, d. [Abraham & Rhoda], b. Mar. 11, 1797 1 194
Levi, s [Sam[ue]ll], b. May 12, 1754 1 263
Levi, s. Sam[ue]ll, d. May 29, 1754 1 272
Levi, s. Sam[ue]ll, b. May 13, 1759 1 263
Lewis M., s. Ebenezer, s. of Col. Ebenezer, s. Samuel, of
Durham, b. Dec. 22, 1783; m. Laura **FOOT**, of
Canton, Oct. 10,. 1805 1 190
Lewis Mills, s. [Ebenezer, Jr.] & Charity, b. Dec. 22, 1783 1 246
Lucia, d. Ebenezer, Jr., b. Feb. 25, 1770 1 246
Lucinda, d. [Capt. Miles], b. July 30, 1772 1 245
Lucretia, d. Andrew, d. Mar. 31, 1813, ae 5 2 395
Lucretia, of Goshen, m. Elihu **CARLISLE**, of Marion, Ala.,
July 28, 1840, by Rev. Grant Powers M 58
Lydia, d. [Samuel & Mary], b. Apr. 3, 1743 1 255
Lydia, m. John **HOW**, Apr. 15, 1766 1 233
Marana, [d. Lewis M. & Laura], b. Mar. 9, 1830 1 190
Margaret, w. Jabez, d. Aug. 26, 1765 1 230
Margaret, d. Jabez, b. Aug. 21, 1766 1 236
Maria, d. [Lewis M. & Laura], b. Dec. 17, 1817 1 190

NORTON, (cont.),	Vol.	Page
Maria E., of Goshen, m. Harvey **JOHNSON**, of Norfolk, May 12, 1852, at the house of C. L. **NORTON**, by Rev. Joshua L. Maynard, of Cornwall	M	81
Marinda, d. [Eben], b. Mar. 13, 1775	1	262
Marrinda, d. [Samuel, Jr.], b. Aug. 23, 1778	1	245
Martha, d. [Aaron], b. Jan. 21, 1780	1	243
Mary, d. Samuell, b. May 20, 1744	1	256
Mary, d. [Samuell], d. Aug. 2, 1748	1	260
Mary, d. [Sam[ue]ll], b. Apr. 20, 1750	1	263
Mary A., m. Nelson D. **FORD**, Sept. 25, 1853, by Lavalette Perrin	M	82
Medad, s. Capt. Miles, b. May 30, 1759	1	245
Mehitable, d. David, b. June 1, 1767	1	236
Miles, s. Ebenezer, b. Mar. 19, 1741	1	268
Miles, Capt., had d. [ ], b. Aug. 22, 1765; d. instantly	1	245
Miles, s. [Capt. Miles], b. Dec. 8, 1774	1	245
Miles, s. Ashbel, b. May 31, 1792	1	248
Mills, [s. Lewis M. & Laura], b. June 22, 1813; d. Feb. 1, 1829	1	190
Nathan, s. [Elisha], b. Jan. 12, 1757	1	263
Noah, s. Jabez, b. Nov. 6, 1769	1	237
Nori, s. [Capt. Miles], b. Feb. 3, 1778	1	245
Olive, d. [Eben], b. Jan. 31, 1758	1	262
Ollive, m. Timothy **BUELL**, Nov. 13, 1777	1	240
Olliver, s. David, b. Mar. 15, 1757	1	273
Pamena, d. Dan[ie]ll, b. May 12, 1779	1	243
Phebe, d. [Samuell, Jr.], b. Aug. 26, 1773	1	245
Phebe, eldest d. Dea. Samuel, d. July 6, [1808], ae 35	2	394
Philo, of Vernon, N. Y., m. Emily **BARTHOLOMEW**, of Goshen, Nov. 14, 1836, by Rev. Grant Powers	M	50
Prudence, m. Jos[eph] **HOW**, Oct. 24, 1768	1	233
Prudence, d. Joshua, b. Oct. 15, 1769	1	238
Rachel, d. Eben, b. June 15, 1752	1	262
Rachel, m. Amasa **COOK**, Mar. 5, 1772	1	233
Reuben, s. Joseph, b. Oct. 16, 1779	1	243
Robert, [s. Lewis M. & Laura], b. Feb. 18, 1822	1	190
Ruth, d. Dan[ie]l, b. Dec. 27, 1764	1	234
Samuel, m. Mary **LUCAS**, Nov. 27, 1740	1	255
Samuel, s. Sam[ue]ll, b. May 19, 1747	1	258
Sam[ue]ll, s. Sam[ue]ll, b. May 19, 1747	1	206
Sam[ue]ll, Jr., m. Elizabeth **LEWIS**, Jan. 1, 1772	1	240
Samuel, Dea. his w. [ ], d. Mar. 5, 1814, ae 71	2	396
Sarah, d. Samuell, b. Oct. 7, 1745	1	257
Sarah, d. Jabez, b. Jan. 7, 1772	1	238
Seth, s. Elisha, b. Aug. 2, 1773	1	239
Seth T., m. Arentia* C. **HUMASON**, Dec. 23, 1845, at the house of Giles **GRISWOLD**, by Lavalette Perrin *("Aurelia" in Hibbard's Hist.)	M	69
Sibill, d.[Ebenezer, Jr.], b. Aug. 15, 1771	1	246
Theodore, s. [Ebenezer, Jr. & Experience], b. Feb. 17, 1775	1	246
Ursula, d. [Capt. Miles], b. Jan. 25, 178-	1	245

	Vol.	Page
NORTON, (cont.),		
Virginia M., m. Daniel G. **KNOX**, July 31, 1851, by Lavalette Perrin	M	79
William, s. David, b. May 30, 1767	1	236
W[illia]m, s. Nathan, b. Apr. 25, 1779	1	243
William, his child d. Oct. 28, [1804], ae 3 d.	2	392
William, s. [Abraham & Rhoda], b. May 15, 1816	1	194
William, s. Abraham, b. May 15, 1816	1	249
William, m. Sarah **GRISWOLD**, b. of Goshen, Mar. 14, 1839, by Nelson Brewster, J. P.	M	55
Zerah, s. Elihu, b. July 17, 1763	1	234
NORVIL, NORVEL, NORVILL, Abigail, w. W[illia]m, d. May 9, 1787	1	247
Anson, s. [William], b. Jan. 1, 1791	1	245
Anson, his w. [ ], d. Dec. 20, 1823, ae 28	2	399
Daniel, d. July 5, 1823, ae 14	2	399
Hiram, m. Sally **MORE**, b. of Goshen, Mar. 10, 1825, by Rev. Joseph Harvey	M	14
John, s. [William], b. May 23, 1788	1	245
Lucy, m. Seth P. **HUNTLEY**, b. of Goshen, Mar. 4, 1838, by Rev. Asahel Gaylord	M	54
Mary, m. John **WILLCOX**, Jr., Mar. 25, 1762	1	225
Nathaniell, m. Mary **BECKWITH**, Jan. 29, 1761	1	225
Nathaniell, s. W[illia]m, b. Nov. 29, 1786	1	245
Nathaniel, his wid. or w. [ ], d. July 6, 1815, ae 77	2	396
Nathaniel, d. July 5, 1816, ae 79	2	397
Sam[ue]ll*, m. Abigail [**STILLMAN**], Apr. 13, 1786 *("William" in Hibbard's Hist.)	1	240
Susan, of Goshen, m. Nicholas **SHELDON**, of Branford, Nov. 22, 1830, by Rev. George Carrington	M	31
William*, m. Abigail [**STILLMAN**], Apr. 13, 1786 *(Arnold copy had "Sam[ue]ll")	1	240
William (?)*, his s. [ ], d. Sept. 22, [1804], ae 5 *(Arnold Copy has "William **NORRIL**")	2	392
-----, Mrs., d. Apr. 28, 1808, ae 84	2	394
OAKS, Charles H., m. Rhoda **MILES**, May 8, 1850, at the house of Augustus **MILES**, by Lavalette Perrin	M	76
OCRID, [see also **OVIATT**], Charlotte, [d. John], b. Jan. 4, 1748	1	246
Diantha, d. [John], b. Sept. 6, 1764	1	246
Elizabeth, [d. John], b. May 8, 1772	1	246
Esther, [d. John], b. Aug. 26, 1766; d. Oct. 26, following	1	246
Huldah, [d. John], b. Dec. 18, 1776	1	246
John, his infant b. Jan. 25, 1768; d. same day	1	246
John, had infant b. July 21, 1772 (1771); d. same day	1	246
John, his infant b. Dec. 12, 1779; d. same day	1	246
Marriana, [d. John], b. June 10, 1781	1	246
Olive, d. [John], b. Dec. 28, 1768	1	246
Ollive, [d. John], b. Jan. 13, 1786	1	246
Rachel, [d. John], b. Sept. 5, 1774	1	246
O'DAY, Daniel, m. Catharine **WELCH**, June 25, 1848, by Rev. Lavalette Perrin, at his house	M	74
O'NEILL, Candace C., [d. John & Emily], b. Sept. 22, 1843	2	5
Edward, [s. John & Emily], b. Oct. 3, 1840	2	5
Emily, [d. John & Emily], b. May 3, 1855	2	5

GOSHEN VITAL RECORDS 49

	Vol.	Page
O'NEILL, (cont.), John, of Goshen, m. Emily HAYDEN, of Litchfield, [ ], 1840, in Litchfield	2	5
John, [s. John & Emily], b. Nov. 5, 1841	2	5
Julia A., [d. John & Emily], b. Apr. 2, 1847	2	5
ORVIS, Roger, m. Ruth HOW, Feb. 27, 1799	1	233
Roger, s. Roger, b. Jan. 22, 1767	1	236
OSBORN, Anna Lucretia, of Goshen, m. Charles C. OSBORN, of Munroe, Sept. 17, 1827, by Rev. Francis H. Case	M	21
Charles C., of Munroe, m. Anna Lucretia OSBORN, of Goshen, Sept. 17, 1827, by Rev. Francis H. Case	M	21
John, his s. [ ], d. May 24, 1805, ae 5	2	392
Mehetable, m. Lemuel* **WALTER**, Oct. [ ], 1769 *("Samuel" in Hibbard's Hist.)	1	233
Ruth C., of Goshen, m. Luther **PIXLEY**, of Great Barrington, Sept. 13, 1829, by Samuel Chapin, J. P.	M	26
Sarah, m. Benjamin **KNIGHT**, Apr. 22, 1823, by Rev. Joseph Harvey	M	9
OVIATT, [see also OCRID], Aaron, [s. Luman & Rhoda], b. Aug. 4, 1810	2	2
Benj[amin], m. Elizabeth **CARTER**, Dec. 8, 1774	1	240
Benjamin, s. [Benjamin], b. Jan. 30, 1780	1	243
Birdsey, [s. Luman & Rhoda], b. Sept. 1, 1796	2	2
Harriet, [d. Luman & Rhoda], b. June 11, 1815	2	2
Harriet, of Goshen, m. Washington **BIGELOW**, of Ohio, Dec. 21, 1837, by Rev. Grant Powers	M	53
Heman, s. Benj[amin], b. Sept. 20, 1775	1	243
Heman, [s. Luman & Rhoda], b. Aug. 26, 1804	2	2
Keziah, [d. Luman & Rhoda], b. May 27, 1800	2	2
Laura, [d. Luman & Rhodah], b. June 11, 1818	2	2
Laura, of Goshen, m. Jonathan **SPAFFORD**, of Ohio, Oct. 6, 1839, by Rev. Epahraim Lyman	M	56
Lucretia, [d. Luman & Aloise], b. Nov. 28, 1822	2	2
Luman, s. [Benjamin], b. Sept. 6, 1777	1	243
Luman, his child d. Oct. 22, 1816, ae 5 m.	2	397
Luman, his w. [ ], d. Jan. 10, 1821, ae 43	2	298
Luman, of Goshen, m. Eloisia **SANFORD**, of Litchfield, Dec. 23, 1821, by Julius Beach, J. P.	M	4
Lyman, [s. Luman & Aloise], b. Sept. 7, 1827	2	2
Marcus, [s. Luman & Rhoda], b. Jan. 15, 1807	2	2
Moses, [s. Luman & Rhoda], b. Mar. 14, 1813	2	2
Nelson, [s. Luman & Rhoda], b. Oct. 9, 1798	2	2
Nelson, [s. Luman & Rhoda], b. Oct. 9, 1798	2	2
Nelson, m. Malinda **HUMPHREY**, b. of Goshen, Oct. 8, 1820, by Rev. Joseph Harvey	M	1
Rhoda, [d. Luman & Rhoda], b. Aug. 21, 1802	2	2
Rhoda, 1st w. Lyman, d. Jan. 10, 1821 in the 43rd y. of her age	2	19
Samuel*, [d.], Jan. 25, 1804, ae 74 *(Arnold Copy has "Samuel **AVIATT**")	2	392
Samuel, [s. Luman & Aliose], b. July 14, 1831	2	2
Sarah L., b. Nov. 28, 1822	2	18
Sarah L., m. James **WADHAMS**, Sept. 25, 1839	2	18

	Vol.	Page
OVIATT, [see also **OCRID**], (cont.),		
Sarah L., m. James **WADHAMS**, b. of Goshen, Sept. 25, 1839, by Rev. Grant Powers	M	56
-----, Mrs., d. Aug. 3, 1821, ae 80	2	298
PACKARD, Affa, m. Worthy **CURTIS**, b. of Goshen, June 25, 1829, by Rev. Grant Powers. Int. Pub.	M	25
PAGE, Julia Ann, of Warren, m. Elias **HART**, of Goshen, Jan. 20, 1830, by Rev. Grant Powers	M	28
PALMER, Charles D., of New Marlborough, Mass., m. Emily **PHILLOW**, of Goshen, May 4, 1831, by Rev. George Carrington	M	33
Charles D., m. Nancy M. **POOLER**, May 29, 1842, by Rev. Chester Colton	M	62
Elizabeth A., m. William T. **CARR**, Sept. 6, 1846, at the house of Samuel **PALMER**, by Lavalette Perrin	M	72
Emily M., of Goshen, m. James L. **FOX**, of Cornwall, Dec. 5, 1847, at the house of William **CARR**, by Rev. Lavalette Perrin	M	74
Hannah C., m. Asaph **HALL**, b. of Goshen, Jan. 29, 1829, by Stephen Mason	M	24
Henry H., m. Experience **SHEVALEAR**, Nov. 15, 1846, by Lavalette Perrin	M	71
Mary, of Goshen, m. Norman C. **BALDWIN**, of Hudson, O., Dec. 17, 1829, by Rev. Grant Powers	M	28
Robert, his child d. July 10, 1816, ae 2	2	397
Samuel, m. Frances J. **POOLER**, b. of Goshen Sept. 23, 1845, by Rev. Chester Colton	M	69
William, his child d. July 29, 1814, ae 2	2	396
PARDY, Antony, of Great Barrington, Mass., m. Charlotte **ROWE**, of Goshen, May 29, 1831, by Rev. Grant Powers	M	34
PARMELEE, PARMELE, PARMELEY, Abraham, m. Mary **STANLEY**, May 8, 1746	1	257
Abraham, s. Abraham, b. Mar. 10, 1749	1	259
Abraham, Jr., d. June 29, 1773	1	235
Abraham, s. N. Stanley, d. Aug. 17, [1808], ae 17	2	394
Abraham, Lieut., his wid. [ ], d. Nov. 20, 1815, ae 90	2	396
Angeline, of Cornwall, m. George **WADHAMS**, of Goshen, Nov. 24, 1836, by Rev. Albert G. Wickmore	M	50
Clarinda, d. Eri, b. Feb. 11, 1764	1	234
Elisha, s. Abram, b. Feb. 22, 1755	1	271
Erastus, d. Apr. 3, 1821, ae 27	2	298
Mary, d. Abram, b. Apr. 15, 1757	1	273
Mary, m. W[illia]m **BEECH**, June 22, 1779	1	240
Nathaniell Stanley, s. Abraham, b. July 28, 1761	1	263
Rhoda, of Goshen, m. Orrin **THOMSON**, of Mansfield, Feb. 25, 1822, by Rev. Joseph Harvey	M	5
Ruth, d. Abraham, b. Mar. 7, 1753	1	270
Seth, s. Abraham, b. Dec. 12, 1768	1	237
Theodore, s. Abraham, b. Mar. 8, 1746/7	1	258
Theodore, s. Abraham, d. Mar. 4, 1750	1	268
Theodore, s. Abraham, b. Apr. 3, 1751	1	268
Theodore, his w. [ ], d. Feb. 3, 1814, ae 57	2	396

	Vol.	Page
PARSONS, [see also **PERSONS**], Lemuel S., m. Lucy P. **STANLEY**, July 14, 1838, by Rev. David L. Parmelee	M	54
PEAS[E], Allen, s. Nath[anie]ll, b. Oct. 12, 1762	1	224
PECK, Leman, of Watertown, m. Rhoda Ann **CARR**, of Goshen, Mar. 11, 1847, by Lavalette Perrin	M	72
Sally, of Goshen, m. Jabez **PRINDLE**, of Alford, Mass., Jan. 8, 1825, by Rev. Arnold Scholfield	M	14
Stiles C., m. Abigail **BALDWIN**, Jan. 26, 1837, by Rev. William Andrews, of South Cornwall	M	50
-----, wid., d. July 22, 1818, ae 82	2	397
PECKHAM, David, m. Mary **POTTER**, Jan. 5, 1823, by Rev. Joseph Harvey	M	7
PENDLETON, Sarah, d. Nov. 7, 1821, ae 27	2	399
PENNOCK, PENNOCH, PINNOCH, PINNOCK, Alexander, s. James, Jr., b. May 4, 1759	1	262
Anne, d. James, b. Aug. 29, 1753	1	271
Herman, s. [James], b. July 7, 1763	1	236
Jeremiah, s. [James], b. Jan. 5, 1760	1	236
Oliver, s. [James], b. Oct. 12, 1757	1	236
Petter, s. James, b. Aug. 12, 1750	1	260
Seleck, s. Jesse, b. Aug. 16, 1766	1	236
William, s. James, b. Feb. 29, 1756	1	236
William, s. [James], b. Feb. last day, 1756	1	271
PERKINS, Charles L., of Litchfield, m. Julia A. **COLBY**, of Goshen, Mar. 11, [probably 1841], by David Osborn	M	59
Christopher, his child d. Aug. 27, 1812, ae 4 m.	2	395
Eli, of Cornwall, m. Emeline **WADHAMS**, of Goshen, Dec. 2, 1840, by Rev. Grant Powers	M	59
Fanny, m. George **BOOTH**, b. of Goshen, Feb. 23, 1823, by Rev. Joseph Harvey	M	8
Frederick, his child d. July 11, 1813, ae 1	2	396
PERSONS, [see also **PARSONS**], Sarah, m. Harvey P. **MERWIN**, May 28, 1850, by Lavalette Perrin, at his house	M	77
PETERS, Joseph, of Warren, m. Elizabeth **BEACH**, of Goshen, June 5, 1821, by Rev. Ananias Dathick, of Warren	M	3
PETTIBONE, Abell, s. Roger, b. Oct. 6, 1754	1	271
Daniel, s. [Samuell], b. May 15, 17[ ]	1	256
Eleanor, d. Roger, b. Sept. 11, 1757	1	263
Eli, m. Phebe **COOK**, Feb. 21, 1751	1	260
Eli, s. Eli, b. Oct. 6, 1764	1	271
Eli, s. Elis b. Oct. 9, 1755	1	271
Elisha, s. Roger, b. June 13, 1760	1	263
Hannah, w. Roger, d. Apr. 29, 1763	1	272
John, s. Lieut. [ ], b. Feb. 22, 1745/6	1	258
Jonathan, m. Mary **PHELPS**, Mar. 11, 1757	1	269
Lois, d. Eli, b. Nov. 25, 1751	1	261
Roger, m. Hannah **COOK**, June 25 O. S., 1752	1	225
Roger, m. Hannah **COOK**, June 28, 1752	1	258
Roger, s. Roger, b. Aug. 28, 1762	1	224
Roger, m. Susannah **TISDILL**, Mar. 15, 1764	1	233
Samuel, s. Samuel, b. Dec. 19, 1740	1	254
Samuel, m. Mrs. Mary **KING**, Apr. 2, 1766	1	233

	Vol.	Page
PHELPS, Abel, Jr., m. Lucia **BRADLEY***, Nov. 20, 1770		
*("**BEARDSLEY**" in Hibbard's Hist.)	1	233
Abigail, m. Elkanah **PHELPS**, Apr. 28, 1762	1	225
Abraham, s. Joel, b. [ ]	1	262
Alexander, s. Abel, Jr., b. July 20, 1768	1	238
Benajah, s. [Abel, Jr.], b. Mar. 14, 1770	1	238
Bildad, s. Beniiman, d. Aug. 28, 1739	1	253
Bildad, s. Benjamin, b. Nov. 15, 1740	1	253
Elijah, s. Abel, b. June 13, 1748	1	259
Elisha, s. Elkanah, b. Sept. 13, 1762	1	224
Elkanah, s. Abel, b. Feb. 3, 1742/3	1	255
Elkanah, m. Abigail **PHELPS**, Apr. 28, 1762	1	225
Emily, of Hector, N. Y., m. Almeran **BEACH**, of Litchfield, Jan. 22, 1832, by Rev. Grant Powers	M	37
Friend, s. Benjamin, b. Dec. 12, 1745	1	257
Jerusha, d. Abel, b. June 28, 1745	1	257
Joel, m. Jerusha **NASH**, Sept. 8, 1757	1	269
Joseph, s. Abell, b. Dec. 7, 1751	1	268
Mabel, d. Benjamin, b. Apr. 24, 1739; d. Sept. 22, 1739	1	253
Mary, d. Abel, b. Mar. 15, 1740	1	253
Mary, m. Jonathan **PETTIBONE**, Mar. 11, 1757	1	269
Mary, m. Sam[ue]l **FRANCIS**, [ ]	1	269
Oliver, s. Elkanah, b. Mar. 17, 1761	1	263
Ruth, m. Jonah **CASE**, June 23, 1763	1	233
Sarah, d. Benja[min], b. June 7, 1743	1	256
PHILLOW*, Emily, of Goshen, m. Charles D. **PALMER**, of New Marlborough, Mass., May 4, 1831, by Rev. George Carrington *("Emily **PHILLON**" in Hibbard's Hist.)	M	33
PIERCE, BIERCE, Angeline, [d. Archibald], b. Feb. 26, 1819	1	193
Angeline, [d. Archibald], b. Feb. 26, 1819	2	2
Angeline, of Goshen, m. Noah W. **BEACH**, of Litchfield, Apr. 7, 1840	M	57
Archibald, s. Archibald, b. May 26, 1817	1	193
Archibald, s. [Archibald], b. Mar. 26, 1817	2	2
Edwin, of Cornwall, m. Amanda **MARTIN**, of Goshen, Jan. 1, 1845, by Rev. Chester Colton	M	66
Emeline, [d. Archibald], b. July 29, 1824	1	193
Emeline, [d. Archibald], b. July 29, 1824	2	2
Emeline, of Goshen, m. Enos B. **PRATT**, of Litchfield, Apr. 18, 1848, at the house of Archibald **BIERCE**, by Lavalette Perrin	M	74
Harriet Eliza, [d. Archibald], b. Mar. 15, 1831	2	2
Leah, m. Peter N. **RANNEY**, b. of Goshen, Sept. 13, 1845, by Rev. David L. Marks	M	70
PINNEO, James B., of New York City, m. Eliza **LYMAN**, of Goshen, Nov. 7, 1832, by Rev. Grant Powers	M	38
PINNOCK, [see under **PENNOCK**]		
PIXLEY, Luther, of Great Barrington, Mass., m. Ruth C. **OSBORN**, of Goshen, Sept. 13, 1829, by Samuel Chapin, J. P.	M	26
PLATT, Lodelia, b. Apr. 4, 1822	2	18
Lodelia, Mrs., m. James **WADHAMS**, Oct. 1, 1850	2	18

	Vol.	Page
PLATT, (cont.),		
William, m. Jane A. **HURD**, b. of Goshen, Mar. 20, 1845, by Rev. Chester Colton	M	67
PLUMB, Ovid, of Millport, N. Y., m. Anner L. **MILES**, of Goshen, July 20, 1852, by Lavalette Perrin at the house of Augustus **MILES**	M	82
Sibble, m. Josiah **DIBBLE**, Mar. 18, 1756	1	269
POOLER, Eliza M., m. Levi **BALDWIN**, Feb. 3, 1847, at the house of Hiram **SAGE**, by Lavalette Perrin	M	71
Frances J., m. Samuel **PALMER**, b. of Goshen, Sept. 23, 1845, by Rev. Chester Colton	M	69
Harriet, m. Hiram **SAGE**, b. of Goshen, Sept. 9, 1840, by Rev. Grant Powers	M	58
Mary Ann, m. Obed M. **HUMPHREY**, b. of Goshen, Oct. 29, 1833, by Rev. Grant Powers	M	42
Nancy M., m. Charles D. **PALMER**, May 29, 1842, by Rev. Chester Colton	M	62
PORTER, John, P., m. Laura Caroline **PRENTISS**, b. of Goshen, July 13, 1837, by Rev. James Beach	M	51
Levi, s. Benjamin, b. Jan. 18, 1781	1	244
Luther Holcom*, s. Mat[t]hew **HOLCOM** & Lydia Porter, b. July 26, 1740; d. Mar. 28, 1741	1	254
Lydia, had s. Luther, b. July 26, 1740; f. Mathew **HOLCOM**, d. Mar. 28, 1741	1	254
Nathaniell, s. Nathan, b. Apr. 11, 1775	1	239
POTTER, Christopher C., of New Marlborough, Mass., m. Esther B. **SMITH**, of Goshen, Aug. 28, 1820, by Rev. Joseph Harvey	M	1
Mary, m. David **PECKHAM**, Jan. 5, 1823, by Rev. Joseph Harvey	M	7
POWERS, Benjamin, of Canaan, m. Nancy **PRATT**, of Goshen, Nov. 25, 1823, by Rev. Joseph Harvey	M	10
George Carrington, [s. Grant & Eliza], b. July 24, 1831	2	2
Samuel, m. Sarah **REID**, Nov. 27, 1854, at the house of Erastus **POWERS**, by Lavalette Perrin	M	84
William Grant, [s. Grant & Eliza], b. Dec. 17, 1829	2	2
PRATT, Caroline, m. Levi **IVES**, Nov. 3, 1784	1	240
Enos B., of Litchfield, m. Emeline **BIERCE**, of Goshen, Apr. 18, 1848, at the house of Archibald **BIERCE**, by Lavalette Perrin	M	74
Honour, d. [Isaac], b. Sept. 1, 1762	1	244
Isaac, m. Mary **BEEKLY***, July 21, 1755 *("**BECKLY**" in Hibbard's Hist.)	1	225
Isaac, Capt., his w. [ ], d. Dec. 11, [1807], ae 75	2	393
Isaac, Capt., d. Sept. 6, 1814, ae 81	2	396
Mary, d. Isaac, b. Oct. 26, 1758	1	224
Nancy, of Goshen, m. Benjamin **POWERS**, of Cannan, Nov. 25, 1823, by Rev. Joseph Harvey	M	10
Sarah, d. [Isaac], b. Apr. 19, 1760	1	224
PRENCHET, Catharine, m. George **PREUNEZ***, May 24, 1852, by Henry Kimberley, J. P. *("**PRENNER**" in Hibbard's Hist.)	M	81

	Vol.	Page
PRENNER*, George, m. Catharine **PRENCHET**, May 24, 1852, by Henry Kimberley *(Arnold Copy has "**PREUNEZ**")	M	81
PRENTICE, PRENTESS, Laura Caroline, m. John H. **PORTER**, b. of Goshen, July 13, 1837, by Rev. James Beach, of Winsted	M	51
Walker, his child d. Apr. 5, 1812, ae 6 m.	2	395
PRESTON, Lois, m. Caleb **BEECH**, Jr., Nov. 19, 1756	1	269
PREUNEZ*, George, M. Catharine **PRENCHET**, May 24, 1852, by Henry Kimberley, J. P. *("**PRENNER**" in Hibbard's Hist.)	M	81
PRICE, Ann S., of Goshen, m. Harvey H. **GROSS**, of Poughkeepsie, N. Y., Aug. 28, 1836, by Rev. Albert G. Wickmore	M	48
Benjamin, his child d. July 16, 1822, ae 8 m.	2	399
Maria, of Goshen, m. Joseph **BUNNELL**, of Cornwall, Mar. 29, 1830, by Rev. Grant Powers	M	29
Marilla L., m. Daniel N. **LUCAS**, Sept. 13, 1840, by David Osborn	M	58
Mary, m. Darius **NEAL**, b. of Goshen, Oct. 22, 1829, by Grant Powers	M	27
Phebe, of Goshen, m. Lewis **SPERRY**, of Torrington, Mar. 29, 1830, by Rev. Grant Powers	M	29
Sarah G., m. Simmons W. **SCOVILLE**, b. of Goshen, Sept. 19, 1837, by Nelson Brewster, J. P.	M	52
PRINCE, Alphonso, m. Melinda **BOWHAM**, (colored), Oct. 27, 1822, by Julius Beach, J. P., at his house	M	6
Alphonso, of Goshen, m. Emmeline **LEWIS**, of Hudson, Jan. 3, 1827, by Rev. Francis H. Case	M	19
George, d. Oct. 31, 1819, ae 25	2	298
Jacob, his child, d. June 24, [1807], ae 10 m.	2	393
Jacob, his child d. July 14 [1807], ae 11 m.	2	393
Jacob, of Goshen, m. Nancy **JONES**, of Warren, Jan. 18, 1833, by Rev. Grant Powers	M	39
Lucina, m. George **ANTHONY**, Feb. 10, 1828, by Samuel Chapin, J. P.	M	22
Mary, of Goshen, m. Benjamin **HILL**, of Torrington, Jan. 5, 1831, by Rev. George Carrington	M	32
PRINDLE, Jabez, of Alford, Mass., m. Sally **PECK**, of Goshen, Jan. 8, 1825, by Rev. Arnold Scholfield	M	14
RANNEY, Peter N., m. Leah **PIERCE**, b. of Goshen, Sept. 13, 1845, by Rev. David L. Marks	M	70
RATHBURN, Ann, of Hartland, m. Caleb **BEACH**, of Winchester, [ ], by Rev. Grant Powers. Recorded Jan. 23, 1832	M	36
REED [see also **REID**], Abby W., m. Gad L. **YALE**, Oct. 16, 1836, by Albert G. Wickmore	M	49
Charles, s. Robert, b. Nov. 13, 1772	1	243
Harriet, of Goshen, m. John F. **THOMSON**, of Canaan, Oct. 11, 1837, by Rev. John Lucky	M	52
Marietta A., of New Haven, m. Abraham **MILLER**, of Litchfield, Aug. 17, 1829, by Grant Powers. Int. Pub.	M	25

GOSHEN VITAL RECORDS 55

	Vol.	Page
REED [see also **REID**], (cont.),		
Olliver, s. [Robert], b. Feb. 28, 1778	1	243
Onney, s. Nathaniell, b. June 20, 1770	1	238
Polly, d. [Robert], b. Nov. 15, 1774	1	243
Rachel C., m. Hiram **GARNER**, b. of Cornwall, Jan. 31, 1825, by Rev. Arnold Scholfield	M	14
Robert Randolph, s. [Robert], b. Mar. 6, 1780	1	243
[**REEVES**], **REVES**, Benj[amin], m. Huldah **HILL**, Jan. 31, 1764	1	233
Mary, d. Osens, b. Dec. 29, 1764	1	234
REID, [see also **REED**], Sarah, m. Samuel **POWERS**, Nov. 27, 1854, at the house of Erastus **POWERS**, by Lavalette Perrin	M	84
[**REYNOLDS**], **RENOLD**, Cynthia, m. Elisha **MAYO**, Feb. 27, 1780	1	240
RICE, [see also **ROYCE**], Dinah, m. Lynus **BEECH**, Oct. 21, 1747	1	258
Sarah, m. Amos **BEECH**, Dec. 24, 1746, by Rev. Mr. Hall	1	258
RICHARDS, **RITCHARDS**, Abijah, [twin with Hanah], s. [Daniel], b. July 7, 1746	1	257
Abijah, s. Sam[ue]ll, b. Nov. 3, 1759	1	262
Caroline, m. George **BEACH**, b. of Goshen, Nov. 25, 1830, by Rev. Bradley Selleck	M	31
Charity, d. Sam[ue]ll, b. June 3, 1757	1	273
Charles, d. July 4, 1817, ae 75	2	397
Clorinda, d. Samuell, b. Mar. 27, 1755	1	271
Clarinda, d. Samuell, d. Apr. 17, 1755	1	272
Elizabeth, m. Asa **HILL**, Mar. 13, 1745	1	257
Enos, d. Nov. 22, 1815, ae 34	2	396
Erastus L., m. Lois **BEACH**, b. of Goshen, Nov. 8, 1840, by Rev. David Osborn	M	58
Hanah, [twin with Abijah], d. [Daniel], b. July 7, 1746	1	257
Lyman, m. Ann **BARTHOLOMEW**, Sept. 14, 1848, at the house of Thomas **BARTHOLOMEW**, by Lavalette Perrin	M	75
Mary, m. John **HILL**, Mar. 1, 1747	1	261
Naomi, m. Caleb **ROOT**, of Canaan, July 7, 1833, by Rev. George Carrington	M	41
Samuell, m. Mary **BROWN**, Feb. 14, 1754	1	269
RICHMOND, Hannah, m. Jno **GOULD**, Dec. 20, 1768	1	233
Jonathan, s. Eph[raim], b. Jan. 20, 1756	1	262
Niles, his child s.b. Oct. 3, 1762	1	224
Rhoda, d. [Ephraim], b. Feb. 26, 1758	1	262
Sarah, m. Jonathan **DEMING**, Dec. 19, 1782	1	240
Silas, m. Hannah **TUTTLE**, Mar. 29, 1762	1	225
Silas, s. Silas, b. Dec. 16, 1768	1	237
RILEY, Appleton, s. John, b. Aug. 24, 1763	1	234
Appleton, d. Nov. 10, 1812, ae 49	2	395
John, m. Lucia **CASE**, Mar. 20, 1762	1	233
John Chester, s. John, b. Apr. 25, 1768	1	237
Sam[ue]l, s. Lieut. John, b. July 20, 1782	1	246
RIPLEY, Elizabeth, d. Samuel, b. Mar. 31, 1780	1	244
John, s. [Samuel], b. July 13, 1782	1	244
RIPP, -----, Mr., d. July 9, 1814, ae 4	2	396

	Vol.	Page
ROBERTS, ROBERT, Ann, m. Erastus **MERWIN**, b. of Goshen, Apr. 24, 1834, by Rev. Grant Powers	M	44
Benjamin, his child d. June 13, [1806], ae 1	2	393
Benjamin, his child d. Nov. 18, [1808], ae 1	2	394
Benjamin, m. Ann **LEAVENWORTH**, b. of Goshen, May 19, 1833, by Rev. Grant Powers	M	41
Harriet, of Goshen, m. George William **THOMSON**, of Waterbury, May 4, 1842, by Rev. Thomas Ellis	M	62
Maria, of Goshen, m. Timothy **CHURCH**, of Waterbury, May 4, 1836, by Rev. A. G. Wickmore	M	47
Peter Moriaty, m. Jo Anna **WOOSTER**, b. of Goshen, Apr. 2, 1823, by Daniel Coe	M	9
Sarah, of Goshen, m. Elijah **CLARK**, of Hartland, Dec. 28, 1831, by Rev. Luther Mead	M	36
Stephen, m. Lucinda **BAILEY**, b. of Goshen, Nov. 6, 1833, by Rev. Aaron Hill	M	42
ROBERTSON, Betsey, of Goshen, m. George **LANPHER**, of Stonington, Jan. 12, 1826, by Alfred Walter, J. P.	M	16
ROBINS, William, m. Jane **BARNEY**, June 24, 1846, by Rev. William Dixon	M	72
ROBINSON, William P., of New Haven, Ill., m. Caroline M. **BUELL**, of Goshen, Aug. 21, 1820, by Rev. Joseph Harvey	M	1
ROBY, Lydia, d. John, b. July 14, 1775	1	244
ROE, [see also **ROWE**], Mary Ann, m. Homer **FREEMAN**, Dec. 3, 1829, by Rev. Grant Powers. Int. Pub.	M	27
ROGERS, Lewis, m. Maria **SIMPSON**, Jan. 18, 1847, by Rev. D. L. Marks	M	72
Sarah, m. Sam[ue]l **KELLOGG**, Jr., Dec. 9, 1780	1	240
ROOT, Caleb, of Canaan, m. Naomi **RICHARDS**, July 7, 1833, by Rev. George Carrington	M	41
John J., of Farmington, m. Fanny **ALLYN**, of Goshen, Mar. 10, 1839, by Rev. Grant Powers	M	55
Lucretia H., m. Nelson **BREWSTER**, Dec. 19, 1827, by Rev. Francis H. Case	M	21
Mary, m. Uri **HILLS**, Mar. 15, 1756	1	269
ROSE, [see also **ROWE**], Phillip, m. Betsey **MIX**, Nov. 16, 1826, by Rev. Francis H. Case	M	18
ROWE, ROWS, [see also **ROE & ROSE**], Betty, m. James **ACKAMAN**, b. of Goshen, Mar. 20, 1831, by Rev. Grant Power	M	33
Charlotte, of Goshen, m. Antony **PARDY**, of Great Barrington, Mass., May 29, 1831, by Rev. Grant Powers	M	34
Phillip, his s. [ ], d. Oct. 8, 1815, ae 3	2	396
Philip, his w. [ ], d. July 19, 1822, ae 35	2	399
Phillip, of Goshen, m. Harriet **SAVOY**, of Sharon, Mar. 27, 1831, by Rev. Grant Powers	M	33
ROYCE, [see also **RICE**], Anna, w. Nath[anie]ll, d. Dec. 13, 1759	1	272
Asa, s. Nathaniell, b. Oct. 25, 1761	1	263
Elisha*, s. Jno, b. July 31, 1768 *(Arnold Copy has "Elisha HOY")	1	238
Huldah, d. John, b. Sept. 5, 1770	1	238

	Vol.	Page
ROYCE, [see also **RICE**], (cont.),		
James, d. [June 6, 1767]	1	235
James, s. Josiah, b. Nov. 6, 1768	1	237
Lidia, d. David, b. Sept. 1, 1754	1	271
Nathaniell, Jr., m. Anne **BOONE**, July 10, 1755	1	269
Nathaniell, m. Eleanor **WRIGHT**, Nov. 5, 1760	1	269
Nathaniell, s. Nathaniell, b. Feb. 10, 1773	1	239
Phebe, m. Samuel **WILLCOX**, July 30, 1753	1	269
Sarah, d. John, b. Apr. 15, 1768	1	237
Thaddeus, s. Nathaniell, b. July 4, 1767	1	237
RUGG, Laura, m. Abner C. **BOTSFORD**, Oct. 13, 1850, at the house of Uri **MARVIN**, by Lavalette Perrin	M	77
SACKETT, John, of Stanford, Dutchess Co., N. Y., m. Jane **BROWN**, of Goshen, Feb. 16, 1834, by Rev. Aaron S. Hill	M	43
SAGE, Hiram, m. Harriet **POOLER**, b. of Goshen, Sept. 9, 1840, by Rev. Grant Powers	M	58
Mary L., m. Henry H. **BEACH**, b. of Goshen, Oct. 8, 1832, by Rev. Grant Powers	M	38
Orrin, d. Aug. 21, 1812, ae 28	2	395
SANFORD, Barthena, d. Phelemon, b. Mar. 2, 1772	1	239
Caroline M., m. Harlow **BUELL**, b. of Goshen, Jan. 28, 1836, by Rev. Grant Powers	M	47
Eloisia, of Litchfield, m. Luman **OVIATT**, of Goshen, Dec. 23, 1821, by Julius Beach, J. P.	M	4
Joseph, d. Oct. 22, 1805, ae 31	2	392
Phebe, d. Philemon, b. Feb. 10, 1777	1	241
Phebe, had d. Rhoda, b. July 9, 1780	1	244
Rhoda, d. Phebe, b. July 9, 1780	1	244
-----, wid. her child d. Mar. 21, 1806, ae 18 m.	2	393
SAUNDERS, John B., of Goshen, m. Phebe **BONNEY**, of Cornwall, Jan. 1, 1833, by Rev. Aaron S. Hill	M	39
SAVOY, Harriet, of Sharon, m. Phillip **ROWE**, of Goshen, Mar. 27, 1831, by Rev. Grant Powers	M	33
SAWYER, Alice Lyman, of Waverly, N. Y., had possession of the **LYMAN** Family bible. Witness J. T. **SAWYER**. Dated Mar. 7, 1907	2	6
SCOVILLE, Elias, of Goshen, m. Armenia A. **CADY**, of Norfolk, Sept. 13, 1836, by Rev. Grant Powers	M	48
Ralph G., m. Mariah E. **WADHAMS**, Sept. 16, 1851, at the house of Lewis **WADHAMS**, by Lavalette Perrin	M	80
Simmons W., m. Sarah G. **PRICE**, b. of Goshen, Sept. 19, 1837, by Nelson Brewster, J. P.	M	52
SEELEY, SEELYE, Jane L., of Goshen, m. James **BLAKE**, of Cornwall, May 4, 1847, by Rev. D. L. Marks	M	72
Jennette, m. Seely **HART**, b. of Goshen, Sept. 27, 1854, by D. W. Lounsbury	M	84
John, m. Abigail **LONG**, May 5, 1777	1	120
John, his d. [ ], d. May 28, 1811, ae 29	2	395
Joseph, m. Abiah A. **CROCKER**, Mar. 26, 1837, by Albert G. Wickmore	M	50
SHELDON, Nicholas, of Branford, m. Susan **NORVIL**, of Goshen, Nov. 22, 1830, by Rev. George Carrington	M	31

	Vol.	Page
SHELDON, (cont.), Roswell, of Southbury, m. Ruth **MUNSON**, of Goshen, Aug. 29, 1827, by Rev. E. Washburn	M	20
Russel, his s. [ ], d. Dec. 6, [1807], ae 7	2	393
SHEPERD, Isaiah, of Litchfield, m. Levinia **WEBSTER**, of Goshen, Oct. 23, 1826, by Rev. Francis H. Case	M	18
SHEVALEAR, [see under **CHAVALIER**]		
SILL, Elisha, M. D., d. Jan. 20, 1808, ae 78	2	394
SIMONS, Jane P., of Sandisfield, Mass., m. Lyman **BENEDICT**, of Winchester, Oct. 25, 1849, by Frederick Marsh	M	75
SIMPSON, Maria, m. Lewis **ROGERS**, Jan. 18, 1847, by Rev. D. L. Marks	M	72
SKINNER, Charlotte L., of Harwinton, m. Bushnell **AUSTIN**, of Goshen, Feb. 6, 1831, by Rev. George Carrington	M	33
SMEDLEY, John, m. Deliverance **HUMPHREY**, Aug. 8, 1753	1	269
SMITH, Archibald, of Goshen, m. Mrs. Oby **BARNUM**, of Cornwall, Feb. 7, 1841, by Rev. David Osborn	M	59
Benjamin M., of Cornwall, m. Caroline **MORRIS**, of Goshen, Mar. 6, 1844, by Rev. Chester Colton	M	65
Calieb*, m. Asenath **MARSHALL**, Mar. 2, 1758 *("Chileab")	1	269
Chilieb, d. Oct. 8, 1808, ae 74	2	394
Cornelia, m. Byron **BAILEY**, Nov. 9, 1820, by Benjamin Sedgewick, J. P.	2	396
David, d. Feb. 21, 1814, ae 40	2	396
Esther B., of Goshen, m. Christopher C. **POTTER**, of New Marlborough, Mass., Aug. 28, 1820, by Rev. Joseph Harvey	M	1
Experience, m. Joseph **NORTON**, May 7, 1779	1	240
Haskell Gilbert m. Lucretia **COLLINS**, May 26, 1851, by Rev. N. S. Wheaton	M	79
John, his child d. [, 1820], ae 8	2	298
Obadiah, d. Apr. 30, 1807, ae 38	2	393
Olive, m. John **WILLOUGHBY**, Jr., Dec. 18, 1753	1	269
Prudence, m. Daniell **WILLIAMS**, Feb. 15, 1765	1	233
Rhoda, d. [Chiliab], b. Jan. 5, 1759	1	262
Rufus, of Norfolk, m. Hannah **LUCAS**, of Goshen, Jan. 14, 1824, by Rev. Joseph Harvey	M	12
Ruth, m. Asa **FRANCIS**, July 9, 1761	1	269
Ruth, m. Charles **WRIGHT**, Nov. 11, 1767	1	225
Sarah, m. Medad **HILL**, Dec. 5, 1751	1	268
Sarah, of Goshen, m. Lyman **HOWE**, of Canaan, Jan. 2, 1840, by Benjamin Sedgwick, J. P.	M	56
Zebina, s. Chiliab, b. Apr. 21, 1760	1	262
-----, Dr. his child d. June 15, 1815, ae 3	2	396
SNOW, Ruth, m. Peris **BONNEY**, s. John & Elizabeth, Apr. 20, 1739, by Rev. Daniel Perkins	1	242
SOPER, Joel, Dr., m. Rachel **HILL**, July 26, 1762	1	255
Phebe, m. Roger* **BEECH**, June 9, 1756 *("Royce"?)	1	269
SPAFFORD, Jonathan, of Ohio, m. Laura **OVIATT**, of Goshen, Oct. 6, 1839, by Rev. Ephraim Lyman	M	56

	Vol.	Page
SPAULDING, Chester, of Sheffield, Mass., m. Emily **BUTTON**, of Goshen, Jan. 25, 1831, by Rev. Grant Powers. Int. Pub.	M	32
SPELMAN, Harriet, of Goshen, m. Cornwall **CLARK**, of Hartland, Oct. 9, 1836, by Albert G. Wickmore	M	49
Sophia, m. Carlton **WADHAMS**, Nov. 27, 1834, by Albert B. Camp	M	45
SPENCER, Diedamus, of Crownpoint, N. Y., m. Phebe **SPENCER**, of Goshen, Nov. 13, 1822, by Rev. Joseph Harvey	M	7
Esther A., m. James S. **LEWIS**, Oct. 12, 1846, by Rev. D. L. Marks	M	71
Laura, niece of John **BEACH**, d. June 8, 1822, ae 23	2	399
Phebe, of Goshen, m. Diedamus **SPENCER**, of Crownpoint, N. Y., Nov. 13, 1822, by Rev. Joseph Harvey	M	7
SPERRY, Lewis, of Torrington, m. Phebe **PRICE**, of Goshen, Mar. 29, 1830, by Rev. Grant Powers	M	29
Sarah, m. William D. **WHITING**, Mar. 27, 1853, by Lavalette Perrin	M	82
SPRING, Marcus R. of Derby, m. Jane **HILL**, of Goshen, July 31, 1845, by Rev. D. L. Marks	M	69
SPUR, Norman, of Sheffield, Mass., m. Esther **IVES**, of Goshen, Aug. 23, 1841, by Rev. Thomas Ellis	M	60
SQUIRE, Clarrendy, [d. Clement], b. July 15, 1783	1	248
Clement, d. May [ ], 1814, ae 64* *(Note says "about 60")	2	396
Content, d. [Clement], b. July 20, 1778	1	248
Justus, m. Eleanor **BALEY**, Dec. 13, 1782	1	240
Luman, s. Justus, b. Sept. 23, 1783	1	244
Mary, m. Nathan **CENTER**, June 22, 1774	1	240
Miles, s. Clement, b. Oct. 25, 1775	1	248
Orren, [s. Clement], b. Apr. 16, 1786	1	248
Oxley, [s. Clement], b. May 12, 1789	1	248
Samuel W., of Wolcottville, m. Almira **CLUMMINGS**, of Goshen, June 26, 1844, by Rev. J. D. Marshall	M	66
Seth, [s. Clement], b. May 21, 1780	1	248
Theron, [s. Clement], b. Nov. 15, 1791	1	248
STANLEY, Anne, d. [William], b. Mar. 1, 1761	1	224
Anne, d. [Earl], b. July 26, 1784	1	246
Earl, s. [Timothy, Jr.], b. Nov. 28, 1752	1	270
Earl, m. Lois **BEECH**, July 8, 1773	1	240
Elisha, s. [Jonathan, Jr.,], b. Jan. 13, 1760	1	273
Eunice, m. Zacheus **GRISWOLD**, Jr., Mar. 13, 1775	1	225
Felix, s. Nathaniell, Jr., b. Jan. 13, 1764	1	224
George, s. [Earl], b. Sept. 18, 1787	1	246
George, s. [Earl], d. Nov. 4, 1788	1	247
Jesse, s. [William], b. Dec. 23, 1757	1	224
Lois, m. Joseph **BALEY**, Mar. 29, 1749	1	261
Lois, d. W[illia]m, b. Jan. 3, 1764	1	224
Lois, d. [Earl], b. Jan. 29, 1777	1	246
Lucy P. m. Lemuel S. **PARSONS**, July 14, 1838, by Rev. David L. Parmelee	M	54
Mary, m. Abraham **PARMELEE**, May 8, 1746	1	257

STANLEY, (cont.), | Vol. | Page
Mary, d. Timothy, Jr., b. Dec. 21, 1750 | 1 | 270
Mary, d. Jonathan, Jr., b. Mar. 24, 1757 | 1 | 273
Mary, m. Giles **GRISWOLD**, Oct. 28, 1762 | 1 | 233
Mary, d. Earl, b. Nov. 21, 1773 | 1 | 246
Mercy, m. Sam[ue]ll **BALDWIN**, Nov. 28, 1744 | 1 | 257
Nathaniel, Jr., m. Sarrah **BALDWIN**, Nov. 6, 1746 | 1 | 257
Norman, s. [Earl], b. July 25, 1780 | 2 | 246
Norman, s. Earl, d. Apr. 26, 1781 | 1 | 247
Norman, 2nd, s. [Earl], b. May 18, 1782 | 1 | 246
Rachel, d. [Earl], b. May 19, 1775 | 1 | 246
Ruth, m. Jacob **WILLIAMS**, Dec. 11, 1746 | 1 | 258
Samuel, s. [Nathaniell, Jr.], b. Sept. 3, 1748; d. same day | 1 | 260
Sarah, d. Nathaniell, Jr., b. Sept. 30, 1747; d. Oct. 9, 1747 | 1 | 260
Sarah, d. [Nathaniell, Jr.], b. Aug. 14, 1749 | 1 | 260
Sarah, m. David **LUEAS**, Apr. 9, 1767 | 1 | 233
Cibil*, d. [Earl], b. Nov. 12, 1778   *("Sybil") | 1 | 246
Thaddeus, s. Timothy, b. Sept. 14, 1769 | 1 | 237
Timothy, m. Mary **BALEY**, June 18, 1750 | 1 | 261
Timothy, his d. [   ], d. Dec. 6, [1807], ae 8 | 2 | 393
W[illia]m, his 1st child, b. Dec. 4, 1756; d. [   ], ae about 28 days | 1 | 224
William, his w. [   ], d. Nov. 15, [1807], ae 72 | 2 | 393
William, d. Feb. 11, 1816, ae 86 | 2 | 397
W[illia]m, m. Amey **BALDWIN**, Mar. 31, 1856*
    *(Probably "1756") | 1 | 225
STARR, Abigail, d. [Ephraim], b. Jan. 24, 1778 | 1 | 241
Anna, d. Ephraim, b. Jan. 3, 1773 | 1 | 241
Ephraim, had Tobey (negro), d. May 12, 1806, ae 76 | 2 | 393
Ephraim, d. Oct. 27, 1809, ae 64 | 2 | 394
Eph[raim]*, m. Hannah **HILLS**, Nov. 13, 1769   *(Written "Eph[raim] **STEER**") | 1 | 233
Esther, m. Harvey **BALDWIN**, M. D., b. of Goshen, Mar. 30, 1842, by Cornelius B. Everist | M | 62
Hannah, d. [Ephraim], b. Nov. 12, 1774 | 1 | 241
Laurepee, d. Eph[raim], b. Aug. 22, 1770 | 1 | 238
Leuice, d. [Ephraim], b. Nov. 9, 1782 | 1 | 242
Sarah, d. [Ephraim], b. May 7, 1776 | 1 | 241
Truman, s. Ephraim, b. June 6, 1780 | 1 | 242
STEER, Ephraim, see Ephraim **STARR** | 1 | 233
STERLING, Isaac H., m. Harriet **EMMONS**, b. of Goshen, Oct. 5, 1823, by Rev. Ashbel Baldwin | M | 10
STETSON, Abel S., m. Sally M. **TAYLOR**, Sept. 10, 1826, by John Lovejoy | M | 17
STEWART, Elizabeth, m. James **HUNTER**, b. of Goshen, Dec. 1, 1843, by Rev. J. D. Marshall | M | 64
[**STILLMAN**], Abigail, m. Sam[ue]ll* **NORVILL**, Apr. 13, 1786
    *("William" in Hibbard's Hist.) | 1 | 240
STODDARD, Jerusha L., of Goshen, m. John T **CLARK**, of Wethersfield, Sept. 17, 1854, by John F. Norton. Int. Pub. | M | 83
-----, wid., d. June 24, 1818, ae 73 | 2 | 397

GOSHEN VITAL RECORDS   61

	Vol.	Page
STREET, [Ebenezer], Mr., d. Feb. 7, [1806], ae 71	2	393
Rachel, wid., d. Dec. 5, 1811, ae 77	2	395
Samuel D., his child d. Oct. 9, 1818, ae 1 d.	2	298
STRONG, George W., m. Harriet T. **TIBBALLS**, b. of Goshen, Sept. 29, 1847, by Frederick Marsh	M	72
William F., m. Sarah Anne **APLEY**, b. of Goshen, Jan. 1, 1834, by Rev. G. Powers	M	42
STUDLEY, Joshua T., of Sharon, m. Abba Ann **CUMMINGS**, of New Preston, July 19, 1855, by Rev. Albert G. Wickmore	M	45
SWEET, Adison, m. Freelove **KIMBERLY**, Dec. 24, 1821, by Rev. Ebenezer Washburn	M	5
TATRO, Anthony, of Winsted, m. Eliza **WADHAMS**, of Goshen, Apr. 6, 1841, by Rev. David Osborn	M	59
Jonathan, of Collinsville, m. Laura E. **WADHAMS**, of Goshen, July 23, 1843, by Rev. J. D. Marshall	M	64
TAYLOR, Sally M., m. Abel S. **STETSON**, Sept. 10, 1826, by John Lovejoy	M	17
-----, Mrs., d. Apr. 1, 1809, ae 96	2	394
THOMAS*, Esther, m. Jeremiah **HURLBURT**, June 23, 1751 *("**THOMSON**" in Hibbard's Hist.)	1	261
THOMSON, Abraham, s. Step[hen], b. Oct. 26, 1762	1	234
Charles, s. Dea. Augustus, d. Nov. 23, 1823, ae 23	2	399
Chloe, d. [Dea.], b. Aug. 11, 1743	1	257
Clarinda, d. James, b. Oct. 18, 1768	1	237
Clarissa, m. Jeffrey **BALLARD**, May 10, 1825, by Rev. Joseph Harvey	M	15
David, m. Hannah **GRISWOLD**, Nov. 26, 1766	1	225
Edward, s. Elisher, b. Sept. 30, 1766	1	236
Elisha, his w. [ ], d. Apr. 17, 1812, ae 78	2	395
Elisha, d. Apr. 24, 1812, ae 82* *(Note says "84 1/2")	2	395
Eliza, of Goshen, m. James **DUNN**, of Newton, N. Y., Apr. 18, 1827, by Rev. Francis H. Case	M	19
Esther*, m. Jeremiah **HURLBURT**, June 23, 1751 *(Arnold Copy has "Esther **THOMAS**")	1	261
George William, of Waterbury, m. Harriet **ROBERTS**, of Goshen, May 4, 1842, by Rev. Thomas Ellis	M	62
Gideon, s. Elisha, b. Feb. 23, 1761	1	224
Hanah, d. Sam[ue]ll, Jr., b. Aug. 25, 1747	1	259
Hannah, d. Jno, b. Mar. 10, 1759	1	262
Henry W., m. Lydia **BUTTON**, Jan. 1, 1826, by Rev. Walter Smith	M	15
Horace J., of Humphreyville, m. Anna **ALLYN**, of Goshen, Mar. 2, 1834, by Rev. Grant Powers	M	43
Ira, s. Jonathan, b. Mar. 24, 1784	1	244
Isaac, m. Mary **HOLBROOK**, b. of Goshen, Jan. 21, 1830, by Rev. Grant Powers	M	28
James, s. Dea. [ ], b. Mar. 17, 1741	1	255
James, m., Ruth **BENTON**, June 2, 1767	1	223
James, his w. [ ], d. May 11, 1813, ae 73	2	396
James, d. Nov. 8, 1817, ae 76	2	397
John, s. Amos, b. May 7, 1743	1	255

THOMSON, (cont.),	Vol.	Page
John, s. Amos, d. July 1, 1747	1	258
John, m. Hannah **HEATON**, Jan. 31, 1754	1	269
John, s. John, b. Feb. 27, 1757	1	273
John, d. Jan. 17, 1812, ae 85	2	359
John F., of Canaan, m. Harriet **REED**, of Goshen, Oct. 11, 1837, by Rev. John Lucky	M	52
Jonathan, s. Elisha, b. Dec. 31, 1756	1	273
Jonathan, m. Anne **LUCAS**, July 13, 1785	1	240
Jonathan B., m. Sarah C. **CRANDALL**, b. of Goshen, Jan. 11, 1846, by Rev. David L. Marks	M	70
Lemuel*, Sr., d. [Dec.] 30, [1807], ae "about 40 about 80" [sic] *("Samuel"?)	2	393
Lois, d. Dr. [ ], b. Mar. 3, 1746/7	1	259
Lois, m. Jared **ABERNETHA**, May 26, 1766	1	233
Louce*, m. David **HURLBUTT**, Mar. 3, 1783 *("Louisa" in Hibbard's)	1	240
Lucy, m. Frederick **HURLBUTT**, b. of Goshen, May 4, 1826, by Elder Eli Barnett	M	17
Mabel, d. Jno, b. Feb. 17, 1763	1	224
Martha, d. Stephen, b. Mar. 11, 1771	1	238
Mary, d. Amos, b. Dec. 6, 1741/2	1	254
Mary, d. [Stephen], b. Feb. 15, 1766	1	237
Mary, d. Stephen, d. July 17, 1766	1	235
Mary, 2nd, d. [Stephen], b. May 10, 1767	1	237
Nancy, of Goshen, m. Rev. Aaron **HUNT**, of Sharon, Apr. 12, 1832, by Rev. Laban Clark	M	37
Orrin, of Mansfield, m. Rhoda **PARMELEE**, of Goshen, Feb. 25, 1822, by Rev. Joseph Harvey	M	5
Rebecca, d. Samuell, Jr. [& Sarah], b. Jan. 29, 1745/6	1	257
Rhoda, d. David, b. Sept. 1, 1761	1	224
Rhoda, b. Sept. 11, 1776; m. Abraham **NORTON**, Nov. 27, 1794	1	194
Ruth, d. Stephen, b. Oct. 10, 1760	1	263
Samuell, Jr., m. Sarah **HOLCOMB**, Oct. 29, 1744	1	257
Samuel, Capt., d. Mar. 26, 1749, ae 79 y. 10 m.	1	260
Samuel*, Sr., d. [Dec.] 30, [1807], ae "about 40 about 80" [sic] *("Lemuel"?)	2	393
Sarah, d. Elihu, b. June 28, 1759	1	262
Sarah, m. Allyn **LUCAS**, Oct. 8, 1780	1	240
Sollomon, s. Elisha, b. Aug. 27, 1764	1	234
Stephen, m. Mary **WALTER**, Jan. 3, 1760	1	269
Step[hen], s. D[ ], b. May 6, 1764	1	234
Stephen, s. Stephen, b. May 6, 1764	1	237
Susannah, d. Jno, b. Feb. 18, 1755	1	271
Susannah, d. Jan. 3, 1820, ae 62	2	298
William Henry, s. David, d. Mar. 10, 1806, ae 14 m.	2	393
TIBBALS, TIBBALLS, TIBELL, Abigail, m. Alfred **APLEY**, b. of Goshen, Jan. 15, 1851, by Frederick Marsh	M	78
Harriet T., m. George W. **STRONG**, b. of Goshen, Sept. 29, 1847, by Frederick Marsh	M	72
Mary*, m. John **WILLOUGHBY**, Oct. 2, 1728 *("Mary **DIBBLE**" in Hibbard's Hist.)	1	256

	Vol.	Page
TIBBALS, TIBBALLS, TIBELL, (cont.), Mary Jane, m. Truman P. **CLARK**, b. of Goshen, Mar. 5, 1849, by Frederick March	M	75
TISDILL, Susannah, m. Roger **PETTIBONE**, Mar. 15, 1764	1	233
TOWNER, TOWRNER, TORNER, Elijah, s. Eph[raim], b. Apr. 3, 1758	1	273
Eph[raim], m. Sarah **WILLCOX**, Oct. 3, 1750	1	268
Ephraim, s. Ephraim [& Sarah], b. Mar. 29, 1752	1	268
Ephraim, d. Dec. 25, 1760	1	272
Ezekiel, s. Eph[raim], b. Mar. 3, 1756	1	273
Laban, s. Ephraim, b. Feb. 2, 1754	1	270
Moses, s. Eph[raim], b. Sept. 15, 1760	1	262
Phebe, m. Arah **WIARD***, Aug. 13, 1740 *("**WARD**" in Hibbard's Hist.)	1	254
Timothy, s. Leban, b. July 18, 1777	1	241
TUTTLE, Amos, s. Timothy, b. Feb. 4, 1744/5	1	257
Aurelia, d. D[ ], b. June 29, 1764	1	234
Calvin, s. Ichabod, b. Aug. 21, 1772	1	238
Clarissa, of Goshen, m. Nehemiah **GRIFFIN**, of Plymouth, Jan. 6, 1830, by Rev. Bradley Selleck	M	28
David, s. Timothy J., b. Dec. 26, 1756	1	224
David, s. [Timothy], d. Oct. 10, 1760	1	272
Deborah, m. Elias **KELLEY**, b. of Goshen, Sept. 23, 1833, by Rev. Grant Powers	M	41
Deliverance, s. [Jonathan], b. Oct. 14, 1753	1	263
Deliverance, s. [Timothy], d. Oct. 8, 1760	1	272
Elisha, s. Timothy, b. Nov. 24, 1746	1	258
Esther, m. Warren **BROWN**, b. of Goshen, Jan. 5, 1840, by Rev. David Osborn	M	57
Esther, m. Amasa **WADHAMS**, b. of Goshen, Mar. 26, 1843, by Rev. Thomas Ellis	M	64
Hannah, d. [Timothy J.], b. Aug. 10, 1758	1	224
Hannah, m. Silas **RICHMOND**, Mar. 29, 1762	1	225
Ichabod, s. Timothy, b. June 23, 1748	1	259
Ichabod, m. Elizabeth **MATTHEWS**, Feb. 20, 1772	1	240
Ichabod, s. Ichabod, b. July 15, 1776	1	241
Ithiel B., of Lee, Mass., m. Rhoda S. **MINER**, of Goshen, Oct. 8, 1823, by Daniel Brayton, Elder. Int. Pub.	M	11
Laura, of Goshen, m. Daniel **DENNIS**, of Stratford, Dec. 10, 1828, by Rev. E. Washburn	M	24
Lois, d. [Timothy J.], b. May 21, 1760	1	224
Luther, s. Ichabod, b. Apr. 8, 1774	1	239
Mary, d. Timothy, b. Dec. 1, 1743	1	256
Mary, of Goshen, m. Ithiel **LOMBARD**, of Belchertown, Mass., Mar. 1, 1840, by Nelson Brewster, J. P.	M	57
Morris, m. Althia **ALLEN**, b. of Goshen, Feb. 3, 1831, by Rev. Grant Powers. Int. Pub.	M	32
Noah, s. Jonathan, b. Mar. 26, 1752	1	263
Samuel B., of Hartford, m. Lucretia C. N. **CARLISLE**, of Goshen, Oct. 2, 1854, by Lavalette Perrin, at the house of Mrs. Myron **NORTON**	M	84
Sarah, d. Step[hen], b. May 23, 1759	1	234
Sarah, d. Eph[raim], b. May 23, 1759 *("Stephen"?)	1	262

	Vol.	Page
TUTTLE, (cont.),		
Sarah Ann, of Goshen, m. James **BURR**, of Norfolk, Oct. 15, 1837, by Rev. John Lucky	M	52
Step[hen], m. Lydia **LYMAN**, Mar. 23, 1758	1	269
Stephen, s. Stephen, b. Aug. 4, 1772	1	238
Thankful, d. [Jonathan], b. May 30, 1759	1	263
Timothy, m. Hanah **WADDAMS**, Jan. 27, 1742/3, by Rev. Mr. Heaton	1	255
Timothy, s. [Jonathan], b. June 10, 1755	1	263
Timothy, d. Oct. 23, 1760	1	272
Tyrannus, his child d. June 15, 1809, ae 3 m.	2	394
Tyrannus, his child d. Aug. 8, 1809, ae 2 1/2	2	394
UTLEY, Erastus, m. Deborah **MORGAN**, b. of Goshen, Dec. 28, 1820, by Rev. Joseph Harvey	M	2
VAIL, David, d. Dec. 10, 1823, ae 49	2	399
Phebe, d. Sept. 11, 1808, ae 8	2	394
VALSON*, Bethiah, m. Jacob **BEECH**, Sept. 19, 1753		
*("**WATSON**" in Hibbard's Hist. of Goshen)	1	269
VARNEY, George A., of New York, m. Juliana **CASE**, of Goshen, Sept. 26, 1830, by Rev. Grant Powers. Int. Pub.	M	30
VEB, Alanson Brooks, [twin with Prudence Cooper], s. Jona[tha]n, b. May 22, 1782	1	244
Prudence Cooper, [twin with Alanson Brooks], d. Jonathan, b. May 22, 1782	1	244
VESPER, Thomas, m. Irena **BRIODY**, b. of Goshen, Oct. 27, 1831, by Rev. Grant Powers	M	35
WADHAMS, WADDAMS, WADAMS, WADHAM, Aaron, s. John, d. Jan. 1, 1776	1	235
Abner H., b. May 29, 1844	2	18
Abraham, s. Jonathan, b. May 11, 1755	1	271
Abraham, s. Jonathan, d. May 30, 1755	1	272
Abraham, s. Jonathan, b. Sept. 24, 1756	1	273
Abraham, m. Trephena **COLLINS**, Jan. 15, 1778	1	240
Albert, d. Apr. 26, 1819, ae 16	2	298
Albert S., b. Oct. 6, 1825	2	18
Amasa, m. Esther **TUTTLE**, b. of Goshen, Mar. 26, 1843, by Rev. Thomas Ellis	M	64
Amos, s. John, b. Apr. 3, 1772	1	238
Ann, m. Homer **COLLINS**, b. of Goshen, Feb. 3, 1825, by Rev. Joseph Harvey	M	13
Anne, m. John **HOY**, Nov. 9, 1760	1	233
Arthur N., b. Sept. 8, 1854	2	18
Arthur N., d. July 12, 1884, in Idaho Territory, ae 30	2	19
Beebe, his s. [ ], d. Mar. 22, 1811, ae 1 1/2	2	395
Birdsey, illeg. child of Louice **WADHAMS**, b. Sept. 10, 1783; father Birdsey **NORTON**	1	244
Burr, b. Sept. 23, 1810	2	18
Burr, d. Aug. 1, 1868, in Yorkville, N. Y., ae 58	2	19
Carlton, m. Sophia **SPELMAN**, Nov. 27, 1834, by Albert B. Camp	M	45
Caroline, m. Hiram **NORTON**, b. of Goshen, Aug. 14, 1822, by Rev. Joseph Harvey	M	5
Catharine, b. May 7, 1816	2	18

	Vol.	Page
WADHAMS, WADDAMS, WADAMS, WADHAM, (cont.),		
Catharine, of Goshen, m. Abner **HARD**, of Milton, Soc., Oct. 30, 1833, by Rev. Grant Powers	M	42
David, s. Seth, b. Mar. 25, 1769	1	238
Dolly E., of Goshen, m. Almeran M. **CARTER**, of Paris, N. Y., Sept. 26, 1836, by Rev. E. Washburn	M	49
Eliza, of Goshen, m. Anthony **TATRO**, of Winsted, Apr. 6, 1841, by Rev. David Osborn	M	59
Elizabeth, d. John, b. June 5, 1769	1	238
Ellen, m. James **BRADLEY**, b. of Goshen, Aug. 30, 1836, by Rev. Grant Powers	M	48
Emeline, of Goshen, m. Eli **PERKINS**, of Cornwall, Dec. 2, 1840, by Rev. Grant Powers	M	59
Frederic L., b. Dec. 4, 1842	2	18
George, of Goshen, m. Angeline **PARMELEE**, of Cornwall, Nov. 24, 1836, by Rev. Albert G. Wickmore	M	50
Hannah, m. Timothy **TUTTLE**, Jan. 27, 1742/3, by Rev. Mr. Horton	1	255
Harriet, of Goshen, m. Isaac H. **McNIEL**, of Newark, N. J., May 13, 1833, by Rev. Grant Powers	M	40
Isaac, s. John, b. Jan. 3, 1767	1	236
Jacob, m. Mary **LEE**, Jan. 10, 1754	1	269
James, b. Feb. 4, 1815	2	18
James, m. Sarah L. **OVIATT**, Sept. 25, 1839	2	18
James, m. Sarah L. **OVIATT**, b. of Goshen, Sept. 25, 1839, by Rev. Grant Powers	M	56
James, m. Mrs. Lodelia **PLATT**, Oct. 1, 1850	2	18
James, d. Oct. [ ], 1882, ae 68	2	19
James S., b. Oct. 10, 1848	2	18
James S., d. Sept. 26, 1870, at Wolcottville, Conn., ae 22	2	19
Jane M., of Goshen, m. Darius B. **COOK**, of Mich., Aug. 11, 1841, by Rev. Thomas Ellis	M	60
Jesse, his child d. June 14, [1804], ae 4	2	392
John, m. Ruth **MARAH**, Jan. 3, 1765	1	225
John, s. John, b. Sept. 18, 1765	1	234
John, his child d. Feb. 1, 1810, ae 1 d.	2	394
John, his two children, d. Sept. 4, 1812, ae 1 d.	2	395
John, Jr., d. Sept. 3, 1814, ae 49	2	396
John, d. Mar. 3, 1816, ae 83	2	397
Jonathan, m. Judeth **HOW**, Aug. 8, 1754	1	269
Jonathan, Ens., s. Jonathan, b. Dec. 4, 1774	1	239
Jonathan, d. Apr. 12, 1812, ae 82	2	395
Jonathan, his wid., d. July 12, 1813, ae 83	2	396
Jonathan, his s. [ ], d. Oct. 23, 1816, ae 3	2	397
Jonathan, his w. [ ], d. Mar. 16, 1819, ae 41	2	298
Jonathan, Jr., m. Ann P. **LUCAS**, b. of Goshen, Feb. 2, 1841, by Cornelius B. Everist	M	61
Laura E., of Goshen, m. Jonathan **TATRO**, of Collinsville, July 23, 1843, by Rev. J. D. Marshall	M	64
Ledelia, d. Mar. 19, 1886, ae 64	2	19
Louisa M., m. Moses **WADHAMS**, b. of Goshen, Oct. 30, 1828, by Rev. Epaphras Goodman	M	23
Lucia, d. Jonathan, b. Nov. 14, 1766	1	236

	Vol.	Page
WADHAMS, WADDAMS, WADAMS, WADHAM, (cont.),		
Lucia Ann, m. Earl **JOHNSON**, Jan. 9, 1833, by Rev. Walter Smith, of Cornwall	M	39
Louice, had Birdsey illeg. child b. Sept. 10, 1783; f. Birdsey **NORTON**	1	244
Lucy, m. John **BEACH**, b. of Goshen, Nov. 9, 1820, by Rev. J. Harvey	M	2
Lydia A., of Goshen, m. Dwight **GALLUP**, of Ledyard, Nov. 19, 1849, at the house of Lewis C. **WADHAMS**, by Lavalette Perrin	M	76
Lyman S., b. Mar. 20, 1819	2	18
Lyman S., d. Apr. 27, 1878, ae 59	2	19
Maria, of Goshen, m. Joseph M. **LAWTON**, of Westfield, Mass., May 19, 1852, by Rev. L. A. McKinstry	M	81
Mariah E., m. Ralph G. **SCOVILLE**, Sept. 16, 1851, at the house of Lewis **WADHAMS**, by Lavalette Perrin	M	80
Martha, Mrs., d. Dec. 29, 1821, ae 39 y.	2	18
Mary, m. John **HOW**, Apr. [ ], 1756	1	269
Mary, m. Watts H. **BROOKS**, b. of Goshen, Apr. 3, 1834, by Rev. Grant Powers	M	44
Mina, d. Abraham, b. Jan. 10, 1779	1	243
Moses, s. Jonathan, b. Sept. 17, 1759	1	262
Moses, m. Anne **COLLINS**, Jan. 9, 1783	1	240
Moses, had child b. Jan. 7, 1784; d. in a few hours	1	244
Moses, his child d. Apr. 30, [1805], ae 2	2	392
Moses, d. Mar. 11, 1823, ae 63	2	399
Moses, m. Louisa M. **WADHAMS**, b. of Goshen, Oct. 30, 1828, by Rev. Epaphras Goodman	M	23
Nancy, d. Seth, b. Oct. 18, 1767	1	236
Nelson, of Goshen, m. Elvira **GRISWOLD**, of Milton, June 13, 1837, by Rev. Grant Powers	M	51
Norman, b. Apr. 14, 1782	2	18
Norman, m. Martha **NORTH**, Dec. 20, 1809	2	18
Norman, his w. [ ], d. Dec. 30, 1821, ae 39	2	399
Norman, m. Philenda **HUNGERFORD**, Aug. 18, 1822	2	18
Norman, Jr., b. June 13, 1827	2	18
Norman, Jr., d. July 21, 1850, ae 23, in California	2	19
Norman, d. Aug. 30, 1860, ae 78	2	18
Obed, s. John, b. May 18, 1775	1	239
Orlo E., b. Aug. 26, 1852	2	18
Phebe, of Goshen, m. Roswell **CARTER**, of Buffalo, N. Y., [Mar.] 15, 1838, by Rev. Grant Powers	M	53
Philinda, Mrs., d. Dec. [ ], 1858, ae 74 y.	2	18
Ruth, w. John, d. Feb. 9, 1801, in the 63rd y. of her age	1	246
Sam[ue]l, m. Lois **DICKENSON**, Mar. 23, 1780	1	240
Sarah L., Mrs., d. Aug. 9, 1849, ae 26	2	19
Seth, s. Noah, b. Nov. 1, 1743	1	257
Seth, m. Anne **CATLING**, June 11, 1767	1	233
Seth, d. Apr. 8, 1817, ae 72	2	397
Solomon, d. Dec. 21, 1821, ae 81	2	399
Tazah Mark*, [b.], May 22, 1778 *(Perhaps "Tazah child of Mark")	1	242
Uri M., b. July 26, 1840	2	18

GOSHEN VITAL RECORDS 67

WADHAMS, WADDAMS, WADAMS, WADHAM, (cont.), Vol. Page
  Uri M., d. Sept. 25, 1863, at Alexandria, Va., ae 23   2   19
WALTER, Alfred, his w. [   ], d. Oct. 25, [1806], ae 25   2   393
  Alfred, his child d. Jan. 12, 1809, ae 5 m.   2   394
  Alfred, his child d. Jan. 14, 1812, ae 1 1/2   2   395
  Charles, m. Julia **LEWIS**, b. of Goshen, Aug. 9, 1829, by
    Rev. Grant Powers. Int. Pub.   M   25
  Daniel, s. [Henry], b. Mar. 19, 1754   1   273
  Elemwell, s. Henry, b. Apr. 30, 1749   1   261
  Elijah, s. William, b. Apr. 29, 1751; d. Feb. 9, 1753   1   268
  Henry, had d. [   ], b. Sept. 2, 1750   1   261
  Ira, s. Lemuel, b. Mar. 11, 1770   1   239
  Joel, s. [William], b. July 1, 1740   1   259
  John, s. Henry, b. Mar. 16, 1752   1   273
  Laura Ann, m. David A. **WOOSTER**, b. of Goshen, Mar. 14,
    1836, by Rev. Grant Powers   M   47
  Lemuel*, m. Mehetable **OSBORN**, Oct. [ ], 1769
    *("Samuel" in Hibbard's Hist.)   1   233
  Lydia, d. [Lemuel], b. Nov. 18, 1772   1   239
  Mary, d. Walter, b. May 27, 1742   1   255
  Mary, m. Stephen **THOMSON**, Jan. 2, 1760   1   269
  Patience, d. [William], b. Dec. 12, 1746; Dec. 21, 1747   1   259
  Patience, m. Lemuel **BASSETT**, Oct. 23, 1773   1   233
  Salla, d. [Lemuel], b. May 22, 1771   1   239
  Stephen, s. [William], b. Dec. 21, 1748   1   259
  William, s. William, b. Aug. 21, 1744   1   259
  -----, wid., d. Dec. 3, 1814, ae 73   2   396
WARD, Arah*, m. Phebe **TOWNER**, Aug., 13, 1740   *(Arnold Copy
    has "Arah **WIARD**")   1   254
  Bethuel, s. [Zenas], b. Apr. 8, 1744   1   256
  Dianthe, d. Arad & Phebe, b. Aug. 9, 1741   *(Arnold Copy
    has "Dianthe **WIARD**")   1   254
  Elisha, d. July 13, [1807], ae 16   2   393
  Mocox, s. Zenas, Nov. 6, 1745   1   257
  Zenas, m. Mary **BATES**, May 24, 1743   1   256
WARNER, Joseph W., of Dover, Dutchess, N. Y., m. Deborah M.
    KELLEY, of Goshen, Mar. 4, 1839, by Rev. John
    Lucky   M   55
WARREN, Cornelia A., m. Edwin **IVES**, May 20, 1847, by Rev.
    William H. Moore   M   72
WASHBURN, Eliza C., m. John H. **COLLINS**, May 12, 1822, by Rev.
    Ebenezer Washburn   M   5
  Melinda A., m. Thaddeus G. **KELLOGG**, b. of Goshen, Sept.
    4, 1822, by David Miller   M   6
WATSON*, Bethiah, m. Jacob **BEECH**, Sept. 19, 1753   *(Arnold
    Copy has "**VALSON**")   1   269
  Lois, m. Job **WILLCOX**, Oct. 26, 1757   1   225
WAY, Phebe, m. Edward **WRIGHT**, b. of Goshen, May 24, 1826, by
    Elder Eli Barnett   M   17
  Sarah, of Goshen, m. Amos **LAMPSON**, of New Milford,
    May 7, 1833, by Rev. Grant Powers   M   40
WEAVER, Elias, s. Jonathan, b. May 4, 1799   1   247

	Vol.	Page
WEBSTER, Amos, of Harwinton, m. Experience **BARNUM**, of Goshen, May 13, 1840, by Rev. Grant Powers	M	57
Cynthia, of Goshen, m. Elias **BUELL**, of Litchfield, May 7, 1828, by Rev. Francis H. Case	M	22
Levinia, of Goshen, m. Isaiah **SHEPEERD**, of Litchfield, Oct. 23, 1826, by Rev. Francis H. Case	M	18
WEDGE, Marinda, d. Stephen, b. Feb. 25, 1774	1	244
Stephen, s. Stephen, b. June 12, 1786	1	244
Temperance, d. Stephen, b. Mar. 28, 1788	1	246
WEEKS, Betsey, of Goshen, m. Rufus **CARRIER**, of Kent, Sept. 24, 1828, by Rev. Silas Ambler	M	23
Deman, of Warren, m. Betsey **HART**, of Goshen, Oct. 17, 1822, by Rev. Joseph Harvey	M	6
WEISLEY, Rufus, m. Caroline **AUSTIN**, b. of Goshen, Nov. 24, 1831, by Rev. George Carrington	M	36
WELCH, Catharine, m. Daniel **O'DAY**, June 25, 1848, by Rev. Lavalette Perrin, at his house	M	74
WELTON, Daniel M., his child d. July 22, [1807], ae 11	2	393
WEST, Dorothy, m. Moses **HARRIS**, Mar. 20, 1746	1	257
WHEELER, Caroline M., m. Wells B. **MORGAN**, Mar. 27, 1852, by Rev. David Miller	M	80
WHITING, Frederick P., of Torrington, m. Mary N. **HILLS**, of Goshen, Feb. 15, 1826, by Rev. Francis H. Case	M	16
John N., of Torrington, m. Laura Ann **HART**, of Goshen, Nov. 5, 1851, by Rev. L. A. McKinstry	M	80
William D., m. Sarah **SPERRY**, Mar. 27, 1853, by Lavalette Perrin	M	82
-----, Mr. his child d. Aug. 22, [1807], ae 6 m.	2	393
WIARD, WYARD, Arah*, Phebe **TOWNER**, Aug. 13, 1740 *("Arah **WARD**" in Hibbard's Hist.)	1	254
David, s. Thomas, b. Dec. 28, 1770	1	244
Dianthe, d. Arad & Phebe, b. Aug. 9, 1741	1	254
Nancy, d. [Thomas], b. Jan. 24, 1773	1	244
Susannah, d. [Thomas], b. Nov. 24, 1775	1	244
Thomas, [twin with], [s. Thomas], b. Apr. 8, 1781	1	244
-----, [twin with Thomas, d. Thomas], b. Apr. 8, 1781	1	244
WILCOX, WILLCOX, Abner, s. Nathaniell, b. Apr. 15, 1754	1	271
Adah, d. Samuell, b. Sept. 15, 1768	1	237
Adna, s. Sam[uel], d. Feb. 15, 1766	1	235
Ami, of Sheffield, m. Abby **WOODRUFF**, of New Hartford, Sept. 2, 1844, at the house of Simeon **LOOMIS**, by Thomas Benedict	M	66
Benjamin, s. Gid[eon], b. Mar. 19, 1760; d. 3 wks. after birth	1	262
Chauncey, of Greenwich, m. Abigail B. **LUDINGTON**, of Goshen, Nov. 6, 1828, by Rev. George Carrington	M	24
D[ ], had child b. Mar. 14, 1767	1	237
Elijah, m. Silena Lamb **BECKWITH**, Mar. 8, 1765	1	233
Elijah, s. Elijah, b. Feb. 2, 1766	1	236
Elijah, s. Elijah, d. Feb. 24, 1766	1	235
Elijah, s. Elijah, b. Feb. [ ], 1766	1	236
Elijah, s. Elijah, d. Mar. [ ], 1766	1	235
Eunice, d. Job, b. Oct. 22, 1766	1	236

	Vol.	Page
WILCOX, WILLCOX, (cont.),		
Eunice, d. Job, b. Oct. 22, 1766	1	237
[E]unice, d. Job, b. Oct. 22, 1766	1	237
Gideon, m. Mary **BLANCHARD**, Nov. 8, 1751	1	261
Gid[eon], d. May 20, 1760	1	272
Heman, s. Job, b. Sept. 10, 1768	1	237
Heman, s. Job, b. Sept. 16, 1768	1	237
Huldah, d. Gideon, b. Aug. 16, 1751	1	261
Isaac, s. John, b. Mar. 13, 1767	1	237
J. Flavil, his child d. Sept. 19, 1808, ae 6	2	394
Jesse, s. Nath[anie]ll, b. July 16, 1757	1	273
Job, m. Lois **WATSON**, Oct. 26, 1757	1	225
Job, s. [Job], b. Oct. 30, 1764	1	236
John, Jr., m. Mary **NORVEL**, Mar. 25, 1762	1	225
Jonah, s. Nath[anie]ll, b. Oct. 12, 1752	1	271
Lois, d. [Job], b. Aug. 4, 1760	1	224
Martin, m. Ruth **IVES**, Mar. 2, 1758	1	269
Martin, s. Elijah, b. Feb. [ ], 1767	1	236
Martin, s. Elijah, b. Apr. 27, 1767	1	236
Martin, d. June 6, 1767	1	235
Mary, w. Gideon, d. Jan. 28, 1758	1	272
Mary, d. Gideon, b. Nov. 4, 1758	1	262
Mary, d. John, Jr., b. Sept. 29, 1764	1	237
Mary, d. Jno, Jr., b. Sept. 29, 1764	1	237
Moses, s. [Job], b. July 2, 1762	1	224
Nathaniel, m. Abigail **HURLBUTT**, Nov. 24, 1748	1	259
Oliver, s. Gid[eon], b. Mar. 20, 1753	1	270
Phebe, d. Sam[ue]ll, b. May 8, 1761	1	263
Phebe, wid., m. Jeremiah **BELCHER**, Oct. 25, 1763	1	225
Ruth, d. Nathaniell, b. Oct. 22, 1749	1	260
Ruth, d. Martin, b. Apr. 9, 1759	1	262
Ruth, w. Martin, d. July 4, 1760	1	272
Ruth, d. [Martin], d. Aug. 6, 1760	1	272
Ruth, d. Samuell, b. Aug. 20, 1767	1	237
Samuel, m. Phebe **ROYCE**, July 30, 1753	1	269
Samuel, s. Sam[ue]ll, b. Aug. 18, 1758	1	273
Sarah, m. Eph[raim] **TOWNER**, Oct. 3, 1750	1	268
Sarah, d. Job, b. Oct. 13, 1758	1	224
Sarah, d. Job, d. Apr. 8, 1767	1	235
Silvanus, s. Samuell, b. July 16, 1771	1	238
Stephen, s. Gid[eon], b. Apr. 19, 1755	1	273
Thomas, s. Samuel, b. May 25, 1769	1	262
Zadock, s. Samuell, b. Nov. 6, 1755	1	271
WILLIAMS, Abigail, d. [Daniell], b. Feb. 14, 1767	1	243
Dan, s. Jacob, d. Aug. 14, 1765	1	235
Daniel, s. Jacob, b. Oct. 17, 1759	1	262
Daniell, m. Prudence **SMITH**, Feb. 15, 1765	1	233
Dan[ie]ll, s. Daniel, b. June 1, 1765	1	234
Dan[ie]ll, s. Dan[ie]ll, b. June 1, 1765	1	243
Elizabeth, d. Jacob, b. Dec. 11, 1747	1	259
Jacob, m. Ruth **STANLEY**, Dec. 11, 1746	1	258
Jacob, s. Jacob, b. June 27, 1752	1	270
Jacob, m. Elizabeth **MERREL**, Aug. 24, 1773	1	233

WILLIAMS, (cont.),	Vol.	Page
Lucia, d. Jacob & Mary, b. Mar. 23, 1757	1	273
Lucia, d. Jacob, d. Jan. 19, 1762	1	272
Luinia, d. Jacob, b. Mar. 12, 1765	1	234
Mary, d. [Daneill], b. Apr. [ ], 1769	1	243
Moses, s. Jacob, b. Apr. 7, 1763	1	234
Moses, s. Jacob, b. Apr. 7, 1764	1	234
Moses, s. Jacob, b. Aug. 22, 1765	1	235
Peter, of Goshen, m. Maria **FITCH**, of Litchfield, Apr. 6, 1823, by Rev. Joseph Harvey	M	9
Prudence, d. Jacob, b. July 13, 1767	1	237
Ruth, d. Jacob, b. Dec. 1, 1749	1	260
Ruth, w. Jacob, d. July 4, 1752	1	272
Sarah, d. Jacob, b. June 2, 1755	1	271
Uri, s. Jacob, Jr., b. Mar. 1, 1774	1	239
WILLIS, Jane, d. Oct. 28, 1820, ae 24	2	298
WILLOUGHBY, WILLOBY, Ambrose, s. [John & Mary], b. Sept. 30, 1743	1	256
Ambrose, s. John, d. Oct. 7, 1751	1	268
Amhurst, s. [John], b. Aug. 5, 1769	1	241
Arnold, s. Vestal, b. Oct. 9, 1771	1	238
David, s. Vestal, b. Dec. 8, 1764	1	236
Eben[eze]r, s. [Vestal*], b. May 6, 1778 *("Westal")	1	248
Huldah, d. [John], b. Mar. 20, 1773	1	241
John, m. Mary **TIBELL***, Oct. 2, 1728 *("**DIBBLE**" in Hibbard's)	M	256
John, s. [John & Mary], b. June 28, 1729	1	256
John, Jr., m. Olive **SMITH**, Dec. 18, 1753	1	269
John, s. Jno, b. Nov. 5, 1754	1	271
John, d. Apr. 25, 1774	1	235
Josiah, s. [John & Mary], b. Aug. 30, 1731	1	256
Josiah, d. Dec. 31, [1804], ae 70	2	392
Lydia, d. [Vestal], b. May 30, 1780	1	248
Mary, d. [John & Mary], b. Aug. 2, 173[ ]	1	255
Mary, d. Jno, b. Feb. 25, 1764	1	234
Nancy, d. Vestel, b. Mar. 18, 1767	1	236
Olive, d. Jno, b. Sept. 2, 1758	1	262
Ruth, d. Vestel*, b. Apr. 18, 1776 *(Written over "Westal")	1	248
Salmon, s. John, b. Sept. 22, 1762	1	224
Samuel, s. [John & Mary], b. Apr. 10, 1741	1	256
Sam[ue]ll, s. John, d. Oct. 9, 1751	1	268
Sam[ue]ll, s. Jno, b. Nov. 22, 1756	1	273
Sarah, d. [Vestel], b. Feb. 11, 1785	1	248
Susannah, d. [Vestel], b. Nov. 11, 1782	1	248
Vestel*, s. Vestel, b. Nov. 20, 1769 *('Westal")	1	237
Westel, s. [John & Mary], b. Mar. 31, 1739	1	256
Westal, m. Ruth **ARNOLD**, June 5, 1764	1	233
William, s. [John & Mary], b. Feb. 25, 1737	1	256
William, s. [Vestel], b. May 14, 1787	1	248
Zerah, s. John, b. Feb. 10, 1767	1	241
WILSON, John, s. [& Sarah], b. Sept. 15, 1784	1	244
Leighton B., d. Apr. 24, 1807, ae 10	2	393
Louice, d. [ ] & Sarah, b. Aug. 21, 1782	1	244

	Vol.	Page
WILSON, (cont.),		
Mary, m. Andrew **BAILEY**, b. of Goshen, Oct. 16, 1845, by Rev. Chester Colton	M	69
WILTON, Stephen, d. Apr. 24, 1805, ae 93	2	392
WIX, Alva, of Warren, m. Amanda **HART**, of Goshen, May 21, 1823, by Rev. Joseph Harvey	M	9
WOODRUFF, Abby, of New Hartford, m. Ami **WILCOX**, of Sheffield, Sept. 2, 1844, at the house of Simeon **LOOMIS**, by Thomas Benedict	M	66
Daniel, his child d. Mar. 20, 1822, ae 10	2	399
WOOSTER, Austin, m. Rebecca A. **ALLYN**, b. of Goshen, Mar. 2, 1845, by Rev. J. D. Marshall	M	67
David, his child d. Jan. 26, 1822, ae 7 m.	2	399
David A., m. Laura Ann **WALTER**, b. of Goshen, Mar. 14, 1836, by Rev. Grant Powers	M	47
Jo Anna, m. Peter Moriaty **ROBERTS**, b. of Goshen, Apr. 2, 1823, by Daniel Coe	M	9
Joseph A., m. Mary M. **HAWKINS**, b. of Goshen, Nov. 19, 1840, by Grant Powers	M	58
Lucy C., m. Philo **HONE***, May 24, 1835, by Rev. Albert G. Wickmore *(**HOWE**"?)	M	46
Mary C., m. Henry H. **CAUKINS**, Dec. 27, 1846, by Rev. D. L. Marks	M	72
Mary E., m. Zebulon C. **LAWTON**, b. of Goshen, Mar. 17, 1845, by Rev. J. D. Marshall	M	67
Newton, of Oxford, m. Lavina **BROWN**, of Goshen, Oct. 1, 1820, by Nathan Emery, Elder	M	1
Polly Ann, d. David, d. Oct. 27, 1821, ae 18	2	399
Sarah E., m. Willard E. **GAYLORD**, May 14, 1851, at the house of Sterling **WOOSTER**, by Lavalette Perrin	M	79
WRIGHT, Abigail, d. Sam[ue]ll, b. Jan. 8, 1757	1	273
Andrew, s. Sam[ue]ll, b. Mar. 11, 1763	1	224
Asaph, s. [John], b. June 15, 1735	1	261
Asaph, s. Jabez, b. Jan. 3, 1772	1	239
Charles, s. [John], b. Sept. 3, 1739	1	261
Charles, m. Ruth **SMITH**, Nov. 11, 1767	1	225
David, s. John, b. Sept. 5, 1746	1	261
Dorcas, d. John, b. Sept. 9, 1733	1	261
Edward, m. Phebe **WAY**, b. of Goshen, May 24, 1826, by Elder Eli Barnett	M	17
Eleanor, m. Nathaniell **ROYCE**, Nov. 5, 1760	1	269
Freedom, s. John, b. July 3, 1749	1	261
Freelove, d. Jabez, b. Jan. 1, 1768	1	237
Jabez, s. [John], b. July 4, 1737	1	261
Jabez, m. Martha **BALDWIN**, Feb. 11 or 12, 1767	1	233
Jabez, d. Mar. 21, 1813, ae 75	2	395
John, had child b. Dec. [ ], 1741; d. Dec. [ ], 1741	1	261
John, s. John, b. Jan. 22, 1743	1	261
Josiah, s. Sam[ue]l, b. Apr. 6, 1753	1	270
Marcy, d. [John], b. Sept. 6, 1751	1	261
Martha, d. Jabez, b. Mar. 24, 1770	1	237
Oliver, s. Sam[ue]ll, b. Sept. 1, 1755	1	271
Oliver, s. Sam[ue]ll, d. Sept. 18, 1755	1	272

	Vol.	Page
WRIGHT, (cont.),		
Ozias, s. Sam[ue]ll, b. Feb. 18, 1759	1	262
Sarah, d. Charles, b. Jan. 28, 1770	1	238
Cybill, d. [Jabez], b. Mar. 4, 1776	1	239
Tyrannus, s. Charles, b. Mar. 22, 1768	1	238
WYARD, [see under **WIARD**]		
YALE, Elisha, m. Rebeckah **NORTH**, Sept. 1, 1762	1	225
Elisha, s. Elisha, b. Dec. 7, 1762	1	224
Elisha, of Canaan, m. Delight **LYMAN**, of Goshen, Nov. 21, 1822, by Rev. Joseph Harvey	M	7
Gad L., m. Abby W. **REED**, of Goshen, Oct. 16, 1836, by Albert G. Wickmore	M	49
NO SURNAME, Nathan, his child d. Jan. 15, 1810, ae 4	2	394
Sarah, d. [ ], b. June 26, 1764	1	234
Uranie, d. Levi, Jr., b. Dec. 6, 1785	1	244

GRANBY VITAL RECORDS
1786-1850

	Vol.	Page
ABBE, ABBY, Harr[i]et, res. Rainbow, d. May 23, 1851, ae 28	1	138
James, of Enfield, m. Harriet **HOLCOMB**, of Granby, June 4, 1844, by I. P. Warren	1	42
ABBOTT, James D., s. Louis D., mechanic & Sarah N., b. July 11, 1849	1	236-7
ABELLS, Franklin L., of Lowell, Mass., m. Esther C. **HOLCOMB**, of Granby, Nov. 15, 1831, by Rev. Asa Cornwall	1	9
ADAIR, Elizabeth, m. Willson **KELLOGG**, b. of Granby, Sept. 8, 1830, by Stephen Crosby	1	4
ADAMS, Almira, m. Jarvis **SPRING**, Apr. 8, 1830, by Ammi Linsley, V. D. M.	1	2
Harvey, shoemaker, ae 23, b. Willington, res. Granby, m. Angeline C. **CHAPIN**, ae 27, of Granby, June 11, 1848, by Rev. Stephen Rushmore	1	226-7
Harvey, shoemaker & Angeline, had d. [ ], b. Oct. 1, 1849	1	248-9
Ida G., d. Harvey, shoemaker, ae 25 & Angeline, ae 30, b. Oct. 27, 1848	1	234-5
James W., merchant, b. Simsbury, res. Tariffville, m. Abigail **BLAKESLEY**, b. Granby, Nov. 8, 1848, by Rev. Ransom Warner	1	238-9
Mary, of Granby, m. Hiram **HUMPHREYS**, of Simsbury, July 18, 1833, by Ammi Linsley, V. D. M.	1	14
Polly M., m. Trumbull **WILCOX**, Sept. 9, 1830, by Isaac Porter	1	4
ADELL, Celecta P., of Granby, m. Joseph E. **THOMAS**, of Waterbury, Nov. 25, 1847, by Rev. Stephen Rushmore	1	55
ADDANY, Sarah, Mrs., m. Noah **PHELPS**, Jan. 12, 1775	TM1	33
ALDEN, Caroline W., ae 20, b. Springfield, res. Granby, m. Benjamin F. **BARKER**, ae 21, b. Granville, Mass., res. Granby, Mar. 26, 1851, by T. A. Savage	1	134
ALDERMAN, Abigail M., m. Milo M. **OWEN**, June 12, 1839, by Rev. Daniel Hemenway	1	30
Almond, b. July 17, 1808	TM1	43
Catharine E., housewife, d. June 15, 1848, ae 22	1	230-1
Chloe H., of East Granby, m. Henry **REMINGTON**, of Suffield, May 31, 1846, by [ ]	1	48
Chloe H., b. E. Granby, res. Granby, d. Sept. 16, 1848, ae 2 1/2	1	244-5
Clyden, mechanic, d. [ ], 1847, ae 33	1	230-1
Cynthia T., of Granby, m. Elisha **ROOT**, of Westfield, Mass., Nov. 30, 1840, by Rev. Daniel Hemenway	1	35
Daniel T., [s. Ephraim], b. Dec. 22, [1786?]	TM1	5
Daniel T., Jr., m. Eliza **GODARD**, b. of Granby, June 1, 1835, by C. Bentley	1	19
Elijah, b. Apr. 11, 1815	TM1	43
Eliza, b. May 15, 1806	TM1	43
George, b. July 9, 1796	TM1	43

ALDERMAN, (cont.),   Vol. Page

	Vol.	Page
Irijah B., m. Annis **ROCKWELL**, Jan. 27, 1831, by Stephen Crosby	1	6
Israel P., farmer, ae 23, b. W. Springfield, res. Chenago, N. Y., m. Caroline **GRIFFIN**, ae 22, b. Granby, res. same, Dec. 23, 1847, by Rev. Miles Olmsted	1	226-7
James H., m. Catharine E. **HOLCOMB**, Aug. 30, 1847	1	226-7
Jane, m. Watson **DEWEY**, b. of Granby, July 8, 1840, by Rev. Chauncey D. Rice	1	34
Laura A., of East Granby, m. Luke **BUSH**, of Westfield, Oct. 22, 1844, by I. B. Clarke	1	43
Mary Ann, m. John C. **CARPENTER**, b. of Granby, Apr. 9, 1849, by Rev. A. L. Loveland	1	58
Mary Ann, ae 25, m. J. C. **CARPENTER**, shoemaker, ae 25, b. of Granby, Apr. 9, 1849, by Rev. A. L. Loveland	1	238-9
Parly, b. July 7, 1794	TM1	43
Phelps, b. July 12, 1813	TM1	43
Ranselear, b. Feb. 15, 1805	TM1	43
Zebena, b. Dec. 6, 1810	TM1	43
Zeriwiah, b. July 5, 1801	TM1	43
ALFORD, B[e]ulah, of Granby, m. George **CLARK** of Granville, Mass., Aug. 27, 1834, by Charles Bentley	1	17
ALLEN, [see also **ALLING**], Caroline, m. William **WILLIAMSON**, Jan. 1, 1847, by Rev. R. G. Thompson, of Tariffville	1	51
Catharine O., of Granby, m. Jonathan P. **THOMPSON**, of Lansing, Mich., Nov. 6, 1850, by Rev. Pliney F. Sanborn	1	62
Catherine O., res. Lansing, Mich., m. Jonathan P. **THOMPSON**, attny. at law, res. Lansing, Mich., Nov. 6, 1851, by Pliny F. Sanborne	1	134
Edward I., s. Marcus, joiner, b. Oct. 16, 1848	1	232-3
Frances Green, d. Truman, Jr. & Lydia A., b. Sept. 11, 1849	1	248-9
Francis Green, d. Jan. 22, 1850, ae 4 m.	1	254-5
Francis Roxana, m. Martin **FANCHER**, Apr. 18, 1838, by Isaac Porter	1	26
Harriet Elizabeth, d. William A., shoemaker & Harriet, b. May 17, 1849	1	232-3
J. O., merchant, ae 23 & Emana G., ae 21, had d. [ ], b. May 8, 1850	1	250-1
James O., m. Emma G. **THOMPSON**, b. of East Granby, Sept. 4, 1849, by Rev. Ralph H. Main, of Tariffville	1	59
James O., merchant, ae 23, b. Enfield, res. Granby, m. Emma G. **THOMPSON**, ae 21, b. New York State, res. Granby, Sept. 4, 1849, by Rev. Ralph H. Main	1	252-3
Josiah C., of Barkhamsted, m. Harriet E. **HAYES**, of Granby, Sept. 12, 1844, by I. P. Warren	1	43
Justus L., shoemaker, b. Simsbury, res. Granby, d. Feb. 25, 1850, ae 34	1	254-5
Justus Luther, m. Alma **HAYES**, b. of Granby, Apr. 16, 1838, by Allen McLean	1	27

	Vol.	Page

ALLEN, [see also **ALLING**], (cont.),
    Luther, shoemaker & Alma, had d. [   ], b. Apr. 16,
        1849   1   232-3
    Samuel D., m. Harriet M. **SHAILOR**, b. of Granby, Mar. 30,
        1835, by Charles Bentley   1   18
    Susan M., m. William **DIBBLE**, b. of Granby, Sept. 7, 1843,
        by Israel B. Warren   1   40
    Truman, m. Electa **HAYES**, b. of Granby, June 12, 1834, by
        Amasa Holcomb   1   21
    Truman, Jr., shoemaker, ae 21, m. Lydia A. **FILLMORE**,
        ae 21, b. of Granby, Apr. 26, 1849, by Rev. A. L.
        Loveland   1   238-9
    Truman, Jr., m. Lydia A. **FILLMORE**, b. of Granby, Apr. 28,
        1849, by Rev. A. L. Loveland   1   58
    William A., m. Harriet L. **KENDALL**, b. of Granby, July 3,
        1848, by Allen McLean   1   56
    William A., shoemaker, ae 29, m. 2nd w. Harriet L.
        KENDALL, ae 28, b. of Granby, July 3, 1848, by
        Rev. Allen McLean   1   226-7
ALLING, [see also **ALLEN**], Marcus B., of Woodbridge, m. Eliza A.
    TAYLOR, of West Granby, Nov. 28, 1844, by
    Rev. Levi Warner   1   44
ANDREWS, ANDRUS, ANDRUSS, Betsey, of Simsbury, m. Leonard
    C. **BACON**, Sept. 8, 1836, by Justus D. Wilcox,
    J. P.   1   22
    Hezekiah A., m. Philura **BACON**, b. of Simsbury, Nov. 2,
        1836, by Rev. J. Shrigley   1   23
    William E., of Farmington, m. Lucy Ann **WILLIAMS**, of
        Granby, July 5, 1835, at the house of John
        WILLIAMS, by Rev. Harvey Ball, of Suffield   1   20
ARMSTRONG, James, of Philadelphia, Pa., m. Annis **LAMPSON**, of
    Granby, June 1, 1831, by Joel Holcomb, J. P.   1   7
ARNOLD, Joseph, of Westfield, Mass., m. Caroline A. **SEARLS**, of
    Granby, May 22, 1844, by I. P. Warren   1   41
ATWOOD, Daniel D., farmer, ae 29 & Permelia M., housewife, ae 25,
    had child b. July 2, 1848   1   222-3
AUSTIN, Thomas H., of Suffield, m. Miranda **MESSENGER**, of
    Granby, June 29, 1840, by Rev. Daniel Hemenway   1   33
AVERY, Horace W., m. Elvina **HAYES**, b. of Granby, Nov. 25, 1841,
    by Rev. Amasa Holcomb, at the house of Phineas
    HAYES   1   36
BABCOCK, Cynthia, d. Benjamin, brass mfgr., colored, ae 29 &
    Frances, housewife, colored, ae 29, b. Nov. 21,
    1847   1   224-5
    Lucy, housewife, b. Wethersfield, res. Granby, d. Dec. 12,
        1848, ae 47   1   244-5
    Robert Primus, s. Benjamin, hostler, colored & Frances,
        colored, b. May 10, 1850   1   250-1
BACON, Arlow, s. [Selah & Balsarah], b. Apr. 25, 1791   TM1   6
    Balsory Lodashi, d. [Selah & Balsarah], b. Aug. 24, 1810   TM1   6
    Edward E., s. Asa, farmer, ae 45 & Sarah, ae 43, b. Apr. [ ],
        1851(?)   (Written "1841")   1   130-1
    Grove, s. [Selah & Balsarah], b. Feb. 9, 1794   TM1   6

	Vol.	Page
BACON, (cont.), Huldah C., of Granby, m. Henry A. **SMITH**, of Blanford, Mass., Jan. 3, 1839, by Justus D. Wilcox, J. P.	1	28
Leonard C., m. Betsey **ANDRUS**, of Simsbury, Sept. 8, 1836, by Justus D. Willcox, J. P.	1	22
Lucius, farmer, ae 23, b. Simsbury, res. Granby, m. Amoret **HAND**, ae 23, b. Blandford, Apr. [ ], 1851, by Rev. John Pegg	1	134
Olive E., m. Albert **RICE**, Oct. 23, 1832, by Isaac Porter	1	12
Philura, m. Hezekiah A. **ANDREWS**, b. of Simsbury, Nov. 2, 1836, by Rev. J. Shrigley	1	23
Salle, d. Selah & Balsarah, b. Jan. 17, 1789	TM1	6
Selah, m. Mrs. Balsarah **BREWER**, Jan. 17, 1786	TM1	6
Selah Austine, s. Selah [& Balsarah], b. Nov. 31 [sic], 1796	TM1	6
Seldon, s. [Selah & Balsarah], b. Oct. 26, 1801	TM1	6
Theron, [s. Selah & Balsarah], b. Jan. 8, 1804	TM1	6
Warren, s. [Selah & Balsarah], b. Apr. 8, 1806	TM1	6
[BAILEY], **BAYLEY**, William H., res. Canton, m. Charlotte **DEBIT**, res. Springfield, Nov. 2, 1848, by Rev. P. F. Sanborn	1	238-9
BANNING, Abner, m. Lucretia **PRATT**, Dec. 7, 1820, by Philander Humphrey, J. P.	TM1	160
Samuel W., merchant, b. Hartland, res. Granby, d. Mar. [ ], 1850, ae 30	1	254-5
BARBER, Orville, of Harwinton, m. Sarah H. **CONE**, of Granby, June 19, 1845, by Rev. James C. Houghton, of Hartland	1	45
BARKER, Benjamin F., ae 21, b. Granville, Mass., res. Granby, m. Caroline W. **ALDEN**, ae 20, b. Springfield, res. Granby, Mar. 26, 1851, by T. A. Savage	1	134
Lucy M., m. Lester **GRIFFIN**, b. of East Granby, Oct. 30, 1844, by I. B. Clarke	1	43
Oliver, m. Hannah **HOLCOMB**, Oct. 29, 1832, by Isaac Porter	1	12
BARLOW, Roland, m. Cleo **GODARD**, Feb. 3, 1831, by Abner Case, J. P.	1	6
Roland, of East Granville, Mass., m. Lavera **KENDALL**, of Granby, Feb. 24, 1841, by C. D. Rice	1	35
Rufus H., m. Alice **HAYES**, Apr. 4, 1837, by Charles Bentley	1	24
BARNARD, Calvin L., of Bloomfield, m. Zilpha G. **HOLCOMB**, of Granby, Oct. 10, 1847, by Rev. Stephen Rushmore	1	54
Harrison, of Simsbury, m. Sally **BLAKESLEY**, of Granby, May 7, 1834, by Rev. D. Hemmenway	1	16
Linnus, peddler, had s. [ ], b. July 21, 1849	1	232-3
BARNES, **BARNS**, Allen, m. Emiline **LOOMISE**, of Southwick, Jan. 3, 1831, by Asa Cornwall	1	5
Allen, farmer & Emelind, had s. [ ], b. Feb. 20, 1849	1	234-5
Betsey, of Granby, m. John **PHELPS**, of East Granville, Mass., Sept. 28, 1840, by Rev. Chauncey D. Rice	1	34
Charles, wheelwright, ae 21 & Lenora, ae 21, had s. [ ], b. Aug. 3, 1849	1	234-5

GRANBY VITAL RECORDS 77

	Vol.	Page
BARNES, BARNS (cont.),		
Emma C., d. Charles, farmer, ae [ ], & Lenora, housewife, b. Sept. 28, 1847 *("ae 11 mos." follows birth date)	1	222-3
Genette E., m. Francis L. **VIETS**, b. of Granby, May 9, 1852, at the house of her father, by George D. Felton	1	66
John R., s. Charles, farmer & Eleanora, b. Aug. 3, 1849	1	248-9
John R., d. June 10, 1850, ae 10 m.	1	254-5
John R., s. Charles & Lenora, b. Mar. 1, 1851	1	130-1
William, Jr., of Windsor, m. Catharine C. **HILLYER**, of Granby, Dec. 25, 1837, by Charles Bentley	1	25
BARNETT, Lucinda, m. Eli R. **DAVIS**, Apr. 15, 1848	1	226-7
BARNEY, Lucy, b. Windsor, d. Feb. 20, 1850, ae 70	1	254-5
BARTHOLOMEW, Augusta, of Granby, m. Selah **WOODRUFF**, of New Hartford, Sept. 15, 1840, by Rev. Chanucey D. Rice	1	34
Ursula, of Granby, m. Azariah S. **FIELDING**, of Hartford, Oct. 28, 1833, by Rev. Charles Bentley	1	15
BARTLETT, BARTLET, Alseda, of Southwick, m. Silas D. **PHELPS**, of Suffield, Mass., May 19, 1834, by Charles Bentley	1	17
Fanny, of Williamsburg, Mass., m. Consider **MORETON**, Jan. 10, 1831, by Asa Cornwall	1	5
BATES, Alvan, of Southampton, Mass., m. Harriet **MORGAN**, of Granby, Sept. 20, 1846, by Rev. James C. Houghton	1	50
Anson, lawyer, ae 51 & Louisa C., ae 31, had d. [ ], b. June 20, 1850	1	250-1
Dolly Louisa, d. Anson, farmer, ae 50 & Louisa C. T., res. East Granby, b. Sept. 18, 1848	1	236-7
Edward W., s. William, farmer, ae 38 & Mary A., ae 38, b. Oct. 26, 1849	1	250-1
Ella E., d. May 2, 1851, ae 10 m.	1	138
Lucretia of Granby, m. James S. **JUDD**, of Southampton, Mass., June 20, 1821, by Daniel B. Holcomb, J. P.	TM1	162
BEACH, Clarissa, m. James **GILLET**, b. of Granby, Apr. 17, 1833, by Ammi Linsley, V. D. M.	1	14
Sidney, shoemaker, had s. [ ], b. Aug. 12, 1849	1	232-3
Sidney, shoemaker, had s. [ ], b. Apr. 6, 1850	1	246-7
BECKWITH, Charles, Dr., m. Mrs. Hellen **TOPPING**, Nov. 17, 1788	TM1	25
Elisha, m. Mrs. Polly **SAUNDERS**, Oct. 2, 1788	TM1	24
BEEBE, BEEBEE, Julia E., of East Windsor, m. Willis **DEWEY**, of East Granby, June 11, 1848, by Rev. A. L. Loveland	1	55
Julia E., ae 22, b. East Windsor, res. Granby, m. Willis **DEWEY**, merchant, ae 31, b. Granby, res. same, June 11, 1848, by Rev. A. L. Loveland	1	226-7
BEERS, William, of Barkhamsted, m. Lucy **DEAN**, of Granby, Sept. 16, 1834, by Charles Bentley	1	17
BEMAN, BEAMAN, Betsey, m. Albert **HAYES**, b. of Granby, Dec. 14, 1834, by Rev. Charles Spear	1	18
Henriette, of Granby, m. Chester A. **MILLER**, of Hartland, Feb. 19, 1849, by Rev. A. B. Pulling	1	58

	Vol.	Page
BEMAN, BEAMAN, (cont.),		
Luman, m. Flora **MESSENGER**, b. of Granby, Mar. 20,		
1842, by Samuel Weed, J. P.	1	36
Sally, m. Seymour **MESSENGER**, b. of Granby, Mar. 21,		
1832, by Nathaniell Pratt, J. P.	1	10
Thomas, of Hartland, m. Jemima **CASE**, of Granby, Apr. 5,		
1840, by Rev. Charles Stearns	1	32
Timothy, farmer, d. Nov. 16, 1850, ae 64	1	138
BENJAMIN, Abigail, m. Anson L. **HOLCOMB**, Mar. 31, 1831, by		
Isaac Porter	1	7
Martha Sybil, m. Rev. William Wallace **HEBBARD**, b. of		
Granby, Jan. 30, 1845, by Rev. John Moore, of		
Hartford	1	44
Polly, m. Charles P. **CLARK**, b. of Granby, Mar. 23, 1836, by		
Rev. James Thrigley	1	21
Rachel, of Granby, m. Dr. Russel **TIFFANY**, of Torringford,		
Nov. 28, 1837, by Charles Bentley	1	25
BENNETT, George, of Windsor, m. Harriet **DAVIS**, of Granby, Mar.		
25, 1847, by Rev. Pliney F. Sanborne	1	52
Joseph, m. Jane **VIZIAN**, Feb. 4, 1844, by Abner Case, J. P.	1	40
BENTON, Sarah, Mrs., of Hartland, m. Harvey **ELKY**, of Granby, Aug.		
12, 1846, by Rev. James C. Houghton	1	49
BIDDLE, Isaiah, of Baltimore, Md., m. Cornelia I. **LATHAM**, of		
Granby, Nov. 22, 1846, by Rev. James C.		
Houghton	1	50
BIDWELL, Edmund, farmer, d. Nov. 29, 1847, ae 46	1	230-1
BIRCH, Amelia Sheridan, d. Thomas & Elleanor, b. Apr. 14, 1850	1	250-1
BLAKESLEY, Abigail, b. Granby, m. James W. **ADAMS**, merchant, b.		
Simsbury, res. Tariffville, Nov. 18, 1848, by Rev.		
Ransom Warner	1	238-9
Sally, of Granby, m. Harrison **BARNARD**, of Simsbury, May		
7, 1834, by Rev. D. Hemmenway	1	16
BLEDENBERGE, Moses, minister, b. Long Island, res. Wolcottville, d.		
Sept. 13, 1848, ae 31	1	244-5
BOHANNA, Bridget, m. Michel **KELLY**, June 8, 1844, by W. W.		
Hubbard	1	42
BORDEN, Tirzah P. of Suffield, m. Orrin **MOORE**, of Granby, Nov.		
29, 1832, by Rev. D. Hemenway	1	13
BOSWOTH, Lewis, of Cabotville, Mass., m. Flavia M. **REED**, of W.		
Granby, Sept. 22, 1842, by Rev. William		
McKender Bangs	1	38
BOUTWELL, Charles H., s. James, laborer, ae 29 & Nancy D., ae 30, b.		
Jan. 31, 1849	1	236-7
BOWERS, Edward H., m. Mary A. **VIETS**, Mar. 15, 1848	1	226-7
Edward H., of Hartford, m. Mary Adelia **VEITS**, of E.		
Granby, Mar. 16, 1848, by Pliney F. Sanborn	1	55
Edward H., s. Edward R., merchant, ae 37 & Celia, ae 31, res.		
Hartford, b. Oct. 23, 1849	1	250-1
BOYLE, William, m. Cornelia T. **VIETS**, b. of Granby, July 11, 1851,		
by H. B. Soule	1	63
William, farmer, ae 19, b. Southwick, res. Granby, m.		
Cornelia T. **VIETS**, ae 20, b. Granby, July 11,		
1851, by W. B. Soule	1	134

	Vol.	Page
BRACE, Fedelia, m. Lucius **ELMER**, b. of Hartford, Dec. 8, 1831, by Stephen Crosby	1	9
BRADBURY, E., m. Eliza **McCAULY**, b. of Simsbury, May 23, 1852, by Rev. John Pegg, Jr.	1	67
BRADFORD, Alvin, m. Abagail B. **HUNT**, b. of Williamsburg, Mass., Mar. 15, 1831, by Rev. Asa Cornwall	1	6
BRADLEY, Eliza, d. William & Mary, b. Dec. 19, 1799	TM1	18
William Hyde, s. [William & Mary], b. Nov. 10, 1801	TM1	18
BREWER, Balsarah, Mrs., m. Selah **BACON**, Jan. 17, 1786	TM1	6
Duane, s. Edwin, manufacturer, ae 36 & Eliza, ae 38, b. Oct. 6, 1849	1	246-7
Logen A., b. Westfield, Mass., res. Granby, d. Jan. 18, 1850, ae 4	1	254-5
BRIDGES, J., pauper, b. Mass., res. Granby, d. June 21, 1851, ae 70	1	138
BROWN, Augustus, s. Justus Brown & Sarah Hays, b. Sept. 20, 1802	TM1	10
B. M., of New York, m. Harriet L. **MESSENGER**, of Granby, May 12, 1850, by Rev. A. B. Pulling	1	61
Benjamin M., farmer, ae 25, m. Harriet L. **MESSENGER**, ae 21, b. New York, res. same, May 12, 1850, by Rev. A. B. Pulling	1	252-3
Charles, s. Wadsworth, laborer, ae 22 & Laura, b. Sept. 18, 1848	1	236-7
Clarissa, Mrs., m. Israel **HALE**, Nov. 3, 1802	TM1	14
Flora M., ae 21, b. Canton, m. James **THOMPSON**, mechanic, ae 25, b. Scotland, res. Thompsonville, May 20, 1851, by Rev. Mr. Stoddard	1	134
Harriet L., d. Wadsworth, laborer & Laura, res. Windsor, b. July 27, 1851	1	132-3
Justice, m. Mary **TOUVEL**, Oct. 9, 1811, by Judah Holcomb, J. P.	TM1	21
Wadsworth, farmer, ae 21, b. E. Granby, res. Granby, m. Laura **LOOMIS**, ae 19, b. E. Granby, res. Granby, Sept. [ ], 1847, by Walther Thrall	1	226-7
BUCKLAND, Nelson, m. Maria **CASE**, of Springfield, Mass., Mar. 16, 1841, by Isaac Porter	1	34
BURKE, BURK, John, pauper, b. Ireland, d. Oct. 12, 1849, ae 35	1	254-5
Mary, pauper, b. Ireland, res. Granby, d. Dec. 2, 1850, ae 48	1	138
BURR, Candace, m. Ruddy **GOSSARD**, Dec. 10, 1802	TM1	21
Lamira, of Granby, m. David **TAYLOR**, of Simsbury, Nov. 21, 1830, by Nathaniel Pratt, J. P.	1	4
BURWELL, John of [Conn.], m. Annis E. **STRONG**, of Granby, May 8, 1845, by I. P. Warren	1	45
BUSH, Luke, of Westfield, m. Laura A. **ALDERMAN**, of East Granby, Oct. 2, 1844, by I. B. Clarke	1	43
William Ter, of Simsbury, m. Susan Jane **CLARK**, of Windsor, Apr. 15, 1838, by Rev. D. Hemenway	1	26
BUTLER, Leander, of Savannah, Ga., m. Lydia **SKINNER**, of Granby, July 19, 1838, by Rev. Daniel Hemenway	1	27
BUTTLES, [see also **BUTTOLPH**], Desire, m. Hiram **CADWELL**, b. of Granby, Dec. 27, 1821, by Joel Holcomb, J. P.	TM1	164
Enoch, farmer, d. Aug. 29, 1849, ae 74	1	254-5
Enoch H., m. Hannah D. **RICE**, July 3, 1832, by Isaac Porter	1	11

80 BARBOUR COLLECTION

	Vol.	Page
BUTTLES, [see also **BUTTOLPH**], (cont.), Levi, of E. Granville, Mass., m. Caroline **HOLCOMB**, of Granby, Apr. 20, 1841, by C. D. Rice	1	35
Ransom, s. Enoch H., millwright, b. [ ], Mar. 1, 1850, [d] [ ], ae 6m.	1	248-9
BUTTOLPH, [see also **BUTTLES**], Affiah, Mrs., m. Capt. Hoadiah **HOLCOMB**, May 28, 1778	TM1	33
Agnes, Mrs., m. Samuel **EVERITT**, Jr., May 24, 1771	TM1	5
Bennoni, s. Joel & Hannah, b. Dec. 28, 1773	TM1	24
Enoch, s. Joel & Hannah, b. Oct. 10, 1775	TM1	24
Hannah, d. Joel & Hannah, b. Apr. 16, 1780	TM1	24
Joel, Sergt., m. Mrs. Hannah **PHELPS**, July 14, 1773	TM1	24
Joel, Sergt., d. Nov. 24, 1786, in the 37th y. of his age	TM1	24
CADWELL, Hiram, m. Desire **BUTTLES**, b. of Granby, Dec. 27, 1821	TM1	164
James M., of Bloomfield, m. Frances W. **PINNEY**, of Granby, Jan. 25, 1852, by Rev. Pliny F. Sanborn	1	66
CAHILL, Thomas, s. John, farmer, ae 23 & Margaret, ae 23, b. Feb. 17, 1850	1	248-9
CAMP, Mary, Mrs., m. Martin **HAYS**, Dec. 25, 1798	TM1	14
CAMPBELL, George, b. Canada, res. Granby, d. Sept. 29, 1847, ae 5	1	230-1
Margaret, b. Lowell, Mass., res. Granby, d. Sept. 11, 1848 (?), ae 2 *("1847"?)	1	230-1
CARMINE, Morris, farmer, b. Ireland, res. Granby, d. Feb. 10, 1849, ae 45	1	244-5
CARPENTER, Amanda T., of Granby, m. William A. **HENDREY**, of New York State, Oct. 8, 1851, by Caleb F. Page	1	66
J. C., shoemaker, ae 25, m. Mary Ann **ALDERMAN**, ae 25, b. of Granby, Apr. 9, 1849, by Rev. A. L. Loveland	1	238-9
John C., m. Mary Ann **ALDERMAN**, b. of Granby, Apr. 9, 1849, by Rev. A. L. Loveland	1	58
CASE, Albert, m. Phebe Eveline **CASE**, Mar. 18, 1834, by Rev. Charles Spear	1	16
Amy, m. Oliver **CASE**, Nov. 10, 1791	TM1	25
Azuah, m. Curtis **CASE**, Oct. 6, 1833, by Rev. David Miller	1	15
Bethual, m. Clemena **GODDARD**, b. of Granby, Sept. 13, 1831, by Rev. Edwin G. Griswold	1	8
Cate, [d. Mirah & Cathirine], b. June 6, 1784; decd [ ]	TM1	76
Cate, [d. Mirah & Cathirine], b. June 9, 1789	TM1	76
Chester, of Canton, m. Rhoda **RUIC**, of Granby, Apr. 29, 1839, by Rev. Davis Stocking	1	29
Chester, of Barkhamsted, m. Mariah **WILCOX**, of Granby, May 10, 1848, by Rev. S. Rushmore	1	55
Chloe P., of Suffield, m. Asa **DIBBLE**, of Granby, Oct. 28, 1849, by Rev. Richard D. Kirby	1	60
Chloe T., of Barkhamsted, m. Joseph F. **GOFF**, of Haddam, Nov. 3, 1834, by Rev. William R. Gould	1	17
Curtis, m. Azuah **CASE**, Oct. 6, 1833, by Rev. David Miller	1	15
Diana, [d. Mirah & Cathirine,] Apr. 29, 1781	TM1	76
Elizer, [d. Mirah & Cathirine], b. Oct. 7, 1787	TM1	76
Eliza Ann, of Granby, m. Charles P. **JOHNSON**, of Hartford, Sept. 9, 1844, by Rev. Levi Warner	1	43
Frances, m. Martha Ann **DIBBLE**, b. of Granby, Oct. 7, 1852, by Caleb F. Page	1	65

GRANBY VITAL RECORDS 81

CASE, (cont.),   Vol.   Page
    Hastings, m. Esther **PRATT**, Aug. 22, 1821, by Isaac Porter   TM1   163
    Hilpha, [child of Job & Mary], b. Jan. 8, 1794   TM1   12
    Hiram, m. Eunice **HIGLEY**, Dec. 4, 1834, by Isaac Porter   1   18
    Jarius, m. Mary T. **HIGLEY**, Oct. 5, 1830, by Isaac Porter   1   4
    Jefferson, [s. Mirah & Cathirine], b. Oct. 9, 1802   TM1   76
    Jemima, of Granby, m. Thomas **BEMAN**, of Hartland, Apr. 5,
        1840, by Rev. Charles Stearns   1   32
    Job, m. Mrs. Mary **HOLCOMB**, Apr. 21, 1784   TM1   12
    Job Warren, [s. Job & Mary], b. Apr. 2, 1787   TM1   12
    Joseph, [s. Mirah & Cathirine], b. Jan. 8, 1797   TM1   76
    Joseph, farmer, b. W. Granby, res. same, d. Feb. 17, 1848,
        ae 49   1   230-1
    Laura, of Granby, m. Lyman **VARY**, of New York, June 3,
        1849, by Rev. N. Scott   1   59
    Lester, [s. Job & Mary], b. Apr. 10., 1789   TM1   12
    Lucretia, m. Justin **HAYES**, Aug. 22, 1821, by Isaac Porter   TM1   162
    Lydia, [d. Mirah & Cathirine], b. Jan. 18, 1786   TM1   76
    Maria, of Springfield, Mass., m. Nelson **BUCKLAND**, Mar.
        16, 1841, by Isaac Porter   1   34
    Mirah, s. [Mirah & Cathirine], b. Sept. 13, 1782;
        decd [   ]   TM1   76
    Mirah, [s. Mirah & Cathirine], b. Mar. 21, 1793   TM1   76
    Nery, [d. Mirah & Cathirine], b. July 3, 1791   TM1   76
    Olive, of Granby, m. Philo **CASE**, of Barkhamsted, Mar. 4,
        1847, by Rev. Thomas Joralds   1   51
    Oliver, m. Amy **CASE**, Nov. 10, 1791   TM1   25
    Phebe Eveline, m. Albert **CASE**, Mar. 18, 1834, by Rev.
        Charles Spear   1   16
    Philo, [s. Job & Mary], b. Mar. 10, 1796   TM1   12
    Philo, of Barkhamsted, m. Olive **CASE**, of Granby, Mar. 4,
        1847, by Rev. Thomas Joralds   1   51
    Philo, merchant, had s. [   ], b. Mar. 12, 1850   1   248-9
    Polly, [d. Job & Mary], b. Dec. 17, 1791   TM1   12
    Rhoda, m. Ovil **MESSENGER**, b. of Granby, June 26, 1838,
        by Rev. Davis Stocking   1   27
    Richard E., m. Caroline A. **DAY**, Nov. 24, 1831, by Isaac
        Porter   1   10
    Sabra, d. Job & Mary, b. Apr. 1, 1785   TM1   12
    Statira, [d. Mirah & Cathirine], b. Dec. 9, 1794   TM1   76
    Statira, [d. Mirah & Cathirine], b. Oct. 18, 1799   TM1   76
    Sybal, Mrs., m. Seth **HILLYER**, Apr. 10, 1783   TM1   14
    Thomas, [s. Mirah & Cathirine], b. July 10, 1805   TM1   76
CAULKINS, Daniel O., of New York City, m. Lydia M. **CLARK**, of
        Granby, July 2, 1835, by Rev. Daniel Hemenway   1   20
CAYTON, Margaret, m. David **SPENCER**, Apr. 26, 1821, by James
        Forward, J. P.   TM1   161
CHANDLER, Albert C., of Pomfret, m. Narcissa P. **DAVIS**, of Granby,
        Mar. 10, 1851, by Rev. Pliny F. Sanborne 1   63
    Albert C., farmer, ae 28, b. Pomfret, res. same, m. Marissa P.
        DAVIS, ae 26, b. Granby, Mar. 10, 1851, by Pliny
        F. Sanborne   1   134

	Vol.	Page
CHAPIN, Angeline C., ae 27, of Granby, m. Harvey **ADAMS**, shoemaker, ae 23, b. Willington, res. Granby, June 11, 1848, by Rev. Stephen Rushmore	1	226-7
Parmenas, of Granby, m. Mrs. Eliza C. **DRAKE**, of Southwick, June 7, 1846, by Rev. James C. Houghton	1	49
Rhoda M., d. Apr. [ ], 1848, ae 35	1	228-9
Sybil M., d. July 14, 1850, ae 36	1	254-5
CHAPMAN, Eunice, m. Ithra **GODARD**, Dec. 5, 1832, by Isaac Porter	1	13
Eunice, of Westfield, Mass., m. Emery **MOORE**, of Montgomery, Mass., Sept. 9, 1845, by Rev. James C. Houghton. Int. Pub. in each of said towns	1	46
Lewis, of Tariffville, m. Almira **SMITH**, of Granby, Oct. 9, 1831, by Rev. Asa Cornwall	1	8
CHISHOLM, William, res. Canada, m. Louisa P. **LATHAM**, b. Granby, res. same, Jan. 15, 1850, by R. Warner	1	252-3
CHITTENDON, Charles, Rev., of Suffield, m. Emily **CORNISH**, of Granby, Mar. 29, 1835, by Rev. Stephen Martiadal. Witnesses Eli **BRONSON**, Nathaniell **KELLOG** & Mary **CORNISH**	1	18
CHURCH, David, m. Emily **HOLCOMB**, Nov. 24, 1829, by Isaac Porter	1	1
Electa, seamstress, d. Feb. 27, 1851, ae 49	1	138
Francis, m. Anson **COOLEY**, b. of Granby, Feb. 12, 1851, by Caleb F. Page	1	65
Francis A., housekeeper, ae 21, b. Granby, res. same, m. [ ], Feb. 8, 1851, by Rev. Mr. Page	1	134
Jane, m. Isaac C. **CROCKER**, b. of Granby, Sept. 1, 1834, by Charles Bentley	1	17
Sophia, of Granby, m. Charles **SWEETSUR**, of Delaware, O., Oct. 31, 1832, by Rev. Asa Cornwall, at the house of Jonathan **CHURCH**	1	12
CHURCHIL[L], Robert, m. wid. Elinor **FULLER**, b. of Granby, Feb. 5, 1822, by James Dibble, J. P.	TM1	164
CLARK, CLARKE, Albert, of Granby, m. Esther J. **WOODRUFF**, of Windsor, [ ], by Stephen Crosby	1	4
Albert, m. Virginia E. **PARKS**, b. of Russell, Mass., Feb. 18, 1850, by Ardon B. Holcomb, J. P.	1	61
Amada, ae 25, b. Hartland, res. same, m. Morgan **COOLEY**, whipmaker, ae 34, b. Granby, res. same, Oct. 11, 1847, by Rev. Alfred White	1	226-7
Andrew, farmer, ae 41 & Caroline V., ae 36, res. Suffield, had s. [ ], b. July 26, 1851	1	132-3
Ceneth, m. Samuel **THOMPSON**, Jr., b. of Granby, Aug. 3, 1820, by Joel Holcomb, J. P.	TM1	160
Charles P., m. Polly **BENJAMIN**, b. of Granby, Mar. 23, 1836, by Rev. James Thrigley	1	21
Chauncey, of Granby, m. Betsey **THRALL**, of Windsor, May 1, 1836, by Rev. D. Hemenway	1	22
Chauncey, farmer, had s. [ ], b. Jan. [ ], 1850, [d.] [ ], ae 7 m.	1	248-9
Chauncey B., d. Feb. 20, 1849, ae 1 1/4	1	242-3

		Vol.	Page

CLARK, CLARKE, (cont.)
Cyrus E., m. Henryette I. JOHNSON, b. of Hartford,
    May 27, 1849, by Rev. A. B. Pulling — 1 — 59
David, m. Lydia **THOMPSON**, b. of Granby, Feb. 6,
    1834, by Rev. D. Hemenway — 1 — 16
Eliphelet, m. Mrs. Lydia **THOMAS**, Sept. 25, 1780 — TM1 — 26
Eliphelet, Jr., s. Eliphelet & Lydia, b. Dec. 1, 1781 — TM1 — 26
Emma M., d. Chester R., farmer, ae 42 & Lucinda M.,
    housewife, ae 36, res. West Granby, b. Aug.
    17, 1847 — 1 — 222-3
Gaylord, farmer & Mary J., res. Windsor, had d. [ ],
    b. May 17, 1851 — 1 — 132-3
George, of Granville, Mass., m. Bulah **ALFORD**, of
    Granby, Aug. 27, 1834, by Charles Bentley — 1 — 17
Howell S., s. Samuel A., farmer, ae 28 & Rhuhama M.,
    ae 25, b. Jan. [ ], 1849 — 1 — 236-7
Huldah, Mrs., m. Joel **HOLCOMB**, b. of Granby, Oct. 8,
    1832, by Rev. Asa Cornwall — 1 — 11
Jonathan, m. Sarah **FILLEY**, b. of Granby, Oct. 18,
    1821, by James Dibble, J. P. — TM1 — 163
Lybias, s. Eliphelet & Lydia, b. Feb. 12, 1783 — TM1 — 26
Lydia M., of Granby, m. Daniel O. **CAULKINS**, of New
    York City, July 2, 1835, by Rev. Daniel
    Hemmenway — 1 — 20
Lyman E., b. Suffield, res. Hartford, m. Jane **JOHNSON**,
    b. Suffield, May [ ], 1849, by Rev. Mr.
    Pulling — 1 — 238-9
Margret, d. Eliphalet & Lydia, b. Jan. 29, 1785 — TM1 — 26
Moses, m. Betsey **WARNER**, Nov. 28, 1821, by Daniel
    Benjamin, J. P. — TM1 — 163
Patty, m. Prince **FOOL** (colored), Nov. [ ], 1783 — TM1 — 35
Ruth Ann, b. Otis, Mass., res. Granby, d. Jan. 18,
    1850, ae 40 — 1 — 254-5
Samuel A., m. Ruhama M. **DIBBLE**, b. of Granby, Apr.
    5, 1843, by J. P. Warren — 1 — 38
Sophia, m. Henry **EMMONS**, b. of Hartland, June 9,
    1835, by Abner Case, J. P. — 1 — 20
Susan Jane, of Windsor, m. William Ter. **BUSH**, of
    Simsbury, Apr. 15, 1838, by Rev. D.
    Hemenway — 1 — 26
Warren, s. Eliphelet & Lydia, b. Oct. 10, 1788 — TM1 — 26
CLEMENS, Willis, m. Mrs. Almira **HARPER**, b. of Granby, Oct.
    14, 1838, by Abner Case, J. P. — 1 — 28
COE, Marietta, see Mariella **CWO** — 1 — 11
COFFIN, Thomas, had s. [ ], b. May 26, 1851 — 1 — 132-3
COGSWELL, Selah, m. Lovena **DIBBLE**, Dec. 30, 1830, by Isaac
    Porter — 1 — 5
COLLINS, Anson A., farmer & Mary A., housewife, had child

	Vol.	Page

COLLINS, (cont.)
    b. July 20, 1848 ("ae 1 mo." follows birth
        date)   1   222-3
    Harvey P., of Hamilton, N. Y., m. Jane P. GODARD,
        of Granby, Mar. 1, 1840, by Rev. Chauncey
        D. Rice   1   34
    Julia, m. Miles FISH, Mar. 17, 1831, by Isaac Porter   1   7

COLTON, Almira, of Granby, m. Davias EMMONS, of East
    Hartland, Nov. 20, 1839, by Rev. Chauncey D.
    Rice   1   34
    Anna, d. [Mrs. Axa], b. Mar. 12, 1789   TM1   32
    Axa, d. [Mrs. Axa], b. July 21, 1784   TM1   32
    Eliza Ann, of Granby, m. Jeremiah EMMONS, of
        Hartland, Oct. 12, 1836, by Charles Bentley   1   23
    Lemuel, s. [Mrs. Axa], b. Mar. 22, 1786   TM1   32
    Mariette, b. Granby, res. same, m. Joseph C. HALY,
        farmer, b. Blandford, Mass., res. same,
        Oct. [ ], 1849   1   252-3
    Marietta H., of Granby, m. Joseph C. HALEY, of
        Blandford, Mass., Oct. 18, 1849, by Samuel
        W. Barnum   1   60
    William, Jr., s. Harmon, joiner, ae 24 & Eliza M.,
        ae 27, b. Aug. 27, 1850   1   130-1

COMB, Nancy, m. Moses WEED, Jr., May 7, 1806   TM1   18

CONE, Caroline, of Granby, m. Sydney S. TULLER, of Simsbury,
        May 8, 1844, by Allen McLean   1   42
    Sarah, b. Barkhamsted, res. Granby, d. Apr. 16, 1849,
        ae 55   1   242-3
    Sarah H., of Granby, m. Orville BARBER, of Harwinton,
        June 19, 1845, by Rev. James C. Houghton, of
        Hartland   1   45

CONNELL, CONNEL, John, m. Mehitabel REED, b. of Granby,
        July 17, 1849, by Rev. A. B. Pulling   1   59
    John, farmer, ae 27, b. Ireland, res. Granby, m.
        Mehitabel REED, ae 42, of Granby, July 17,
        1849, by Rev. A. P. Pulling   1   238-9
    William, farmer, b. Ireland, res. Granby, d. Nov.
        15, 1848, ae 50   1   242-3

CONVERSE, Joseph P., Dr., of Enfield, m. Mary CORNISH, of
    Granby, June 11, 1840, by Rev. Daniel
    Hemenway   1   33

COOK, Charles, m. Mary LEWIS, Sept. 10, 1837, by Isaac Porter   1   25
    Mary Ann, d. Charles & Ellen, b. Mar. 19, 1850   1   250-1

COOLEY, COOLE, COOLY, Anson, m. Candice HOLCOMB, b.
    of Granby, Nov. 9, 1836, by Charles Bentley   1   23
    Anson, m. Francis CHURCH, b. of Granby, Feb. 12,
        1851, by Caleb F. Page   1   65
    Candice, housekeeper, d. May 3, 1850, ae 35   1   254-5

	Vol.	Page
COOLEY, GOOLE, COOLY, (cont.)		
Cynthia, d. Anson, farmer & Candace, b. Apr. 12, 1849	1	234-5
Cynthia, d. July 21, 1849, ae 3 1/2 m.	1	244-5
Doris, [d. Ens. Noah & Lois], b. May 3, 1776; d. July 18, 1778	TM1	23
Dorris, [d. Ens. Noah & Lois], b. Sept. 7, 1782	TM1	23
Eunice, m. William **DEWEY**, b. of Granby, Nov. 30, 1837, by Charles Bentley	1	25
Forrest, [s. Ens. Noah & Lois], b. Oct. 27, 1778	TM1	23
Forest, m. Dorothy **GRIFFIN**, b. of Granby, June 4, 1835, by C. Bentley	1	19
Lucina, Mrs. of Granville, m. Moses **SIBLEY**, Jr., of Westfield, Mass., Dec. 12, 1843, by I. P. Warren	1	40
Mary, Mrs., m. Asa **COSSIT**, Nov. 30, 1777	TM1	35
Mary, m. Daniel **HAYES**, 2nd, Mar. 29, 1835, by Abner Case, J. P.	1	19
Morgan, whipmaker, ae 34, b. Granby, res. same, m. Amada **CLARKE**, ae 25, b. Hartland, res. same, Oct. 11, 1847, by Rev. Alfred White	1	226-7
Morgan, whipmaker, ae 34 & Arhada M., housewife, ae 25, had child b. July 23, 1848	1	222-3
Morgan, farmer & Rhoda, had s. [ ], b. May 17, 1850	1	250-1
Noah, Ens., m. Lois **HOLCOMB**, July [ ], 1772	TM1	23
Parly, [child of Ens. Noah & Lois], b. Dec. 4, 1780	TM1	23
Pattee, [d. Ens. Noah & Lois], b. May 5, 1785	TM1	23
Philetus, m. Mrs. Bernice **REED**, Feb. 13, 1844, by I. P. Warren	1	40
Phytas, [s. Ens. Noah & Lois], b. May 14, 1773	TM1	23
Sherman, m. Diana **DAY**, Oct. 4, 1830, by [ ]	1	4
COPLEY, Alexander, [s. Thomas & Mary], b. Nov. 22, 1790	TM1	32
Belinde, [twin with Lucende, d. Thomas & Mary], b. Oct. 1, 1780	TM1	32
Bildad, [s. Thomas & Mary], b. Jan. 22, 1778; d. Mar. 5, 1782	TM1	32
Bildad, [s. Thomas & Mary], b. Apr. 1, 1786	TM1	32
Ebenezer, [s. Thomas & Mary], b. Dec. 19, 1787	TM1	32
Lucende, [twin with Belinde, d. Thomas & Mary], b. Oct. 1, 1780	TM1	32
Oliver, [s. Thomas & Mary], Dec. 27, 1776	TM1	32
Thomas, m. Mrs. Mary **HOLCOMB**, July 11, 1774	TM1	32
Thomas, Jr., [s. Thomas & Mary], b. Apr. 11, 1775; d. Mar. 3, 1782	TM1	32
Thomas, [s. Thomas & Mary], b. Sept. 26, 1782	TM1	32
CORNISH, Emily, of Granby, m. Rev. Charles **CHITTENDON**, of Suffield, Mar. 29, 1835, by Rev. Stephen Martiadal. Witness: Eli Bronson, Nathaniell Kellog & Mary Cornish	1	18

CORNISH, (cont.)

	Vol.	Page
Franklin, s. [Joseph & Abiah], b. Aug. 16, 1796; d. same day	TM1	14
Joseph, m. Mrs. Abiah **OWEN**, July 11, 1793	TM1	14
Joseph, s. Joseph & Abiah, b. Nov. 14, 1793	TM1	14
Mary, of Granby, m. Joseph P. **CONVERSE** (Dr.), of Enfield, June 11, 1840, by Rev. Daniel Hemenway	1	33
Morton, m. Mary R. **HOLCOMB**, Oct. 21, 1840, by Rev. Daniel Hemenway	1	33
Phebe, Mrs., m. Gurdon **GOOLD**, May 12, 1790	TM1	29
Virgel, s. [Joseph & Abiah], b. July 28, 1798	TM1	14
Virgil, m. Chloe **HOLCOMB**, Dec. 25, 1821, by Isaac Porter	TM1	164

CORNWALL, Stephen N., m. Cordelia E. **REED**, Sept. 5, 1832, by

	Vol.	Page
Isaac Porter	1	12
Stephen W., manufacturer, b. Berlin, res. Granby, d. Dec. 17, 1849, ae 42	1	254-5

COSSETT, COSSIT, COSSITT, Abigail, m. John **GAINS**, Dec.

	Vol.	Page
22, 1830, by Isaac Porter	1	5
Alma, d. [Asa & Mary], b. Dec. 10, 1780	TM1	35
Asa, m. Mrs. Mary **COOLE**, Nov. 30, 1777	TM1	35
Asa, s. [Asa & Mary], b. May 24, 1783	TM1	35
Cyrus, blacksmith, d. Nov. 19, 1850, ae 45	1	138
Eli, [s. Silus], b. June 7, 1788	TM1	33
Epaphus, s. Silus, b. Jan. 6, 1784	TM1	33
Hailo G., [child of Silus], b. May 1, 1797	TM1	33
Henry D., [s. Silus], b. May 3, 1801	TM1	33
James Shepid, [s. Silus], b. May 21, 1795	TM1	33
John, [s. Silus], b. Oct. 30, 1790	TM1	33
Laura, b. Suffield, res. Granby, married, d. Mar. 30, 1848, ae 67	1	230-1
Mary, m. Ezekiel **HAYS**, July 17, 1783	TM1	75
Mary, m. Joshua R. **JEWETT**, June 19, 1820, by James Dibble, J. P.	TM1	160
Mary Levinia, d. [Asa & Mary], b. Feb. 1, 1786	TM1	35
Mindall, Mrs., m. Rufus **GOSSARD**, Mar. 9, 1786	TM1	76
Monimia, d. [Asa & Mary], b. Mar. 5, 1788	TM1	35
Moses, farmer, ae 40 & Chloe, ae 35, had child, b. June 7, 1848	1	220-1
Nancy, [d. Silus], b. Dec. 27, 1808	TM1	33
Polley, d. [Asa & Mary], b. Dec. 16, 1790	TM1	35
Reubin, m. Mrs. Laura **GILLET**, Jan. 31, 1832, by Abner Case, J. P.	1	10
Ruth, m. Stephen **PERRING**, Feb. 2, 1769	TM1	24
Samuel Cole, [s. Asa & Mary], b. Oct. 20, 1778	TM1	35
Sarah, Jr., [d. Silus], b. Nov. 15, 1792	TM1	33
Silus, Jr., [s. Silus], b. July 14, 1786	TM1	33

	Vol.	Page
COSSETT, COSSIT, COSSITT, (cont.)		
Timothy, Capt., d. May 26, 1795, in the 65th y. of his age	TM1	36
COWDING, Amos H., of Hartland, m. Harriett HOLCOMB, of Granby, [Sept.] 25, 1839, by Rev. Albert Case, of Charleston, S. C.	1	30
COWDRY, Phelps, of Hartland, m. Emily HOLCOMB, of Granby, Sept. 4, 1833, by Rev. Charles Bentley	1	15
Vesta, b. Hartland, res. Granby, m. Milo WILCOX, farmer, ae 22, b. Granby, res. same, July 4, 1850, by Rev. Amasa Holcomb	1	252-3
William W., m. Mary C. KASSON, Mar. 31, 1830, by Isaac Porter	1	2
COWLES, Desire, housekeeper, b. Long Island, res. Granby, d. Dec. 10, 1850, ae 69	1	138
Mary Ann, of Granby, m. Obadiah W. WILCOX, of Hartland, Sept. 15, 1840, by Rev. Daniel Hemenway	1	33
Seth, m. Harriet FOX, b. of Westfield, Mass., Sept. 21, 1831, by Joel Holcomb, J. P.	1	7
William B., m. Esther M. HARGEE, of Granby, Dec. 24, 1834, by Rev. Daniel Hemmenway	1	18
CRAW, Daniel T., m. Charlotte P. HOSMER, b. of Granby, Nov. 3, 1845, by Rev. I. S. Dennis	1	47
CROCKER, Esther, of Granville, m. Samuel GILLET, of Westfield, Jan. 13, 1847, by Hiram F. Chapin, J. P.	1	51
Isaac C., m. Jane CHURCH, b. of Granby, Sept. 1, 1834, by Charles Bentley	1	17
CULVER, Jerusha, had d. Mariah, b. June 28, 1798	TM1	29
Mariah, d. Jerusha CULVER, b. June 28, 1798	TM1	29
CUSHMAN, John, m. Candace GODARD, b. of Granby, June 3, 1846, by John S. Hayes, J. P.	1	48
John, had s. [ ], b. Apr. 17, 1851	1	130-1
Marcus, m. Mary J. DIBBLE, b. of Granby, Nov. 28, 1849, by Samuel W. Barnum	1	61
Marcus, blacksmith, m. Mary Ann DIBBLE, b. of Granby, Nov. 28, 1849, by Joseph Barnum	1	252-3
Milton, m. Clarissa RICE, May 31, 1821, by Philander Humphrey, J. P.	TM1	162
Simeon M. 2nd, m. Amelia RICE, May 29, 1821, by Isaac Porter	TM1	162
Thomas E., d. Aug. 20, 1848, ae 19 m.	1	244-5
CWO*, Mariella, m. Elijah S. SMITH, of Southwick, Mass., June 4, 1832, by Daniel Hemingway *("Marietta COE"?)	1	11
DAILEY, Orrin, of Waterbury, m. Dinanthee HUBBARD, of Granby, Jan. 2, 1837, by Charles Bentley	1	23

	Vol.	Page
DANIELS, Starling, of Hartland, m. Levicy HAYES, of Granby, Mar. 27, 1836, by Abner Case, J. P.	1	21
DARROW, Edwin I., of New York City, m. Lucy P. GAY, of Granby, June 28, 1854, by Rev. D. Hemenway	1	69
DAVIS, DAVICE, Eli R., m. Lucinda BARNETT, Apr. 15, 1848	1	226-7
Frederic, laborer, ae 40 & Juliana, ae 38, had s. [ ], b. July 14, 1849	1	232-3
Harriet, of Granby, m. George BENNETT, of Windsor, Mar. 25, 1847, by Rev. Pliney F. Sanborne	1	52
Howard R., travelling merchant, d. Sept. 17, 1847, ae 27	1	230-1
John E., m. Janette EDGERTON, b. of Granby, Nov. 1, 1846, by Rev. Pliney F. Sanborn	1	50
John E., travelling merchant, d. June 5, 1848, ae 29	1	230-1
Lamira, ae 20, m. Lyman GRIFFIN, laborer, ae 20, b. of Granby, June 30, 1850, by Rev. Ardon B. Holcomb	1	252-3
Lorilla, [child of Silas & Matilda], b. Aug. 1, 1791	TM1	35
Marissa P., ae 26, b. Granby, m. Albert C. CHANDLER, farmer, ae 28, b. Pomfret, res. same, Mar. 10, 1851, by Pliny F. Sanborne	1	134
Metildah, d. [Silas & Metilda], b. Aug. 3, 1789	TM1	35
Myra, m. Chauncey GRIFFIN, b. of Granby, June 30, 1850, by Ardon B. Holcomb, J. P.	1	62
Narcissa P., of Granby, m. Albert C. CHANDLER, of Pomfret, Mar. 10, 1851, by Rev. Pliny F. Sanborne	1	63
Philip C., trunk peddler, b. Granby, res. E. Granby, d. Feb. 28, 1849, ae 23	1	244-5
Samuel A., d. Sept. 30, 1847, ae 7	1	230-1
Silas, m. Metilda GRIFFEN, Sept. 21, 1788	TM1	35
Silas, s. [Silas & Metilda], b. Jan. 5, 1793	TM1	35
DAY, Alva, s. Luis & Sebrah, b. Feb. 7, 1781	TM1	31
Bliss, [s. Timothy & Eunice], b. Mar. 21, 1793	TM1	26
Caroline A., m. Richard E. CASE, Nov. 24, 1831, by Isaac Porter	1	10
Denman D., m. Elizabeth R. GILLET, of Granby, Oct. 30, 1834, by Rev. Daniel Hemmenway	TM1	18
Diana, m. Sherman COOLEY, Oct. 4, 1830, by [ ]	1	4
Flavia, d. Timothy & Eunice, b. Oct. 2, 1789	TM1	26
Horatio, s. Capt. Luis & Sebrah, b. June 19, 1779	TM1	31
Julia, of Granby, m. Horace GRAVES, of Windsor, Apr. 27, 1840, by Rev. Daniel Hemenway	1	33
Luis, Jr., [s. Luis & Sebrah], b. Sept. 21, 1787	TM1	31
Mun[n], s. Luis & Sebrah, b. Sept. 9, 1783	TM1	31
Norman, of Springfield, m. Jane E. REED, of Granby, Nov. 27, 1845, by Rev. Levi Warner	1	46
Sebrah, [d. Luis &eSabrah], b. Nov. 17, 1791	TM1	31
Seth, s. Luis & Sebrah, b. Sept. 27, 1785	TM1	31

	Vol.	Page
DAY, (cont.)		
Solomon, [s. Luis & Sebrah], b. Feb. 12, 1790	TM1	31
Timothy, m. Mrs. Eunic[e] HALE, Jan. [ ], 1778	TM1	26
Timothy, Jr., [s. Timothy & Eunice], b. Sept. 11, 1791	TM1	26
W[illia]m, m. Ruth MESSENGER, b. of Granby, Jan. 3, 1841, by Chauncey D. Rice	1	34
DEAN, Alpheus, m. Selina SEGAR, b. of Granby, Sept. [ ], 1830, by Decius Humphrey, J. P.	1	3
Ellen, d. William & Ellen, b. Aug. 31, 1849	1	250-1
Fidelia C., of Granby, m. John C. STEADMAN, of Charleston, O., Apr. 4, 1852, by Caleb F. Page	1	67
Hannah E., m. Ebenezer L. POMEROY, Nov. 9, 1847	1	226-7
Lucy, of Granby, m. William BEERS, of Barkhamsted, Sept. 16, 1834, by Charles Bentley	1	17
Ruth H., d. Timothy, laborer, ae 38 & Betsey, housewife, ae 35, b. Feb. 23, 1848	1	220-1
Timothy, m. Betsey HOLCOMB, b. of Granby, Apr. 22, 1847, by Ardon B. Holcomb, J. P.	1	51
DEBIT, Charlotte, res. Springfield, m. William H. BAYLEY, res. Canton, Nov. 28, 1848, by Rev. P. F. Sanborn	1	238-9
DEWEY, Ann Gertrude, d. Jan. 10, 1848, ae 5	1	228-9
Eli, farmer, ae 34 & Dolly, ae 34, had s. [ ], b. July 14, 1851	1	130-1
Eli, farmer & Dolly, had s. [ ], b. [ ]	1	234-5
Ella Jane, d. Oct. 28, 1847, ae 1	1	228-9
Eva L., d. Wilson, mechanic & Minerva, b. Mar. 23, 1849	1	232-3
Isaac, Jr., m. Sophia GRIFFIN, b. of Granby, July 23, 1837, by Rev. Shaler J. Hillyer	1	24
Jane Isabella, d. Dec. 30, 1847, ae 7	1	228-9
John, m. Julia HAYS, Nov. 6, 1821, by Isaac Porter	TM1	163
Julia, m. Elam MESSENGER, June 4, 1834, by Isaac Porter	1	17
Lovisa, Mrs. of Granby, m. Dea. Timothy STONE, of Henrietta, N. Y., Oct. 7, 1849, by Samuel W. Barnum	1	60
Maria A., of Granby, m. Simeon F. KELSEY, of Bloomfield, Aug. 24, 1842, by Rev. Alfred Gates	1	37
Rhoda A., m. Willis MESSENGER, Jan. 14, 1834, by Rev. Charles Spear	1	15
Samuel, m. Sabra HOLCOMB, Nov. 29, 1820, by Isaac Porter	TM1	160
Samuel, farmer, d. Jan. 28, 1850, ae 61	1	254-5
Susan, m. Franklin B. REED, Sept. 30, 1841, by Isaac Porter	1	35
Watson, m. Jane ALDERMAN, b. of Granby, July 8, 1840, by Rev. Chauncey D. Rice	1	34

BARBOUR COLLECTION

	Vol.	Page
DEWEY, (cont.)		
William, m. Eunice **COOLEY**, b. of Granby, Nov. 30, 1837, by Charles Bentley	1	25
William, farmer & Eunice, had s. [ ], b. June 10, 1849	1	232-3
Willis, of East Granby, m. Julia E. **BEEBE**, of East Windsor, June 11, 1848, by Rev. A. L. Loveland	1	55
Willis, merchant, ae 31, b. Granby, res. same, m. Julia E. **BEEBEE**, ae 22, b. East Windsor, res. Granby, June 11, 1848, by Rev. A. L. Loveland	1	226-7
DEWOLF, Duty, [d. Joseph], b. Nov. 6, 1790	TM1	2
Eli Gibbens, [s. Joseph], b. Mar. 19, 1799	TM1	2
Elisabeth Gibbins, [d. Joseph], b. Feb. 24, 1795	TM1	2
Henry Champion, [s. Joseph], b. Aug. 3, 1781	TM1	2
Horatio, [s. Joseph], b. May 31, 1793	TM1	2
Joseph, [s. Joseph], b. Apr. 6, 1787	TM1	2
Louisa, d. [Joseph], b. Mar. 27, 1797	TM1	2
Ruhamah, d. [Joseph], b. June 8, 1783	TM1	2
Sally, d. [Joseph], b. Mar. 10, 1789	TM1	2
Tenford Robinson, [child of Joseph], b. June 5, 1785	TM1	2
DIBBLE, DIBOL, Asa, of Granby, m. Chloe P. **CASE**, of Suffield, Oct. 28, 1849, by Rev. Richard D. Kirby	1	60
Calvin B., m. Lura **HAYES**, b. of Granby, Oct. 3, 1837, by Charles Bentley	1	25
Catharine, ae 21, b. Southwick, res. Granby, m. Erastus **OWEN**, farmer, ae 29, b. Granby, res. same, Jan. 31, 1850, by Mr. Lamberton	1	252-3
Charlotte E., of Southwick, Mass., m. Drayton **PHELPS**, of Granby, Oct. 19, 1851, by Caleb F. Page	1	66
Clement, s. [Dea. Benjamin], b. Dec. 5, 1799	TM1	5
Cleopatra, Mrs., m. Miles **GOSSARD**, Feb. 4, 1789	TM1	21
Diana, ae 20, b. Granby, res. same, m. Nelson **TALMADGE**, farmer, ae 23, b. Southwick, res. same, Dec. 21, 1847, by Rev. Alfred White	1	226-7
Dianah L., of Granby, m. Nelson **TALMADGE**, of Southwick, Dec. 1, 1847, by Alfred White	1	54
Doroty, [d. Dea. Benjamin], b. Nov. 16, 1796	TM1	5
George H., farmer & merchant, ae 25 & Emma E., housewife, ae 21, had child, b. July 14, 1848	1	220-1
Israll, [s. Dea. Benjamin], b. Oct. 16, 1794	TM1	5
James M., m. Jerusha **SPRING**, Jan. 9, 1822, by Isaac Porter	TM1	164
Jerusha M., of Granby, m. Emerson L. **HOLCOMB**, of New Britain, Apr. 20, 1851, by Caleb F. Page	1	65
Jerusha M., ae 20, b. Granby, m. Emerson L. **HOLCOMB**, mechanic, ae 21, res. New		

	Vol.	Page

DIBBLE, DIBOL, (cont.)
    Britain, Apr. 20, 1851, by [ ]   1   134
    Julia M., of Granby, m. James B. **HOSKINS**, of
      Simsbury, Dec. 29, 1850, by Caleb F. Page   1   65
    Julia M., seamstress, ae 20, b. Granby, res. same,
      m. [ ], Dec. 27, 1851, by Rev. Mr. Paige   1   134
    Louisa, ae 20, b. Granby, res. same, m. Lewis **FRENCH**,
      farmer, ae 25, b. Granville, Mass., res.
      Granby, Nov. 9, 1847, by Rev. Mr. Brockway   1   226-7
    Lovena, m. Selah **COGSWELL**, Dec. 30, 1830, by Isaac
      Porter   1   5
    Lovisa, d. Philander, farmer, ae 43 & Julia, ae 38, b. July
      23, 1850   1   248-9
    Mariett, of Granby, m. Martin **TULLER**, of Simsbury,
      May 19, 1836, by J. Shrigley   1   22
    Martha Ann, m. Frances **CASE**, b. of Granby, Oct. 7,
      1852, by Caleb F. Page   1   65
    Martha Melissa, d. Willis, peddler, ae 33 & Rhoda, ae
      33, b. Feb. [ ], 1850   1   250-1
    Mary Ann, m. Marcus **CUSHMAN**, blacksmith, b. of
      Granby, Nov. 28, 1849, by Joseph Barnum   1   252-3
    Mary J., m. Marcus **CUSHMAN**, b. of Granby, Nov. 28,
      1849, by Samuel W. Barnum   1   61
    Mary L., d. July 8, 1851, ae 11 m.   1   138
    Paulina C., m. Moses **STEBBINS**, b. of Granby, Oct.
      2, 1838, by Amasa Holcomb   1   27
    R. Seymour, m. Cornelia I. **STEVENS**, b. of Granby,
      Mar. 14, 1849, by Rev. Pliney F. Sanborn   1   58
    Ruhama M., m. Samuel A. **CLARK**, b. of Granby, Apr.
      5, 1843, by J. P. Warren   1   38
    Sarah, [d. Dea. Benjamin], b. Apr. 10, 1792   TM1   5
    Seymour R., farmer, ae 20, m. Cornelia G. **STEVENS**,
      ae 20, of Granby, Mar. 14, 1849, by Rev.
      Pliney F. Sanborn   1   240-1
    Sophia O., of Granby, m. Edward W. **JOHNSON**, of
      East Windsor, Dec. 31, 1850, by Caleb F.
      Page   1   65
    Sophia O., ae 25, b. Granby, m. Edward W. **JOHNSON**,
      ae 24, b. Windsor, res. same, Dec. 31, 1851,
      by Caleb F. Page   1   134
    Wealthy, m. Daniel **PURPLE**, Dec. 25, 1844, by I. P.
      Warren   1   44
    William, m. Susan M. **ALLEN**, b. of Granby, Sept. 7,
      1843, by Israel B. Warren   1   40
DICKINSON, Abel S., m. Hellen L. **HOLCOMB**, Sept. 13, 1852,
    by Rev. A. S. Loveland   1   67
    Aurelias, of Hartford, m. Frances Maria **GALPIN**, of
      Durham, May 17, 1830, by Isaac Porter   1   2

	Vol.	Page
DICKINSON, (cont.)		
Friend, of Amherst, Mass., m. Betsey HAYES, of Granby, Oct. 3, 1833, by Rev. Charles Bentley	1	15
DILLON, Martha Ann, of New Hartford, m. Freeman POWERS, of Westfield, Mass., Aug. 8, 1843, by Ardon B. Holcomb, J. P.	1	39
DOLAN, James, farmer, b. Ireland, res. Granby, d. Jan. 9, 1849, ae 64	1	242-3
DORMAN, Daniel W., m. Caroline E. SMITH, June 30, 1844, by Rev. W. N. Hebbard	1	42
DRAKE, Anna, of Southwick, m. Stephen C. RUSSELL, of Springfield, Oct. 13, 1842, by Abner Case, J. P.	1	37
Eliza C., Mrs. of Southwick, m. Parmenas CHAPIN, of Granby, June 7, 1846, by Rev. James C. Houghton	1	49
Lucretia, of New Hartford, m. John VADAKIN, of Granby, Nov. 25, 1832, by Rev. D. Hemenway	1	13
Susan M., m. Ralph SEYMOUR, b. of New Hartford, Sept. 29, 1833, by Rev. Daniel Hemmenway	1	15
DRAPER, Lewis, of Springfield, Mass., m. Eunetia E. FILLMORE, of Granby, May 7, 1845, by I. P. Warren	1	45
DRIVER, Ellen, d. W[illia]m, laborer, ae 30 & Ellen, ae 29, b. Sept. 16, 1848	1	236-7
DUDLEY, DUDLY, Isaac, s. Silvenos & Lois, b. June 22, 1784	TM1	22
Joseph, [s. Silvenus & Lois], b. Apr. 1790	TM1	22
Marcy, d. Silvenus & Lois, b. June 18, 1786	TM1	22
Salvenus, m. Loyes TAYLOR, Nov. 28, 1782	TM1	22
DYER, George J., [s. Joseph & Eunice], b. Jan. 9, 1802	TM1	51
Henry, [s. Joseph & Eunice], b. Jan. 3, 1788	TM1	51
John, [s. Joseph & Eunice], b. Sept. 11, 1798; d. Sept. 15, 1798	TM1	51
Joseph, b. Mar. 17, 1758; m. Eunice HOLCOMB, Apr. 27, 1784	TM1	51
Joseph, Jr., [s. Joseph & Eunice], b. Jan. 3, 1790; d. Jan. [ ], 1795	TM1	51
Joseph, 2nd, [s. Joseph & Eunice], b. Aug. 18, 1795	TM1	51
Joseph, b. London, Eng., res. Granby, d. Nov. 11, 1848, ae 91	1	242-3
Nancy, [d. Joseph & Eunice], b. Dec. 20, 1799	TM1	51
Polly, [d. Joseph & Eunice], b. Aug. 15, 1791	TM1	51
Thomas, [s. Joseph & Eunice], b. Apr. 17, 1785	TM1	51
EATON, Shepard, m. Ann KELLOGG, Sept. 11, 1831, by Isaac Porter	1	8
EDGERTON, Diantha A., m. Thomas S. GOULD, b. of Granby, Oct. 1, 1845, by Rev. Levi Warner	1	46

GRANBY VITAL RECORDS 93

	Vol.	Page
EDGERTON, (cont.)		
Janette, m. John E. DAVIS, b. of Granby, Nov. 1, 1846, by Rev. Pliney F. Sanborn	1	50
Josephus, m. Lorenda REED, b. of Granby, Feb. 7, 1830, by Joab Griffin, Jr., J. P.	1	3
EDSON, Merrick, m. Eunice Clarissa HINE, Sept. 15, 1835, by Isaac Porter	1	20
EDWARDS, Arnold, m. Lovisa Pamela HAYES, b. of Granby, July 4, 1832, at Judah Hays, by Asa Cornwall	1	11
EGGLESTON, Edward, jeweller, ae 26, b. Barkhamsted, res. New York, m. Betsey PRATT, ae 23, Nov. 29, 1849, by Rev. A. B. Pulling	1	252-3
Edward F., of Pleasant Valley, m. Betsey E. PRATT, of West Granby, Nov. 29, 1849, by Rev. A. B. Pulling	1	61
Martha E., m. William H. NOBLE, b. of Westfield, Sept. 3, 1850, by Ardon B. Holcomb, J. P.	1	62
Nathaniel, of Hartford, m. Emily HILLYER, of Granby, May 1, 1821, by Isaac Porter	TM1	161
ELKEY, ELKY, Harvey, of Granby, m. Mrs. Sarah BENTON, of Hartland, Aug. 12, 1846, by Rev. James C. Houghton	1	49
Jane A., had child b. [ ] 1848?]	1	222-3
Starling, farmer, colored & Lorinda ELKEY, colored, had illeg. twins, b. July [ ], 1850 ("ae 1 m." follows birth date)	1	248-9
ELLIS, Deborah, d. Capt. William & Deborah, b. Oct. 27, 1782	TM1	27
ELLSWORTH, Clara, pauper, b. Simsbury, res. Granby, d. Dec. 12, 1850, ae 80	1	138
ELMER, Lucius, m. Fidelia BRACE, b. of Hartford, Dec. 8, 1831, by Stephen Crosby	1	9
EMMONS, Davias, of East Hartland, m. Almira COLTON, of Granby, Nov. 20, 1839, by Rev. Chauncey D. Rice	1	34
Henry, m. Cophia CLARK, b. of Hartland, June 9, 1835, by Abner Case, J. P.	1	20
Jeremiah, of Hartland, m. Eliza Ann COLTON, of Granby, Oct. 12, 1836, by Charles Bentley	1	23
ENO, Elisabeth, w. James, d. Oct. 7, 1679; bd. in Old Windsor	1	143
James, m. Elisabeth HOLCOMBE, wid. Thomas, Aug. 5, 1658	1	143
ENSIGN, Samuel, of Hartford, m. Mary E. GORDON, of Granby, [Nov. 29, 1832], by Rev. D. Hemenway	1	13
EVENS, Hannah, m. Richard ROCK[W]ELL, Nov. 21, 1831, by Rev. Asa Cornwall	1	9
EVERITT, Flora Agnes, [d. Samuel, Jr. & Agnes], b. May 9, 1776	TM1	5
Revel Gordon, [s. Samuel, Jr. & Agnes], b. May 21, 1774	TM1	5
Samuel, Jr., m. Mrs. Agnes BUTTOLPH, May 24, 1771	TM1	5

	Vol.	Page

EVERITT, (cont.)
   Samuel Harlow, [s. Samuel, Jr. & Agnes], b. Apr. 15,
      1772 — TM1 — 5
EWING, C. A., d. J. F., physician, ae 34 & Amelia, ae 30, b. June
      13, 1850 — 1 — 248-9
FAIRCHILD, FAIRCHIELD, Jane, of Granby, m. J. Newton
   KENDALL, of Alabama, July 23, 1840, by
   Rev. Chauncey D. Rice — 1 — 34
   Robert, of Williamsburg, Mass., m. Olive NICHOLS,
   of Chesterfield, Mass., Sept. 6, 1831, by Rev.
   Asa Cornwall — 1 — 7
FANCHER, John M., s. Sherman, carriage maker, b. Oct. 8, 1848 — 1 — 232-3
   Martin, m. Francis Roxana ALLEN, Apr. 18, 1838, by
   Isaac Porter — 1 — 26
   Susan E., d. Mar. 15, 1851, ae 5 — 1 — 138
FARNHAM, Ruth, d. Amasa, farmer, ae 41 & Mary An[n],
   housewife, ae 35, res. West Granby, b. Aug.
   20, 1847 — 1 — 222-3
   Warren, m. Marilla HOLCOMB, Nov. 28, 1821, by
   Isaac Porter — TM1 — 163
FIELD, Betsey, d. Robert & Dinah, b. Aug. 23, 1776 — TM1 — 23
   Job, s. Robert & Dinah, b. May 5, 1784 — TM1 — 23
   Joseph Lambson, s. Roberd & Dinah, b. Aug. 24, 1767 — TM1 — 23
   Robard, m. Mrs. Dinah LAMBSON, Nov. 26, 1766 — TM1 — 23
   Robert, s. Robert & Dinah, b. Apr. 15, 1781 — TM1 — 23
   Silettee, d. Robard & Dinah, b. Mar. 1, 1772 — TM1 — 23
FIELDING, Azariah S., of Hartford, m. Ursula
   BARTHOLOMEW, of Granby, Oct. 28,
   1833, by Rev. Charles Bentley — 1 — 15
   Philo, of Hartford, m. Hannah T. HOSMER, of Granby,
   Nov. 25, 1829, by Stephen Crosby — 1 — 1
FILLEY, Sarah, m. Jonathan CLARK, b. of Granby, Oct. 18,
   1821, by James Dibble, J. P. — TM1 — 163
FILLMORE, Abigail S., of Granby, m. Horace E. WRIGHT, of
   Springfield, Mass., Apr. 2, 1844, by I. P.
   Warren — 1 — 41
   Eunetia E., of Granby, m. Lewis DRAPER, of
   Springfield, Mass., May 7, 1845, by I. P.
   Warren — 1 — 45
   Lydia A., m. Truman ALLEN, Jr., b. of Granby, Apr.
   28, 1849, by Rev. A. L. Loveland — 1 — 58
   Lydia A., ae 21, m. Truman ALLEN, Jr., shoemaker, ae
   21, b. of Granby, Apr. 26, 1849, by Rev. A.
   L. Loveland — 1 — 238-9
FISH, Miles, m. Julia COLLINS, Mar. 17, 1831, by Isaac Porter — 1 — 7
FLETCHER, Alsinda, [d. Ephraim & Margrit], b. Sept. 27, 1783 — TM1 — 5
   Assenath, [d. Ephraim & Margrit], b. Oct. 26, 1781 — TM1 — 5
   Eber, farmer, ae 48 & Deborah, ae 33, had d. [ ],

	Vol.	Page

FLETCHER, (cont.)
b. Aug. 11, 1849	1	234-5
Ephraim, m. Mrs. Margrit HOLCOMB, June 30, 1768	TM1	5
Ephraim, [s. Ephraim & Margrit], b. Mar. 20, 1770	TM1	5
Hannah, [d. Ephraim & Margrit], b. Feb. 12, 1777	TM1	5
Lois, [d. Ephraim & Margrit], b. Oct. 25, 1785	TM1	5
Lucense, d. Eber, farmer, ae 50 & Deborah, ae 34, b. Aug. 4, 1849	1	248-9
Margaret A., [d. Ephraim & Margrit], b. Oct. 20, 1772	TM1	5
Sabrina, [d. Ephraim & Margrit], b. Mar. 6, 1779	TM1	5
Sarah, [d. Ephraim & Margrit], b. Apr. 24, 1788	TM1	5
Thadeus, [twin with Zacheus, s. Ephraim & Margrit], b. Feb. 3, 1775	TM1	5
Virgil, of Windsor, m. Charlotte ROCKWELL, of Granby, Feb. 7, 1839, by Rev. D. Hememway	1	29
Zacheus, [twin wtih Thadeus, s. Ephraim & Margrit], b. Feb. 3, 1775	TM1	5

FOOL, Abigail, [d. Prince & Patty], b. Mar. 17, 1801 — TM1 — 35
Betse, d. Prince & Patty, colored, b. Feb. 12, 1790 — TM1 — 35
George W., [s. Prince & Patty], colored, b. Jan. 18, 1796 — TM1 — 35
Hester, [d. Prince & Patty], b. Mar. 31, 1799 — TM1 — 35
Olle, d. Prince & Patty, colored, b. Aug. 7, 1785 — TM1 — 35
Patty, d. Prince & Patty, colored, b. Aug. 11, 1792 — TM1 — 35
Philop, [s. Prince & Patty], colored, b. Apr. 31, 1783 — TM1 — 35
Prince, m. Patty CLARK, (colored), Nov. [ ], 1783 — TM1 — 35

FORD, Adonijah, m. Mrs. Martha HOLCOMB, Jr., Aug. 24, 1772 — TM1 — 27
Adonijah, Jr., [s. Adonijah & Martha], b. July 17, 1775 — TM1 — 27
Almon, [s. Adonijah & Martha], b. Apr. 12, 1785 — TM1 — 27
Alvin, [s. Adonijah & Martha], b. Sept. 16, 1789 — TM1 — 27
Elisabeth, [d. Adonijah & Martha], b. Mar. 29, 1781 — TN1 — 27
Martha, [d. Adonijah & Martha], b. Aug. 4, 1778 — TM1 — 27
Orpah, [child of Adonijah & Martha], b. Nov. 14, 1791 — TM1 — 27
Ruth, [d. Adonijah & Martha], b. July 15, 1787 — TM1 — 27

FORWARD, Dan, [s. Dan], b. July 12, 1812 — TM1 — 43
Unelia, [child of Dan], b. Nov. 22, 1809 — TM1 — 43
Wadsworth, [s. Dan], b. Jan. 1, 1807 — TM1 — 43
Walter, [s. Dan], b. Apr. 23, 1805 — TM1 — 43

FOWLER, Clarissa M., m. Adison HARGER, Nov. 10, 1841, by Rev. Daniel Hemenway — 1 — 36
Lyman, of West Springfield, Mass., m. Loisa King VADAKIN, of Granby, Mar. 12, 1833, by Rev. Daniel Hemenway — 1 — 14
Sally, m. William RICHARDSON, Oct. 16, 1831, by Abner Case, J. P. — 1 — 9

FOX, Albert, shoemaker, res. Granby & Lucy L., had d. [ ], b. Sept. 8, 1849 — 1 — 248-9
Crispus, farmer, d. Apr. 11, 1849, ae 95 — 1 — 242-3
Harriet, m. Seth COWLES, b. of Westfield, Mass., Sept.

	Vol.	Page
FOX, (cont.)		
21, 1831, by Joel Holcomb, J. P.	1	7
Horace, laborer, b. Bolton, res. Granby, d. Dec. 27, 1848, ae 37	1	246-7
Sophia, m. Thomas GILLET, b. of Granby, Dec. 11, 1832, by Nathaniel Pratt, J. P.	1	13
FRENCH, Lewis, farmer, ae 25, b. Granville, Mass., res. Granby, m. Louis DIBBLE, ae 20, of Granby, Nov. 9, 1847, by Rev. Mr. Brockway	1	226-7
Philip N., of Southwick, Mass., m. Cyrene WINCHELL, of Granby, May 24, 1833, by Rev. Daniel Hemenway	1	14
FRERY, Noble D., of Springfield, m. Mary KENDALL, of Granby, Oct. 30, 1845, by Rev. Levi Warner	1	46
FULLER, Elinor, wid., m. Robert CHURCHIL[L], b. of Granby, Feb. 5, 1822, by James Dibble, J. P.	TM1	164
GAINES, GAINS, Calvin, mechanic, b. Enfield, res. Granby, d. Feb. 18, 1851, ae 81	1	138
John, m. Abigail COSSETT, Dec. 22, 1830, by Isaac Porter	1	5
John, farmer, d. May 22, 1851, ae 71	1	138
Lucy, b. Hartland, res. Granby, d. June 14, 1848, ae 71	1	228-9
GALPIN, Frances Maria, of Durham, m. Aurelias DICKINSON, of Hartford, May 17, 1830, by Isaac Porter	1	2
Grace I., d. Joseph A., sash maker, ae 25 & Caroline N., housewife, ae 23, b. Jan. 26, 1848	1	220-1
Joseph, whip maker & Caroline, had d. [ ], b. Aug. 8, 1849	1	250-1
Joseph A., m. Caroline M. GODARD, b. of Granby, May 17, 1847, by Rev. Pliney F. Sanborn	1	52
Mary A., d. Joseph A., manufacturer, ae 28 & Caroline N., ae 26, b. Aug. 10, 1850[?]	1	130-1
GARDNER, Joseph, of Russel, Mass., m. Lovina PHELPS, of Westfield, Mass., May 21, 1832, by Asa Cornwall	1	10
GAY, Alfred, of East Granby, m. Jane S. THRALL, of Windsor, Nov. 26, 1846, by Rev. Pliney F. Sanborn	1	51
Alfred, farmer, ae 27 & Jane S., ae 34, res. Windsor, had s. [ ], b. July 30, 1850	1	250-1
Lucy P., of Granby, m. Edwin I. DARROW, of New York City, June 28, 1854, by Rev. D. Hemenway	1	69
Walter Newton, s. Alfred, farmer, ae 25 & Jane S., housewife, ae 31, b. Nov. 22, 1847	1	224-5
GIBBS, Julia M., of Manchester, m. Henry JOHNSON, Jr., of Hartford, Feb. 8, 1852, by Rev. Pliny F. Sanborn	1	66
GIDDINGS, Louisa A., m. Ebenezer K. MASON, b. of Southwick,		

	Vol.	Page

GIDDINGS, (cont.)
    Mass., May 23, 1844, by Ardon B. Holcomb,
      J. P.   1   41

GILLEN, Hugh, m. Mary M. **GILLETT**, Nov. 27, 1844, by I. P.
    Warren   1   44

GILLETT, GILLET, GILLETTE, Abigail, housekeeper, b.
    Southwick, res. Granby, d. Mar. [ ], 1851, ae
    72   1   138
    Adaline, m. Leonard **GODARD**, Mar. 10, 1830, by Isaac
      Porter   1   1
    Almon, of Southwick, Mass., m. Carolin **SKINNER**,
      of Granby, Sept. 21, 1831, by Isaac Porter   1   8
    Buckland, [s. Thomas B. & Rhoda], b. May 3, 1779   TM1   5
    Calvin, [s. Ephraim], b. Jan. 22, 1786   TM1   5
    Caroline, m. Theodore I. **HILLYER**, Apr. 5, 1845, by
      I. P. Warren   1   45
    Curtis, m. Mrs. Louis **STEER**, b. of Southwick, Mass.,
      Nov. 27, 1833, by Rev. Charles Spear   1   15
    Denis, [s. Thomas B. & Rhoda], b. Feb. 20, 1789   TM1   5
    Edwin, m. Jane **LEWIS**, b. of Granby, Apr. 4, 1841,
      by Rev. Daniel Hemenway   1   35
    Elizabeth R., m. Denman D. **DAY**, Oct. 30, 1834, by
      Rev. Daniel Hemmenway   1   18
    Elmira S., m. Wilson **GODARD**, Nov. 3, 1840, by Rev.
      John Higby   1   34
    Emeline, of Granville, Mass., m. Elisha I. **MALISON**,
      of Sandisfield, Mass., Mar. 14, 1840, by
      Abner Case, J. P.   1   31
    Ephraim, Jr., [s. Ephraim], b. Jan. 12, 1784   TM1   5
    Eunice, [d. Thomas B. & Rhoda], b. Jan. 6, 1777   TM1   5
    Eunice, m. Harmon **HAYES**, Nov. 5, 1828, by Joab
      Griffin, Jr., J. P.   1   3
    Frederick, m. Naoma **TINKER**, b. of Granville, Mass.,
      Jan. 24, 1837, by Abner Case, J. P.   1   23
    Gideon, [s. Thomas B. & Rhoda], b. Apr. 14, 1781   TM1   5
    Henry, m. Betsey **HOLCOMB**, b. of Granby, Mar. 31,
      1831, by Rev. Asa Cornwall   1   6
    Henry, had d. [ ], b. July 24, 1851   1   132-3
    Henry C., of Southwick, m. Adah H. **GODARD**, of
      Granby, Dec. 7, 1837, by Isaac Porter   1   25
    Hosea, b. Oct. 18, 1788   TM1   10
    James, m. Clarissa **BEACH**, b. of Granby, Apr. 17, 1833,
      by Ammi Linsley, V. D. M.   1   14
    Jemime, [d. Thomas B. & Rhoda], b. July 21, 1791   TM1   5
    Justin, [s. Thomas B. & Rhoda], b. Sept. 14, 1784   TM1   5
    Justus P., of Windsor, m. Julia **VEITS**, of Granby,
      Oct. 31, 1832, at the house of Benoni Veits,
      by Rev. Asa Cornwall   1   12

98   BARBOUR COLLECTION

	Vol.	Page
GILLETT, GILLET, GILLETTE, (cont.)		
Laura, Mrs., m. Reubin **COSSIT**, Jan. 31, 1832, by Abner Case, J. P.	1	10
Lura A., m. John **PETTIBONE**, b. of Granby, May 21, 1854, by Rev. Henry H. Bates, of Tariffville	1	69
Mary M., m. Hugh **GILLEN**, Nov. 27, 1844, by I. P. Warren	1	44
Merton A., s. Austin, farmer & Lucinda, res. Windsor, b. Jan. 9, 1851	1	132-3
Olive, farmer's daughter, d. Sept. 25, 1847, ae 1 1/2	1	230-1
Rhoda, [d. Thomas B. & Rhoda], b. July 6, 1775	TM1	5
Ruth, [d. Thomas B. & Rhoda], b. Apr. 14, 1793	TM1	5
Samuel, of Westfield, m. Esther **CROCKER**, of Granville, Mass., Jan. 13, 1847, by Hiram F. Chapin, J. P.	1	51
Sibbel M., of Granville, m. Oliver S. **GRANGER**, of Suffield, Oct. 11, 1838, by Abner Case, J. P.	1	28
Thankfull, [d. Thomas B. & Rhoda], b. Feb. 22, 1795	TM1	5
Thomas, [s. Thomas B. & Rhoda], b. Nov. 30, 1786	TM1	5
Thomas, m. Sophia **FOX**, b. of Granby, Dec. 11,, 1832, by Nathaniel Pratt, J. P.	1	13
Thomas B., m. Mrs. Rhoda **TAYLOR**, June 30, 1774	TM1	5
Thomas E., s. Thomas, farmer, ae 41 & Julia, ae 34, b. Nov. 25, 1851	TM1	130-1
Wilson, m. Laura E. **SPELMAN**, b. of Granby, Nov. 7, 1848, by Hiram F. Chapin, J. P.	1	57
GLAZIER, Orphia, Mrs., m. Silas **HODGE**, Sept. 2, 1832, by Abner Case, J. P.	1	11
GODARD, GODDARD, GOSSARD, Achsa, [child of Archilus & Rebisah], b. Sept. 20, 1813	TM1	10
Achsa, d. Achillis, m. John I. **WRIGHT**, Oct. 7, 1839, by Rev. Charles Stearns	1	31
Adah, d. June [ ], 1849, ae 103	1	244-5
Adah H., of Granby, m. Henry C. **GILLET**, of Southwick, Dec. 7, 1837, by Isaac Porter	1	25
Affiah, [child of Nicholas & Mary], b. Apr. 6, 1778	TM1	12
Alden, s. [Rufus & Mindall], b. Nov. 12, 1804	TM1	76
Amelia, d. Aug. 14, 1847, ae 19	1	228-9
Amelia, d. Aug. 14, 1848	1	242-3
Anna, [d. Nicola[s] & Mary], b. Jan. 21, 1776	TM1	12
Ansel, s. [Rufus & Mindall], b. May 11, 1795	TM1	76
Archelus, s. [Ebenezer, Jr. & Achsah], b. Jan. 3, 1788	TM1	6
Archilus, m. Mrs. Rebisah **MESSENGER**, Feb. 11, 1808	TM1	10
Asenath, m. Orlando **PEASE**, Dec. 20, 1832, by Isaac Porter	1	13
Austin, [s. Lieut. Martin & Abigal], b. Mar. 5, 1795	TM1	22
Candace, m. John **CUSHMAN**, b. of Granby, June 3, 1846, by John S. Hayes, J. P.	1	48

	Vol.	Page
GODARD, GODDARD, GOSSARD, (cont.)		
Candia, d. Levi, b. Nov. 18, 1791	TM1	75
Caroline M., m. Joseph A. **GALPIN**, b. of Granby, May 17, 1847, by Rev. Pliney F. Sanborn	1	52
Caroline S., m. Horace **ROCKWELL**, of Windsor, Nov. 3, 1848, by A. L. Loveland	1	56
Clarassa, d. Levi, b. Feb. 11, 1788	TM1	75
Clemena, m. Bethual **CASE**, b. of Granby, Sept. 13, 1831, by Rev. Edwin G. Griswold	1	8
Cleo, m. Roland **BARLOW**, Feb. 3, 1831, by Abner Case, J. P.	1	6
Curtis, s. [Rufus & Mindall], b. Nov. 10, 1789	TM1	76
Dan, s. Levi, b. Nov. 2, 1783	TM1	75
Denis, s. [Rufus & Mindall], b. Sept. 1, 1787	TM1	76
Deotus, s. [Nicolas & Mary], b. Dec. 18, 1786	TM1	12
Deziah, [d. Nicolas & Mary], b. Nov. [ ], 1784	TM1	12
Ebenezer, Jr., m. Mrs. Achsah **HAYS**, July 7, 1784	TM1	6
Ebenezer, m. Sarah **MOORE**, b. of Granby, Apr. 2, 1833, by Joab Griffin, J. P.	1	14
Eli, s. [Lieut. Marten] & Abigal, b. Dec. 15, 1778	TM1	22
Elias, [s. Moses], b. June 23, 1785; d. [ ]	TM1	36
Eliza, m. Daniel T. **ALDERMAN**, Jr., b. of Granby, June 1, 1835, by C. Bentley	1	19
Fidelia, m. Aaron C. **TERRY**, Oct. 27, 1831, by Isaac Porter	1	9
Flora, m. Forrest **REED**, Nov. 4, 1830, by Isaac Porter	1	5
Harriet, m. Milton **PHELPS**, Jan. 11, 1831, by Isaac Porter	1	6
Horatio, farmer, ae 21, m. Lorenda E. **HAYES**, ae 19, b. of Granby, July 3, 1851, by Rev. Nelson Scott	1	134
Ichabod, [s. Moses], b. Feb. 6, 1790; d. [ ]	TM1	36
Isaac, m. Polly **GODARD**, Nov. 14, 1821, by Isaac Griffin, 2nd, J. P.	TM1	163
Ithra, m. Eunice **CHAPMAN**, Dec. 5, 1832, by Isaac Porter	1	13
James, [s. Moses], b. Dec. 6, 1792	TM1	36
James, m. Sophia P. **HAYES**, b. of Granby, Oct. 27, 1846, by Rev. James C. Houghton	1	50
James F., s. James, blacksmith, ae 29 & Sophia P., ae 29, b. Dec. 28, 1848	1	234-5
Jane, of Granby, m. J. Leroy **ROOT**, of Granville, Mass., Apr. 17, 1837, by H. B. Soule	1	63
Jane, b. Apr. 17, 1851	1	130-1
Jane, seamstress, ae 19, b. Granby, res. same, m. [ ], Apr. 17, 1851, by Rev. Mr. Soule	1	134
Jane P., of Granby, m. Harvey P. **COLLINS**, of Hamilton, N. Y., Mar. 1, 1840, by Rev. Chauncey D. Rice	1	34

	Vol.	Page
GODARD, GODDARD, GOSSARD, (cont.)		
Jedediah, [s. Moses], b. Aug. 2, 1774; d. [ ]	TM1	36
Jethra, s. [Rufus & Mindall], b. July 7, 1807	TM1	76
Joab, s. [Rufus & Mindall], b. June 13, 1800	TM1	76
Jula, [child of Nicolas & Mary], b. Dec. 10, 1789	TM1	12
Kezia, d. Moses, b. Mar. 11, 1770	TM1	36
Laura, of Granby, m. Henry C. **REED**, of Hartford, Dec. 6, 1848, by A. L. Loveland	1	56
Laura, ae 36, m. Henry C. **REED**, carpenter, ae 29, b. of Granby, [ ], by Rev. A. L. Loveland	1	238-9
Leonard, m. Adaline **GILLET**, Mar. 10, 1830, by Isaac Porter	1	1
Linda, d. Levi, b. Sept. 28, 1793	TM1	75
Lucy, d. [Rufus & Mindall], b. Apr. 6, 1793	TM1	76
Maranda, m. Moses **WATERS**, Apr. 8, 1835, by Abner Case, J. P.	1	19
Marten, Jr., s. Lieut. Marten & Abigal, b. July 8, 1776	TM1	22
Marvin, s. [Archilus & Rebisah], b. Aug. 26, 1811	TM1	10
Mary, [d. Nicolas & Mary], b. Feb. 10, 1781	TM1	12
Mary E., d. George, farmer, ae 36 & Mary P., housewife, ae 30, b. Aug. 5, 1847	1	224-5
Mary Melissa, m. Albert **KIMBAL**, of Bangor, Me., May 24, 1838, by Charles Bentley	1	27
Miles, [s. Moses], b. June 2, 1778	TM1	36
Miles, m. Mrs. Cleopatra **DIBOL**, Feb. 4, 1789	TM1	21
Moses, Jr., [s. Moses], b. Feb. 21, 1772	TM1	36
Murton, m. Loisa **PRATT**, b. of Granby, Sept. 8, 1836, by Charles Bentley	1	22
Nancy, d. Miles [& Cleopatra], b. Apr. 5, 1802	TM1	21
Nicolas, m. Mrs. Mary **GRANGER**, Oct. 22, 1772	TM1	12
Oran, [child of Moses], b. Dec. 22, 1780	TM1	36
Orin, s. Miles [& Cleopatra], b. Oct. 18, 1800	TM1	21
Orin, m. Minerva **HOLCOMB**, b. Dec. 4, 1821, by Daniel Benjamin, J. P.	TM1	163
Oren, s. Orren, farmer & sawyer, ae 49 & Minerva, ae 46, b. Aug. 20, 1848	1	234-5
Patty, d. [Archilus & Rebisah], b. Feb. 25, 1809	TM1	10
Patty, m. Stanley **WEED**, June 7, 1830, by Isaac Porter	1	3
Permelia, of Granby, m. Henry C. **PORTER**, of East Hartford, Dec. 11, 1838, by Rev. Davis Stocking	1	28
Peter, s. Lieut. Martin & Abigail, b. Apr. 22, 1784	TM1	22
Philetus, s. [Levi], b. Dec. 31, 1781	TM1	75
Philo, s. Lieut. Martin & Abigal, b. May 20, 1782	TM1	22
Pliney, s. [Lieut. Marten] & Abigal, b. Oct. 10, 1780	TM1	22
Polly, m. Isaac **GODDARD**, Nov. 14, 1821, by Isaac Griffin, 2nd, J. P.	TM1	163
Rebeckah, d. [Rufus & Mindall], b. Aug. 13, 1797	TM1	76

	Vol.	Page
GODARD, GODDARD, GOSSARD, (cont.)		
Rebec[c]a, of Granby, m. Ebenezer OSBORN, of Mass.,		
[Sept.] 7, 1840, by Rev. Charles Stearns	1	32
Ruddy, [d. Moses], b. Apr. 17, 1783	TM1	36
Ruddy, m. Candace BURR, Dec. 10, 1802	TM1	21
Rufus, m. Mrs. Mindall COSSIT, Mar. 9, 1786	TM1	76
Samuel, s. Lieut. Martin & Abigal, b. May 1, 1786	TM1	22
Semantha, m. Chauncey HOLCOMB, Sept. 13, 1831, by Isaac Porter	1	8
Sophia, m. Jabez HOLCOMB, [ ], 1792	1	141
Sophia, m. Uri HOLCOMB, Apr. 26, 1831, by Isaac Porter	1	7
Starling, s. [Ebenezer, Jr. & Achsah], b. June 20, 1785	TM1	6
Starling, s. Ruddy & Candace, b. Nov. 22, 1803	TM1	21
Submit, [d. Moses, b. Dec. 19, 1775	TM1	36
Theron, [s. Lieut. Martin & Abigal], b. Dec. 15, 1792	TM1	22
Truman, [s. Nicolas & Mary], b. Oct. 2, 1791	TM1	12
Warren, [s. Lieut. Martin & Abigal], b. June 15, 1790	TM1	22
Wilson, m. Elmira S. GILLET, Nov. 3, 1840, by Rev. John Higby	1	34
GOFF, Joseph F., of Haddam, m. Chloe T. CASE, of Barkhamsted, Nov. 3, 1834, by Rev. William R. Gould	1	17
GOODMAN, Ozar D., of New Haven, m. Mary A. JEWETT, of Granby, Aug. 26, 1852, by Caleb F. Page	1	68
GOODRICH, Catharine, m. Ardon B. HOLCOMB, Oct. 12, 1828, by Isaac Porter	1	7
Catharine, m. Ardon B. HOLCOMB, Oct. 12, 1828, by Rev. Isaac Porter	1	213
Eliger, of Chatham, m. Sophia PRATT, of Granby, May 13, 1821, by Joab Griffin, J. P.	TM1	161
Emillia, housekeeper, d. Apr. 4, 1851, ae 43	1	138
John H., s. Elizur, farmer, ae 37 & Clarinda, ae 33, b. Mar. 28, 1851	1	130-1
Marion, d. Hezekiah, shoe maker, ae 37 & Sarah Ann, ae 27, b. May 13, 1850	1	248-9
Mellisant, married, d. Dec. 27, 1847, ae 71	1	228-9
Sophia, of Granby, see Sophia KING, [of Granby]	1	36
Sophronia, d. Apr. 3, 1851, ae 35	1	138
GORDON, Loisa C., of Granby, m. David L. RISING, of Westfield, Mass., July 4, 1838, by Rev. D. Wright	1	28
Mary E., of Granby, m. Samuel ENSIGN, of Hartford, [Nov. 29, 1832], by Rev. D. Hemenway	1	13
GORHAM, Betsey, m. Hollister F. Marsh, b. of Chester, Mass., Nov. 17, 1839, by Rev. A. C. Washburn	1	31
GORMAN, John, laborer, b. Ireland, res. Granby, d. June 24, 1849, ae 18	1	246-7
GOULD, GOOLD, Caroline M., m. Jacob P. MERROW, b. of		

	Vol.	Page
GOULD, GOOLD, (cont.)		
East Granby, July 28, 1846, by Rev. Pliney F. Sanborn	1	49
Chancy, s. David & Rebeckah, b. Feb. 25, 1787	TM1	22
George S., [s. Gurdon & Phebe], b. Dec. 7, 1799	TM1	29
Gurdon, m. Mrs. Phebe **CORNISH**, May 12, 1790	TM1	29
Gurdon C., [s. Gurdon & Phebe], b. Mar. 10, 1791	TM1	29
James, s. David [& Rebeckah], b. July 28, 1790	TM1	22
James H., [s. Gurdon & Phebe], b. Dec. 10, 1793	TM1	29
Janny, [child of David & Rebeckah], b. Feb. 11, 1792	TM1	22
Joseph A., [s. Gurdon & Phebe], b. Aug. 16, 1792	TM1	29
Mary E., of East Granby, m. W[illia]m H. **MERROW**, of Hartford, June 1, 1847, by Rev. Pliney F. Sanborn	1	52
Phebe C., [d. Gurdon & Phebe], b. Aug. 8, 1804	TM1	29
Thomas S., m. Diantha A. **EDGERTON**, b. of Granby, Oct. 1, 1845, by Rev. Levi Warner	1	46
GOWDRY, [see also **GOWDY**], Hannah, m. Sylvester **PARKS**, Feb. 28, 1832, at the house of Daniel Hayes, by Rev. Asa Cornwall	1	10
GOWDY, [see also **GOWDRY**], Mary An[n], of Windsor, m. William W. **WARE**, Aug. 23, 1840, by Rev. Daniel Hemenway	1	33
GRANGER, Asahel, m. Louisa Ana **LOOMIS**, b. of Southwick, Mass., Nov. 23, 1830, by Rev. Asa Cornwall	1	4
Dorcus, w. Josiah, d. Mar. 23, 1806	TM1	12
Lois, m. Silas **ORSBURN**, Jan. 31, 1822, by Isaac Porter	TM1	164
Mary, Mrs., m. Nic[h]olas **GOSSARD**, Oct. 22, 1772	TM1	12
Oliver S., of Suffield, m. Sibbel M. **GILLET**, of Granville, Oct. 11, 1838, by Abner Case, J. P.	1	28
GRANT, Lyman, of East Windsor, m. Sarah Jane **HOSMER**, of Granby, June 6, 1830, by Ebenezer Everitt, V. D. M.	1	3
GRAVES, Erastus, of Williamsburgh, Mass., m. Elizabeth R. **STRONG**, of Granby, Sept. 18, 1844, by I. P. Warren	1	43
Horace, of Windsor, m. Julia **DAY**, of Granby, Apr. 27, 1840, by Rev. Daniel Hemenway	1	33
GRAY, Elisabeth, b. Suffield, res. same, d. Jane. 20, 1849, ae 100	1	244-5
GREEN, Howard J., m. Cordelia M. **REED**, Nov. 28, 1850, by Caleb F. Page	1	64
GRIFFIN, GRIFFEN, GRIFFINS, Abraham, m. Mehitabel **MOOR**, Dec. 4, 1788	TM1	35
Abraham, Jr., [s. Abraham & Mehitabel], b. Sept. 13, 1790	TM1	35
Adaline, d. Milton, farmer, ae 37 & Adaline, ae 31, b. Oct. 27, 1850	1	130-1
Adaline, b. Granby, res. West Granby, d. Oct. 27, 1850,		

GRANBY VITAL RECORDS 103

	Vol.	Page
GRIFFIN, GRIFFEN, GRIFFINS, (cont.)		
ae 37	1	138
Alice Josephine, d. Richardson, farmer, ae 37 & Juliann, ae 33, b. May 23, 1849	1	234-5
Aralza, of Suffield, m. Annie T. VEITS, of Granby, Nov. 26, 1834, by Rev. Daniel Hemmenway	1	18
Benjamin F., s. Gilbert, farmer & Harriet N., b. July 13, 1850	1	250-1
Caroline, ae 22, b. Granby, res. same, m. Israel P. ALDERMAN, farmer, ae 23, b. W. Springfield, res. Chenago, N. Y., Dec. 23, 1847, by Rev. Miles Olmsted	1	226-7
Chauncey, m. Myra DAVIS, b. of Granby, June 30, 1850, by Ardon B. Holcomb, J. P.	1	62
Deborah, [d. Stephen & Deborah], b. Jan. 14, 1781	TM1	29
Dorothy, m. Forest COOLEY, b. of Granby, June 4, 1835, by C. Bentley	1	19
Emma Adaline, d. Milton, farmer & Adaline, housewife, b. Oct. 17, 1847, [d. [ ], ae 10 m.]	1	222-3
Erastus, [s. Abraham & Mehitabel], b. Dec. 22, 1797	TM1	35
Eugene, s. Henry, farmer, ae 26 & Harriet M., ae 23, b. Apr. 4, 1849	1	234-5
Gilbert, blacksmith, b. Granby, res. West Granby, d. Dec. 7, 1850, ae 33	1	138
Hannah, [d. Stephen], b. Sept. 26, 1764	TM1	29
Harriett N., Mrs. m. Milton GRIFFIN, b. of Granby, Apr. 25, 1852, by Caleb F. Page	1	68
Henry, farmer, ae 24, m. Harriet M. VIETS, ae 21, b. of Granby, Oct. 21, 1847, by Rev. Miles N. Olmsted	1	226-7
Homer, m. Susan GRIFFIN, b. of Granby, May [ ], 1843, by Rev. William McKendee Bangs	1	39
Horace, of Oswego, N. Y., m. Luna C. HOLCOMB, of Granby, June 3, 1849, at the house of Orator Holcomb, by Rev. Amasa Holcomb	1	58
Howard, m. Eliza MARBLE, May 6, 1840, by Isaac Porter	1	32
Isaac, [s. Stephen], b. Apr. 6, 1772; d. Oct. 22, 1775	TM1	29
Isaac, [s. Stephen], b. Mar. 10, 1777	TM1	29
Jefferson, s. Homer, farmer, ae 25 & Susan, housewife, ae 25, b. June 27, 1848	1	224-5
Jeptha, [child of Abraham & Mehitabel], b. July 30, 1772* *("1792"?)	TM1	35
Lester, m. Lucy M. BARKER, b. of East Granby, Oct. 30, 1844, by I. B. Clarke	1	43
Lovisa, d. Mar. 26, 1849, ae 73	1	242-3
Lyman, farmer, ae 49 & Harriet, ae 35, had d. [ ], b. Mar. 15, 1849	1	232-3

GRIFFIN, GRIFFEN, GRIFFINS, (cont.)

	Vol.	Page
Lyman, laborer, ae 20, m. Lamira **DAVIS**, ae 20, b. of Granby, June 30, 1850, by Rev. Ardon B. Holcomb	1	252-3
Margaret C., d. Philo Z., farmer & Betsey A., housewife, b. Apr. 6, 1848, [d. [ ], ae 4 m.	1	222-3
Mary, m. Almon **OWEN**, b. of Granby, May 26, 1835, by C. Bently	1	19
Metilda, m. Silas **DAVICE**, Sept. 21, 1788	TM1	35
Mercy, [d. Stephen], b. Nov. 27, 1767	TM1	29
Milo J., s. Appolos, farmer, ae 28 & Martha A., ae 25, b. June 28, 1849	1	234-5
Milton, m. Mrs. Harriett N. **GRIFFIN**, b. of Granby, Apr. 25, 1852, by Caleb F. Page	1	68
Morton, farmer & Lorinda M., had s. [ ], b. Nov. 14, 1850; d. [ ], ae 8 1/2 m.	1	132-3
Moses, mechanic, ae 24, b. New Haven, res. Hartford, m. Lucy **LAMB**, ae 26, of Granby, June 3, 1849, by Samuel Weed	1	238-9
Oliver, [s. Stephen & Deborah], b. Feb. 12, 1788	TM1	29
Philo, m. Betsey Ann **STEVENS**, b. of Granby, Dec. 26, 1833, by Rev. D. Hemmenway	1	16
Philo Z., farmer, ae 45 & Betsey Ann, ae 41, had s. [ ], b. Oct. 27, 1850	1	130-1
Rhoda, m. Hiram **WILCOX**, b. of Granby, July 13, 1837, by Amasa Holcomb	1	24
Richardson, m. Julianna **VEITS**, of Granby, Apr. 13, 1837, by Rev. Daniel Hemenway	1	24
Samuel, [s. Stephen & Deborah], b. Oct. 1, 1783; d. Oct. 8, 1785	TM1	29
Samuel, [s. Stephen & Deborah], b. Mar. 30, 1785	TM1	29
Sarah, [d. Stephen], b. Aug. 26, 1765	TM1	29
Sarah, d. Mar. 6, 1851, ae 48	1	138
Sophia, m. Isaac **DEWEY**, Jr., b. of Granby, July 23, 1837, by Rev. Shaler J. Hillyer	1	24
Stephen, [s. Stephen], b. Dec. 14, 1769	TM1	29
Stephen, m. Mrs. Deborah **HIGLEY**, Aug. 17, 1779	TM1	29
Susan, m. Homer **GRIFFIN**, b. of Granby, May [ ], 1843, by Rev. William McKendee Bangs	1	39
Timothy, [s. Stephen], b. Apr. 23, 1774	TM1	29
Virgil D., of Granby, m. Esther E. **MILLER**, of Southampton, Mass., Nov. 30, 1842, by Ardon B. Holcomb, J. P.	1	38
Walter, of Granby, m. Eunice E. **MOORE**, of Southwick, Mass., Aug. 12, 1840, by Rev. Daniel Hemenway	1	33
W[illia]m R., farmer & Lathama, had s. [ ], s.b.	1	236-7

	Vol.	Page
GRISWOLD, GRISWOULD, Adaline, m. Avery PARSONS, b. of Windsor, May 1, 1839, by Rev. Daniel Hemenway	1	30
Alexander H., m. Lucy SKINNER, b. of Granby, May 3, 1821, by Allen McLean	TM1	161
Alexander H., m. Mrs. Mahetable PHELPS, b. of Granby, Feb. 12, 1846, by Cornelius B. Everest	1	47
Almira, m. James Hiram HOLCOMB, Feb. 15, 1821, by James Dibble, J. P.	TM1	161
Arthur, farmer, b. Windsor, res. same, d. June 11, 1850, ae [ ]	1	254-5
Charles, of Windsor, m. Lovisa HOLCOMB, of Granby, Aug. 31, 1846, by Rev. James C. Houghton	1	49
Charlotte N., of Granby, m. Edwin HOLCOMB, of Simsbury, July 4, 1847, by Hiram F. Chapin, J. P.	1	53
Chancy, [s. David & Lois], b. Feb. 11, 1797	TM1	25
Cynthia, m. William SMITH, May 18, 1821, by Isaac Porter	TM1	162
David, m. Mrs. Lois HIGLEY, July 16, 1772	TM1	25
David, Jr., s. David & Lois, b. Mar. 22, 1773	TM1	25
George, of Granby, m. Charity HOLCOMB, of Simsbury, May 30, 1847, by Hiram F. Chapin, J. P.	1	52
George D., laborer, ae 44 & Charlotte, housewife, ae 40, had child b. May 27, 1848	1	220-1
George D., laborer, ae 45 & Charlotte, ae 42, had s. [ ], b. June 19, 1850	1	246-7
Huldah, d. David & Lois, b. July 8, 1782	TM1	25
Ira, s. David & Lois, b. May 31, 1777	TM1	25
James M., m. Catharine M. PHELPS, b. of E. Granby, Nov. 30, 1843, by I. B. Clark	1	41
Jared, of Hartford, m. Mary ROBBINS, of Granby, Jan. 1, 1831, by Stephen Crosby	1	5
Julia, m. Sewall T. MACK, b. of Granby, Oct. 30, 1832, by Ammi Linsley, V. D. M.	1	12
Lois, Jr., d. David & Lois, b. May 4, 1775	TM1	25
Olive, d. David & Lois, b. Jan. 3, 1780	TM1	25
Pliney, s. David & Lois, b. Dec. 27, 1785	TM1	25
Virgil H., m. Esther F. PHELPS, b. of East Granby, Nov. 30, 1843, by I. B. Clark	1	41
Warhan, of Hartford, m. Delia A. THOMPSON, of Granby, Feb. 1, 1831, by Rev. Augustus Bolles	1	6
HACK, Harriet E., d. Henry, shoemaker, ae 22 & Adeline, ae 25, b. Jan. 15, 1851	1	130-1
Harriet Eliza, d. July 24, 1851, ae 7 m.	1	138

	Vol.	Page

HACK, (cont.)
 Susan, m. Homer **LAMPSON**, Mar. 13, 1845, by Rev. L.
  Warner   1   45
HAGEN, Addison, manufacturer, ae [ ] & Clarissa, had d. [ ], b.
  Sept. 11, 1849   1   236-7
HALE, Diana, d. [Israel & Clarissa], b. Sept. 20, 1803   TM1   14
 Eunic[e], Mrs., m. Timothy **DAY**, Jan. [ ], 1778   TM1   26
 Israel, m. Mrs. Clarissa **BROWN**, Nov. 3, 1802   TM1   14
HALEY, HALY, Joseph C., of Blandford, Mass., m. Marietta H.
  COLTON, of Granby, Oct. 18, 1849, by
  Samuel W. Barnum   1   60
 Joseph C., farmer, b. Blandford, Mass., res. same,
  m. Mariette **COLTON**, b. Granby, res. same,
  Oct. [ ], 1849   1   252-3
HAMLIN, Leander B., medical student, b. Burlington, Conn., res.
  E. Granby, d. Sept. 2, 1849, ae 20   1   254-5
HAND, Amoret, ae 23, b. Blandford, res. Granby, m. Lucius
  BACON, farmer, ae 23, b. Simsbury, res.
  Granby, Apr. [ ], 1851, by Rev. John Pegg   1   134
HARGEE, Esther M., m. William B. **COWLES**, Dec. 24, 1834, by
  Rev. Daniel Hemmenway   1   18
HARGER, Adison, m. Clarissa M. **FOWLER**, Nov. 10, 1841, by
  Rev. Daniel Hemenway   1   36
HARPER, Almira, Mrs., m. Willis **CLEMENS**, b. of Granby, Oct.
  14, 1838, by Abner Case, J. P.   1   28
HART, Amanda, of Barkhamsted, m. Frederick M. **HOLCOMB**, of
  Granby, Dec. 16, 1845, by Rev. James C.
  Houghton   1   47
HARTLAND, Newell, laborer, d. May 22, 1849, ae 34   1   246-7
HARVEY, Erastus W., m. Candace **PRATT***, b. of Hartford, Apr.
  11, 1836, by Rev. D. Hemenway *(In pencil
  "PEARL")   1   22
HASKINS, Anna, of Granvill, m. Harley **MOOR**, of Granby, Nov.
  30, 1820, by Daniel Benjamin, J. P.   TM1   160
HATCH, Josiah T., of East Granville, m. Lucelia **HAYES**, of
  Granby, Feb. 12, 1836, by Charles Bentley   1   21
HATH, Solomon, m. Elizabeth **HUMPHREY**, b. of Simsbury, Feb.
  9, 1821, by James Dibble, J. P.   TM1   161
HAWLEY, Elisabeth, Mrs., m. Simeon **HAYS**, Mar. 22, 1790   TM1   26
 Ursula, of Canton, m. Aaron H. **WHEELER**, of West
  Springfield, Mass., Feb. 19, 1833, by Rev. D.
  Hemenway   1   13
HAYDEN, Oliver, farmer, ae 42 & Jane O., ae 37, res. Windsor,
  had d. [ ], b. Apr. 30, 1849   1   236-7
HAYES, HAYS, HAY, Achsah, Mrs., m. Ebenezer **GOSSARD**, Jr.,
  July 7, 1784   TM1   6
 Addison, s. Harlow, farmer, b. Oct. 12, 1849   1   248-9
 Albert, m. Betsey **BEAMAN**, b. of Granby, Dec. 14,

GRANBY VITAL RECORDS 107

	Vol.	Page
HAYES, HAYS, HAY, (cont.)		
1834, by Rev. Charles Spear	1	18
Albert, joiner, ae 34 & Sophrona, ae 29, had d. [ ], b. Mar. 28, 1849	1	232-3
Alice, m. Rufus H. BARLOW, Apr. 4, 1837, by Charles Bentley	1	24
Alice A., d. Milton & Alvira, b. Mar. 13, 1851	1	130-1
Alice O., of Granby, m. Frederick F. MELLEN, of E. Marion, Ga., Dec. 12, 1850, by Caleb F. Page	1	65
Alice O., ae 23, b. Granby, res. Georgia, m. George F. MELLEN, school teacher, ae 29, b. Brookfield, res. Georgia, Dec. 12, 1851, by Rev. Mr. Page	1	134
Alma, m. Justus Luther ALLEN, b. of Granby, Apr. 16, 1838, by Allen McLean	1	27
Amasa, m. Olive LAMBSON, Nov. 23, 1791	TM1	75
Anson Byron, [s. Levi & Ruhamah], b. Nov. 25, 1801	TM1	22
Benjamin Sheldon, s. [Benjamin & Hannah], b. Jan. 14, 1804	TM1	40
Betsey, of Granby, m. Friend DICKINSON, of Amherst, Mass., Oct. 3, 1833, by Rev. Charles Bentley	1	15
Caroline, ae 18, m. William HELA, machinist, ae 24, b. New Hartford, res. same, Sept. [ ], 1848, by Rev. Mr. Pulling	1	238-9
Caroline A., of Granby, m. William C. HEALY, of New Hartford, Sept. 13, 1848, by Rev. A. B. Pulling	1	56
Caroline Almira, d. James R., farmer & Almira, b. Sept. 12, 1848	1	232-3
Catharine A., m. Seymour L. SPELLMAN, b. of Granby, Oct. 5, 1851, by H. B. Soule	1	64
Collins E., m. Mary Ann KENDALL, b. of Granby, Sept. 15, 1847, by Rev. Stephen Rushmore	1	53
Collins E., farmer, ae 25, m. Mary Ann KENDALL, ae 21, b. of Granby, Sept. 15, 1847, by Rev. Stephen Rushmore	1	226-7
Collins E., farmer, d. Mar. 15, 1849, ae 26	1	244-5
Daniel, 2nd, m. Mary COOLEY, Mar. 29, 1835, by Abner Case, J. P.	1	19
Deziah Miranda, m. Charles PETTIBONE, Mar. 29, 1822, by Isaac Porter	TM1	165
Dudley, farmer, d. May 25, 1849, ae 61	1	242-3
Edward, m. Rhoda KENDALL, Aug. 5, 1839, by Isaac Porter	1	30
Edwin P., m. Mary E. TAYLOR, Nov. 23, 1831, by Isaac Porter	1	10
Electa, m. Truman ALLEN, b. of Granby, June 12, 1834, by Amasa Holcomb	1	21

	Vol.	Page

HAYES, HAYS, HAY, (cont.)

Elihu, m. Helen LANE, May 5, 1841, by Rev. C. D. Rice	1	35
Eliza, m. Linus HAYES, b. of Granby, July 22, 1849, by Rev. A. B. Pulling	1	59
Elisa, ae 21, m. Linus HAYES, farmer, ae 28, b. of Granby, July [ ], 1849, by Rev. Mr. Pulling (Her 2nd m.)	1	238-9
Elmina, of Granby, m. Lyman LOOMISE, of Westfield, Mar. 26, 1846, at the house of Phineas Hayes, by Rev. Amasa Holcomb	1	49
Elvina, m. Horace W. AVERY, b. of Granby, Nov. 25, 1841, by Rev. Amasa Holcomb, at the house of Phinehas Hayes	1	36
Ezekiel, m. Mary COSSIT, July 17, 1783	TM1	75
Ezekiel, s. [Ezekiel & Mary], b. Apr. 14, 1786	TM1	75
Flora, d. Benjamin & Hannah, b. Sept. 8, 1794	TM1	40
Gaylor, s. [Ezekiel & Mary], b. Dec. 29, 1790	TM1	75
George, m. Caroline WILLCOX, Aug. 29, 1832, by Isaac Porter	1	11
George, clothier, had s. [ ], b. Apr. 3, 1849	1	232-3
Harmon, s. [Amasa & Olive], b. May 23, 1795	TM1	75
Harmon, m. Eunice GILLET, Nov. 5, 1828, by Joab Griffin, Jr., J. P.	1	3
Harriet, of Granby, m. Orrin MOOR, of Southwick, Mar. 30, 1830, by Smith Dayton, Elder. Witnesses: Electa Hayes, Ursula Moor, Maria Hays & Phinehas Hays	1	1
Harriet E., of Granby, m. Josiah C. ALLEN, of Barkhamsted, Sept. 12, 1844, by I. P. Warren	1	43
Harvey, d. Oct. 19, 1849, ae 15	1	254-5
Hilpah, d. Seth, b. Mar. 16, 1782	TM1	26
Julia, m. John DEWEY, Nov. 6, 1821, by Isaac Porter	TM1	163
Julius, farmer, ae 44 & Sophia, ae 40, had s. [ ], b. Mar. 7, 1849	1	234-5
Justin, m. Lucretia CASE, Aug. 22, 1821, by Isaac Porter	TM1	162
Lester, s. Marten & Mary, b. Oct. 5, 1799	TM1	14
Levi, m. Ruhamah PARSONS, Dec. 14, 1786	TM1	22
Levi Loring, s. Levi & Ruhamah, b. Aug. 29, 1788	TM1	22
Levicy, of Granby, m. Starling DANIELS, of Hartland, Mar. 27, 1836, by Abner Case, J. P.	1	21
Lewis, had d. [ ], b. Nov. 22, 1850	1	130-1
Linus, farmer, ae 28, m. Elisa HAYES, ae 21, b. of Granby, July [ ], 1849, by Rev. Mr. Pulling	1	238-9
Linus, m. Eliza HAYES, b. of Granby, July 22, 1849, by Rev. A. B. Pulling	1	59
Looisa, d. Jan. 12, 1849, ae 68	1	242-3

	Vol.	Page
HAYES, HAYS, HAY, (cont.)		
Lorenda E., ae 19, m. Horatio **GODARD**, farmer, ae 21, b. of Granby, July 3, 1851, by Rev. Nelson Scott	1	134
Lovisa Pamela, m. Arnold **EDWARDS**, b. of Granby, July 4, 1832, at Judah Hays, by Asa Cornwall	1	11
Lucelia, of Granby, m. Josiah T. **HATCH**, of East Granville, Feb. 12, 1836, by Charles Bentley	1	21
Lura, m. Calvin B. **DIBBLE**, b. of Granby, Oct. 3, 1837, by Charles Bentley	1	25
Margaret A., d. Edwin G., joiner, b. Oct. 7, 1848	1	232-3
Margaret D., of West Granby, m. Alexander **McKINLEY**, of Washington, Pa., Apr. 27, 1852, by Rev. John Pegg, Jr.	1	67
Maria, of Granby, m. Royal **PROUTY**, of Windsor, Oct. 26, 1836, by Amasa Holcomb	1	24
Marietta, of Granby, m. William **VANDEVEER**, of Westfield, Mass., May 23, 1844, by I. P. Warren	1	41
Marilla, m. James H. **VIETS**, b. of Granby, Oct. 11, 1849, by Rev. A. B. Pulling	1	60
Marilla, ae 23, m. James H. **VIETS**, farmer, ae 26, b. of Granby, Oct. 11, 1849, by Rev. A. B. Pulling	1	252-3
Martha, m. Alvin **HUMPHREY**, Apr. 24, 1833, by Isaac Porter	1	14
Marten, m. Mrs. Mary **CAMP**, Dec. 25, 1798	TM1	14
Marvin C., s. Milton, farmer & Elvira, housewife, b. Mar. 19, 1848 (ae "5 mo" follows birth date)	1	222-3
Mary, d. [Ezekiel & Mary], b. Apr. 15, 1784	TM1	75
May E., of Granby, m. John **LEVIT**, of New York City, Oct. 26, 1851, by H. B. Soule	1	64
Mehitabel, d. Seth, b. Sept. 14, 1786	TM1	26
Melissa, d. Seth, b. Oct. 26, 1783	TM1	26
Millee, d. [Amasa & Olive], b. Jan. 15, 1798	TM1	75
Nancy, m. Sereno **MESSENGER**, b. of Granby, May 2, 1831, by Nathaniel Pratt, J. P.	1	10
Orlen Persons, s. Levi & Ruhamah, b. May 9, 1790	TM1	22
Rachel, d. Nov. 27, 1849, ae 77 (1848?)	1	242-3
Rosannah, [d. Levi & Ruhamah], b. Aug. 28, 1797	TM1	22
Roxey, Mrs., m. Sedosa **WILLCOX**, Dec. 2, 1784	TM1	25
Rozetta, Mrs., m. Roger **MOOR**, Dec. 4, 1786	TM1	12
Ruhamah, d. Levi & Ruhamah, b. Dec. 1, 1792	TM1	22
Salley, d. [Ezekiel & Mary], b. Dec. 12, 1794	TM1	75
Sarah, had illeg. s. Augustus **BROWN**, b. Sept. 20, 1802; f. Justus **BROWN**	TM1	10
Seth, s. Seth, b. Mar. 23, 1788	TM1	26
Sheldon, s. Benjamin [& Hannah], b. Feb. 17, 1797;		

	Vol.	Page
HAYES, HAYS, HAY, (cont.)		
d. May 4, 1803	TM1	40
Simeon, m. Mrs. Elizabeth HAWLEY, Mar. 22, 1790	TM1	26
Sophia P., m. James GODARD, b. of Granby, Oct. 27, 1846, by Rev. James C. Houghton	1	50
Theodore Dwight, m. Louisa HOLCOMB, Nov. 3, 1830, by Isaac Porter	1	5
Theodosia, Mrs., m. Maj. Chauncy PETIBONE, May 21, 1780	TM1	29
Timothy, d. Feb. 25, 1849, ae 9	1	242-3
Wales Vore, [s.] Lewis, farmer, b. July 11, 1849	1	232-3
William, farmer, d. Mar. 28, 1849, ae 23	1	242-3
William L., farmer, ae 23, m. Eliza C. VIETS, ae 19, b. of Granby, Apr. 20, 1848, by Rev. Miles N. Olmsted	1	226-7
William L., s. William L., farmer, b. Nov. 13, 1849	1	248-9
William S., m. Mary O. SPERRY, b. of Granby, Sept. 19, 1842, by Ardon B. Holcomb, J. P.	1	37
Zaccheus, m. Sabra PETTIBONE, Apr. 9, 1833, by Isaac Porter	1	14
HAYNES, Clarissa, [d. Asa & Mary], b. Nov. 26, 1810	TM1	14
Ellen C., m. Alfred PETTIBONE, b. of Tariffville, Nov. 17, 1851, by Caleb F. Page	1	64
Ellen C., m. Alfred PETTIBONE, tinner, b. Granby, res. Simsbury, Nov. 17, 1851, by Rev. Caleb F. Page	1	134
Julia, [d. Asa & Mary], b. May 2, 1815	TM1	14
Mariah, d. Asa & Mary, b. Jan. 31, 1808	TM1	14
HEALY, HELA, William C., of New Hartford, m. Caroline A. HAYES, of Granby, Sept. 13, 1848, by Rev. A. B. Pulling	1	56
William, machinist, ae 24, b. New Hartford, res. same, m. Caroline HAYES, ae 18, Sept. [ ], 1848, by Rev. Mr. Pulling	1	238-9
HENDREY, William A., of New York State, m. Amanda T. CARPENTER, of Granby, Oct. 8, 1851, by Caleb F. Page	1	66
HEBBARD, William Wallace, Rev., m. Martha Sybil BENJAMIN, b. of Granby, Jan. 30, 1845, by Rev. John Moore, of Hartford	1	44
HIGGINS*, Ruth K., of Granby, m. Samuel WHITE, of Suffield, Sept. 26, 1850, by Rev. Nelson Scott *("HIGLEY" on p. 134)	1	63
HIGLEY, Asa, Jr., m. Elisa PRATT, b. of Granby, Sept. 16, 1834, by Charles Bentley	1	17
Deborah, Mrs., m. Stephen GRIFFEN, Aug. 17, 1779	TM1	29
Diana, m. Luke MASON, b. of Simsbury, Mar. 13, 1831, by Rev. Asa Cornwall	1	6

	Vol.	Page
HIGLEY, (cont.)		
Eunice, m. Hiram CASE, Dec. 4, 1834, by Isaac Porter	1	18
Henry E., of Marion, Ia., m. Mary N. MORGAN, of Granby, July 29, 1845, by Rev. James C. Houghton	1	46
Lois, Mrs., m. David GRISWOULD, July 16, 1772	TM1	25
Marilla, d. Orson, butcher, ae 44 & Lucy, ae 27, b. Jan. 13, 1849	1	234-5
Mary T., m. Jarius CASE, Oct. 5, 1830, by Isaac Porter	1	4
Roxsena, Mrs., m. Abel HOLCOMB, 2nd, Feb. 11, 1790	TM1	33
Ruth, ae 29, b. Granby, res. Suffield, m. Samuel WHITE, ae 35, b. Suffield, res. same, Sept. 25, 1850, by Rev. Nelson Scott	1	134
Ruth K., see Ruth K. HIGGINS	1	63
Sally, m. Ansel HUMPHREY, Apr. 16, 1822, by Isaac Porter	TM1	165
Sarah C., m. Albert KENDALL, b. of Granby, Nov. 9, 1840, by Rev. Chauncey D. Rice	1	34
Theodosia, m. Waldo REED, b. of Granby, Oct. 19, 1837, by Charles Bentley	1	25
HILLYER, Alma, d. [Seth & Sybal], b. May 12, 1799	TM1	14
Andrew A., m. Nancy HOLCOMB, Oct. 2, 1838, by Charles Bentley	1	29
Betsey, wid., m. Hezekiah HOLCOMB, b. of Granby, June 21, 1821, by James Dibble, J. P.	TM1	162
Catharine C., of Granby, m. William BARNES, Jr., of Windsor, Dec. 25, 1837, by Charles Bentley		
Chauncey H., d. Sept. 24, 1847, ae 8	1	25
Cleo, d. [Seth & Sybal], b. May 6, 1799	1	228-9
Emily, of Granby, m. Nathaniel EGGLESTON, of Hartford, May 1, 1821, by Isaac Porter	TM1	14
Harrit, d. [Seth & Sybal], b. Feb. 1, 1797	TM1	161
Harriet P., d. Mar. 29, 1849, ae 34	TM1	14
Horace, Dr., m. Mrs. Anna HOLCOMB, Sept. 22, 1796	1	242-3
Horace, Jr., [s. Dr. Horace & Anna], b. Nov. 29, 1797	TM1	26
Horace, Dr., d. Apr. 27, 1812	TM1	26
Lora, d. [Seth & Sybal], b. Sept. 7, 1792	TM1	26
Maltby G., m. Irene Amorett JEWETT, Nov. 20, 1821, by Isaac Porter	TM1	14
Maria, [twin with Miranda], [d. Dr. Horace & Anna], b. Sept. 29, 1802	TM1	163
Miranda, [twin with Maria, d. Dr. Horace & Anna], b. Sept. 20, 1802	TM1	26
Miranda, m. Thomas WILLCOX, May 18, 1830, by Isaac Porter	TM1	26
Rhoda S., [d. Dr. Horace & Anna], b. Nov. 11, 1811	1	2
Sally, d. [Seth & Sybal], b. Sept. 9, 1794	TM1	26
	TM1	14

BARBOUR COLLECTION

	Vol.	Page
HILLYER, (cont.)		
Seth, m. Mrs. Sybal **CASE**, Apr. 10, 1783	TM1	14
Seth, s. Seth & Sybal, b. June 17, 1788	TM1	14
Shaler, [s. Dr. Horace & Anna], b. Dec. 12, 1799	TM1	26
Sybal, d. Seth & Sybal, b. May 19, 1796	TM1	14
Theodore I., m. Caroline **GILLETT**, Apr. 5, 1845, by I. P. Warren	1	45
HIND, Mary, m. Levi **MERRIMAN**, Apr. 23, 1821, by Daniel Benjamin, J. P.	TM1	161
HINE, Eunice Clarissa, m. Merrick **EDSON**, Sept. 15, 1835, by Isaac Porter	1	20
HINMAN, Samuel, farmer, had s. [ ], b. July 16, 1850	1	248-9
HINSDALE, Elizabeth R., m. Charles I. **PERKINS**, July 24, 1839, by Rev. Daniel Hemenway	1	30
HOADLEY, John B., of Auburn, O., m. Caroline A. **OWEN**, of Granby, May 13, 1847, by Rev. Pliney F. Sanborn	1	52
HODGE, Silas, m. Mrs., Orphia **GLAZIER**, Sept. 2, 1832, by Abner Case, J. P.	1	11
HOLCOMB, HOLCOMBE, Abel, 2nd, m. Mrs. Roxsena **HIGLEY**, Feb. 11, 1790	TM1	33
Abigail, [d. Thomas & Elisabeth], b. Jan. 6, 1638	1	143
Abijah, [s. Jabez & Sophia], b. Apr. 10, 1806	1	141
Adaline, m. William H. **SPENCER**, July 3, 1844, by I. P. Warren	1	42
Alanson, of Ill., m. Mrs. Aurora **SEARLS**, of Granby, Dec. 7, 1845, by Rev. James C. Houghton	1	47
Albert, farmer & sawyer, ae 37 & Adeline, ae 31, had child s.b. [ ]	1	234-5
Alfred, farmer, ae 21, b. Granby, res. same, m. Lovinia **HOLLISTER**, weaver, ae 22, b. Glastonbury, res. Granby, Mar. 5, 1849, by Rev. Mr. Smith, of Glastonbury	1	238-9
Alfred, farmer, had s. [ ], b. Jan. [ ], 1850, [d. [ ], ae 7 m.	1	248-9
Alfred Goodrich, [s. Ardon B. & Catharine], b. Sept. 20, 1830	1	213
Almanzer*, [s. Jabez & Sophia], b. Nov. 30, 1816; d. Apr. 4, 1845 *(Perhaps "Almanyer")	1	141
Almira, d. John, whip maker, ae 26 & Lydia, ae 27, b. Mar. 10, 1850	1	248-9
Alson, [s. Ozias & Ruth], b. May 18, 1791	TM1	27
Alson, farmer, ae 36 & Candis A., housewife, ae 25, res. West Granby, had child b. July 13, 1848	1	222-3
Alson, farmer, ae 38 & Candace, ae 28, had d. [ ], b. July 22, 1850	1	248-9
Alvira Merriam, illeg. s. Nathan **HOLCOMB**, farmer, ae 35 & Margaret **WHITE**, ae 27, b. Aug.		

	Vol.	Page

HOLCOMB, HOLCOMBE, (cont.)

25, 1848	1	234-5
Amasa, b. June 18, 1787; m. Mrs. Gillet KENDALL, Nov. 10, 1808	TM1	40
Amos, apprentice, b. Granville, Mass., res. Granby, d. Jan. 26, 1848, ae 17	1	228-9
Ann, d. Apr. 5, 1849, ae 16	1	244-5
Anna, Jr., d. Judah & Anna, b. Jan. 25, 1774[5]	TM1	22
Anna, Mrs., m. Dr. Horace HILLYER, Sept. 22, 1796	TM1	26
Anson L., m. Abigail BENJAMIN, Mar. 31, 1831, by Isaac Porter	1	7
Ardon B., m. Catharine GOODRICH, Oct. 12, 1828, by Isaac Porter	1	7
Ardon B., m. Catharine GOODRICH, Oct. 12, 1828, by Rev. Isaac Porter	1	213
Ardon I., m. Clarissa HOLCOMB, Oct. 11, 1829, by Joab Griffin, Jr., J. P.	1	3
Asenath, housekeeper, d. Apr. 6, 1851, ae 69	1	138
Augustin, s. [Nahum & Rebeckah], b. Jan. 31, 1797; d. May 11, 1837, at Sterling, Mass. Left one child William Frederic, b. Apr. 2, 1817	TM1	49
Aurillia, Mrs., m. Grove HOLCOMB, Mar. 10, 1775	TM1	12
Bashabe, [child of Caleb & Mercy], b. Mar. 8, 1780	TM1	29
Benajah, [s. Thomas & Elisabeth], b. June 23, 1644 who remained in Windsor & from whom came most of those who now live in Poquonnoc	1	143
Bethuel, farmer, d. Apr. 26, 1848, ae 72	1	228-9
Betsey, m. Henry GILLET, b. of Granby, Mar. 31, 1831, by Rev. Asa Cornwall	1	6
Betsey, m. Warren STILES, May 10, 1831, by Isaac Porter	1	7
Betsey, m. Timothy DEAN, b. of Granby, Apr. 22, 1847, by Ardon B. Holcomb, J. P.	1	51
Caleb, m. Mrs. Mercy WINCHEL, Dec. 25, 1776	TM1	29
Caleb, [s. Caleb & Mercy], b. May 16, 1786; d. Apr. 6, 1788	TM1	29
Caleb, [s. Caleb & Mercy], b. Jan. 23, 1789	TM1	29
Candice, m. Anson COOLEY, b. of Granby, Nov. 3, 1836, by Charles Bentley	1	23
Carleton, m. Ann Eliza WILCOX, b. of Granby, May 27, 1847, by Alfred White	1	52
Caroline, of Granby, m. Levi BUTTLES, of E. Granville, Mass., Apr. 20, 1841, by C. D. Rice	1	35
Catharine E., m. James H. ALDERMAN, Aug. 30, 1847	1	226-7
Chandler, of Southwick, Mass., m. Juliet P. MORE, of Granby, Mar. 25, 1834, by Rev. Charles Bentley	1	16
Charity, of Simsbury, m. George GRISWOLD, of		

HOLCOMB, HOLCOMBE, (cont.)

	Vol.	Page
Granby, May 30, 1847, by Hiram F. Chapin, J. P.	1	52
Charles, of Simsbury, m. Emeline HOLCOMB, of Granby, Apr. 29, 1829, by Rev. Ransom Warner, of Simsbury	1	22
Charles, 2nd, farmer, ae 43 & Chloe, ae 33, had twins, s.b. Feb. 4, 1849	1	236-7
Charles H., d. May 19, 1848, ae 1 1/4	1	230-1
Chauncey, m. Semantha GODDARD, Sept. 13, 1831, by Isaac Porter	1	8
Chancey, m. Polly HOLCOMB, b. of Granby, Mar. 8, 1843, by Allen McLean	1	38
Chauncey, farmer, ae 51, of Granby, m. 3rd w. Alma WELLS, ae 43, b. West Hartford, res. Granby, May 8, 1849, by Rev. Horace Bushnell	1	238-9
Chauncey Pettibone, [s. Thomas & Clarinda], b. Dec. 11, 1803	1	213
Chloe, m. Virgil CORNISH, Dec. 25, 1821, by Isaac Porter	TM1	164
Clarinda Gunilda, [d. Thomas & Clarinda], b. Oct. 7, 1817	1	213
Clarissa, m. Ardon I. HOLCOMB, Oct. 11, 1829, by Joab Griffin, Jr., J. P.	1	3
Clarissa, m. Sereno W. HOLCOMB, b. of Granby, Oct. 10, 1837, by Charles Bentley	1	25
Climena, [d. Jabez & Sophia], b. Aug. 11, 1799	1	141
Curtis, [s. Increase & Mary], b. Mar. 26, 1795	TM1	35
Deborah, [d. Thomas & Elisabeth], b. Oct. 15, 1646; d. [ ]	1	143
Deborah, [d. Thomas & Elisabeth], b. Mar. 23, 1652	1	143
Draten, s. Grove & Aurillia, b. Oct. 30, 1796	TM1	12
Edwin, of Simsbury, m. Charlotte N. GRISWOLD, of Granby, July 4, 1847, by Hiram F. Chapin, J. P.	1	53
Edwin L., m. Lucy G. WHITE, b. of Granby, Oct. 23, 1854, by William H. Hebbard	1	69
Eliza, of Granby, m. Sylvanus STONE, of New Britain, Jan. 6, 1851, by Caleb F. Page	1	65
Elisa, ae 40, b. Granby, m. Sylvanus STONE, paper box maker, res. New Britain, Jan. 6, 1851, by Rev. Caleb F. Page	1	134
Elisabeth, wid. Thomas, m. James ENO, Aug. 5, 1658; d. Oct. 7, 1679; bd. in Old Windsor	1	143
Ella A., d. Lester H., carriage maker, ae 26, & Abegail, housewife, ae 26, b. June 22, 1848	1	220-1
Emeline, of Granby, m. Charles HOLCOMB, of		

GRANBY VITAL RECORDS 115

	Vol.	Page
HOLCOMB, HOLCOMBE, (cont.)		
Simsbury, Apr. 29, 1829, by Rev. Ransom Warner, of Simsbury	1	22
Emerson L., of New Britain, m. Jerusha M. DIBBLE, of Granby, Apr. 20, 1851, by Caleb F. Page	1	65
Emerson L., mechanic, ae 21, res. New Britain, m. Jerusha M. DIBBLE, ae 20, b. Granby, Apr. 20, 1851, by [ ]	1	134
Emily, m. David CHURCH, Nov. 24, 1829, by Isaac Porter	1	1
Emily, of Granby, m. Phelps COWDRY, of Hartland, Sept. 4, 1833, by Rev. Charles Bentley	1	15
Emma, d. Feb. 9, 1851, ae 7	1	138
Est[h]er, m. Orwin TERRY, Nov. 17, 1830, by Isaac Porter	1	5
Esther C., of Granby, m. Franklin L. ABELLS, of Lowell, Mass., Nov. 15, 1831, by Rev. Asa Cornwall	1	9
Eugene S., s. Albert & Adaline E., b. Apr. 30, 1851	1	130-1
Eunice, b. Oct. 19, 1763; m. Joseph DYER, Apr. 27, 1784	TM1	51
Experience A., d. Apr. 15, 1851, ae 61	1	138
Fanny, had d. [ ], b. Dec. 10, 1851	1	132-3
Fidelia, d. [Nahum & Rebeckah], b. Aug. 8, 1795	TM1	49
Franklin Porteus, [s. Thomas & Clarinda], b. Jan. 3, 1813	1	213
Frederick M., of Granby, m. Amanda HART, of Barkhamsted, Dec. 16, 1845, by Rev. James C. Houghton	1	47
Gaylord, farmer, b. W. Granby, res. same, d. Mar. 8, 1848, ae 58	1	228-9
Gaylord G., farmer, d. July 1, 1849, ae 50	1	246-7
George C., farmer, d. June 25, 1849, ae 50	1	246-7
Goodsel, farmer, d. May 7, 1849, ae 33	1	244-5
Grove, m. Mrs. Aurillia HOLCOMB, Mar. 10, 1795	TM1	12
Hannah, m. Oliver BARKER, Oct. 29, 1832, by Isaac Porter	1	12
Hannah, wid., m. Jacob HOLCOMB, Nov. 9, 1836, by Isaac Porter	1	23
Hannah, ae 20, m. Lucius WALDRON, peddler, ae 24, b. Simsbury, res. same, Sept. [ ], 1848, by Rev. Mr. Pulling	1	238-9
Hannah E., m. Alexander A. POMEROY, Dec. 25, 1821, by Sameul Griswold	TM1	164
Hannah E., of Granby, m. Lucius W. MOSES, of Simsbury, Nov. 22, 1848, by Rev. A. B. Pulling	1	57
Hannah M., m. Owen RUICK, b. of Granby, July 10, 1848, by Rev. A. B. Pulling	1	56

HOLCOMB, HOLCOMBE, (cont.)

	Vol.	Page
Harlow, s. Hoadiah & Affiah, b. Mar. 28, 1788	TM1	33
Harriett, of Granby, m. Amos H. COWDING, of Hartland, [Sept.] 25, 1839, by Albert Case, of Charleston, S. C.	1	30
Harriet, of Granby, m. James ABBE, of Enfield, June 4, 1844, by I. P. Warren	1	42
Hellen, d. [Nahum & Rebeckah], b. Apr. 29, 1805	TM1	49
Hellen L., m. Abel S. DICKINSON, Sept. 13, 1852, by Rev. A. S. Loveland	1	67
Henry Albert, s. Edwin, laborer, ae 21 & Ursula, housewife, ae 19, b. June 4, 1848	1	220-1
Henry Lyman, [s. Thomas & Clarinda], b. Aug. 22, 1808	1	213
Hezekiah, m. wid. Betsey HILLYER, b. of Granby, June 21, 1821, by James Dibble, J. P.	TM1	162
Hoadiah, Capt., m. Mrs. Affiah BUTTOLPH, May 28, 1778	TM1	33
Hoadiah Anson, s. Hoadiah [& Affiah], b. Dec. 27, 1792	TM1	33
Homar, s. Increase & Mary, b. Feb. 1, 1791	TM1	35
Increase, m. Mrs. Mary READ, June 2, 1789	TM1	35
Irena, m. Wilson REED, b. of Granby, Mar. 13, 1838, by Rev. Davis Stocking	1	26
Jabez, b. Sept. 29, 1765; m. Sophia GODARD, [ ],1792	1	141
Jabez, d. July 20, 1843	1	141
Jacob, m. wid. Hannah HOLCOMB, Nov. 9, 1836, by Isaac Porter	1	23
James Hiram, m. Almira GRISWOLD, Feb. 15, 1821, by James Dibble, J. P.	TM1	161
Joel, m. Mrs. Huldah CLARKE, b. of Granby, Oct. 8, 1832, by Rev. Asa Cornwall	1	11
John, of Springfield, Mass., is supposed to be s. of Jonathan HOLCOMBE	1	143
Jonathan, [s. Thomas & Elisabeth], b. Mar. 23, 1652; d. Sept. 13, 1656 (It is supposed that John HOLCOMBE, of Springfield, Mass., was his son)	1	143
Jonathan, s. Hoadiah & Affiah, b. Nov. 7, 1783	TM1	33
Joshua, [s. Thomas & Elisabeth], b. Sept. 27, 1640	1	143
Joshua, went to Simsbury & from him came the "Falls HOLCOMBS" known as the "Scotland HOLCOMBS"	1	143
Judah, m. Anna HUBBARD, June 30, 1774	TM1	22
Lemuel, [s. Jabez & Sophia], b. May 21, 1808	1	141
Lois, m. Ens. Noah COOLEY, July [ ], 1772	TM1	23
Louisa, m. Theodore Dwight HAYES, Nov. 3, 1830, by Isaac Porter	1	5
Lovisa, of Granby, m. Charles GRISWOLD, of Windsor, Aug. 31, 1846, by Rev. James C. Houghton	1	49

GRANBY VITAL RECORDS

	Vol.	Page
HOLCOMB, HOLCOMBE, (cont.)		
Lucinda, of Granby, m. Luther **REED**, of Simsbury, Dec. 1, 1839, by Charles Stearns	1	31
Lucius Harvey, s. Harvey & Rosannah, b. Oct. 23, 1842	1	213
Luna C., of Granby, m. Horace **GRIFFINS**, of Oswego, N. Y., June 3, 1849, at the house of Orator Holcomb, by Rev. Amasa Holcomb	1	58
Lyman, s. Ozias & Ruth, b. Jan. 12, 1789	TM1	27
Mahala, [d. Jabez & Sophia], b. May 27, 1810	1	141
Mahala, m. George **SPRING**, Nov. 10, 1835, by Isaac Porter	1	21
Margrit, Mrs., m. Ephraim **FLETCHER**, June 30, 1768	TM1	5
Margaret, had d. [ ], d. Oct. [ ], 1848, ae 3 m.	1	244-5
Maria, m. Rolland **HOLCOMB**, Dec. 30,1829, by John Willey, J. P.	1	1
Maria, of Granby, m. Phelps **HUMPHREYS**, of Hartland, Jan. 2, 1834, by Rev. D. Hemmenway	1	16
Mariett, m. Sylvester **NOBLE**, June 27, 1821, by Isaac Porter	TM1	162
Mariett, m. Sanford R. **OLCOTT**, Sept. 12, 1837, by Rev. Daniel Hemenway	1	24
Marilla, [d. Jabez & Sophia], b. Sept. 29, 1796	1	141
Marilla, m. Warren **FARNHAM**, Nov. 28, 1821, by Isaac Porter	TM1	163
Martha, Jr., Mrs., m. Adonijah **FORD**, Aug. 24, 1772	TM1	27
Martha Ellen, [d. Ardon B. & Catharine], b. Feb. 5, 1829	1	213
Martin M., m. Permelia **ROWLEY**, of Blandford, Sept. 6, 1847, by Peter I. Jewett, J. P.	1	53
Mary, Mrs., m. Thomas **COPLEY**, July 11, 1774	TM1	32
Mary, Mrs., m. Job **CASE**, Apr. 21, 1784	TM1	12
Mary, farming, d. Feb. 10, 1848, ae 78	1	228-9
Mary Ann, m. Elijah H. **KENDAL**, b. of Granby, Oct. 22, 1835, by Charles Bentley	1	20
Mary Isabella, d. Charles, farmer & Chloe, b. Sept. 24, 1850	1	132-3
Mary P., of Granby, m. Eliakim **STILES**, of Southwick, Mass., Oct. 5, 1820, by Daniel B. Holcomb, J. P.	TM1	160
Mary R., m. Morton **CORNISH**, Oct. 21, 1840, by Rev. Daniel Hemenway	1	33
Melissa, [d. Jabez & Sophia], b. Dec. 23, 1803; d. Feb. 2, 1855	1	141
Mercy, d. Caleb & Mercy, b. Mar. 6, 1778	TM1	29
Millicia, [d. Increase & Mary], b. July 24, 1793	TMM	35
Millisent, d. Judah & Anna, b. Nov. 22, 1776	1	22
Milo, s. [Nahum & Rebeckah], b. May 12, 1803	TM1	49
Milton, s. [Nahum & Rebeckah], b. Apr.21, 1793	TM1	49

	Vol.	Page
HOLCOMB,HOLCOMBE, (cont.)		
Minerva, m. Orin **GODARD**, Dec. 4, 1821, by Daniel Benjamin, J. P.	TM1	163
Miriam, of Granby, m. Elijah **JONES**, of Barkhamsted, Feb. 6, 1839, by Charles Bentley	1	29
Nahum, m. Rebeckah **MOOR**, d. Shadrach, of Southwick, Nov. 26, 1789	TM1	49
Nahum, [s. Nahum & Rebeckah], b. July 4, 1809; d. Aug. 27, 1871, at West Granby. Left one son Samuel Frederic, b. Dec. 15, 1855	TM1	49
Nahum, Jr., m. Sabra **HOLCOMB**, Apr. 27, 1830, by Isaac Porter	1	2
Nahum, farmer, ae 43 & Sabra A., ae 39, had d. [ ], b. Sept. 25, 1849	1	248-9
Nahum, farmer, res. West Granby, d. Mar. 11, 1851, ae 88	1	138
Nancy, d. [Hoadiah & Affiah], b. Mar. 2, 1795; d. [ ], 1811	TM1	33
Nancy, m. Andrew A. **HILLYER**, Oct. 2, 1838, by Charles Bentley	1	29
Nancy G., m. Edward P. **THOMPSON**, Sept. 1, 1841, by Rev. Daniel Hemenway	1	36
Nancy R., of Granby, m. Asa **HOSKINS**, of Simsbury, Oct. 19, 1846, by Allen McLean	1	50
Nathan G., m. Mrs. Margaret **WHITE**, Aug. 24, 1848, by A. L. Loveland	1	56
Nathan G., farmer, ae 35, b. Granby, res. same, m. Margaret **WHITE**, house keeper, ae 27, b. Ireland, res. Granby, Sept. 20, 1848, by Rev. Mr. Loveland	1	238-9
Nathaniel, [s. Thomas & Elisabeth], b. Nov. 4, 1648; who went to Simsbury and finally to Salmon Brook, most of the Bushy Hill, Hungary, West and North Granby **HOLCOMBES** or **HOLCOMBS**	1	143
Noah, m. Trifene **YOUNGS**, Feb. 1, 1785	TM1	24
Orlen, s. Ozias & Ruth, b. Aug. 20, 1794	TM1	27
Ozias, Jr., m. Mrs. Ruth **PIRKINS**, Jan. 1, 1788	TM1	27
Polly, m. Chancey **HOLCOMB**, b. of Granby, Mar. 8, 1843, by Allen McLean	1	38
Rachel L., of Granby, m. Pliny **MOSES**, of Simsbury, Apr. 24, 1834, by Allen McLean	1	16
Richard Erskine, [s. Thomas & Clarinda], b. Sept. 28, 1824	1	213
Roger, farmer, d. Nov. 25, 1847, ae 71	1	228-9
Rolland, m. Maria **HOLCOMB**, Dec. 30, 1829, by John Willey, J. P.	1	1
Sabra, [d. Jabez & Sophia], b. May 26, 1793	1	141

	Vol.	Page
HOLCOMB, HOLCOMBE, (cont.)		
Sabra, m. Samuel **DEWEY**, Nov. 29, 1820, by Isaac Porter	TM1	160
Sabra, m. Nahum **HOLCOMB**, Jr., Apr. 27, 1830, by Isaac Porter	1	2
Sabra A., housekeeper, d. Sept. 29, 1849, ae 39	1	254-5
Sally, of Granville, Mass., m. Reuben **WARNER**, of Southwick, Mass., Dec. 9, 1838, by Abner Case, J. P.	1	28
Samuel Frederic, [s. Nahum], b. Dec. 15, 1855	TM1	49
Sarah, [d. Thomas & Elisabeth], b. Aug. 14, 1642	1	143
Sarah, d. Noah & Trifene, b. Jan. 11, 1786	TM1	24
Sarah, d. Abel & Roxenah, b. Jan. 1, 1791	TM1	33
Sarah, of Granby, m. Hiram **JONES**, of Hartland, May 20, 1835, by Abner Case, J. P.	1	19
Sireno, s. Hoadiah & Affiah, b. Oct. 10, 1785	TM1	33
Sereno W., m. Clarissa **HOLCOMB**, b. of Granby, Oct. 10, 1837, by Chares Bentley	1	25
Sophia, d. [Amasa & Gillet], b. Sept. 12, 1810	TM1	40
Sophia, [w. Jabez], d. July 24, 1851	1	141
Sophia, d. [ ], ae 78	1	138
Starr, s. [Nahum & Rebeckah], b. Sept. 7, 1801	TM1	49
Susanah, d. [Nahum & Rebeckah], b. Feb. 22, 1799	TM1	46
Susanna, m. Oren H. **LEE**, Sept. 26, 1821, by Isaac Porter	TM1	163
Thomas, of Dorchester, Mass., on May 14, 1634, was made a Freeman, Sept. [ ], 1635, sold house and lands to Richard **JONES**, of Dorchester, Mass. In 1640, his name appears as owner of house and lands in Windsor, Conn. and at Poquonnoc. d. Sept. 7, 1657	1	143
Thomas, s. Noah & Trifene, b. Apr. 8, 1787	TM1	24
Thomas, m. Clarinda **PETTIBONE**, Jan. 3, 1803, by Rev. Isaac Porter	1	213
Thomas Guernsey, [s. Thomas & Clarinda], b. Dec. 5, 1805	1	213
Uri, m. Sophia **GODDARD**, Apr. 26, 1831, by Isaac Porter	1	7
Ursille, [child of Caleb & Mercy], b. Jan. 15, 1784	TM1	29
Vashti, of Granby, m. Capt. Redeout **MOOR**, of Hartland, July 15, 1821, by [Samuel Griswold]	TM1	162
Warren, s. Judah & Anna, b. Sept. 22, 1778	TM1	22
Weston, [s. Jabez & Sophia], b. Aug. 28, 1801	1	141
Wilbor Sylvester, s. Sylvester, farmer, ae 38 & Sarah, housewife, ae 26, b. Apr. 20, 1848	1	222-3
W[illia]m Frederic, [s. Augustine], b. Apr. 2, 1827	TM1	49
W[illia]m Frederic, Dr., of New York, b. Apr. 2, 1827, at		

	Vol.	Page

HOLCOMB, HOLCOMBE, (cont.)
    Sterling, Mass., a descendant of Nathaniel H.,
    Nathaniel, 2nd, David, 1st, Reuben, Nahum,
    Augustine (**HOLCOMBE** entries recorded by
    Dr. William Frederic **HOLCOMBE**, of New
    York, Aug. 10, 1872   1   143
    Zilpha G., of Granby, m. Calvin L. **BARNARD**, of
    Bloomfield, Oct. 10, 1847, by Rev. Stephen
    Rushmore   1   54
    ------, or **HOLCOMB**, appears first on record in America
    at Boston, Mass.   1   143
HOLLISTER, Lovinia, weaver, ae 22, b. Glastonbury, res.
    Granby, m. Alfred **HOLCOMB**, farmer, ae
    21, b. Granby, res. same, Mar. 5, 1849, by
    Rev. Mr. Smith, of Glastonbury   1   238-9
HOLMES, Cyrus, s. Robert, tavernkeeper & Ellen, b. Sept. 16,
    1849   1   250-1
    Cyrus, d. Sept. 17, 1849, ae 1 d.   1   254-5
    James, m. Mary **McRAY**, of Simsbury, July 24, 1837,
    by Rev. Daniel Hemenway   1   24
HORSFIELD, Elizabeth, of Granby, m. John **McCARTNEY**, of
    Windsor, Sept. 21, 1854, by Rev. Henry H.
    Bates, of Tariffville   1   69
HOSKINS, Asa, of Simsbury, m. Nancy R. **HOLCOMB**, of
    Granby, Oct. 19, 1846, by Allen McLean   1   50
    Diadama, of Granby, m. Henry **SPENCER**, of Simsbury,
    Dec. 30, 1821, by Joel Holcomb, J. P.   TM1   164
    James B., of Simsbury, m. Julia M. **DIBBLE**, of Granby,
    Dec. 29, 1850, by Caleb F. Page   1   65
HOSMER, Charlotte P., m. Daniel T. **CRAW**, b. of Granby, Nov.
    3, 1845, by Rev. I. S. Dennis   1   47
    Hannah T., of Granby, m. Philo **FIELDING**, of Hartford,
    Nov. 25, 1829, by Stephen Crosby   1   1
    Sarah Jane, of Granby, m. Lyman **GRANT**, of East
    Windsor, June 6, 1830, by Ebenezer Everitt,
    V. D. M.   1   3
HUBBARD, Anna, m. Judah **HOLCOMB**, June 30, 1774   TM1   22
    Dinanthee, of Granby, m. Orrin **DAILEY**, of
    Waterbury, Jan. 2, 1837, by Charles Bentley   1   23
HUGGINS, HUGINS, Charlotte R., m. Willis **WILCOX**, b. of
    Granby, June 17, 1839, by Allen McLean   1   30
    Lucius, blacksmith, had s. [   ], b. July 15, 1849   1   232-3
    Lucius, had s. [   ], b. Jan. 22, 1851   1   130-1
HUGH, Jane, pauper, had illeg. s. [   ], b. Mar. 18, 1850   1   248-9
HUGHES, Lydia Ann, m. Isaac **JONES**, Mar. 28, 1852, by Watson
    Dewey, J. P.   1   67
HULL, Jane, b. Chester, Mass., m. Zenas C. **LEFFINGWELL**, b.
    Chester, Mass., Mar. 26, 1851, by Pliny F.

	Vol.	Page
HULL, (cont.)		
Sanborne	1	134
HUMPHREY, HUMPHREYS, Alvin, m. Martha HAYES, Apr. 24, 1833, by Isaac Porter	1	14
Ansel, m. Sally HIGLEY, Apr. 16, 1822, by Isaac Porter	TM1	165
Elizabeth, m. Solomon HATH, b. of Simsbury, Feb. 9, 1821, by James Dibble, J. P.	TM1	161
Hannah A., d. W[illia]m, farmer, ae 26 & Roxana, housewife, ae 25, b. May 24, 1848	1	222-3
Hiram, of Simsbury, m. Mary ADAMS, of Granby, July 18, 1833, by Ammi Linsley, V. D. M.	1	14
Phelps, of Hartland, m. Maria HOLCOMB, of Granby, Jan. 2, 1834, by Rev. D. Hemmenway	1	16
William, of Bloomfield, m. Roxana PRATT, of Granby, Apr. 6, 1842, by Isaac Porter	1	37
William, farmer & Roxey, had d. [ ], b. [ ]	1	234-5
HUNT, Abagail B., m. Alvin BRADFORD, b. of Williamsburg, Mass., Mar. 15, 1831, by Rev. Asa Cornwall	1	6
Sullivan, m. Cinderilla SPERRY, b. of Granby, May 11, 1843, by Ardon B. Holcomb, J. P.	1	39
W[illia]m Morgan, d. Nov. 28, 1847, ae 1	1	228-9
HUTCHINSON, Hisana, d. Jonathan, b. May 9, 1789	TM1	6
Temperance C., of Mansfield, m. William Orson RUICK, of Granby, July 25, 1847, by Rev. Stephen Rushmore	1	53
JACKSON, Anson, pedlar, b. East Haddam, res. Granby, colored, d. Sept. 2, 1847, ae 35	1	230-1
David, farmer's son, colored, d. Sept. 6, 1847, ae 6	1	230-1
Hope, m. Susan SANS, b. of Granby, June 13, 1830, by Joe Holcomb, J. P.	1	3
King Hope, farmer, colored, ae 47 & Susan, colored, ae 40, had child, b. Apr. 4, 1849	1	236-7
Thankful, pauper, colored, res. Simsbury, d. Oct. 3, 1849	1	254-5
Thomas, pauper, colored, b. Simsbury, res. Granby, d. May 17, 1851, ae 62	1	138
JACOBSON, R. Hopewell, farmer, colored, ae 46, & Susan, housewife, colored, ae 39, had child b. Feb. [ ], 1848	1	224-5
JEWETT, JEWIT, JEWITT, JEWET, Betsey, [d. Joshua R. & Sibyl], b. Apr. 1, 1801	TM1	40
Erastus, joiner, b. Granby, res. Hartford, m. Nanuad E. PINNEY, b. Granby, res. Hartford, June 6, 1849, by Rev. Ranson Warner	1	238-9
Frederick William, s. Joseph & Jane, b. Nov. 25, 1790	TM1	26
George, [s. Joshua R. & Sibyl], b. May 10, 1799	TM1	40
Helen F., ae 20, of Granby, m. Pliney PRATT, merchant, ae 24, b. Granby, res. Springfield, Mass., Feb. 5, 1849, by Rev. R. Warner	1	238-9

JEWETT, JEWIT, JEWITT, JEWET, (cont.)

	Vol.	Page
Irene Amorett, m. Maltby G. HILLYER, Nov. 20, 1821, by Isaac Porter	TM1	163
Joseph, Dr., m. Mrs. Jane PETIBONE, Oct. 18, 1785	TM1	26
Joseph Franklin, s. Joseph & Jane, b. Aug. 22, 1788	TM1	26
Joshua R., b. Aug. 14, 1771, at Lyme; m. Sibyl PETIBONE, Mar. 20, 1796, by Rev. Isaac Porter	TM1	40
Joshua R. & Sibyl, had 2nd s. [ ], b. Feb. 24, 1803; d. same day, ae 9 hrs.	TM1	40
Joshua R., m. Mary COSSIT, June 19, 1820, by James Dibble, J. P.	TM1	160
Julia, [d. Joshua R. & Sibyl], b. Sept. 13, 1804	TM1	40
Juliett(?) M., m. Gustus PHELPS, Jan. 25, 1821, by Isaac Porter	TM1	160
Mary A., of Granby, m. Ozar D. GOODMAN, of New Haven, Aug. 26, 1852, by Caleb F. Page	1	68
Peter I., organ builder, b. Hillsdale, Mo., res. Granby, d. Oct. 16, 1847, ae 46	1	228-9
Polley, d. Zebdiel Rogers & Zibiah, b. June 15, 1787	TM1	29
Sibyl H., [d. Joshua R. & Sibyl], b. Mar. 28, 1797	TM1	40
Zebdiel Rogers, m. Mrs. Zibiah ROE, Apr. 15, 1787	TM1	29

JOHNSON, Charles P., of Hartford, m. Eliza Ann CASE, of

Granby, Sept. 9, 1844, by Rev. Levi Warner	1	43
Edward W., of East Windsor, m. Sophia O. DIBBLE, of Granby, Dec. 31, 1850, by Caleb F. Page	1	65
Edward W., ae 24, b. Windsor, res. same, m. Sophia O. DIBBLE, ae 25, b. Granby, Dec. 31, 1851, by Caleb F. Page	1	134
Henryette I., m. Cyrus E. CLARK, b. of Hartford, May 27, 1849, by Rev. A. B. Pulling	1	59
Henry, Jr., of Hartford, m. Julia M. GIBBS, of Manchester, Feb. 8, 1852, by Rev. Pliny F. Sanborn	1	66
Jane, b. Suffield, m. Lyman E. CLARK, b. of Suffield, res. Hartford, May [ ], 1849, by Rev. Mr. Pulling	1	238-9
L. F., had s. [ ], b. [ ], [d.], ae 10 d.	1	246-7
Layfayette, physician & Sarah, had s. [ ], b. Aug. 9, 1849	1	236-7
Lorenzo, of Westfield, Mass., m. Eliza Ann POMEROY, of Granville, Mass., Oct. 20, 1850, by Ardon B. Holcomb, J. P.	1	62
Polly, house laborer, b. E. Windsor, res. Granby, d. Mar. 20, 1849, ae 71	1	244-5
Sarah M., b. Windsor, res. same, d. Jan. 18, 1850, ae 26	1	254-5

JONES, Abijah, s. Levi, b. Mar. 3, 1792   TM1   23
Elijah, of Barkhamsted, m. Miriam HOLCOMB, of

	Vol.	Page
JONES, (cont.)		
Granby, Feb. 6, 1839, by Charles Bentley	1	29
Hiram, of Hartland, m. Sarah HOLCOMB, of Granby, May 20, 1835, by Abner Case, J. P.	1	19
Isaac, m. Lydia Ann HUGHES, Mar. 28, 1852, by Watson Dewey, J. P.	1	67
Lucy, [d. Levi], b. June 14, 1795	TM1	36
Rodah, d. Levi, b. Apr. 14, 1789	TM1	23
Rodah, [d. Levi], b. Apr. 14, 1790	TM1	36
JUDD, James S., of Southampton, Mass., m. Lucretia BATES, of Granby June 20, 1821, by Daniel B. Holcomb, J. P.	TM1	162
KASSON, Mary C., m. William W. COWDRY, Mar. 31, 1830, by Isaac Porter	1	2
KELLOGG, Ann, d. Oliver [& Molley], b. Dec. 14, 1790; d. Jan. 18, 1793	TM1	75
Ann, m. Shepard EATON, Sept. 11, 1831, by Isaac Porter	1	8
Anna, d. Oliver [& Molley], b. Sept. 25, 1789; d. Sept. 27, 1789	TM1	75
Eunice, of Southwick, Mass.; m. Amos I. LARNARD of Westfield, Mass., Sept. 21, 1831, by Joel Holcomb, J. P.	1	8
Jeptha, s. Oliver [& Ann], b. Jan. 6, 1793	TM1	75
Oliver, m. Mrs. Molley WEBSTER, June 18, 1788	TM1	75
Oliver, Jr., [s. Oliver & Ann] b. May 12, 1797	TM1	75
Thalia, d. Oliver [& Ann], b. Mar. 21, 1795	TM1	75
Willson, m. Elizabeth ADAIR, b. of Granby, Sept. 8, 1830, by Stephen Crosby	1	4
KELLY, James, s. Michael, farmer, ae [ ] & Bridget, housewife, b. Jan. 1, 1848 (*ae 8 mos. "follows birth date)	1	222-3
Michel, m. Bridget BOHANNA, June 8, 1844, by W. W. Hubbard	1	42
KELSEY, Simeon F., of Bloomfield, m. Maria A. DEWEY, of Granby, Aug. 24, 1842, by Rev. Alfred Gates	1	37
KENDALL, KENDAL, Albert, m. Sarah C. HIGLEY, b. of Granby, Nov. 9, 1840, by Rev. Chauncey D. Rice	1	34
Amy, d. May 27, 1849, ae 52	1	242-3
Elam, m. Harriet M. REED, Mar. 24, 1831, by Smith Dayton, Elder	1	6
Elijah H., m. Mary Ann HOLCOMB, b. of Granby, Oct. 22, 1835, by Charles Bentley	1	20
Gillet, Mrs., m. Amasa HOLCOMB, Nov. 10, 1808	TM1	40
Harriet L., m. William A. ALLEN, b. of Granby, July 3, 1848, by Allen McLean	1	56
Harriet L., ae 28, m. William A. ALLEN, shoemaker, ae		

	Vol.	Page

KENDALL, KENDAL, (cont.)
    29, b. of Granby, July 3, 1848, by Rev. Allen
      McLean   1   226-7
    J. Newton, of Alabama, m. Jane **FAIRCHILD**, of
      Granby, July 23, 1840, by Rev. Chauncey D.
      Rice   1   34
    Joanna D., ae 23, m. George **NICHOLS**, school teacher,
      ae 25, b. Bainbridge, N. Y., res. Granby, Oct.
      [ ], 1848, by Rev. Mr. Pulling   1   238-9
    Joanna D., of Granby, m. George A. **NICHOLS**, of
      Bainbridge, N. Y., Nov. 26, 1848, by Rev. A.
      B. Pulling   1   57
    Lavera, of Granby, m. Roland **BARLOW**, of East
      Granville, Mass., Feb. 24, 1841, by C. D. Rice   1   35
    Mary, of Granby, m. Noble D. **FRERY**, of Springfield,
      Oct. 30, 1845, by Rev. Levi Warner   1   46
    Mary Ann, m. Collins E. **HAYES**, b. of Granby, Sept.
      15, 1847, by Rev. Stephen Rushmore   1   53
    Mary Ann, ae 21, m. Collins E. **HAYES**, farmer, ae 25,
      b. of Granby, Sept. 15, 1847, by Rev. Stephen
      Rushmore   1   226-7
    Mercia A., of Granby, m. Aldsom **MORSE**, of Pa., Oct.
      6, 1840, by Rev. Chauncey D. Rice   1   34
    Rhoda, m. Edward **HAYES**, Aug. 5, 1839, by Isaac
      Porter   1   30
KENT, Selah M., farmer, ae 33 & Betsey, ae 30, had child s.b. [ ]   1   234-5
KEYS, Emma Jane, b. Granville, Mass., res. Granby, d. Aug. 13,
    1848, ae 2   1   230-1
KILBOURN, Lyman, m. Hapalonia **LOOMIS**, Sept. 4, 1842, by
    Edmund Holcomb, J. P.   1   37
KIMBAL, Albert, of Bangor, Me., m. Mary Melissa **GODARD**,
    May 24, 1838, by Charles Bentley   1   27
KING, Achsah, m. Alfred **SEYMOUR**, b. of Granville, Mass.,
    Jan. 5, 1838, by Abner Case, J. P.   1   26
    Elizabeth, of Springfield, Mass., m. Stephen W.
      PETTIBONE, of Canton, May 6, 1835, by C.
      Bentley   1   19
    John, had d. [ ], b. July 27, 1851   1   130-1
    Lucy, Mrs., m. Sylvanus **LAMBSON**, Mar. 15, 1794   TM1   75
    Sophia, formerly Sophia **GOODRICH**, of Granby, m.
      Harvey **SIKES**, of Suffield, Mass., Jan. 23,
      1842, by Joshua R. Jewitt, J. P.   1   36
    Susan, b. Suffield, res. same, d. Sept. 20, 1848, ae 80   1   242-3
    Thadeus, farmer, ae 50, b. Suffield, res. Enfield, m.
      Philura **MESSENGER**, ae 25, b. Granby, Jan.
      10, 1850, by Rev. A. B. Pulling   1   252-3
KNIGHT, Jane, ae 33, b. England, res. Granby, m. Edward
    PICKFORD, carpet weaver, ae 66, b.

	Vol.	Page
KNIGHT, (cont.)		
England, res. Granby, July 2, 1848, by Rev. Ranson Warner	1	226-7
Stephen, pauper, d. May [ ], 1850, ae 60	1	254-5
KNOX, Emeline, m. Lial **RIGGS**, May 24, 1846, by John S. Hayes, J. P.	1	48
John T., of East Granby, m. Fanny M. **PROUT**, of East Granby, Mar. 30, 1842, by Rev. David L. Marks. Witnesses: G. L. Harman & E. A. Spencer	1	36
LAMB, Lucy, ae 26, of Granby, m. Moses **GRIFFIN**, mechanic, ae 24, b. New Haven, res. Hartford, June 3, 1849, by Samuel Weed	1	238-9
LAMPSON, LAMBSON, Alson, [s. Samuel & Elisabeth], b. Aug. 15, 1798	TM1	25
Annis, of Granby, m. James **ARMSTRONG**, of Philadelphia, Pa., June 1, 1831, by Joel Holcomb, J. P.	1	7
Cephas, s. [Sylvanus & Lucy], b. Mar. 31, 1797	TM1	75
Chauncy, [s. Samuel & Elisabeth], b. Mar. 17, 1794	TM1	25
David, s. Samuel & Elisabeth, b. Dec. 7, 1782	TM1	25
Dinah, Mrs., m. Robard **FIELD**, Nov. 26, 1766	TM1	23
Elisabeth, d. Samuel & Elisabeth, b. Nov. 1, 1784	TM1	25
Ezekiel, [s. Sylvanus & Lucy], b. June 20, 1795	TM1	75
Homer, m. Susan **HACK**, Mar. 13, 1845, by Rev. L. Warner	1	45
Joseph, s. Elnathan, b. Apr. 2, 1774	TM1	25
Lydia, Mrs., m. Ewins **WRIGHT**, Oct. 23, 1788	TM1	33
Lydia, of Barkhamsted, m. Drayton **LOOMIS**, of Granby, June 20, 1838, by Allen McLean	1	27
Olive, m. Amasa **HAYS**, Nov. 23, 1791	TM1	75
Reuben, [s. Samuel & Elisabeth], b. May 5, 1791	TM1	25
Samuel, m. Mrs. Elisabeth **SLAUGHTER**, Sept. 17, 1781	TM1	25
Samuel, Jr., s. Samuel & Elisabeth, b. Aug. 15, 1788	TM1	25
Sarah J., d. Homer, farmer, b. Jan. [ ], 1850, [d. [ ], ae 5 m.	1	248-9
Sylvanus, m. Mrs. Lucy **KING**, Mar. 15, 1794	TM1	75
Sylvenus, s. Sylvenus & Lucy, b. Apr. 24, 1794	TM1	75
LANE, Helen, m. Elihu **HAYES**, May 5, 1841, by Rev. C. D. Rice	1	35
LARNARD, Amos I., of Westfield, Mass., m. Eunice **KELLOGG**, of Southwick, Mass., Sept. 21, 1831, by Joel Holcomb, J. P.	1	8
LATHAM, Betsey M., m. Joseph E. **PINNEY**, May 2, 1832, by Isaac Porter	1	11
Chester, s. Seymour, mechanic & Caroline, b. Mar. 17, 1849	1	232-3
Cornelia I., of Granby, m. Isaiah **BIDDLE**, of Baltimore,		

	Vol.	Page

LATHAM, (cont.)
    Md., Nov. 22, 1846, by Rev. James C.
        Houghton   1   50
    George H., laborer, d. May 28, 1849, ae 32   1   246-7
    Louisa P., b. Granby, res. same, m. William
        CHISHOLM, res. Canada, Jan. 15, 1850, by
        R. Warner   1   252-3
LATIMER, Dexey, m. Philip M. MORGAN, b. of Canton, Sept.
    16, 1840, by Rev. Daniel Hemenway   1   33
LAUGHLIN, Allen, carpet weaver, b. Ireland, res. Granby,
    d. Oct. 29, 1850, ae 70   1   138
[LEAVITT], LEVETTE, LEVIT, John, of New York City, m.
    May E. HAYES, of Granby, Oct. 26, 1851, by
    H. B. Soule   1   64
    Layette, colored, b. Feb. 11, 1848 ("ae 6 m." follows
        birth date)   1   222-3
LEE, Charles, of Southwick, Mass., m. Aurelia SMITH, of Suffield,
    Mar. 15, 1846, by Oliver Owen, J. P.   1   47
    Martha, ae 23, b. Granby, m. Alfred L. LOVELAND,
    minister, ae 25, b. Glastonbury, res. Norwich,
    Oct. [ ], 1851, by Rev. Turner Hart   1   134
    Oren H., m. Susanna HOLCOMB, Sept. 26, 1821, by
        Isaac Porter   TM1   163
LEFFINGWELL, Zenas C., b. Chester, Mass., m. Jane HULL, b.
    Chester, Mass., Mar. 26, 1851, by Pliny F.
    Sanborne   1   134
LEWIS, LUIS, Adaline S., of Granby, m. Julius R. NEWELL, of
    East Windsor, July 20, 1840, by Rev. Daniel
    Hemenway   1   33
    Gabrial, s. Hezekiah & Lydia, b. Dec. 19, 1788   TM1   27
    Jane, m. Edwin GILLET, b. of Granby, Apr. 4, 1841,
        by Rev. Daniel Hemenway   1   35
    Mary, m. Charles COOK, Sept. 10, 1837, by Isaac Porter   1   25
    Ruth, house lady, b. Bloomfield, res. Granby, d. Apr. 8,
        1849, ae 97   1   244-5
LINCOLN, Daniel, laborer, ae 29, & Semantha, ae 19, had d. [ ],
    b. May 2, 1849   1   236-7
LINDSLEY, William, of Chester, Mass., m. Mrs. Florana L.
    VIETS, of Tariffville, Mar. 14, 1852, by Rev.
    R. H. Bowles   1   66
LLOYD, Nancy C., of Westfield, Mass., m. Charles S. WARNER,
    of East Hartford, Oct. 20, 1839, by Abner
    Case, J. P.   1   31
LOCHRAEL, Janet, Mrs., m. James TAYLOR, b. of Simsbury,
    Jan. 1, 1832, by Stephen Crosby   1   9
LOMBARD, Sarah Ann, of Chicopee, Mass., m. James M.
    WOOLCOTT, of West Springfield, Mass.,
    Sept. 16, 1849, by Samuel W. Barnum. Int.

	Vol.	Page

LOMBARD, (cont.)
    Pub.   1   60
LOOMIS, LOOMISE, Drayton, of Granby, m. Lydia **LAMPSON**,
    of Barkhamsted, June 20, 1838, by Allen
    McLean   1   27
Drayton, farmer, ae 40 & Lydia, ae 38, had d. [   ],
    b. July 15, 1850   1   248-9
Emiline, of Southwick, m. Allen **BARNES**, Jan. 3, 1831,
    by Asa Cornwall   1   5
Hapalonia, m. Lyman **KILBOURN**, Sept. 4, 1842, by
    Edmund Holcomb, J. P.   1   37
Harrison, of Southwick, Mass., m. Charlotte H. **PECK**,
    of Granby, Nov. 15, 1831, by Ammi Linsley,
    V. D. M.   1   9
Laura, ae 19, b. E. Granby, res. Granby, m. Wadsworth
    BROWN, farmer, ae 21, b. E. Granby, res.
    Granby, Sept. [   ], 1847, by Walter Thrall   1   226-7
Louisa Ana, m. Asahel **GRANGER**, b. of Southwick,
    Mass., Nov. 23, 1830, by Rev. Asa Cornwall   1   4
Lyman, of Westfield, m. Elmina **HAYES**, of Granby,
    Mar. 26, 1846, at the house of Phineas Hayes,
    by Rev. Amasa Holcomb   1   49
LOVELAND, Alfred L., minister, ae 25, b. Glastonbury, res.
    Norwich, m. Martha **LEE**, ae 23, b. Granby,
    Oct. [   ], 1851, by Rev. Turner Hart   1   134
LYMAN, Quartus F., m. Phyphena **WRIGHT**, b. of East Hampton,
    Mass., Nov. 7, 1832, by Ashel Gaylord   1   12
McCARTNEY, John, of Windsor, m. Elizabeth **HORSFIELD**, of
    Granby, Sept. 21, 1854, by Rev. Henry H.
    Bates, of Tariffville   1   69
McCAULY, Eliza, m. E. Bradbury, b. of Simsbury, May 23, 1852,
    by Rev. John Pegg, Jr.   1   67
MACK, Sewall T., m. Julia **GRISWOLD**, b. of Granby, Oct. 30,
    1832, by Ammi Linsley, V. D. M.   1   12
McKAFFERY, Hough, farmer, d. Oct. 24, 1848, ae 50   1   242-3
McKENDRICK, Robert, manufacturer, ae 20, b. Scotland, res.
    Simsbury, m. Emely **YATES**, ae 19, b.
    England, res. Granby, Mar. 5, 1849, by Rev.
    Mr. Thompson   1   240-1
McKENNY, Jennet, d. Robert, farmer & Emily, b. Sept. 3, 1849   1   250-1
McKINLEY, Alexander, of Washington, Pa., m. Margaret D.
    HAYES, of West Granby, Apr. 27, 1852, by
    Rev. John Pegg, Jr.   1   67
McRAY, Mary, of Simsbury, m. James **HOLMES**, July 24, 1837,
    by Rev. Daniel Hemenway   1   24
McWHINNEE, Mary, of Simsbury, m. James **MINTRI**, Dec. 31,
    1835, by Rev. D. Hemmenway   1   21
MAHONY, Timy, farmer, had d. [   ], b. Feb. 10, 1851   1   132-3

	Vol.	Page

MALISON, Elisha I., of Sandisfield, Mass., m. Emeline **GILLET**,
of Granville, Mass., Mar. 14, 1840, by Abner
Case, J. P.   1   31

MANN, MAN, [see also **MUNN**], Delorah, d. May 7, 1787, in the
68th y. of her age   TM1   24

MANNERING, Granville, b. New Jersey, state pauper, d. June 21,
1851, ae 6 m.   1   138

MANY(?), Patrick, farmer, b. Ireland, res. Granby, d. Dec. 27,
1848, ae 70   1   242-3

MARBLE, Eliza, m. Howard **GRIFFIN**, May 6, 1840, by Isaac
Porter   1   32

MARK, Julia, pauper, d. May 30, 1850, ae [ ]   1   254-5

MARSH, Hollister F., m. Betsey **GORHAM**, b. of Chester, Mass.,
Nov. 17, 1839, by Rev. A. C. Washburn   1   31

MASON, Ebenezer K., m. Louisa A. **GIDDINGS**, b. of Southwick,
Mass., May 23, 1844, by Ardon B. Holcomb,
J. P.   1   41

Luke, m. Diana **HIGLEY**, b. of Simsbury, Mar. 13,
1831, by Rev. Asa Cornwall   1   6

MELLEN, [see also **MOLLEN**], Frederick F., of E. Marion, Ga.,
m. Alice O. **HAYES**, of Granby, Dec. 12,
1850, by Caleb F. Page   1   65

George F., school teacher, ae 29, b. Brookfield, res.
Georgia, m. Alice O. **HAYES**, ae 23, b.
Granby, res. Georgia, Dec. 12, 1851, by Rev.
Mr. Page   1   134

MERRIAM, MERIAM, [see also **MERRIMAN**], Alvira, d. Oct.
[ ], 1848, ae 2 m.   1   242-3

Benjamin, farmer, d. Jan. 13, 1849, ae 79   1   242-3

Henry Edward, s. Henry, merchant, ae 34 & Julia M., b.
May 27, 1849   1   236-7

Lucretia, weaver, b. Meriden, res. Granby, d. May 28,
1848, ae 72   1   228-9

MERRIMAN, [see also **MERRIAM**], Lester, m. Susan Jane
VIETS, July 10, 1832, by Isaac Porter   1   11

Levi, m. Mary **HIND**, Apr. 23, 1821, by Daniel
Benjamin, J. P.   TM1   161

MERROW, Jacob P., m. Caroline M. **GOULD**, b. of East Granby,
July 28, 1846, by Rev. Pliney F. Sanborn   1   49

Joseph G., s. John G., painter, ae 31 & Lucy, ae
20, b. Dec. 7, 1850   1   130-1

W[illia]m H., of Hartford, m. Mary E. **GOULD**, of East
Granby, June 1, 1847, by Rev. Pliney F.
Sanborn   1   52

MERWIN, Henry, farmer & Matilda, had s. [ ], b. Mar. 5, 1851   1   132-3

MESSENGER, Abigail, d. Jan. 18, 1849, ae 85   1   242-3

Celista, of Granby, m. Samuel N. **REID**, of Suffield,
Dec. 8, 1840, by Rev. Daniel Hemenway   1   35

	Vol.	Page

MESSENGER, (cont.)
Elam, m. Julia **DEWEY**, June 4, 1834, by Isaac Porter	1	17
Enos L., d. Apr. 13, 1849, ae 13	1	242-3
Flora, m. Luman **BEMAN**, b. of Granby, Mar. 20, 1842, by Samuel Weed, J. P.	1	36
Harriet L., of Granby, m. B. M. **BROWN**, of New York, May 12, 1850, by Rev. A. B. Pulling	1	61
Harriet L., ae 21, b. New York, res. same, m. Benjamin M. **BROWN**, farmer, ae 25, May 12, 1850, by Rev. A. B. Pulling	1	252-3
Luke, farmer, d. Apr. 27, 1850, ae 30	1	254-5
Matilda, d. Aug. 20, 1848, ae 79	1	242-3
Miranda, of Granby, m. Thomas H. **AUSTIN**, of Suffield, June 29, 1840, by Rev. Daniel Hemenway	1	33
Ovil, m. Rhoda **CASE**, b. of Granby, June 26, 1838, by Rev. Davis Stocking	1	27
Philura, ae 25, b. Granby, m. Thadeus **KING**, farmer, ae 50, b. Suffield, res. Enfield, Jan. 10, 1850, by Rev. A. B. Pulling	1	252-3
Rebisah, Mrs. m. Archilus **GOSARD**, Feb. 11, 1808	TM1	10
Ruth, m. W[illia]m **DAY**, b. of Granby, Jan. 3, 1841, by Chauncey D. Rice	1	34
Sereno, m. Nancy **HAYES**, b. of Granby, May 2, 1831, by Nathaniel Pratt, J. P.	1	10
Seymour, m. Sally **BEMAN**, b. of Granby, Mar. 21, 1832, by Nathaniell Pratt, J. P.	1	10
Willis, m. Rhoda A. **DEWEY**, Jan. 14, 1834, by Rev. Charles Spear	1	15
Willis, farmer, had d. [ ], b. Aug. 2, 1848	1	232-3

MILLER, Chester A., of Hartland, m. Henriette **BEMAN**, of
Granby, Feb. 19, 1849, by Rev. A. B. Pulling	1	58
Esther E., of Southampton, Mass., m. Virgil D. **GRIFFIN**, of Granby, Nov. 30, 1842, by Ardon B.Holcomb, J. P.	1	38
John, of Southampton, Mass., m. Sophronia **TULLER**, of Granby, Sept. 4, 1844, by Allen McLean	1	42

MILLS, Jared C., d. Jan. 24, 1848, ae 3 1 230-1

MINOR, Julia, m. Hiram **SAGE**, Mar. 27, 1833, by Abner Case, J. P. 1 13

MINTRI, James, m. Mary **McWHINNEE**, of Simsbury, Dec. 31, 1835, by Rev. D. Hemmenway 1 21

MOLLEN, [see also **MELLEN**], George, farmer, b. Greece, res. Granby, d. Jan. 13, 1849, ae 65 1 242-3

MONROE, Martha M., m. Willington G. **WHIPPLE**, b. of Westfield, Mass., May 19, 1847, by Rev. Pliney F. Sanborn 1 52

MOORE, MOOR, [see also **MORE**], Emery, of Montgomery,

	Vol.	Page

MOORE, MOOR, (cont.)
    Mass., m. Eunice **CHAPMAN**, of Westfield,
      Mass., Sept. 9, 1845, by Rev. James C.
      Houghton. Int. Pub. in each of said towns   1   46
    Eunice E., of Southwick, Mass., m. Walter **GRIFFIN**, of
      Granby, Aug. 12, 1840, by Rev. Daniel
      Hemenway   1   33
    Fanny, [d. Roger & Rosetta], b. Jan. 15, 1790   TM1   12
    Harley, of Granby, m. Anna **HASKINS**, of Granvill,
      Nov. 30, 1820, by Daniel Benjamin, J. P.   TM1   160
    Harriet, [d. Roger & Rosetta], b. July 9, 1792   TM1   12
    Helen C., m. David B. **WILLCOX**, Nov. 25, 1829, by
      Isaac Porter   1   1
    Homer, s. Roger & Rosetta, b. July 23, 1787   TM1   12
    Mary, m. Moses **WEED**, Jr., Sept. 30, 1813   TM1   18
    Mary Jane, of Southwick, m. Edmund **NOBLE**, of West
      Springfield, Nov. 3, 1847, by Alfred White.
      Int. Pub. Southwick   1   54
    Mehitabel, m. Abraham **GRIFFEN**, Dec. 4, 1788   TM1   35
    Miach, pauper, d. Feb. 22, 1851, ae 80   1   138
    Orrin, of Southwic, m. Harriet **HAYES**, of Granby, Mar.
      30, 1830, by Smith Dayton, Elder. Witnesses:
      Electa Hayes, Ursula Moor, Maria Hays &
      Phinehas Hays   1   1
    Orrin, of Granby, m. Tirzah P. **BORDEN**, of Suffield,
      Nov. 29, 1832, by Rev. D. Hemenway   1   13
    Rebeckah, d. Shadrach, of Southwick, m. Nahum
      HOLCOMB, Nov. 26, 1789   TM1   49
    Redeout, Capt., of Hartland, m. Vashti **HOLCOMB**, of
      Granby, July 15, 1821, by [Samuel Griswold]   TM1   162
    Roger, m. Mrs. Rozetta **HAYS**, Dec. 4, 1786   TM1   12
    Roger Sherman, [s. Roger & Rosetta], b. Aug. 18,
      1795; d. Nov. 15, 1800   TM1   12
    Rozittee Mariah, [d. Roger & Rosetta], b. Jan. 5, 1798;
      d. Nov. 7, 1800   TM1   12
    Sarah, m. Ebenezer **GODARD**, b. of Granby, Apr. 2,
      1833, by Joab Griffin, J. P.   1   14

MORE, [see also **MOORE**], Juliet P., of Granby, m. Chandler
    HOLCOMB, of Southwick, Mass., Mar. 25,
    1834, by Rev. Charles Bentley   1   16

MORETON, Consider, m. Fanny **BARTLET**, of Williamsburg,
    Mass., Jan. 10, 1831, by Asa Cornwall   1   5

MORGAN, Harriet, of Granby, m. Alvan **BATES**, of Southampton,
    Mass., Sept. 20, 1846, by Rev. James C.
    Houghton   1   50
    Mary N., of Granby, m. Henry E. **HIGLEY**, of Marion,
      Ia., July 29, 1845, by Rev. James C. Houghton   1   46
    Philip M., m. Dexey **LATIMER**, b. of Canton, Sept. 16,

	Vol.	Page
MORGAN, (cont.)		
1840, by Rev. Daniel Hemenway	1	33
Samuel, of Springfield, m. Elizabeth R. REED, of		
Granby, June 15, 1847, by Allen McLean	1	54
MORSE, MOSS, Aldsom, of Pa., m. Mercia A. KENDALL, of		
Granby, Oct. 6, 1840, by Rev. Chauncey D. Rice	1	34
James, of Granby, m. Jane SIMSON, of Tariffville, July 13, 1851, by H. B. Soule	1	63
Lydia Ann, d. W[illia]m L., laborer, ae 45 & Catharine, ae 25, b. Dec. 12, 1848	1	236-7
Lydia Ann, d. Dec. 28, 1848, ae 16 d.	1	246-7
MOSES, Lucius W., of Simsbury, m. Hannah E. HOLCOMB, of Granby, Nov. 22, 1848, by Rev. A. B. Pulling	1	57
Pliny, of Simsbury, m. Rachel L. HOLCOMB, of Granby, Apr. 24, 1834, by Allen McLean	1	16
MUNN, MUN, [see also MANN], Caterine, [d. Gustus & Ester], b. Dec. 2, 1781	TM1	22
	TM1	22
Gustus, m. Ester PHELPS, June 20, 1781	TM1	22
John G., [s. Gustus & Ester], b. Mar. 29, 1785	1	130-1
MURRAY, MURRY, Joanna, had s. [ ], b. May 30, 1851		
John, farmer, b. Canada, res. Granby, d. Jan. 12, 1849, ae 80	1	242-3
NASH, Oliver, of Williamsburgh, Mass., m. Julia A. STRONG, of Granby, May 27, 1846, by Rev. James C. Houghton	1	48
NELSON, Horatio K., of West Suffield, m. Martha J. STEVENS, of Granby, Dec. 5, 1850, by Rev. P. F. Sanborn	1	62
NEWELL, Julius R., of East Windsor, m. Adaline S. LEWIS, of Granby, July 20, 1840, by Rev. Daniel Hemenway	1	33
NICHOLS, Elisabeth Joanna, d. George A., farmer & Joanna, b. Sept. 11, 1849	1	248-9
George, school teacher, ae 25, b. Bainbridge, N. Y., res. Granby, m. Joanna D. KENDALL, ae 23, Oct. [ ], 1848, by Rev. Mr. Pulling	1	238-9
George A., of Bainbridge, N. Y., m. Joanna D. KENDALL, of Granby, Nov. 26, 1848, by Rev. A. B. Pulling	1	57
Olive, of Chesterfield, Mass., m. Robert FAIRCHIELD, of Williamsburg, Mass., Sept. 6, 1831, by Rev. Asa Cornwall	1	7
NOBLE, Edmund, of West Springfield, m. Mary Jane MOORE, of Southwick, Nov. 3, 1847, by Alfred White. Int. Pub. Southwick	1	54
Phinehas W., of Harrington, m. Chloe OWEN, of	1	1

	Vol.	Page
NOBLE, (cont.)		
Sylvester, m. Mariett HOLCOMB, June 27, 1821, by Isaac Porter	TM1	162
William H., m. Martha E. EGGLESTON, b. of Westfield, Sept. 3, 1850, by Ardon B. Holcomb, J. P.	1	62
O'DONNELL, James, illeg. s. Susan, pauper, ae 25, b. Apr. 14, 1850	1	248-9
Susan, pauper, ae 25, had James, illeg. s., b. Apr. 14, 1850	1	248-9
OLCOTT, Ann Elisa, d. Sept. 28, 1849, ae 4 1/3 (1848?)	1	242-3
George S., d. Sept. 28, 1849, ae 1 1/4 (1848?)	1	242-3
Sanford R., m. Mariett HOLCOMB, Sept. 12, 1847, by Rev. Daniel Hemenway	1	24
Sanfor[d] R., harness maker, ae 38 & Margette, ae 33, had s. [ ], b. July 18, 1851	1	130-1
OSBORN, ORSBURN, Ebenezer, of Mass., m. Rebeca GODDARD, of Granby, [Sept.] 7, 1840, by Rev. Charles Stearns	1	32
Silas, m. Lois GRANGER, Jan. 31, 1822, by Isaac Porter	TM1	164
OSDEN, Joseph W., m. Charlotte SANDERS, Oct. 13, 1841, by Isaac Porter	1	35
OTIS, Elisa Jane, d. Abner L., machinist, ae [ ] & Almira, housewife, b. Jan. 1, 1848 ("ae 8 m." follows birth date)	1	222-3
OWEN, Abby Amanda, d. Chauncey, farmer, ae 34 & Fanny, ae 28, b. June 20, 1849	1	234-5
Abiah, Mrs., m. Joseph CORNISH, July 11, 1793	TM1	14
Almon, m. Mary GRIFFIN, b. of Granby, May 26, 1835, by C. Bently	1	19
Caroline A., of Granby, m. John B. HOADLEY, of Auburn, O., May 13, 1847, by Rev. Pliney F. Sanborn	1	52
Chloe, of Windsor, m. Phinehas W. NOBLE, of Harrington, Dec. 10, 1829, by Stephen Crosby	1	1
Ella Jane, d. Erastus, farmer, ae 31 & Catherine E., ae 22, b. Nov. 11, 1850	1	130-1
Erastus, farmer, ae 29, b. Granby, res. same, m. Catharine DIBBLE, ae 21, b. Southwick, res. Granby, Jan. 31, 1850, by Mr. Lamberton	1	252-3
Milo M., m. Abigail M. ALDERMAN, of Granby, June 12, 1839, by Rev. Daniel Hemenway	1	30
PARKER, Miron, s. Wells, farmer, ae 31 & Syntha, ae 35, b. Oct. 1, 1849	1	250-1
Seth W., farmer, ae 32, res. East Granby, had s. [ ], b. June 25, 1851	1	132-3
PARKS, Sylvester, m. Hannah GOWDRY, Feb. 28, 1832, at the		

	Vol.	Page

PARKS, (cont.)
                house of Daniel Hayes, by Rev. Asa Cornwall   1   10
    Virginia E., m. Albert **CLARK**, b. of Russell, Mass.,
        Feb. 18, 1850, by Ardon B. Holcomb, J. P.,   1   61
PARMALEE, Sylvester, m. Charlotte **WILCOX**, b. of Granby,
        Apr. 24, 1839, by Rev. Davis Stocking   1   29
PARSONS, PERSONS, Avery, m. Adaline **GRISWOLD**, b. of
        Windsor, May 1, 1839, by Rev. Daniel
        Hemenway   1   30
    Charles Brownson, s. Erastus & Clarissa, b. Jan.
        12, 1812   TM1   21
    Clarisse, d. Erastus [& Clarissa], b. Mar. 20, 1814   TM1   21
    Ruhamah, m. Levi **HAYS**, Dec. 14, 1786   TM1   22
PEARL, Candace, m. Erastus W. **HARVEY**, b. of Hartford, Apr.
        11, 1836, by Rev. D. Hemenway   1   22
PEASE, Orlando, m. Asenath **GODARD**, Dec. 20, 1832, by Issac
        Porter   1   13
PECK, Charlotte H., of Granby, m. Harrison **LOOMISE**, of
        Southwick, Mass., Nov. 15, 1831, by Ammi
        Linsley, V. D. M.   1   9
PERCY, PERCEY, Leonard, laborer, colored, ae 40 & Nancey,
        housewife, colored, ae 28, had child, b. Mar.
        1, 1848   1   220-1
    Marcia, [twin with Martin], d. Leonard, laborer,
        colored, ae 43, & Nancy, colored, ae 38, b.
        Apr. 6, 1850   1   246-7
    Martin, [twin with Marcia], s. Leonard, laborer, colored,
        ae 43, & Nancy, ae 38, b. Apr. 6, 1850   1   246-7
PERKINS, PIRKINS, Charles I., m. Elizabeth R. **HINSDALE**,
        July 24, 1839, by Rev. Daniel Hemenway   1   30
    Ruth, Mrs., m. Ozias **HOLCOMB**, Jr., Jan. 1, 1788   TM1   27
PERRIN, PERRING, Clarrace, [child of Elisha & Rhoda], b.
        Dec. 22, 1775   TM1   22
    Elijah, [s. Elisha & Rhoda], b. Nov. 25, 1773   TM1   22
    Elisha, m. Rhoda **PERRING**, May 7, 1771   TM1   22
    Fradrick, s. Stephen & Ruth, b. June 6, 1779   TM1   24
    Lucinda, d. Stephen & Ruth, b. July 20, 1782   TM1   24
    Mary, [d. Elisha & Rhoda], b. May 15, 1782   TM1   22
    Phebe, d. Stephen & Ruth, b. June 13, 1776   TM1   24
    Rachael, [d. Elisha & Rhoda], b. May 6, 1777   TM1   22
    Ranna, s. Stephen & Ruth, b. Feb. 12, 1774   TM1   24
    Rhoda, m. Elisha **PERRING**, May 7, 1771   TM1   22
    Ruth, d. Stephen & Ruth, b. Oct. 16, 1769   TM1   24
    Stephen, m. Ruth **COSSIT**, Feb. 2, 1769   TM1   24
    Stephen, s. Stephen & Ruth, b. Nov. 3, 1771   TM1   24
    Stephen, d. Aug. 20, 1787, in the 41st y. of his age   TM1   24
    Westover, [s. Elisha & Rhoda], b. Jan. 7, 1780   TM1   22
PERRO, Peter, servant, colored, b. Africa, res. [   ], d.

	Vol.	Page

PERRO, (cont.)

Sept. 24, 1848, ae 100	1	242-3

PERSONS, [see under **PARSONS**]

PETERSON, Caroline, colored, ae 17, had illeg child b. [ ]	1	220-1
Caroline, colored, had illeg. s. John **SANDS**, b. Aug. 12, 1850; f. Hilton **SANDS**, farmer, colored	1	130-1
Caroline, ae 21, b. Windsor, res. Granby, m. Hilton **SANDS**, farmer, ae 49, b. Granby, res. same, Oct. 25, 1851, by Ardon B. Holcomb	1	134

PETTIBONE, PETIBONE, Alfred, m. Ellen C. **HAYNES**, b. of

Tariffville, Nov. 17, 1851, by Caleb F. Page	1	64
Alfred, tinner, b. Granby, res. Simsbury, m. Ellen C. **HAYNES**, Nov. 17, 1851, by Rev. Caleb F. Page	1	134
Bitsy, [d. Maj. Chauncy & Theodosia], b. Mar. 5, 1783	TM1	29
Charles, m. Deziah Miranda **HAYES**, Mar. 29, 1822, by Isaac Porter	TM1	165
Chauncy, Maj., m. Mrs. Theodosia **HAYS**, May 21, 1780	TM1	29
Chauncy, Jr., [s. Maj. Chauncy & Theodosia], b. July 19, 1787	TM1	29
Clarindia, [d. Maj. Chauncy & Theodosia], b. Jan. 19, 1781	TM1	29
Clarinda, m. Thomas **HOLCOMB**, Jan. 3, 1803, by Rev. Isaac Porter	1	213
Elisabeth, d. Nov. 5, 1848, ae 24	1	242-3
Harrit, [d. Maj. Chauncy & Theodosia], b. Oct. 2, 1785	TM1	29
Hector Doratus, [s. Maj. Chauncy & Theodosia], b. Aug. 27, 1791	TM1	29
Jane, Mrs., m. Dr. Joseph **JEWETT**, Oct. 18, 1785	TM1	26
John, m. Lura A. **GILLETTE**, b. of Granby, May 21, 1854, by Rev. Henry H. Bates, of Tariffville	1	69
Lemira Theodosha, [d. Maj. Chauncy & Theodosia], b. Mar. 20, 1778* *("1798"?)	TM1	29
Miles Demetrus, [s. Maj. Chauncy & Theodosia], b. Aug. 28, 1793	TM1	29
Ozias, Col. had negroes Earl, b. Nov. 24, 1784; Jube, b. June 28, 1788; Rhoda, b. Aug. 24, 1791. Affidavits made before Judah Holcomb, J. P.	TM1	27
Ozias, Col, had negro servant Erastus **PERSONS**, Charles Brownson **PERSONS**, s. of Erastus & Clarissa, was b. Jan. 12, 1812 and Clarissa, d., b. Mar. 20, 1814	TM1	21
Ralph Hiram, [s. Maj. Chauncy & Theodosia], b. May 16, 1796	TM1	29
Rolling, [s. Maj. Chauncy & Theodosia], b. July 13, 1789	TM1	29
Sabra, m. Zaccheus **HAYES**, Apr. 9, 1833, by Isaac Porter	1	14

GRANBY VITAL RECORDS 135

	Vol.	Page
PETTIBONE, PETIBONE, (cont.)		
Stephen W., of Canton, m. Elizabeth **KING**, of Springfield, Mass., May 6, 1835, by C. Bentley	1	19
Sibyl, b. Mar. 21, 1779, at Granby; m. Joshua R. **JEWETT**, Mar. 20, 1796, by Rev. Isaac Porter	TM1	40
PHELPS, Alamena, Mrs., m. Samuel **WINCHELL**, b. of Windsor, June 17, 1838, by Rev. Daniel Hemenway	1	27
Alva, d. [Levi], b. Feb. 21, 1788	TM1	31
Amillison, d. Levi, b. May 24, 1773	TM1	31
Catharine L., d. Rholand, farmer, & Emeline, res. Windsor, b. Oct. 19, 1851	1	132-3
Catharine M., m. James M. **GRISWOLD**, b. of E. Granby, Nov. 30, 1843, by I. B. Clark	1	41
Charles N., farmer's son, d. Sept. 13, 1847, ae 12	1	230-1
Corintha, m. Alexander **WINCHELL**, Mar. 15, 1833, by Abner Case	1	13
Dan, s. Noah & Sarah, b. July 27, 1791	TM1	33
Drayton, of Granby, m. Charlotte E. **DIBBLE**, of Southwick, Mass., Oct. 19, 1851, by Caleb F. Page	1	66
Esther, m. Gustus **MUN[N]**, June 20, 1781	TM1	22
Esther F., m. Virgil H. **GRISWOLD**, b. of East Granby, Nov. 30, 1843, by I. B. Clark	1	41
Francis, of Windsor, m. Jane M. **SPERRY**, of Bloomfield, Dec. 31, 1837, by Rev. Daniel Hemmenway	1	26
Griswould, s. Levi, b. Apr. 20, 1792	TM1	31
Gustus, m. Juliett(?) M. **JEWETT**, Jan. 25, 1821, by Isaac Porter	TM1	160
Hannah, Mrs., m. Sergt. Joel **BUTTOLPH**, July 14, 1773	TM1	24
Ira, s. Levi, b. June 11, 1782	TM1	31
Isaac, m. Mrs. Sarah **PHELPS**, b. of Granby, July 24, 1837, by Charles Bentley	1	24
Isabella, d. Charles, Inn keeper & Eliza Ann, b. Aug. 25, 1850	1	132-3
James, farmer, b. Windsor, res. same, d. Apr. 23, 1850, ae 19	1	254-5
John, of East Granville, Mass., m. Betsey **BARNES**, of Granby, Sept. 28, 1840, by Rev. Chauncey D. Rice	1	34
Levi, [s. Noah & Sarah], b. Mar. 10, 1782; d. Nov. 8, 1782	TM1	33
Levi Curtis, [s. Levi], b. Dec. 25, 1779	TM1	31
Lovice, d. Noah & Sarah, b. Mar. 10, 1782	TM1	33
Lovina, of Westfield, Mass., m. Joseph **GARDNER**, of Russel, Mass., May 21, 1832, by Asa Cornwall	1	10

PHELPS, (cont.)

	Vol.	Page
Lydia, d. Noah & Sarah, b. Aug. 20, 1784	TM1	33
Mary, d. Levi, b. Aug. 31, 1777	TM1	31
Mary, m. Hiram **RICE,** Mar. 9, 1831, by Abner Case,J.P	1	6
Mahetable, Mrs., m. Alexander H. **GRISWOLD,** b. of Granby, Feb. 12, 1846, by Cornelius B. Everest	1	47
Milton, m. Harriet **GODARD,** Jan. 11, 1831, by Isaac Porter	1	6
Noah, m. Mrs. Sarah **ADDANY,** Jan. 12, 1775	TM1	33
Noah, s. Noah & Sarah, b. Feb. 19, 1778	TM1	33
Oliver, s. Noah & Sarah, b. Dec. 12, 1779	TM1	33
Orin, farmer, b. Suffield, res. same, d. May 1, 1849, ae 75	1	242-3
Phebe, d. Levi, b. Oct. 29, 1785	TM1	31
Saloma, housekeeper, b. Suffield, res. Granby, d. July 1, 1848, ae 75	1	228-9
Sarah, d. Noah & Sarah, b. Oct. 2, 1775	TM1	33
Sarah, Mrs., m. Isaac **PHELPS,** b. of Granby, July 24, 1837, by Charles Bentley	1	24
Silas D., of Suffield, Mass., m. Alseda **BARTLETT,** of Southwick, May 19, 1834, by Charles Bentley	1	17
Warren, s. Noah & Sarah, b. Mar. 24, 1787	TM1	33
Willis, m. Betsey **RUIC,** Aug. 21, 1831, by Abner Case, J. P.	1	8
Willis, farmer, had s. [ ], [d.[ ], ae 1 m.	1	248-9

PICKFORD, Edward, carpet weaver, ae 66, b. England, res. Granby, m. 2nd w. Jane **KNIGHT,** ae 33, b. England, res. Granby, July 2, 1848, by Rev. Ranson Warner 1 226-7

PINNEY, Allen, of Simsbury, m. Eleanor H. **PINNEY,** of Granby, Dec. 23, 1834, by Rev. Daniel Hemmenway 1 18

Eleanor H., of Granby, m. Allen **PINNEY,** of Simsbury, Dec. 23, 1834, by Rev. Daniel Hemmenway 1 18

Eunice G., b. Simsbury, res. Granby, d. Feb. 9, 1849, ae 79 1 246-7

Frances W., of Granby, m. James M. **CADWELL,** of Bloomfield, Jan. 25, 1852, by Rev. Pliny F. Sanborn 1 66

Jerasco B., s. Rensalaer, farmer & Parletta, res. Windsor, b. Apr. 12, 1849 1 236-7

Joseph E., m. Betsey M. **LATHAM,** May 2, 1832, by Isaac Porter 1 11

Mary, d. Aug. 21, 1848, ae 37 1 244-5

Nanuad E., b. Granby, res. Hartford, m. Erastus **JEWETT,** joiner, b. Granby, res. Hartford, June 6, 1849, by Rev. Ransom Warner 1 238-9

	Vol.	Page
POMEROY, POMORY, Alexander A., m. Hannah E. HOLCOMB, Dec. 25, 1821, by Samuel Griswold	TM1	164
Ebenezer, L., m. Hannah E. DEAN, Nov. 9, 1847	1	226-7
Eliza Ann, of Granville, Mass., m. Lorenzo JOHNSON, of Westfield, Mass., Oct. 20, 1850, by Ardon B. Holcomb, J. P.	1	62
Jerusha*, Mrs., m. Thomas SPRING, July 9, 1795 *(Line drawn through name)	TM1	12
Sarah, m. Alfred SMITH, Dec. 15, 1844, by Oliver Owen, J. P.	1	44
PORTER, Henry C., of East Hartford, m. Permelia GODARD, of Granby, Dec. 11, 1838, by Rev. Davis Stocking	1	28
Isaac, Rev., m. Mary SMAWLEY, (Mrs.), Oct. 20, 1794	TM1	49
Richard, s. [Isaac & Mary], b. July 16, 1803	TM1	49
POST, Clarissa Mariah, [d. Joseph], b. July 7, 1805	TM1	36
Hannah, d. Jan. 24, 1850, ae 93	1	254-5
John Elizur, s. [Joseph], b. Jan. 16, 1811	TM1	36
Lorenzo, s. [Joseph], b. Dec. 26, 1807	TM1	36
POWERS, Freeman, of Westfield, Mass., m. Martha Ann DILLON, of New Hartford, Aug. 8, 1843, by Ardon B. Holcomb, J. P.	1	39
PRATT, Almrin, m. Lavinia A. VIETS, b. of Granby, Nov. 10, 1840, by Rev. Daniel Hemenway	1	35
Betsey, ae 23, m. Edward EGGLESTON, jeweller, ae 26, b. Barkhamsted, res. New York, Nov. 29, 1849, by Rev. A. B. Pulling	1	252-3
Betsey E., of West Granby, m. Edward F. EGGLESTON, of Pleasant Valley, Nov. 29, 1849, by Rev. A. B. Pulling	1	61
Candace*, m. Erastus W. HARVEY, b. of Hartford, Apr. 11, 1836, by Rev. D. Hemenway *(In Pencil "Candace PEARL")	1	22
Elisa, m. Asa HIGLEY, Jr., b. of Granby, Sept. 16, 1834, by Charles Bentley	1	17
Esther, m. Hastings CASE, Aug. 22, 1821, by Isaac Porter	TM1	163
Frank D., s. Nathaniel P., shoemaker, ae 25 & Laura L., housewife, ae 27, b. Sept. 1, 1847	1	220-1
Frederic W., s. Perkins, shoemaker & Laura, b. May 3, 1849	1	232-3
Jane, m. Eber RUIC, b. of Granby, May 2, 1843, by I. P. Warren	1	39
Loisa, m. Murton GODARD, b. of Granby, Sept. 8, 1836, by Charles Bentley	1	22
Lucretia, m. Abner BANNING, Dec. 7, 1820, by Philander Humphrey, J. P.	TM1	160

PRATT, (cont.)

	Vol.	Page
Pliney, merchant, ae 24, b. Granby, res. Springfield, Mass., m. Helen F. JEWETT, ae 20, of Granby, Feb. 5, 1849, by Rev. R. Warner	1	238-9
Pliney, merchant, ae 25 & Hellen, ae 21, res. Springfield, had s. [ ], b. June 22, 1850	1	246-7
Polly, m. Thadeus WHITNEY, Feb. 11, 1844, by Abner Case, J. P.	1	40
Roxana, of Granby, m. William HUMPHREY, of Bloomfield, Apr. 6, 1842, by Isaaac Porter	1	37
Sophia, of Granby, m. Eliger GOODRICH, of Chatham, May 13, 1821, by Joab Griffen, J. P.	TM1	161
Wadsworth, m. Elonora ROSE, b. of Hartford, Mar. 22, 1840, by Abner Case, J. P.	1	32
William, farmer, b. Saybrook, res. Granby, d. Feb. 26, 1850, ae 99	1	254-5
PRESTON, Hiram, of Ozan(?), N. Y., m. Esther K. VEITS, of Granby, Oct. 17, 1834, by Rev. Daniel Hemmenway	1	18
PROUT, Fanny M., m. John T. KNOX, b. of East Granby, Mar. 30, 1842, by Rev. David L. Marks, Witnesses: G. L. Harman, E. A. Spencer	1	36
PROUTY, Royal, of Windsor, m. Maria HAYES, of Granby, Oct. 26, 1836, by Amasa Holcomb	1	24
PROVIN, William, m. Abby WELLER, of Westfield, Aug. 26, 1847, by Peter I. Jewett, J. P.	1	53
PURPLE, Daniel, m. Wealthy DIBBLE, Dec. 25, 1844, by I. P. Warren	1	44
RAYMOND, Harriet, m. Lewis A. WARREN, b. of Westfield, Mass., Feb. 24, 1850, by Rev. A. B. Pulling	1	61
REED, REID, Amoret, farmer, b. Southwick, Mass., res. Granby, d. Feb. 27, 1849, ae 47	1	244-5
Bernice, Mrs., m. Philetus COOLEY, Feb. 13, 1844, by I. P. Warren	1	40
Chester, s. Allen & Sylvia, b. Aug. 23, 1815	TM1	83
Cordelia E., m. Stephen N. CORNWALL, Sept. 5, 1832, by Isaac Porter	1	12
Cordelia M., m. Howard J. GREEN, Nov. 28, 1850, by Caleb F. Page	1	64
Edmund, s. Allen & Sylvia, b. Oct. 28, 1813	TM1	83
Elizabeth R., of Granby, m. Samuel MORGAN, of Springfield, June 15, 1847, by Allen McLean	1	54
Ella J., d. Wilbert, farmer & Henrietta, b. [ ]	1	250-1
Flavia M., of W. Granby, m. Lewis BOSWORTH, of Cabotville, Mass., Sept. 22, 1842, by Rev. William McKender Bangs	1	38
Forrest, m. Flora GODDARD, Nov. 4, 1830, by Isaac Porter	1	5

GRANBY VITAL RECORDS 139

	Vol.	Page
REED, REID, (cont.)		
Franklin B., m. Susan DEWEY, Sept. 30, 1841, by Isaac Porter	1	35
Harriet M., m. Elam KENDAL, Mar. 24, 1831, by Smith Dayton, Elder	1	6
Henry C., of Hartford, m. Laura GODARD, of Granby, Dec. 6, 1848, by A. L. Loveland	1	56
Henry C., joiner & Laura, had d. [ ], b. Apr. 21, 1850	1	248-9
Henry C., carpenter, ae 29, m. Laura GODARD, ae 36, b. of Granby, [ ], by Rev. A. L. Loveland	1	238-9
Jane E., of Granby, m. Norman DAY, of Springfield, Nov. 27, 1845, by Rev. Levi Warner	1	46
Julia, of Granby, m. John C. SMITH, of Suffield, Mar. 20, 1851, by Caleb F. Page	1	65
Lorenda, m. Josephus EDGERTON, b. of Granby, Feb. 7, 1830, by Joab Griffin, Jr. J. P.	1	3
Lucia(?) A., of Granby, m. Josiah SMITH, of Springfield, Mass., Apr. 2, 1839, by Rev. Davis Stocking	1	29
Lucian, carriage maker, had d. [ ], b. June 3, 1849	1	232-3
Lucian, had s. [ ], b. Jan. 1, 1851	1	130-1
Luther, of Simsbury, m. Lucinda HOLCOMB, of Granby, Dec. 1, 1839, by Charles Stearns	1	31
Mary, Mrs., m. Increase HOLCOMB, June 2, 1789	TM1	35
Mary Ann, d. Allen & Sylvia, b. Dec. 28, 1811	TM1	83
Mehitabel, m. John CONNEL, b. of Granby, July 17, 1849, by Rev. A. B. Pulling	1	59
Mehitabel, ae 42, b. Granby, res. same, m. John CONNELL, farmer, ae 27, b. Ireland, res. Granby, July 17, 1849, by Rev. A. P. Pulling	1	238-9
Samuel N., of Suffield, m. Celista MESSENGER, of Granby, Dec. 8, 1840, by Rev. Daniel Hemenway	1	35
Waldo, m. Theodosia HIGLEY, b. of Granby, Oct. 19, 1837, by Charles Bentley	1	25
Willis, m. Eliza RICE, b. of Granby, Apr. 29, 1850, by Rev. R. G. Thompson, of Tariffville	1	64
Willis, farmer, m. 2nd w. Eleza RICE, b. of Granby, Apr. 29, 1850, by [ ]	1	252-3
Wilson, m. Irena HOLCOMB, b. of Granby, Mar. 13, 1838, by Rev. Davis Stocking	1	26
REMINGTON, Henry, of Suffield, m. Chloe H. ALDERMAN, of East Granby, May 31, 1846, by [ ]	1	48
REYNOLDS, Josiah, weaver, d. Mar. 10, 1851, ae 86	1	138
[RHOADES], ROADS, Alfred, had s. [ ], b. June 2, 1851	1	132-3
RICE, Albert, m. Olive E. BACON, Oct. 23, 1832, by Isaac Porter	1	12
Alice E., d. Levi, farmer, ae 33 & Lydia, b. Nov. 20, 1851	1	130-1

	Vol.	Page
RICE, (cont.)		
Amelia, m. Simeon CUSHMAN, 2nd, May 29, 1821, by Isaac Porter	TM1	162
Clarissa, m. Milton CUSHMAN, May 31, 1821, by Philander Humphrey, J. P.	TM1	162
Deziah, [d. Jonah], b. Mar. 6, 1790	TM1	24
Elisha, [s. Jonah], b. Jan. 13, 1787	TM1	24
Eliza, m. Willis REED, b. of Granby, Apr. 29, 1850, by Rev. R. G. Thompson, of Tariffville	1	64
Eleza, m. Willis REED, farmer, b. of Granby, Apr. 29, 1850, by [ ]	1	252-3
Frances, wid., d. May 21, 1849, ae 82	1	242-3
Hannah D., m. Enoch H. BUTTLES, July 3, 1832, by Isaac Porter	1	11
Hiram, m. Mary PHELPS, Mar. 9, 1831, by Abner Case, J. P.	1	6
Jonah, Jr., [s. Jonah], b. Jan. 17, 1778	TM1	24
Mary A., d. [ ], ae 6	1	254-5
Richard, [s. Jonah], b. Oct. 21, 1780	TM1	24
Silas, [s. Jonah], b. Apr. 15, 1783	TM1	24
RICHARDSON, William, m. Sally FOWLER, Oct. 16, 1831, by Abner Case, J. P.	1	9
RIGGS, Lial, m. Emeline KNOX, May 24, 1846, by John S. Hayes, J. P.	1	48
RISING, Aretus, cigar box maker, ae 23, b. Suffield, res. same, m. Lucinda SEARLE, ae 19, b. Hartland, res. Granby, July 4, 1849, by Rev. George Felten	1	238-9
David L., of Westfield, Mass., m. Loisa C. GORDON, of Granby, July 4, 1838, by Rev. D. Wright	1	28
ROBBINS, Chloe, b. Farmington, res. Granby, married, d. Aug. 21, 1847, ae 75	1	230-1
Harriet N., Mrs., of Ashfield, Mass., m. Nathan W. STEELE, of New Britain, Apr. 19, 1846, by Rev. James C. Houghton	1	48
Mary, of Granby, m. Jared GRISWOLD, of Hartford, Jan. 1, 1831, by Stephen Crosby	1	5
ROBY, ROBEE, Almira How, [d. Mrs. Elisabeth], b. Nov. 27, 1801	TM1	3
Amherst, [s. Mrs. Elisabeth], b. Sept. 15, 1794	TM1	3
Aralya, farming, b. Granby, res. W. Granby, d. Feb. 25, 1848, ae 47	1	228-9
Betsey Hillyer, [d. Mrs. Elisabeth], b. Aug. 26, 1784	TM1	3
Celesta Dean, [d. Mrs. Elisabeth], b. Nov. 17, 1807	TM1	3
Daniel Hillyer, [s. Mrs. Elisabeth], b. Nov. 12, 1786	TM1	3
Elisabeth, Mrs., had Betsey Hillyer, b. Aug. 26, 1784; Daniel Hillyer, b. Nov. 12, 1786; Philetus Hillyer, b. Jan. 25, 1789; Lois, b. Sept. 6, 1791; Lament, b. Jan. 14, 1793; Amherst, b.		

	Vol.	Page
ROBY, ROBEE, (cont.)		
Sept. 15, 1795; Almira How, b. Nov. 27, 1801		
& Celesta Dean, b. Nov. 17, 1807	TM1	3
Lament, [d. Mrs. Elisabeth], b. Jan. 14, 1793	TM1	3
Lois, [d. Mrs. Elisabeth], b. Sept. 6, 1791	TM1	3
Philetus Hillyer, [s. Mrs. Elisabeth], b. Jan. 25, 1789	TM1	3
ROCHE, James, farmer & Bridget, MU[ ], res. Ireland, had illeg.		
child b. Feb. 12, 1849	1	234-5
ROCKWELL, Annis, m. Irijah B. ALDERMAN, Jan. 27, 1831,		
by Stephen Crosby	1	6
Charlotte, of Granby, m. Virgil FLETCHER, of		
Windsor, Feb. 7, 1839, by Rev. D. Hemenway	1	29
Horace, of Windsor, m. Caroline S. GODARD, Nov. 3,		
1848, by A. L. Loveland	1	56
Richard, m. Hannah EVENS, of Granby, Nov. 21, 1831,		
by Rev. Asa Cornwall	1	9
ROE, Zibiah, Mrs., m. Zebdiel Rogers JEWETT, Apr. 15, 1787	TM1	29
ROOT, Elisha, of Westfield, Mass., m Cynthia T. ALDERMAN, of		
Granby, Nov. 30, 1840, by Rev. Daniel		
Hemenway	1	35
J. Leroy, of Granville, Mass., m. Jane GODARD, of		
Granby, Apr. 17, 1837, by H. B. Soule	1	63
Noah, farmer, d. May 11, 1848, ae 47	1	230-1
ROSE, Elonora, m. Wadsworth PRATT, b. of Hartford, Mar. 22,		
1840, by Abner Case, J. P.	1	32
ROWLEY, Permelia, of Blandford, m. Martin M. HOLCOMB,		
Sept. 6, 1847, by Peter I. Jewett, J. P.	1	53
RUICK, RUIC, Betsey, m. Willis PHELPS, Aug. 21, 1831, by		
Abner Case, J. P.	1	8
Eber, m. Jane PRATT, b. of Granby, May 2, 1843, by I.		
P. Warren	1	39
Hannah, ae 37, b. Granby, res. W. Granby, m. 2nd h.		
Owen RUICK, farmer, ae 50, of Granby, July		
10, 1848, by Rev. Mr. Pulling	1	226-7
Maria Candis, d. Eber, blacksmith, b. May 1, 1849	1	232-3
Owen, m. Hannah M. HOLCOMB, b. of Granby, July		
10, 1848, by Rev. A. B. Pulling	1	56
Owen, farmer, ae 50, of Granby, m. 2nd w. Hannah		
RUICK, ae 37, b. Granby, res. W. Granby,		
July 10, 1848, by Rev. Mr. Pulling	1	226-7
Rhoda, of Granby, m. Chester CASE, of Canton, Apr.		
29, 1839, by Rev. Davis Stocking	1	29
William A., s. Henry, farmer, ae 23 & Mary, ae 23, b.		
Jan. 10, 1851	1	130-1
William Orson, of Granby, m. Temperance C.		
HUTCHINSON, of Mansfield, July 25, 1847,		
by Rev. Stephen Rushmore	1	53
RUSSELL, John, of Granby, m. Lucinda SANDERS, of Stafford,		

	Vol.	Page

RUSSELL, (cont.)
    Sept. 24, 1848, by Hiram F. Chapin, J. P.   1   57
  Stephen C., of Springfield, m. Anna **DRAKE**, of
    Southwick, Oct. 13, 1842, by Abner Case,
    J. P.   1   37
SACKETT, Jane, m. Elijah **WHEATON**, b. of Westfield, Mass.,
    June 1, 1843, by Israel P. Warren   1   39
SAGE, Hiram, m. Julia **MINOR**, Mar. 27, 1833, by Abner Case,
    J. P.   1   13
SANBORN, SANBORNE, Charles G., [twin with Chester], s. P. F.,
    clergyman, ae 28 & Caroline G., ae 22, b.
    Oct. 2, 1848   1   236-7
  Charles G., s. [   ], clergyman, d. May 12, 1849,
    ae 7 m.   1   244-5
  Chester, [twin with Charles G.], s. P. F., clergyman, ae
    28 & Caroline G., ae 22, b. Oct. 2, 1848   1   236-7
  Chester, s. [   ], clergyman, d. May 8, 1849, ae 7 m.   1   244-5
    P. F., minister, ae 29 & Caroline, ae 23, had d. [   ],
    b. July 7, 1850   1   250-1
SANDERS, [see under SAUNDERS]
SANDS, SANS, Hilton, farmer, ae 49, b. Granby, res. same, m.
    Caroline **PETERSON**, ae 21, b. Windsor, res.
    Granby, Oct. 25, 1851, by Ardon B. Holcomb   1   134
  John, illeg, s. Caroline **PETERSON** (colored), b. Aug.
    12, 1850; f. Hilton SANDS, farmer, (colored)   1   130-1
  Susan, m. Hope **JACKSON**, b. of Granby, June 13,
    1830, by Joe Holcomb, J. P.   1   3
SANFORD, Joseph D. F., m. Mary I. **SMITH**, b. of Granby,
    Oct. 22, 1835, by Charles Bentley   1   20
SANS, [see under SANDS]
SAUNDERS, SANDERS, Charlotte, m. Joseph W. **OSDEN**, Oct.
    13, 1841, by Isaac Porter   1   35
  Lucinda, of Stafford, m. John **RUSSELL**, of Granby,
    Sept. 24, 1848, by Hiram F. Chapin, J. P.   1   57
  Polly, Mrs., m. Elisha **BECKWITH**, Oct. 2, 1788   TM1   24
SEARLS, SEARLE, Aurora, Mrs., of Granby, m. Alanson
    HOLCOMB, of Ill., Dec. 7, 1845, by Rev.
    James C. Houghton   1   47
  Caroline A., of Granby, m. Joseph **ARNOLD**, of
    Westfield, Mass., May 22, 1844, by I. P.
    Warren   1   41
  Emeline T., of Granby, m. Chauncey **TRASK**, of
    Deerfield, Mass., Oct. 9, 1839, by Rev. Albert
    Case, of Charleston, S. C.   1   30
  Lucinda, ae 19, b. Hartland, res. Granby, m. Aretus
    RISING, cigar box maker, ae 23, b. Suffield,
    res. same, July 4, 1849, by Rev. George
    Felten   1   238-9

GRANBY VITAL RECORDS 143

	Vol.	Page
SEERS, Dotia, m. Edmund TAYLOR, b. of Williamsburg, Mass., Mar. 14, 1821, by Joel Holcomb, J. P.	TM1	161
SEGAR, Selina, m. Alpheus DEAN, b. of Granby, Sept. [ ], 1830, by Decius Humphrey, J. P.	1	3
SEYMOUR, Alfred, m. Achsah KING, b. of Granville, Mass., Jan. 5, 1838, by Abner Case, J. P.	1	26
Julia, d. Apr. 23, 1849, ae 7 y. 9 m.	1	244-5
Ralph, m. Susan M. DRAKE, b. of New Hartford, Sept. 29, 1833, by Rev. Daniel Hemmenway	1	15
SHAILOR, Harriet M., m. Samuel D. ALLEN, b. of Granby, Mar. 30, 1835, by Charles Bentley	1	18
SHERIDAN, Georgianna, d. T. M., daguerreotypist, ae 30 & Martha H., ae 31, b. Apr. 8, 1849	1	236-7
T. M., tailor, res. Windsor & Martha A., res. Windsor, had s. [ ], b. May 8, 1851	1	132-3
SHERWOOD, Charles W., s. Walter W., ae 23 & Ellen E., ae 24, res. New York State, b. Nov. 13, 1848	1	232-3
SIBLEY, Moses, Jr., of Westfield, Mass., m. Mrs. Lucina COOLEY, of Granville, Dec. 12, 1843, by I. P. Warren	1	40
SIKES, Harvey, of Suffield, Mass., m. Sophia KING, formerly Sophia GOODRICH, of Granby, Jan. 23, 1842, by Joshua R. Jewit, J. P.	1	36
SIMONS, Isabel, d. Silas, shoemaker, ae 54 & Sarah, ae 48, b. Mar. 26, 1850	1	250-1
Jane, of Tariffville, m. James MOSS, of Granby, July 13, 1851, by H. B. Soule	1	63
SKINNER, Carolin, of Granby, m. Almon GILLET, of Southwick, Mass., Sept. 21, 1831, by Isaac Porter	1	8
Harvey, farmer, d. [ ], ae 64	1	244-5
Lucy, m. Alexander H. GRISWOLD, b. of Granby, May 3, 1821, by Allen McLean	TM1	161
Lydia, of Granby, m. Leander BUTLER, of Savannah, Ga., July 19, 1838, by Rev. Daniel Hemenway	1	27
Mary D., d. Dwight T., farmer, ae 32 & Sarah, ae 32, b. Sept. 8, 1848	1	236-7
SLAUGHTER, Elisabeth, Mrs., m. Samuel LAMBSON, Sept. 17, 1781	TM1	25
SMART, Rhoda C., ae 58, m. 2nd h. Thomas SMART, ae 62, b. England, res. Granby, June [ ], 1849, by Rev. Amasa Holcomb	1	238-9
Thomas, of Tariffville, m. Mrs. Rhoda C. STRONG, of Granby, June 3, 1849, by Rev. Amasa Holcomb	1	58
Thomas, ae 62, b. England, res. Granby, m. 2nd w. Rhoda C. SMART, ae 58, June [ ], 1849, by Rev. Amasa Holcomb	1	238-9

	Vol.	Page
SMAWLEY, Mary, Mrs., m. Rev. Isaac PORTER, Oct. 20, 1794	TM1	49
SMITH, Alfred, m. Sarah POMEROY, Dec. 15, 1844, by Oliver Owen, J. P.	1	44
Almira, of Granby, m. Lewis CHAPMAN, of Tariffville, Oct. 9, 1831, by Rev. Asa Cornwall	1	8
Aurelia, of Suffield, m. Charles LEE, of Southwick, Mass., Mar. 15, 1846, by Oliver Owen, J. P.	1	47
Caroline E., m. Daniel W. DORMAN, June 30, 1844, by Rev. W. N. Hebbard	1	42
David, farmer, b. Suffield, res. Granby, d. Jan. 15, 1848, ae 40	1	228-9
Elijah S., of Southwick, Mass., m. Mariella CWO*, June 4, 1832, by Daniel Hemingway *("Marietta COE"?)	1	11
Henry A., of Blanford, Mass., m. Huldah C. BACON, of Granby, Jan. 3, 1839, by Justus D. Wilcox, J. P.	1	28
John, s. John, farmer & Mary, b. Oct. 1, 1847 ("ae 10 m." follows birth date)	1	222-3
John, farmer, ae 50, b. Ireland, res. Granby, m. Mary YEH, ae 25, b. Ireland, res. Granby, Nov. 23, 1847, by Rev. W. N. Hebbard	1	226-7
John C., of Suffield, m. Julia REED, of Granby, Mar. 20, 1851, by Caleb F. Page	1	65
Josiah, of Springfield, Mass., m. Lucia(?) A. REED, of Granby, Apr. 2, 1839, by Rev. Davis Stocking	1	29
Mary I., m. Joseph D. F. SANFORD, b. of Granby, Oct. 22, 1835, by Charles Bentley	1	20
Sidney, m. Rebecca STEVENS, b. of E. Granby, Feb. 13, 1843, by I. B. Clark	1	41
Sidney, farmer, ae 35 & Sarah, ae 22, had d. [ ], b. Jan. [ ], 1850	1	250-1
William, m. Cynthia GRISWOLD, May 18, 1821, by Isaac Porter	TM1	162
William, s. John, farmer, ae 47 & Mary, ae 28, res. Ireland, b. Feb. 20, 1849	1	234-5
SPELMAN, SPELLMAN, Laura E., m. Wilson GILLETT, b. of Granby, Nov. 17, 1848, by Hiram F. Chapin, J. P.	1	57
Seymour L., m. Catharine A. HAYES, b. of Granby, Oct. 5, 1851, by H. B. Soule	1	64
SPENCER, David, m. Margaret CAYTON, Apr. 26, 1821, by James Forward, J. P.	TM1	161
Henry, of Simsbury, m. Diadama HOSKINS, of Granby, Dec. 30, 1821, by Joel Holcomb, J. P.	TM1	164
William H., m. Adaline HOLCOMB, July 3, 1844, by I. P. Warren	1	42

GRANBY VITAL RECORDS 145

	Vol.	Page
SPERRY, Cinderilla, m. Sullivan HUNT, b. of Granby, May 11, 1843, by Ardon B. Holcomb, J. P.	1	39
Jane M., of Bloomfield, m. Francis PHELPS, of Windsor, Dec. 31, 1837, by Rev. Daniel Hemmenway	1	26
Mary O., m. William S. HAYES, b. of Granby, Sept. 19, 1842, by Ardon B. Holcomb, J. P.	1	37
SPRING, Albert, s. [Thomas & Jerusha], b. Sept. 15, 1807	TM1	12
Aurora, [d. Thomas & Jerusha], b. May 29, 1796(?) *("1798"?)	TM1	12
George, m. Mahala HOLCOMB, Nov. 10, 1835, by Isaac Porter	1	21
Gerrose, [child of Ephraim], b. Sept. 29, 1806	TM1	10
James Hubert, d. Jan. 21, 1850, ae 9	1	254-5
Jarvis, m. Almira ADAMS, Apr. 8, 1830, by Ammi Linsley, V. D. M.	1	2
Jerusha, [d. Thomas & Jerusha], b. Mar. 14, 1801	TM1	12
Jerusha, m. James M. DIBBLE, Jan. 9, 1822, by Isaac Porter	TM1	164
Julia or Juliana, [d. Ephraim], b. July 23, 1797	TM1	10
Juliana, see Julia SPRING	TM1	10
Juli[us], [s. Ephraim], b. May 24, 1795	TM1	10
Lewis C., s. George, farmer, ae 40 & Alice, ae 38, b. Jan. 21, 1851	1	130-1
Mariah, [d. Thomas & Jerusha], b. June 14, 1803; d. Jan. 7, 1804	TM1	12
Mariah, d. [Thomas & Jerusha], b. Nov. 19, 1804	TM1	12
Nancy E., [d. Ephraim], b. Aug. 24, 1804	TM1	10
Thomas, m. Mrs. Jerusha POMORY*, July 9, 1795 *(Line drawn through name)	TM1	12
Thomas, [s. Thomas & Jerusha], b. May 13, 1796(?) *(Conflicts with birth of Aurora)	TM1	12
Thomas & Jerusha, had d. [ ], b. Mar. 23, [1800?]; d. on her 3rd day	TM1	12
Wilson B., [s. Ephraim], b. Mar. 31, 1808	TM1	10
STAN[N]ARD, Joseph, farmer, b. Windsor, res. same, d. Oct. 28, 1849, ae 68	1	242-3
Josiah, farmer, b. Haddam, res. Windsor, d. Oct. 27, 1848, ae 72	1	244-5
STEBBINS, Betsey, b. Guilford, Vt., res. Simsbury, d. Sept. 19, 1848, ae 55	1	242-3
Moses, m. Paulina C. DIBBLE, b. of Granby, Oct. 2, 1838, by Amasa Holcomb	1	27
STEDMAN, STEADMAN, Jara M., m. Mariah WILSON, May 4, 1848, by Rev. S. Rushmore	1	55
Jary, farmer, ae 19, m. Maria WILSON, ae 19, b. of Granby, May 4, 1848, by Rev. [ ] Bushnell	1	226-7
John C., of Charleston, O., m. Fidelia C. DEAN, of		

	Vol.	Page
STEDMAN, STEADMAN, (cont.)		
Granby, Apr. 4, 1852, by Caleb F. Page	1	67
STEELE, Chester, s. Chester, farmer, ae 29 & Candace, ae 29,		
res. West Hartford, b. June 15, 1850	1	250-1
Chester, d. June 16, 1850, ae 1 d.	1	254-5
Nathan W., of New Britain, m. Mrs. Harriet N.		
ROBBINS, of Ashfield, Mass., Apr. 19, 1846,		
by Rev. James C. Houghton	1	48
STEER, Louis*, Mrs., m. Curtis GILLET, b. of Southwick, Mass.,		
Nov. 27, 1833, by Rev. Charles Spear		
*("Lois"?)	1	15
STEVENS, Betsey Ann, m. Philo GRIFFIN, b. of Granby, Dec. 26,		
1833, by Rev. D. Hemmenway	1	16
Cornelia G., ae 20, m. Seymour R. DIBBLE, farmer,		
ae 20, b. of Granby, Mar. 14, 1849, by Rev.		
Pliney F. Sanborn	1	240-1
Cornelia I., m. R. Seymour DIBBLE, b. of Granby, Mar.		
14, 1849, by Rev. Pliney F. Sanborn	1	58
Martha J., of Granby, m. Horatio K. NELSON, of West		
Suffield, Dec. 5, 1850, by Rev. P. F. Sanborn	1	62
Rebecca, m. Sidney SMITH, b. of E. Granby, Feb. 13,		
1843, by I. B. Clark	1	41
STILES, Eliakim, of Southwick, Mass., m. Mary P. HOLCOMB,		
of Granby, Oct. 5, 1820, by Daniel B.		
Holcomb, J. P.	TM1	160
Warren, m. Betsey HOLCOMB, May 10, 1831, by Isaac		
Porter	1	7
STOCKEN, Charles H., of New Hartford, m. Jane M.		
WINCHELL, of Granby, [Nov. 29, 1832], by		
Rev. D. Hemenway	1	13
STONE, Sylvanus, of New Britain, m. Eliza HOLCOMB, of		
Granby, Jan. 6, 1851, by Caleb F. Page	1	65
Sylvanus, paper box maker, res. New Britain, m.		
2nd w. Elisa HOLCOMB, ae 40, b. Granby,		
Jan. 6, 1851, by Rev. Caleb F. Page	1	134
Timothy, Dea. of Henrietta, N. Y., m. Mrs. Lovisa		
DEWEY, of Granby, Oct. 7, 1849, by Samuel		
W. Barnum	1	60
STRATTON, Phineh(?), s. Marten, decd. & Hannah, b. May 24,		
1786	TM1	24
STRONG, Annis E., of Granby, m. John BURWELL, of [Conn.],		
May 8, 1845, by I. P. Warren	1	45
Asa, farmer, d. Aug. 4, 1848, ae 69	1	242-3
Elizabeth R., of Granby, m. Erastus GRAVES, of		
Williamsburgh, Mass., Sept. 18, 1844, by I. P.		
Warren	1	43
Julia A., of Granby, m. Oliver NASH, of Williamsburgh,		
Mass., May 27, 1846, by Rev. James C.		

	Vol.	Page
STRONG, (cont.)		
Houghton	1	48
Rhoda C., Mrs. of Granby, m. Thomas SMART, of Tariffville, June 3, 1849, by Rev. Amasa Holcomb	1	58
SWANEY, Benjamin, [s. Benjamin], b. Dec. 17, 1779	TM1	76
James, [twin with Nancy], s. [Benjamin], b. Aug. 1, 1792; d. June 11, 1793	TM1	76
John, [s. Benjamin], b. Apr. 28, 1782 (Written "decd. b. Apr. 28, 1782*)	TM1	76
John, [s. Benjamin], d. Dec. 19, [1793]	TM1	76
Mehitabel, d. Benjamin, b. Sept. 26, 1775	TM1	76
Nancy, [twin with James], d. [Benjamin], b. Aug. 1, 1792	TM1	76
Rebekah, [d. Benjamin], b. July 14, 1789	TM1	76
Rosannah, [d. Benjamin], b. Sept. 27, 1777	TM1	76
Salley, [d. Benjamin], b. May 28, 1787	TM1	76
Temperance, [d. Benjamin], b. June 14, 1784	TM1	76
SWEETSUR, Charles, of Delaware, O., m. Sophia CHURCH, of Granby, Oct. 31, 1832, by Rev. Asa Cornwall, at the house of Jonathan Church	1	12
TAFT, Henry C., d. Aug. 31, 1849, ae 2	1	254-5
TALMADGE, Nelson, of Southwick, m. Dianah L. DIBBLE, of Granby, Dec. 1 1847, by Alfred White	1	54
Nelson, farmer, ae 23, b. Southwick, res. same, m. Diana DIBBLE, ae 20, b. Granby, res. same, Dec. 21, 1847, by Rev. Alfred White	1	226-7
TAYLOR, David, of Simsbury, m. Lamira BURR, of Granby, Nov. 21, 1830, by Nathaniel Pratt, J. P.	1	4
Edmund, m. Dotia SEERS, b. of Williamsburg, Mass., Mar. 14, 1821, by Joel Holcomb, J. P.	TM1	161
Eliza A., of West Granby, m. Marcus B. ALLING, of Woodbridge, Nov. 28, 1844, by Rev. Levi Warner	1	44
James, m. Mrs. Janet LOCHRAEL, b. of Simsbury, Jan. 1, 1832, by Stephen Crosby	1	9
Loyes, m. Salvenus DUDLY, Nov. 28, 1782	TM1	22
Mary E., m. Edwin P. HAYES, Nov. 23, 1831, by Isaac Porter	1	10
Rhoda, Mrs., m. Thomas B. GILLET, June 30, 1774	TM1	5
TER BUSH, William of Simsbury, m. Susan Jane CLARK, of Windsor, Apr. 15, 1838, by Rev. D. Hemenway	1	26
TERRY, Aaron C., m. Fidelia GODDARD, Oct. 27, 1831, by Isaac Porter	1	9
Caroline, of Granby, m. Samuel W. VIETS, of Windsor, June 27, 1849, by Rev. A. B. Pulling	1	59
Caroline, ae 19, of Granby, m. Samuel W. VIETS,		

	Vol.	Page

TERRY, (cont.)
  mechanic, ae 24, b. Windsor, res. Suffield,
   June 27, 1849, by A. P. Pulling   1   238-9
 Orwin, m. Ester **HOLCOMB**, Nov. 17, 1830, by Isaac
   Porter   1   5
THOMAS, Joseph E., of Waterbury, m. Celecta P. **ADELL**, of
   Granby, Nov. 25, 1847, by Rev. Stephen
   Rushmore   1   55
 Lydia, Mrs., m. Eliphelet **CLARK**, Sept. 25, 1780   TM1   26
THOMPSON, THOMSON, Delia A., of Granby, m. Warhan
   GRISWOLD, of Hartford, Feb. 1, 1831, by
   Rev. Augustus Bolles   1   6
 Edward P., m. Nancy G. **HOLCOMB**, Sept. 1, 1841, by
   Rev. Daniel Hemenway   1   36
 Eliza Ann, d. Leander, laborer, colored & Ellen,
   b. Oct. 20, 1849   1   248-9
 Emma G., m. James O. **ALLEN**, b. of East Granby, Sept.
   4, 1849, by Rev. Ralph H. Main, of Tariffville   1   59
 Emma G., ae 21, b. New York State, res. Granby, m.
   James O. **ALLEN**, merchant, ae 23, b.
   Enfield, res. Granby, Sept. 4, 1849, by Rev.
   Ralph H. Main   1   252-3
 James, mechanic, ae 25, b. Scotland, res. Thompsonville,
   m. Flora M. **BROWN**, ae 21, b. Canton, May
   20, 1851, by Rev. Mr. Stoddard   1   134
 Jonathan P., of Lansing, Mich., m. Catharine O. **ALLEN**,
   of Granby, Nov. 6, 1850, by Rev. Pliney F.
   Sanborn   1   62
 Jonathan P., attny. at law, res. Lansing, Mich., m.
   Catherine O. **ALLEN**, res. Lansing, Mich.,
   Nov. 6, 1851, by Pliny F. Sanborne   1   134
 Leander, [s. Sipio & Charlot], b. Apr. 24, 1814   TM1   76
 Lydia, m. David **CLARK**, b. of Granby, Feb. 6, 1834,
   by Rev. D. Hemenway   1   16
 Margaret, d. Leander, laborer, colored, ae 37, & Ellen,
   housewife, colored, ae 24, b. [   ]   1   220-1
 Mary C., d. Edward P., wheelwright, ae 30 & Mary S.,
   ae 25, b. Mar. 26, 1849   1   236-7
 Samuel, Jr., m. Ceneth **CLARK**, b. of Granby, Aug. 3,
   1820, by Joel Holcomb, J. P.   TM1   160
 Sipio R., [s. Sipio & Charlot], b. Feb. 16, 1812   TM1   76
 William N., jeweller, b. Granby, res. Hartford, d. Feb.
   14, 1848, ae 24   1   230-1
THRALL, Betsey, of Windsor, m. Chauncey **CLARK**, of Granby,
   May 1, 1836, by Rev. D. Hemenway   1   22
 Jane S., of Windsor, m. Alfred **GAY**, of East Granby,
   Nov. 26, 1846, by Rev. Pliney F. Sanborn   1   51
TIFFANY, Russel, Dr. of Torringford, m. Rachel **BENJAMIN**, of

	Vol.	Page
TIFFANY, (cont.)		
Granby, Nov. 28, 1837, by Charles Bentley	1	25
TINKER, Naoma, m. Frederick **GILLET**, b. of Granville, Mass.,		
Jan. 24, 1837, by Abner Case, J. P.	1	23
TOHILL, Bridget, d. John & Mary, b. Mar. 10, 1850	1	250-1
Ellen, d. Sept. 28, 1847, ae 8 m.	1	230-1
James, s. John, laborer, ae 31 & Mary, housewife, ae 26, b. July 11, 1848	1	224-5
TOPPING, Hellen, Mrs., m. Dr. Charles **BECKWITH**, Nov. 17, 1788	TM1	25
TOUVEL, Mary, d. Josiah & Pelsey*, b. Apr. 18, 1804 *("Betsey")	TM1	21
Mary, m. Justice **BROWN**, Oct. 9, 1811, by Judah Holcomb, J. P.	TM1	21
TOWNSEND, Edward, m. Juliann **WHEELER**, Nov. 3, 1842, by Charles T. Hillyer, J. P.	1	38
TRASK, Chauncey, of Deerfield, Mass., m. Emeline T. **SEARLS**, of Granby, Oct. 9, 1839, by Rev. Albert Case, of Charleston, S. C.	1	30
TREADWELL, Frances M., of Stockbridge, Mass., m. Henry O. **WARREN**, of Farmington, Sept. 24, 1848, by Hiram F. Chapin, J. P.	1	57
TULLER, Martin, of Simsbury, m. Mariett **DIBBLE**, of Granby, May 19, 1836, by J. Shrigley	1	22
Sidney, had s. [ ], b. Jan. [ ], 1851	1	130-1
Sydney S., of Simsbury, m. Caroline **CONE**, of Granby, May 8, 1844, by Allen McLean	1	42
Sophronia, of Granby, m. John **MILLER**, of Southampton, Mass., Sept. 4, 1844, by Allen McLean	1	42
TUMEY, Winney, pauper, res. Enfield, had illeg., s. [ ], b. June 2, 1850	1	248-9
TWEELY, John, farmer, b. Scotland, res. Granby, d. Oct. 13, 1848, ae 70	1	242-3
VADAKIN, John, of Granby, m. Lucretia **DRAKE**, of New Hartford, Nov. 25, 1832, by Rev. D. Hemenway	1	13
Judah, s. Henry J., teamster & Merinda, res. Windsor, b. Oct. 12, 1849	1	250-1
Loisa King, of Granby, m. Lyman **FOWLER**, of West Springfield, Mass., Mar. 12, 1833, by Rev. Daniel Hemenway	1	14
VANDEVEER, William, of Westfield, Mass., m. Marietta **HAYES**, of Granby, May 23, 1844, by I. P. Warren	1	41
VAN NESS, Georgianna Kate, d. Edward & Catherine, b. Dec. 12, 1849	1	250-1
VARY, Lyman, of New York, m. Laura **CASE**, of Granby, June 3, 1849, by Rev. N. Scott	1	59

	Vol.	Page
VIETS, VEITS, Albert, s. Judah D., wheelwright, ae 24 & Caroline, ae 21, b. Dec. 9, 1847	1	224-5
Alfred W., s. George W., farmer & Adaline, b. Sept. 30, 1850; [d.] [ ], ae 11 m.	1	132-3
Annie T., of Granby, m. Aralza **GRIFFIN**, of Suffield, Nov. 26, 1834, by Rev. Daniel Hemmenway	1	18
Chatahrine, d. [Luke], b. Nov. 22, 1783	TM1	14
Chloe, d. [Luke], b. May 19, 1793	TM1	14
Cornelia T., m. William **BOYLE**, b. of Granby, July 11, 1851, by H. B. Soule	1	63
Cornelia T., ae 20, b. Granby, m. William Boyle, farmer, ae 19, b. Southwick, res. Granby, July 11, 1851, by W. B. Soule	1	134
Eliza C., ae 19, m. William L. **HAYES**, farmer, ae 23, b. of Granby, Apr. 20, 1848, by Rev. Miles N. Olmsted	1	226-7
Esther, d. [Luke], b. Jan. 22, 1790	TM1	14
Esther K., of Granby, m. Hiram **PRESTON**, of Ozan(?), N. Y., Oct. 17, 1834, by Rev. Daniel Hemmenway	1	18
Fanny, d. Dan, farmer, ae 24 & Caroline, ae 24, b. Feb. 23, 1850	1	250-1
Florana L., Mrs. of Tariffville, m. William **LINDSLEY**, of Chester, Mass., Mar. 14, 1852, by Rev. R. H. Bowles	1	66
Francis L., m. Genette E. **BARNES**, b. of Granby, May 9, 1852, at the house of her father, by George D. Felton	1	66
George, [s. Luke], b. June 23, 1786; d. Apr. 10, 1787	TM1	14
George, s. [Luke], b. Feb. 12, 1788	TM1	14
Harriet M., ae 21, m. Henry **GRIFFIN**, farmer, ae 24, b. of Granby, Oct. 21, 1847, by Rev. Miles N. Olmsted	1	226-7
James H.,m. Marilla **HAYES**, b. of Granby, Oct. 11, 1849, by Rev. A. B. Pulling	1	60
James H., farmer, ae 26, m. Marrilla **HAYES**, ae 23, b. of Granby, Oct. 11, 1849, by Rev. A. B. Pulling	1	252-3
James H., farmer, ae 27 & Marilla, ae 24, res. Suffield, had s. [ ], b. Jan. 8, 1851	1	132-3
John, s. [Luke], b. Mar. 1, 1782	TM1	14
Julia, of Granby, m. Justus P. **GILLET**, of Windsor, Oct. 31, 1832, at the house of Benoni Veits, by Rev. Asa Cornwall	1	12
Julianna, m. Richardson **GRIFFIN**, Apr. 13, 1837, by Rev. Daniel Hemenway	1	24
Keziah, d. [Luke], b. Nov. 12, 1777	TM1	14
Keziah, b. Simsbury, res. Granby, housekeeper, d.		

GRANBY VITAL RECORDS 151

	Vol.	Page
VIETS, VEITS, (cont.)		
Nov. 22, 1850, ae 93	1	138
Lavinia A., m. Almvin **PRATT**, b. of Granby, Nov. 10, 1840, by Rev. Daniel Hemenway	1	35
Luke, s. [Luke], b. Aug. 2, 1780	TM1	14
Mary A., m. Edward H. **BOWERS**, Mar. 15, 1848	1	226-7
Mary Adelia, of E. Granby, m. Edward H. **BOWERS**, of Hartford, Mar. 16, 1848, by Pliney F. Sanborn	1	55
Roger, s. [Luke], b. Oct. 28, 1791	TM1	14
Rosannah, d. [Luke], b. Dec. 4, 1778	TM1	14
Samuel W., of Windsor, m. Caroline **TERRY**, of Granby, June 27, 1849, by Rev. A. B. Pulling	1	59
Samuel W., mechanic, ae 24, b. Windsor, res. Suffield, m. Caroline **TERRY**, ae 19, of Granby, June 27, 1849, by A. P. Pulling	1	238-9
Susan Jane, m. Lester **MERRIMAN**, July 10, 1832, by Isaac Porter	1	11
VINING, Dan, s. John W., [s. of Dan], b. Nov. 28, 1804	TM1	12
Elmon, tinner, b. Simsbury, res. same, d. Nov. 11, 1848, ae 70	1	242-3
VIZIAN, Jane, m. Joseph **BENNETT**, Feb. 4, 1844, by Abner Case, J. P.	1	40
WALDRON, Lucius, peddler, ae 24, b. Simsbury, res. same, m. Hannah **HOLCOMB**, ae 20, Sept. [ ], 1848, by Rev. Mr. Pulling	1	238-9
WALTER, Josephas, farmer, d. Sept. 16, 1848, ae 75	1	242-3
WARD, John, farmer, b. Ireland, res. Granby, d. Jan. 11, 1849, ae 60	1	242-3
WARE, Daniel, cooper, b. Enfield, Conn., res. Granby, d. Feb. 2, 1849, ae 76	1	246-7
William W., m. Mary An[n] **GOWDY**, of Windsor, Aug. 23, 1840, by Rev. Daniel Hemenway	1	33
WARNER, Betsey, m. Moses **CLARK**, Nov. 28, 1821, by Daniel Benjamin, J. P.	TM1	163
Charles S., of East Hartford, m. Nancy C. **LLOYD**, of Westfield, Mass., Oct. 20, 1839, by Abner Case, J. P.	1	31
Reuben, of Southwick, Mass., m. Sally **HOLCOMB**, of Granville, Mass., Dec. 9, 1838, by Abner Case, J. P.	1	28
WARREN, Henry O., of Farmington, m. Frances M. **TREADWELL**, of Stockbridge, Mass., Sept. 24, 1848, by Hiram F. Chapin, J. P.	1	57
Lewis A., m. Harriet **RAYMOND**, b. of Westfield, Mass., Feb. 24, 1850, by Rev. A. B. Pulling	1	61
WATERS, Moses, m. Maranda **GODARD**, Apr. 8, 1835, by Abner Case, J. P.	1	19
WATSON, Thomas, m. Lucy **WETHERBY**, b. of Southwick,		

BARBOUR COLLECTION

WATSON, (cont.)

	Vol.	Page
Mass., Mar. 1, 1848, by Lewis Holcomb, J. P.	1	54
WEBSTER, Molley, Mrs., m. Oliver KELLOGG, June 18, 1788	TM1	75
WEED, Benjamin, Jr., [s. Benjamin], b. Jan. 25, 178[ ]	TM1	6
Betsy, [d. Benjamin], b. Nov. 1[5?], [ ]	TM1	6
Dan, [s. Moses], b. Aug. 6, 1792	TM1	35
David, [s. Moses], b. June 23, 1789	TM1	35
David, d. May 22, 1811	TM2	last page
Deborah, had d. Harriet L., b. July 24, 18[ ]	TM1	6
Florence, d. Daniel, farmer, b. July 29, 1849	1	232-3
Lucius, [s. Moses, Jr. & Mary], b. Mar. 24, 1816	TM1	18
Mehitabel, d. Mar. 17, 1814	TM2	last page
Minerva, of Granby, m. William WILCOX, of Farmington, O., Nov. 2, 1851, by Rev. A. B. Pulling	1	64
Moses, Jr., m. Nancy COMB, May 7, 1806	TM1	18
Moses, Jr., m. 2nd w. Mary MOORE, Sept. 30, 1813	TM1	18
Moses, d. Jan. 10, 1829	TM2	last page
Nancy, w. Moses, d. June 24, 1812	TM1	18
Nancey, d. June 24, 1812	TM2	last page
Nancey, d. Mar. 13, 1825	TM2	last page
Noris, d. Mar. 10, 1825	TM2	last page
Polly, [d. Moses], b. Oct. 20, 1785	TM1	35
Ransley, s. [Moses, Jr. & Nancy], b. Feb. 13, 1808	TM1	18
Risha, [child Benjamin], b. Aug. 17, [ ]	TM1	6
Samuel, farmer, ae 52 & Maria A., housewife, ae 35, res. W. Granby, had child b. Sept. 6, 1847	1	222-3
Samuel, [s. Benjamin], b. Feb. 12, [ ]	TM1	6
Stanly, s. [Moses, Jr. & Nancy], b. Nov. 30, 1806	TM1	18
Stanley, m. Patty GODARD, June 7, 1830, by Isaac Porter	1	3
WELLER, Abby, of Westfield, m. William PROVIN, Aug. 26, 1847, by Peter I. Jewett, J. P.	1	53
WELLS, Alma, ae 43, b. West Hartford, res. Granby, m. Chauncey HOLCOMB, farmer, ae 51, b. Granby, res. same, May 8, 1849, by Rev. Horace Bushenll	1	238-9
WETHERBY, Lucy, m. Thomas WATSON, b. of Southwick, Mass., Mar. 1, 1848, by Lewis Holcomb, J. P.	1	54
WHEATON, Elijah, m. Jane SACKETT, b. of Westfield, Mass., June 1, 1843, by Israel P. Warren	1	39
WHEELER, Aaron H., of West Springfield, Mass., m. Ursula HAWLEY, of Canton, Feb. 19, 1833, by Rev. D. Hemenway	1	13

GRANBY VITAL RECORDS 153

	Vol.	Page
WHEELER, (cont.)		
Juliann, m. Edward **TOWNSEND**, Nov. 3, 1842, by Charles T. Hillyer, J. P.	1	38
WHIPPLE, Willington G., m. Martha M. **MONROE**, b. of Westfield, Mass., May 19, 1847, by Rev. Pliney F. Sanborn	1	52
WHITE, Jane, pauper, had illeg. child, b. [ ]	1	222-3
Lucy G., m. Edwin L. **HOLCOMB**, b. of Granby, Oct. 23, 1854, by William H. Hubbard	1	69
Margaret, Mrs., m. Nathan G. **HOLCOMB**, Aug. 24, 1848, by A. L. Loveland	1	56
Margaret, ae 27, had illeg., s. Alvira **MERRIAM**, b. Aug. 25, 1848; f. Nathan **HOLCOMB**, farmer, ae 35	1	234-5
Margaret, housekeeper, ae 27, b. Ireland, res. Granby, m. Nathan G. **HOLCOMB**, farmer, ae 35, b. Granby, res. same, Sept. 20, 1848, by Rev. Mr. Loveland	1	238-9
Mary Elizabeth, d. Alfred, clergyman & Roxana C., b. Aug. 18, 1848	1	234-5
Samuel, ae 35, b. Suffield, res. same, m. 2nd w. Ruth **HIGLEY**, ae 29, b. Granby, res. Suffield, Sept. 25, 1850, by Rev. Nelson Scott	1	134
Samuel, of Suffield, m. Ruth K. **HIGGINS***, of Granby, Sept. 26, 1850, by Rev. Nelson Scott *("**HIGLEY**" in tabulated form)	1	63
WHITNEY, Thadeus, m. Polly **PRATT**, Feb. 11, 1844, by Abner Case, J. P.	1	40
WILCOX, WILLCOX, Adeliza, d. Hiram, farmer & distiller, ae 47 & Rhoda, ae 35, b. Oct. 28, 1849	1	234-5
Ann Eliza, m. Carleton **HOLCOMB**, b. of Granby, May 27, 1847, by Alfred White	1	52
Candae, d. Ledose & Roxey, b. Mar. 21, 1786	TM1	25
Carlos, m. Sophronia **WILCOX**, b. of Granby, Sept. 3, 1840, by Rev. Charles Stearns	1	32
Caroline, m. George **HAYES**, Aug. 29, 1832, by Isaac Porter	1	11
Charlotte, m. Sylvester **PARMALEE**, b. of Granby, Apr. 24, 1839, by Rev. Davis Stocking	1	29
Sintha, d. Ledosa & Roxey, b. Dec. 10, 1787	TM1	25
Daniel, s. [Ledosa & Roxey], b. Feb. 20, 1798	TM1	25
David B., m. Helen C. **MOOR**, Nov. 25, 1829, by Isaac Porter	1	1
Edwin, merchant, ae 28, b. Canton, res. same, m. Jerusha **WILCOX**, ae 21, b. Granby, res. same, Dec. 18, 1851, by Rev. Lucius King	1	134
Eliza, ae 22, m. Wells **WILCOX**, farmer, ae 27, b. of Granby, Dec. 18, 1851, by Rev. Lucius King	1	134

	Vol.	Page
WILCOX, WILLCOX, (cont.)		
Flora, m. Jerry **WILLCOX,** Jan. 25, 1832, by Isaac Porter	1	10
Harlow, s. [Ledosa & Roxey], b. Nov. 29, 1791	TM1	25
Hiram, m. Rhoda **GRIFFIN,** b. of Granby, July 13, 1837, by Amasa Holcomb	1	24
Jeremiah, carriage maker, d. Sept. 7, 1849, ae 28	1	254-5
Jerry, m. Flora **WILLCOX,** Jan. 25, 1832, by Isaac Porter	1	10
Jerusha, ae 21, b. Granby, res. same, m. Edwin **WILCOX,** merchant, ae 28, b. Canton, res. same, Dec. 18, 1851, by Rev. Lucius King	1	134
Mariah, of Granby, m. Chester **CASE,** of Barkhamsted, May 10, 1848, by Rev. S. Rushmore	1	55
Milo, of Ohio, m. Roxey L. **WILCOX,** of Granby, Aug. 20, 1848, by Rev. A. B. Pulling	1	56
Milo, farmer, ae 22, b. Granby, res. same, m. Vesta **COWDRY,** b. Hartland, res. Granby, July 4, 1850, by Rev. Amasa Holcomb	1	252-3
Obadiah W., of Hartland, m. Mary Ann **COWLES,** of Granby, Sept. 15, 1840, by Rev. Daniel Hemenway	1	33
Ovid, s. Ledose & Roxe, b. Mar. 3, 1780	TM1	25
Roxey, d. Ledosa & Roxey], b. Apr. 13, 1794	TM1	25
Roxey L., of Granby, m. Milo **WILCOX,** of Ohio, Aug. 20, 1848, by Rev. A. B. Pulling	1	56
Sedosa, m. Mrs. Roxey **HAYS,** Dec. 2, 1784	TM1	25
Sophronia, m. Carlos **WILCOX,** b. of Granby, Sept. 3, 1840, by Rev. Charles Stearns	1	32
Thomas, m. Miranda **HILLYER,** May 18, 1830, by Isaac Porter	1	2
Trumbull, m. Polly M. **ADAMS,** Sept. 9, 1830, by Isaac Porter	1	4
Wells, farmer, ae 27, m. Eliza **WILCOX,** ae 22, b. of Granby, Dec. 18, 1851, by Rev. Lucius King	1	134
William, of Farmington, O., m. Minerva **WEED,** of Granby, Nov. 2, 1851, by Rev. A. B. Pulling	1	64
Willis, m. Charlotte R. **HUGINS,** b. of Granby, June 17, 1839, by Allen McLean	1	30
WILKISSON, Merila, b. Apr. 7, 1780	TM1	26
WILLIAMS, Lucy Ann, of Granby, m. William E. **ANDRUSS,** of Farmington, July 5, 1835, at the house of John Williams, by Rev. Harvey Ball, of Suffield	1	20
WILLIAMSON, William, m. Caroline **ALLEN,** Jan. 1, 1847, by Rev. R. G. Thompson, of Tariffville	1	51
WILSON, Maria, ae 19, m. Jary **STEDMAN,** farmer, ae 19, b. of Granby, May 4, 1848, by Rev. [ ] Bushnell	1	226-7
Mariah, m. Jara M. **STEDMAN,** May 4, 1848, by Rev.		

GRANBY VITAL RECORDS   155

	Vol.	Page
WILSON, (cont.)		
S. Rushmore	1	55
WINCHELL, WINCHEL, Alexander, m. Corintha PHELPS, Mar.		
15, 1833, by Abner Case	1	13
Cyrene, of Granby, m. Philip N. FRENCH, of		
Southwick, Mass., May 24, 1833, by Rev.		
Daniel Hemenway	1	14
Jane M., of Granby, m. Charles H. STOCKEN, of New		
Hartford, [Nov. 29, 1832], by Rev. D.		
Hemenway	1	13
Mercy, Mrs., m. Caleb HOLCOMB, Dec. 25, 1776	TM1	29
Samuel, m. Mrs. Alamena PHELPS, b. of Windsor,		
June 17, 1838, by Rev. Daniel Hemenway	1	27
WOOLCOTT, James M., of West Springfield, Mass., m. Sarah Ann		
LOMBARD, of Chicopee, Mass., Sept. 16,		
1849, by Samuel W. Barnum. Int. Pub.	1	60
WOODRUFF, Esther J., of Windsor, m. Albert CLARK, of		
Granby, [ ], by Stephen Crosby	1	4
Selah, of New Hartford, m. Augusta BARTHOLOMEW,		
of Granby, Sept. 15, 1840, by Rev. Chauncey		
D. Rice	1	34
WRIGHT, Ewins, m. Mrs. Lydid LAMBSON, Oct. 23, 1788	TM1	33
Horace E., of Springfield, Mass., m. Abigail S.		
FILLMORE, of Granby, Apr. 2, 1844, by I.		
P. Warren	1	41
John I., m. Achsa GODDARD, d. Achillis, Oct. 7, 1839,		
by Rev. Charles Stearns	1	31
Lydia, [d. Ewins & Lydia], b. Mar. 3, 1789	TM1	33
Phyphena, m. Quartus F. LYMAN, b. of East Hampton,		
Mass., Nov. 7, 1832, by Asahel Gaylord	1	12
Polly, [d. Ewins & Lydia], b. Apr. 3, 1792	TM1	33
YATES, Emely, ae 19, b. England, res. Granby, m. Robert		
McKENDRICK, manufacturer, ae 20, b.		
Scotland, res. Simsbury, Mar. 5, 1849, by Rev.		
Mr. Thompson	1	240-1
YEH(?), Mary, ae 25, b. Ireland, res. Granby, m. John SMITH,		
farmer, ae 50, b. Ireland, res. Granby, Nov.		
23, 1847, by Rev. W. N. Hebbard	1	226-7
YOUNGS, Trifene, m. Noah HOLCOMB, Feb. 1, 1785	TM1	24

GREENWICH VITAL RECORDS
1640 - 1848

	Vol.	Page
ABBOT, David, b. Aug. 11, 1742; m. Rachel **JAMES**, Oct. 3, 1762, by [ ]	1	89-90
David, b. Aug. 11, 1742; m. Rachel **JAMES**, Oct. 3, 1762	ER	225*
David, [s. David & Rachel], b. July 9, 1763	1	89-90
David, [s. David & Rachel], b. July 9, 1763	ER	225*
ADAMS, ADDAMS, Alfred, m. Hannah **SCOTT**, [July] 10, [1834], by J. Mann	1	193
Edwin N., [s. John & Mary], b. July 7, 1807	1	99
Elizabeth, d. John, b. Apr. 17, 1727	1	50
Elizabeth, d. John, b. Apr. 17, 1727	ER	183
Frances, of Greenwich, m. Charles G. **ROWELSON**, of New York, Sept. 2, 1838, by Rev. William Biddle, of Stamford	1	201
John, s. John, b. Jan. 22, 1724	1	50
John, s. John, b. Jan. 22, 1724	ER	183
John, [s. William & Patience], b. Oct. 23, 1762	1	89-90
John, b. Apr. 17, 1779; m. Mary **HOBBY**, Feb. 27, 1804; d. Oct. 2, 1825	1	99
John A., [s. John & Mary], b. Aug. 7, 1814	1	99
Jonathan, s. John, b. Nov. 6, 1719	ER	182
Jonathan, s. John, b. Nov. 19, 1719	1	50
Joseph H., [s. John & Mary], b. Jan. 1, 1817	1	99
Laura, of Greenwich, m. Andrew B. **HATHAWAY**, of Norwalk, Nov. 7, 1843, by Rev. Adrian Parker, of Stamford	1	212
Marilda H., [d. John & Mary], b. Sept. 15, 1809	1	99
Mary E., [d. John & Mary], b. May 23, 1805	1	99
Phebe, of Greenwich, m. Joseph **YOUNG**, of Stamford, Nov. 5, 1838, by Rev. William Riddle, of Stamford	1	202
Samuel, s. John, b. June 10, 1717	1	50
Samuell, s. John, b. June 10, 1718	ER	182
Sarah, d. John, b. Aug. 6, 1721	1	50
Sarah, d. John, b. Aug. 6, 1721	1	182
Sarah K., [d. John & Mary], b. Aug. 10, 1812	1	99
Susan C., [d. John & Mary], b. Dec. 25, 1810	1	99
William, m. Patience **RATHBURN**, Mar. 25, 1759, by Rev. Abraham Todd	1	89-90
ADDINGTON, Ebenezer, [s. John], b. Sept. 8, 1758	1	111
Ebenezer, [s. John], b. Sept. 8, 1758	ER	226

	Vol.	Page
ADDINGTON, (cont.)		
Elizabeth, [d. John], b. Sept. 7, 1754	1	111
Elizabeth, [d. John], b. Sept. 7, 1754	ER	226
Hannah, [d. John], b. July 17, 1747	1	111
Hannah, [d. John], b. July 17, 1747	ER	226
Henry, [s. John], b. Sept. 13, 1752	1	111
Henry, [s. John], b. Sept. 13, 1752	ER	226
John, [s. John], b. Sept. 8, 1743	1	111
John, [s. John], b. Sept. 8, 1743	ER	226
John, Jr., m. Elizabeth **HAYS**, d. Abraham, July 2, 1769	1	122
John, [s. John, Jr. & Elizabeth], b. Mar. 11, 1772	1	122
Lemuel, [s. John, Jr. & Elizabeth], b. Feb. 10, 1774	1	122
Sarah, [d. John], b. Aug. 15, 1750	1	111
Sarah, [d. John], b. Aug. 15, 1750	ER	226
Thomas, [s. John], b. Aug. 17, 1745; d. Sept. 9, 1752	1	111
Thomas, [s. John], b. Aug. 17, 1745; d. Sept. 9, 1752	ER	226
Thomas, [s. John, Jr. & Elizabeth], b. Sept. 22, 1770	1	122
William, [s. John], b. Oct. 9, 1756	1	111
William, [s. John], b. Oct. 9, 1756	ER	226
AIXLE, AUXLE, Ann, m. Richard **WALTTERS**, Aug. 25, 1772, by Jonathan Hoitt	1	47
An[n]a, m. Richard **WALTERS**, Aug. 25, 1722, by Jonathan Hoitt	ER	189
ALEXANDER, John, of Bedford, m. Susan **KNAPP**, of Stanwich, Feb. 2, [1823], by Platt Buffett	1	169
ALTHOUSE, Zachariah, m. Eliza **MEAD**, [Dec.] 12, [1830], by E. S. Raymond	1	185
AMBLER, Sarah, d. July 23, 1736	CP	103
William, d. July 21, 1736	CP	103
ANDERSON, Abigail Jane, m. David T. **PLATT**, b. of Greenwich, May 1, 1842, by B. M. Yarrington, at Glenville	1	208
John P., of Cortlandt, N. Y., m. Mary **MEAD**, of Greenwich, Dec. 3, [probably 1842], by Noah Coe	1	210
Purdy, m. Mary **SHAMPENIRE**, Oct. 9, 1848, by Rev. Daniel Vail, Portchester	1	217
William, m. Abigail **LYON**, d. Thomas, Oct. 16, 1716, by Rev. Christopher Bridge	1	48
William, m. Abigail **LYON**, d. Thomas, Oct. 16, 1716, by Rev. Christopher Bridge	ER	177
William, s. William [& Abigail], b. Dec. 15, 1717	1	48
William, s. William [& Abigail], b. Dec. 15, 1717	ER	477
ANDMAN, George, m. Hannah **PECK** (colored), b. of Greenwich, Dec. 18, 1839, by Rev. Platt Buffett	1	205
ANNAN, Samuel, of Fishkill, Dutchess Co., N. Y., m. Sarah H. **SEYMOUR**, of Greenwich, Jan. 29, [1823], by Isaac Lewis	1	168

	Vol.	Page

AUGDEN, [see under OGDEN]
AUSTIN, Eliza, of Stanwich, m. Daniel MILES, of Greenwich,
    Feb. 1, 1824, by Platt Buffett   1   171
  Elizabeth, of Greenwich, m. Frederick WRIGHT, of
    Mass., Dec. 16, 1832, by Rev. Platt Buffett, of
    Stanwich   1   189
AUXLE, [see under AIXLE]
AVERY, Abraham, [s. Peter], b. July 1, 1774   1   121
  Elizabeth, [d. Peter], b. Nov. 6, 1761   1   121
  Elizabeth, d. Peter, m. Aaron DENTON, Nov. 5, 1788,
    by Amos Mead   1   142
  Elizabeth, m. Purdy TOWNSEND, b. of Greenwich,
    Dec. 12, 1821, by Joshua Ferris, J. P.   1   167
  Emeline, [d. Israel Knapp], b. June 21, 1807   1   154
  Gertrude, [d. Peter], b. Aug. 11, 1770   1   121
  Hannah, [d. Peter], b. July 13, 1760   1   121
  Ira, [s. Peter], b. July 21, 1772   1   121
  Israel Knapp, s. Peter, b. Aug. 30, 1782   1   121
  Israel Knapp, s. [Israel Knapp], b. Mar. 2, 1809   1   154
  John, [s. Peter], b. Nov. 11, 1763   1   121
  Mary Elizabeth, d. Israel Knapp, b. Oct. 30, 1804   1   154
  Matilda, d. [Israel Knapp & Sally], b. Aug. 18, 1811   1   154
  Peter, [s. Peter], b. Oct. 19, 1768   1   121
  Rachal, [d. Peter], b. Oct. 21, 1765   1   121
  Reuben, [s. Peter], b. Mar. 1, 1776   1   121
  Sally, w. Israel Knapp, d. June 5, 1814   1   154
  Sally Hobby, [d. Israel Knapp & Sally], b. Sept. 11, 1813   1   154
  Walter, s. Peter, b. Jan. 4, 1779   1   121
AYRES, Joseph, of Stamford, m. Nancy Ann YOUNG, of
    Greenwich, Feb. 10, 1839, by Rev. Platt
    Buffett   1   203
BANEY, John, m. Delia Ann LOUNSBURY, b. of Greenwich, Feb.
    26, 1843, by Chauncey Wilcox   1   211
BANKS, Abigail, d. Joseph, b. Jan. 23, 1707   1   46
  Abigail, d. Joseph, b. Jan. 23, [ ]   ER   146
  Abigail, [d. Daniel], b. July 23, 1721   1   95
  Abigail, d. [Daniel], b. July 23, 1721   ER   186
  Anne, d. James, b. July 3, 1785   1   154
  Catharine, d. James, b. Jan. 20, 1783   1   154
  Charity, [d. Daniel, Jr. & Rachel], b. Mar. 9, 1753   ER   233
  Daniel, [s. Daniel], b. Jan. 23, 1723; d. July 25, [ ]   1   95
  Daniel, [s. Daniel], b. Jan. 33[sic], 1723; d. July 25, 1759   1   186
  Daniel, Jr., m. Rachel HOBBY, Aug. 14, 1747   1   233
  Daniel, Jr., m. Rachal HOBBY, [ ] 14, 1747   ER   96
  Daniel, Jr. & w. Rachal, had child, b. Dec. 1, 1747   1   96
  Daniel, [s. Daniel, Jr. & Rachel], b. Dec. 1, 1747   ER   233
  Daniel, Jr. & w. Rachal, had child, b. Sept. 20, 1749   1   96
  Daniel, Jr. & w. Rachal, had child b. May 27, 1751   1   96

BARBOUR COLLECTION

	Vol.	Page
BANKS, (cont.)		
Daniel, Jr. & w. Rachal, had child b. Mar. 9, 1753	1	96
Daniel, Jr. & w. Rachal, had child, b. May 27, 1756	1	96
Daniel, Jr. & w. Rachal, had child, b. Aug. 9, 1757	1	96
Daniel, Jr., d. July 25, 1759	1	96
Daniel, Jr, d. July 25, 1759	ER	233
David, [s. Daniel, Jr. & Rachel], b. May 27, 1751	ER	233
David, [s. Obadiah & Elizabeth], b. Dec. 23, 1760	1	95
David, m. Marilda PECK, May 10, [1821], by Rev. David Peck	1	165
Elizabeth, d. James, b. June 25, 1777	1	154
George, of Rye, m. Mary Ann SANTIERS, of Greenwich, Sept. 23, [1821], by Isaac Lewis	1	165
Hannah, d. Joseph, b. Oct. 27, 1704	1	46
Hannah, d. Joseph, b. Oct. 27, 1704	ER	146
Hannah, d. James, b. Jan. 10, 1773	1	154
Jacob, s. James, b. Jan. 12, 1790; d. Nov. 29, 1794	1	154
James, m. Elizabeth HULSTED, Jan. 6, 1833, by E. S. Raymond	1	188
Jonathan, m. Phebe Ann HOPSON, b. of Greenwich, Oct. 22, 1845, by Rev. Geo[rge] Waterbury	1	214
Joseph, s. Joseph, b. Jan. 14, 1708/9	1	46
Joseph, s. Joseph, b. Jan. 14, 1708/9	ER	146
Joshua, [s. Obadiah & Elizabeth], b. Feb. 23, 1759	1	95
Lydia, [d. Daniel], b. July 2, 1726	1	95
Lydia, d. [Daniel], b. July 2, 1726	ER	186
Lydea, d. Daniell, m. [ ], Feb. 16, 1754, by Rev. Mr. Todd	1	70
Lydea, d. Dan[ie]l, m. [ ] SMITH, Jr., Feb. 16, 1754, by Rev. Mr. Todd	ER	246
Lydia, [d. Daniel, Jr. & Rachel], b. Aug. 9, 1757	ER	233
Mary, d. [Joseph], b. June 27, 1710	1	46
Mary, d. [Joseph], b. June 27, 1710	ER	146
Mary, d. James, b. Apr. 5, 1779; d. Oct. [ ], 1781	1	154
Mary, m. Jonathan FINCH, b. of Greenwich, [Nov.] 17, [1839], by Rev. D. B. Booth, of Stanwich	1	205
Obadiah, [s. Daniel], b. Aug. 21, 1724	1	95
Obadiah, s. [Daniel], b. Aug. 21, 1724	ER	186
Obadiah, m. Eliza[be]th SMITH, d. Daniel, Sept. 1, 1755, by [ ]	1	95
Obadiah, [s. Obadiah & Elizabeth], b. Jan. 12, 1757	1	95
Painpey(?), m. Catharine FLORENCE, Mar. 24, 1842, by Rev. D. B. Butts	1	207
Phebe, d. James, b. Aug. 31, 1787; d. Jan. [ ], 1793	1	154
Ruth, [d. Daniel], b. June [ ], 1730	1	95
Ruth, d. [Daniel], b. June [ ], 1730	ER	186
Sally, m. Thomas SEYMOUR, Dec. 14, 1831, by E. S. Raymond	1	187

GREENWICH VITAL RECORDS 161

	Vol.	Page
BANKS, (cont.)		
Samuel, [s. Daniel, Jr. & Rachel], b. May 27, 1755	ER	233
Sanford, m. Elizabeth Jane READ, b. of Greenwich, Dec. 21, 1829, by C. Wilcox, of North Greenwich	1	183
Sarah, [d. Daniel, Jr. & Rachel], b. Sept. 20, 1749	ER	233
Sarah, d. James, b. Mar. 2, 1781; d. May [ ], 1781	1	154
William, s. James, b. Apr. 15, 1775; d. Aug. [ ], 1777	1	154
BAREMORE, Maria, m. Stephen SMITH, b. of Greenwich, Sept. 26, 1830, by Rev. Platt Buffett, of Stanwich	1	184
BARKER, [see under BUNKER]		
BARNES, BARNS, Eliza Ann, m. W[illia]m Benson SHERWOOD, Aug. 28, [1831], by J. Mann	1	186
John, of New York, m. Julia STUVETS, of Old Greenwich, July 17, 1833, by Rev. John Ellis, of Stamford. Int. Pub.	1	191
BAXTAR, [see also BUXTON], John, m. Martha CLOSE, Jan. 25, 1731/2 by Joshua Knapp, J. P.	1	58
[BEAY], BEYEA, James, [s. Peter], b. Oct. 15, 1764	1	72
Martha, [d. Peter], b. Aug. 17, 1762	1	72
Samuel, [s. Peter], b. Sept. 20, 1768	1	72
BEEBE, Anna, m. Samuel JESSUP, of the Cos Mill, b. of Greenwich, June 30, 1839, by B. M. Farrington	1	204
BELCHER, Anna Augusta, m. Barton Fowler WHITE, b. of Greenwich, Nov. 27, 1823, by Isaac Lewis	1	170
Elizabeth M., of Greenwich, m. Joseph W. STRONG, of Peekskell, N. Y., Sept. 3, 1821, by Rev. Isaac Lewis	1	165
Henry, m. Grace FERRIS, b. of Greenwich, Aug. 17, 1834, by Rev. Edwin Hall, of Norwalk	1	193
BELDING, Sarah, d. Benjamin, m. Ebenezer HOWE, June 6, 1774, by Rev. Mr. Murdock	1	132
BETTS, A[a]ron, [s. Silas & Elizabeth], b. Jan. 22, 1755; d. Apr. 19, 1755	ER	227*
An[n], [twin with Elizabeth, d. Silas & Elizabeth], b. Dec. 6, 1744	ER	227*
Catharine, m. Charles BURTREE, Mar. 27, 1842, by Rev. J. W. Alvord	1	208
Elizabeth, [twin with An[n], d. Silas & Elizabeth], b. Dec. 6, 1744; d. Jan. 5, 1745	ER	227*
Elizabeth, [d. Silas & Elizabeth], b. May 26, 1746	ER	227*
Elizabeth, [w. Silas], d. Apr. 29, 1759	ER	227*
Hannah, [d. Silas & Elizabeth], b. Feb. 16, 1748; d. Sept. 10, 1758	ER	227*
John, Jr., of Norwalk, m. Hannah BURWELL, of Greenwich, d. [ ], decd. [ ], 1703, by Sam[ue]l Peck, J. P.	LR1	3

BARBOUR COLLECTION

	Vol.	Page
BETTS, (cont.)		
John, Jr., of Norwalk, m. Hannah BURWELL, d. John, decd., of Greenwich, Apr. 13, 1708, by Samuel Peck, J. P.	ER	160
Lucy, [d. Silas & Elizabeth], b. Aug. 17, 1750	ER	227*
Lucy, [d. Silas & Elizabeth], b. Sept. 16, 1752	ER	227*
Silas, m. Elizabeth LOCKWOOD, d. Gershom, Jan. 15, 1743/4, by Mr. Todd	ER	227*
Silas, [s. Silas & Elizabeth], b. Sept. 1, 1752	ER	227*
William A., m. Mary W. MARSHALL, b. of Greenwich, May 12, 1847, by Rev. B. M. Yarrington	1	216
BEYEA, [see under BEAY]		
BIRGE, Chester, m. Hannah C. MEAD, June 9, 1831, by Chauncey Wilcox	1	187
BISHOP, Alfred, m. Mary FERRIS, b. of Greenwich, Oct. 11, 1821, by Rev. Daniel Smith, of Stamford	1	166
BIXLEY, Alfred, m. Thirza OLMSTEAD, [Nov.] 5, [1834], by J. Mann	1	194
BLAKE, Elizabeth, [d. William & Abigail], b. Aug. 11, 1761	1	97
William, m. Abigail REYNOLDS, d. David, decd., Mar. 26, 1756	1	97
William, [s. William & Abigail], b. Sept. 11, 1758	1	97
BOSTWICK, Hannah, wid. Merryday & d. Capt. Elnathan HANFORD, of Norwalk, m. [ ] PEROTT, s. James, of St. Martins, in the Fields, City of Westminster, Kingdom of Great Britain, Feb. 15, 1764, by Rev. Abraham Todd	1	124
BOURDEAU, Louisa, m. John Jay TRACY, b. of Greenwich, Nov. 23, 1845, by Rev. Benjamin M. Yarrington, Int. Pub.	1	215
BOUTON, Daniel, of Rye, Westchester Co., m. Hahalo HITCHCOCK, of Horseneck, Fairfield Co., Nov. 14, 1827, by Rev. John Ellis, of Stamford	1	177
BOWEN, William, m. Sabrina BUNNELL, b. of Greenwich, Dec. 24, 1845, by Rev. Peter C. Oakely	1	215
BOWERS, John, Lieut., d. Mar. 17, 1690	LR1	448
John, Lieut., d. Mar. 17, 1694/5	ER	85
BRIGGS, Alva, m. Hannah L. KNAPP, b. of Greenwich, Jan. 1, 1843, by D. B. Butts	1	210
Amey, m. Nathaniel FERRIS, b. of Stanwich, May 30, 1830, by Platt Buffett, of Stanwich	1	183
Deborah Ann, m. Reuben O. FREDAND, b. of Greenwich, Mar. 5, 1823, by Henry Hoit, Jr.	1	169
Lydia Ann, of Greenwich, m. James BUCKHOUT, of Rye, N. Y., Apr. 18, 1824, by Rev. Henry Wait. Evangelist of North Baptist Church, Stamford	1	171

	Vol.	Page
BRITT, James, of North Castle, N. Y., m. Rebecca BRUNDAGE, of Greenwich, Dec. 30, [1829], by E. S. Raymond	1	183
BRONSON, Maria, b. July 31, 1773, in Haverstraw, N. Y.; m. Silas DAVIS, of Greenwich, Feb. 24, 1794, at Toppin, N. Y.	1	75
BROWN, Abigall, m. John QUICK, Oct. 1, 1735, by Rev. Abraham Todd	1	61
Abigal, m. John QUICK, Oct. 1, 1735, by Abraham Toodd	ER	215
Abigail, [d. Edmund], b. Nov. 29, 1755	1	83
Abigail, [d. Edmund], b. Nov. 29, 1755	ER	246
Abigail, d. Thomas [& Abigail], b. Oct. 1, 1781	1	139
Anngenette, m. Silas LOUNSBURY, Oct. 1, 1834, by C. Wilcox	1	194
Barabelle, m. Clarisa DAVIS, b. of Greenwich, May 4, 1824, by Rev. Henry Wait	1	171
Bezalelle, m. Clarasa DAVIS, b. of Greenwich, May 4, 1824, by Rev. Henry Hoit, of Stamford	1	133
Charity, [d. Ebenezer & Deborah], b. Dec. 11, 1760	1	94
Charlott[e], m. Harvey HUBBARD, b. of Greenwich, May 9, 1832, by Rev. Platt Buffett, of Stanwich	1	190
David, d. Mar. 13, 1813	1	99
Deborah, b. Sept. 1, 1772	1	127
Deborah, m. Jonathan RUNDLE, May 2, 1799, by Rev. Nathaniel Finch, Jr.	1	127
Dinah, m. Jeffery FELMETTE, Sept. 20, 1830, by Elijah Hebard	1	186
Ebenezer, m. Deborah HOBBY, Jan. 24, 1757	1	94
Electa, m. Benjamin HUSTED, Jr., b. of Greenwich, May 13, 1844, by Chauncey Wilcox	1	212
Elizabeth, [d. Ebenezer & Deborah], b. Apr. 8, 1759	1	94
Francis J., of Greenwich, m. Jonah C. BRUNDAGE, of Rye, N. Y., Mar. 6, 1842, by Rev. Charles F. Pelton	1	209
Hannah, m. Ebenezer MEAD, Dec. 3, 1717	LR1	447
Hannah, m. Ebenezer MEAD, Jr., Dec. 12, 1717	1	60
Hannah, m. Ebenezer MEAD, Jr., Dec. 12, 1717	ER	180
Hannah, [d. Edmund], b. Feb. 17, 1763	1	83
Hannah, [d. Edmund], b. Feb. 17, 1763	ER	246
Jackson D., of Somerstown, N. Y., m. Julia E. FINCH, of Greenwich, Feb. 23, 1842, by Rev. D. B. Butts	1	207
John, [s. Edmund], b. Mar. 14, 1760	1	83
John, [s. Edmund], b. Mar. 14, 1760	ER	246
John, s. Thomas [& Abigail], b. Nov. 9, 1783	1	139
John K., m. Angeline A. LYON, Dec. 20, [1824], by		

	Vol.	Page

BROWN, (cont.)

Platt Buffett	1	171
Joseph, of Rye, N. Y., m. Eliza **PURDY**, of Greenwich, Jan. 4, 1838, by Chauncey Wilcox	1	198
Mary, [d. Edmund], b. Apr. 27, 1758	1	83
Mary, [d. Edmund], b. Apr. 27, 1758	ER	246
Mary, m. Frederick **SHERWOOD**, Sept. 7, 1834, by Chauncey Wilcox	1	193
Narah*, [d. Edmund], b. June 6, 1754 *(Sarah?)	ER	246
Nehemiah, of Rye, Westchester Co., N. Y., m. Pamela H. **SANFORD**, of Greenwich, Sept. 21, 1823, by Isaac Lewis	1	169
Rachal, m. Benjamin **MEAD**, June 20, 1716	ER	177
Rachel, m. Benjamin **MEAD**, June 27, 1716	LR1	447
Rachall, of Poundridge, but now residing with Mrs. Mills; m. Daniel **MERRETT**, of North Castle, Apr. 19, 1826, at the house of wid. Mills, by Platt Buffett	1	173
Rachel, of Greenwich, m. Jeremiah **PLATT**, of Rye, N. Y., Dec. 10, 1827, by P. Buffett	1	178
Sarah, [d. Edmund], b. June 6, 1754	1	83
Sarah*, [d. Edmund], b. June 6, 1754 *(Arnold Copy has "Narah")	ER	246
Sarah, [d. Ebenezer & Deborah], b. Nov. 7, 1757	1	94
Thomas, m. Abigail **HOLLY**, of Stamford, d. Frank, Dec. 9, 1780, by Rev. Mr. Dibble	1	139
Thomas, d. Oct. 2, 1783, ae 37 y.	1	139

BRUNDAGE, Harrison, of North Castle, m. Mary E. **PURDY**, of Greenwich, Feb. 16, 1837, by C. Wilcox — 1   203

Jonah C., of Rye, N. Y., m. Frances J. **BROWN**, of Greenwich, Mar. 6, 1842, by Rev. Charles F. Pelton	1	209
Rebecca, of Greenwich, m. James **BRITT**, of North Castle, N. Y., Dec. 30, [1829], by E. S. Raymond	1	183
Sarah, of Greenwich, m. William **HUBBARD**, of Somers, N. Y., Nov. 23, 1835, by Platt Buffett	1	196

BRUSH, Asa N., m. Mary R. **CLOSE**, Feb. 28, 1831, by Joel Mann   1   185

Benjamin, 3rd, m. Clarissa **SACKETT**, b. of Greenwich, Oct. 5, 1829, by Rev. Platt Buffett, of Stanwich	1	182
Clarissa, m. William **SMITH**, b. of Greenwich, Jan. 10, 1837, by Noah Coe	1	197
Deborah, m. Reuben **FINCH**, b. of Greenwich, Feb. 13, 1822, by Platt Buffet	1	167
Elizabeth, m. David **DAYTON**, b. of Stanwich, Mar. 6, 1827, by Rev. Platt Buffett	1	174
Hannah, d. Stephen, b. Nov. 7, 1728	1	58

	Vol.	Page
BRUSH, (cont.)		
Han[n]ah, d. Stephen, b. Nov. 10, 1728	ER	201
Joseph, m. Sarah A. **MEAD**, Mar. 18, 1823, by Isaac Lewis	1	169
Joshua, s. Joseph, b. June 11, 1717	LR1	449
Joshua, s. John, b. June 11, 1717	ER	180
Mary, Jr., d. Benjamin, m. John **MEAD**, Jr., Aug. 25, 1754, by Rev. Benjamin Strong	1	117
Mary, Jr., d. Benjamin, m. John **MEAD**, Jr., Aug. 25, 1754, by Rev. Benjamin Strong	ER	246
Platt, m. Maria **CLOSE**, b. of Stanwich, Dec. 20, 1826, by Platt Buffett	1	174
Rachal, of Stanwich, m. Thomas **RUNDLE**, of Somers, N. Y., Dec. 4, 1823, by Platt Buffitt	1	170
Rebecca A., of Greenwich, m. John L. C. **COIT**, of Stamford, Jan. 3, 1843, by D. B. Butts	1	211
Richard, s. Richard, b. Dec. 19, 1727	1	65
Richard, s. Richard, b. Dec. 19, 1727	ER	196
BUCKHOUT, James, of Rye, N. Y., m. Lydia Ann **BRIGGS**, of Greenwich, Apr. 18, 1824, by Rev. Henry Wait. Evangelist of North Baptist Church, Stamford	1	171
BUDSON, Hannah, d. Thomas, of North Castle, Westchester, Co., N. Y., m. Joseph **SACKETT**, of Greenwich, Apr. 28, 1751, by Rev. Samuel Sackett, of Bedford	1	119
Hannah, d. Thomas, of North Castle, in Westchester, Cty., Province of New York, m. Joseph **SACKETT**, of Greenwich, Apr. 28, 1751, by Rev. Samuel Sackett, of Bedford	ER	238
BUFFETT, Edwin S., m. Susan **SMITH**, b. of Greenwich, Aug. 3, 1846, by Rev. Platt Buffett	1	216
Elacissa, of Greenwich, m. Rev. Samuel **HOWE**, of Hopewell, Ontario Co., N. Y., Aug. 20, 1835, by Rev. Platt Buffett	1	195
Mary E., of Greenwich, m. Henry **DURANT** (Rev.), of Acton, Mass.,Dec. 10, 1833, by Platt Buffett	1	191
BULL, Elnathan, Rev. of Cincinnatus, N. Y., m. Electa H. **RITCH**, of Greenwich, Sept. 14, 1839, by Rev. P. S. Holly, of Sandis Falls, Mass.	1	204
BULLARD, Elizabeth, m. George **WEBB**, June 19, 1832, by J. Mann	1	190
BULLIS, BULLES, [see also **CULLIS**], Abraham, 2nd s. [Thomas & Margret], b. Feb. 17, 1736/7	1	49
Abraham, s. Thomas [& Margaret], b. Feb. 17, 1736/7	ER	212
Charles, s. John [& Mary], b. Nov. 8, 1723	ER	186
Effum, d. Thomas [& Margret], b. Nov. 11, 1737	1	49
Efsum(?), d. Thomas [& Margaret], b. Nov. 11, 1737	ER	212

	Vol.	Page
BULLIS, BULLES, (cont.)		
Felip, s. Thomas [& Margret], b. May 25, 1734	1	49
John*, m. Mary GORMAN, Mar. 8, 1720/1 (CULLIS?)	ER	186
John, s. John [& Mary], b. July 15, 1722	ER	186
Petter, s. Thomas, b. May 25, 1734	ER	212
Thomas, m. Margret ROBERSON, July 11, 1733, by Ebenezer Mead, J. P.	1	49
Thomas, m. Margaret ROBERSON, July 11, 1733, by Ebenezer Mead, J. P.	ER	212
BUNKER*, Anna, of Greenwich, m. Nehemiah HOYT, of Stamford, Mar. 14, 1826, by Platt Buffett *(BARKER?)	1	173
BUNNELL, Sabrina, m. William BOWEN, b. of Greenwich, Dec. 24, 1845, by Rev. Peter C. Oakely	1	215
BURKHEART, Jane, m. Obadiah LOUDON, Oct. 15, 1831, by E. S. Raymond	1	186
BURLEY, Ebenezer, s. [John & Hannah], b. Aug. 18, 1725	1	49
Ebenezer, s. [John & Hannah], b. Aug. 18, 1725	ER	190
John, m. Hannah WHELPLEY, Feb. 20, 1723	1	49
John, m. Hannah WHELPLY, Feb. 20, 1723	ER	190
BURNS, Mary, m. Charles OWENS, b. of Greenwich, Dec. 3, 1835, by Platt Buffett	1	196
Matilda, m. William McGURNE, b. of Greenwich, June 6, 1841, by Rev. E. T. Ball	1	207
Sarah, m. David WILSON, b. of Greenwich, Mar. 25, 1840, by Rev. Platt Buffett	1	207
BURTIS, Peter A., had negroes Francis, s. Peg, b. Oct. 7, 1798, Charles, s. Peg, b. Apr. 30, 1801, Henry, s. Peg. b. June 19, 1804 & Rhoda, d. Dol, b. May 25, 1804	1	162
BURTREE, Charles, m. Catharine BETTS, Mar. 27, 1842, by Rev. J. W. Alvord	1	208
BURWELL, Hannah, of Greenwich, d. [ ], decd, m. John BETTS, Jr., of Norwalk, [ ], 1703, by Sam[uel] Peck, J. P.	LR1	3
Hannah, d. John, decd., of Greenwich, m. John BETTS, Jr., of Norwalk, Apr. 13, 1708, by Samuel Peck, J. P.	ER	160
John, d. May 1, 1698	ER	71
John, d. May 7, [ ]	LR1	448
BUSH, Charity, made affidavit Jan. 26, 1760, that Mary JONES, (wid.) gave birth to son Frederick Harding JONES, on Nov. 28, 1759, and she was at her house the summer before last with Mr. Hardin JONES of N. C., whom she called husband	1	92
Charlotte, d. David [& Sarah], b. May 26, 1784	1	151
Cull, m. Lilly [ ], Feb. 21, 1832, in Harrison, Co. of Westchester, N. Y., by E. S. Raymond	1	187

GREENWICH VITAL RECORDS   167

	Vol.	Page
BUSH, (cont.)		
Cull, Jr., m. Dinah **CHARITY**, Aug. 17, 1834, b. of Greenwich, by Rev. Edwin Hall, of Norwalk	1	193
David, m. wid. Sarah **ISAACS**, (wid. Capt. Benjamin), of Norwalk, Apr. 9, 1777, by Rev. Mr. Lemming	1	151
David, had negroes Phillis, d. Petience, b. Apr. 6, 1789, Milly, d. Patience, b. Apr. 12, 1791, Rose, d. Patience, b. May 15, 1793, Lucy, d. Patience, b. Aug. 27, 1795 & Nancy, d. Patience, b. Apr. 10, 1798 & Cull, s. Patience, b. Apr. 2, 1801	1	145
David, had negroes Jack, s. Candis, b. Mar. 18, 1802 & Hester, d. Candis, b. Jan. 6, 1807	1	145
Fanny, d. David [& Sarah], b. Jan. 1, 1782	1	151
Fanny, of Greenwich, s. Jordan **COLES**, of Brooklyn, N. Y., [Dec.] 11, [1827], by Rev. Ambrose S. Todd, of Stamford	1	177
Gilbert, m. Thurza Ann **SMITH**, (colored), b. of Greenwich, Feb. 16, 1847, by Rev. B. M. Yarrington	1	217
Grace, d. David [& Sarah], b. Apr. 5, 1788	1	151
Justus, d. Nov. 23, 1760	1	112
Justus Luke, s. David [& Sarah], b. Dec. 5, 1777	1	151
Mary, made affidavit Jan. 26, 1760, that Mary **JONES**, (wid.) gave birth to a son Frederick Harding **JONES**, Nov. 28, 1759, and she was at her house summer before last with Mr. Hardin **JONES**, of N. C., whom she called husband	1	92
Mary, Jr., made affidavit Jan. 26, 1760, that Mary **JONES**, (wid.), gave birth to son Frederick Harding **JONES**, b. Nov. 28, 1759 and she was at her house summer before last with Mr. Hardin **JONES**, of N. C., whom she called husband	1	92
Ralph Isaac, s. David [& Sarah], b. Oct. 29, 1779	1	151
Ruth, d. Justus, m. Dr. Amos **MEAD**, Jan. 1, 1753, by Rev. Mr. Todd	1	73
Ruth, d. Justus, m. Dr. Amos **MEAD**, Jan. 1, 1753, by Rev. Mr. Todd	ER	241
Samuell, had negroes Bob, s. Mose, b. Dec. 23, 1785, Tack, s. Mose, b. Nov. [ ], 1787, Ellen, d. Jude, b. Nov. 25, 1793 & Jack, s. Ellen, b. Apr. 2, 1814	1	150
William, Dr. his negroes Platt, b. July [ ], 1789, Candis, b. July [ ], 1791, Diana, b. Apr. 9, 1793 & Rose, b. Jan. 21, 1795	1	147
BUTLER, BUTTLER, Abigail, m. Daniel **MARSHALL**, June 23, 1703	1	52

	Vol.	Page
BUTLER, BUTTLER, (cont.)		
Abigail, m. Daniell **MARSHILL**, June 23, 1703	ER	141
Elisabeth, m. Benjamin **KNAP[P]**, Apr. 18, 1700	ER	124
Elizabeth, m. Benjamin **KNAP[P]**, Feb. 28, 1700/1	LR1	449
Easter, m. Jonathan **MEAD**, cooper, Dec. 7, 1713	ER	173
Easther, m. Nathan **MEAD**, cooper, Dec. [ ]	LR1	446
Rebeckah, m. Daniel **SMITH**, Apr. 25, 1706, by Rev. Joseph Morgan	ER	155
Rebeckah, m. Daniel **SMITH**, Apr. 25, 1706, by Rev. Joseph Morgan	LR1	458
BUTTIS, Mary, m. Jonathan **DATON**, Aug. 13, 1718	LR1	456
BUTTON, Philander, m. Julia Ann **MEAD**, b. of Greenwich, Oct. 11, 1843, by N. Coe	1	211
BUTTS, Ann Wallace, m. William Henry **WILSON**, b. of Greenwich, Jan. 3, 1847, by Rev. B. M. Yarrington	1	216
BUXTON*, [see also **BAXTAR**], John, m. Martha **CLOS[E]**, Jan. 25, 1731/2, by Joshua Knapp, J. P. *(**BAXTER?**)	ER	204
CANFIELD, Deborah, had d. Sarah, b. Jan. 28, 1778	1	136
Sarah, d. Deborah, b. Jan. 28, 1778	1	136
CAREY, Archibald **THOMSON**, s. Leteshe, alias **MARSHALL**, b. Mar. 26, 1776	1	138
Hannah Danford, d. Leteshe, alias **MARSHALL**, b. May 24, 1779	1	138
Leteshe, alias **MARSHALL**, had s. Archibald **THOMSON**, b. Mar. 26, 1776	1	138
Leteshe, alias **MARSHALL** had d. Hannah **DANFORD**, b. May 24, 1779	1	138
CARGILL, John, of Stamford, m. Jemima **STUDWELL**, of Greenwich, June 22, 1828, by Rev. N. C. Saxton	1	180
CARHEART, Ann Eliza, m. John B. **WILLSON**, Oct. 10, 1837, by E. S. Raymond	1	198
CARPENTER, Jasper W., m. Allace **OWENS**, b. of Greenwich, Oct. 16, 1842, by Samuel Close, J. P.	1	209
CARTER, Joseph, m. Sarah Elizabeth **WATSON**, b. of Greenwich, Feb. 7, 1843, by Chauncey Wilcox	1	211
CASTIEN, CAUSTIEN, Joseph, [s. Samuel], b. Apr. 22, 1749	1	103
Joseph, [s. Samuel], b. Apr. 22, 1749	ER	236
Sarah, [d. Samuel], b. Nov. 2, 1752	1	103
Sarah, [d. Samuel], b. Nov. 2, 1752	ER	236
Susan, [d. Samuel], b. Aug. 23, 1759	ER	236
Susanna, [d. Samuel], b. Aug. 23, 1759	1	103
CHAPMAN, Daniel, m. Elizabeth [ ], Aug. 25, 1744	ER	229
Daniel, m. Elizabeth [ ], Aug. [ ]	1	109
Elizabeth, [twin with Hannah], d. Daniel & Elizabeth b. Oct. 16, 1759	1	109

	Vol.	Page
CHAPMAN, (cont.)		
Elizabeth, [twin with Hannah, d. Daniel & Elizabeth], b. Oct. 16, 1759	ER	229
Hannah, [twin with Elizabeth, d. Daniel & Elizabeth], b. Oct. 16, 1759	1	109
Hannah, [twin with Elizabeth, d. Daniel & Elizabeth], b. Oct. 16, 1759	ER	229
Jeremiah, [s. Daniel & Elizabeth], b. Mar. 25, 1745	1	109
Jeremiah, [s. Daniel & Elizabeth], b. Mar. 25, 1745	ER	229
Mary, [d. Daniel & Elizabeth], b. May 22, 1753	1	109
Mary, [d. Daniel & Elizabeth], b. May 22, 1753	ER	229
Phebe, [d. Daniel & Elizabeth], b. Nov. 2, 1761	1	109
Phebe, [d. Daniel & Elizabeth], b. Nov. 2, 1761	ER	229
Sarah, [d. Daniel & Elizabeth], b. Dec. 17, 1752	1	109
Sarah, [d. Daniel & Elizabeth], b. Dec. 17, 1752	ER	229
Titus, [s. Daniel & Elizabeth], b. Oct. 9, 1756	1	109
Titus, [s. Daniel & Elizabeth], b. Oct. 9, 1756	ER	229
CHARITY, Dinah, m. Cull BUSH, Jr., Aug. 17, 1834, b. of Greenwich, by Rev. Edwin Hall, of Norwalk	1	193
CHARRAND, Elizabeth, m. Gerlando MUNSIGLINA, b. of New York City, Apr. 23, 1837, by Rev. Ambrose S. Todd, of Stamford	1	215
CILLEY, CELLY, [see also SEELY], Thomas, m. Hannah WILLSON, July 29, 1751, by Joshua Knapp, J. P.	1	61
Thomas*, m. Hannah WILLSON, July 29, 1731, by Joshua Knapp, J. P. *(Written "Thomas CILLEY")	ER	203
Thomas, see Thomas CILLEY	ER	203
CLAP[P], Zachariah, m. Sarah HUSTED, b. of Greenwich, Mar. 13, 1833, by Rev. Platt Buffett, of Stanwich	1	189
CLARK, Eliza, m. Lewis SCOTT, [July] 10, [1834], by J. Mann	1	193
Jay L., m. Caroline R. LANE, b. of Greenwich, Feb. 22, 1847, by Rev. B. M. Yarrington	1	216
John Latham*, s. John, b. Aug. 4, 1776 *(John Latham CLOCK"?)	1	163
Lockwood E., m. Eliza MEAD, b. of Greenwich, Feb. 3, 1845, by N. Coe	1	213
Ruel Jones Morton, of Northampton, Mass., m. Hetty Elizabeth LOUNSBURY, of Conn., Sept. 17, 1843, by Rev. S. W. Scofield	1	211
CLOCK(?), John Latham, s. John, b. Aug. 4, 1776 *(Arnold copy has "CLARK")	1	163
CLOSE, CLOES, CLOOS, CLOOSE, Abigail, m. John KNAP[P], Jan. 14, 1730/1, by Joshua Knap[p], J. P.	1	58
Abigail, m. John KNAPP, Jan. 14, 1730/1, by Joshua Knap[p], J. P.	ER	202

CLOSE, CLOES, CLOOS, CLOOSE, (cont.)

	Vol.	Page
Abraham H., m. Ann MEAD, b. of Greenwich, June 22, 1835, by Rev. Platt Buffett	1	195
Adle*, m. Rachaell E. MEAD, Oct. 6, 1834, by Samuel Close, J. P. *(Odle?)	1	194
Beniamin, s. Beniamin, b. Mar. 6, 1712	1	51
Beniaman, s. Beniamin, b. Mar. 6, 1712	ER	171
Caroline H., m. James SMITH, Nov. 23, 1831, by Chauncey Wilcox	1	187
Caroline Hobbie, [d. Samuel & Eliza], b. Sept. 19, 1812; m. James SMITH, of Ridgefield, Conn., [ ]; d. May 17, 1835	1	118
Charlotte, m. Horton O. KNAPP, b. of Greenwich, Nov. 24, 1836, by C. Wilcox	1	198
David, s. Solomon, b. Feb. 12, 1742/3	1	57
David, s. Solomon, b. Feb. 12, 1742/3	ER	201
Debrow, d. Solomon, b. Aug. 20, 1733	1	57
Debrow, d. Solomon, b. Aug. 20, 1733	ER	201
Elizabeth, d. Joseph, b. July 11, 1684	LR1	457
Elizabeth, d. Joseph, b. July 11, 1704	ER	136
Elizabeth, d. Beniamin, b. Sept. 19, 1716	1	51
Elizabeth, d. Beniamin, b. Sept. 19, 1716	ER	171
Elizabeth, d. Benjamin, m. Jonathan LOCKWOOD, June 24, 1733	1	107
Elizabeth, d. Benjamin, m. Jonathan LOCKWOOD, June 24, 1733	ER	212
Emily L., m. Silas D. MEAD, b. of Greenwich, Sept. 29, 1840, by C. Wilcox	1	206
Eunice, d. Joseph, m. Gideon PECK, Oct. 4, 1781, by Rev. Jonathan Murdock	1	132
George Washington, [s. Samuel & Eliza], b. Apr. 1, 1816; m. Esther SMITH, d. Col. William, of Flushing. L. I., Mar. 4, 1845	1	118
Gideon, m. Mary Ann INGERSOLL, b. of Greenwich, Nov. 25, 1838, by Darius Mead	1	202
Hannah, [d. Thomas & Hannah], b. Jan. 11, 1730	1	98
Hannah, d. [Thomas & Hannah], b. Jan. 11, 1730	ER	201
Han[n]ah, d. Solomon, b. Apr. 25, 1736	1	57
Hannah, d. Sellomon, b. Apr. 25, 1736	ER	201
Hannah, d. Thomas, m. Theophilus LOCKWOOD, Dec. 17, 1749	1	83
Hannah, d. Thomas, m. Theophilus LOCKWOOD, Dec. 17, 1749	ER	236
Hannah, d. Sam[ue]ll, decd, m. Peter MEAD, Jr., s. Peter, Nov. 19, 1777	1	129
Hannah, wid, Thomas, d. Apr. 8, 1780	1	104
Hannah, m. Lewis MEAD, b. of Greenwich, Feb. 1, 1826, by Platt Buffett	1	173

GREENWICH VITAL RECORDS 171

	Vol.	Page
CLOSE, CLOES, CLOOS, CLOOSE, (cont.)		
Henry, m. Abigail Jane HOBBY, b. of Greenwich, Sept. 9, 1845, by Rev. Peter C. Oakley	1	213
Isaac O., m. Sarah Ann PURDY, b. of Greenwich, Aug. 21, 1844, by Chauncey Wilcox	1	212
John, s. Solomon, b. Sept. 13, 1737	ER	201
John, s. Solomon, b. Sept. 15, 1737	1	57
Jonathan, s. Beniamin, b. Feb. 3, 1719	ER	171
Jonathan, s. Beniamin, b. Feb. 3, 1719/20	1	51
Joseph, s. Joseph, b. Sept. 20, 1682	LR1	457
Joseph, s. Joseph, b. Sept. 20, 1702	ER	136
Maria, m. Platt BRUSH, b. of Stanwich, Dec. 20, 1826, by Platt Buffett	1	174
Martha, d. Benjamin, b. Oct. 26, 1714	1	51
Martha, d. Beniamin, b. Oct. 26, 1714	ER	171
Martha, m. John BAXTAR, Jan. 25, 1731/2, by Joshua Knapp, J. P.	1	58
Martha, m. John BUXTON*, Jan. 25, 1731/2, by Joshua Knapp, J. P. *(BAXTER)	ER	204
Mary, [d. Beniamin], b. Apr. 22, 1727	1	51
Mary, d. [Beniamin], b. Apr. 22, 1727	ER	171
Mary Amanda, of Greenwich, m. Jerem[i]ah PALMER, of Bedford, N. Y., Aug. 25, 1840, by D. B. Butts	1	206
Mary R., m. Asa N. BRUSH, Feb. 28, 1831, by Joel Mann	1	185
Nathaniel, twin with Thomas, s. Joseph, b. Feb. 7, 1719/20	ER	136
Nathaniel, s. Beniamin, b. May 5, 1722	1	51
Nathaniel, s. Beniamin, b. May 5, 1722	ER	171
Nathaniell, s. Solomon, b. Feb. 1, 1731/2	1	57
Nathaniell, s. Solomon, b. Feb. 1, 1731/2	ER	201
Nathaniell, s. Beniamin, b. Mar. 5, 1735	1	51
Nathaniel, s. Beniamin, b. Mar. 6, 1735	ER	171
Nathaniell, s. Beniamin, b. Mar. 6, 1735	1	61
Nathaniell, s. Beniamin, b. Mar. [ ], 1735	ER	215
Phebe, [d. Thomas & Hannah], b. June 29, 1738	1	98
Phebe, [d. Thomas & Hannah], b. June 29, 1738	ER	201
Phebe, m. [Joseph]* LYON, Jr., Feb. 24, 1758 *(Supplied from Mead's History)	1	100
Polly Ann, m. Conklin HUSTED, b. of Greenwich, Apr. 28, 1834, by Rev. Platt Buffett, of Stanwich	1	192
Rachall, d. Joseph, b. Oct. [ ], bp. [ ] 4, [ ]	LR1	457
Rachall, d. [Joseph], b. Oct. 11, 1715	ER	136
Reachell, m. David KNAP[P], Nov. 7, 1735, by Rev. Abraham Todd	ER	215
Rachal E., m. David B. MEAD, Dec. 16, 1838, by Noah Coe	1	203

	Vol.	Page
CLOSE, CLOES, CLOOS, CLOOSE, (cont.)		
Rebeckah, d. Joseph, b. May 21, 1693	LR1	457
Rebecca, d. Joseph, b. May 21, 1723	ER	137
Rebeckah*, m. David **KNAP[P]**, Nov. 7, 1735, by Rev. Abraham Todd *(Rachel?)	1	65
Rebecca Rosina, [d. Samuel & Eliza], b. June 14, 1821; m. Capt. Thomas **MAYO**, Aug. 24, 1858	1	118
Reuben, s. Benjamin, b. Feb. 9, 1717/18	1	51
R[e]uben, s. Beniamin, b. Feb. 9, 1717/18	ER	171
Ruth, d. [Thomas & Hannah], b. Aug. 2, 1735	1	98
Ruth, [d. Thomas & Hannah], b. Aug. 2, 1735	ER	201
Ruth, d. Thomas, m. Timothy **KNAPP**, Sept. 14, 1751	1	99
Ruth, d. Thomas, m. Timothy **KNAPP**, Sept. 14, 1751	ER	238
Sam[ue]ll, s. Beniamin, b. July 31, 1724	1	51
Samuel, s. Beniamin, b. July 31, 1724	ER	171
Samuel, s. Henry **MEAD**, b. Feb. 10, 1783; m. Eliza **HOBBIE**, Oct. 24, 1811	1	118
Samuel O., m. Sarah J. **REYNOLDS**, b. of Greenwich, May 18, [probably 1842], by Rev. D. W. Butts	1	209
	LR1	457
Sarah, d. Joseph, b. Oct. 29, 1689* *(1712?)	ER	136
Sarah, d. Joseph, b. Oct. 29, 1712	1	98
Sarah, [d. Thomas & Hannah], b. Mar. 13, 1733	ER	201
Sarah, d. [Thomas & Hannah], b. Mar. 13, 1733	1	67
Sarah, m. David **MEAD**, May 21, 1734	ER	213
Searah, m. David **MEAD**, May 21, 1734	1	57
Sarah, d. Solomon, b. Feb. 12, 1738/9	ER	201
Sarah, d. Solomon, b. Feb. 12, 1738/9		
Sarah, d. Thomas, m. Jesse **PARSONS**, Oct. 25, 1755, by Rev. Mr. Feeks	1	94
Shadrach J., m. Hannah E. **REYNOLDS**, Apr. 6, 1847, by Chauncey Wilcox	1	217
	LR1	457
Solloman, s. Joseph, b. June 23, 1686* *(1706?)	ER	136
Sollomon, s. Joseph, b. June 23, 1706	1	57
Solomon, s. Solomon, b. May 22, 1730	ER	201
Solomon, s. Solomon, b. May 22, 1730		
Thomas, twin with Nathaniel, s. Joseph, b. Feb. 7, 1719/20	ER	136
	1	98
Thomas, m. Hannah **LYON**, May 6, 1729	ER	201
Thomas, m. Hannah **LYON**, May 6, 1729	1	98
Thomas, [s. Thomas & Hannah], b. Apr. 1, 1740	ER	201
Thomas, [s. Thomas & Hannah], b. Apr. 1, 1740	1	98
Thomas, d. Nov. last day, 1764, in the 59th y. of his age	ER	201
Thomas, d. Nov. 1, 1764, in the 59th y. of his age		
Thomas, m. Hannah **LYON**, d. Joseph, of White Plains, Westchester Co., Sept. 30, 1765, by Rev. Mr. Sackett, of Crampond	1	118
Tomcens*, s. Solomon, b. Mar. 27, 1744 *(Tompkins)	1	57

	Vol.	Page
CLOSE, CLOES, CLOOS, CLOOSE, (cont.)		
Tomcans, s. Solomon, b. Mar. 27, 1744	ER	201
COE, Edward, s. Jonathan [& Esther], b. Aug. 25, 1758	1	134
Edward, s. Jonathan [& Esther], b. Aug. 25, 1758	ER	238
Elizabeth E., of Greenwich, m. Chaunc[e]y GOODRICH, of New York, Aug. 22, 1843, by N. Coe	1	211
John, s. Jonathan [& Esther], b. Mar. 6, 1752	1	134
John, s. Jonathan [& Esther], b. Mar. 6, 1752	ER	238
Jonathan, m. Esther **GREEN**, d. Reuben, May 26, 1751	1	134
Jonathan, m. Esther **GREEN**, d. Reuben, May 26, 1751	ER	238
Mary, d. Jonathan [& Esther], b. July 6, 1756	1	134
Mary, d. Jonathan [& Esther], b. July 6, 1756	ER	238
Reuben, s. Jonthan [& Esther], b. July 23, 1754	1	134
Reuben, s. Jonathan [& Esther], b. July 23, 1754	ER	238
COIT, John L. C., of Stamford, m. Rebecca A. **BRUSH**, of Greenwich, Jan. 3, 1843, by D. B. Butts	1	211
COLES, Jordan, of Brooklyn, N. Y., m. Fanny **BUSH**, of Greenwich, [Dec.] 11, [1827], by Rev. Ambrose S. Todd, of Stamford	1	177
COLLINS, Joanna, m. John E. **KNAPP**, [Nov.] 17, [1835], by J. Mann	1	196
COMINGS, George W., m. Harriet **MILES**, Apr. 5, 1835, by Chauncey Wilcox	1	195
CONKLING, Jacob, s. [ ], b. Nov. 14, 1753, in Bedford New Purchase	1	74
Jacob, s. Jacob, b. Nov. 14, 1753, in Bedford New Purchase, in the Province of New York	ER	242
Neville, Jr., m. Joshua **SMITH**, May 22, 1766, by Rev. Mr. Todd	1	118
Silvanus, [s.], b. July 11, 1761	1	74
Sylvanus, [s. Jacob], b. July 11, 1761	ER	242
-----, s. [ ], b. Nov. 14, 1753, in Bedford New Purchase, in Province of New York	1	70
COOKE, Elizabeth, of New York, m. Elias B. **STEVENS**, of Danbury, Feb. 15, 1843, by Chauncey Wilcox	1	211
CORNALL, Samuel Douglass, s. James G., b. Dec. 2, 1839	1	207
COX, Henry, m. Margaret **SWAN**, Dec. 13, 1835, by J. Mann	1	197
CRAFT, William H., m. Ann Eliza **STRONG**, b. of Greenwich, Dec. 20, 1841, by Rev. Charles F. Pelton	1	208
CROMWELL, Phebe, m. David R. **FIELD**, Oct. 6, 1830, by E. S. Raymond	1	184
CULLIS, [see also **BULLIS**], Charles, s. John [& Mary], b. Nov. 2, 1723	LR1	445
John*, m. Mary **GORMAN**, Mar. 8, 1720/1 *(Probably "John BULLIS")	LR1	445
John, s. [John & Mary], b. July 15, 1722	LR1	445
CURKUN*, John, m. Rachell **KNAPP**, Nov. 21, 1731, by Joshua		

	Vol.	Page
CURKUN*, (cont.)		
Knapp, J. P. ***(CURTAIN?)**		
John, m. Rachell **KNAPP**, [ ], by Joshua Knapp, J. P.	1	62
CURRY, Benjamin, [s. William & Abigail], b. July 21, 1753	ER	203
Benjamin, [s. William & Abigail], b. July 21, 1753	1	69
Elizabeth, [d. William & Abigail], b. Dec. 1, 1743	ER	226
Elizabeth, [d. William & Abigail], b. Dec. 1, 1743	1	69
Joseph, [s. William & Abigail], b. Jan. 5, 1750/1	ER	226
Joseph, [s. William & Abigail], b. Jan. 5, 1750/1	1	69
William, [s. William & Abigail], b. June 24, 1747	ER	226
William, [s. William & Abigail], b. June 24, 1747	1	69
CURTAIN, [see under **CURKUN**]	ER	226
CURTIS, CURTISE, Jerusha, m. Nathaniel **PECK**, Jr., Oct. 9, 1746		
Jerusha, m. Nathaniel **PECK**, Jr., Oct. 9, 1746	1	81-2
Sarah, m. Nathaniel **LOCKWOOD**, Oct. 8, [ ], by Rev. Abraham Todd	ER	230
Sarah, m. Nathaniel **LOCKWOOD**, Oct. 8, [ ], by Rev. Abraham Todd	CP	107
Solomon, Jr., of Stratford, m. Frances Sarah **MERRETT**, of Greenwich, Sept. 26, [1821], by Isaac Lewis	ER	236
DANFORD, Hannah, d. Leteshe **CAREY**, alias **MARSHALL**, b. May 24, 1779	1	165
DARBY, Hannah, [d. John], b. Nov. 8, 1717	1	138
Hannah, d. John, b. Nov. 23, 1717	LR1	3
John, s. John, b. Sept. 8, 1714	ER	174
John, s. John, b. Aug. 8, [ ], bp. Mar. 3, 1715	ER	174
Samuel, s. [John], b. Mar. 9, 1715/16	LR1	3
DARROW, Azariah, [s. Isaac & Hannah], b. Nov. 13, 1768	ER	174
Isaac, m. Hannah **MEAD**, d. Peter, Dec. 20, 1764, by Rev. Abrahm Todd	1	120
Isaac, [s. Isaac & Hannah], b. Sept. 20, 1765; d. Dec. 7, 1765	1	120
Susanna, [d. Isaac & Hannah], b. Oct. 8, 1766	1	120
DAVENPORT, Joseph, m. Elizabeth **JACKSON**, b. of Greenwich, (colored), Sept. 3, 1839, by Noah Coe	1	120
DAVIS, Abraham Benson, [s. Silas & Maria], b. Sept. 15, 1803	1	204
Ann Maria, [d. Silas & Maria], b. May 7, 1806	1	75
Arthur, s. Stephen, Jr. [& Bethiah], b. May 23, 1793	1	75
Clarasa, m. Bezallelle **BROWN**, b. of Greenwich, May 4, 1824, by Rev. Henry Hoit, of Stamford	1	155
Clarisa, m. Barabelle **BROWN**, b. of Greenwich, May 4, 1824, by Rev. Henry Wait	1	133
Edward DeNoyelles, [s. Silas & Maria], b. Aug. 12, 1815	1	171
Elisha, [s. Silas & Maria], b. Dec. 28, 1810	1	75
Elisha, of New York City, m. Alice M. **RITCH**, of	1	75

	Vol.	Page
DAVIS, (cont.)		
Greenwich, May 17, 1841, by B. M. Yarrington	1	207
Emeline J., [d. Silas & Maria], b. July 30, 1808	1	75
Henry, [s. Silas & Maria], b. Jan. 8, 1797	1	75
Henry, m. Abigaill Jane LYON, Feb. 28, 1819, by Rev. Drake Wilson. Witnesses: Seth Lyon, Fitch Lyon, Elias Lyon	1	205
Josiah, s. Stephen, Jr. [& Bethiah], b. Feb. 23, 1795	1	155
Laura, d. Stephen, Jr. [& Bethia], b. Feb. 9, 1789	1	155
Lockwood C., m. Rebecca FERRIS, Oct. 12, 1834, by Darius Mead	1	194
Lucretia, m. Reuben HOLMES, Apr. 28, 1799	1	112
Lucy, m. Jabez MEAD, Jr., Jan. 4, 18[ ], by Isaac David, D. D.	1	160
Sally, d. Stephen, Jr. [& Bethiah], b. Feb. 5, 1797	1	155
Sarah Jane, m. Albert KNAPP, b. of Greenwich, Feb. 24, 1834, by Rev. Robert Dauis	1	192
Silas, b. Oct. 21, 1773, in Greenwich; m. Maria BRONSON, of Haverstraw, N. Y., Feb. 24, 1794, at Toppin, N. Y.	1	75
Silas, Jr., [s. Silas & Maria], b. Apr. 4, 1813	1	75
Stephen, Jr., m. Bethiah MEAD, d. Nehemiah, Jan. 24, 1788, by Rev. Isaac Lewis	1	155
Thomas Jefferson, [s. Silas & Maria], b. May 7, 1801	1	75
Walter, [s. Silas & Maria], b. Dec. 20, 1794	1	75
William, s. Stephen, Jr. [& Bethia], b. Dec. 24, 1790	1	155
William, m. Ruth M. FLETCHER, b. of Greenwich, May 23, 1824, by Isaac Lewis	1	171
William B., [s. Silas & Maria], b. Mar. 25, 1799	1	75
DAY, Elias, m. Amey FINCH, d. Nathaniel, May 30, 1772, by Rev. Abraham Todd	1	138
Elizabeth, d. Elias [& Amey], b. Dec. 28, 1772	1	138
P. C., of Iowa Territory, m. Zetta MEAD, of Greenwich, July 9, [1839], by Noah Coe	1	204
DAYTON, DATON, Amy, m. Benoni RUNDLE, b. of Greenwich, Dec. 28, 1831, by Rev. Platt Buffett, of Stanwich	1	187
Anna A., m. Reuben D. LOCKWOOD, b. of Greenwich, July 3, 1842, by Rev. D. B. Butts, of Stanwich	1	209
David, m. Elizabeth BRUSH, b. of Stanwich, Mar. 6, 1827, by Rev. Platt Buffett	1	174
Jonathan, m. Mary BUTTIS, Aug. 13, 1718	LR1	456
Joseph, s. Jonathan [& Mary], b. May 11, 1719	LR1	456
Sarah, of Stanwick, m. William WOOD, of New York, Dec. 30, 1821, by Platt Buffett	1	167
DEAN, Isaac, of North Stamford, m. Charlotte LOCKWOOD, of Vermont, but residing in Stanwich, Nov. 23,		

	Vol.	Page

DEAN, (cont.)
    1825, by Platt Buffett   1   172
DEMILL, William John, s. [Peter], b. Sept. 17, 1800   1   141
DENTON, [see also DUNTON], Aaron, m. Elizabeth AVERY, d.
    Peter, Nov. 5, 1788, by Amos Mead   1   142
    Evert, s. Aaron [& Elizabeth], b. Feb. 14, 1789   1   142
    Humphrey, Jr., m. Ruth Mariah PECK, b. of Greenwich,
        Nov. 2, 1845, by Rev. Ebenezer Mead   1   214
    Peter, s. Solomon, b. Dec. 24, 1759   1   143
DOWNS, Seth P., m. Amey SCOFIELD, Sept. 21, 1835, by E. S.
    Raymond   1   196
DUNTON, [see also DENTON], Julia, m. Lewis SCOTT, Nov. 24,
    1837, by James Jarman   1   199
DURANT, Henry, Rev. of Acton, Mass., m. Mary E. BUFFET, of
    Greenwich, Dec. 10, 1833, by Platt Buffett   1   191
EDGELL, [see under EDGITT]
EDGITT, EDGELL, Addam*, [s. William & Abigail], b. June 8,
    1756   *(Arnold Copy has "Addam
    EDGELL")   1   78
    Adam*, [s. William & Abigail], b. [ ] *(Arnold
        copy has "Adam EDGELL")   1   78
    Elizabeth*, [d. William & Abigail], b. Nov. 26, 1754
        *(Arnold copy has "Elizabeth EDGELL")   1   78
    Mary*, [d. William & Abigal], b. Apr. 25, 1750
        *(Arnold copy had "Mary EDGELL")   1   78
    Mattathias*, [s. William & Abigail], b. Jan. 29, 1748, in
        Penn. *(Arnold copy has Mattathias
        EDGELL")   1   78
    Peter*, [s. William & Abigal], b. Feb. 15, 1758
        *(Arnold copy has "Peter EDGELL")   1   78
    William*, [s. William & Abigail], b. July 28, 1751
        *(Arnold copy has "William EDGELL")   1   78
    William*, m. Abigail HOBBY, d. John, Mar. 16, 1758
        *(Arnold copy has "William EDGELL")   1   77
EDWARDS, William, m. Elizabeth HOLLY, [Jan.] 1, [1835], by J.
    Mann   1   195
ELDREDGE, Lewis, of New York, m. Susan MEAD, of
    Greenwich, Apr. 29, [1822], by Isaac Lewis   1   168
ENNIS, Alexander, of Rye, m. Allin JOURDAN, of Stanwick, Jan.
    30, 1821, by Platt Buffet   1   165
FAIRCHILD, James H., m. Ann MINER, Sept. 7, 1822, by Isaac
    Lewis   1   168
[FANCHER], FINCHER, David, [twin with Hannah, s. Joseph], b.
    Mar. 4, 1742/3   ER   218
    Elizabeth, [d. Joseph], b. Dec. 21, 1746   ER   218
    Ezekiel, [s. Joseph], b. May 24, 1753   ER   218
    Hannah, [twin with David, d. Joseph], b. Mar. 4, 1742/3   ER   218
    Jabez, [s. Joseph], b. Feb. 23, 1748/9   ER   218

	Vol.	Page
[FANCHER], FINCHER, (cont.)		
Jeremiah, [s. Joseph], b. Nov. 19, 1744	ER	218
Jesse, [s. Joseph], b. Jan. 14, 1739/40	ER	218
Joseph, [s. Joseph], b. Feb. 22, 1737/8	ER	218
William, [s. Joseph], b. Jan. 30, 1750/1	ER	218
FARNAM, David H., of New Haven, m. Cornelia MEAD, of Chester, Oct. 20, 1845, by Ebenezer Mead	1	214
FELMETTE*, James, m. Eliza HUSTED, Oct. 20, 1824, by Isaac Lewis *(FELMEN?)	1	171
Jeffery, m. Dinah BROWN, Sept. 20, 1830, by Elijah Hebard	1	186
FERRILL, FERRELL, Mindwell, m. Joseph RUNDALL, Apr. 15, 1729, by Justice Mead, J. P.	1	66
Mindwell, m. Joseph RUNDALL, Apr. 15, 1729, by Justice Mead, J. P.	ER	199
FERRIS, FERIS, Abigail, wid., m. Josiah FERRIS, July 7, 1753, by Nathaniel Peck, J. P.	1	86
Abigail, wid., m. Josiah FERRIS, July 7, 1753, by Nathaniel Peck, J. P.	ER	241
Abigail, w. Josiah, d. Dec. 16, 1760	1	86
Abigail, w. Josiah, d. Dec. 16, 1760	ER	241
Abigail, d. Oliver [& Abigail], b. Feb. 24, 1785	1	140
Angelina Adelia, [d. Nathaniel & Jerusha], b. Feb. 10, 1805	1	147
Ann, m. William H. LOCKWOOD, b. of Greenwich, July 8, 1838, by Thomas Payne	1	201
Ann, m. Jonathan JESSUP, b. of Greenwich, Dec. 23, 1838, by Rev. Edw[ar]d Oldrin, of Stamford	1	203
Beniamin, m. Rodi FERRIS, Nov. 11, 1731, by Joshua Knapp, J. P.	1	62
Beniamin, m. Rodi FERRIS, Nov. 11, 1731, by Joshua Knapp, J. P.	ER	203
Benson, s. Oliver [& Abigail], b. Mar. 21, 1794	1	140
Caroline, m. Joseph O. KEELER, Oct. 15, 1834, by C. Wilcox	1	194
Charles, m. Margaret Ritch LOCKWOOD, b. of Greenwich, Oct. 13, 1839, by Noah Coe	1	204
Claridia*, d. Peetar [& Mary], b. Aug. 27, 1729 *(Claudia?)	ER	183
Claudia, s. [Peetar & Mary], b. Aug. 27, 1729	1	53
David, [twin with Hannah, s. Joseph], b. Mar. 4, 1742/3	1	69
Debra, d. John [& Mariah], b. Apr. 14, 1730	1	59
Debra, d. John [& Seariah], b. Apr. 14, 1730	ER	190
Edwin Washington, s. [Nathaniel & Jerusha], b. July 5, 1811	1	147
Elizabeth, d. James, Jr., b. Dec. 1, 1716	1	50
Elizabeth, d. James, Jr., b. Dec. 1, 1716	ER	177
Elizabeth, [d. Joseph], b. Dec. 27, 1746	1	69

FERRIS, FERIS, (cont.)

	Vol.	Page
Elizabeth, d. Oliver [& Abigail], b. Feb. 1, 1781	1	140
Ezekiel, [s. Joseph], b. May 24, 1753	1	69
Grace, m. Henry BELCHER, b. of Greenwich, Aug. 17, 1834, by Rev. Edwin Hall, of Norwalk	1	193
Hannah, d. [James, Sr.], b. Aug. 17, 1710	ER	121
Hannah, d. [James, Sr.], b. Aug. [ ], 1710	LR1	454
Han[n]ah, m. Joseph MARSHALL, Jr., July 24, 1731, by Joshua Knapp, J. P.	1	61
Hannah, m. Joseph MARSHALL, Jr., July 24, 1731, by Joshua Knapp, J. P.	ER	203
Hannah, [twin with David, d. Joseph], b. Mar. 4, 1742/3	1	69
Hannah, d. James, m. John Wood PALMER, June 6, 1776, by Rev. Mr. Seward	1	133
Henry, m. Eliza MEAD, [Apr.] 4, [1833], by J. Mann	1	191
Isaiah, s. John [& Mariah], b. May 7, 1728	1	59
Jabez, [s. Joseph], b. Feb. 23, 1748/9	1	69
James, s. James, Sr., b. Dec. 18, 1699	ER	121
James, s. James, Sr., b. Dec. 18, 1699	LR1	454
James, s. James, Jr., b. Mar. 22, 1720	1	50
James, s. James, Jr., b. Mar. 22, 1720	ER	177
James, m. Abigail Jane SHERWOOD, May 13, 1821, by Rev. Nathaniel Finch, Jr.	1	165
James W., m. Deborah P. QUINTARD, b. of Greenwich, Jan. 5, 1846, by Rev. S. B. S. Bissell	1	214
Jeremiah, [s. Joseph], b. Nov. 19, 1744	1	69
Jerusha, [w. Nathaniell], b. May 14, 1770; d. Sept. 12, 1815	1	147
John, m. Abigail HOIGHT, of Norwalk, Feb. 13, 1695, by Capt. Umstead, Com	ER	98
John, m. Abigaill HOIGHT, of Norwalk, Dec. 13, 1695, by Capt. Umstead	LR1	447
John, Jr., m. Mariah* MEAD, Feb. 27, 1722/3, by Rev. Mr. Sacet *("Sarah" in Mead's Hist.)	1	59
John, Jr., m. Seariah* MEAD, Feb. 27, 1722/3, by Rev. Mr. Sacitt *(Sarah)	ER	190
John, s. John, Jr. [& Mariah], b. Nov. 7, 1723	1	59
John, s. John [& Seariah], b. Nov. 7, 1723	ER	190
Joseph, [s. Joseph], b. Feb. 22, 1737/8	1	69
Joseph, [s. Joseph], b. Jan. 14, 1740/1	1	69
Josiah, s. John [& Mariah], b. July 12, 1726	1	59
Josiah, s. John [& Seariah], b. July 12, 1726	ER	190
Josiah, m. wid. Abigail FERRIS, July 7, 1753, by Nathaniel Peck, J. P.	1	86
Josiah, m. wid, Abigail FERRIS, July 7, 1753, by Nathaniel Peck, J. P.	ER	241
Josiah, m. Mary PECK, d. Eliphalet, Nov. 3, 1762	1	86
Josiah, m. Mary PECK, d. Eliphalet, Nov. 3, 1762	ER	241

	Vol.	Page
FERRIS, FERIS, (cont.)		
Julia A. L., m. Petrus V. T. **JESSUP**, b. of Greenwich, Jan. 20, 1839, by Rev. Edw[ar]d Oldrin	1	202
Julia Ann, m. Jefferson **JANE**, b. of Stanwich, Mar. 28, 1836, by Platt Buffett	1	197
Letta, d. Oliver [& Abigail], b. Apr. 16, 1792	1	140
Levina, m. Walter **LOCKWOOD**, Dec. 4, 1837, by James Jarman	1	199
Lockwood, m. Samanthia **MEAD**, b. of Greenwich, Nov. 29, 1843, by N. Coe	1	212
Lucy, of Greenwich, m. James **SPERREAR**, of New Milford, Dec. 1, 1822, by Rev. Daniel Peck	1	168
Martha, m. Benjamin **MEAD**, Nov. 18, 1728, by Rev. Mr. Munson	1	59
Martha, m. Beniamin **MEAD**, Nov. 18, 1728, by Rev. Mr. Munson	ER	198
Mary, d. [James, Sr.], b. Oct. [ ], 1708	LR1	454
Meary, d. Peetar [& Mary], b. May 8, 1727	ER	183
Mary, d. Oliver [& Abigail], b. Aug. 24, 1802	1	140
Mary, m. Alfred **BISHOP**, b. of Greenwich, Oct. 11, 1821, by Rev. Daniel Smith, of Stamford	1	166
Mary, m. Warren **PALMER**, b. of Greenwich, Nov. 13, 1823, by W[illia]m Knapp, J. P.	1	170
Mary Ann, m. Rufus **LOUNSBURY**, Feb. 22, 1832, by E. S. Raymond	1	187
Mary P., m. Stephen T. **JACKSON**, Aug. 29, 1822, by Rev. Sam[ue]l D. Ferguson. Witnesses: William P. Reynolds, Shadrack Finch	1	168
Mearcey, [d. Peetar & Mary], b. May 8, 1727	1	53
Nathaniel, s. James, Sr., b. Mar. 31, 1702	LR1	454
Nathaniel, s. James, Sr., b. Mar. 31, 1702	ER	121
Nathaniel, b. Jan. 24, 1774; m. Jerusha **GRAHAM**, Feb. 26, 1804	1	147
Nathaniel, m. Amey **BRIGGS**, b. of Stanwich, May 30, 1830, by Platt Buffett, of Stanwich	1	183
Nathaniel Peck, s. [Nathaniel & Jerusha], b. Mar. 12, 1807	1	147
Nelson, [s. Nathaniel & Jerusha], b. Apr. 1, 1809	1	147
Oliver, [s. Josiah & Abigail], b. Nov. 22, 1753	1	86
Oliver, [s. Josiah & Abigail], b. Nov. 22, 1753	ER	241
Oliver, of Greenwich, m. Abigail **LOCKWOOD**, d. Enos, Feb. 10, 1779, by Rev. Mr. Burrit	1	140
Peter, s. Joseph, d. Jan. 23, 1690, in the 31st y. of his age	ER	74
Peter, s. Joseph, d. June 23, 1690, in the 31st y. of his age	LR1	448
Peetar, m. Mary **TUCKER**, Aug. 6, 1719	1	53
Peetare, m. Mary **TUCKER**, Aug. 6, 1719	ER	183
Peetar, s. Peetar [& Mary], b. Apr. 21, 1726	1	53

FERRIS, FERIS, (cont.)

	Vol.	Page
Peetar, s. Peetar [& Mary], b. Apr. 21, 1726	ER	183
Rebecca, m. Lockwood C. **DAVIS**, Oct. 12, 1834, by Darius Mead	1	194
Rodi, m. Benjamin **FERRIS**, Nov. 11, 1731, by Joshua Knapp, J. P.	1	62
Rodi, m. Beniamin **FERRIS**, Nov. 11, 1731, by Joshua Knapp, J. P.	ER	203
Ruth, m. Samuell **PECK**, Nov. 27, 1686, by Jonathan Bell, Com.	LR1	454
Ruth, m. Samuel **PECK**, Nov. 27, 1686, by Jonathan Bell, Com	ER	55
Ruth, m. Joseph **RENOLLS**, Mar. 5, 1721/2, by Samuell Peck, J. P.	1	55
Ruth, m. Joseph **RENOLLS**, Mar. 5, 1721/2, by Samuell Peck, J. P.	ER	188
Samuel, s. James, Sr., b. Sept. 21, 1706	ER	121
Samuel, s. James, Sr., b. Sept. 21, 1706	LR1	454
Samuell, s. Peetar, [& Mary], b. Dec. 10, 1720	1	53
Samuell, s. Peetar [& Mary], b. Dec. 10, 1720	ER	183
Samuel, of Stanwich, m. Phebe **HOPSON**, member of the Church of East Greenwich, Jan. 15, 1822, by Platt Buffett	1	167
Samuel, m. Frances Louisa **LOCKWOOD**, b. of Greenwich, Jan. 12, 1847, by Rev. B. M. Yarrington	1	216
Searah, d. John [& Seariah], b. May 7, 1728	ER	190
Sarah, d. James, m. [ ], May 24, 1751, by Rev. Abraham Todd	1	89-90
Sarah, d. James, m. James **MEAD**, May 24, 1751, by Rev. Abraham Todd	ER	238
Sarah, [d. Josiah & Abigail], b. Mar. 3, 1756; d. Dec. 29, 1759	1	86
Sarah, [d. Josiah & Abigail], b. Mar. 3, 1756	ER	241
Sarah, [d. Josiah & Abigail], d. Dec. 29, 1759	ER	241
Sarah, [d. Josiah & Mary], b. July 10, 1764	1	86
Sarah, [d. Josiah & Mary], b. July 10, 1764	ER	241
Sarah, d. Oliver [& Abigail], b. July 8, 1779	1	140
Sarah, m. Martin **SHERWOOD**, b. of Greenwich, Nov. 2, 1823, by John Ellis	1	171
Susan, m. Seth P. **QUINTARD**, b. of Greenwich, Dec. 23, 1822, by Rev. John Noyes	1	168
Timothie, s. Peetar [& Mary], b. Nov. 3, 1722	1	53
Timothy, s. Peetar [& Mary], b. Nov. 3, 1722	ER	183
William, [s. Joseph], b. Jan. 30, 1750/1	1	69
William A., of New Orleans, La., m. Susan Knapp **TITUS**, of Greenwich, Oct. 3, 1836, by Rev. Joseph H. Nichols	1	199

GREENWICH VITAL RECORDS

	Vol.	Page
FERRIS, FERIS, (cont)		
William E., m. Julia A. ROBBINS, b. of Greenwich, Mar. 18, 1845, by Noah Coe	1	213
William Edgar, s. [Nathaniel & Jerusha], b. Mar. 12, 1814	1	147
FIELD, David R., m. Phebe CROMWELL, Oct. 6, 1830, by E. S. Raymond	1	184
FINCH, Abigail, d. Joseph, b. Mar. 9, 1721/2	1	46
Abigail, d. Joseph, b. Mar. 9, 1721/2	ER	144
Amos, m. Alice SMITH, b. of Stanwich, Nov. 29, 1829, by Rev. Platt Buffett, of Stanwich	1	182
Emey*, d. [Nathaniel & Hannah], b. Sept. 17, 1736 *(Amey)	1	54
Amey, d. Nathaniel, m. Elias DAY, May 30, 1772, by Rev. Abraham Todd	1	138
Anna, d. [Benjamin & Elizabeth], b. May 19, 1717/18	ER	179
Anna, d. Benjamin & Elizabeth, b. Mar. 19, 1717/18	LR1	450
Benjamin, m. Elizabeth PALMER, Apr. 16, 1717	LR1	450
Benjamin, m. Elizabeth PALMER, Apr. 18, 1717	ER	179
Beniamin, m. Susana PEAT, Dec. 23, 1727, by Samuel Peck, J. P.	1	54
Beniamin, m. Susana PEAT, Dec. 23, 1727, by Sam[ue]ll Peck, J. P.	ER	196
Caleb, s. Nathaniel & Hannah, b. Sept. 7, 1744	1	54
David, s. Nath[anie]l [& Anne], b. July 3, 1787	1	139
David Isaac, [s. Gilbert P. & Martha], b. June 2, 1841	1	85
Ebenezer, s. Joseph, b. Dec. 8, 1714	1	46
Ebenezer, s. Joseph, b. Dec. 8, 1714	ER	144
Ebenezer, b. Dec. 8, 1714	LR1	457
Eliza, b. Apr. 6, 1720	LR1	457
Eliza, d. William [& Rachel], b. Dec. 14, 1798	1	161
Elizabeth, d. Joseph, b. Feb. 27, 1703/4	1	46
Elizabeth, d. Joseph, b. Feb. 27, 1703/4	ER	144
Elizabeth, m. Ebenezer KNAP[P], Jan. 7, 1724, by Rev. Mr. Sackett	1	50
Elizabeth, m. Ebenezer KNAP[P], Jan. 7, 1724, by Rev. Mr. Sacet	ER	191
Ezekiel, s. Joseph, b. June 11, 1712	1	46
Ezekiel, s. Joseph, b. June 11, 1712	ER	144
Fanny, d. William [& Rachel], b. June 28, 1790	1	161
Frances Cecelia, [d. Gilbert P. & Martha], b. Dec. 17, 1829	1	85
Gilbert P., b. June 30, 1799; m. 2nd w. Martha* PECK, [ ], *(Allathea?)	1	85
Gilbert P., m. Allathea PECK, Apr. 8, 1827, by David Peck	1	176
Gilbert P., [s. Gilbert P. & Martha], b. Oct. 27, 1831	1	85
Gilbert Peck, m. Frances Cecelia MEAD, Dec. 22, 1822,		

BARBOUR COLLECTION

	Vol.	Page
FINCH, (cont.)		
by Isaac Lewis	1	168
Griffen, s. William [& Rachel], b. Oct. 15, 1796	1	161
Hannah, d. Joseph, b. Mar. 10, 1716/17	1	46
Hannah, d. Joseph, b. Mar. 10, 1716/17	ER	144
Hannah, d. Nathaniel [& Hannah], b. Oct. 11, 1733	1	54
Hannah, d. Nath[anie]l [& Anne], b. Dec. 22, 1778	1	139
Hannah M., m. Arba SMITH, b. of Greenwich, Dec. 24, 1833, by Rev. Platt Buffett, of Stanwich	1	191
Hannah Rundall, [d. Gilbert P. & Martha], b. Dec. 17, 1823	1	85
Henry, s. William [& Rachel], b. Apr. 30, 1793	1	161
Hester Ann, [d. Gilbert P. & Martha], b. Jan. 31, 1828	1	85
Isaac, b. Mar. 10, 1716	LR1	457
Jabez, s. Joseph, b. Feb. 8, 1718/19	1	46
Jabez, s. Joseph, b. Feb. 8, 1718/19	ER	144
Jacob, s. Isack, b. Feb. 24, 1706/7	ER	158
Jacob, s. Isaac, b. Feb. 24, 1706/7	LR1	447
James, s. Timothy, b. Feb. 4, 1782	1	115
James, [s. Gilbert P. & Martha], b. Apr. 22, 1843	1	85
Jared, s. Timothy, b. Nov. 24, 1785	1	115
Job., b. Mar. 8, 1718	LR1	457
Joel, s. Timothy, b. Feb. 1, 1778; d. Feb. 8, 1778	1	115
Joel, s. Timothy, b. May 27, 1780	1	115
Jonathan, [s. Timothy & Rebecca], b. Aug. 28, 1767	1	115
Jonathan, m. Mary BANK, b. of Greenwich, [Nov.] 17, [1839], by Rev. D. B. Booth, of Stanwich	1	205
Joseph, b. Sept. 16, 1707	LR1	457
Joseph, s. Joseph, b. Sept. 16, 1709	1	46
Joseph, s. Joseph, b. Sept. 16, 1709	ER	144
Joseph, [s. Timothy & Rebecca], b. Apr. 1, 1771	1	115
Julia E., of Greenwich, m. Jackson D. BROWN, of Somerstown, N. Y., Feb. 23, 1842, by Rev. D. B. Butts	1	207
Marth Peck, [d. Gilbert P. & Martha], b. Apr. 23, 1834	1	85
Mary, [d. Timothy & Rebecca], b. Jan. 16, 1772	1	115
Mary Elizabeth, [d. Gilbert P. & Martha], b. Sept. 16, 1845	1	85
Mary Reynolds, m. Silas WOOD, b. of Greenwich, Nov. 30, 1825, by Platt Buffett	1	172
Nathaniel, b. Oct. 5, 1706	LR1	457
Nathaniel, s. Joseph, b. Oct. 25, 1706	1	46
Nathaniel, s. Joseph, b. Oct. 25, 1706	ER	144
Nathaniel, m. Hannah KNAP[P], d. Timothy, Sept. 17, 1732	1	54
Nathaniel, s. [Nathaniel & Hannah], b. Oct. 22, 1738	1	54
Nathaniel, s. Timothy, b. Jan. 12, 1776	1	115
Nathaniel, m. Anne HIBBARD, d. Jonathan, Mar. 23,		

	Vol.	Page
FINCH, (cont.)		
1778, by Rev. Jonathan Murdock	1	139
Nathaniel, Jr., s. Nath[anie]l [& Anne], b. Aug. 2, 1780	1	139
Rachel, w. William, had s. Daniel TAYLOR, b. Oct. 13, 1774; f. Joshua TAYLOR, Jr.	1	161
Rachal, m. Thadeus LOCKWOOD, b. of Stanwich, Jan. 29, 1824, by Rev. Platt Buffett	1	170
Rebeccah, d. [Benjamin & Elizabeth], b. Aug. 28, 1720	LR1	450
Rebecca, d. [Benjamin & Elizabeh], b. Aug. 28, 1720	ER	179
Rebecca, [d. Timothy & Rebecca], b. Jan. 30, 1766	1	115
Rebecca Knapp, [d. Gilbert P. & Martha], b. May 16, 1838	1	85
Reuben, m. Deborah BRUSH, b. of Greenwich, Feb. 13, 1822, by Platt Buffet	1	167
Rhoda, [d. Timothy & Rebecca], b. Nov. 20, 1774	1	115
Ruth, w. Timothy, d. Sept. 18, 1761	1	96
Ruth, [d. Timothy & Rebecca], b. Feb. 18, 1769	1	115
Sabin, [s. Gilbert P. & Martha], b. Mar. 26, 1836	1	85
Sally, d. W[illia]m [& Rachel], b. Aug. 6, 1784	1	161
Sarah, b. June 11, 1712	LR1	457
Silas, [s. Gilbert P. & Martha], b. Oct. 4, 1839	1	85
Thomas Smith, [s. Gilbert P. & Martha], b. Nov. 5, 1825	1	85
Timothy, s. [Nathaniel & Hannah], b. Aug. 12, 1742	1	54
Timothy, m. Rebecca WARING, June 16, 1763	1	115
Timothy, [s. Timothy & Rebecca], b. Mar. 3, 1764	1	115
Titus, s. [Nathaniel & Hannah], b. Jan. 30, 1748	1	54
W[illia]m, Jr., s. William [& Rachel], b. Mar. 9, 1787	1	161
Zabud, s. Nath[anie]l [& Anne], b. July 19, 1782	1	139
-----, b. Feb. 27, 1704/5	LR1	457
FINCHER, [see under FANCHER]		
FINLEY, John H., of New York City, m. Sarah G. WILLSON, of Greenwich, Mar. 29, 1838, by E. S. Raymond	1	200
FISK, Jerusha, [twin with Rebecca, d. [ ], b. Aug. 24, 174[ ]	1	64
Jonathan, m. Abigall MEAD, Apr. 23, 1738, by Rev. Mr. Todd	1	59
Jonathan, m. Abigell MEAD, Apr. 23, 1738, by Rev. Mr. Todd	ER	
Jonathan, s. Jonathan [& Abigall], b. Aug. 13, 1739	1	219
Jonathan, s. Jonathan [& Abigell], b. Aug. 13, 1739	ER	59
Rebecca, [twin with Jerusha, d. [ ],b. Aug. 24, 174[ ]	1	219
FITCH, Amy, d. Taber [& Amy], b. Mar. 2, 1789	1	64
Anne, d. Taber [& Amy], b. Jan. 5, 1795	1	130
Elizabeth, d. Taber [& Amy], b. May 4, 1786	1	130
Jabez*, m. Amy KNAPP, d. Capt. Israel, May 22, 1780 *(Arnold copy had "Taber")	1	130
Lydia, d. Taber & Amy], b. July 21, 1791	1	130
Lydia, d. Taber [& Amy], d. Nov. 7, 1807	1	130
Sam[ue]ll Mills, s. [Taber & Amy], b. Feb. 4, 1783	1	130

	Vol.	Page
FITCH, (cont.)		
Sarah, d. Taber [& Amy], b. Apr. 29, 1784	1	130
Taber*, m. Amy KNAPP, d. Capt. Israel, May 22, 1780 *("Jabez" in Mead's Hist.)	1	130
Thomas Marshall, s. Taber [& Amy], b. Oct. 20, 1797	1	130
FLEELAND, Deborah Ann, wid., m. Sylvester STILES, b. of Stanwich, May 3, 1829, by Rev. Platt Buffett, of Stanwich	1	182
FLETCHER, Hannah, m. Daniel HOWARD, b. of Greenwich, Jan. 16, 1825, by Isaac Lewis	1	171
Israel Avery, s. William & Mary Elizabeth, b. June 16, 1824	1	146
Joseph Denton, [s. William & Mary Elizabeth], b. Jan. 7, 1826	1	146
Julia Catharine, [d. William & Mary Elizabeth], b. Feb. 7, 1828	1	146
Mandana, m. Elias Smith MEAD, b. of Greenwich, Feb. 18, 1824, by Isaac Lewis, Jr.	1	170
Ruth M., m. William DAVIS, b. of Greenwich, May 23, 1824, by Isaac Lewis	1	171
FLOOD, Phebe Ann, m. Michael B. LOCKWOOD, Nov. 30, 1843, by Rev. Chaunc[e]y Wilcox	1	212
Sarah, m. William PURDY, b. of Greenwich, Dec. 19, 1841, by Rev. C. Wilcox	1	208
FLORENCE, Catharine, m. Painpey BANKS, Mar. 24, 1842, by Rev. D. B. Butts	1	207
Rebecca, m. Drake MARSHALL, [May] 21, [1832], by J. Mann	1	190
Sarah, m. Zebulon TAYLOR, June 10, 1821, by Rev. Nathaniel Finch, Jr.	1	165
FOSTER, James H., m. Phebe Jane WATSON, Dec. 17, 1840, by Chauncey Wilcox	1	206
FOWLER, Phebe, m. James REYNOLDS, May 24, 1731	1	106
Phebe, m. James REYNOLDS, May 24, 1731	ER	202*
FRANCIS, Ann Maria, of New York, m. Joshua KNAPP, of Greenwich, [Feb.] 6, [1828], by Isaac Lewis	1	179
FREDAND, Reuben O., m. Deborah Ann BRIGGS, b. of Greenwich, Mar. 5, 1823, by Henry Hoit, Jr.	1	169
FROST, Stoddard J., of Norwalk, m. Mary HUBBARD, of Stanwich, May 16, [1826], by Platt Buffett	1	174
GARDINER, Mary, m. Jabez M. HOBBY, b. of Greenwich, June 29, 1834, by Samuel Close, J. P	1	193
GASSNER, Daniel D., of New York, m. Mary P. JESSUP, of Greenwich, July 16, 1835, by Rev. Daniel Smith, of Stamford	1	195
GERALDS, Merrett, m. Betsey SHERWOOD, b. of Greenwich, Mar. 7, 1842, by Rev. C. Wilcox, of New York	1	209

GREENWICH VITAL RECORDS

	Vol.	Page
GERMAN, [see under JARMAN]		
GININS, [see under JENNINGS]		
GOODRICH, Chauncey, of New York, m. Elizabeth E. COE, of Greenwich, Aug. 22, 1843, by N. Coe	1	211
GORMAN, Mary, m. John BULLIS, Mar. 8, 1720/1	ER	186
Mary, m. John CULLIS*, Mar. 8, 1720/1 *(BULLIS?)	LR1	445
GRAHAM, Jerusha, m. Nathaniel FERRIS, Feb. 26, 1804	1	147
GRANGER, Abigail, d. Daniel, b. Nov. 21, 1731	1	64
Abigall, d. Daniel, b. Nov. 21, 1731	ER	203
GREEN, Allen, m. Mary JOHNSON, [Nov.] 10, [1828], by Ebenezer S. Raymond	1	180
Allen, m. Rachal GREEN (colored), b. of Greenwich, Oct. 24, 1839, by Noah Coe	1	204
Benjamin, [s. Benjamin], b. Sept. 1, 1765	ER	234
Benjamin, m. Mary GREEN, Nov. 16, 1841, by E. S. Raymond	1	208
Caleeb, s. Caleb & Mary, b. Sept. 30, 1764	1	113
Daniel, [s. Benjamin], b. Dec. 26, 1752	ER	234
Elizabeth, [d. Benjamin], b. July 21, 1750	ER	234
Esther, d. Reuben, m. Jonathan COE, May 26, 1751	1	134
Esther, d. Reuben, m. Jonathan COE, May 26, 1751	ER	238
Lydia, [d. Benjamin], b. Jan. 4, 1755	ER	234
Mary, m. Benjamin GREEN, Nov. 16, 1841, by E. S. Raymond	1	208
Phebe, [d. Benjamin], b. Feb. 23, 1761	ER	234
Rachal, m. Allen GREEN, (colored), b. of Greenwich, Oct. 24, 1839, by Noah Coe	1	204
Reuben, m. Mary MERRITT, Sept. 19, 1731, by Joshua Knapp, J. P.	1	61
R[e]ubin, m. Mary MERRIT, Sept. 19, 1731, by Joshua Knapp, J. P.	ER	203
Sally, m. James WILSON, Feb. 21, 1828, by Ebenezer Raymond	1	179
William, [s. Benjamin], b. June 22, 1748	ER	234
GRIGGS, GREGG, GRIGG, Ann, made affidavit Jan. 26, 1760, that Mary JONES, (wid.), gave birth to son Frederick Harding JONES, b. Nov. 28, 1759, and she was at her house the summer before last with Mr. Hardin JONES, of N. C., whom she called husband	1	92
Elizabeth, wid. Capt. Henry, d. June 9, 1847, ae 80 y. 3 m. 23 d.	1	217
Henry, had negroes Abbe, d. Flora, b. Apr. 5, 1784, Pena, d. Flora, b. Dec. 22, 1788 & Charles, s. Flora, b. Mar. 13, 1793	1	145
John, s. Alexander, b. Oct. 22, 1790	1	169
GRISWOLD, Samuel S., D. D. of New York, m. Sarah SMITH, of Stanwich, Oct. 18, 1836, by Rev. Joseph H.		

	Vol.	Page
GRISWOLD, (cont.)		
Nichols	1	199
HAEM, G. Susanah, m. James **MEAD**, [ ] 25, 1719/20, by Rev.		
Richard Sackett	ER	185
HAIGHT, [see also **HOYT**], Gerrard, s. Sarah, b. Jan. 6, 1762	1	126
Lewis, of New York City, m. Mary **WILSON**, of		
Greenwich, Mar. 29, 1838, by E. S. Raymond	1	200
Sarah, had s. Gerrard, b. Jan. 6, 1762	1	126
Theodore, m. Mary Mc**CAY**, b. of Greenwich, Nov. 14,		
1837, by C. Wilcox	1	198
HALLIGAN, John, m. Sarah Ann **PALMER**, [Jan. 2, 1842], by		
Thomas Payne	1	209
HALLOCK, Benjamin F., of New York, m. Sally **HOBBY**, of		
Greenwich, [June] 19, [1826], by Isaac Lewis	1	174
HALSEY, Mary Ann, m. William **REYNOLDS**, b. of Greenwich,		
Feb. 23, 1836, by Platt Buffett	1	197
HANCOCK, Ellen, m. Riley **SHERWOOD**, b. of Greenwich, Dec.		
24, [1826], by Ebenezer S. Raymond	1	174
HANFORD, Hannah, see Hannah **BOSTWICK**	1	124
HARDY, HARDEY, HERDY, Hannah, m. Samuel **RUNDALL**,		
Mar. 1, 1715, by Ebenezer Mead, J. P.	1	56
Hannah, m. Samuel **RANDALL**, Mar. 1, 1715, by		
Ebenezer Mead, J. P.	ER	175
Ruth, m. John **MEAD**, Oct. 27, 1681, by Richard Laws,		
Com.	ER	40
Ruth, m. John **MEAD**, Oct. 27, 1681, by Richard Lanes,		
Com.	LR1	454
HATHAWAY, Andrew B., of Norwalk, m. Laura **ADAMS**, of		
Greenwich, Nov. 7, 1843, by Rev. Adrian		
Parker, of Stamford	1	212
HAYES, HAYS, Abraham, [s. Abraham], b. Dec. 14, 1743	1	111
Abraham, [s. Abraham], b. Dec. 14, 1743	ER	218
Anne, d. Charity, b. July 28, 1792	1	158
Charity, [d. Abraham], b. June 9, 1756	1	111
Charity, [d. Abraham], b. June 9, 1756	ER	218
Charity, had d. Anne, b. July 28, 1792 & s. Henry, b.		
July 24, 1794	1	158
Elizabeth, [d. Abraham], b. Feb. 14, 1749	1	111
Elizabeth, [d. Abraham], b. Feb. 14, 1749	ER	218
Elizabeth, d. Abraham, m. John **ADDINGTON**, Jr., July		
2, 1769	1	122
Es[t]her, [child of Abraham], b. Aug. 3, 1753	ER	218
Est[h]er, [d. Abraham], b. Aug. 30, 1753	1	111
Hannah, [d. Abraham], b. Dec. 26, 1746	1	111
Hannah, [d. Abraham], b. Dec. 26, 1746	ER	218
Henry, s. Charity, b. July 24, 1794	1	158
Rachall, [d. Abraham], b. Jan. 13, 1738	1	111
Rachel, [d. Abraham], b. Jan. 13, 1738	ER	218

	Vol.	Page
HENDERSON, William, s. Lieut, James & Elizabeth (EMMONS), b. Sept. 12, 1767	1	123
HERDY, [see under HARDY]		
HEWES, Edward Payson, m. Mary Elizabeth NEWMAN, Jan. 4, 1841, by Thomas Payne	1	206
HEWIT, Ann, m. Sam[[ue]ll MEAD, Dec. 6, 1716, by Ebenezer Mead, J. P.	LR1	423
HIBBARD, Anne, d. Jonathan, m. Nathaniel FINCH, Mar. 23, 1778, by Rev. Jonathan Murdock	1	139
Gideon, [s. Jonathan], b. Jan. 16, 1760	1	96
Jonathan, had child b. Mar. 18, 1756	1	96
Jonathan, had child b. Mar. 17, 1758	1	96
Jonathan, had child b. May 16, 1760?	1	96
[Nath]aniel, twin with Smith, s. Jonathan, b. Nov. 14, 1764	1	96
Ruth, see Ruth FINCH	1	96
Ruth M., b. Feb. 14, 1786; m. Obadiah MEAD, June 22, 1809, by Rev. Isaac Lewis, D. D.	1	152
Smith, twin with [Nath]aniel, s. Jonathan, b. Nov. 14, 1764	1	96
HITCHCOCK, John, m. Mindwell RUNDALL, d. Joseph, July 8, 1756, by Rev. Abraham Todd	1	101
Joseph, [s. John & Mindwell], b. Oct. 29, 1759	1	101
Louisa, m. Aroe KNAPP, b. of Greenwich, May 10, 1841, by B. M. Yarrington	1	207
Mahalo, of Horseneck, Fairfield Co., m. Daniel BOUTON, of Rye, Westchester Co., Nov. 14, 1827, by Rev. John Ellis, of Stamford	1	177
Thomas, s. [John & Mindwell], b. Aug. 30, 1757	1	101
Thomas, m. Clemence REYNOLDS, d. William, of Poundridge, Feb. 26, 1784	1	136
HOBBY, HABBY, HOBBIE, Abigail, d. John, b. Mar. 30, 1732/3	ER	179
Abigail, d. John, m. William EDGELL*, Mar. 16, 1758 *(EDGITT)	1	77
Abigail Jane, m. Henry CLOSE, b. of Greenwich, Sept. 9, 1845, by Rev. Peter C. Oakely	1	213
Amos, m. Harriet MOSHIER, Apr. 15, 1823, by Isaac Lewis	1	169
Amy, d. Benjamin [& Amy], b. Oct. 3, 1764	1	128
Annah, m. Andrew MEAD, Nov. 26, 1788, by Rev. Isaac Lewis	1	153
Benjamin, m. Amy MEAD, wid. Ebenezer, Jr., Feb. 25, 1763	1	128
Benjamin, s. Benjamin [& Amy], b. June 4, 1763	1	128
David, blacksmith, m. Hannah SEYMOUR, d. Samuel, Sept. 5, 1768	1	122
David, [s. David, blacksmith & Hannah], b. Feb. 3, 1769	1	122
David, Col. had negroes Orison, s. Cyrus, b. Aug. 2, 18		

	Vol.	Page
HOBBY, HABBY, HOBBIE, (cont.)		
1801 & Allen, s. Cyrus, b. Apr. 5, 1805	1	149
Deborah, m. Ebenezer **BROWN**, Jan. 24, 1757	1	94
Drake, [s. David, blacksmith & Hannah], b. Feb. 5, 1771	1	122
Ebenezer, s. [Jonathan & Sarah], b. Feb. 8, 1718/19	ER	170
Eliza, b. Dec. 14, 1795; m. Samuel **CLOSE**, s. Henry Mead, Oct. 24, 1811	1	118
Eunice Rebecca, m. Stephen H. **SEAMAN**, Oct. 23, 1833, by J. Mann	1	192
Fanny O., m. Alfred A. **REYNOLDS**, b. of Greenwich, [Jan.] 15, [1839], by N. Coe	1	202
Hannah, d. [John & Hannah], b. Nov. 19, 1720	ER	179
Jabez M., m. Mary **GARDINER**, b. of Greenwich, June 29, 1834, by Samuel Close, J. P.	1	193
Jemima, [d. Capt. Joseph], b. May 25, 1768	1	148
Jemima, d. Capt. Joseph, m. Benjamin **HOLMES**, s. Reuben, Aug. 16, 1785	1	148
John, m. Hannah **MEAD**, Mar. 16, 1716/17	ER	179
John, s. [John & Hannah], b. Jan. 18, 1717/18	ER	179
John, s. John, d. Dec. 11, 1726	ER	179
John, s. John, b. Nov. 4, 1739	ER	179
Jonathan, m. Sarah **MEAD**, Dec. 12, 1711	ER	170
Jonathan, s. Jonathan [& Sarah], b. Oct. [ ], 1714	ER	170
Joseph, s. [Jonathan & Sarah], b. Dec. 23, 1716	ER	170
Martha, m. Charles **THOMAS**, Oct. 29, 1718, by Rev. Richard Sackett	1	47
Martha, m. Charles **THOMAS**, Oct. 29, 1718, by Rev. Richard Sackett	ER	183
Martha, d. [John & Hannah], b. Jan. 12, 1730/1	ER	179
Martha, d. Martha, b. Feb. 6, 1751	ER	179
Martha, had d. Martha, b. Feb. 6, 1751	ER	179
Mary, b. Feb. 14, 1774; m. John **ADAMS**, Feb. 27, 1804	1	99
Mary E., m. Gales **SELLECK**, b. of Greenwich, [Mar.] 11, [1845], by S. B. S. Bissell	1	213
Mary Jerusha, m. Jabez **MEAD**, 3rd, Nov. 11, [1833], by J. Mann	1	192
Phebe, d. John, b. Sept. 11, 1737	ER	179
Polly, m. Nehemiah **MEAD**, 3rd, Mar. 27, 1803, by Rev. Isaac Lewis, D. D.	1	155
Rachall, d. John [& Hannah], b. Dec. 21, 1726	ER	179
Rachel, m. Daniel **BANKS**, Jr., [ ], 14, 1747	1	96
Rachel, m. Daniel **BANKS**, Jr., Aug. 14, 1747	ER	233
Rebecca, d. [John & Hannah], b. Mar. 30, 1721	ER	179
Reuben, m. Hannah **HUSTED**, b. of Greenwich, [Jan.] 22, [1839], by [N. Coe]	1	202
Sally, of Greenwich, m. Benjamin F. **HALLOCK**, of New York, [June] 19, [1826], by Iaac Lewis	1	174

	Vol.	Page
HOBBY, HABBY, HOBBIE, (cont.)		
Sarah, d. John [& Hannah], b. Dec. 25, 1724	ER	179
Sarah, d. John, b. May 11, 1735	ER	179
Sarah, d. Jonathan, m. Thaddeus **MEAD**, July 7, 1754	1	83
Sarah, d. Jonathan, m. Thaddeus **MEAD**, July 7, 1754	ER	246
Sarah, m. Jabez **MEAD**, Jr., Apr. 5, 1757	1	98
Sarah, d. Benjamin [& Amy], b. Nov. 8, 1768	1	128
Sarah*, d. Francis, of Stamford, m. Reuben **RUNDALL**, Jr., Dec. 23, 1781, by Rev. Mr. Dibble *("Sarah **HOLLY**" in Mead's Hist.)	1	133
Squier, s. Benjamin [& Amy], b. Apr. 2, 1766	1	128
Susana, d. John [& Hannah], b. Feb. 7, 1728	ER	179
Thomas, s. John [& Hannah], b. Jan. 6, 1722/3	ER	179
Thomas, Sr., d. Aug. 6, 1732	ER	179
Thomas, Col., d. July 30, 1798	1	158
HOLLINS*, Isaac, s. Stephen, b. Mar. 5, 1702 *(**HOLMES**?)	ER	136
HOLLIS, William, m. Maria **SCOFIELD**, b. of Stanwich, Jan. 21, 1824, by Rev. Platt Buffett	1	170
HOLLOWAY, W[illia]m H., of North Castle, m. Louisa **TODD**, of Stanwich, Sept. 21, 1845, by Rev. Chauncey Wilcox	1	214
HOLLY, Abigaill, d. John, b. Mar. 30, 1732/3	LR1	438
Abigail, of Stamford, d. Frank, m. Thomas **BROWN**, Dec. 9, 1780, by Rev. Mr. Dibble	1	139
Ebenezer, s. [Jonathan & Sarah], b. Feb. 8, 1718/19	LR1	442
Elizabeth, m. William **EDWARDS**, [Jan.] 1, [1835], by J. Mann	1	195
Hannah, d. [John & Hannah], b. Nov. 19, 1720	LR1	438
Isaac, m. Abigail Elizabeth **LYON**, b. of Greenwich, Sept. 20, 1826, by Platt Buffett	1	174
John, m. Hannah **MEAD**, Mar. 16, 1716/17	LR1	438
John, s. [John & Hannah], b. Jan. 13, 1717/18	LR1	438
John, [s. John & Hannah], d. Dec. 11, 1726	LR1	438
John s. John, b. Nov. 4, 1739	LR1	438
Jonathan, m. Sarah **MEAD**, Dec. 12, 1711	LR1	442
Jonathan, s. Jonathan [& Sarah], b. Oct. 6, 1714	LR1	442
Joseph, s. [Jonathan & Sarah], b. Dec. 23, 1716	LR1	442
Martha, d. [John & Hannah], b. Jan. 12, 1730	LR1	438
Martha, d. John, [ ]	LR1	438
Phebe, d. [John], b. Sept. 11, 1737	LR1	438
Rachell, d. [John & Hannah], b. Dec. 21, 1726	LR1	438
Rebecca, d. [John & Hannah], b. Mar. 30, 1721	LR1	438
Samantha R., m. Nehemiah **HOW[E]**, [May] 16, 1831, by J. Mann	1	190
Sarah, d. [John & Hannah], b. Dec. [ ], 1724	LR1	438
Sarah, d. John, b. Aug. 11, 1735	LR1	438
Sarah*, d. Francis, of Stamford, m. Reuben **RUNDALL**, Jr., Dec. 23, 1781, by Rev. Mr. Dibble		

	Vol.	Page

HOLLY, (cont.)

	Vol.	Page
*(Arnold copy has "Sarah HOBBY")	1	133
Stephen, m. Emeline E. REYNOLDS, b. of Greenwich, Jan. 13, 1829, by Rev. Platt Buffett, of Stanwich	1	181
Susanna, d. [John & Hannah], b. Feb. 7, 1728	LR1	438
Thomas, s. John [& Hannah], b. Jan. 6, 1722/3	LR1	438
Thomas, Sr., d. Aug. 6, 1732	LR1	438

HOLMES, Abigail, d. Isaac, b. Mar. 6, 1730; m. Samuel MILLS,

	Vol.	Page
s. Samuel, [ ]	1	135
Abigail, d. Isaac, b. Mar. 6, 1730; m. Samuell MILLS, s. Samuel [ ]	ER	233
Abigail, [d. Epenetus & Sarah], b. May 11, 1757	1	71
Abigail, [d. Epenetus & Sarah], b. May 11, 1757	ER	277*
Abraham, [s. Reuben & Mary (d. Thomas BROWN), b. Aug. 3, 1761	1	115
Azel, [s. Epenetus & Sarah], b. May 6, 1751	1	71
Azel, [s. Epenetus & Sarah], b. May 6, 1751	ER	227*
Benjamin, [s. Reuben & 2nd w. Ruth (d. John WOOD), b. May 28, 1764	1	115
Benjamin, b. May 28, 1764	1	148
Benjamin, s. Reuben, m. Jemima HOBBY, d. Capt. Joseph, Aug. 16, 1785	1	148
Betsey, m. Eben[eze]r MEAD, Jr., Oct. 28, 1807	1	157
Caleb, m. Bythena MEAD, [Sept. 23, 1834], by J. Mann	1	193
Caleb Knapp, s. Benjamin [& Jemima], b. Apr. 23, 1788	1	148
Charles Knapp, s. [Benjamin & Jemima], b. Oct. 4, 1799	1	148
Edward Wood, [s. Reuben & Lucretia], b. Jan. 31, 1800	1	112
Edward Wood, [s. Reuben & Lucretia], d. June 25, 1810	1	112
Edward Wood, [s. Reuben & Lucretia], b. Nov. 5, 1810	1	112
Eliza, [d. Reuben & Lucretia], b. June 15, 1819	1	112
Elizabeth, d. [Jonathan & Sarah], b. Oct. 9, 1714	LR1	414
Epenetus, s. [Jonathan], b. Oct. 30, 1722	LR1	414
Epenetus, m. Sarah MEAD, d. Caleb, Feb. 3, 1743/4	1	71
Epenetus, m. Sarah MEAD, d. Caleb, Feb. 9, 1743/4	ER	227*
Ezra, m. Martha OWENS, b. of Greenwich, Sept. 30, [1821], by Rev. David Peck	1	166
Henry, s. Benjamin [& Jemima], b. Dec. 14, 1794	1	148
Isaac*, s. Stephen, b. Mar. 5, 1702 *(Arnold copy has "Isaac HOLLINS")	ER	136
Isaac, s. Stephen, b. Mar. 5, 1720 [Arnold note: "This is a mistake", shoud be "1702"]	1	57
Israel, [s. Reuben & 2nd w. Ruth (d. John WOOD), b. Dec. 20, 1768	1	115
Jane, [d. Reuben & Lucretia], b. Jan. 28, 1809	1	112
Jemima, m. John RICH, Feb. 17, 1741, by Rev. Abraham Todd	1	61
Jonathan, m. Sarah SEELEY, July 29, 1707	LR1	414

HOLMES, (cont.)

	Vol.	Page
Jonathan, s. Jonathan [& Sarah], b. Feb. 27, 1716/17	LR1	414
Jonathan, [s. Epenetus & Sarah], b. Sept. 28, 1746	1	71
Jonathan, [s. Epenetus & Sarah], b. Sept. 28, 1746	ER	227*
Jotham, [s. Reuben & 2nd w. Ruth (d. John **WOOD**), b. Dec. 22, 1767	1	115
Latham, s. Benjamin [& Jemima], b. Mar. 27, 1786	1	148
Lucretia, [d. Reuben & Lucretia], b. Oct. 6, 1806	1	112
Martha, d. Jonathan [& Sarah], b. Sept. 22, 1711	LR1	414
Mary, d. Isaac, m. Andrew **WORDEN**, Nov. 28, 1759	1	95
Mary, [d. Reuben & 2nd w. Ruth (d. John **WOOD**), b. Jan. 4, 1763	1	115
Mary, d. Benjamin [& Jemima], b. July 29, 1790	1	148
Mary, [d. Reuben & Lucretia], b. May 11, 1804	1	112
Monro Warren, [s. Reuben & Lucretia], b. July 4, 1822	1	112
Phebe Ann, [d. Reuben & Lucretia], b. Aug. 31, 1813	1	112
Phebe Ann, [d. Reuben & Lucretia], d. Oct. 9, 1820	1	112
Rachel, d. [Jonathan & Sarah], b. Feb. 24, 1719/20	LR1	414
Reuben, s. Reuben & 2nd w. Ruth (d. John **WOOD**), b. Aug. 11, 1772	1	115
Reuben, m. Lucretia **DAVIS**, Apr. 28, 1799	1	112
Reuben Augustus, [s. Reuben & Lucretia],b. Jan. 10,1817	1	112
Ruth, [d. Reuben & 2nd w. Ruth (d. John **WOOD**), b. Dec. 20, 1766	1	115
Ruth, d. Benjamin [& Jemima], b. June 12, 1792	1	148
Ruth, [d. Reuben & Lucretia], b. Nov. 13, 1815; d. Nov. 20, 1815	1	112
Sarah, d. [Jonathan & Sarah], b. Mar. 22, 1708	LR1	414
Sarah, w. Jonathan, d. Feb. 11, 1726/7	LR1	414
Sarah, [d. Epenetus & Sarah], b. Nov. 6, 1744	1	71
Sarah, [d. Epenetus & Sarah], b. Nov. 6, 1744	ER	227*
Silas, [s. Reuben & 2nd w. Ruth (d. John **WOOD**), b. Feb. 16, 1770	1	115
Squire, [s. Epenetus & Sarah], b. Mar. 5, 1760	1	71
Squire, [s. Epenetus & Sarah], b. Mar. 5, 1760	ER	227*
Stephen, m. [ ], Feb. 24, 1717, by Ebenezer Mead, J. P.	LR1	446
Stephen, m. Martha **MEAD**, Feb. 27, 1717/18, by Ebenezer Mead, J. P.	ER	182
Stephen, [d. Reuben & 2nd w. Ruth (d. John **WOOD**), b. Oct. 18, 1765	1	115
Stephen Knapp, s. Benjamin [& Jemima], b. Nov. 18, 1801	1	148
Susan, d. Benjamin [& Jemima], b. June 7, 1797	1	148
Susana, d. Jonathan [& Sarah], b. Feb. 10, 1724/5	LR1	414
Susanna, [d. Reuben & Mary (d. Thomas **BROWN**)], b. July 14, 1759	1	115
William, [s. Reuben & Lucretia], b. Dec. 20, 1801	1	112

	Vol.	Page
HOLMES, (cont.)		
William, m. Ang[e]line Amey MEAD, July 6, 1823, by Isaac Lewis	1	169
HOPKINS, Lawrence, of New York, m. Sarah Lewis MEAD, of Greenwich, May 20, 1828, by Isaac Lewis	1	180
HOPSON, Phebe, member, of the Church of West Greenwich, m. Samuel FERRIS, of Stanwich, Jan. 15, 1822, by Platt Buffett	1	167
Phebe Ann, m. Jonathan BANKS, b. of Greenwich, Oct. 22, 1845, by Rev. Geo[rge] Waterbury	1	214
HOWARD, Daniel, m. Hannah FLETCHER, b. of Greenwich, Jan. 16, 1825, by Isaac Lewis	1	171
Harriet, m. Patrick McGURRAN, Feb. 22, 1822, by William Knapp, J. P.	1	167
HOWE, HOW, Abigail, d. Isaac, m. Deliverance MEAD, Jan. 11, 1758	ER	226
Abigail, m. Deliverence MEAD, Jan. 11, 1759	1	111
Barthana, d. Ebenezer [& Sarah], b. Apr. 11, 1783	1	132
Betsey, d. Isaac [Jr. & Lucy], b. Sept. 24, 1782	1	130
Cornelia, d. Isaac [& Lucy], b. Mar. 15, 1797	1	130
Ebenezer, m. Sarah BELDING, d. Benjamin, June 6, 1774, by Rev. Mr. Murdock	1	132
Ebenezer, s. Ebenezer [& Sarah], b. Aug. 17, 1775	1	132
Elizabeth, d. Isaac [& Elizabeth], b. Mar. 16, 1708	ER	133-4
Elizabeth, d. Ebenezer [& Sarah], b. May 17, 1780	1	132
Elizabeth, d. Isaac, b. Mar. 16, 17[ ]	LR1	452
Esther, d. Isaac [& Lucy], b. Apr. 3, 1786	1	130
Isaac, m. Elizabeth WATERBERY, June 1, 1701/2	ER	133
Isaac, m. Elizabeth WATERBURY, June 2, 1701/2	LR1	452
Isaac, s. Isaac [& Elizabeth], b. Jan. 8, 1710/11	ER	134
Isaac, s. Isaac, b. Jan. 9, 1710/11	LR1	452
Isaac, Jr., m. Lucy MEAD, d. Nehemiah, May 8, 1778	1	130
Isaac, d. Oct. 8, 1779	1	130
Isaac, Jr., s. Isaac [& Lucy], b. Jan. 29, 1793	1	130
John, had d. [ ], b. Apr. 3, 1716	ER	173
John, s. John, b. June 4, 17[ ]	ER	173
Jonas, [s. Isaac & Lucy], b. Aug. 24, 1787	1	130
Keziah, d. Isaac, m. Abraham MEAD, Jr., Jan. 3, 1765, by Rev. Abraham Todd	1	113
Keziah, d. Isaac, m. Abraham MEAD, Jr., Jan. 3, 1765, by Rev. Abraham Todd	1	156
Keziah, [twin with Rachal, d. Isaac & Lucy], b. Mar. 28, 1784	1	130
Laura, [d. Isaac, Jr. & Lucy], b. Oct. 10, 1780; d. July 22, 1789	1	130
Laura, d. Isaac [& Lucy], b. Apr. 12, 1789	1	130
Lucy, d. Isaac [& Lucy], b. Mar. 5, 1791	1	130
Nathaniel, s. John, b. Jan. 27, 170[ ]	LR1	454

	Vol.	Page
HOWE, HOW, (cont.)		
Nathaniel, s. [Isaac & Elizabeth], b. June 12, 1702/3	ER	133
Nathaniel, 1st s. [Isaac & Elizabeth], b. June 12, 1702/3	LR1	452
Nathaniel, s. John, b. Jan. 27, 1713/14	ER	173
Nehemiah, s. [Isaac & Lucy], b. Jan. 8, 1795	1	130
Nehemiah, m. Samantha R. HOLLY, [May] 16, 1831, by J. Mann	1	190
Rachal, [twin with Keziah, d. Isaac & Lucy], b. Mar. 28, 1784	1	130
Sally, d. Isaac, Jr. [& Lucy], b. Aug. 18, 1779	1	130
Sam[ue]ll, s. Isaac [& Lucy], b. Mar. 20, 1799; d. Dec. 17, 1801	1	130
Samuel, Rev. of Hopewell, Ontario Co., N. Y., m. Elacissa BUFFETT, of Greenwich, Aug. 20, 1835, by Rev. Platt Buffett	1	195
Sarah, d. [Isaac & Elizabeth], b. Oct. 8, [ ]; d. Dec. 24, 1704	ER	133
Sarah, d. [Isaac & Elizabeth], b. Oct. 8, [ ]; d. Dec. 24, 1704	LR1	452
Sarah, d. Ebenezer [& Sarah], b. Nov. 4, 1777	1	132
Sarah, m. Mark MEAD, 2nd, b. of Greenwich, this day [Nov. 12, 1845], by Mark Mead, V. D. M.	1	214
HOYT, HOIT, HOIGHT, [see also HAIGHT], Abigail, of Norwalk, m. John FERRIS, Feb. 13, 1695, by Capt. Umstead, Com.	ER	98
Abigaill, of Norwalk, m. John FERRIS, Dec. 13, 1695, by Capt. Umstead	LR1	447
George, s. Billy & Sally, b. Aug. 28, 1813	1	148
Nehemiah, of Stamford, m. Anna BUNKER*, of Greenwich, Mar. 14, 1826, by Platt Buffett *(BARKER?)	1	173
Nehemiah, of Stamford, m. Lavina KNAPP, of Greenwich. June 8, 1836, by Platt Buffett	1	197
Rachel, of Stanwich, m. Allen MEAD, of West Greenwich, Nov. 29, 1822, by Platt Buffet	1	168
Sarah Ann, of Stamford, m. Aaron SNOW (Rev.), of Eastbury, Conn., May 7, 1841, by Rev. D. B. Butts	1	207
HUBBARD, Abraham, m. Amey PALMER, b. of Greenwich, Feb. 11, 1828, by Platt Buffett	1	179
Elmaretta, m. Lewis Augustus MERRETT, [Sept.] 23, [1834], by J. Mann	1	193
Harvey, m. Charlott BROWN, b. of Greenwich, May 9, 1832, by Rev. Platt Buffett, of Stanwich	1	190
Mary, of Stanwich, m. Stoddard J. FROST, of Norwalk, May 16, [1826], by Platt Buffett	1	174
William, of Somers, N. Y., m. Sarah BRUNDAGE, of Greenwich, Nov. 23, 1835, by Platt Buffett	1	196

	Vol.	Page
HUESTIS, [see also HUSTED], Caleb, m. Ann WILSON, b. of Greenwich, May 23, [1830], by E. S. Raymond	1	184
HUGH, Robert, m. Polly RICH, b. of Greenwich, Nov. 1, 1827, by Ebenezer J. Raymond	1	176
HULSTED, [see also HUSTED], Elizabeth, m. James BANKS, Jan. 6, 1833, by E. S. Raymond	1	188
HURLEY, Elizabeth, d. Samuel [& Elizabeth], b. Mar. 8, 1727	ER	190
Elizabeth, d. Samuel [& Elizabeth], b. Mar. 29, 1727	1	49
Samuell, m. Elizabeth WHITTNE, May 8, 1723, by Samuel Peck, J. P.	1	49
Samuell, m. Elizabeth WHITTNE, May 8, 1723, by Samuel Peck, J. P.	ER	190
HURTELL, Emily, m. Lyman B. TRIPP, b. of North Castle, Dec. 25, 1840, by Rev. C. Wilcox	1	206
HUSTED, HEUSTED, HUESTEAD, [see also HUESTIS], Abigaile, m. Abraham WANSHER, Dec. 7, 1721	1	47
Abigaile, m. Abraham WANSHER, Dec. 7, 1721	ER	187
Abigail, d. Moses [& Susana], b. June 1, 1734	1	64
Abigal, d. Moses [& Susana], b. June 1, 1734	ER	194
Augustus W., of Greenwich, m. Nancy E. HUSTED, of Venice, Caydge Co., N. Y., [Jan.] 21, [1839], by N. Coe	1	202
Benjamin, Jr., m. Electa BROWN, b. of Greenwich, May 13, 1844, by Chauncey Wilcox	1	212
Benjamin W., m. Rachel P. LYON, b. of Greenwich, [Dec.] 24, [1827], by Isaac Lewis	1	178
Catharine, m. Major LOCKWOOD, May 21, 1833, by C. Wilcox	1	191
Conklin, m. Polly Ann CLOSE, b. of Greenwich, Apr. 28, 1834, by Rev. Platt Buffett, of Stanwich	1	192
Cynthia Elizabeth, m. Sanford MEAD, Feb. 25, 1833, by J. Mann	1	189
David, of Greenwich, m. Elizabeth SMITH, of North Castle, N.Y., Feb. 23, 1842, by B. M. Yarrington	1	208
Eliza, m. James FELMETTE, Oct. 20, 1824, by Isaac Lewis	1	171
Hannah, m. Reuben HOBBY, b. of Greenwich, [Jan.] 22, [1839], by [N. Coe]	1	202
Hannah E., of Greenwich, m. Robert MYERS, of Herkimer, N. Y., Oct. 18, 1841, by Thomas Payne	1	208
Lucy, wid., her negroes James, s. Kate, b. Jan. 6, 1795 & Julia Ann, d. Lib., b. June 30, 1798	1	147
Lucy, wid. Moses, Jr., d. July 30, 1796	1	149
Lydia H., of Greenwich, m. Robert SCOTT, of New York, Jan. 20, 1834, by Platt Buffett	1	192

	Vol.	Page
HUSTED, HEUSTED, HUESTEAD, (cont.)		
Mary E., m. Nathaniel HUSTED, Jr., b. of Greenwich, Dec. 3, 1821, by Isaac Lewis	1	167
Moses, m. Susana MEAD, Sept. 5, 1726, by Rev. Richard Sackit	1	64
Moses, m. Susana MEAD, Sept. 5, 1726, by Rev. Richard Sackit	ER	194
Moses, s. Moses [& Susana], b. July 5, 1728	1	64
Moses, s. Moses [& Susana], b. July 5, 1728	ER	194
Nancy E., of Venice Caydge Co., N. Y., m. Augustus W. HUSTED, of Greenwich, [Jan.] 21, [1839], by [N. Coe]	1	202
Nathaniel, Jr., m. Mary E. HUSTED, b. of Greenwich, Dec. 3, 1821, by Isaac Lewis	1	167
Sarah, m. Zacchariah CLAP[P], b. of Greenwich, Mar. 13, 1833, by Rev. Platt Buffett, of Stanwich	1	189
Sarah M., m. Augustus MEAD, Sept. 12, 1832, by J. Mann	1	188
Silas, m. Martha MEAD, b. of Greenwich, May 20, 1839, by Chauncey Wilcox	1	203
Susana, d. Moses [& Susana], b. Apr. 1, 1731	1	64
Susana, d. Moses [& Susana], b. Apr. 1, 1731	ER	194
INGERSOLL, Mary Ann, m. Gideon CLOSE, b. of Greenwich, Nov. 25, 1838, by Darius Mead	1	202
ISAACS, Esther, d. Capt. Benjamin, decd., of Norwalk, m. William KNAPP, Dec. 19, 1784, by Rev. Eben Dibble	1	152
Sarah, wid. Capt. Benjamin, of Norwalk, m. David BUSH, Apr. 9, 1777, by Rev. Mr. Lemming	1	151
JACKSON, Elizabeth, m. Joseph DAVENPORT, (colored), b. of Greenwich, Sept. 3, 1839, by Noah Coe	1	204
Stephen T., m. Mary P. FERRIS, Aug. 29, 1822, by Rev. Sam[ue]l D. Ferguson. Witnesses: William P. Reynolds, Shadrack Finch	1	168
JAMES, Rachel, b. [ ], 1744; m. David ABBOT, Oct. 3, 1762	1	89-90
Rachel, b. [ ], 1744; m. David ABBOT, Oct. 3, 1762	ER	225*
JAMESON, James, m. Lavina WILSON, Dec. 23, 1832, by E. S. Raymond	1	188
JANE, Edwin W., m. Cynthia J. TAYLOR, Mar. 17, 1842, by Rev. Charles F. Pelton	1	209
Jefferson, m. Julia Ann FERRIS, b. of Stanwich, Mar. 28, 1836, by Platt Buffett	1	197
JARMAN, GERMAN, Abigail*, d. Peter, b. Aug. 26, 1779 *(Arnold copy has "Abigail GERMAN")	1	142
Caleb, s. Peter, b. Nov. 6, 1776	1	142
Charles, m. Patty MERRELL, June 2, 1836, by James Jarman	1	199
Mary, d. Peter, b. Oct. 4, 1781	1	142

	Vol.	Page
JENNINGS, JININS, Ann, of England, d. Mar. 4, 1841, at the house of James G. Cornell	1	207
John, m. Mary WINTON, Jan. 18, 1725/6, by Joshua Knapp, J. P.	1	63
John, m. Mary WINTAN, Feb. 18, 1731/2, by Joshua Knapp, J. P.	ER	204
JESSUP, Ann Augusta, of Greenwich, m. Lewis Augustus READ, of New York, Dec. 22, 1845, by Rev. Pater C. Oakley	1	215
Hannah Mariah, m. Henry Lockwood KNAPP, Jan. 5, 1840, by Thomas Payne	1	205
Jonathan, m. Ann FERRIS, b. of Greenwich, Dec. 23, 1838, by Rev. Edw[ar]d Oldrin, of Stamford	1	203
Julia A., of Greenwich, m. Rufus SMITH, of Norwalk, Jan. 2, 1842, by [Thomas Payne]	1	209
Mary P., of Greenwich, m. Daniel D. GASSNER, of New York, July 16, 1835, by Rev. Daniel Smith, of Stamford	1	195
Petrus V. T., m. Julia A. L. FERRIS, b. of Greenwich, Jan. 20, 1839, by Rev. Edw[ar]d Oldrin	1	202
Samuel, of the Cos Mill, m. Anna BEEBE, b. of Greenwich, June 30, 1839, by B. M. Farrington	1	204
JOHNS, Delila A., m. Charles TIMPANNY, b. of Greenwich, Dec. 17, 1839, by Noah Coe	1	205
JOHNSON, Mary, m. Allen GREEN, [Nov.] 10, [1828], by Rev. Ebenezer S. Raymond	1	180
JONES, Frederick Harding, s. Mary (WHITING) & Harding, decd., of Newburn, Carven Co., N. C., b. Nov. 28, 1759, at the home of Justus Bush, of Greenwich. 7 witnesses	1	92
Mary, d. Beniamin, m. Sackett REYNOLDS, Nov. 21, 1760	1	97
JOURDAN, Allin, of Stanwick, m. Alexander ENNIS, of Rye, Jan. 30, 1821, by Platt Buffet	1	165
KEELER, Ezra, of Kartright, Co. of Deleware, N. Y., m. Mary SHERWOOD, of Greenwich, Nov. 18, 1827, by Isaac Lewis	1	176
Joseph O., m. Caroline FERRIS, Oct. 15, 1834, by C. Wilcox	1	194
Mary E., m. Aaron SEELEY, b. of Danbury, Aug. 13, 1838, by Rev. Chauncey Wilcox	1	201
KETCHUM, Beniamin, s. [Beniamin], b. July 7, 1738	1	51
Beniamin, s. [Beniamin], b. July 7, 1738	ER	193
Benjamin, Jr., s. Benjamin & Rose, b. July 7, 1739	CP	108
Benjamin, Jr., s. Benjamin & Rose, b. July 7, 1739	ER	219
Debora, d. [Beniamin], b. Apr. 20, 1730	1	51
Debroa, d. [Beniamin], b. Apr. 20, 1730	ER	193

	Vol.	Page
KETCHUM, (cont.)		
Mary, d. Joshua, of Huntington, L. I., m. Josiah UTTER, Feb. 4, 1779	1	137
Rachall, d. Beniamin, b. Aug. 29, 1727	ER	193
Rebeckah, d. Beniamin, b. Aug. 29, 1727	1	51
Richard, s. Benjamin, b. Mar. 7, 1733	ER	193
Richard, s. Beniamin, b. Mar. 7, 1734	1	51
Ros[e], d. Beniamin, b. Aug. 21, 1736	1	51
Rose, d. Beniamin, b. Aug. 21, 1736	ER	193
Samuell, s. Beniamin, b. [ ], 2, 1725	1	51
Samuel, s. Beniamin, b. Oct. 2, 1725	ER	193
Titus, s. [Beniamin], b. Sept. 21, 1741	1	51
Titus, s. [Beniamin], b. Sept. 21, 1741	ER	193
Titus, s. Beniamin, b. Oct. 23, 174[ ]	1	63
KITCHELL, Margaret, wid. Robert, d. Apr. 26, 1682	ER	40
Margaret, wid. Robert, [ ], Apr. 26, 1682	LR1	448
KNAPP, KNAP, Abigail, w. Joshua, b. June 1, 1710	1	58
Abigail, w. John, b. June 1, 1710	ER	159
Abigail, w. John, b. June 1, 1710	ER	202
Abigail(?), d. Timothie [& Elizabeth], b. Jan. 26, 1712	LR1	449
Abigail, d. John [& Abigail], b. Feb. 5, 1733/4	1	58
Abigall, d. John [& Abigail], b. Feb. 5, 1733/4	ER	202
Albert, m. Sarah Jane DAVIS, b. of Greenwich, Feb. 24, 1834, by Rev. Robert Dauis	1	192
Amanda Lamina, m. George A. SMITH, Oct. 7, 1838, by Noah Coe	1	201
Amos, s. Caleb, b. May 1, 1742	ER	219
Amos, s. Caleb, b. June 1, 1742; m. Mary SMITH, d. John, Jan. 22, 1763	1	100
Amos, s. Caleb, b. June 1, 1742; m. Mary SMITH, d. John, Jan. 22, 1763	ER	225*
Amos, m. Mary SMITH, d. John, Jan. 22, 1763	ER	219
Amy, d. Caleb, [& Clemens], b. Nov. 23, 1726	ER	185
Amy, m. [ ] MEAD, Jr., Jan. 13, 1748, by Rev. Abraham Todd	1	81-2
Amy, m. Ebenezer MEAD, Jr., Jan. 13, 1748, by Rev. Abraham Todd	ER	234
Amy, d. Capt. Israel, m. Taber* FITCH, May 22, 1780 *("Jabez" in Mead's Hist.)	1	130
Aroe, m. Louisa HITCHCOCK, b. of Greenwich, May 10, 1841, by B. M. Yarrington	1	207
Benjamin, had d. [ ], b. [ ] & another ch., [ ], b. [ ]	LR1	449
Benjamin, m. Elisabeth BUTLER, Apr. 18, 1700	ER	124
Benjamin, m. Elizabeth BUTTLER, Feb. 28, 1700/1	LR1	449
Benjamin, s. Benjamin [& Elizabeth], b. Mar. 17, 1704	LR1	449
Beniamin, s. [Benjamin & Elisabeth], b. Apr. 17, 1704	ER	124
Beniamin, m. Susanah MILLIAR, June 3, 1731, by Rev.		

KNAPP, KNAP, (cont.)

	Vol.	Page
John Tenant	ER	202*
Beniamin, m. Susanah **MILLARD**, June 3, 1731, by Rev. John Tennant	1	65
Beniamin, s. Beniamin [& Susanah], b. Feb. 27, 1731/2	1	65
Beniamin, s. Beniamin [& Susanah], b. Feb. 27, 1731/2	ER	203
Benjamin, [s. Justus & Sarah], b. Sept. 16, 1764	1	110
Benjamin, [s. Justus & Sarah], b. Sept. 16, 1764	ER	216
Burr, of Stamford, m. Phebe **MERRELL**, of Greenwich, Sept. 7, [1840], by Noah Coe	1	206
Caleb, m. Sarah **RUNDALL**, Apr. 1, 1697	ER	121
[Caleb], m. Sarah [**RUNDALL**], Apr. 1, [ ]	LR1	4
Caleb, s. Caleb, b. Nov. 11, 1698	LR1	4
Caleb, s. [Caleb & Sarah], b. Nov. 11, 1698	ER	121
Caleb, s. Caleb & Clemence, b. Nov. 9, 1724	1	68
Caleb, s. Caleb & Clemens, b. Nov. 9, 1724	ER	185
Charity, d. Caleb & Clemence, b. Dec. 5, 1733	1	68
Charity, d. Caleb & Clemens, b. Dec. 5, 1733	ER	186
Charity, m. Joseph **LOCKWOOD**, b. of Greenwich, Nov. 10, 1751, by Rev. Abraham Todd	1	84
Charity, m. Joseph **LOCKWOOD**, b. of Greenwich, Nov. 10, 1751, by Rev. Abraham Todd	ER	238
Charles, s. Caleb, b. Feb. 24, 1700	ER	121
Charles, s. Caleb, b. July 15, 1705	LR1	4
Clemens, d. Caleb & Clemens, b. Dec. 31, 1722	ER	185
Daniel, s. [Benjamin & Elisabeth], b. Apr. 20, 1714	ER	124
David, s. [Benjamin], b. Apr. [ ]	LR1	449
David, s. Benjamin [& Elizabeth], b. Feb. 19, 1709/10	LR1	449
David, s. Benjamin [& Elisabeth], b. Feb. 19, 1709/10	ER	124
David, s. David [& Rebeckah], b. Oct. 22, 1735	1	65
David, s. David [& Reachell], b. Oct. 22, 1735	ER	215
David, m. Rebeckah* **CLOSE**, Nov.* 7, 1735, by Rev. Abraham Todd. *("Jan." & Rachel" in Mead's Hist.)	1	65
David, m. Reachell **CLOSE**, Nov. 7, 1735, by Rev. Abraham Todd	LR1	215
Deborah, d. Caleb, b. Aug. 25, 1710	ER	4
Deborah, d. [Caleb & Sarah], b. Aug. 25, 1710	ER	121
Deborah, d. Joseph, b. Oct. 21, 1731	1	58
Deobera, d. Joseph, b. Oct. 22, 1731	ER	203
Ebenezer, m. Elizabeth **FINCH**, Jan. 7, 1724, by Rev. Mr. Sackett	1	50
Ebenezer, m. Elizabeth **FINCH**, Jan. 7, 1724, by Rev. Mr. Sacet	ER	191
Ebenezer, s. Ebenezer [& Elizabeth], b. May 23, 1730	1	50
Elizabeth, had s. William, b. Sept. 17, [ ]	1	131
Elizabeth, d. Timothie [& Elizabeth], b. Aug. 22, 1710	ER	123
Elizabeth, d. Timothie [& Elizabeth], b. Aug. 22, 1710	LR1	449

GREENWICH VITAL RECORDS 199

	Vol.	Page
KNAPP, KNAP, (cont.)		
Elizabeth, w. Timothie, d. June 17, 1712	LR1	449
Elizabeth, w. Timothie, d. June 17, 1713	ER	123
Elizabeth, d. Benjamin [& Elisabeth], b. Feb. 18, 1716	ER	124
Elizabeth, m. Nathan MEAD, Jan. 2, 1717/18	ER	181
Elizabeth, m. Nathan MEAD, Jan. 2, 1717/18	LR1	445
Elizabeth, d. Caleb & Clemence, b. Dec. 31, 1722	1	68
Elizabeth, d. Joseph, b. Aug. 26, 1723	ER	203
Elizabeth, d. Ebenezer [& Elizabeth], b. Oct. 14, 1725	1	50
Elizabeth, d. Ebenezer [& Elizabeth], b. Oct. 14, 1725	ER	191
Elizabeth, d. Ebenezer [& Elizabeth], b. May 23, 1730	ER	191
Elizabeth, d. [Beniamin & Susanah], b. June 23, 1733	1	65
Elizabeth, d. Beniamin [& Susanah], b. June 23, 1733	ER	203
Elizabeth, d. Joseph, b. Aug. 26, 1733	1	58
Elizabeth, [d. Timothy & Ruth], b. Aug. 20, 1765	1	99
Elizabeth, [d. Timothy & Ruth], b. Aug. 20, 1765	ER	238
Elizabeth, d. William [& Esther], b. Nov. 9, 1786	1	152
Elizabeth C., m. Caleb PURDY, Feb. 12, 1833, by Chauncey Wilcox	1	189
Elizabeth Huggford, d. Israel, decd., m. John MACKAY Jr., [ ]	1	157
Elnathan, [s. Justus & Sarah], b. Aug. 5, 1761	1	110
Elnathan, [s. Justus & Sarah], b. Aug. 5, 1761	ER	216
Esther Rebecca, d. William [& Esther], b. Nov. 28, 1794	1	152
Ezekial, s. Ebenezer [& Elizabeth], b. Dec. 22, 1734	1	50
Ezekiel, s. Ebenezer [& Elizabeth], b. Dec. 22, 1734	ER	191
Hannah, d. Timothie, b. June 12, 1717	ER	180
Hannah, d. Timothy, m. Nathaniel FINCH, Sept. 17, 1732	1	54
Hannah, d. Caleb & Clemence, b. Jan. 20, 1735/6	1	68
Hannah, d. Caleb & Clemens, b. Jan. 22, 1735/6	ER	186
Hannah, d. Ebenezer [& Elizabeth], b. [ ] 21, 1739/40	1	50
Hannah, d. Ebenezer [& Elizabeth], b. Feb. 21, 1739/40	ER	191
Hannah L., m. Alva BRIGGS, b. of Greenwich, Jan. 1, 1843, by D. B. Butts	1	210
Harriet, m. Geo[rge] A. PALMER, [Sept.] 9, [1834], by J. Mann	1	193
Henry, [s. Justus & Sarah], b. Aug. 25, 1763	1	110
Henry, [s. Justus & Sarah], b. Aug. 25, 1763	ER	216
Henry Lockwood, m. Hannah Mariah JESSUP, Jan. 5, 1840, by Thomas Payne	1	205
Horton O., m. Charlotte CLOSE, b. of Greenwich, Nov. 24, 1836, by C. Wilcox	1	198
Isaac(?), s. Benjamin, b. Nov. 22, [ ]	LR1	449
Isaac, m. Rebecca RENOLLS, Jan. 29, 1727/8, by Ebenezer Mead, J. P.	1	54
Isaack, m. Rebecca RENOLLS, Jan. 29, 1727/8, by Ebnear Mead, J. P.	ER	198

KNAPP, KNAP, (cont.)	Vol.	Page
Isaac, s. Isaac [& Rebecca], b. May 27, 1729	1	54
Isaac, s. Isaack [& Rebecca], b. May 27, 1729	ER	198
Isaac, m. Theodotia MEAD, b. of Greenwich, Nov. 25, 1839, by Chauncey Wilcox	1	205
Isaac W., m. Nancy WILSON, b. of Greenwich, Sept. 15, 1841, by Thomas Payne	1	207
Israel, s. Timothie [& Elizabeth], b. Dec. 13, 1705	ER	123
Isareal, s. Timothie [& Elizabeth], b. Dec. 13, 1705	LR1	449
Israel, [s. Timothy & Ruth], b. Nov. 7, 1763	1	99
Israel, [s. Timothy & Ruth], b. Nov. 17, 1763	ER	238
Israel, had negroes Jenny, d. Nelly, b. June 25, 1789, James, s. Nelly, b. Mar. 14, 1791 & Nero, s. Prue, b. June 9, 1815	1	144
James, s. Benjamin [& Elisabth], b. Nov. 28, 1711	ER	124
John, had d. [ ], b. [ ]	1	58
John, had d. [ ], b. [ ]	ER	202
John, s. Joshua, b. Mar. 1, 1708	1	58
John, s. Joshua, b. Mar. 1, 1708	ER	159
John, s. Joshua, b. Mar. 1, 1708	ER	202
John, m. Abigail CLOSE, Jan. 14, 1730/1, by Joshua Knap, J. P.	1	58
John, m. Abigail CLOSE, Jan. 14, 1730/1, by Joshua Knap[p], J. P.	ER	202
John, s. John [& Abigail], b. Nov. 24, 1731	1	58
John, s. John [& Abigail], b. Nov. 24, 1731	ER	202
John E., m. Joanna COLLINS, [Nov.] 17, [1835], by J. Mann	1	196
Joseph, m. Elizabeth RENOLDS, Mar. 16, 1684, by Jonathan Bell, Com.	LR1	447
Joseph, s. Benjamin [& Elisabeth], b. Dec. 13, 1707	ER	124
Joseph, s. Benjamin [& Elizabeth], b. Dec. 18, 1708	LR1	449
Joseph, s. Joseph, b. July 11, 1736	1	58
Joseph, [twin with Ruth, s. Joseph], b. July 11, 1736	ER	203
Joshua, m. Elizabeth RENOLDS, Mar. 16, 1687, by Jonathan Bell, Com.	ER	60
Joshua, s. Benjamin [& Elizabeth], b. Dec. 12, 1705	ER	124
Joshua, s. Benjamin [& Elizabeth], b. Dec. 12, 17[0]6	LR1	449
Joshua, s. John [& Abigail], b. Jan. 20, 1735/6	1	58
Joshua, of Greenwich, m. Ann Maria FRANCIS, of New York, [Feb.] 6, [1828], by Isaac Lewis	1	179
Julia Ann, m. Drake MEAD, b. of Greenwich, Sept. 8, 1828, by Rev. Ambrose S. Todd, of Stamford	1	181
Justus*, s. Caleb & Clemens, b. Apr. 1, 1731 *(Arnold copy has "Titus")	ER	186
Justus, s. John [& Abigail], b. Jan. 19, 1735/6	ER	202
Justus, b. Jan. 19, 1736; m. Sarah [ ]	1	110
Justus, b. Jan. 19, 1736	ER	216

GREENWICH VITAL RECORDS 201

	Vol.	Page
KNAPP, KNAP, (cont.)		
Justus, [s. Justus & Sarah], b. Oct. 11, 1756	1	110
Justus, [s. Justus & Sarah], b. Oct. 11, 1756	ER	216
Katharine, d. Timothy, m. Jacob LOCKWOOD, July 28, 1765	1	121
Lavina, of Greenwich, m. Nehemiah HOIT, of Stamford, June 8, 1836, by Platt Buffett	1	197
Martha, d. [Benjamin & Elisabeth], b. Feb. 28, 1700/1	ER	124
Martha, d. [Benjamin & Elizabeth], b. [ ], 1702	LR1	449
Martha, m. Joseph PALMER, Feb. 29, 1719/20, by Rev. Zachary Sacket	LR1	412
Mary, d. [Benjamin & Elizabeth], b. Aug. 22, [ ]	LR1	449
Mary, d. Timothie [& Elizabeth], b. Apr. 6, 1708	ER	123
Mary, d. Timothie [& Elizabeth], b. Apr. 6, 1708	LR1	449
Mary, d. Caleb & Clemence, b. Nov. 23, 1726	1	68
Mary, [d. Timothy & Ruth], b. Jan. 6, 1752	1	99
Mary, [d. Timothy & Ruth], b. Jan. 6, 1752	ER	238
Mary, d. Capt. Israel, m. Stephen MEAD, June 23, 1755, by Rev. Mr. Todd	1	105
Mary Ann, of Greenwich, m. William Alexander RAYNOR, of New York, Mar. 28, 1827, by Isaac Lewis	1	174
Matthew, [s. Timothy & Ruth], b. Feb. 8, 1756	1	99
Matthew, [s. Timothy & Ruth], b. Feb. 8, 1756	ER	238
Melicent, m. James W. SMITH, Apr. 18, 1842, by Rev. C. Wilcox	1	209
Mills, s. Caleb [& Clemens], b. Feb. 7, 1728/9	ER	185
Nathaniel, s. Caleb, b. Feb. 21, 1700	LR1	4
Nehemiah, s. Caleb, b. Oct. 15, 1714	LR1	4
Nehemiah, s. Caleb [& Sarah], b. Oct. 15, 1714	ER	121
Peeter, s. Caleb & Clemence, b. Apr. 4, 1731	1	68
Phinehas, s. David [& Rebeckah], b. July 30, 1739	1	65
Phinehas, s. David [& Reachell], b. July 30, 1739	ER	215
Prudence, d. Timothie [& Elizabeth], b. Jan. 26, 1712/13	ER	123
R-----, d. [Benjamin & Elisabeth], b. Aug. 22, 1702	ER	124
Rachell, m. John CURKIN, [ ], by Joshua Knapp, J. P.	ER	203
Rachell, m. John CURKUN, Nov. 21, 1731, by Joshua Knapp, J. P.	1	62
Rachel, d. David, m. Jesse MEAD, Dec. 10, 1760	1	116
Reacheall Cloos, d. David [& Reachell], b. Nov. 25, 1741	ER	215
Rachall Close, d. David [& Rebeckah], b. Nov. 26, 1741	1	65
Rebeckah, d. [Timothie & Elizabeth], b. Sept. 24, 1701	ER	123
Rebeckah, d. [Timothie & Elizabeth], b. Sept. 24, 1701	LR1	449
Rebecca, m. Jacob RUNDALL, Apr. 1, 1728, by Rev. Mr. Munson	1	57
Rebecca, m. Jacob RUNDALL, Apr. 5, 1729, by Rev. Mr. Munson	ER	199
Rebecca*, m. Nathaniel LOCKWOOD, Dec. 6, 1733,		

KNAPP, KNAP, (cont.)

	Vol.	Page
by Mr. Todd *("Ruth" in Mead's Hist.)	1	48
Rebeckah, d. David [& Rebeckah], b. July 18, 1737	1	65
Rebeckah, d. David [& Reachell], b. July 18, 1737	ER	215
Rebecca, m. Theophilus PECK, Jr., July 5, 1753	1	72
Rebecca, m. Theophilus PECK, Jr., July 5, 1753	ER	241
Rebecca Bush, [d. William & Esther], b. Dec. 14, 1791; d. Aug. 20, 1793	1	152
Reuben, s. Ebenezer [& Elizabeth], b. Apr. 6, 1737	ER	191
Reuben, s. Ebenezer [& Elizabeth], b. Aug. 6, 1737	1	50
Rueamah, d. Timothie, b. Aug. 12, 1717	LR1	451
Ruth, d. [Timothie & Martha], b. Feb. 24, 1714/15	ER	123
Ruth, d. [Timothie & Martha], b. Feb. 24, 1714/15	LR1	449
Ruth, m. Nathaniel LOCKWOOD, Dec. 6, 1733, by Mr. Tode	ER	212
Ruth, d. Joseph, b. July 11, 1735	1	58
Ruth, [twin with Joseph, d. Joseph], b. July 11, 1736	ER	203
Ruth, [d. Timothy & Ruth], b. Nov. 27, 1757	1	99
Ruth, [d. Timothy & Ruth], b. Nov. 27, 1757	ER	238
Ruth, [d. Uriah], b. Sept. 26, 1761	1	106
Sally William, d. William [& Esther], b. Nov. 17, 1789	1	152
Samuell, s. Caleb & Clemence, b. Feb. 7, 1728/9	1	68
Samuell, s. Isaac [& Rebecca], b. June 24, 1731	1	54
Sam[ue]ll, s. Isaac [& Rebecca], b. June 24, 1731	ER	198
Samuell, s. Benjamin [& Susanah], b. May 19, 1735	1	65
Samuell, s. Beniamin [& Susanah], b. May 19, 1735	ER	203
Sarah, d. Caleb, b. June 27, 1708	LR1	4
Sarah, d. Caleb [& Sarah], b. June 27, 1708	ER	121
Sarah, m. Peter RENOLDS, May 15, 1712, by Rev. Richard Sacket	LR1	446
Sarah, m. Peter RENOLLS, Jan. 14, 1718/19, by Rev. Richard Sackett	ER	183
Sarah, d. Caleb & Clemens, b. Oct. 9, 1720	ER	185
Sarah, d. Caleb & Clemence, b. Oct. 29, 1720	1	68
Sarah, m. William RUNDLE, Apr. 12, 1722, by Rev. Mr. Sacet	1	52
Sarah, m. William RUNDALL, Apr. 12, 1722, by Rev. Mr. Jacit	ER	188
Sarah, d. [Ebenezer & Elizabeth], b. Feb. 20, 1727/8	1	50
Sarah, d. Ebenezer [& Elizabeth], b. Feb. 20, 1727/8	ER	191
Sarah, [w. Justus], b. Sept. 11, 1737	1	110
Sarah, w. Justus, b. Sept. 11, 1737	ER	216
Sarah, d. Charles, of Stamford, m. Nathaniel MEAD, Jan. 22, 1756, by Rev. Mr. Wells, of Stamford	1	105
Sollomon, s. [Uriah], b. Dec. 19, 1757	1	106
Susan, of Stanwich, m. John ALEXANDER, of Bedford, Feb. 2, [1823], by Platt Buffett	1	169
Susan Isaac, d. William [& Esther], b. Oct. 24, 1796	1	152

	Vol.	Page

KNAPP, KNAP, (cont.)

	Vol.	Page
Thomas, [s. Timothy & Ruth], b. Jan. 7, O. S. 1754	1	99
Thomas, [s. Timothy & Ruth], b. Jan. 7, N. S. 1754	ER	238
Timothie, m. Elizabeth SEAMOR, Mar. 16, 1699, by Capt. Umsted, J. P.	ER	123
Timothie, m. Elizabeth STRONGE(?)*, Mar. 16, 1699, by Capt. Umstead, J. P. *(SEYMOUR)	LR1	449
Timothie, s. Timothie [& Elizabeth], b. Aug. 9, 1703; d. Apr. 22, 1706	ER	123
Timothie, s. Timothie [& Elizabeth], b. Aug. 9, 1703; d. Apr. 22, 1706	LR1	449
Timothie, m. Martha WEEKS, Feb. 13, 1713, by Sam[ue]l Hoit, J. P.	LR1	449
Timothie, m. Martha WEEKS, Feb. 16, 1713/14, by Sam[ue]ll Hoit, J. P.	ER	123
Timothy, s. Caleb, b. Jan. 27, 1717	LR1	4
Timothy, s. Caleb [& Sarah], b. Jan. 27, 1717/18	ER	121
Timothy, m. Ruth CLOSE, d. Thomas, Sept. 14, 1751	1	99
Timothy, m. Ruth CLOSE, d. Thomas, Sept. 14, 1751	ER	238
Timothy, [s. Timothy & Ruth], b. Dec. 20, 1759	1	99
Timothy, [s. Timothy & Ruth], b. Dec. 20, 1759	ER	238
Titus*, s. Caleb & Clemens, b. Apr. 1, 1731 *("Justus" in Mead's Hist.)	ER	186
William, s. Elizabeth, b. Sept. 17, [ ]	1	131
William, [s. Justus & Sarah], b. Jan. 5, 1759	1	110
William, [s. Justus & Sarah], b. Jan. 5, 1759	ER	216
William, m. Esther ISAACS, d. Capt. Benjamin, of Norwalk, decd., Dec. 19, 1784, by Rev. Eben Dibble	1	152
William, had negroes, George, s. Milla, b. Dec. 13, 1792; Jenny, d. Milla, b. Jan. 18, 1795; Eleanor, d. Milla, b. Dec. 13, 1798; Rachal, d. Milla, b. May 23, 1800; & Alfred, s. Milla, b. Mar. 15, 1804	1	144
William, s. William [& Esther], b. Jan. 17, 1794	1	152
William, s. William [& Eather], d. Jan. 28, 1794	1	152
William Bush, s. William [& Esther], b. June 13, 1788; d. Feb. 15, 1789	1	152
LaBREE, Lawrence, of Patterson, N. J., m. Amey MEAD, formerly of Greenwich, Sept. 25, 1836, by Rev. Joseph H. Nichols	1	199
LANE, Alanson, m. Anna PURDY, b. of Greenwich, Aug. 12, 1835, by Chauncey Wilcox	1	196
Caroline R., m. Jay L. CLARK, b. of Greenwich, Feb. 22, 1847, by Rev. B. M. Yarrington	1	216
Hannah, m. Josiah LANE, Dec. 16, 1837, by James Jarman	1	199
Josiah, m. Hannah LANE, Dec. 16, 1837, by James		

	Vol.	Page
LANE, (cont.)		
Jarman	1	199
LAWRENCE, Joseph F., of Greensbury, m. Susan REYNOLDS, of Greenwich, Jan. 11, 1843, by Noah Coe	1	210
LEANE, [see under LEONE]		
LENT, Gilbert, m. Abigail S. SACKETT, [Feb. 15, 1836], by J. Mann	1	197
LEONE, LEANE, [see also LYON], Abigail, m. David MEAD, Dec. 16, 1707, by Ebenezer Mead, J. P.	LR1	4
Abigail*, m. David MEADE, Dec. 16, 1707, by Ebenezer Mead, J. P. *("Abigail LYON?")	ER	159
LEWIS, Isaac, had negro DENNIS, s. Fanny, b. June 27, 1810	1	79-80
Margaret Mariah, of Greenwich, m. Harvey Prindle PECK, of Hartford, Nov. 26, 1823, by Isaac Lewis	1	170
LIVINGSTON, E. Ridley, m. Ophelia Mariah MEAD, [July] 29, [1833], by J. Mann	1	191
LOCKWOOD, Abigail, [d. Gershom], b. Apr. 16, 1746	1	81-2
Abigail, [d. Gershom, Jr.], b. Apr. 16, 1746	ER	219
Abigail, d. Enos, m. Oliver FERRIS, Feb. 10, 1779, by Rev. Mr. Burrit	1	140
Abram, [s. Gershom], b. Oct. 6, 1759	1	81-2
Abram, [s. Gershom, Jr.], b. Oct. 6, 1759	ER	219
Alexander, m. Mary Elizabeth POT[T]S, b. of Stanwich, Nov. 17, 1825, by Platt Buffett	1	172
Anna, [d. Jonathan & Elizabeth], b. Mar. 12, 1734	1	107
Arnea, [child of Jonathan & Elizabeth], b. Mar. 12, 1734	ER	212
Betsey*, [d. Jeremiah], b. Jan. 17, 1763 *(Or "Elizabeth")	1	122
Catharine, d. Samuel, m. Joseph MEAD, Dec. 10, 1755	1	93
Catharine, [d. Jacob & Katharine], b. Aug. 17, 1771	1	121
Charles, [s. Jacob & Katharine], b. May 8, 1766	1	121
Charles, Jr., m. Deborah LOCKWOOD, b. of Greenwich, Nov. 27, 1821, by Isaac Lewis	1	166
Charlotte, of Vermont but residing in Stanwich, m. Isaac DEAN, of North Stamford, Nov. 23, 1825, by Platt Buffett	1	172
David, [s. Theophilus & Hannah], b. Feb. 18, 1763	1	83
David, [s. Theophilus & Hannah], b. Feb. 18, 1763	ER	236
Deborah, [d. Jonathan & Elizabeth], b. Apr. 6, 1750; lived almost a month	1	107
Deborah, [d. Jonathan & Elizabeth], b. Apr. 6, 1750; lived almost a month	ER	212
Deborah, [d. Jonathan & Elizabeth], b. July 28, 1755	1	107
Deborah, [d. Jonathan & Elizabeth], b. July 28, 1755	ER	212
Deborah, m. Charles LOCKWOOD, Jr., b. of Greenwich, Nov. 27, 1821, by Isaac Lewis	1	166
Denison A., m. Clarissa STUDWELL, b. of Greenwich,		

GREENWICH VITAL RECORDS 205

	Vol.	Page
LOCKWOOD, (cont.)		
Jan. 27, 1833, by Rev. Platt Buffett, of Stanwich	1	189
Dorcas, [d. Jonathan & Elizabeth], b. Feb. 19, 1748	1	107
Dorcas, [d. Jonathan & Elizabeth], b. Feb. 19, 1748	ER	212
Drusilla, [d. Abraham], b. May 28, 1770	1	123
Edmond, [s. Jonathan & Elizabeth], b. July 6, 1757	1	107
Edmund, m. Mary Ann **NEWMAN**, Nov. 9, 1842, by Farnam Knowlton	1	210
Edward, [s. Jonathan & Elizabeth], b. July 6, 1757	ER	212
Eli, [s. Gershom], b. [ ], 1757	1	81-2
Eli, [s. Gershom, Jr.], b. [ ], 1757	ER	219
Eliphalet, [s. Joseph & Charity], b. Mar. 23, 1753	1	84
Eliphalet, [s. Joseph & Charity], b. Mar. 23, 1753	ER	238
Eliza, [d. Gershom, Jr.], b. Jan. 9, 1739; d. [ ]	ER	219
Eliz[a], [d. Gershom, Jr.], b. Sept. 24, 1768	ER	219
Eliz[abeth], [d. Gershom], b. Jan. 9, 1739; d. [ ]	1	81-2
Elizabeth, [d. Jonathan & Elizabeth], b. Feb. 14, 1741	1	107
Elizabeth, [d. Jonathan & Elizabeth], b. Feb. 14, 1741	ER	212
Elizabeth, d. Gershom, m. [ ], Jan. 15, 1743/4, by Mr. Todd	CP	108
Elizabeth, d. Gershom, m. Silas **BETTS**, Jan. 15, 1743/4, by Mr. Todd	23	227*
Eliz[abeth], [d. Gershom], b. Sept. 24, 1768	1	81-2
Elizabeth, see Betsey **LOCKWOOD**	1	122
Frances Louisa, m. Samuel **FERRIS**, b. of Greenwich, Jan. 12, 1847, by Rev. B. M. Yarrington	1	216
Gershom, [s. Gershom], b. Feb. 9, 1753	1	81-2
Gershom, s. Gershom, of Coscob, b. Feb. 9, 1753	1	120
Gershom, [s. Gershom, Jr.], b. Feb. 9, 1753	ER	219
Gershom, s. Gershom, of Cos Cob, b. Feb. 9, 1753	ER	241
Hanford, m. [ ] **NASH**, b. of Greenwich, Oct. 6, 1830, at the house of James Nash, by Rev. Daniel J. Wright	1	185
Hannah, d. Gershom, b. Sept. 20, 1710	LR1	452
Hannah, d. Gershom, b. Sept. 20, 1710	ER	137
Hannah, d. [Nathaniel & Rebecca], b. May 25, 1741	1	48
Hannah, d. Nathaniel, b. May 25, 1741	ER	212
Hannah, [d. Gershom], b. Apr. 16, 1744	1	81-2
Hannah, [d. Gershom, Jr.], b. Apr. 16, 1744	ER	219
Hannah, w. Nathaniel, Jr., d. Nov. 9, 1749	CP	107
Hannah, w. Nathaniel, Jr., d. Nov. 9, 1749	ER	236
Hannah, [d. Theophilus & Hannah], b. Feb. 9, 1752	1	83
Hannah, [d. Theophilus & Hannah], b. Feb. 9, 1752	ER	236
Henry, m. Fanny **MEAD**, Dec. 4, 1837, by James Jarman	1	199
Hezekiah, s. Gershom, b. June 29, 1706	LR1	452
Hezekiah, s. Gershom, b. June 29, 1706	ER	137
Israel, [s. Theophilus & Hannah], b. Nov. 28, 1755	1	83

LOCKWOOD, (cont.)

	Vol.	Page
Israel, [s. Theophilus & Hannah], b. Nov. 28, 1755	ER	236
Jabez, s. Gershom, s. Lieut, [ ], decd., b. Jan. 18, 1702/3	LR1	452
Jabez, 1st s. Gershom, s. of Lieut. [ ], b. Jan. 18, 1702/3	ER	137
Jacob, m. Katharine **KNAPP**, d. Timothy, July 28, 1765	1	121
James, colored had d. Mary, b. Feb. 12, 1813; s. William, b. Feb. 25, 1815 & d. Luta, b. July 23, 1817	1	140
Jared, [s. Joseph & Charity], b. July 7, 1758	1	84
Jared, [s. Joseph & Charity], b. July 7, 1758	ER	238
Jerusha, [d. Nathaniel & Sarah], b. Dec. 12, 1756	CP	107
Jerusha, [d. Nathaniel & Sarah], b. Dec. 12, 1756	ER	236
John, [s. Theophilus & Hannah], b. Apr. 26, 1754	1	83
John, [s. Thoephilis & Hannah], b. Apr. 26, 1754	ER	236
John, [s. Gershom], b. [ ], 1762	1	81-2
Jno, [s. Gershom, Jr.], b. [ ], 1762	ER	219
Jonathan, Lieut, & J. P., d. May 12, 1683	LR1	448
Jonathan, Jr., s. Lieut, [ ] decd., d. Nov. 9, 1689	ER	71
Jonathan, Jr., s. [Lieut. Jonathan & J. P.], d. Nov. 9, 1689	LR1	448
Jonathan, m. Elizabeth **CLOSE**, d. Benjamin, June 24, 1733	1	107
Jonathan, m. Elizabeth **CLOSE**, d. Benjamin, June 24, 1733	ER	212
Jonathan, [s. Jonathan & Elizabeth], b. Aug. 24, 1745; lived 1 y. 5 m.	1	107
Jonathan, [s. Jonathan & Elizabeth], b. Aug. 24, 1745; d. 1 y. 5 m. after birth	ER	212
Jonathan, [s. Jonathan & Elizabeth], b. Apr. 1, 1751	1	107
Jonathan, [s. Jonathan & Elizabeth], b. Apr. 1, 1751	ER	212
Joseph, m. Charity **KNAPP**, b. of Greenwich, Nov. 10, 1751, by Rev. Abraham Todd	1	84
Joseph, m. Charity **KNAPP**, b. of Greenwich, Nov. 10, 1751, by Rev. Abraham Todd	ER	238
Joseph, [s. Joseph & Charity], b. Jan. 9, 1755	1	84
Joseph, [s. Joseph & Charity], b. Jan. 9, 1755	ER	238
Lebni, s. Gershom, b. May 30, 1708	LR1	452
Libni, s. Gershom, b. May 30, 1708	ER	137
Lucy Ann, [d. Theophilus & Hannah], b. Jan. 22, 1769	1	83
Lucy Ann, [d. Theophilus & Hannah], b. Jan. 22, 1769	ER	236
Major, m. Sarah H. **MILLS**, Dec. 26, 1827, by Rev. Lyman Andrus	1	180
Major, m. Catharine **HUSTED**, May 21, 1833, by C. Wilcox	1	191
Margaret Ritch, m. Charles **FERRIS**, b. of Greenwich, Oct. 13, 1839, by Noah Coe	1	204
Mary, d. [Gershom], b. Nov. 6, 1712	LR1	452

GREENWICH VITAL RECORDS

	Vol.	Page
LOCKWOOD, (cont.)		
Mary, 2nd, d. Gershom, b. Nov. 6, 1712	ER	137
Mary, [d. Gershom], b. Feb. 24, 1742	1	81-2
Mary, [d. Gershom, Jr.], b. Feb. 24, 1742	ER	219
Mary, [d. Jonathan & Elizabeth], b. June 13, 1743	1	107
Mary, [d. Jonathan & Elizabeth], b. June 13, 1743	ER	212
Michael B., m. Phebe Ann **FLOOD**, Nov. 30, 1843, by Rev. Chauncy Wilcox	1	212
Nancy, m. Alen **STUDWELL**, b. of Greenwich, Feb. 15, 1825, by Rev. Henry Hoit, Jr., of Stamford	1	172
Nathan, s. Gershom, b. July 23, 1704	LR1	452
Nathan, s. Gershom, b. July 28, 1704	ER	137
Nathaniel, Jr., m. Hannah **MEAD**, Nov. [ ], [ ], by Rev. Abraham Todd	ER	236
Nathaniel, Jr., b. Dec. 2, 1727; d. Dec. 22, 1758	CP	107
Nathaniel, Jr., b. Sept. 2, 1727*; d. Dec. 22, 1758 *(Arnold copy has "1827")	ER	236
Nathaniel, m. Rebecca* **KNAP[P]**, Dec. 6, 1733, by Mr. Todd *("Ruth" in Mead's Hist.)	1	48
Nathaniel, m. Ruth **KNAP[P]**, Dec. 6, 1733, by Mr. Tode	ER	212
Nathaniell, s. Nathaniel, b. Mar. 3, 1744	ER	212
Nathaniel, s. Nathaniel [& Rebecca], b. Mar. 3, 1744/5	1	48
Nathaniel, Jr., m. Hannah **MEAD**, [ ], by Rev. Abraham Todd	CP	107
Nathaniel, m. Sarah **CURTIS**, Oct. 8, [ ], by Rev. Abraham Todd	CP	107
Nathaniel, m. Sarah **CURTIS**, Oct. 8,[ ], by Rev. Abraham Todd	ER	236
Phinehas, [s. Jacob & Katharine], b. Nov. [ ], 1769	1	121
Rebecca, d. Jeremiah, m. James **SHERWOOD**, Dec. [ ], 1767	1	103
Reuben D., m. Anna A. **DAYTON**, b. of Greenwich, July 3, 1842, by Rev. D. B. Butts, of Stanwich	1	209
Ruth, d. Nathaniel [& Rebecca], b. June 28, 1738	1	48
Ruth, d. Nathaniell [& Ruth], b. June 28, 1738	ER	212
Ruth, [d. Theophilus & Hannah], b. Apr. 4, 1750	1	83
Ruth, [d. Theophilus & Hannah], b. Apr. 4, 1750	ER	236
Ruth, [d. Nathaniel & Sarah], b. May 16, 1754	CP	107
Ruth, [d. Nathaniel & Sarah], b. May 16, 1754	ER	236
Sally, of Greenwich, m. John **PARSONS**, of Sharon, Litchfield Co., Oct. 30, [1821], by Isaac Lewis	1	166
Sally Ann, of Greenwich, m. John B. **STOKEM**, of Norwalk, May 27, [1827], by Isaac Lewis	1	176
Sarah, [d. Jonathan & Elizabeth], b. June 17, 1735; d. in 2 m.	1	107
Sarah, [d. Jonathan & Elizabeth], b. June 17, 1735; d. in 2 m.	ER	212
Sarah, [d. Jonathan & Elizabeth], b. Jan. 29, 1736	1	107

BARBOUR COLLECTION

	Vol.	Page
LOCKWOOD, (cont.)		
Sarah, 2nd, [d. Jonathan & Elizabeth], b. Jan. 29, 1736	ER	212
Sarah, [d. Nathaniel & Sarah], b. Feb. 16, 1752	CP	107
Sarah, [d. Nathaniel & Sarah], b. Feb. 16, 1752	ER	236
Sarah, [d. Gershom], b. July 3, 1764	1	81-2
Sarah, [d. Gershom, Jr.], b. July 8, 1764	ER	219
Sarah, of Greenwich, m. William P. **REYNOLDS**, of Chester Co. of Warren, N. Y., May 27, 1823, by Platt Buffett	1	171
Shubael, [s. Jacob & Katharine], b. Dec. 21, 1768	1	121
Stephen, [s. Jeremiah], b. June 24, 1760	1	122
Susannah, [d. Jonathan & Elizabeth], b. Apr. 12, 1739	1	107
Susanna, [d. Jonathan & Elizabeth], b. Apr. 12, 1739	ER	212
Thadeus, m. Rachal **FINCH**, b. of Stanwich, Jan. 29, 1824, by Rev. Platt Buffett	1	170
Theodosia, [child of Jonathan & Elizabeth], b. May 28, 1753	1	107
Theodosia, [d. Jonathan & Elizabeth], b. May 28, 1753	ER	212
Theophilus, m. Hannah **CLOSE**, d. Thomas, Dec. 17, 1749	1	83
Theophilus, m. Hannah **CLOSE**, d. Thomas, Dec. 17, 1749	ER	236
Theophilus, [s. Theophilus & Hannah], b. Feb. 6, 1759	1	83
Theophilus, [s. Theophilus & Hannah], b. Feb. 6, 1759	ER	236
Thomas, [s. Theophilus & Hannah], b. Jan. 22, 1761	1	83
Thomas, [s. Theophilus & Hannah], b. Jan. 22, 1761	ER	236
Walter, m. Levina **FERRIS**, Dec. 4, 1837, by James Jarman	1	199
William H., m. Ann **FERRIS**, b. of Greenwich, July 8, 1838, by Thomas Payne	1	201
LOUDON, Allen, m. Elizabeth **REUTSCHARTS**, b. of Greenwich, Dec. 20, 1837, by Chauncey Wilcox	1	198
Obadiah, m. Jane **BURKHEART**, Oct. 15, 1831, by E. S. Raymond	1	186
Sary M., m. William **SNIFFIN**, b. of Greenwich, Aug. 1, 1844, by Rev. Chauncey Wilcox	1	212
LOUNSBURY, Delia Ann, m. John **BANEY**, b. of Greenwich, Feb. 26, 1843, by Chauncey Wilcox	1	211
Hetty Elizabeth, of Conn., m. Ruel Jones Morton **CLARK**, of Northampton, Mass., Sept. 17, 1843, by Rev. S. W. Scofield	1	211
Rufus, m. Mary Ann **FERRIS**, Feb. 22, 1832, by E. S. Raymond	1	187
Silas, m. Anngenette **BROWN**, Oct. 1, 1834, by C. Wilcox	1	194
LYON, [see also **LEONE**], Abigail, d. Thomas, m. William **ANDERSON**, Oct. 16, 1716, by Rev. Christopher Bridge	1	48

GREENWICH VITAL RECORDS

	Vol.	Page
LYON, (cont.)		
Abigail, d. Thomas, m. William **ANDERSON**, Oct. 16, 1716, by Rev. Christopher Bridge	ER	177
Abigail Elizabeth, m. Isaac **HOLLY**, b. of Greenwich, Sept. 20, 1826, by Platt Buffett	1	174
Abigaill Jane, m. Henry **DAVIS**, Feb. 28, 1819, by Rev. Drake Wilson. Witnesses: Seth Lyon, Fitch Lyon, Elias Lyon	1	205
Angeline A., m. John K. **BROWN**, Dec. 20, [1824], by Platt Buffett	1	171
Augustus, m. Sarah Amanda **MILLS**, Dec. 7, 1820, by Rev. Benjamin Griffin	1	165
Benjamin Westly*, [s. James], b. Apr. 15, 1764	1	102
*(Woolsey?)	ER	236
Benjamin Woolsey, [s. James], b. Apr. 15, 1764		
Benjamin Woolsey, had negroes Plato, b. Nov. 1, 1798 & Anthony, b. Dec. 3, 1795	1	159
Daniell, m. Elizabeth **MARSHALL**, Aug. 26, 1736, by James Reynolls, J. P.	1	67
Daniell, m. Elizabeth **MARSHALL**, Aug. 26, 1736, by Jeames Reynolds, J. P.	ER	216
	ER	216
Daniell, [s. Daniell & Elizabeth], b. Dec. 12, 1736	1	67
Daniell, s. [Daniell & Elizabeth], b. Dec. 20, 1736	1	102
Daniel, [s. James], b. Dec. 20, 1756	ER	236
Daniel, [s. James], b. Dec. 20, 1756	1	102
David, [s. James], b. July 19, 1754	ER	236
David, [s. James], b. July 19, 1754	1	46
Elizabeth, d. [John], b. June 12, 1718	ER	173
Elizabeth, d. [John], b. June 12, 1718	1	102
Elizabeth, [d. James], b. Jan. 10, 1762	ER	236
Elizabeth, [d. James], b. Jan. 10, 1762	1	98
Hannah, m. Thomas **CLOSE**, May 6, 1729	ER	201
Hannah, m. Thomas **CLOSE**, May 6, 1729		
Hannah, d. Joseph, of White Plains, Westchester Co., m. Thomas **CLOSE**, Sept. 30, 1765, by Rev. Mr. Sackett, of Crampond	1	118
Isaac, m. Amelia **MEAD**, b. of Greenwich, Dec. 9, 1828, by Chauncey Wilcox	1	181
Isaac, m. Eliza **MEAD**, of Greenwich, Nov. 17, 1840, by Noah Coe	1	206
	1	46
James, s. [John], b. May 31, 1720	ER	173
James, s. [John], b. May 31, 1720	1	102
James, s. [James], b. Dec. 19, 1749	ER	236
James, [s. James], b. Dec. 19, 1749	1	46
John, s. John, b. Nov. 18, 1713	ER	173
John, s. John, Jr., b. Nov. 18, 1713		
[Joseph]*, Jr., m. Phebe **CLOSE**, Feb. 24, 1758	1	100

	Vol.	Page

LYON, (cont.)
Joseph Close, [s. & Phebe], b. Sept. 18, 1758	1	100
Mary, [d. James], b. Feb. 25, 1758	1	102
Mary, [d. James], b. Feb. 25, 1758	ER	236
Mary, m. James McMILLAN, b. of Greenwich, Feb. 25, 1826, by Isaac Lewis	1	173
Purdy, m. [ ] MERRETT, July 19, 1840, by John Smith	1	206
Rachel P., m. Benjamin W. HUSTED, b. of Greenwich, [Dec.] 24, [1827], by Isaac Lewis	1	178
Rodger, s. John, b. Dec. 13, 1715	1	46
Roger, s. John, b. Dec. 13, 1715	ER	173
Ruth, d. Thomas, decd., m. Abraham MEAD, s. Elnathan, b. of Greenwich, Nov. 1, 1753	1	114
Ruth, d. Thomas, decd., m. Abraham MEAD, s. Elnathan, Nov. 1, 1753, b. of Greenwich	ER	215
Sarah, [d. James], b. Dec. 16, 1751	1	102
Sarah, [d. James], b. Dec. 16, 1751	ER	236
Sarah, colored had children, Henry, b. Oct. 25, 1808, John, b. Feb. 19, 1809, Tamour, b. Nov. [ ], 1811, Deborah, b. Mar. 3, 1814, Margarett, b. Feb. 3, 1818 & Charles, b. May 13, 1820	1	101
W[illia]m L., Capt. of New York City, m. Catharine MEAD, of Greenwich, May 25, 1840, by Noah Coe	1	207

McGURNE, William, m. Matilda BURNS, b. of Greenwich, June 6, 1841, by Rev. E. T. Ball 1 207

McGURRAN, Patrick, m. Harriet HOWARD, Feb. 22, 1822, by William Knapp, J. P. 1 167

MACKAY, McCAY, MACAY, Donold, s. John, Jr. [& Elizabeth Huggford], b. Sept. 6, 1802 1 157
Hugh, s. John, Jr. [& Elizabeth Huggford], b. June 12, 1797	1	157
John, Jr., m. Elizabeth Huggford KNAPP, d. Israel, decd., [ ]	1	157
Julia, d. William*, Jr., b. Aug. 14, 1806 *(John?)	1	157
Katharine, m. Thomas PHILLIPS, Mar. 6, 1832, by Chauncey Wilcox	1	190
Margaret, d. John, Jr. [& Elizabeth Huggford], b. July 29, 1800	1	157
Mary*, d. John, Jr. [& Elizabeth Huggford], b. Oct. 12, 1804 *(Perhaps twin with William)	1	157
Mary, m. Theodore HAIGHT, b. of Greenwich, Nov. 14, 1837, by C. Wilcox	1	198
William*, s. William, Jr., b. Oct. 12, 1804 *(Perhaps twin with Mary, dau. of John)	1	157

McMILLAN, James, m. Mary LYON, b. of Greenwich, Feb. 25, 1826, by Isaac Lewis 1 173

GREENWICH VITAL RECORDS 211

	Vol.	Page
MARSHALL, MARSHELL, Abigail, [d. Daniel & Abigail], ae 6 y., Feb. 1, last [ ]	1	52
Abigall, d. [Daniell], ae 6 y., Feb. [ ], last [ ]	ER	141
Amey, [d. Joseph], b. Nov. 28, 1718	1	55
Amey, [d. Joseph], b. Nov, 28, 1718	ER	141
Daniel, m. Abigail BUTTLER, June 23, 1703	1	52
Daniell, m. Abigail BUTTLER, June 23, 1703	ER	141
Daniel, s. [Daniel & Abigail], b. Jan. 28, 1703/4	1	52
Daniell, s. [Daniell & Abigail], b. Jan. 28, 1703/4	ER	141
David, s. John, b. Jan. 31, 1706/7	ER	141
David, s. John, b. Jan. 31, 1706/7	LR1	458
Debrow, [s. Joseph], b. Feb. 4, 1708	1	55
Debrow, d. [Joseph], b. Feb. 4, 1708	ER	141
Deborah, [d. , Jr. & Sarah], b. Oct. 9, 1739	1	87-8
Deborah, [d. , Jr. & Sarah], b. Oct. 9, 1739	ER	204
Drake, m. Rebecca FLORENCE, [May] 21, [1832], by J. Mann	1	190
Elihu, s. John, b. June 4, 1710	LR1	458
Elihu, s. John, b. June 4, 1710	ER	141
Elizabeth, d. John, b. Oct. 6, 1708	ER	141
Elizabeth, d. John, b. Oct. 6, 1708	LR1	458
Elizabeth, m. Daniell LYON, Aug. 26, 1736, by James Reynolls, J. P.	1	67
Elizabeth, m. Daniell LYON, Aug. 26, 1736, by Jeames Reynolds, J. P.	ER	216
Freelove, [d. Daniel & Abigail], ae 8 y., Mar. 23,last [ ]	1	52
Freelove, d. [Daniel], ae 8 y., Mar. 23, last [ ]	ER	141
Hannah, [d. Daniel & Abigail], ae 1 y., Aug. 6, last [ ]	1	52
Hanah, [d. Daniell], ae 1 y., Aug. 6, last [ ]	ER	141
Hannah, d. John, [Jr.], b. Dec. 25, 1704/5	LR1	458
Hannah, d. John, Jr., b. Dec. 25, 1704/5	ER	141
Hannah, [d. [ ], Jr. & Sarah], b. Nov. 18, 1733; d. Feb. 28, 1744	1	87-8
Hannah, [d.], Jr. & Sarah], b. Nov. 18, 1733; d. Feb. 28, 1744	ER	204
Henry, [s.], Jr. & Sarah], b. Apr. 30, 1744	1	87-8
Henry, [s.], Jr. & Sarah], b. Apr. 30, 1744	ER	204
Ichabod, s. John, b. Feb. 23, 1717/18	LR1	458
Ichabod, s. John, b. Feb. 23, 1717/18	ER	141
Jehu, s. John, b. Sept. 24, 1714	ER	141
John, s. John, Jr., b. May [ ]	LR1	458
John, s. John, Jr., b. May [ ], 17[ ]	ER	141
John, Jr., m. [ ]ember 10, [ ]	LR1	458
John, s. John, b. Sept. 24, 1714	LR1	458
John, Jr., m. Sarah MARSHALL, Jan. [ ], 1731/2, by Joshua Knapp, J. P,	1	63
John, m. Serah MARSHELL, Jan. [ ], 1731/2, by Joshua Knapp, J. P.	ER	204

	Vol.	Page
MARSHALL, MARSHELL, (cont.)		
[John]*, Jr., m. Sarah MARSHALL, d. Joseph, Jan. 10, 1732, by Joshua Knapp, J. P. *(Supplied from Mead's Hist.)	1	87-8
[John]*, Jr., m. Sarah MARSHALL, d. Joseph, Jan. 10, 1732, by Joshua Knapp, J. P. *(Supplied from Mead's Hist.)	ER	204
John, [s.], Jr. & Sarah], b. Apr. 18, 1732	1	87-8
John, [s.], & Sarah], b. Apr. 18, 1732	ER	204
Joseph, [s. Joseph], b. July 30, 1705	1	55
Joseph, s. [Joseph], b. July 30, 1705	ER	141
Joseph, Jr., m. Han[n]ah FERRIS, July 24, 1731, by Joshua Knapp, J. P.	1	61
Joseph, Jr., m. Hannah FERRIS, July 24, 1731, by Joshua Knapp, J. P.	ER	203
Joseph, [s. , Jr. & Sarah], b. July 2, 1746	1	87-8
Joseph, [s. , Jr. & Sarah], b. July 2, 1746	ER	204
Justus, [s. , Jr. & Sarah], b. Sept. 4, 1735	1	87-8
Justus, [s. , Jr. & Sarah], b. Sept. 4, 1735	ER	204
Lebbeus, s. Jeremiah & Mary (HIBBARD), b. Sept. 15, 1768	1	96
Lettishe, [child of [ ], Jr. & Sarah], b. Jan. 27, 1742	ER	204
Letteshe, [d. , Jr. & Sarah], b. Jan. 28, 1742	1	87-8
Marsey*, m. Daniell OGDEN, Nov. 8, 1734, by Rev. Abraham Todd *("Mary" in Mead's Hist.)	ER	213
Marcy, m. Daniell OGDEN, Nov. 8, 1754, by Rev. Abraham Todd	1	67
Mariah, [d. Daniel & Abigail], ae 4 y., Aug. 6, last [ ]	1	52
Mary, d. John, b. Jan. 11, 1711/12	ER	141
Mary, [d. Joseph], b. Nov. 8, 1720	1	55
Mary, d. [Joseph], b. Nov. 8, 1720	ER	141
Mary, [d. , Jr. & Sarah], b. Apr. 30, 1750	1	87-8
Mary, [d. , Jr. & Sarah], b. Apr. 30, 1750	ER	204
Mary Jane, found under Woolsey LYON's horse shed (so called), supposed to have been born Sept. 25, 1833	1	216
Mary W., m. William A. BETTS, b. of Greenwich, May 12, 1847, by Rev. B. M. Yarrington	1 LR1	216
Mercy, d. John, Jan. 11, 1711/12	LR1	458
Michajah, s. John, b. June 17, 1723	ER	458
Michaiah, s. John, b. June 17, 1723/4		141
Nathaniell, s. Daniel [& Abigail], ae 22 y., May 27, last [ ]	1 ER	52
Nathaniell, s. Daniell, ae 22 y., May 27, last [ ]	ER	141
Neamiah, s. [Daniell], ae 4 y., Aug. 6, last [ ]	ER	141
Rebeccah, d. Daniell, ae 5 m., about May 25, 1727	1	141
Rebeckah, [d. Daniel & Abigail], ae 5 m. [ ]	1	52
Ruth, m. Abraham NICKOLLS, Dec. 6, 1722	ER	49

GREENWICH VITAL RECORDS 213

	Vol.	Page
MARSHALL, MARSHELL, (cont.)		
Ruth, m. Abraham NICKALLS, Dec. 6, 1722	ER	189
Samuell, [s. Daniel & Abigail], ae 12 y., Mar. 6, last [ ]	1	52
Samuell, s. [Daniel], ae 12 y., Mar. 6, last [ ]	ER	141
Samuell, decd, & w. Mary, had s. [ ], b. Sept. 2, 1713; d. within 24 hr.	1	56
Samuell, decd. & Mary, had s. [ ], b. Sept. 23, 1713; d. 24 h. after birth	ER	172
Sarah, [d. Joseph], b. July 19, 1703	1	55
Sarah, d. [Joseph], b. July 19, 1703	ER	141
Sarah, m. John MARSHALL, Jr., Jan. [ ], 1731/2, by Joshua Knapp, J. P.	1	63
Serah, m. John MARSHALL, Jan. [ ], 1731/2, by Joshua Knapp, J. P.	ER	204
Sarah, d. Joseph, m. [ ] MARSHALL, Jr., Jan. 10, 1732, by Joshua Knapp, J. P.	1	87-8
Sarah, d. Joseph, m. [ ] MARSHALL, Jr., Jan. 10, 1732, by Joshua Knapp, J. P.	ER	204
Sarah, [d. [ ], Jr. & Sarah], b. Sept. 12, 1737	1	87-8
Sarah, d. [ ], Jr. & Sarah], b. Sept. 12, 1737	ER	204
Sarah, made affidavit Jan. 26, 1760, that Mary JONES (wid.) gave birth to son Frederick Harding JONES, b. Nov. 28, 1759, and she was at her house the summer before last with Mr. Hardin JONES, of N. C., whom she called husband	1	92
Seth, m. Fanny MORRELL, b. of Greenwich, Jan. 7, 1828, by Rev. John Ellis, of Stamford	1	178
Stephen, m. Ann Genette YOUNG, b. of Greenwich, Apr. 29, 1838, by Rev. Platt Buffett	1	200
Susannah, [d. Joseph], b. July 7, 1727	1	55
Susannah, d. [Joseph], b. July 7, 1727	ER	141
Thadeus, [s. Joseph], b. Nov. 2, 1707	1	55
Thadeus, s. [Joseph], b. Nov. 2, 1707	ER	141
Thomas, [s. Daniel & Abigail], ae 21 y., Aug. 6 last [ ]	1	52
Thomas, s. [Daniell], ae 21 y., Aug. 6, last [ ]	ER	141
Zaccheus, s. John, b. Apr. 11, 1716	LR1	458
Zacheus, s. John, b. Apr. 11, 1716	ER	141
MARTIN, Hue, m. Abigaill RENOLS, July 8, 1731, by Samuel Peck, J. P.	1	63
Hue, m. Abigell RENELS, July 8, 1731, by Sam[ue]ll Peck, J. P.	ER	203
James, s. Hue [& Abigaill], b. Dec. 24, 1731	1	63
James, s. Hue [& Abigell], b. Dec. 24, [ ]	ER	203
MATHEWS, John, m. Susan MEAD, Jan. 19, 1839, by N. Coe	1	202
MAYHEW, [see also MAYO], Thomas, of Maine, m. Mary H. MEAD, of Greenwich, Dec. 25, 1842, by Noah Coe	1	210
MAYO, [see also MAYHEW], Thomas, Capt., m. Rebecca Rosina		

MAYO, (cont.)

	Vol.	Page
CLOSE, [d. Samuel & Eliza], Aug. 24, 1858	1	118
MEAD, MEADE, Aaron, [s. Silas & Mary], b. July 11, 1751	1	71
Aaron, [s. Silas & Mary], b. July 11, 1751	ER	229
Abigail, d. Ebenezer, b. Sept. 13, 1705	LR1	450
Abigail, d. Ebenezer, b. Sept. 13, 1705	ER	144
Abigail, d. [David], b. July 17, 1710	ER	159
Abigail, [d. David & Abigail], b. [ ], 17, 1710	LR1	4
Abigail, d. Joseph, b. Aug. 16, 1729	1	120
Abigail, d. Josiah, b. Aug. 16, 1729; had s. John, b. Jan. 24, 1753	ER	241
Abigall, m. Jonathan FISK, Apr. 23, 1738, by Rev. Mr. Todd	1	59
Abigell, m. Jonathan FISK, Apr. 23, 1738, by Rev. Mr. Todd	ER	219
Abigail, d. John, b. Jan. 24, 1753	1	120
Abigail, [d. Nathaniel & Prudence], b. Mar. 28, 1757	1	125
Abigail, [d. Nathaniel & Prudence], b. Mar. 28, 1757	ER	229
Abigail, Jr., made affidavit Jan. 26, 1760, that Mary JONES, (wid.), gave birth to son Frederick Harding JONES, b. Nov. 28, 1759, and she was at her house the summer before last with Mr. Hardin JONES, of N. C., whom she called husband	1	92
Abigail, [d. Nathaniel, 3rd], b. May 26, 1766	1	123
Abigail, [d. Jesse & Rachel], b. Mar. 31, 1767	1	116
Abigail, [d. Zenas], b. Dec. 21, 18[ ]	CP	108
Abigail, m. Jonas MEAD, 2nd, [Aug.] 14, [1832], by J. Mann	1	190
Abner, [s. Silas & Mary], b. Feb. 24, 1750	1	71
Abner, [s. Silas & Mary], b. Feb. 24, 1750	ER	229
Abraham, s. [Ebenezer, Jr. & Hannah], b. Dec. 5, 1721	1	60
Abraham, s. [Ebenezer, Jr. & Hannah], b. Dec. 5, 1721	ER	180
Abraham, s. Elnathan, b. May 22, 1733; m. Ruth LYON, d. Thomas, decd, Nov. 1, 1753, (b. of Greenwich)	1	114
Abraham, s. Elnathan, b. May 22, 1735; m. Ruth LYON, d. Thomas, decd., Nov. 1, 1753, b. of Greenwich	ER	215
Abraham, Jr., [s. Abraham & Ruth], b. Aug. 26, 1754	1	114
Abraham, Jr., s. [Abraham & Ruth], b. Aug. 26, 1754	ER	215
Abraham, Jr., m. Keziah HOW, d. Isaac, Jan. 3, 1765, by Rev. Abraham Todd	1	113
Abraham, Jr., m. Keziah HOWE, d. Isaac, Jan. 3, 1765, by Rev. Abraham Todd	1	156
Adaline, d. Daniel Smith [& Rachal], b. Aug. [ ]	1	165
Adaline, d. Daniel Smith [& Rachal], d. Aug. [ ]	1	164
Adaline, d. Daniel Smith [& Rachall], b. Oct. 3, 1807	1	164

GREENWICH VITAL RECORDS 215

	Vol.	Page
MEAD, MEADE, (cont.)		
Alice, [d. Silas & Mary], b. Nov. 21, 1755	1	71
Alice, [d. Silas & Mary], b. Nov. 21, 1755	ER	229
Allen, of West Greenwich, m. Rachel HOIT, of Stanwich, Nov. 29, 1822, by Platt Buffet	1	168
Alma, d. Jared [& Lydia], b. July 26, 1783	1	128
Almira, d. Eben[eze]r, Jr. [& Lotte], b. Sept. 15, 1801	1	157
Alsa, [child of John, Jr. & Mary, Jr.], b. Aug. 24, 1774	1	117
Alvah, m. Jane Augusta RUNDLE, b. of Greenwich, Dec. 21, 1825, by Isaac Lewis	1	172
Alvin, s. Jared [& Lydia], b. Nov. 30, 1794	1	128
Alvin, m. Eliza PECK, Dec. 18, 1821, by Rev. Isaac Lewis	1	91
Alvin, m. Eliza PECK, b. of Greenwich, Dec. 18, 1821, by Isaac Lewis	1	167
Amelia, m. Isaac LYON, b. of Greenwich, Dec. 9, 1828, by Chauncey Wilcox	1	181
Amos, s. [Ebenezer, Jr. & Hannah], b. Feb. 22, 1730	1	60
Amos, s. [Ebenezer, Jr. & Hannah], b. Feb. 22, 1730	ER	180
Amos, Dr., m. Ruth BUSH, d. Justus, Jan. 1, 1753, by Rev. Mr. Todd	1	73
Amos, Dr., m. Ruth BUSH, d. Justus, Jan. 1, 1753, by Rev. Mr. Todd	ER	241
Amos, had negroes York, b. July 4, 1784, Eber, b. May 8, 1786, Cuff, b. June 17, 1786, Flora, b. Dec. 17, 1787, Rose, d. Milly, b. Jan. 17, 1790 & Lewis, d. Job, b. June 21, 1791	1	141
Amos, s. Richard [& Rachal], b. May 29, 1799	1	137
Amy, wid. Ebenezer, Jr., m. Benjamin HOBBY, Feb. 25, 1763	1	128
Amy, d. Ebenezer, b. June 7, 1789	1	110
Amey, formerly of Greenwich, m. Lawrence LaBREE, of Patterson, N. J., Sept. 25, 1836, by Rev. Joseph H. Nichols	1	199
Amey, d. Jabez, Jr. [& Lucy], b. Mar. 11, 18[ ]	1	160
Andrew, [s. Titus & Rachall], b. May 26, 1755	1	74
Andrew, [s. Titus & Rachall], b. May 26, 1755	ER	246
Andrew, Jr., s. Nehemiah, b. Aug. 23, 1782	1	153
Andrew, m. Annah HOBBY, Nov. 26, 1788, by Rev. Isaac Lewis	1	153
Angeline Amy, grand daughter [Ebenezer], b. June 9, 1807	1	110
Angeline Amy, grand daughter of Ebenezer, b. June 9, 1817	1	160
Angline Amey, m. William HOLMES, July 6, 1823, by Isaac Lewis	1	169
Ann, d. Sam[ue]ll [& Ann], b. Jan. 22, 1718/19	LR1	423
Ann, [d. Peter & Hannah], b. May 12, 1757	1	104

MEAD, MEADE, (cont.)

	Vol.	Page
Ann, [d. Peter & Hannah], b. May 12, 1757	ER	228
Ann, [twin with Mary, d. John, Jr. & Mary], b. Dec. 11, 1759	ER	246
Ann, [twin with Mary, d. John & Mary, Jr.], b. Dec. 31, 1759	1	117
Ann, m. Abraham H. CLOSE, b. of Greenwich, June 22, 1835, by Rev. Platt Buffett	1	195
Anne, [d. Eliphalet & Ann], b. Dec. [ ], 1762	1	108
Anne, [d. Jesse & Rachel], b. Sept. 24, 1776	1	116
Anne, d. Peter [& Hannah], b. Aug. 17, 1787	1	129
Augustus, m. Sarah M. HUSTED, Sept. 12, 1832, by J. Mann	1	188
Benjamin, s. Benjamin, b. Mar. 18, 1701	LR1	447
Benjamin, s. Benjamin, b. Mar. 18, 1701	ER	177
Benjamin, m. Rachal BROWN, June 20, 1716	ER	177
Benjamin, m. Rachal BROWN, June 27, 1716	LR1	447
Beniamin, m. Martha FERRIS, Nov. 18, 1728, by Rev. Mr. Munson	1	59
Beniamin, m. Martha FERRIS, Nov. 18, 1728, by Rev. Mr. Munson	ER	198
Beniamin, s. Beniamin [& Martha], b. Apr. 15, 1729	1	59
Beniamin, s. Beniamin [& Martha], b. Aug. 15, 1729	ER	198
Benjamin, [s. John, Jr. & Mary, Jr.], b. June 26, 1770	1	117
Benjamin, [s. John, Jr. & Mary], b. June 26, 1770	ER	246
Benjamin, [s. John, Jr. & Mary, Jr.], d. Oct. [ ], 1776	1	117
Benjamin, s. John, Jr. [& Mary], d. Oct. [ ], 1776	ER	246
Benjamin, s. Edmund [& Theodosia], b. Apr. 24, 1780	1	129
Benjamin, d. Oct. 22, 1703	1	146
Benjamin, Jr., s. Obadiah [& Ruth M.], b. Feb. 4, 1811	1	152
Benjamin, m. Hannah H. MEAD, [Sept.] 16, [1835], by J. Mann	1	196
Benjamin C., m. Mary Elizabeth RITCH, b. of Greenwich, June 27, [1839], by Noah Coe	1	204
Bethiah, [s. Nathaniel & Sarah], b. Dec. 27, 1769	1	105
Bethiah, d. Nehemiah, m. Stephen DAVIS, Jr., Jan. 24, 1788, by Rev. Isaac Lewis	1	155
Bythena, m. Caleb HOLMES, [Sept. 23, 1834], by J. Mann	1	193
Caleb, s. Ebenezer, b. Jan. 14, 1693/4	ER	144
Caleb, s. Ebenezer, b. Jan. 14, 1693/4	LR1	450
Caleb, m. Hannah RUNDALL, Dec. 2, 1736, by Rev. Mr. Todd	1	68
Caleb, m. Hannah RUNDELL, Dec. 2, 1736/7, by Rev. Mr. Todd	ER	216
Caleb, s. Caleb [& Hannah], b. Sept. 7, 1737	1	68
Caleb, s. Caleb [& Hannah], b. Sept. 7, 1737	ER	216
Calvin, [s. Silas & Mary], b. Aug. 1, 1760	1	71

MEAD, MEADE, (cont.)

	Vol.	Page
Calvin, [s. Silas & Mary], b. Aug. 1, 1760	ER	
Catharine, of Greenwich, m. W[illia]m L. LYON, Capt. of New York City, May 25, 1840, by Noah Coe	1	229 207
Charity, [d. Peter & Hannah], b. July 27, 1763	1	104
Charity, [d. Peter & Hannah], b. July 29, 1763	ER	228
Charles, s. Sam[ue]ll [& Ann], b. Mar. 22, 1720/1	LR1	423
Charles, [s. Jonas], b. Feb. 4, 1812	1	149
Charles, m. Rachal E. SACKETT, Dec. 31, 1838, by Noah Coe	1	203
Charles, m. Elizabeth THOMSON, b. of Greenwich, Nov. 28, 1842, by Chauncey Wilcox	1	210
Cornelia, of Chester, m. David H. FARNAM, of New Haven, Oct. 20, 1845, by Ebenezer Mead	1	214
Cornelia Graham, [d. Alvin & Eliza], b. Mar. 12, 1828	1	91
Cyrus, s. Peter [& Hannah], b. Jan. 2, 1784; d. Sept. 27, 1784	1	129
Cyrus, s. Peter [& Hannah], b. Aug. 11, 1789	1	129
Demares, [child Nathaniel & Prudence], b. Apr. 24, 1761	1	125
Demas, [s. Nathaniel & Prudence], b. Apr. 24, 1761	ER	229
Daniel, [s. Abraham & Ruth], b. May 1, 1758	1	114
Daniel, [s. Abraham & Ruth], b. May 1, 1758	ER	215
Daniel S., m. Huldah MEAD, [Nov.] 26, [1832], by J. Mann	1	188
Daniel Smith, [s. Jared & Lydia], b. Nov. 20, 1778	1	128
Daniel Smith, s. Daniel Smith, [& Rachal], b. Apr. 9, [ ]	1	164
Daniel Smith, m. Rachal MEAD, d. Joshua, Jan. 16, 1806, by Isaac Lewis, D. D.	1	164
Darius, [s. [ ], Jr. & Amy], b. Jan. 31, 1751; d. Mar. 22, 1751	1	81-2
Darius, [s. Ebenezer, Jr. & Amy], b. Jan. 31, 1751; d. Mar. 22, 1751	ER	234
Darius, [s. Eliphalet & Ann], b. Jan. 22, 1768	1	108
David, s. Ebenezer, b. Oct. 10, 1701	ER	144
David, s. Ebenezer, b. Oct. 10, 1701	LR1	450
David, m. Abigail LEENE, Dec. 16, 1707, by Ebenezer Mead, J. P.	LR1	4
David, m. Abigail LEONE, Dec. 16, 1707, by Ebenezer Mead, J. P.	ER	159
David, s. David [& Abigail], b. Sept. 1, 1708	LR1	4
David, s. David, b. Sept. 1, 1708	ER	159
David, m. Sarah CLOOS, May 21, 1734	1	67
David, m. Searah CLOES, May 21, 1734	ER	213
David, s. David [& Sarah], b. Dec. 11, 1736	1	67
David, s. David [& Searah], b. Dec. 11, 1736	ER	213
David, [s. Nathaniel & Prudence], b. Oct. 27, 1747	1	125

	Vol.	Page
MEAD, MEADE, (cont.)		
David, [s. Nathaniel & Prudence], b. Oct. 27, 1747	ER	229
David B., m. Rachal E. CLOSE, Dec. 16, 1838, by		
Noah Coe	1	203
Debbe, d. Peter [& Hannah], b. Apr. 28, 1785	1	129
Deborah, 2nd d. [Samuell], b. Jan. 11, 1703/4	ER	101
Deborah, 2nd d. [Sam[ue]ll], b. Jan. 11, 1703/4	LR1	453
Deborah, d. Abraham, Jr. [& Keziah], b. Jan. 14, 1766; d.		
Sept. 22, 1766	1	156
Deborah, [d. Jehiel], b. Sept. 11, 1766	1	105
Deborah, d. Abraham, Jr. [& Keziah], b. May 6, 1767	1	156
Deliverence, s. [Ebenezer, Jr. & Hannah], b. May 4, 1728	1	60
Deliverance, s. [Ebenezer, Jr. & Hannah], b. May 4, 1728	ER	180
Deliverance, m. Abigail HOW, d. Isaac, Jan. 11, 1758	ER	226
Deliverence, m. Abigail HOW, Jan. 11, 1759	1	111
Demiss, [child of Jesse & Rachel], b. Sept. 26, 1761	1	116
Drake, m. Julia Ann KNAPP, b. of Greenwich, Sept. 8,		
1828, by Rev. Ambrose S. Todd, of Stamford	1	181
Ebenetus, [s. Nathaniel & Prudence], b. Apr. 12, 1759	ER	229
Ebenezer, s. Ebenezer, b. Oct. 25, 1692; d. May 3, 1775,		
in the 83rd y. of his age	1	128
Ebenezer, s. Ebenezer, b. Oct. 25, 1692	LR1	450
Ebenezer, s. Ebenezer, b. Oct. 25, 1692	ER	144
Ebenezer, m. Hannah BROWN, Dec. 3, 1717	LR1	447
Ebenezer, Jr., m. Hannah BROWN, Dec. 12, 1717	1	60
Ebenezer, Jr., m. Hannah BROWN, Dec. 12, 1717	ER	180
Ebenezer, s. [Ebenezer, Jr. & Hannah], b. Oct. 8, 1718	1	60
Ebenezer, s. [Ebenezer, Jr. & Hannah], b. Oct. 8, 1718	ER	180
Ebenezer, s. [Ebenezer & Hannah], b. Oct. 8, 1718	LR1	447
Ebenezer, m. Ruth RENOLLS, wid. of John, July 16,		
1735, by Rev. Abraham Todd	1	64
Ebenezer, Jr., m. Amy KNAPP, Jan. 13, 1748, by Rev.		
Abraham Todd	ER	234
Ebenezer, [s. [ ], Jr. & Amy], b. Dec. 12, 1748	1	81-2
Ebenezer, [s. Ebenezer, Jr. & Amy], b. Dec. 12, 1748	ER	234
Ebenezer, [s. Ebenezer, Jr.], b. Mar. 3, 1778	1	110
Ebenezer, Jr., s. Gen Ebenezer, m. Lotte MEAD, Nov.		
29, 1798, by Rev. Dr. Isaac Lewis	1	157
Eben[eze]r, 3rd, s. Eben[eze]r, Jr. [& Lotte], b. Aug.		
6, 1803	1	157
Eben[eze]r, Jr., m. Betsey HOLMES, Oct. 28, 1807	1	157
Edmond, [s. [ ] & Sarah], b. July 5, 1756	1	89-90
Edmund, [s. James & Sarah], b. July 5, 1756	ER	238
Edmund, s. Jonas, m. Theodosia MEAD, d. Benjamin,		
Jr., Feb. 22, 1775	1	129
Edward, [s. Thaddeus & Sarah], b. Sept. 25, 1757	1	83
Edward, [s. Thaddeus & Sarah], b. Sept. 25, 1757	ER	246
Edward, m. Susanna Ann Eliza MERRELL, [Dec.] 24,		

GREENWICH VITAL RECORDS 219

	Vol.	Page
MEAD, MEADE, (cont.)		
[1832], by Joel Mann	1	188
Edwin, s. Daniel Smith [& Rachal], b. Oct. 27, [ ]	1	164
Elias Smith, m. Mandana **FLETCHER**, b. of Greenwich, Feb. 18, 1824, by Isaac Lewis, Jr.	1	170
Eliphalet, s. Benjamin, b. Mar. 14, 1704	ER	177
Eliphalet, s. Benjamin, b. Mar. 14, 1704	LR1	447
Eliphalet, m. Ann **RUNDALL**, Dec. 13, 1761	1	108
Eliza, [d. Zenas], b. Jan. 21, 18[ ]	CP	108
Eliza, m. Zachariah **ALTHOUSE**, [Dec.] 12, [1830], by E. S. Raymond	1	185
Eliza, m. Henry **FERRIS**, [Apr.] 4, [1833], by J. Mann	1	191
Eliza, m. Isaac **LYON**, Nov. 17, 1840, by Noah Coe	1	206
Eliza, m. Lockwood E. **CLARK**, b. of Greenwich, Feb. 3, 1845, by N. Coe	1	213
Elizabeth, d. Benjamin, b. Nov. 2, 1705	LR1	447
Elizabeth, d. Benjamin, b. Nov. 2, 1705	ER	177
Elizabeth, 3rd d. [Samuell], b. Apr. 5, 1708	ER	101-2
Elizabeth, 3rd d. [Sam[ue]ll], b. Apr. 5, 1709	LR1	453
Elizabeth, m. Reuben **REYNOLLS**, Mar. 19, 1734/5, by Rev. Mr. Todd	1	66
Elizabeth, m. Ruben **REYNOLDS**, Mar. 19, 1734/5, by Rev. Mr. Todd	ER	215
Elizabeth, d. [Beniamin], b. Oct. [ ], 1737	1	60
Elizabeth, d. [Beniamin], b. Oct. [ ], 1737	ER	205
Elizabeth, [d. Deliverence & Abigail], b. Apr. 19, 1760	1	111
Elisabeth, [d. Deliverance & Abigail], b. Apr. 19, 1760	ER	226
Elizabeth, [d. John, Jr. & Mary, Jr.], b. Jan. 29, 1764	1	117
Elizabeth, [d. John, Jr. & Mary], b. Jan. 29, 1764	ER	246
Elizabeth, [d. Jesse & Rachel], b. June 10, 1772	1	116
Elkanah, m. Jane **MEAD**, b. of Greenwich, Mar. 4, 1839, by Noah Coe	1	203
Ellan, [s. John, Jr. & Mary], b. Aug. 24, 1774	ER	246
Elnathan, 2nd s. [Samuel], b. Feb. 11, 1697/8	ER	101
Elnathan, 2nd s. [Sam[ue]ll], b. Feb. 11, 1697/8	LR1	453
Elsey, d. Zaccheus, m. Job **MEAD**, May 7, 1797, by Rev. Platt Buffitt	1	153
Emeline, d. Eben[eze]r, Jr. [& Lotte], b. July 30, 1805	1	157
Enoch, [s. [ ], Jr. & Amy], b. Apr. [ ], 1756	1	81-2
Enoch, [s. Ebenezer, Jr. & Amy], b. Apr. [ ], 1756	ER	234
Enoch, s. Eben[eze]r, Jr. [& Betsey], b. Sept. 22, 1809	1	157
Enos, [s. Abraham & Ruth], b. May 3, 1761	1	114
Enos, [s. Abraham & Ruth], b. May 3, 1761	ER	215
Epenetus, [s. Nathaniel & Prudence], b. Apr. 12, 1759	1	125
Epenetus, see also Ebenetus		
Ephraim, [s. Deliverence & Abigail], b. Mar. 15, 1775	1	111
Ephraim, [s. Deliverance & Abigail], b. Mar. 15, 1775	ER	226
Esbon, [s. Abraham & Ruth], b. Jan. 26, 1757	1	114

MEAD, MEADE, (cont.)

	Vol.	Page
Esbon, [child of Abraham & Ruth], b. Jan. 26, 1757	ER	215
Esther, d. Abraham, Jr. [Keziah], b. Dec. 20, 1773	1	156
Eunice, Jr., [d. Abraham & Ruth], b. Oct. 9, 1755	1	114
Eunice, Jr., [d. Abraham & Ruth], b. Oct. 9, 1755	ER	215
Eunice, wid. & wid. Sarah REYNOLDS, jointly made affidavit Jan. 26, 1760, that they had assisted in the birth of a son Frederick Harding JONES, to wid. Mary (WHITING) JONES, b. Nov. 28, 1759, at the home of Justus Bush of Greenwich	1	92
Eunice, of Greenwich, m. Alfred REYNOLDS, of Stamford, Jan. 5, 1831, by Rev. Platt Buffett, of Stanwich	1	185
Ezra, s. Timothy [& Martha], b. Oct. 9, 1737	1	48
Ezra, s. Timothy [& Martha], b. Oct. 9, 1737	ER	192
Fanny, m. Henry LOCKWOOD, Dec. 4, 1837, by James Jarman	1	199
Francis, s. Silas, Jr. [& Sarah], b. Jan. 7, 1805	1	146
Frances Cecelia, m. Gilbert Peck FINCH, Dec. 22, 1822, by Isaac Lewis	1	168
Gideon, s. [Beniamin], b. Apr. 18, 1741	1	60
Gideon, s. [Beniamin], b. Apr. 18, 1741	ER	205
Gilbard, s. James, b. Nov. 3, 1726/7	CP	106
Gillbard, s. James [& Susanah], b. Nov. 3, 1726/7	ER	185
Grace W., m. Cornelius MINOR, b. of Greenwich, Dec. 13, 1842, by B. M. Yarrington	1	210
Halsey, [s. Nathaniel & Prudence], b. Jan. 31, 1755	1	125
Halsey, [s. Nathaniel & Prudence], b. Jan. 31, 1755	ER	229
Hannah, d. [Jonathan, cooper & Easter], b. Sept. 2, [ ]	ER	173
Hannah, d. Nathan, cooper [& Easther], b. Sept. [ ]	LR1	446
Hannah, m. Nathaniel LOCKWOOD, Jr., Nov. [ ], by Rev. Abraham Todd	ER	236
Hannah, m. Nathaniel LOCKWOOD, Jr., [ ], by Rev. Abraham Todd	CP	107
Hannah, d. Ebenezer, b. Nov. 8, 1698	LR1	450
Hannah, d. Ebenezer, b. Nov. 8, 1698	ER	144
Hannah, eldest, d. [Samuell], b. Sept. 29, 1701	ER	101
Hannah, eldest d. [Sam[ue]ll], b. Sept. 29, 1701	LR1	453
Hannah, d. Ebenezer, b. Feb. 28, 1708	LR1	450
Hannah, m. John HOBBY, Mar. 16, 1716/17	ER	179
Hannah, m. John HOLLY*, Mar. 16, 1716/17 *("HOBBY" in Mead's Hist.)	LR1	438
Hannah, d. [Ebenezer, Jr. & Hannah], b. Dec. 5, 1734	1	60
Hannah, d. [Ebenezer, Jr. & Hannah], b. Dec. 5, 1734	ER	180
Hannah, m. Peter MEAD, July 29, 1744, by Rev. Mr. Todd	1	104
Hannah, m. Peter MEAD, July 29, 1744, by Rev. Mr.		

MEAD, MEADE, (cont.)

	Vol.	Page
Todd	ER	228
Hannah, [d. Peter & Hannah], b. Nov. 9, 1745	1	104
Hannah, [d. Peter & Hannah], b. Nov. 9, 1745	ER	228
Hannah, [d. [ ], Jr. & Amy], b. Mar. 7, 1752	1	81-2
Hannah, [d. Ebenezer, Jr. & Amy], b. Mar. 7, 1752	ER	234
Hannah, [d. Nathaniel & Prudence], b. Feb. 25, 1753	1	125
Hannah, [d. Nathaniel & Prudence], b. Feb. 25, 1753	ER	229
Hannah, d. Jabez, Jr. & Sarah, b. Sept. 29, 1757	1	98
Han[n]ah, [d. Nathaniel 3rd], b. Mar. 28, 1764	1	123
Hannah, d. Peter, m Isaac DARROW, Dec. 20, 1764, by Rev. Abraham Todd	1	120
Hannah, [d. Seth & Deborow], b. June 8, 1765	1	117
Hannah, [d. Deliverence & Abigail], b. Aug. 10, 1765	1	111
Hannah, [d. Deliverance & Abigail], b. Aug. 10, 1765	ER	226
Hannah, [d. Ebenezer, Jr.], b. Dec. 1, 1773; d. June 4, 1795	1	110
Hannah, d. Jared [& Lydia], b. May 25, 1788	1	128
Hannah, d. Ebenezer, d. June 4, 1795	1	110
Hannah, d. Eben[eze]r, d. June 4, 1796	1	160
Hannah, d. Eben[eze]r, Jr. [& Lotte], b. Feb. 19, 1800	1	157
Hannah, w. Jonas, d. Mar. 12, 1814	1	149
Hannah, m. Seeley MEAD, b. of Greenwich, Oct. 10, 1826, by Isaac Lewis	1	174
Hannah C., m. Chester BIRGE, June 9, 1831, by Chauncey Wilcox	1	187
Hannah H., m. Benjamin MEAD, [Sept.] 16, [1835], by J. Mann	1	196
Hannah Hibbard, [d. Jonas & Hannah], b. June 9, 1813	1	149
Hardy, [s. Titus & Rachell], b. Dec. 8, 1768	1	74
Hardy, [s. Titus & Rachall], b. Dec. 8, 1768	ER	246
Harriet, m. Bradley REDFIELD, b. of Greenwich, Jan. 4, 1824, by Isaac Lewis	1	170
Henry, m. Abigail M. SMITH, b. of Greenwich, Jan. 16, 1828, by Platt Buffett	1	179
Henry, [s. Zenas], b. Aug. 13, 18[ ]	CP	108
Hezekiah, s. Jonathan, b. Aug. 30, 1705	LR1	456
Hezekiah, s. Jonathan, b. Aug. 30, 1706	ER	70
Huldah, [d. Deliverence & Abigail], b. Feb. 26, 1773	1	111
Huldah, [d. Deliverance & Abigail], b. Feb. 26, 1773	ER	226
Huldah, d. Nehemiah, b. Jan. 27, 1777	1	153
Huldah, m. Hezekiah PRAY, Dec. 28, 1807, by Rev. Isaac Lewis, D. D.	1	156
Huldah, m. Daniel S. MEAD, [Nov.] 26, 1832], by J. Mann	1	188
Ira, [s. Titus & Rachell], b. Oct. 10, 1770	1	74
Ira, [s. Titus & Rachell], b. Oct. 10, 1770	ER	246
Isack, s. Jonathan, b. Nov. 8, 1698	ER	70

MEAD, MEADE, (cont.)

	Vol.	Page
Isaac, s. Jonathan, b. Nov. 8, 1698	LR1	456
Isaac, s. Isaac, b. Mar. 1, 1723	1	56
Isaac, s. Isaac, b. Mar. 1, 1723	ER	190
Isaac, s. Abraham, Jr. [& Keziah], b. Dec. 8, 1770	1	156
Isaac, of Genoa, N. Y., m. Susan MEAD, of Greenwich, Oct. 18, 1837, by Rev. Joseph H. Nichols	1	200
Israel, [s. Stephen & Mary], b. Mar. 18, 1760	1	105
Israel, [s. Nathaniel & Prudence], b. Aug. 3, 1763	1	125
Israel, [s. Nathaniel & Prudence], b. Aug. 3, 1763	ER	229
Jabez, s. Ebenezer, b. June 10, 1700	LR1	450
Jabez, s. Ebenezer, b. June 10, 1700	ER	144
Jabez, Jr., m. Sarah HOBBY, Apr. 5, 1757	1	98
Jabez, [s. Titus & Rachell], b. May 26, 1764	1	74
Jabez, [s. Titus & Rachall], b. May 26, 1764	ER	246
Jabez, [s. Deliverence & Abigail], b. Feb. 15, 1767	1	111
Jabez, [s. Deliverance & Abigail], b. Feb. 15, 1767	ER	226
Jabez, [s. Deliverence & Abigail], b. Aug. 22, 1777	1	111
Jabez, [s. Deliverance & Abigail], b. Aug. 22, 1777	ER	226
Jabez, s. Ebenezer, b. Nov. 7, 1785	1	110
Jabez, Jr., m. Lucy DAVIS, Jan. 4, 18[ ], by Isaac Davis, D. D.	1	160
Jabez, 3rd, s. Jabez, Jr. [& Lucy], b. Dec. 21, 18[ ]	1	160
Jabez, 3rd, m. Mary Jerusha HOBBY, Nov. 11, [1833], by J. Mann	1	192
Jabez Hobby, s. Nehemiah, 3rd [& Polly], b. Feb. 10, 1804	1	155
James, s. Jonathan, b. Mar. 11, 1696	ER	70
James, s. Jonathan, b. [ ], 11, 1696	LR1	456
James, s. [James & Susannah], b. Sept. 26, 17[ ]	CP	106
James, m. Susannah [ ], [ ] 25, 1719/20, by Rev. Richard Sackett	CP	106
James, m. Susanah HAEM[ ]G, [ ] 25, 1719/20, by Rev. Richard Sackett	ER	185
James, s. James [& Susanah], b. Sept. 26, 1722	ER	185
James, d. Mar. 3, 1726/7	CP	106
James, d. Mar. 3, 1726/7	ER	185
James, s. Timothy [& Martha], b. Aug. 25, 1730	1	48
James, s. Timothy [& Martha], b. Aug. 25, 1730	ER	192
James, m. Sarah FERRIS, d. James, May 24, 1751, by Rev. Abraham Todd	ER	238
James, m. Deborah Ann PALMER, b. of Greenwich, Dec. 19, 1821, by Isaac Lewis	1	167
Jane, m. Elkanah MEAD, b. of Greenwich, Mar. 4, 1839, by Noah Coe	1	203
Jared, s. Daniel Smith, [& Rachal], b. July 25, [ ]	1	164
Jared, m. Lydia SMITH, d. Daniel, Dec. 10, 1775	1	128
Jared, had negro Prue, d. Lib, b. Aug. 16, 1790,		

	Vol.	Page

MEAD, MEADE, (cont.)

	Vol.	Page
Lucy, d. Lib. b. July 18, 1792, Joe, s. Prue, b. Sept. 8, 1812 & Dorcas, d. Lucy, b. Aug. 22, 1822? (struck over in original manuscript and is unreadable)	1	144
Jared, s. Jared [& Lydia], b. Sept. 28, 1791	1	128
Jared, had formerly negro Lucy, d. Prudence, b. Mar. 4, 1818	1	150
Jehiel, [s. Jehiel], b. May 4, 1768	1	105
Jemime, d. Ebenezer, b. Oct. 12, 1711	LR1	450
Jemime, d. Ebenezer, b. Oct. 12, 1711	ER	144
Jesse, m. Rachel **KNAPP**, d. David, Dec. 10, 1760	1	116
Jesse, [s. Jesse & Rachel], b. Oct. 22, 1774	1	116
Job, m. Elsey **MEAD**, d. Zaccheus, May 7, 1797, by Rev. Platt Buffitt	1	153
John, m. Ruth **HARDEY**, Oct. 27, 1681, by Richard Laws, Com.	ER	40
John, m. Ruth **HARDEY**, Oct. 27, 1681, by Richard Lanes, Com.	LR1	454
John, 1st s. [John & Ruth], b. Oct. 7, 1682	ER	40
John, 1st s. [John & Ruth], b. Oct. 7, 1682	LR1	454
John, s. Samuel, b. Feb. 11, 1703/4	ER	101
John, 4th s. [Sam[ue]ll], b. Feb. 14, 1703/4	LR1	453
John, s. Abigail, b. Jan. 24, 1753	ER	241
John, Jr., m. Mary **BRUSH**, Jr., d. Benjamin, Aug. 25, 1754, by Rev. Benjamin Strong	1	117
John, Jr., m. Mary **BRUSH**, Jr., d. Benjamin, Aug. 25, 1754, by Rev. Benjamin Strong	ER	246
John, [s. John, Jr. & Mary, Jr.], b. Sept. 18, 1755	1	117
John, [s. John, Jr. & Mary], b. Sept. 18, 1755	ER	246
John, 3rd, s. Nehemiah, b. May 14, 1794	1	153
John, s. Nehemiah, d. Jan. 15, 1815	1	153
Jonas, s. [Ebenezer, Jr. & Hannah], b. Dec. 25, 1723	1	60
Jonas, d. Sept. 14, 1783	1	89-90
Jonas, s. Jonas, decd. [& Sarah], b. Apr. 13, 1784	1	89-90
Jonas, m. Jan. 2, 1809, [ ]	1	149
Jonas, 2nd, m. Abigail **MEAD**, [Aug.] 14, [1832], by J. Mann	1	190
Jonathan, s. [Nathan, cooper & Easther], b. [ ] 10,[ ]	LR1	446
Jonathan, s. Jonathan, b. Sept. 15, 1689	ER	70
Jonathan, s. Jonathan, b. Sept. 15, 1689	LR1	456
Jonathan, cooper, m. Easter **BUTTLER**, Dec. 7, 1713	ER	173
Jonathan, s. [Jonathan & Easter], b. [ ] 10, 1715	ER	173
Jonathan, [s. Abraham & Ruth], b. Nov. 25, 1759	1	114
Jonathan, [s. Abraham & Ruth], b. Nov. 25, 1759	ER	215
Jonathan, [s. Nathaniel & Prudence], b. Sept. 27, 1766	1	125
Jonathan, [s. Nathaniel & Prudence], b. Sept. 27, 1766	ER	229
Joseph, m. Catharine **LOCKWOOD**, d. Samuel, Dec.		

MEAD, MEADE, (cont.)

	Vol.	Page
10, 1755	1	93
Joseph, [s. Joseph & Catharine], b. Jan. 4, 1758	1	93
Joseph, [s. Seth & Deborow], b. Dec. 18, 1760	1	117
Joseph G., m. Mary W. TAGTON, b. of Greenwich, Jan. 17, 1840, by Noah Coe	1	205
Joshua, [s. Nathaniel & Prudence], b. May 16, 1751	1	125
Joshua, [s. Nathaniel & Prudence], b. May 16, 1751	ER	229
Josiah, [s. Nathaniel 3rd], b. Oct. 9, 1761	1	123
Julia, [d. Zenas], b. June 26, 18[ ]	CP	108
Julia, m. Isaac PECK, b. of Greenwich, Sept. 7, [1840], by Noah Coe	1	206
Julia Ann, m. Philander BUTTON, b. of Greenwich, Oct. 11, 1843, N. Coe	1	211
Junius, s. [Ebenezer, Jr. & Hannah], b. Dec. 25, 1723	ER	180
Lemuel, [s. Abraham & Ruth], b. Apr. 1, 1763	1	114
Lemuel, [s. Abraham & Ruth], b. Apr. 1, 1763	ER	215
Lewis, m. Hannah CLOSE, b. of Greenwich, Feb. 1, 1826, by Platt Buffett	1	173
Lotte, d. Daniel Smith [& Rachal], b. Mar. [ ]	1	164
Lottie, [d. Jared & Lydia], b. Jan. 14, 1777	1	128
Lotte, m. Ebenezer MEAD, Jr., s. Gen. Ebenezer, Nov. 29, 1798, by Rev. Dr. Isaac Lewis	1	157
Lotte, w. Eben[eze]r, Jr., d. May 26, 1807	1	157
Lotte, d. Eben[eze]r, Jr. [& Betsey], b. Feb. 20, 1812	1	157
Lucinda, m. Benjamin REYNOLDS, b. of Greenwich, Jan. 3, 1842, by Darius Mead	1	208
Luckner, s. Peter [& Hannah], b. May 17, 1793	1	129
Lucy, d. Nehemiah, m. Isaac HOWE, Jr., May 8, 1778	1	130
Lucy, d. Abraham, Jr. [& Keziah], b. May 14, 1779; d. Oct. 8, 1780	1	156
Lucy, d. Abraham, Jr. [& Keziah], b. Sept. 12, 1781; d. Aug. 20, 1783	1	156
Lucy, d. Abraham [& Keziah], b. May 18, 1786	1	156
Lucy Mumford, d. Andrew [& Annah], b. Sept. 8, 1809	1	153
Lucy Mumford, m. Titus MEAD, b. of Greenwich, Feb. 25, 1838, by Noah Coe	1	200
Lydia, [d. Nathaniel & Sarah], b. Mar. 1, 1757	1	105
Lydia, d. Jared [& Lydia], b. Aug. 11, 1781	1	128
Lydia Adelia, [d. Daniel Smith & Rachal], b. June [ ]	1	164
Lydia Ann, d. Eben[eze]r, Jr. [& Betsey], b. Aug. 8, 1813	1	157
Lyman, [s. Zenas], b. Mar. 26, 1824	CP	108
Mariah, m. John FERRIS, Jr., Feb. 27, 1722/3, by Rev. Mr. Sacet	1	59
Mark, s. Jonas [& Sarah], b. Nov. 6, 1782	1	89-90
Mark, 2nd, m. Sarah HOW, b. of Greenwich, this day [Nov. 12, 1845], by Mark Mead, V. D. M.	1	214

	Vol.	Page
MEAD, MEADE, (cont.)		
Martha, d. Jonathan, b. Dec. 11, 1693	ER	70
Martha, m. Stephen **HOLMES**, Feb. 27, 1717/18, by Ebenezer Mead, J. P.	ER	182
Martha, d. Timothy [& Martha], b. Sept. 6, 1726	1	48
Martha, d. Timothy [& Martha], b. Sept. 6, 1726	ER	192
Martha, d. Beniamin, b. July 18, 1732	1	60
Martha, d. Beniamin, b. July 18, 1732	ER	204
Martha, d. Ebenezer, b. Sept. 12, 1775	1	110
Martha, d. Jonathan, b. Dec. 11, 1793	LR1	456
Martha, d. Jabez, Jr. [& Lucy], b. Sept. 5, 18[ ]	1	160
Martha, m. Silas **HUSTED**, b. of Greenwich, May 20, 1839, by Chauncey Wilcox	1	203
Martin, [s. Titus & Rachell], b. Oct. 15, 1773	1	74
Martin, [s. Titus & Rachell], b. Oct. 15, 1773	ER	246
Mary, d. Jonathan, b. May 22, 1704	ER	70
Mary, d. Jonathan, b. May 22, 1704	LR1	456
Mary, d. [Beniamin], b. Sept. 29, 1743	1	60
Mary, d. [Beniamin], b. Sept. 29, 1743	ER	205
Mary, m. Silas **MEAD**, Aug. 7, 1745	1	71
Mary, m. Silas **MEAD**, Aug. 7, 1745	ER	229
Mary, [d. Peter & Hannah], b. Apr. 23, 1747	1	104
Mary, [d. Peter & Hannah], b. Apr. 23, 1747	ER	228
Mary, [d. Obadiah & Lois], b. Aug. 10, 1757	1	105
Mery, [d. Seth & Deborah], b. Feb. 19, 1758	1	117
Mary, [d. Stephen & Mary], b. Apr. 30, 1758	1	105
Mary, [d. Thaddeus & Sarah], b. Aug. 19, 1759	1	83
Mary, [d. Thaddeus & Sarah], b. Aug. 19, 1759	ER	246
Mary, [twin with Ann], d. [John, Jr. & Mary], b. Dec. 11, 1759	ER	246
Mary, [twin with Ann, d. John, Jr. & Mary, Jr.], b. Dec. 31, 1759	1	117
Mary, [d. Silas & Mary], b. June 20, 1762	1	71
Mary, [d. Silas & Mary], b. June 20, 1762	ER	229
Mary, [d. Deliverence & Abigail], b. Mar. 25, 1771	1	111
Mary, [d. Deliverance & Abigail], b. Mar. 25, 1771	ER	226
Mary, [d. Jehiel], b. Mar. 7, 1773	1	105
Mary, d. Peter, Jr. & Hannah, b. Aug. 17, 1778	1	129
Mary, w. John [Jr.], d. Oct. 28, 1784	ER	246
Mary, w. John, d. Dec. 28, 1784	1	117
Mary, of Greenwich, m. John P. **ANDERSON**, of Cortlandt, N. Y., Dec. 3, [probably 1842], by Noah Coe	1	210
Mary Ann, [d. John, Jr. & Mary, Jr.], b. May 5, 1766	1	117
Mary Ann, [d. John, Jr. & Mary], b. May 5, 1766	ER	246
Mary Ann, d. Obadiah [& Ruth M.], b. Sept. 8, 1814	1	152
Mary Ann, of Greenwich, m. George **SULLIVAN**, of Rye, N. Y., Mar. 22, 1838, by Rev. C.		

	Vol.	Page

MEAD, MEADE, (cont.)

Wilcox	1	200
Mary Elizabeth, d. Eben[eze]r, Jr. [& Betsey], b. Aug. 13, 1808	1	157
Mary Elizabeth, of Greenwich, m. J. Ralph SACKETT, of New York, Feb. 28, 1843, by Noah Coe	1	213
Mary H., of Greenwich, m. Thomas MAYHEW, of Maine, Dec. 25, 1842, by Noah Coe	1	210
Mary Husted, m. Willis Jarvis MERRETT, [Oct.] 10, [1831], by Joel Mann	1	186
Mary Jane, m. Charles PORTER, b. of Greenwich, Aug. 1, 1838, by Rev. Chauncey Wilcox	1	201
Mahetable, d. Nehemiah, b. Dec. 1, 1784	1	153
Melancton Wood, [s. Alvin & Eliza], b. July 12, 1826	1	91
Mercy, d. Samuel, m. Reuben MEAD, Dec. 22, 1742	CP	104
Michael, s. [Jonathan & Easter], b. Sept. 4, 1718	ER	173
Michael, s. [Nathan, cooper & Easther], b. Sept. [ ], 1718	LR1	446
Nancee, d. Eliphalet, b. Apr. 6, 1729	1	61
Nancee, d. Eliphalet, b. Apr. 6, 1749	ER	236
Nancy, [d. Ebenezer, Jr.], b. Sept. 12, 1771	1	110
Nancy, d. Ebenezer, d. May 18, 1813	1	110
Nancy, [d. Ebenezer], d. May 12, 1813	1	160
Nathan, m. Elizabeth KNAP[P], Jan. 2, 1717/18	ER	181
Nathan, m. Elizabeth KNAP[P], Jan. 2, 1717/18	LR1	445
Nathan, cooper, m. Easther BUTTLER, Dec. [ ]	LR1	446
Nathaniel, s. David, b. Oct. [ ], 1714, at Greenwich; m. Prudence WOOD, d. Joseph, of Huntington, Nassau Island, N. Y., Mar. 27, 1745	1	125
Nathaniel, s. David, of Greenwich, b. Oct. 13, 1714; m. Prudence WOOD, d. Joseph, of Huntington, N. Y., Mar. 27, 1745	ER	229
Nathaniel, [s. Nathaniel & Prudence], b. Mar. 7, 1745/6	1	125
Nathaniel, [s. Nathaniel & Prudence], b. Mar. 7, 1745/6	ER	229
Nathaniel, m. Sarah KNAPP, d. Charles, of Stamford, Jan. 22, 1756, by Rev. Mr. Wells, of Stamford	1	105
Nathaniel, [s. Nathaniel, 3rd], b. Nov. 4, 1768	1	123
Nehemiah, [s. Nathaniel & Sarah], b. Dec. 7, 1771	1	105
Nehemiah, 3rd, s. Nehemiah, b. Aug. 21, 1779	1	153
Nehemiah, 3rd, m. Polly HOBBY, Mar. 27, 1803, by Rev. Isaac Lewis, D. D.	1	155
Nehemiah E., m. Phebe MERRITT, Dec. 7, 1829, by Chauncey Wilcox	1	183
Nehemiah Edgar, s. Nehemiah, 3rd [& Polly], b. Feb. 13, 1806; d. June 30, 1808	1	155
Nehemiah Edgar, s. Nehemiah, 3rd [& Polly], b. Aug. 1, 1808	1	155

MEAD, MEADE, (cont.)

	Vol.	Page
Noah, s. Jonas [& Sarah], b. Oct. 21, 1780	1	89-90
Obediah, s. [Benjamin & Rachal], b. Feb. 20, 1718	ER	177
Obadiah, s. [Benjamin & Rachal], b. Feb. 20, 1718	LR1	447
Obadiah, m. Lois **TODD**, d. Rev. Mr. Todd, Nov. [ ], 1756	1	105
Obadiah, d. Apr. 27, 1759	1	105
Obadiah, [s. Nathaniel & Sarah], b. Jan. 25, 1768	1	105
Obadiah, b. Mar. 10, 1785; m. Ruth M. **HIBBARD**, June 22, 1809, by Rev. Isaac Lewis, D. D.	1	152
Oliver, [s. Joseph & Catharine], b. Mar. 4, 1760	1	93
Oliver, s. Abraham, Jr. [& Keziah], b. May 13, 1776; d. Dec. 21, 1777	1	156
Ophelia Mariah, m. E. Ridley **LIVINGSTON**, [July] 29, [1833], by J. Mann	1	191
Pa-----, s. [Dr. Amos & Ruth], b. Sept. 5, 1753	1	73
Peter, 3rd s. [Samuell], b. Oct. 2, 1699	ER	101
Peter, 3rd s. [Sam[ue]ll], b. Oct. 2, 1699	LR1	453
Peter, s. Samuel [& Ann], b. May 22, 1717	LR1	423
Peter, m. Hannah MEAD, July 29, 1744, by Rev. Mr. Todd	1	104
Peter, m. Hannah MEAD, July 29, 1744, by Rev. Mr. Todd	ER	228
Peter, [s. Peter & Hannah], b. Jan. 4, 1755	1	104
Peter, [s. Peter & Hannah], b. Jan. 4, 1755	ER	228
Peter, Jr., s. Peter, m. Hannah **CLOSE**, d. Sam[ue]ll, decd., Nov. 19, 1777	1	129
Peter, s. Peter [& Hannah], b. Dec. 25, 1780	1	129
Phebe, [d. Obadiah & Lois], b. Dec. 22, 1758	1	105
Polly, d. Jesse [& Rachel], b. Apr. 6, 1782	1	116
Polly, d. Nehemiah, b. July 3, 1797	1	153
Rachel, d. Jonathan, [ ]	ER	70
Rachal, d. Jonathan, b. Nov. 22, 1707	LR1	456
[Rachel, d. Jonathan], b. Nov. 22, 1708	ER	71
Rachall, d. [Benjamin & Rachal], b. May 30, 1717	LR1	447
Rechall, d. [Benjamin & Rachal], b. May 30, 1717	ER	177
Rachell, d. [Beniamin], b. Apr. 29, 1745	1	60
Rachall, d. [Beniamin], b. Aug. 29, 1745	ER	205
Rachal, m. Edmon **PERLEE*** , Jan. 29, 1747 *(**PURDY**)	1	66
Rachall, m. Edmund **PURDEE**, June 29, 1747	ER	233
Rachal, [d. Peter & Hannah], b. Dec. 23, 1752	1	104
Rachal, [d. Peter & Hannah], b. Dec. 23, 1752	ER	223
Rachal, [d. Deliverence & Abigail], b. Aug. 25, 1763	1	111
Rachall, [d. Deliverance & Abigail], b. Aug. 25, 1763	ER	226
Rachel, [d. Jesse & Rachel], b. Sept. 8, 1764	1	116
Rachall, [d. Nathaniel & Sarah], b. Feb. 17, 1766	1	105
Rachall, [d. Titus & Rachell], b. Oct. 3, 1766	1	74
Rachall, [d. Titus & Rachall], b. Oct. 3, 1766	ER	246

	Vol.	Page
MEAD, MEADE, (cont.)		
Rachal, m. Richard MEAD, June 27, 1798	1	137
Rachel, d. Joshua, m. Daniel Smith MEAD, Jan. 16, 1806, by Isaac Lewis, D. D.	1	164
Rachaell E., m. Adle CLOSE, Oct. 6, 1834, by Samuel Close J. P.	1	194
Rachal Elizabeth, d. Daniel Smith [& Rachal], b. [ ]	1	164
Ralph Peck, [s. Alvin & Eliza], b. Oct. 8, 1822	1	91
Rebeckah, m. Abraham RUNDLE, Mar. 31, 1721, by Sam[ue]ll Peck, J. P.	1	46
Rebeckah, m. Abraham RUNDLE, Mar. 31, 1721, by Sam[ue]ll Peck, J. P.	ER	186
Rebecca, [d. Jesse & Rachel], b. Sept. 23, 1769	1	116
Reuben, m. Mercy MEAD, d. Samuel, Dec. 22, 1742	CP	104
Reuben, [s. Reuben [& Mercy], b. Mar. 22, 1743	CP	104
Reuben, [& w. Mercy], had s. [ ] , b. Dec. 11, 1744	CP	104
Richard, s. [Dr. Amos & Ruth], b. Sept. 5, 1753	ER	241
Richard, s. Amos, m. Sarah MEAD, d. Nehemiah, Jan. 3, 1776	1	137
Richard, m. 2nd w. Rachal MEAD, June 27, 1798	1	137
Richard, had negroes Wright, s. Flora, b. Oct. 13, 1805 & Ralph, s. Fanny, b. Mar. 26, 1805	1	141
Robert, [s. Deliverence & Abigail], b. Nov. 22, 1768	1	111
Robert, [s. Deliverance & Abigail], b. Nov. 22, 1768	ER	226
Roger, s. Nehemiah, b. Sept. 1, 1789	1	153
Ruama, d. Ebenezer, b. Mar. 2, 1784	1	110
Ruth, made affidavit Jan. 26, 1760, that Mary JONES, (wid) gave birth to son Frederick Harding JONES, b. Nov. 28, 1759, and she was at her house the summer before last with Mr. Hardin JONES, of N. C., whom she called husband	1	92
Ruth, [d. Abraham & Ruth], b. Jan. 21, 1764	ER	215
Ruth, [d. Abraham & Ruth], b. Jan. 21, 1764	1	114
Ruth Elizabeth, d. Richard [& Rachal], b. Feb. 28, 1801	1	137
Sally Lewis, [d. Nehemiah, 3rd [& Polly], b. Feb. 4, 1811	1	155
Samanthia, m. Lockwood FERRIS, b. of Greenwich, Nov. 29, 1843, by N. Coe	1	212
Sam[ue]ll, s. Sam[ue]ll, b. May 3, 1696	ER	101
Sam[ue]ll, s. Sam[ue]ll, b. May 8, 1696	LR1	453
Sam[ue]ll, m. Ann HEWIT, Dec. 6, 1716, by Ebenezer Mead, J. P.	LR1	423
Samuel, [s. Joseph & Catharine], b. Sept. 21, 1756	1	93
Sanford, s. Peter [& Hannah], b. Dec. 20, 1803	1	139
Sanford, m. Cynthia Elizabeth HUSTED, Feb. 25, 1833, by J. Mann	1	189
Sarah, d. Jonathan, b. Oct. 11, 1691	ER	70
Sarah, d. Jonathan, b. Oct. 11, 1691	LR1	456

MEAD, MEADE, (cont.)

	Vol.	Page
Sarah, d. Ebenezer, b. Oct. 19, 1695	ER	144
Sarah, d. Ebenezer, b. Oct. 19, 1695	LR1	450
Sarah, d. [Benjamin], b. June 3, 1702	ER	177
Sarah, d. Benjamin, b. June 3, 1702	LR1	447
Sarah, m. Jonathan HOBBY, Dec. 12, 1711	ER	170
Sarah, m. Jonathan HOLLY, Dec. 12, 1711 *(Probably HOBBY")	LR1	442
Seariah, m. John FERRIS, Jr., Feb. 27, 1722/3, by Rev. Mr. Sacitt	ER	190
Serah, d. David [& Searah], b. Feb. 21, 1734/5	ER	213
Sarah, d. [Beniamin], b. Aug. 10, 1735	1	60
Sarah, d. [Beniamin], b. Aug. 10, 1735	ER	204
Sarah, d. David [& Sarah], b. Feb. 21, 1735/6	1	67
Sarah, d. Caleb, m. Epenetus HOLMES, Feb. 3, 1743/4	1	71
Sarah, d. Caleb, m. Epenetus HOLMES, Feb. 9, 1743/4	ER	227*
Sarah, [d. Thaddeus & Sarah], b. Dec. 24, 1755	1	83
Sarah, [d. Thaddeus & Sarah], b. Dec. 24, 1755	ER	246
Sarah, [d. Nathaniel & Sarah], b. Nov. 1, 1756	1	105
Sarah, [d. Deliverence & Abigail], b. Nov. 7, 1761	1	111
Sarah, [d. Deliverance & Abigail], b. Nov. 7, 1761	ER	226
Sarah, [d. Titus & Rachell], b. Mar. 27, 1762	1	74
Sarah, [d. Titus & Rachall], b. Mar. 27, 1762	ER	246
Sarah, [d. Peter & Hannah], b. Aug. 1, 1765	1	104
Sarah, [d. Peter & Hannah], b. Aug. 1, 1765	ER	228
Sarah, d. Nehemiah, m. Richard MEAD, s. Amos, Jan. 3, 1776	1	137
Sarah, w. Richard, d. Nov. 29, 1777	1	137
Sarah, d. Edmund [& Theodosia], b. Aug. 17, 1782	1	129
Sarah, wid. Jonas, d. Mar. 30, 1785	1	89-90
Sarah, d. Deliverence, decd., m. Silas MEAD, Jr., June 10, 1790, by Rev. Isaac Lewis	1	146
Sarah, d. Silas, Jr. [& Sarah], b. June 4, 1794	1	146
Sarah, d. Richard [& Rachal], b. Jan. 9, 1803	1	137
Sarah, [d. Jonas], b. Mar. 20, 1810; d. Mar. 16, 1811	1	149
Sarah A., m. Joseph BRUSH, Mar. 18, 1823, by Isaac Lewis	1	169
Sarah Lewis, of Greenwich, m. Lawrence HOPKINS, of New York, May 20, 1828, by Isaac Lewis	1	180
Sarah M., m. Selah SAVAGE, b. of Greenwich, Sept. 3, 1838, by Rev. C. Wilcox	1	201
Seeley, m. Hannah MEAD, b. of Greenwich, Oct. 10, 1826, by Isaac Lewis	1	174
Seth, [s. Seth & Deborow], b. Oct. 1, 1762	1	117
Seth, d. Sept. 27, 1765	1	117
Seth, s. John, Jr. [& Mary, Jr.], b. May 21, 1779	1	117
Seth, s. [John, Jr. & Mary], b. May 26, 1779	ER	246
Shadrach, [s. Titus & Rachall], b. Jan. 15, 1758	1	7

MEAD, MEADE, (cont.)

	Vol.	Page
Shadrach, [s. Titus & Rachall], b. Jan. 15, 1758	ER	246
Sileas, s. [Ebenezer, Jr. & Hannah], b. May 21, 1720	1	60
Selics, s. [Ebenezer, Jr. & Hannah], b. May 21, 1720 *(Silas)	ER	180
Silas, m. Mary MEAD, Aug. 7, 1745	1	71
Silas, m. Mary MEAD, Aug. 7, 1745, by [ ]	ER	229
Silas, [s. Silas & Mary], b. Feb. 7, 1748	1	71
Silas, [s. Silas & Mary], b. Feb. 7, 1748	ER	229
Silas, Jr., m. Sarah MEAD, d. Deliverence, decd., June 10, 1790, by Rev. Isaac Lewis	1	146
Silas D., m. Emily L. CLOSE, b. of Greenwich, Sept. 29, 1840, by C. Wilcox	1	206
Silas Harvey, s. Silas, Jr. [& Sarah], b. Dec. 12, 1796	1	146
Silas Marvin, s. Daniel Smith [& Rachal], b. Oct. 5, [ ]	1	164
Selvanus, s. [Beniamin], b. Jan. 19, 1739	1	60
Salvenus, s. [Beniamin], b. Jan. 19, 1739	ER	205
Silvanus, m. Sibell WOOD, d. Jonah, of Huntington, Nassau Island, June 2, 1763	1	112
Smith, [s. Nathaniel, 3rd], b. Dec. 15, 1756	1	123
Solomon, s. [Ebenezer, Jr. & Hannah], b. Dec. 25, 1725	1	60
Solomon, s. [Ebenezer, Jr. & Hannah], b. Dec. 25, 1725	ER	180
Solomon, [s. James & Sarah], b. July 17, 1754	ER	238
Solomon, [s. [ ] & Sarah], b. July 17, 1754	1	89-90
Solomon, s. Edmund [& Theodosia], b. Apr. 28, 1778	1	129
Sophia, d. Richard [& Sarah], b. Jan. 31, 1777	1	137
Stephen, s. Timothy [& Martha], b. Apr. 23, 1734	1	48
Stephen, s. Timothy [& Martha], b. Apr. 23, 1734	ER	192
Stephen, m. Mary KNAPP, d. Capt. Israel, June 23, 1755, by Rev. Mr. Todd	1	105
Stephen, [s. Stephen & Mary], b. Feb. 19, 1756	1	105
Susan, of Greenwich, m. Lewis ELDREDGE, of New York, Apr. 29, [1822], by Isaac Lewis	1	168
Susan, of Greenwich, m. Isaac MEAD, of Genoa, N. Y., Oct. 18, 1837, by Rev. Joseph H. Nichols	1	200
Susan, m. John MATHEWS, Jan. 19, 1839, by N. Coe	1	202
Susannah, d. Ebenezer, b. Feb. 28, 1708/9	ER	144
Susannah, d. James, b. Apr. 13, 1724	CP	106
Susanah, d. James [& Susanah], b. Apr. 13, 1724	ER	185
Susana, m. Moses HUSTED, Sept. 5, 1726, by Rev. Richard Sackit	1	64
Susana, m. Moses HUSTED, Sept. 5, 1726, by Rev. Richard Sackit	ER	194
Susanna, w. Isaac, d. Mar. 1, 1732	1	56
Susanah, w. Isaac, d. Mar. 1, 1732	ER	190
Tameson, s. Timothy [& Martha], b. Nov. 26, 1739	1	48
Tameson, d. Timothy [& Martha], b. Nov. 26, 1739	ER	192
Thaddeus, s. Beniamin [& Martha], b. Nov. 16, 1730	1	59

MEAD, MEADE, (cont.)

	Vol.	Page
Thaddeus, s. Beniamin [& Martha], b. Nov. 16, 1730	ER	198
Thaddeus, m. Sarah **HOBBY**, d. Jonathan, July 7, 1754	1	83
Thaddeus, m. Sarah **HOBBY**, d. Jonathan, July 7, 1754	ER	246
Theodosia, [d. Nathaniel & Prudence], b. July 6, 1749	1	125
Theodosia, [d. Nathaniel & Prudence], b. July 6, 1749	ER	229
Theodosia, d. Benjamin, Jr., m. Edmund **MEAD**, s. Jonas, Feb. 22, 1775	1	129
Theodotia, m. Isaac **KNAPP**, b. of Greenwich, Nov. 25, 1839, by Chauncey Wilcox	1	205
Thomas, s. [Dr. Amos & Ruth], b. Apr. 7, 1755	1	73
Thomas, 2nd s. [Dr. Amos & Ruth], b. Apr. 7, 1755	ER	241
Timothie, s. Jonathan, b. Apr. 22, 1701	ER	70
Timothy, s. Jonathan, b. Apr. 22, 1701	LR1	456
Timothy, m. Martha **WEEKS**, Feb. 28, 1723/4, by Rev. Richard Sackett	1	48
Timothie, m. Martha **WEEK**, Feb. 28, 1723/4, by Rev. Richard Sacket	ER	191-2
Timothy, s. Timothy & Martha, b. Jan. 7, 1724/5	1	48
Timothy, s. Timothy & Martha, b. Jan. 7, 1724/5	ER	192
Titus, m. Rachall **RUNDALL**, June 13, 1754	1	74
Titus, m. Rachall **RUNDALL**, June 13, 1754	ER	246
Titus, [s. Titus & Rachell], b. Nov. 26, 1759	1	74
Titus, [s. Titus & Rachall], b. Nov. 26, 1759	ER	246
Titus, m. Lucy Mumford **MEAD**, b. of Greenwich, Feb. 25, 1838, by Noah Coe	1	200
Walter, s. John, Jr. [& Mary], b. Apr. 21, 1782	ER	246
Walter, s. [John, Jr. & Mary, Jr.], b. June 21, 1782	1	117
Warren Barker, [s. Alvin & Eliza], b. Sept. 16, 1824	1	91
Whitman, [s. Silvanus & Sibell], b. July 17, 1765	1	112
William, s. [Beniamin], b. Oct. 15, 1747	1	60
William, [s. Beniamin], b. Oct. 15, 1747	ER	205
William Augustus, s. Nehemiah, 3rd [& Polly], b. May 10, 1813	1	155
W[illia]m H., m. Abigail J. **REYNOLDS**, Mar. 7, 1831, by J. Mann	1	185
William L. M., s. Matthew, b. Aug. 28, 1809	1	107
Zabadiah, s. [Benjamin & Rachal], b. Aug. 16, 1720	ER	177
Zabadiah, s. [Benjamin & Rachal], b. Aug. 16, 1720	LR1	447
Zaccheus, [s. Peter & Hannah], b. Dec. 30, 1759	1	104
Zaccheus, [s. Peter & Hannah], b. Dec. 30, 1759	ER	228
Zaccheus, s. Job [& Elsey], b. Jan. 2, 1798	1	153
Zachariah, s. Nehemiah, b. Feb. 6, 1792	1	153
Zebulon, s. Timothy [& Martha], b. Oct. 5, 1729	1	48
Zebulon, s. Timothy [& Martha], b. Oct. 5, 1729	ER	192
Zenas, [s. Deliverence & Abigail], b. Dec. 10, 1779	1	111
Zenas, [s. Deliverance & Abigail], b. Dec. 10, 1779	ER	226
Zetta, of Greenwich, m. P. C. **DAY**, of Iowa Territory,		

	Vol.	Page

MEAD, MEADE, (cont.)

	Vol.	Page
July 9, [1839], by Noah Coe	1	204
Zopher, s. Abraham, Jr. [& Keziah], b. Nov. 22, 1768	1	156
-----, Jr., m. Amy KNAPP, Jan. 13, 1748, by Rev. Abraham Todd	1	81-2

MERRELL, Patty, m. Charles **JARMAN,** June 2, 1836, by James

	Vol.	Page
Jarman	1	199
Phebe, of Greenwich, m. Burr KNAP[P], of Stamford, Sept. 7, [1840], by Noah Coe	1	206
Susanna Ann Eliza, m. Edward MEAD, [Dec.] 24, [1832], by Joel Mann	1	188

MERRITT, MERRET, MERRETT, Daniel, s. Ebenezer [&

	Vol.	Page
Cynthia], b. Oct. 19, 1784	1	134
Daniel, of North Castle, m. Rachall **BROWN,** of Poundridge, but now residing with Mrs. Mills, Apr. 19, 1826, at the house of wid. Mills, by Platt Buffett	1	173
Ebenezer, m. Cynthia **WILLIS,** d. John, Aug. 17, 1783	1	134
Elijah, m. Maria **MINOR,** of Greenwich, Jan. 4, 1829, by C. Wilcox	1	181
Frances Sarah, of Greenwich, m. Solomon **CURTISE,** Jr., of Stratford, Sept. 26, [1821], by Isaac Lewis	1	165
Jotham, m. Elizabeth **PAGE,** d. Benjamin, Nov. 12, 1838, by Rev. Joseph H. Nichols	1	202
Lewis Augustus, m. Elmaretta **HUBBARD,** [Sept.] 23, [1834], by J. Mann	1	193
Mary, m. Reuben **GREEN,** Sept. 19, 1731, by Joshua Knapp, J. P.	1	61
Mary, m. Rubin **GREEN,** Sept. 19, 1731, by Joshua Knapp, J. P.	ER	203
Nathan, Jr., had negroes Charles, s. Peg, b. May 11, 1791 & Tack, s. Peg, b. Feb. 14, 1793	1	150
Phebe, m. Nehemiah E. **MEAD,** Dec. 7, 1829, by Chauncey Wilcox	1	183
Robert, s. Witman (colored), b. July 5, 1737	1	117
Robert, colored had children Charles, b. Nov. 4, 1829, Margaret, b. Oct. 10, 1831, Saunders, b. Dec. 21, 1833, & Susan, b. Aug. 2, 1836	1	101
Willis, s. Ebenezer [& Cynthia], b. Mar. 12, 1786	1	134
Willis Jarvis, m. Mary Husted **MEAD,** [Oct.] 10, [1831], by Joel Mann	1	186
-----, m. Purdy **LYON,** July 19, 1840, by John Smith	1	206

MILES, Daniel, of Greenwich, m. Eliza **AUSTIN,** of Stanwich,

	Vol.	Page
Feb. 1, 1824, by Platt Buffett	1	171
Harriet, m. George W. **COMINGS,** Apr. 5, 1835, by Chauncey Wilcox	1	195

MILLARD*, Susanah, m. Beniamin **KNAPP,** June 3, 1731, by Rev.

	Vol.	Page
MILLARD*, (cont.)		
John Tennant *(MILLER?)	1	65
MILLER, MILLIAR, Maria, d. Ceaser & Lib (negro), b. Sept. 4, 1803	1	93
Susanah, m. Beniamin KNAPP, June 3, 1731, by Rev. John Tenant	ER	202*
MILLS, Abigail, d. Samuel [& Abigail], b. Feb. 12, 1747	1	135
Abigail, d. Samuel [& Abigail], b. Feb. 12, 1747	ER	233
Charlotte, d. Sam[ue]ll, Jr. & Deborah], b. Dec. 1, 1780	1	143
Clemence, d. Samuel [& Abigail], b. Dec. 19, 1770	1	135
Clemence, d. Samuel [& Abigail], b. Dec. 19, 1770	ER	233
Deborah, w. Samuel, Jr., d. Feb. 9, 1791	1	143
Floyd, m. Margaret WILSON, b. of Greenwich, [ ], 16, 1843, by D. B. Butts	1	213
Hannah, d. Samuel [& Abigail], b. Nov. 8, 1764	1	135
Hannah, d. Samuel [& Abigail], b. Nov. 8, 1764	ER	233
John, s. Samuel [& Abigail], b. Nov. 23, 1762	1	135
John, s. Samuel [& Abigail], b. Nov. 23, 1762	ER	233
Lydia, d. Samuel [& Abigail], b. Jan. 25, 1749	ER	233
Lydia, d. Samuel [& Abigail], b. Feb. 25, 1749	1	135
Mary, d. Samuel [& Abigail], b. Jan. 14, 1758	1	135
Mary, d. Samuel [& Abigail], b. Jan. 14, 1758	ER	233
Olla*, d. Samuel, Jr. [& Deborah], b. Aug. 11, 1787 *("Olivia" in Mead's Hist.)	1	143
Samuel, s. Samuel, b. Dec. 2, 1724; m. Abigail HOLMES, d. Isaac, [ ]	1	135
Samuell, s. Samuell, b. Dec. 23, 1724; m. Abigail HOLMES, d. Isaac, [ ]	ER	233
Samuel, s. Samuel [& Abigail], b. Dec. 8, 1751	ER	233
Samuel, s. Samuel [& Abigail], b. Dec. 28, 1751	1	135
Samuel, Jr., of Greenwich, m. Deborah VEAL, d. Joseph, of Cortland Manor, June 15, 1778, by Rev. Mr. Mills, of Bedford	1	143
Sam[ue]ll, 3rd, s. Sam[ue]ll, Jr. [& Deborah], b. Sept. 19, 1783	1	143
Sarah, d. Samuel [& Abigail], b. Dec. 30, 1755	1	135
Sarah, d. Samuel [& Abigail], b. Dec. 30, 1755	ER	233
Sarah, d. Samuel, Jr. [& Deborah], b. Sept. 26, 1785	1	143
Sarah Amanda, m. Augustus LYON, Dec. 7, 1820, by Rev. Benj[ami]n Griffin	1	165
Sarah H., m. Major LOCKWOOD, Dec. 26, 1827, by Rev. Lyman Andrus	1	180
MINOR, MINER, Adaline, m. Nelson D. SCOFIELD, Oct. 14, [1832], by Stephen Waring, J. P.	1	188
Ann, m. James H. FAIRCHILD, Sept. 7, 1822, by Isaac Lewis	1	168
Cornelius, m. Grace W. MEAD, b. of Greenwich, Dec. 13, 1842, by B. M. Yarrington	1	210

	Vol.	Page
MINOR, MINER, (cont.)		
Maria, m. Elijah MERRITT, Jan. 4, 1829, by C. Wilcox	1	181
MITCHELL, Harriet, of Greenwich, m. Henry SMITH, of New York, Dec. 12, 1824, by Noble W. Thomas, Elder	1	171
MOE, Sarah, m. John PURDY, b. of Greenwich, Jan. 6, 1833, by Chauncey Wilcox	1	189
MONROE, Elizabeth, m. William WOOL (colored), b. of Greenwich, Mar. 23, 1833, by Rev. Platt Buffett, of Stanwich	1	191
MO[O]RE, Charles, colored, d. Sept. 24, 1821	1	132
MORGAN, Abraham, s. Joseph [& Sary], b. Nov. 10, 1706	ER	107
Abraham, s. Joseph [& Sary], b. Nov. 10, 1706	LR1	453
Dorothy, d. Joseph & Sary, b. July 24, 1697	ER	107
Dorothy, d. Joseph & Sary, b. July 24, 1697	LR1	453
Mary, d. Joseph [& Sary], b. Mar. 8, 1707/8; d. Nov. 20, 1708	ER	107
Mary, d. [Joseph & Sary], b. Mar. 8, 1707/8; d. Nov. 20, 1708	LR1	453
Nathaniel, s. [Joseph & Sary], b. Sept. 17, 1699	ER	107
Nathaniel, s. [Joseph & Sary], b. Sept. 17, 1699	LR1	453
Sarah, 2nd d. [Joseph & Sary], b. Aug. 22, 1698	ER	107
Sarah, d. [Joseph & Sary], b. Aug. 22, 1698	LR1	453
MORRELL, Fanny, m. Seth MARSHALL, b. of Greenwich, Jan. 7, 1828, by Rev. John Ellis, of Stamford	1	178
MOSHIER, MOSIER, Harriet, m. Amos HOBBY, Apr. 15, 1823, by Isaac Lewis	1	169
James, m. Louisa TIMPANNY, Dec. 3, 1835, by James Jarman	1	199
MUNSIGLINO, Gerlando, m. Elizabeth CHARRAND, b. of New York City, Apr. 23, 1837, by Rev. Ambrose S. Todd, of Stamford	1	215
MYERS, Robert, of Herkimer, N. Y., m. Hannah E. HUSTED, of Greenwich, Oct. 18, 1841, by Thomas Payne	1	208
NASH, Ann, m. William Henry SHERWOOD, b. of Greenwich, Oct. 3, 1838, by Thomas Brewer	1	201
Dorcas, of Greenwich, m. Benjamin SANDS, of New Castle, N. Y., Oct. 9, 1833, by Chauncey Wilcox	1	192
-----, m. Hanford LOCKWOOD, b. of Greenwich, Oct. 6, 1830, at the house of James Nash, by Rev. Daniel J. Wright	1	185
NEWMAN, Ann Augusta, m. Ebenezer PURDY, b. of Greenwich, Oct. 14, 1840, by Daniel B. Butts	1	206
Mary Ann, m. Edmund LOCKWOOD, Nov. 9, 1842, by Farnam Knowlton	1	210
Mary Elizabeth, m. Edward Payson HEWES, Jan. 4, 1841, by Thomas Payne	1	206

	Vol.	Page
NICHOLAS, John, m. Mary **SELLECK**, d. Silas, Feb. [ ], 1765	1	123
John, [s. John & Mary], b. Sept. 23, 1769	1	123
Sarah, [d. John & Mary], b. Dec. 18, 1765	1	123
Silas, [s. John & Mary], b. Nov. 14, 1767	1	123
[NICHOLS], NICKOLLS, NICKALLS, NICOLLS, Abraham, m.		
Ruth **MARSHALL**, Dec. 6, 1722	1	49
Abraham, m. Ruth **MARSHALL**, Dec. 6, 1722	ER	189
James, s. [Abraham & Ruth], b. Dec. 19, 1723	1	49
James, s. [Abraham & Ruth], b. Dec. 19, 1723	ER	189
John, s. Abraham [& Ruth], b. Jan. 18, 1732	1	49
John, s. Abraham [& Ruth], b. Jan. 18, 1732	ER	189
Robert, s. Abraham [& Ruth], b. Mar. 16, 1729	1	49
Robert, s. Abraham [& Ruth], b. Mar. 16, 1729	ER	189
Thomas, s. Abraham [& Ruth], b. May 1, 1726	1	49
Thomas, s. Abraham [& Ruth], b. May 1, 1726	ER	189
NUTT, David, [s. Robert], b. Sept. 15, 1767	1	114
Elizabeth, [d. Robert], b. Feb. 9, 1759	1	114
Henry, [s. Robert], b. Feb. 15, 1770	1	114
Mary, [d. Robert], b. Oct. 6, 1773	1	114
Rachall, [d. Robert], b. Nov. 21, 1771	1	114
William, [s. Robert], b. Mar. 5, 1766	1	114
OGDEN, Daniell, m. Marsey **MARSHALL**, Nov. 8, 1734, by Rev.		
Abraham Todd	ER	213
Daniell, s. [Daniell & Marsey], b. Aug. 21, 1735	ER	213
Daniell, m. Marcy **MARSHALL**, Nov. 8, 1754, by Rev.	1	67
Abraham Todd		
Daniell, s. [Daniell & Marcy], b. Aug. 21, 1755	1	67
Elizabeth, d. [Daniell & Marcy], b. Sept. 9, 1739*		
*(1759?)	1	67
Elizabeth, d. [Daniell & Marsey], b. Sept. 9, 1739	ER	213
Marsey, d. Daniell [& Marcy], b. Apr. 1, 1757	1	67
Mersey, d. Daniell [& Marsey], b. Apr. 5, 1737	ER	213
OLMSTEAD, OLMSTED, Cornelia, m. John **SACKETT**, b. of		
Greenwich, Jan. 9, 1829, by Rev. John M.		
Smith. Witness: Daniel Olmsted	1	182
Thirza, m. Alfred **BIXLEY**, [Nov.] 5, [1834], by J. Mann	1	194
OWENS, OWEN, Allace, m. Jasper W. **CARPENTER**, b. of		
Greenwich, Oct. 16, 1842, by Samuel Close, J.		
P.	1	209
Charles, m. Mary **BURNS**, b. of Greenwich, Dec. 3,		
1835, by Platt Buffett	1	196
Martha, m. Ezra **HOLMES**, b. of Greenwich, Sept. 30,		
[1821], by Rev. David Peck	1	166
Sarah, m. Abraham **ROWEL**, Dec. 4, 1837, by James		
Jarman	1	199
PAGE, Afelia F., of Greenwich, m. George J. **SMITH**, of Stamford,		
Oct. 28, 1839, by B. M. Farrington	1	204
Benjamin, m. Mary B. **WARING**, b. of Greenwich, Sept.		

	Vol.	Page

PAGE, (cont.)

	Vol.	Page
Sept. 13, 1845, by Rev. Benjamin M. Yarrington, Int. Pub.	1	215
Elizabeth, d. Benjamin, m. Jotham **MERRETT**, Nov. 12, 1838, by Rev. Joseph H. Nichols	1	202

PALMER, PALMORE, PALMOUR, PALIMER, Abigail, [d.

	Vol.	Page
Levy & Sarah], b. Aug. 21, 1796	1	151
Albert, [s. Levy & Sarah], b. Sept. 9, 1805	1	151
Amey, m. Abraham **HUBBARD**, b. of Greenwich, Feb. 11, 1828, by Platt Buffett	1	179
Asa, s. John Wood [& Hannah], b. Mar. 7, 1785	1	133
Daniell, s. John [& Hannah], b. Nov. 18, 1740	1	62
Daniell, s. John [& Hannah], b. Nov. 28, 1740	ER	202*
Daniell, s. John, b. Nov. 28, 1740	ER	223*
Deborah Ann, m. James **MEAD**, b. of Greenwich, Dec. 19, 1821, by Isaac Lewis	1	167
Edward, [s. Levy & Sarah], b. Oct. 8, 1799	1	151
Elial, [child of Levy & Sarah], b. Aug. 27, 1793	1	151
Elizabeth, m. Benjamin **FINCH**, Apr. 16, 1717	LR1	450
Elizabeth, m. Benjamin **FINCH**, Apr. 18, 1717	ER	179
Elizabeth, [d. Dr. Nehemiah], b. Dec. 16, 1753	1	121
Elizabeth, [d. Dr. Nehemiah], b. Dec. 16, 1753	ER	238
Ephraim, s. Ephraim & Sarah, b. Oct. 24, 1677	LR1	453
Easter, d. [ ], decd. of Frogneck, Westchester Cty., m. Messinger **PALMER**, of Greenwich, Oct. 27, 1755, by Rev. Mr. Bostwick, of Jamaica, L. I.	1	71
Ferris, s. John Wood [& Hannah], b. Aug. 25, 1789	1	133
Francis, m. John **WEED**, b. of Greenwich, Jan. 26, 1834, by Rev. Platt Buffett, of Stanwich	1	192
Geor[ge] A., m. Harriet **KNAPP**, [Sept.] 9, [1834], by J. Mann	1	193
Hannah, d. John [& Hannah], b. Oct. 1, 1731	1	62
Hannah, d. John [& Hannah], b. Oct. 10, 1731	ER	202*
Hette, d. John Wood [& Hannah], b. Nov. 19, 1792	1	133
Isaac, [s. Dr. Nehemiah], b. Nov. 25, 1760	1	121
Isaac, [s. Dr. Nehemiah], b. Nov. 25, 1760	ER	238
Jemima, d. John [& Hannah], b. Oct. 22, 1738	1	62
Jemine, d. John [& Hannah], b. Oct. 23, [ ]	ER	202*
Jeremah, of Bedford, N. Y., m. Mary Amanda **CLOSE**, of Greenwich, Aug. 25, 1840, by D. B. Butts	1	206
John, m. Hannah **SMITH**, Feb. 16, 1730/1, by Joshua Knapp, J. P.	1	62
John, m. Hannah **SMITH**, Feb. 16, 1730/1, by Joshua Knapp, J. P.	ER	202*
John, [& w. Hannah had s. [ ], b.], Jan. 18, 1732/3	1	62
John, had s. [ ], b. Jan. 19, 1732/3	ER	202*
John Wood, m. Hannah **FERRIS**, d. James, June 6, 1776,		

	Vol.	Page
PALMER, PALMORE, PALMOUR, PALIMER, (cont.)		
1776, by Rev. Mr. Seward	1	133
Joseph, m. Martha **KNAP[P]**, Feb. 29, 1719/20, by Rev. Zachary Sacket	LR1	412
Joshua, s. Joseph [& Martha], b. Mar. 22, 1720/1	LR1	412
Levy, b. Sept. 9, 1763; m. Sarah **RUNDLE**, Jan. 4, 1787, by Rev. William Seward	1	151
Levy, [s. Levy & Sarah], b. Oct. 18, 1789	1	151
Ledea*, m. Samuel **RENOLLS**, Jan. 26, 1727/8		
*(Rebecca)	1	54
Messenger, s. John Wood [& Hannah], b. Apr. 11, 1777	1	133
Messinger, of Greenwich, m. Easter **PALMER**, d. [ ], decd. of Frogneck, Westchester Cty., Oct. 27, 1755, by Rev. Mr. Bostwick, of Jamaica, L. I.	1	71
Nathan, s. John [& Hannah], b. Nov. 29, 1736	1	62
Nathan, s. John [& Hannah], b. Nov. 29, 1736	ER	202*
Nathaniell, s. [John, Jr.], b. June 22, 1755	1	63
Nathaniell, [s. John, Jr.], b. June 22, 1755	ER	226
Nehemiah, [s. Dr. Nehemiah], b. July 24, 1751	1	121
Nehemiah, [s. Dr. Nehemiah], b. July 24, 1751	ER	238
Oliver, s. John Wood [& Hannah], b. May 3, 1779	1	133
Peter, s. William, b. July 23, 1703	ER	85-6
Peter, s. William, b. July 23, 1703	LR1	448
Phebe, d. William, b. July 4, 179[ ]	ER	85
Phebe, d. William, b. July 4, [ ]	LR1	448
Ralph, s. John Wood [& Hannah], b. Sept. 12, 1787	1	133
Rebaca, m. Samuell **RENOLLS**, Jan. 26, 1727/8	ER	198
Rebeccah, d. John [& Hannah], b. Oct. 31, 1742	1	62
Rebecca, d. John [& Hannah], b. Oct. 31, 1742	ER	202*
Rebecca, d. John, b. Oct. 31, 1742	ER	223*
Rebecca, d. John, Jr., b. Mar. 18, 1743	1	63
Rebecca, d. John, Jr., b. Mar. 18, 1743	ER	226
Sally, [d. Levy & Sarah], b. Jan. 14, 1788	1	151
Sarah, d. [John & Hannah], b. Jan. 18, 1732/3	1	62
Sarah, d. [John & Hannah], b. Jan. 28, 1734/5	ER	202*
Sarah Ann, m. John **HALLIGAN**, [Jan. 2, 1842], by Thomas Payne	1	209
Sibbel Wood, d. John Wood [& Hannah], b. Apr. 18, 1781	1	133
Warren, m. Mary **FERRIS**, b. of Greenwich, Nov. 13, 1823, by W[illia]m Knapp, J. P.	1	170
William, s. William, b. Nov. 6, 1694	ER	85
William, s. William, b. Nov. 6, 1694	LR1	448
PARDEE, [see also **PURDY**], Mary, Mrs. of New Haven, m. Nathaniell **PECK**, Dec. 4, 1722, by Samuel Bishop, J. P.	1	79-80
PARSONS, Eliphaz, [s. Jesse & Sarah], b. Apr. 6, 1768	1	94
Hannah, [d. Jesse & Sarah], b. Oct. 23, 1765		94

	Vol.	Page

PARSONS, (cont.)
Jesse, m. Sarah CLOSE, d. Thomas, Oct. 25, 1755, by
    Rev. Mr. Feeks — 1 — 94
Jesse, [s. Jesse & Sarah], b. Sept. 12, 1758 — 1 — 94
John, of Sharon, Litchfield Co., m. Sally LOCKWOOD,
    of Greenwich, Oct. 30, [1821], by Isaac Lewis — 1 — 166
Parmenus, [s. Jesse & Sarah], b. May 12, 1771 — 1 — 94
Phebe, [d. Jesse & Sarah], b. June 22, 1763 — 1 — 94
Phebe, [d. Jesse & Sarah], d. Nov. 29, 1835 — 1 — 94
Theophilus, [s. Jesse & Sarah], b. June 29, 1756 — 1 — 94
Tryphena, [d. Jesse & Sarah], b. Apr. 23, 1761 — 1 — 94
PEACOCK, Sarah, of Greenwich, m. Stephen UNDERHILL, of
    Long Island, Sept. 3, 1823, by Isaac Lewis — 1 — 169
PEAT, Susana, m. Beniamin FINCH, Dec. 23, 1727, by Samuel
    Peck, J. P. — 1 — 54
Susana, m. Beniamin FINCH, Dec. 23, 1727, by
    Sam[ue]ll Peck, J. P. — ER — 196
PECK, Aaron, [s. Samuel], b. May 3, 1757 — 1 — 84
Aaron, [s. Samuel], b. May 3, 1757 — ER — 239
Abraham, s. Theophilus, m. Hannah PURDY, d. Caleb,
    of Rye, Dec. 6, 1770 — 1 — 124
Abraham, [s. Abraham & Hannah], b. Apr. 30, 1779 — 1 — 124
Abraham, d. Feb. 3, 1792 — 1 — 124
Allathea, m. Gilbert P. FINCH, Apr. 8, 1827, by David
    Peck — 1 — 176
Amey, d. David [& Amy], b. Aug. 12, 1777 — 1 — 131
Amy, w. David, d. Jan. 31, 1793 — 1 — 131
Amy Eliza, [d. Benoni & Huldah], b. Sept. 11, 1821 — 1 — 131
Anna, d. Robert [& Ann], b. June 21, [   ] — 1 — 164
Anne, d. Abraham [& Hannah], b. Sept. 30, 1783 — 1 — 124
Anne, d. David, b. Apr. 30, 1785 — 1 — 131
Arad, s. Solomon, m. Eliza STEPHENS, of New York,
    d. of Ruleaf, Sept. 3, 1833 — 1 — 131
Benjamin, of Greenwich, m. Deborah SACKETT, of
    Hanover, on Cortlandts Manor, Nov. 11, 1766 — 1 — 102
Benjamin, [s. Benjamin & Hannah], b. May 20, 1773[sic] — 1 — 102
Benjamin, m. Hannah READ, Aug. 12, 1774 — 1 — 102
Benoni, s. David [& Amy], b. Oct. 5, 1790 — 1 — 131
Benoni, s. David, b. Nov. 5, 1790; m. Huldah [   ],
    Dec. 2, 1812 — 1 — 131
Charlotte, [d. Theophilus, Jr. & Rebecca], b. Nov.
    4, 1768 — 1 — 72
Charlotte, [s. Theophilus, Jr. & Rebecca], b. Nov. 4,
    1768 — ER — 241
Charlotte, [twin with Rebecca, d. David & Amy], b.
    Jan. 21, 1793 — 1 — 131
Clare, d. Gideon [& Eunice], b. May 29, 1783 — 1 — 132
Cornelius, 3rd s. [Benoni & Huldah], b. Sept. 30, 1827 — 1 — 131

PECK, (cont.)

	Vol.	Page
David, s. [Samuel & Ruth], b. Dec. 15, [16]94	ER	55
David, 4th s. [Samuell & Ruth], b. Dec. 15, 1694	LR1	454
David, [s. Theophilus, Jr. & Rebecca], b. Feb. 14, 1754	1	72
David, [s. Theophilus, Jr. & Rebecca], b. Feb. 14, 1754	ER	241
David, m. Amy RUNDALL, d. Reuben, Aug. 12, 1773	1	131
David, s. David [& Amy], b. May 13, 1775	1	131
David, 3rd, 2nd s. [Benoni & Huldah], b. Feb. 16, 1825	1	131
Deborah, [d. Benjamin & Deborah], b. Feb. 5, 1768	1	102
Deborah, w. Benjamin, d. July 14, 1769	1	102
Deborah, d. David [& Amy], b. Sept. 15, 1788	1	131
Deborah M., m. Eliphalet PECK, 2nd, Jan. 25, 1824, by Rev. David Peck	1	170
Edward A., only s. [Arad & Eliza], b. Oct. 22, 1834	1	131
Elias, s. Robert [& Ann], b. Jan. 5, [ ]	1	164
Eliphalet, s. [Theophilus, Jr. & Rebecca], b. May 18, 1774	1	72
Eliphalet, [s. Theophilus, Jr. & Rebecca], b. May 18, 1774	ER	241
Eliphalet, 2nd, m. Deborah M. PECK, Jan. 25, 1824, by Rev. David Peck	1	170
Eliza, m. Alvin MEAD, Dec. 18, 1821, by Rev. Isaac Lewis	1	91
Eliza, m. Alvin MEAD, b. of Greenwich, Dec. 18, 1821, by Isaac Lewis	1	167
Elizabeth, [d. Nathaniell & Mary], b. June 19, 1724; d. July 1, 1724	1	79-80
Elizabeth, [d. Nathaniell & Mary], b. Dec. 28, 1737	1	79-80
Elizabeth, [d. Nathaniel, Jr. & Jerusha], b. May 8, 1757	1	81-2
Elizabeth, [d. Nathaniel, Jr. & Jerusha], b. May 8, 1757	ER	230
Elizabeth, [d. Samuel, Jr. & Hannah], b. Apr. 11, 1763	1	103
Elizabeth, d. [Abraham & Hannah], b. Sept. 26, 1771; d. Oct. 31, 1772, ae 1 y. 1 m. 4 d.	1	124
Elizabeth, wid. Theophilus, d. Nov. 17, 1783, in the 80th y. of her age	1	135
Elizabeth, d. Israel [& Levine], b. Dec. 5, 1786; d. Dec. 6, 1786	1	135
Elizabeth, [twin with Eunice, d. Gideon & Eunice], b. June 20, 1793	1	132
Elizabeth, d. Israel [& Levine], b. May 20, 1797; d. Jan. 14, 1802	1	135
Ephraim, [s. Nathaniel, Jr. & Jerusha], b. Jan. 5, 1755	1	81-2
Ephraim, [s. Nathaniel, Jr. & Jerusha], b. Jan. 5, 1755	ER	230
Esther, d. David [& Amy], b. Nov. 25, 1781	1	131
Esther, d. [Abraham & Hannah], b. Aug. 26, 1786	1	124
Eunice, [twin with Elizabeth, d. Gideon & Eunice], b. June 20, 1793	1	132
Eunice, w. Gideon, d. Apr. 12, 1801	1	132

BARBOUR COLLECTION

	Vol.	Page
PECK, (cont.)		
Fanny, d. Gideon [& Eunice], b. Jan. 23, 1785	1	132
George, [s. Nathaniell & Mary], b. Jan. 4, 1743	1	79-80
Gideon, [s. Theophilus, Jr. & Rebecca], b. Sept. 3, 1756	ER	241
Gideon, [s. Theophilus, Jr. & Rebecca], b. Sept. 4, 1756	1	72
Gideon, m. Eunice **CLOSE**, d. Joseph, Oct. 4, 1781, by Rev. Jonathan Murdock	1	132
Gideon, Jr., s. Gideon [& Eunice], b. Nov. 23, 1791	1	132
Gilbert, s. [Theophilus, Jr. & Rebecca], b. Apr. 26, 1763	1	72
Gilbert, [s. Theophilus, Jr. & Rebecca], b. Apr. 26, 1763	ER	241
Hannah, [d. Samuel], b. Apr. 16, 1755	1	84
Hannah, [d. Samuel], b. Apr. 16, 1755	ER	239
Hannah, [d. Samuel, Jr. & Hannah], b. June 8, 1770	1	103
Hannah, [d. Benjamin & Hannah], b. Feb. 21, 1775	1	102
Hannah, d. Abraham [& Hannah], b. May 14, 1776	1	124
Hannah, 1st d. [Benoni & Huldah], b. Sept. 13, 1813	1	131
Hannah, of Greenwich, m. Jesse L. **SHERWOOD**, of New York, July 28, 1823, by Rev. David Smith, of Stamford	1	169
Hannah, m. George **ANDMAN** (colored), b. of Greenwich, Dec. 18, 1839, by Rev. Platt Buffett	1	205
Harvey Prindle, of Hartford, m. Margaret Mariah **LEWIS**, of Greenwich, Nov. 26, 1823, by Isaac Lewis	1	170
Hezekiah, [s. Nathaniell & Mary], b. Feb. 9, 1732/3; d. [ ], 1733	1	79-80
Hezekiah, [s. Nathaniel, Jr. & Jerusha], b. Sept. 26, 1752	ER	230
Isaac, [s. Nathaniell & Mary], b. Jan. 2, 1731/2; d. [ ], 1732	1	79-80
Isaac, 6th, 1st s. [Benoni & Huldah], b. May 4, 1815	1	131
Isaac, m. Julia **MEAD**, b. of Greenwich, Sept. 7, [1840], by Noah Coe	1	206
Israel, s. Theoophilus, b. Apr. 9, 1750; m. Levine **PURDY**, of Rye, May 30, 1782	1	135
Israel, s. Israel [& Levine], b. Mar. 8, 1783	1	135
Israel, s. Israel [& Levine], d. May 1, 1793	1	135
Israel, Jr., s. Israel [& Levine], b. Dec. 7, 1794	1	135
Jabez, [s. Samuel, Jr. & Hannah], b. May 12, 1768	1	103
James, [s. Benjamin & Hannah], b. Mar. 11, 1777	1	102
Jared, [s. Samuel, Jr. & Hannah], b. Feb. 27, 1773	1	103
Jeremiah, s. [Samuel & Ruth], b. Dec. 29, 1690	ER	55
Jeremiah, 2nd s. [Samuel & Ruth], b. Dec. 29, 1690	LR1	454
Jonathan, [s. Nathaniell & Mary], b. Sept. 23, 1740	1	79-80
Joseph, s. [Samuel & Ruth], b. May 1, [16]92	ER	55
Joseph, 3rd s. [Samuell & Ruth], b. May 1, 1692	LR1	454
Joshua, [s. Nathaniell & Mary], b. May 12, 1730	1	79-80
Lavina, d. Abraham [& Hannah], b. July 9, 1773	1	124

GREENWICH VITAL RECORDS 241

	Vol.	Page
PECK, (cont.)		
Levina, d. Israel [& Levine], b. Mar. 20, 1791	1	135
Lewis, s. Robert [& Ann], b. Dec. 15, [ ]	1	164
Marilda, m. David **BANKS**, May 10, [1821], by Rev. David Peck	1	165
Martha, b. May 15, 1803; m. Gilbert P. **FINCH**, [ ]	1	85
Mary, [d. Nathaniell & Mary], b. Dec. 12, 1727	1	79-80
Mary, [d. Nathaniel, Jr. & Jerusha], b. Aug. 6, 1747	1	81-2
Mary, d. Nathaniel, Jr. & Jerusha], b. Aug. 6, 1747	ER	230
Mary, [d. Samuel], b. Nov. 13, 1752	1	84
Mary, [d. Samuel], b. Nov. 13, 1752	ER	239
Mary, w. Capt. Nathaniel, d. Jan. 6, 1758	1	79-80
Mary, d. Eliphalet, m. Josiah **FERRIS**, Nov. 3, 1762	1	86
Mary, d. Eliphalet, m. Josiah **FERRIS**, Nov. 3, 1762	ER	241
Mary, d. David [& Amy], b. Sept. 9, 1779	1	131
Molly, d. Robert [& Ann], b. Dec. 21, [ ]	1	164
Nathaniel, s. [Samuel & Ruth], b. Aug. 15, 1697	ER	55
Nathaniel, 5th s. [Samuell & Ruth], b. Aug. 15, 1697	LR1	454
Nathaniell, m. Mrs. Mary **PARDEE**, of New Haven, Dec. 4, 1722, by Samuel Bishop, J. P.	1	79-80
Nathaniel, [s. Nathaniell & Mary], b. June 2, 1725	1	79-80
Nathaniel, Jr., m. Jerusha **CURTIS**, Oct. 9, 1746	1	81-2
Nathaniel, Jr., m. Jerusha **CURTIS**, Oct. 9, 1746	ER	230
Nathaniel, [s. Nathaniel, Jr. & Jerusha], b. May 10, 1750	1	81-2
Nathaniel, [s. Nathaniel, Jr. & Jerusha], b. May 10, 1750	ER	230
Nehemiah, s. Israel [& Levine], b. Dec. 2, 1784	1	135
Polly, d. Gideon [& Eunice], b. Sept. 6, 1786	1	132
Rachel, [d. Samuel, Jr. & Hannah], b. Aug. 19, 1775	1	103
Rachel, d. Israel [& Levine], b. Oct. 28, 1787	1	135
Rebeckah, [d. Nathaniel, Jr. & Jerusha], b. Sept. 26, 1752	1	81-2
Rebecca, [d. Theophilus, Jr. & Rebecca], b. Aug. 1, 1771	1	72
Rebecca, [d. Theophilus, Jr. & Rebeca], b. Aug. 1, 1771	ER	241
Rebecca, [twin with Charlotte, d. David & Amy], b. Jan. 21, 1793	1	131
Rhoda, 2nd d. [Benoni & Huldah], b. Apr. 17, 1818	1	131
Robert, s. Robert [& Ann], b. Nov. 1, [ ]	1	164
Ruth, d. Theophilus, of Greenwich, m. Caleb **PURDY**, of Rye, Apr. 25, 1771	1	136
Ruth, d. Theophilus, Jr. [& Rebecca], b. Dec. 20, 1777	1	72
Ruth, d. Theophilus, Jr. [& Rebecca], b. Dec. 20, 1777	ER	241
Ruth Mariah, m. Humphrey **DENTON**, Jr., b. of Greenwich, Nov. 2, 1845, by Rev. Ebenezer Mead	1	214
Samuel, m. Ruth **FER[R]IS**, Nov. 27, 1686, by Jonathan Bell, Com.	ER	55
Samuell, m. Ruth **FER[R]IS**, Nov. 27, 1686, by Jonathan Bell, Com.	LR1	454
Samuel, 1st s. [Samuel & Ruth], b. Mar. [ ], 1688	ER	55

	Vol.	Page
PECK, (cont.)		
Samuell, s. [Samuell & Ruth], b. Mar. [ ], 1688	LR1	454
Samuel, [s. Nathaniell & Mary], b. Jan. 19, 1744;		
d. [ ], 1744	1	79-80
Samuel, Jr., m. Hannah **SHERWOOD**, Apr. 29, 1762	1	103
Samuel, [s. Samuel, Jr. & Hannah], b. Dec. 22, 1765	1	103
Sarah, 4th d. [Benoni & Huldah], b. Jan. 31, 1827	1	131
Solomon, [s. Theophilus, Jr. & Rebecca], b. Nov. 25, 1763	1	72
Solomon, [s. Theophilus, Jr. & Rebecca], b. Nov. 25, 1765	ER	241
Thankful, [d. Nathaniell & Mary], b. Aug. 17, 1736	1	79-80
Theophilus, s. Theophilus, Jr. [& Rebecca], d. [ ]	1	72
Theophilus, s. Theophilus, Jr. [& Rebecca], d. [ ]	ER	241
Theophilus, Jr., m. Rebecca **KNAPP**, July 5, 1753	1	72
Theophilus, Jr., m. Rebecca **KNAPP**, July 5, 1753	ER	241
Theophilus, s. [Theophilus, Jr. & Rebecca], b. Dec. 7, 1758	1	72
Theophilus, [s. Theophilus, Jr. & Rebecca], b. Dec. 8, 1758	ER	241
Theophilus, d. Nov. 7, 1783, in the 82nd y. of his age	1	135
Theophilus, s. David [& Amy], b. Jan. 24, 1784; d. June 6, 1784	1	131
Theophilus, s. David [& Amy], b. Aug. 16, 1787; d. Sept. 19, 1787	1	131
Theophilus, s. Gideon [& Eunice], b. Apr. 6, 1795	1	132
Thomas, s. [Theophilus, Jr. & Rebecca], b. July 4, 1761	1	72
Thomas, [s. Theophilus, Jr. & Rebecca], b. July 4, 1761	ER	241
Yale, [s. Nathaniell & Mary], b. Oct. 27, 1739; d. [ ], 1739	1	79-80
PERLEE, [see also **PARDEE** & **PURDY**], Edmond, m. Rachal **MEAD**, Jan. 29, 1747	1	66
Mary, d. [Edmond & Rachal], b. Dec. 11, 1750	1	66
Semanthe, d. [Edmond & Rachal], b. July 20, 1749	1	66
[PERROT], PERATT, Amelia, [twin with Ann, d. [ ] & Hannah], b. June 27, 1767, bp. by Rev. Ebenezer Dibble	1	124
Ann, [twin with Amelia, d. [ ] & Hannah], b. June 27, 1767; bp. by Rev. Ebenezer Dibble	1	124
Clarissa, [d. [ ] & Hannah], b. Nov. 7, 1765; bp. by Rev. Ebenezer Dibble	1	124
James, [twin with John, s. [ ] & Hannah], b. Nov. 9, 1770; bp. by Rev. Ebenezer Dibble	1	124
John, [twin with James, s. [ ] & Hannah, b. Nov. 9, 1770; bp. by Rev. Ebenezer Dibble	1	124
------, s. James, of St. Martins in the Fields City of Westminister, Kingdom of Great Britain, m. Hannah **BOSTWICH**, wid. Merryday, d.		

	Vol.	Page
[PERROT], PERATT, (cont.)		
Capt. Elnathan HANFORD, of Norwalk, Feb. 15, 1764, by Rev. Abraham Todd	1	124
PHILLIPS, Thomas, m. Katharine MACAY, Mar. 6, 1832, by Chauncey Wilcox	1	190
William, m. Mary STRICKLAND, Jan. 19, 1837, by James Jarman	1	199
PINTO, Daniell, s. Abraham & Sarah, b. [ ]	CP	103
PLATT, David T., m. Abigail Jane ANDERSON, b. of Greenwich, May 1, 1842, by B. M. Yarrington, at Glenville	1	208
Jeremiah, of Rye, N. Y., m. Rachel BROWN, of Greenwich, Dec. 10, 1827, by P. Buffet	1	178
PORTER, Charles, m. Mary Jane MEAD, b. of Greenwich, Aug. 1, 1838, by Rev. Chauncey Wilcox	1	201
POTTS, POTS, Abraham, s. Thomas, b. Aug. 24, 1719	1	68
Mary Elizabeth, m. Alexander LOCKWOOD, b. of Stanwich, Nov. 17, 1825, by Platt Buffett	1	172
PRAY, Hezekiah, m. Huldah MEAD, Dec. 28, 1807, by Rev. Isaac Lewis, D. D.	1	156
Hezekiah, d. July 10, 1829, in the 58th y. of his age	1	156
Horatio Nelson, s. Hezekiah [& Huldah], b. Mar. 25, 1811	1	156
John Jay, s. Hezekiah [& Huldah], b. July 2, 1800, in Albany	1	156
PUGSLEY, Deborah, of Greenwich, m. Jesse SLAUSON, of Rye, N. Y., Mar. 13, 1832, by Rev. E. Washburn	1	187
PURDY, PERDEE, [see also PARDEE & PERLEE], Anna, m. Alanson LANE, b. of Greenwich, Aug. 12, 1835, by Chauncey Wilcox	1	196
Caleb, of Rye, m. Ruth PECK, d. Theophilus, of Greenwich, Apr. 25, 1771	1	136
Caleb, s. Caleb [& Ruth], b. Jan. 18, 1774	1	136
Caleb, d. Oct. 14, 1783, in the 41st y. of his age	1	136
Caleb, m. Elizabeth C. KNAPP, Feb. 12, 1833, by Chauncey Wilcox	1	189
Ebenezer, m. Ann Augusta NEWMAN, b. of Greenwich, Oct. 14, 1840, by Daniel B. Butts	1	206
Edmund, m. Rachall MEAD, June 29, 1747	ER	233
Elias, s. Caleb [& Ruth], b. Mar. 27, 1780	1	136
Eliza, of Greenwich, m. Joseph BROWN, of Rye, N. Y., Jan. 4, 1838, by Chauncey Wilcox	1	198
Eliza Ann, m. George W. TAYLOR, b. of Greenwich, Dec. 31, 1843, by Rev. C. Wilcox	1	212
Hannah, d. Caleb, of Rye, m. Abraham PECK, s. Theophilus, Dec. 6, 1770	1	124
John, m. Sarah MOE, b. of Greenwich, Jan. 6, 1833, by Chauncey Wilcox	1	189

	Vol.	Page

PURDY, PERDEE, (cont.)
   Levine, d. [   ], of Rye, b. Feb. 19, 1755; m. Israel

	Vol.	Page
PECK, s. Theophilus, May 30, 1782	1	135
Mary, [d. Edmund & Rachall], b. Dec. 11, 1750	ER	233
Mary E., of Greenwich, m. Harrison **BRUNDAGE**, of		
North Castle, Feb. 16, 1837, by C. Wilcox	1	203
Ruth, d. Caleb [& Ruth], b. Feb. 8, 1772	1	136
Sementhe, [d. Edmund & Rachall], b. July 20, 1749		
(Samantha)	ER	233
Sarah, d. Caleb [& Ruth], b. June 16, 1776	1	136
Sarah Ann, m. Isaac O. **CLOSE**, b. of Greenwich, Aug.		
21, 1844, by Chauncey Wilcox	1	212
Solomon, s. Solomon, Jr., b. Nov. 30, 1762	1	71
William, m. Sarah **FLOOD**, b. of Greenwich, Dec. 19,		
1841, by Rev. C. Wilcox	1	208
QUICK, John, m. Abigail **BROWN**, Oct. 1, 1735, by Rev.		
Abraham Todd	1	61
John, m. Abiga[i]l **BROWN**, Oct. 1, 1735, by Abraham		
Toodd	ER	215
QUINTARD, Deborah P., m. James W. **FERRIS**, b. of Greenwich,		
Jan. 5, 1846, by Rev. S. B. S. Bissell	1	214
Seth P., m. Susan **FERRIS**, b. of Greenwich, Dec. 23,		
1822, by Rev. John Noyes	1	168
RATHBURN, Patience, m. William **ADDAMS**, Mar. 25, 1759, by		
Rev. Abraham Todd	1	89-90
Rebecca, m. Caleb **WILLIS**, Dec. 28, 1758, by Rev.		
Abraham Todd	1	89-90
RAYMOND, Henry, m. Charlotte M. **RUSSELL**, b. of Greenwich,		
Feb. 13, 1842, by Noah Coe	1	208
RAYNOR, William Alexander, of New York, m. Mary Ann		
KNAPP, of Greenwich, Mar. 28, 1827, by		
Isaac Lewis	1	174
READ, Elizabeth Jane, m. Sanford **BANKS**, b. of Greenwich, Dec.		
21, 1829, by C. Wilcox, of North Greenwich	1	183
Hannah, m. Benjamin **PECK**, Aug. 12, 1774	1	102
Lewis Augustus, of New York City, m. Ann Augusta		
JESSUP, of Greenwich, Dec. 22, 1845, by		
Rev. Peter C. Oakley	1	215
REDFIELD, Bradley, m. Harriet **MEAD**, b. of Greenwich, Jan. 4,		
1824, by Isaac Lewis	1	170
REUTSCHARTS, Elizabeth, m. Allen **LOUDON**, b. of		
Greenwich, Dec. 20, 1837, by Chauncey		
Wilcox	1	198
REYNOLDS, RENYALLS, RENYOLLS, RENOLLS, RENELS,		
REYNOLLS, Abigail, d. Joseph, b. Apr. 3, 1701	ER	120
Abigail, d. [Joseph], b. Apr. 3, 1701	LR1	441
Abigall, m. David **RENOLDS**, Nov. 4, 1720, by Rev.		
Richard Sacket	LR1	432

GREENWICH VITAL RECORDS 245

REYNOLDS, RENYALLS, RENYOLLS, RENOLLS, RENELS, REYNOLLS, (cont.)

	Vol.	Page
Abigail, m. David RENOLLS, Nov. 24, 1720, by Rev. Richard Sackett	ER	186
Abigaill, d. David, b. Mar. 9, 1724	1	53
Abigaill, d. Daved, b. Mar. 9, 1724	ER	180
Abigaill, m. Hue MARTIN, July 8, 1731, by Samuel Peck, J. P.	1	63
Abigell, m. Hue MARTIN, July 8, 1731, by Sam[ue]ll Peck, J. P.	ER	203
Abigall, d. Joseph, b. May 25, 1735	1	54
Abigail, d. David, decd., m. William BLAKE, Mar. 26, 1756	1	97
Abigail J., m. W[illia]m H. MEAD, Mar. 7, 1831, by J. Mann	1	185
Abraham, s. David, b. Sept. 19, 1731	1	53
Abraham, s. David, b. Sept. 19, 1731	ER	180
Abraham, [s. John & Joanna], b. May 11, 1760	1	119
Adaline, m. Charles RUNDLE, b. of Greenwich, Jan. 17, 1836, by Rev. Platt Buffett	1	197
Alfred, of Stamford, m. Eunice MEAD, of Greenwich, Jan. 5, 1831, by Rev. Platt Buffett, of Stanwich	1	185
Alfred A., m. Fanny O. HOBBY, b. of Greenwich, [Jan.] 15, [1839], by N. Coe	1	202
Alpheas, [s. John & Joanna], b. May 11, 1760	ER	223*
Ambrose, m. Amey M. REYNOLDS, June [ ], [1831], by J. Mann	1	186
Amey M., m. Ambrose REYNOLDS, June [ ], [1831], by J. Mann	1	186
Augustus L., m. Julia R. SMITH, b. of Stanwich, June 1, 1830, by Rev. Platt Buffett, of Stanwich	1	184
Benajah, s. [Joseph], b. Mar. 26, 1705	ER	120
Benjamin, s. [Joseph], b. Mar. 26, 1706	LR1	441
Beniamin, s. David, b. Nov. 27, 1728	1	53
Beniamin, s. David, b. Nov. 27, 1728	ER	180
Benjamin, s. [Sackett & Mary], b. Apr. 10, 1770	1	97
Benjamin, m. Lucinda MEAD, b. of Greenwich, Jan. 3, 1842, by Darius Mead	1	208
Charles, s. [James & Phebe], b. Sept. 1, 1736	ER	202*
Clemence, d. William, of Poundridge, m. Thomas HITCHCOCK, Feb. 26, 1784	1	136
David, s. David, b. Sept. 19, 1717	1	53
David, s. Daved, b. Sept. 19, 1717	ER	180
David, m. Abigall RENOLDS, Nov. 4, 1720, by Rev. Richard Sacket	LR1	432
David, m. Abigaill RENOLLS, Nov. 24, 1720, by Rev. Richard Sackett	ER	186

	Vol.	Page
REYNOLDS, RENYALLS, RENYOLLS, RENOLLS, RENELS, REYNOLLS, (cont.)		
David, Jr., d. Oct. 12, 1745	ER	180
David, Jr., d. Oct. 14, 1745	1	53
Deborah, d. Ebenezer, b. Feb. 3, 1705	ER	152
Deborah, d. David, b. Feb. 24, 1734/5	1	53
Deborah, d. David, b. Feb. 24, 1734/5	ER	180
Deborah, [d. Ebenezer,]	LR1	4
Dorcas, [d. James & Phebe], b. Sept. 9, 1756	1	106
Dorcas, d. [James & Phebe], b. Sept. 9, 1756	ER	202*
Ebenezer, had s. [ ], b. [ ], 27, [ ]	LR1	4
Ebenezer, [s. Ebenezer], b. Mar. 6, 170[6]/7	LR1	4
Ebenezer, s. [Ebenezer], b. Mar. 6, 1706/7	ER	152
Ebenezer, had s. [ ], b. Jan. 27, 1715/16	ER	152
Ebenezer, s. Ebenezer, Jr., b. Oct. 25, 1731	1	63
Ebenezer, s. Ebenezer, Jr., b. Oct. 25, 1731	ER	203
Elizabeth, m. Joseph KNAP[P], Mar. 16, 1684, by Jonathan Bell, Com.	LR1	447
Elizabeth, m. Joshua KNAP[P], Mar. 16, 1687, by Jonathan Bell, Com.	ER	60
Elizabeth, d. Joseph, b. Apr. 18, 1713	LR1	441
Elizabeth, d. Joseph, b. Aug. 18, 1717	ER	120
Elizabeth, d. David, b. Oct. 1, 1733	1	53
Elizabeth, d. David, b. Oct. 1, 1733	ER	180
Elizabeth, [d. John & Joanna], b. Apr. 5, 1742	1	119
Elizabeth, [d. John & Joanna], b. Apr. 5, 1742	ER	223*
Elizabeth, [d. Sackett & Mary], b. Apr. 11, 1765	1	97
Emeline E., m. Stephen HOLLY, b. of Greenwich, Jan. 13, 1829, by Rev. Platt Buffett, of Stanwich	1	181
Frances, s. Nathaniel, b. Jan. 8, 1731	1	66
Francis, s. Nathaniell, b. Jan. 8, 1731	ER	200
Gerardres, [s. John & Joanna], b. Oct. 17, 1748	1	119
Gerardus, [s. John & Joanna], b. Oct. 17, 1748	ER	223*
Gideon, of Lewisburg, N. Y., m. Mrs. Abiah SMITH, of Greenwich, Feb. [ ], 1846, by Rev. B. M. Yarrington. Int. Pub.	1	216
Gideon T., of Lewisburg, N. Y., m. Emily Louisa SMITH, of Greenwich, Oct. 13, 1846, by Rev. B. M. Yarrington. Int. Pub.	1	216
Hannah, [d. Sackett & Mary], b. July 26, 1767	1	97
Hannah E., m. Shadrach J. CLOSE, Apr. 6, 1847, by Chauncey Wilcox	1	217
Hephzibah, [d. James & Phebe], b. Sept. 18, 1744	1	106
Hephzibah, d. [James & Phebe], b. Sept. 18, 1744	ER	202*
Isaac, s. [Joseph], b. June 15, 1711	ER	120
Jacob, s. Joseph [& Ruth], b. Jan. 16, 1734	1	55
Jacob, s. Joseph, b. Jan. 16, 1734	ER	188
Jacob, [s. John & Joanna], b. May 23, 1756	1	119

REYNOLDS, RENYALLS, RENYOLLS, RENOLLS, RENELS, REYNOLLS, (cont.)

	Vol.	Page
Jacob, [s. John & Joanna], b. May 23, 1756	ER	223*
James, s. James, b. July 6, 1700	ER	114
James, s. James, b. July 6, 1700	LR1	456
James, m. Phebe **FOWLER**, May 24, 1731	1	106
James, m. Phebe **FOWLER**, May 24, 1731, by [ ]	ER	202*
James, [s. James & Phebe], b. Jan. 1, 1746	1	106
James, s. [James & Phebe], b. Jan. 1, 1746	ER	202*
Jemima, d. David, b. July 27, 1726	1	53
Jemima, d. David, b. July 27, 1726	ER	180
Jemima, [d. James & Phebe], b. Feb. 9, 1741	1	106
Jemima, d. [James & Phebe], b. Feb. 9, 1741	ER	202*
Joanna, [d. John & Joanna], b. Dec. 11, 1753	1	119
Joanna, [d. John & Joanna], b. Dec. 11, 1753	ER	223*
John, s. [Joseph], b. May 23, 1708	ER	120
John, s. [Joseph], b. May 23, 1708	LR1	441
John, s. Peter, b. Aug. 16, 1727	1	59
John, s. Peter, b. Aug. 16, 1727	ER	196
John, s. Joseph, m. Ruth **RENOLLS**, Nov. 19, 1729, by Rev. Mr. Munson	1	60
John, s. Joseph, m. Ruth **RENALLS**, Nov. 19, 1729, by Rev. Mr. Munson	ER	199
John, s. John [& Ruth], b. Nov. 7, 1732	1	60
John, s. John [& Ruth], b. Nov. 7, 1732	ER	199
John, m. Joanna **WINENT**, Feb. 16, 1740	1	119
John, m. Joanna **WINENS**, Feb. 16, 1740	ER	223*
John, [s. John & Joanna], b. Oct. 29, 1750	1	119
John, [s. John & Joanna], b. Oct. 29, 1750	ER	223*
Jonathan, m. Newell(?) **RICE**(?), Dec. 4, 1682, by Richard Laws, Com.	LR1	448
Jonathan, m. Newell **RIDE**, Dec. 7, 1682, by Richard Laws, Com.	ER	40
Jonathan, m. Rebeccah **SEYMOUR**, Apr. 13, 1700/1, by Stephen Buckingham	LR1	450
Jonathan, m. Rebeckah **SEAMORE**, Apr. 13, 1704, by Stephen Buckingham	ER	145
Joseph, with his family [in pencil "removed to Crumb Elbow, Dutchess Co., N. Y."]	ER	120
Joseph, s. Joseph, b. May 5, 1699	LR1	441
Joseph, s. Joseph, b. May 15, 1699	ER	120
Joseph, m. Ruth **FER[R]IS**, Mar. 5, 1721/2, by Samuel Peck, J. P.	1	55
Joseph, m. Ruth **FERRIS**, Mar. 5, 1721/2, by Samuel Peck, J. P.	ER	188
Joseph, s. Joseph [& Ruth], b. Aug. 27, 1727	1	55
Joseph, s. Joseph [& Ruth], b. Aug. 27, 1727	ER	188
Joshua, [s. John & Joanna], b. Nov. 30, 1743	1	119

REYNOLDS, RENYALLS, RENYOLLS, RENOLLS, RENELS, REYNOLLS, (cont.)

	Vol.	Page
Joshua, [s. John & Joanna], b. Nov. 30, 1743	ER	223*
Joshua, m. Rachel REYNOLDS, b, of Greenwich, Jan. 9, [1822], by Isac Lewis	1	167
Josiah, [s. Joseph], b. July 15, 1703	LR1	441
Justus, [s. James & Phebe], b. Apr. 9, 1748	1	106
Justus, s. [James & Phebe], b. Apr. 9, 1748	ER	202*
Justus, [s. Sackett & Mary], b. July 26, 1761	1	97
Lydiah, d. [Ebenezer], b. [ ], 1709	LR1	4
Lidiah, d. [Ebenezer], b. Mar. 1, 1709/10	ER	152
Mary, d. James, b. Feb. 9, 1703/4	LR1	456
Mary, d. James, b. Feb. 9, 1704/5	ER	114
Mary, [d. James & Phebe], b. June 30, 1732	1	106
Mary, d. [James & Phebe], b. June 30, 1732	ER	202*
Mary, [d. Sackett & Mary], b. Feb. 1, 1763	1	97
Nathaniel, s. James, b. Feb. 20, 1702/3	ER	114
Nathaniel, s. James, b. Feb. 20, 1702/3	LR1	456
Nathaniell, s. Nathaniell, b. Dec. 8, 1729	1	66
Nathaniel, s. Nathaniell, b. Dec. 8, 1729	ER	200
Nehemiah, s. [Joseph], b. Apr. 3, 1709	LR1	441
Nehemiah, s. [Joseph], b. Apr. 8, 1709	ER	120
Peter, s. Peter [& Sarah], b. Dec. 14, [ ]	LR1	446
Peter, m. Sarah KNAP[P], May 15, 1712, by Rev. Richard Sacket	LR1	446
Peter, m. Sarah KNAP[P], Jan. 14, 1718/19, by Rev. Richard Sackett	ER	183
Peter, s. Peter [& Sarah], b. Dec. 14, 1719	ER	183
Phebe, [d. James & Phebe], b. June 27, 1734	1	106
Phebe, d. [James & Phebe], b. June 27, 1734	ER	202*
Rachel, m. Joshua REYNOLDS, b. of Greenwich, Jan. 9, [1822], by Isaac Lewis	1	167
Rebecca, d. Samuell, decd. & Ledea, b. Nov. 4, [ ]	1	54
Rebecca, d. Samuell, decd. & Rebecca, b. Nov. 4, [ ]	ER	198
Rebeccah, d. [Jonathan & Rebeccah], b. Feb. 12, 1701/2	LR1	450
Rebeckah, d. [Jonathan & Rebeckah], b. Feb. 12, 1704	ER	145
Rebecca, m. Isaac KNAP[P], Jan. 29, 1727/8, by Ebenezer Mead, J. P.	1	54
Rebecca, m. Isaack KNAPP, Jan. 29, 1727/8, by Ebnear Mead, J. P.	ER	198
Rebecca, [d. James & Phebe], b. Oct. 27, 1738	1	106
Rebecca, d. [James & Phebe], b. Oct. 27, 1738	ER	202*
Reuben, s. [Joseph], b. June 15, 1711	LR1	441
Reubin, s. [Joseph], b. Dec. 4, 1713/14 [sic]	ER	120
Reuben, m. Elizabeth MEAD, Mar. 19, 1734/5, by Rev. Mr. Todd	1	66
R[e]uben, m. Elizabeth MEAD, Mar. 19, 1734/5, by Rev. Mr. Todd	ER	215

	Vol.	Page
REYNOLDS, RENYALLS, RENYOLLS, RENOLLS, RENELS, REYNOLLS, (cont.)		
Reuben, s. Reuben & Elizabeth, b. Mar. 14, 1735/6	1	66
R[e]uben, s. R[e]uben & Elizabeth, b. Mar. 14, 1735/6	ER	215
Rodah, d. Joseph [& Ruth], b. Nov. 8, 1731	1	55
Rodah, d. Joseph [& Ruth], b. Nov. 8, 1731	ER	188
Rosanna, d. Joseph [& Ruth], b. Sept. 6, 1724	ER	188
Rosanna, d. Joseph [& Ruth], b. Dec. 6, 1724	1	55
Roxanna, d. Ebenezer, b. Feb. 3, [ ]	LR1	4
Ruth, d. Joseph [& Ruth], b. Dec. 13, 1722	1	55
Ruth, d. Joseph [& Ruth], b. Dec. 13, 1722	ER	188
Ruth, m. John **REYNOLDS**, s. Joseph, Nov. 19, 1729, by Rev. Mr. Munson	1	60
Ruth, m. John **RENALLS**, s. Joseph, Nov. 19, 1729, by Rev. Mr. Munson	ER	199
Ruth, d. John [& Ruth], b. Sept. 28, 1730	1	60
Ruth, d. John [& Ruth], b. Sept. 28, 1730	ER	199
Ruth, wid. of John, m. Ebenezer **MEAD**, July 16, 1735, by Rev. Abraham Todd	1	64
Sackett, s. Timothie [& Elizabeth], b. Mar. [ ], 1738	CP	104
Sackett, m. Mary **JONES**, d. Beniamin, Nov. 21, 1760	1	97
Samuell, d. Mar. 6, [ ]	1	54
Samuell, d. Mar. 6, [ ]	ER	198
Sam[ue[]ll, s. [Joseph], b. July 15, 1703	ER	120
Samuel, m. Ledea* **PALLMER**, Jan. 2, 1727/8 *(Rebecca)	1	54
Samuell, m. Rebaca **PALLMER**, Jan. 26, 1727/8	ER	198
Samuell, s. Joseph [& Ruth], b. Aug. 8, 1729	1	55
Samuell, s. Joseph [& Ruth], b. Aug. 8, 1729	ER	188
Sarah, d. James, b. [ ], 25, 1692	LR1	456
Sarah, d. James, b. [ ], 25, 1698	ER	114
Sarah, [d. James & Phebe], b. Sept. 1, 1736	1	106
Sarah, d. David, b. Aug. 7, 1740	1	59
Sarah, d. David, b. Aug. 7, 1740	ER	223*
Sarah, [d. John & Joanna], b. Apr. 15, 1746	1	119
Sarah, [d. John & Joanna], b. Apr. 15, 1746	ER	223*
Sarah, wid. & Eunice **MEAD**, wid., jointly made affidavit Jan. 26, 1760, that they had assisted in the birth of a son Frederick Harding **JONES**, to wid. Mary **(WHITING) JONES**, b. Nov. 28, 1759, at the home of Justus Bush, of Greenwich	1	92
Sarah J., m. Samuel O. **CLOSE**, b. of Greenwich, May 18, [probably 1842], by Rev. D. W. Butts	1	209
Sophia, [d. James & Phebe], b. Sept. 25, 1754	1	106
Sophia, d. [James & Phebe], b. Sept. 25, 1754	ER	202*
Susan, of Greenwich, m. Joseph F. **LAWRENCE**, of Greensbury, Jan. 11, 1843, by Noah Coe	1	210

REYNOLDS, RENYALLS, RENYOLLS, RENOLLS, RENELS, REYNOLLS, (cont.)

	Vol.	Page
Timothie, m. Elizabeth [ ], by Jeames Renolds, J. P.	CP	104
Warren, of Poundridge, m. Sarah SCOFIELD, of Stanwich, Nov. 18, 1821, by Platt Buffett	1	166
William, [s. James & Phebe], b. Jan. 18, 1751	1	106
William, s. [James & Phebe], b. Jan. 18, 1751	ER	202*
William, m. Mary Ann HALSEY, b. of Greenwich, Feb. 23, 1836, by Platt Buffett	1	197
William P., of Chester, Co. of Warren, N. Y., m. Sarah LOCKWOOD, of Greenwich, May 27, 1823, by Platt Buffett	1	171

RICE, Newell(?), m. Jonathan RENOLDS, Dec. 4, 1682, by
Richard Laws, Com.	LR1	448
-----, b. Feb. 26, 1755	1	104

RICH, [see under RITCH]

RIDE(?), Newell (?), m. Jonathan RENOLDS, Dec. 7, 1682, by
Richard Laws, Com.	ER	40

RITCH, RICH, Alice M., of Greenwich, m. Elisha DAVIS, of New
York City, May 17, 1841, by B. M. Yarrington	1	207
Electa H., of Greenwich, m. Rev. Elnathan BULL, of Cincinnatus, N. Y., Sept. 14, 1839, by Rev. P. S. Holly, of Sandis Falls, Mass.	1	204
Elizabeth, [d. Thomas], b. Mar. 13, 1755	1	107
Elizabeth, [d. Thomas], b. Mar. 13, 1755	ER	219
Henry, [s. Thomas], b. Jan. 3, 1742	1	107
Hervy, [s. Thomas], b. Jan. 3, 1742	ER	219
John, s. Thomas, b. May 4, 1718	1	51
John, s. Thomas, b. May 4, 1718	ER	176
John, m. Jemima HOLMES, Feb. 17, 1741, by Rev. Abraham Todd	1	61
Martha, [d. Thomas], b. Oct. 7, 1745	1	107
Martha, [d. Thomas], b. Oct. 7, 1745	ER	219
Mary, [d. Thomas], b. Nov. 9, 1739	1	107
Mary, [d. Thomas], b. Nov. 9, 1739	ER	219
Mary Elizabeth, m. Benjamin C. MEAD, b. of Greenwich, June 27, [1839], by Noah Coe	1	204
Polly, m. Robert HUGH, b. of Greenwich, Nov. 1, 1827, by Ebenezer J. Raymond	1	176
Ruth, d. Thomas, b. Mar. 8, 1720	1	51
Ruth, d. Thomas, b. Mar. 8, 1720	ER	176
Ruth, [d. Thomas], b. Nov. 24, 1749	1	107
Ruth, [d. Thomas], b. Nov. 24, 1749	ER	219
Thomas, s. Thomas, b. Apr. 24, 1716	1	51
Thomas, s. Thomas, b. Apr. 24, 1716	ER	176
Thomas, m. [ ], Jan. 10, 1739	1	107
Thomas, m. [ ], Jan. 11, 1739	ER	219

GREENWICH VITAL RECORDS 251

	Vol.	Page
ROBBINS, Julia A., m. William E. FERRIS, b. of Greenwich, Mar. 18, 1845, by Noah Coe	1	213
ROBERSON, Marg[a]ret, m. Thomas BULLES, July 11, 1733, by Ebenezer Mead, J. P.	1	49
Margaret, m. Thomas BULLIS, July 11, 1733, by Ebenezer Mead, J. P.	ER	212
ROWEL, Abraham, m. Sarah OWEN, Dec. 4, 1837, by James Jarman	1	199
Hiram P., m. Delia Ann WILCOX, b. of Fairfield, June 30, 1825, by Rev. S. Martindale	1	172
ROWELSON, Charles G., of New York, m. Frances ADDAMS, of Greenwich, Sept. 2, 1838, by Rev. William Biddle, of Stamford	1	201
RUNDLE, RUNDALL, Abigail, d. Joseph, b. May 23, 1735	ER	215
Abraham, m. Rebeckah MEAD, Mar. 31, 1721, by Sam[ue]ll Peck, J. P.	1	46
Abraham, m. Rebeckah MEAD, Mar. 31, 1721, by Sam[ue]ll Peck, J. P.	ER	186
Eme*, d. William [& Sarah], b. Oct. 22, 1730 *(Amy)	1	52
Eme*, d. William [& Sarah], b. Oct. 22, 1730 *(Amy)	ER	188
Amy, d. Reuben, m. David PECK, Aug. 12, 1773	1	131
Amy, d. Jonathan [& Deborah], b. Nov. 6, 1803	1	127
Amy, [d. Jonathan & Deborah], d. Dec. 5, 1829, in the 93rd* y. of her age *(26th?)	1	127
Ann, d. Sam[ue]ll [& Hannah], b. Oct. 28, 1739	1	56
Ann, d. Sam[ue]ll [& Hannah], b. Oct. 28, 1739	ER	175
Ann, m. Eliphalet MEAD, Dec. 13, 1761	1	108
Anna B., d. Jonathan [& Deborah], b. Feb. 21, 1813	1	127
Benoni, m. Amy DAYTON, b. of Greenwich, Dec. 28, 1831, by Rev. Platt Buffett, of Stanwich	1	187
Charles, s. William [& Sarah], b. June 1, 1728	1	52
Charles, s. William [& Sarah], b. June 1, 1728	ER	188
Charles, m. Adaline REYNOLDS, b. of Greenwich, Jan. 17, 1836, by Rev. Platt Buffett, of Stanwich	1	197
David B., s. Jonathan [& Deborah], b. Apr. 12, 1801	1	127
David N., s. Nathaniel, b. June 20, 1790	1	127
Deborah J., d. Jonathan [& Deborah], b. Feb. 21, 180[ ]	1	127
Elizabeth, d. William [& Sarah], b. June 22, 1723	1	52
Elizabeth, d. William [& Sarah], b. June 22, 1723	ER	188
Elizabeth, d. Joseph [& Mindwell], b. Oct. 4, 1733	1	66
Elizabeth, d. Joseph [& Mindwell], b. Oct. 4, 1733	ER	199
Ezera, s. Sam[ue]ll [& Hannah], b. Jan. 10, 1725	1	56
Ezra, s. Sam[ue]ll [& Hannah], b. Jan. 10, 1725	ER	175
Han[n]ah, d. [Samuell & Hannah], b. Apr. 16, 1716	1	56
Hannah, d. Sam[ue]ll & Hannah, b. Apr. 16, 1716	ER	175
Hannah, m. Caleb MEAD, Dec. 2, 1736, by Rev. Mr. Todd	1	68
Hannah, m. Caleb MEAD, Dec. 2, 1736/7, by Rev. Mr.		

	Vol.	Page

RUNDLE, RUNDALL, (cont.)
Todd	ER	216
Jacob, m. Rebecca **KNAPP**, Apr. 1, 1728, by Rev. Mr. Munson	1	57
Jacob,m. Rebecca **KNAPP**, Apr. 5, 1729, by Rev. Mr. Munson	ER	199
Jacob & w. Rebecca had d. [ ], b. Mar. 28, 1729/30	ER	199
Jacob, s. Jacob [& Rebecca], b. Aug. 2, 1731	1	57
Jacob, s. Jacob, b. Aug. 2, 1731	1	64
Jacob, s. Jacob [& Rebecca], b. Aug. 2, 1731	ER	199
Jacob, s. Jacob, b. Aug. 2, 1731	ER	203
Jane Augusta, m. Alvah **MEAD**, b. of Greenwich, Dec. 21, 1825, by Isaac Lewis	1	172
Jonathan, b. Mar. 21, 1775	1	127
Jonathan, m. Deborah **BROWN**, May 2, 1799, by Rev. Nathaniel Finch, Jr.	1	127
Joseph, m. Mindwell **FERRELL**, Apr. 15, 1729, by Justice Mead, J. P.	1	66
Joseph, m. Mindwell **FERRILL**, Apr. 15, 1729, by Justice Mead, J. P.	ER	199
Joseph, s. Joseph [& Mindwell], b. June 9, 1730	1	66
Joseph, s. Joseph [& Mindwell], b. June 9, 1730	ER	199
Josiah, s. Reuben, Jr. [& Sarah], b. Oct. 6, 1783	1	133
Margaret B., d. Jonathan [& Deborah], b. Dec. 3, 1810	1	127
Mindwell, d. Joseph [& Mindwell], b. Feb. 6, 1731	1	66
Mindwell, d. Joseph [& Mindwell], b. Feb. 6, 1731	ER	199
Mindwell, d. Joseph, m. John **HITCHCOCK**, July 8, 1756, by Rev. Abraham Todd	1	101
Nathaniell, s. Sam[ue]ll [& Hannah], b. May 1, 1728; d. Apr. 25, 1726 [sic]	1	56
Nathaniel, s. [Samuell & Hannah], b. May 1, 1728; d. Apr. 25, 1726	ER	175
Rachall, m. Titus **MEAD**, June 13, 1754	1	74
Rachall, m. Titus **MEAD**, June 13, 1754	ER	246
Rachall Ann, of Greenwich, m. Joseph Waring **THIRSTON**, of North Castle, Sept. 26, 1837, by C. Wilcox	1	198
Readen, s. Jonathan [& Deborah], b. May 15, 1808	1	127
Rebecca, d. Sam[ue]ll [& Hannah], b. Feb. 26, 1718	ER	175
Rebeccah, d. Sam[ue]ll [& Hannah], b. Feb. 26, 1718/19	1	56
Rebecca, d. Jacob [& Rebecca], b. Mar. 28, 1729/30	1	57
Reuben, s. Sam[ue]ll [& Hannah], b. July 14, 1735	1	56
R[e]uben, s. Sam[ue]ll [& Hannah], b. July 14, 1735	ER	175
Reuben, Jr., m. Sarah **HOBBY***, d. Francis, of Stamford, Dec. 23, 1781, by Rev. Mr. Dibble *("HOLLY" in Mead's Hist.)	1	133
Reuben, d. Feb. 11, 1815	1	127
Samuell, m. Hannah **HERDY**, Mar. 1, 1715, by Ebenezer		

GREENWICH VITAL RECORDS 253

	Vol.	Page
RUNDLE, RUNDALL, (cont.)		
Mead, J. P.	1	56
Samuel, m. Hannah HARDY, Mar. 1, 1715, by Ebenezer		
Mead, J. P.	ER	175
Sam[ue]ll, s. Sam[ue]ll [& Hannah], b. Sept. 23, 1720	1	56
Sam[ue]ll, s. Sam[ue]ll [& Hannah], b. Sept. 23, 1720	ER	175
Sarah, m. Caleb KNAP[P], Apr. 1, 1697	ER	121
Sarah, m. [Caleb KNAP[P], Apr. 1, [ ]	LR1	4
Sarah, [d. Abraham & Rebeckah], b. Jan. 28, 1721/2	1	46
Sarah, d. Abraham [& Rebeckah], b. Jan. 28, 1721/2	ER	186
Sarah, d. William [& Sarah], b. Aug. 10, 1726	1	52
Sarah, d. William [& Sarah], b. Aug. 10, 1726	ER	188
Sarah, b. Jan. 2, 1766; m. Levy PALMER, Jan. 4, 1787,		
by Rev. William Seward	1	151
Thomas, of Somers, N. Y., m. Rachal BRUSH, of		
Stanwich, Dec. 4, 1823, by Platt Buffitt	1	170
William, m. Sarah KNAP[P], Apr. 12, 1722, by Rev. Mr.		
Sacet	1	52
William, m. Sarah KNAP[P], Apr. 12, 1722, by Rev. Mr.		
Jacit	ER	188
William, d. May 19, 1733	1	52
William, d. May 19, 1733	ER	188
William, s. William, decd. [& Sarah], b. June 22, 1733	1	52
William, s. William, decd. [& Sarah], b. June 22, 1733	ER	188
RUNYAN, Henry B., of Haverstraw, m. Fanny SELLECK, of		
Greenwich, Apr. 21, 1839, by N. Coe. Int.		
Pub.	1	203
RUSSELL, Charlotte M., m. Henry RAYMOND, b. of Greenwich,		
Feb. 13, 1842, by Noah Coe	1	208
SACKETT, SACKET, Abigail, d. Richard & Elizabeth, b. Nov. 29,		
[eve next], 1722	ER	173
Abigail S., m. Gilbert LENT, [Feb. 15, 1836], by J.		
Mann	1	197
Clarissa, m. Benjamin BRUSH, 3rd, b. of Greenwich,		
Oct. 5, 1829, by Rev. Platt Buffett, of		
Stanwich	1	182
Daniel, [s. Joseph & Hannah], b. Sept. 23, 1768	1	119
Daniel, [s. Joseph & Hannah], b. Sept. 23, 1768	ER	238
Deborah, [d. Joseph & Hannah], b. Feb. 4, 1765;		
d. same month 20th day	1	119
Deborah, [d. Joseph & Hannah], b. Feb. 4, 1765;		
d. same month 20th day	ER	238
Deborah, of Hanover on Cortlandts Manor, m. Benjamin		
PECK, of Greenwich, Nov. 11, 1766	1	102
Elizabeth, d. Richard, b. Mar. 27, [eve next], 1715	ER	172
Elizabeth, w. Nathaniel, d. May 1, 1758	1	112
J. Ralph, of New York, m. Mary Elizabeth MEAD, of		
Greenwich, Feb. 28, 1843, by Noah Coe	1	213

	Vol.	Page

SACKETT, SACKET, (cont.)
James, [s. Joseph & Hannah], b. Jan. 14, 1762 — 1 — 119
James, [s. Joseph & Hannah], b. Jan. 14, 1762 — ER — 238
John, s. Richard, b. Nov. 14, 1713; d. Nov. next day
    [15], 1713 — ER — 172
John, m. Cornelia **OLMSTED**, b. of Greenwich, Jan.
    9, 1829, by Rev. John M. **SMITH**. Witness:
    Daniel Olmsted — 1 — 182
Joseph, of Greenwich, m. Hannah **BUDSON**, d. Thomas,
    of North Castle, Westchester Co., N. Y., Apr.
    23, 1751, by Rev. Samuel Sackett, of Bedford — 1 — 119
Joseph, of Greenwich, m. Hannah **BUDSON**, d. Thomas,
    of North Castle, in Westchester Cty., Province
    of New York, Apr. 28, 1751, by Rev. Samuel
    Sackett, of Bedford — ER — 238
Joseph, [s. Joseph & Hannah], b. Nov. 2, 1758 — 1 — 119
Joseph, [s. Joseph & Hannah], b. Nov. 2, 1758 — ER — 238
Justus, had negroes Charles, s. Hager, b. Sept. 16, 18[ ]
    & Silva, d. Hager, b. Mar. 29, 18[ ] — 1 — 160
Mary, d. Richard, b. Dec. 28, [eve next], [ ] — ER — 172
Mary Ann, of Greenwich, m. Charles H. **SEAMAN**, of
    New York, Aug. 26, 1840, by Noah Coe — 1 — 206
Nathaniel, s. Richard & Elizabeth, b. June 8, 1720 — ER — 172
Nathaniel, [s. Joseph & Hannah], b. Oct. 8, 1763 — 1 — 119
Nathaniel, [s. Joseph & Hannah], b. Oct. 8, 1763 — ER — 238
Rachal E., m. Charles **MEAD**, Dec. 31, 1838, by Noah
    Coe — 1 — 203
Richard & Elizabeth, had s. [ ], b. Feb. 11, [eve
    following 1724/5] — ER — 173
Richard, [s. Joseph & Hannah], b. June 7, 1754 — 1 — 119
Richard, [s. Joseph & Hannah], b. June 7, 1754 — ER — 238
Samuel, [s. Joseph & Hannah], b. Aug. 4, 1766 — 1 — 119
Samuel, [s. Joseph & Hannah], b. Aug. 4, 1766 — ER — 238
Solomon, [s. Joseph & Hannah], b. Jan. 4, 1760 — 1 — 119
Solomon, [s. Joseph & Hannah], b. Jan. 4, 1760 — ER — 238
Thomas, [s. Joseph & Hannah], b. Jan. 31, 1756;
    d. Feb. 27, 1763 — 1 — 119
Thomas, [s. Joseph & Hannah], b. Jan. 31, 1756;
    d. Feb. 27, 1763 — ER — 238
SANDS, Benjamin, of New Castle, N. Y., m. Dorcas **NASH**, of
    Greenwich, Oct. 9, 1833, by Chauncey Wilcox — 1 — 192
SANFORD, Pamela R., of Greenwich, m. Nehemiah **BROWN**, of
    Rye, Westchester Co., N. Y., Sept. 21, 1823,
    by Isaac Lewis — 1 — 169
SANTIERS, Mary Ann, of Greenwich, m. George **BANKS**, of Rye,
    Sept. 23, [1821], by Isaac Lewis — 1 — 165
SAVAGE, Harriet N., m. Noah **SMITH**, Sept. 2, 1839, by Rev. C.
    Wilcox — 1 — 204

	Vol.	Page
SAVAGE, (cont.)		
Selah, m. Sarah M. MEAD, b. of Greenwich, Sept. 3, 1838, by Rev. C. Wilcox	1	201
SCOFIELD, Amey, m. Seth P. DOWNS, Sept. 21, 1835, by E. S. Raymond	1	196
Edward, m. Eliza STIVERS, b. of Greenwich, Nov. 22, 1827, by Isaac Lewis	1	177
Maria, m. William HOLLIS, b. of Stanwich, Jan. 21, 1824, by Rev. Platt Buffett	1	170
Mary, m. Roger SOUTHERLAND, Apr. 20, 1758	1	76
Mary, m. Roger SOUTHERLAND, Apr. 20, 1758	ER	226
Nelson D., m. Adaline MINOR, Oct. 14, [1832], by Stephen Waring, J. P.	1	188
Sarah, of Stanwich, m. Warren REYNOLDS, of Poundridge, Nov. 18, 1821, by Platt Buffett	1	166
SCOTT, Hannah, m. Alfred ADAMS, [July] 10, [1834], by J. Mann	1	193
Lewis, m. Eliza CLARK, [July], 10, [1834], by J. Mann	1	193
Lewis, m. Julia DUNTON, Nov. 24, 1837, by James Jarman	1	199
Peeter, s. Peeter, b. Feb. 8, 1731	1	62
Peetar, s. Peetar, b. Feb. 8, 1731	ER	202
Robert, of New York, m. Lydia H. HUSTED, of Greenwich, Jan. 20, 1834, by Platt Buffett	1	192
SEAMAN, Charles H., of New York m. Mary Ann SACKETT, of Greenwich, Aug. 26, 1840, by Noah Coe	1	206
Stephen H., m. Eunice Rebecca HOBBY, Oct. 23, 1833, by J. Mann	1	192
SEARS, Sarah, d. May 11, 1756	1	72
SECAR, Mary Ann CLARK, m. Frederick SHERWOOD, b. of Greenwich, June 6, 1842, by B. M. Yarrington	1	208
SEELEY, Aaron, m. Mary E. KEELER, b. of Danbury, Aug. 13, 1838, by Rev. Chauncey Wilcox	1	201
Sarah, m. Jonathan HOLMES, July 29, 1707	LR1	414
Walter, m. Rachal Ann SMITH, b. of Greenwich, Dec. 6, 1842, by B. M. Yarrington	1	210
SELLECK, Fanny, of Greenwich, m. Henry B. RUNYAN, of Haverstraw, Apr. 21, 1839, by N. Coe. Int. Pub.	1	203
Gales, m. Mary E. HOBBY, b. of Greenwich, [Mar.] 11, [1845], by S. B. S. Bissell	1	213
Mary, d. Silas, m. John NICHOLAS, Feb. [ ], 1765	1	123
SEWARD, Electa, d. Rev. W[illia]m, b. May [ ], 178[ ]	1	125
Hannah, d. Rev. W[illia]m, b. Mar. 2, 1782	1	125
Philander, s. Rev. W[illia]m, b. June 6, 17[ ]	1	125
Philander, [s. Rev. William], b. Oct. 10, 1773	1	125
Philander, s. Rev. William, d. Sept. 26, 1776	1	125
Rebecca Ann, d. Rev. W[illia]m, b. Jan. 24, 177[ ]	1	125
William, [s. Rev. William], b. May 31, 178[ ]	1	125

	Vol.	Page

SEYMOUR, SEAMORE, SEAMOR, Delia R., of Greenwich, m.
James TILLOT, of Fishkill, Dec. 15, 1828, by
Albert Judson — 1 — 181
Drake, [s. Samuel], b. Feb. 4, 1757 — 1 — 109
Drake, [s. Samuel], b. Feb. 4, 1757 — ER — 241
Elizabeth*, m. Timothie KNAP[P], Mar. 16, 1699,
by Capt. Umstead, J. P. *(Arnold copy has
"Elizabeth STRONGE") — LR1 — 449
Elizabeth, m. Timothie KNAP[P], Mar. 16, 1699, by
Capt. Umsted, J. P. — ER — 123
Elizabeth, [d. Samuel], b. May 9, 1755 — 1 — 109
Elizabeth, [d. Samuel], b. May 9, 1755 — ER — 241
Hannah, [d. Samuel], b. Oct. 3, 1753 — 1 — 109
Hannah, [d. Samuel], b. Oct. 3, 1753 — ER — 241
Hannah, d. Samuel, m. David HOBBY, blacksmith, Sept.
5, 1768 — 1 — 122
Rebeccah, m. Jonathan RENOLDS, Apr. 13, 1700/1, by
Stephen Buckingham — LR1 — 450
Rebeckah, m. Jonathan RENOLS, Apr. 13, 1704, by
Stephen Buckingham — ER — 145
Sabrina, [d. Samuel], b. Oct. 6, 1761 — 1 — 109
Sabrina, [d. Samuel], b. Oct. 6, 1761 — ER — 241
Sabrina, of Greenwich, m. Peter J. TILLOTT, of
Fishkill, Dutchess Co., N. Y., Oct. 23, [1821],
by Isaac Lewis — 1 — 166
Sarah H., of Greenwich, m. Samuel ANNAN, of Fishkill,
Dutchess Co., N. Y., Jan. 29, [1823], by Isaac
Lewis — 1 — 168
Thomas, m. Sally BANKS, Dec. 14, 1831, by E. S.
Raymond — 1 — 187
William, [s. Samuel], b. Apr. 13, 1758 — 1 — 109
William, [s. Samuel], b. Apr. 13, 1758 — ER — 241
SHAMPENISE, Mary, m. Purdy ANDERSON, Oct. 9, 1848, by
Rev. Daniel Vail, Portchester — 1 — 217
SHERWOOD, Abigail Jane, m. James FERRIS, May 13, 1821, by
Rev. Nathaniel Finch, Jr. — 1 — 165
Betsey, m. Merrett GERALDS, b. of Greenwich, Mar. 7,
1842, by Rev. C. Wilcox, of New York — 1 — 209
Frederick, m. Mary Ann Clark SECAR, b. of Greenwich,
June 6, 1842, by B. M. Yarrington — 1 — 208
Frederick A., m. Mary BROWN, Sept. 7, 1834, by
Chauncey Wilcox — 1 — 193
Hannah, m. Samuel PECK, Jr., Apr. 29, 1762 — 1 — 103
James, m. Rebecca LOCKWOOD, d. Jeremiah, Dec.
[ ], 1767 — 1 — 103
Jared, [s. James & Rebecca], b. Feb. 1, 1772 — 1 — 103
Jesse L., of New York m. Hannah PECK, of Greenwich,
July 28, 1823, by Rev. David Smith, of

	Vol.	Page

SHERWOOD, (cont.)
Stamford 1 169
Martin, m. Sarah FERRIS, b. of Greenwich, Nov. 2,
  1823, by John Ellis 1 171
Mary, [d. James & Rebecca], b. Sept. 11, 1768 1 103
Mary, of Greenwich, m. Ezra KEELER, of Kartright,
  Co. of Deleware, N. Y., Nov. 18, 1827, by
  Isaac Lewis 1 176
Nancy, [d. James & Rebecca], b. Oct. 7, 1770 1 103
Riley, m. Ellen HANCOCK, b. of Greenwich,
  Dec. 24, [1826], by Ebenezer S. Raymond 1 174
W[illia]m Benson, m. Eliza Ann BARNS, Aug. 28,
  [1831], by J. Mann 1 186
William Henry, m. Ann NASH, b. of Greenwich, Oct. 3,
  1838, by Thomas Brewer 1 201
SLAGLE, Samuel, m. Mary Ann WILSON, Jan. 4, 1836, by James
  Jarman 1 199
SLATER, Jeremiah, m. Leatitia STUDWELL, b. of Greenwich,
  Jan. 17, 1830, by David Peck, Elder 1 183
SLAUSON, Jesse, of Rye, N. Y., m. Deborah PUGSLEY, of
  Greenwich, Mar. 13, 1832, by Rev. E.
  Washburn 1 187
SMITH, Abiah, Mrs., of Greenwich, m. Gideon REYNOLDS, of
  Lewisburg, N. Y., Feb. [ ], 1846, by Rev. B.
  M. Yarrington. Int. Pub. 1 216
Abigail, d. Daniel, b. Jan. 7, 1725 LR1 458
Abigail, d. Daniel [& Rebeckah], b. June 13, 1725 ER 155
Abigail M., m. Henry MEAD, b. of Greenwich, Jan. 16,
  1828, by Platt Buffett 1 179
Alice, m. Amos FINCH, b. of Stanwich, Nov. 29, 1829,
  by Rev. Platt Buffett, of Stanwich 1 182
Ann, [d. Peter], b. Aug. 25, 1758 1 126
Arba, m. Hannah M. FINCH, b. of Greenwich, Dec. 24,
  1833, by Rev. Platt Buffett, of Stanwich 1 191
Beniamin, [s. Beniamin], b. Dec. 26, 1725 1 51
Beniamin, s. [Beniamin], b. Dec. 26, 1725 ER 189
Caroline Hobbie, [w. James], d. May 17, 1835 1 118
Charlotte, [d. Peter], b. Dec. 12, 1768; d. Dec. 12, same
  month 1 126
Daniel, m. Rebeckah BUTLER, Apr. 25, 1706, by Rev.
  Joseph Morgan ER 155
Daniel, m. Rebeckah BUTLER, Apr. 25, 1706, by Rev.
  Joseph Morgan LR1 458
Daniel, s. Daniel [& Rebeckah], b. Sept. 2, 1716 ER 155
Daniel, s. Daniel, b. Sept. [ ], 1716 LR1 458
Daniel, s. [Beniamin], b. May 15, 1735 ER 189
Daniel, [s. Peter], b. Dec. 23, 1772 1 126
David, [s. Beniamin], b. May 15, 1735 1 51

SMITH, (cont.)

	Vol.	Page
Debery, [child of Beniamin], b. Dec. 22, 1722*		
*(1723 in Mead's Hist.)	ER	189
Deberry, [s. Beniamin], b. Dec. 22, 1723	1	51
Elizabeth, d. Daniel [& Rebeckah], b. May 5, 1732	ER	155
Elizabeth, d. Daniel, b. May 5, 1732	LR1	458
Elizabeth, [d. John, school-master], b. Apr. 24, 1739	1	100
Elizabeth, [d. John, school-master], b. Apr. 24, 1739	ER	219
Eliza[be]th, d. Daniel, m. Obadiah BANKS, Sept.1, 1755	1	95
Elizabeth, of North Castle, N. Y., m. David HUSTED, of Greenwich, Feb. 23, 1842, by B. M. Yarrington	1	208
Emily Louisa, of Greenwich, m. Gideon T. REYNOLDS, of Lewisburg, N. Y., Oct. 13, 1846, by Rev. B. M. Yarrington. Int. Pub.	1	216
Esther, d. Col. William, of Flushing, L. I., m. George Washington CLOSE, [s. Samuel & Eliza], Mar. 4, 1845	1	118
George A., m. Amanda Lamina KNAPP, Oct. 7, 1838, by Noah Coe	1	201
George J., of Stamford, m. Afelia F. PAGE, of Greenwich, Oct. 28, 1839, by B. M. Farrington	1	204
Gold, of Stamford, m. Sarah STOCKDELL, of Greenwich, Oct. 21, [1821], by Isaac Lewis	1	166
Hannah, d. Daniel [& Rebeckah], b. Nov. 15, 1710	ER	155
Hannah, d. Daniel [& Rebeckah], b. Nov. 15, 1710	LR1	458
Hannah, d. Beniamin, b. Oct. 20, 1722	1	51
Han[n]ah, d. Beniamin, b. Oct. 20, 1722	ER	189
Hannah, m. John PALMER, Feb. 16, 1730/1, by Joshua Knapp, J. P.	1	62
Hannah, m. John PALMER, Feb. 16, 1730/1, by Joshua Knapp, J. P.	ER	202*
Hannah, [d. John, school-master], b. Mar. 24, 1741	1	100
Hannah, [d. John, school-master], b. Mar. 24, 1741	ER	219
Henry, of New York, m. Harriet MITCHELL, of Greenwich, Dec. 12, 1824, by Noble W. Thomas, Elder	1	171
James, [s. Peter], b. Apr. 10, 1771	1	126
James, m. Caroline H. CLOSE, Nov. 23, 1831, by Chauncey Wilcox	1	187
James, of Ridgefield, Conn., m. Caroline Hobbie CLOSE, [d. Samuel & Eliza], by [ ]	1	118
James W., m. Melicent KNAPP, Apr. 18, 1842, by Rev. C. Wilcox, of New York	1	209
Jasper, s. Jasper & Rosanna, b. July 11, 1764	1	110
Jobe, [s. Beniamin], b. Oct. 27, 1737	1	51
Jobe, s. [Beniamin], b. Oct. 27, 1737	ER	189

	Vol.	Page
SMITH, (cont.)		
John, s. Daniel [& Rebeckah], b. Apr. 10, 1723	ER	155
John, s. Daniel, b. Apr. 10, 1723	LR1	458
John, m. 2nd w. Abigail [ ], Mar. 28, 1745	1	100
John, m. 2nd w. Abigail [ ], Mar. 28, 1745	ER	219
Joshua, s. Daniel [& Rebeckah], b. June 10, 1728	ER	155
Joshua, s. Daniel, b. June 10, 1728	LR1	458
Joshua, m. Neville CONKLING, Jr., May 22, 1766, by Rev. Mr. Todd	1	118
Julia R., m. Augustus L. REYNOLDS, b. of Stanwich, June 1, 1830, by Rev. Platt Buffett, of Stanwich	1	184
Lydea, d. [ ], Jr. & Lydea], b. Dec. 8, 1754	ER	246
Lydia, d. Daniel, m. Jared MEAD, Dec. 10, 1775	1	128
Mary, d. Daniel, b. Feb. 16, 1720/1	LR1	458
Mary, d. Daniel [& Rebeckah], b. Feb. 18, 1721	ER	155
Mary, [d. Beniamin], b. Sept. 13, 1732	1	51
Mary, d. [Beniamin], b. Sept. 13, 1732	ER	189
Mary, d. [John & Abigail], b. Aug. 9, 1746	1	100
Mary, d. [John & Abigail], b. Aug. 9, 1746	ER	219
Mary, d. John, m. Amos KNAPP, s. Caleb, Jan. 22, 1763	1	100
Mary, d. John, m. Amos KNAPP, Jan. 22, 1763	ER	219
Mary, d. John, m. Amos KNAPP, s. Caleb, Jan. 22, 1763	ER	225*
Mary, [d. Peter], b. Apr. 5, 1765	1	126
Neville, w. Joshua, d. Sept. 24, 1766	1	118
Noah, m. Harriet N. SAVAGE, Sept. 2, 1839, by Rev. C. Wilcox	1	204
Peter, [s. Beniamin], b. Feb. 3, 1729/30	1	51
Peter, s. [Beniamin], b. Feb. 30 [sic], 1729/30	ER	189
Peter, [s. Peter], b. June 11, 1757	1	126
Rachal Ann, m. Walter SEELEY, b. of Greenwich, Dec. 6, 1842, by B. M. Yarrington	1	210
Rebeckah, d. Daniel [& Rebeckah], b. Mar. 5, 1706/7	ER	155
Rebeckah, d. Daniel [& Rebeckah], b. Mar. 5, 1706/7	LR1	458
Rufus, of Norwalk, m. Julia A. JESSUP, of Greenwich, Jan. 2, 1842, by [Thomas Payne]	1	209
Ruth, d. Daniel, b. Jan. 4, 1718	LR1	458
Ruth, d. Daniel [& Rebeckah], b. Jan. 4, 1718/19	ER	155
Sarah, d. Daniel [& Rebeckah], b. July 7, 1714	ER	155
Sarah, d. Daniel, b. July 7, 1714	LR1	458
Sarah, [d. Peter], b. Nov. 26, 1760	1	126
Sarah, of Stanwich, m. Samuel S. GRISWOLD, D. D., of New York, Oct. 18, 1836, by Rev. Joseph H. Nichols	1	199
Solomon, [s. Beniamin], b. Mar. 15, 1740	1	51
Solomon, s. [Beniamin], b. Mar. 15, 1740	ER	189
Stephen, m. Maria BAREMORE, b. of Greenwich, Sept. 26, 1830, by Rev. Platt Buffett, of Stanwich	1	184

	Vol.	Page

SMITH, (cont.)
Susan, m. Edwin S. **BUFFETT**, b. of Greenwich, Aug. 3,
    1846, by Rev. Platt Buffett — 1 — 216
Susanna, [d. Peter], b. Mar. 1, 1767 — 1 — 126
Thurza Ann, m. Gilbert **BUSH** (colored), b. of
    Greenwich, Feb. 16, 1847, by Rev. B. M.
    Yarrington — 1 — 217
Walter, [s. Peter], b. Dec. 31, 1774 — 1 — 126
William, m. Clarissa **BRUSH**, b. of Greenwich, Jan. 10,
    1837, by Noah Coe — 1 — 197
Zada, [d. Peter], b. Apr. 21, 1763 — 1 — 126
-----, Jr., m. Lydea **BANKS**, d. Dan[ie]l, Feb. 16, 1754,
    by Rev. Mr. Todd — ER — 246

SNIFFEN, SNIFFIN, Robert, m. Elizabeth **TAYLOR**, July 28,
    1821, by Rev. David Peck — 1 — 165
William, m. Sary M. **LOUDON**, b. of Greenwich, Aug.
    1, 1844, by Rev. Chauncey Wilcox — 1 — 212

SNOW, Aaron, Rev., of Eastbury, Conn., m. Sarah Ann **HOIT**,
    of Stamford, May 7, 1841, by Rev. D. B.
    Butts — 1 — 207

SOUTHERLAND, [see under **SUTHERLAND**]

SPERREAR, James, of New Milford, m. Lucy **FERRIS**, of
    Greenwich, Dec. 1, 1822, by Rev. Daniel Peck — 1 — 168

STATE, Addam, [s. Addam], b. June 8, 1756 — ER — 234
Elizabeth, [d. Addam], b. Nov. 26, 1754 — ER — 234
Mary, [d. Addam], b. Apr. 25, 1750 — ER — 234
Mattattis, [s. Addam], b. Jan. 29, 1748, in Penn. — ER — 234
Peter, [s. Addam], b. Feb. 15, 1758 — ER — 234
William, [s. Addam], b. July 28, 1751 — ER — 234

STEPHENS, [see also **STEVENS**], Eliza, of New York, d. Ruleaf,
    m. Arad **PECK**, s. Solomon, Sept. 3, 1833 — 1 — 131

STEVENS, [see also **STEPHENS**], Elias B., of Danbury, m.
    Elizabeth **COOKE**, of New York, Feb. 15,
    1843, by Chauncey Wilcox — 1 — 211

STILES, Sylvester, m. Deborah Ann **FLEELAND** (wid.), b. of
    Stanwich, May 3, 1829, by Rev. Platt Buffett,
    of Stanwich — 1 — 182

STIVERS, Eliza, m. Edward **SCOFIELD**, b. of Greenwich, Nov.
    22, 1827, by Isaac Lewis — 1 — 177

STOCKDELL, Sarah, of Greenwich, m. Gold **SMITH**, of
    Stamford, Oct. 21, [1821], by Isaac Lewis — 1 — 166

STOKEM, John B., of Norwalk, m. Sally Ann **LOCKWOOD**, of
    Greenwich, May 27, [1827], by Isaac Lewis — 1 — 176

STRICTLAND, Mary, m. William **PHILLIPS**, Jan. 19, 1837, by
    James Jarman — 1 — 199

STRONG, Ann Eliza, m. William H. **CRAFT**, b. of Greenwich,
    Dec. 20, 1841, by Rev. Charles F. Pelton — 1 — 208
Elizabeth*, m. Timothie **KNAP[P]**, Mar. 16, 1699, by

	Vol.	Page
STRONG, (cont.)		
Capt. Umstead, J. P. *(Probably "Elizabeth SEYMOUR")	LR1	449
Joseph W., of Peekskell, N. Y., m. Elizabeth M. BELCHER, of Greenwich, Sept. 3, 1821, by Rev. Isaac Lewis	1	165
STUDWELL, STUDDWELL, Alen, m. Nancy LOCKWOOD, b. of Greenwich, Feb. 15, 1825, by Rev. Henry Hoit, Jr., of Stamford	1	172
Clarissa, m. Denison A. LOCKWOOD, b. of Greenwich, Jan. 27, 1833, by Rev. Platt Buffett, of Stanwich	1	189
Jemima, of Greenwich, m. John CARGILL, of Stamford, June 22, 1828, by Rev. N. C. Saxton	1	180
Leatitia, m. Jeremiah SLATER, b. of Greenwich, Jan. 17, 1830, by David Peck, Elder	1	183
Nathaniel, s. Thomas, b. June 14, 1707	LR1	446
Nathaniel, s. Thomas, b. June 14, 1707	ER	158
Thomas, s. Thomas, b. Mar. 31, 1709	LR1	446
Thomas, s. Thomas, b. Mar. 31, 1709	ER	158
Thomas, Jr., s. Thomas & Jemima, b. Sept. 20, 1732	1	124
Thomas, Jr., s. Thomas & Jemima, b. Sept. 20, 1732	ER	205
STUVETS, Julia, of Old Greenwich, m. John BARNES, of New York, July 17, 1833, by Rev. John Ellis, of Stamford. Int. Pub.	1	191
SULLIVAN, George, of Rye, m. Mary Ann MEAD, of Greenwich, Mar. 22, 1838, by Rev. C. Wilcox	1	200
SUNDERLIN, [see under SUTHERLAND]		
[SUTHERLAND], SOUTHERLAND, SOUTHERLIN,		
SUNDERLIN, Abigail, w. Rodger, d. July 25, 1757	1	76
Abigail, w. Rodger, d. July 25, 1757	ER	226
Abigail, [d. Roger & Mary], b. Sept. 7, 1759	1	76
Abigail, [d. Roger & Mary], b. Sept. 7, 1759	ER	226
Hannah, [d. Roger], b. Mar. 15, 1751	1	76
Hannah, [d. Roger & Abigail], b. Mar. 15, 1751	ER	226
Joseph, [s. Rodger], b. Jan. 19, 1749	1	76
Joseph, [s. Roger & Abigail], b. Jan. 19, 1749	ER	226
Mary, [d. Roger & Mary], b. June 24, 1761	1	76
Mary, [d. Roger & Mary], b. June 24, 1761	ER	226
Rodger, [s. Rodger], b. Mar. 16, 1743	1	76
Rodger, [s. Roger & Abigail], b. Mar. 16, 1743	ER	226
Roger, m. Mary SCOFIELD, Apr. 20, 1758	1	76
Roger, m. Mary SCOFIELD, Apr. 20, 1758	ER	226
Samuel, [s. Rodger], b. Jan. 27, 1747	1	76
Samuel, [s. Roger & Abigail], b. Jan. 27, 1747	ER	226
Sarah, [d. Roger & Mary], b. Jan. 26, 1763	1	76
Sarah, [d. Roger & Mary], b. Jan. 26, 1763	ER	226
Silas, [s. Rodger], b. Feb. 5, 1755	1	76

	Vol.	Page
[SUTHERLAND], SOUTHERLAND, SOUTHERLIN, SUNDERLIN, (cont.)		
Silas, [s. Roger & Abigail], b. Feb. 5, 1755	ER	226
Stephen, [s. Rodger], b. Apr. 5, 1753	1	76
Stephen, [s. Roger & Abigail], b. Apr. 5, 1753	ER	226
William, [s. Rodger], b. Mar. 16, 1745	1	76
William, [s. Roger & Abigail], b. Mar. 16, 1745	ER	226
SWAN, Margaret, m. Henry COX, Dec. 13, 1835, by J. Mann	1	197
SAGTON, Mary W., m. Joseph G. MEAD, b. of Greenwich, Jan. 17, 1840, by Noah Coe	1	205
SAYLOR, Cynthia J., m. Edwin W. JANE, Mar. 17, 1842, by Rev. Charles F. Pelton	1	209
Daniel, s. Joshua, Jr. & Rachel FINCH, [w. of William], b. Oct. 13, 1774	1	161
Elizabeth, m. Robert SNIFFEN, July 28, 1821, by Rev. David Peck	1	165
George W., m. Eliza Ann PURDY, b. of Greenwich, Dec. 31, 1843, by Rev. C. Wilcox	1	212
Jonathan, [s. Jonathan], b. Feb. 21, 1755	1	116
Jonathan, [s. Jonathan], b. Feb. 21, 1755	ER	242
Nathaniel, [s. Jonathan], b. Oct. 21, 1753	1	116
Nathaniel, [s. Jonathan], b. Oct. 21, 1753	ER	242
Zebulon, m. Sarah FLORENCE, June 10, 1821, by Rev. Nathaniel Finch, Jr.	1	165
THACHER, Stephen, m. Zeulima TOWNSEND, [ ]	1	121
Townsend, [s. Stephen & Zeulima], b. Mar. 2, 1768	1	121
THIRSTON, Joseph Waring, of North Castle, m. Rachall Ann RUNDLE, of Greenwich, Sept. 26, 1837, by C. Wilcox	1	198
THOMAS, Charles, m. Martha HOBBY, Oct. 29, 1718, by Rev. Richard Sackett	1	47
Charles, m. Martha HOBBY, Oct. 29, 1718, by Rev. Richard Sackett	ER	183
Charles, s. Charles [& Martha], b. Aug. 11, 1722	1	47
Charles, s. Charles [& Martha], b. Aug. 11, 1722	ER	183
Elizabeth, d. Charles [& Martha], b. Apr. 6, 1724	1	47
Elizabeth, d. Charles [& Martha], b. Apr. 26, 1724	ER	183
John, s. [Charles & Martha], b. June 5, 1725	1	47
John, s. [Charles & Martha], b. June 5, 1725	ER	183
Martha, d. Charles [& Martha], b. July 10, 1721	1	47
Martha, d. [Charles & Martha], b. July 10, 1721	ER	183
Sarah, [d. Charles [& Martha], b. Nov. 1, 1730	1	47
Sarah, d. Charles [& Martha], b. Nov. 5, 1730	ER	183
THOMSON, Archibald, s. Leteshe CAREY, alias MARSHALL; b. Mar. 26, 1776	1	138
Elizabeth, m. Charles MEAD, b. of Greenwich, Nov. 28, 1842, by Chauncey Wilcox	1	210
TILLOT, TILLOTT, James, of Fishkill, m. Delia R. SEYMOUR,		

	Vol.	Page
TILLOT, TILLOTT, (cont.)		
of Greenwich, Dec. 15, 1828, by Albert Judson	1	181
Peter J., of Fishkill, Dutchess Co., N. Y., m. Sabrina SEYMOUR, of Greenwich, Oct. 23, [1821], by Isaac Lewis	1	166
TIMPANNY, Charles, m. Delila A. JOHNS, b. of Greenwich, Dec. 17, 1839, by Noah Coe	1	205
Louisa, m. James MOSIER, Dec. 3, 1835, by James Jarman	1	199
TITUS, Frederick, s. Isaac & Hannah (HAYS), Jr., b. Jan. 29, 1768; b. "with an apparent defect on his left ear"	1	111
Susan Knapp, of Greenwich, m. William A. FERRIS, of New Orleans, La., Oct. 3, 1836, by Rev. Joseph H. Nichols	1	199
TODD, Abraham, [s. Abraham], b. Dec. 21, 1738	1	108
Abraham, [s. Abraham], b. Dec. 21, 1738	ER	204
Han[n]ah, [d. Abraham], b. Aug. 12, 1734	1	108
Hannah, [d. Abraham], b. Nov. 18, 1741	1	108
Hannah, [d. Abraham], b. Nov. 18, 1741	ER	204
Jonah, [s. Abraham], b. Aug. 12, 1734	ER	204
Lois, [d. Abraham], b. May 13, 1732	1	108
Lois, [d. Abraham], b. May 13, 1732	ER	204
Lois, d. Rev. [ ], m. Obadiah MEAD, Nov. [ ], 1756	1	105
Louisa, of Stanwich, m. W[illia]m H. HOLLOWAY, of North Castle, Sept. 21, 1845, by Rev. Chauncey Wilcox	1	214
Mabell, [d. Abraham], b. Nov. 21, 1744	1	108
Mabell, [d. Abraham], b. Nov. 21, 1744	ER	204
Mary, [d. Abraham], b. Feb. 10, 1751	1	108
Mary, [d. Abraham], b. Feb. 10, 1751	ER	204
Oliver, [s. Abraham], b. Oct. 25, 1748	1	108
Oliver, [s. Abraham], b. Oct. 25, 1748	ER	204
TOWNSEND, Purdy, m. Elizabeth AVERY, b. of Greenwich, Dec. 12, 1821, by Joshua Ferris, J. P.	1	167
Zeulima, m. Stephen THACHER, [ ]	1	121
TRACY, John Jay, m. Louisa BOURDEAU, b. of Greenwich, Nov. 23, 1845, by Rev. Benjamin M. Yarrington. Int. Pub.	1	215
TREEN, Benjamin, [s. Benjamin], b. Sept. 1, 1765	1	120
Daniel, [s. Benjamin], b. Dec. 26, 1752	1	120
Elizabeth, [d. Benjamin], b. July 21, 1750	1	120
Lydia, [d. Benjamin], b. Jan. 4, 1755	1	120
Phebe, [d. Benjamin], b. Feb. 23, 1761	1	120
William, [s. Benjamin], b. June 22, 1748	1	120
TRIPP, Lyman B., m. Emily HURTELL, b. of North Castle, Dec. 25, 1840, by Rev. C. Wilcox	1	206
TUCKER, Mary, m. Peetar FER[R]IS, Aug. 6, 1719	1	53

	Vol.	Page
TUCKER, (cont.)		
Mary, m. Peetare **FER[R]IS**, Aug. 6, 1719	ER	183
UNDERHILL, Stephen, of Long Island, m. Sarah **PEACOCK**, of Greenwich, Sept. 3, 1823, by Isaac Lewis	1	169
UTTER, Elizabeth, d. Josiah [& Mary], b. Apr. 13, 1783	1	137
Henry, s. Josiah [& Mary], b. Nov. 22, 1779	1	137
Josiah, m. Mary **KETCHUM**, d. Joshua **KETCHUM**, of Huntington, L. I., Feb. 4, 1779	1	137
Josiah, s. Josiah [& Mary], b. May 5, 1781	1	137
VALENTINE, VALLENTINE, Elizabeth, [d. David], b. Oct. 13, 1759	1	78
Jonathan Dibble, [s. David], b. Aug. 23, 1761	1	78
Mary Ann, [d. David], b. Oct. 14, 1757	1	78
Scudder, [s. David], b. Sept. 19, 1755, in Stamford	1	78
VEAL, Deborah, d. Joseph, of Cortland Manor, m. Samuel **MILLS**, Jr. of Greenwich, June 15, 1778, by Rev. Mr. Mills, of Bedford	1	143
WAKEMAN, A[a]ron C., of South Salem, Westchester Co., N. Y., m. Nancy G. **WILLSON**, of Greenwich, May 10, 1837, by E. S. Raymond	1	198
WALTERS, WALTTERS, Ann, d. [Richard & Ann], b. Feb. 28, 1726/7	1	47
Ann, d. Richard [& Anna], b. Feb. 28, 1726/7	ER	189
Daniell, s. Richard [& Ann], b. Mar. 7, 1725	1	47
Daniell, s. [Richard & Anna], b. Mar. 7, 1725	ER	189
Hannah, d. Richard [& Ann], b. Feb. 14, 1723	1	47
Han[n]ah, d. Richard [& Anna], b. Feb. 14, 1723	ER	189
Richard, b. Mar. 19, 1690	LR1	456
Richard, b. Mar. 19, 1690/1	ER	75
Richard, m. Ann **AUXLE**, Aug. 25, 1722, by Jonathan Hoitt	1	47
Richard, m. An[n]a **AIXLE**, Aug. 25, 1722, by Jonathan Hoitt	ER	189
WANSHER, Abraham, m. Abigaile **HUESTEAD**, Dec. 7, 1721	1	47
Abraham, m. Abigaile **HEUSTED**, Dec. 7, 1721	ER	187
Moses, s. [Abraham & Abigaile], b. Oct. 25, 1722	1	47
Moses, s. [Abraham & Abigaile], b. Oct. 25, 1722	ER	187
WARING, Mary B., m. Benjamin **PAGE**, b. of Greenwich, Sept. 13, 1845, by Rev. Benjamin M. Yarrington. Int. Pub.	1	215
Rebecca, m. Timothy **FINCH**, June 16, 1763	1	115
WATERBURY, WATERBERY, Elizabeth, m. Isaac **HOW**, June 1, 1701/2	ER	133
Elizabeth, m. Isaac **HOW**, June 2, 1701/2	LR1	452
WATSON, Phebe Jane, m. James H. **FOSTER**, Dec. 17, 1840, by Chauncey Wilcox	1	206
Sarah Elizabeth, m. Joseph **CARTER**, b. of Greenwich, Feb. 7, 1843, by Chauncey Wilcox	1	211

GREENWICH VITAL RECORDS 265

	Vol.	Page
WEBB, George, m. Elizabeth BULLARD, June 19, 1832, by J. Mann	1	190
Hannah, [d. Richard], b. Jan. 3, 1774	1	125
Milla, [d. Richard], b. Feb. 14, 1763	1	125
Richard, [s. Richard], b. Dec. 28, 1776	1	125
WEED, John, m. Francis PALMER, b. of Greenwich, Jan. 26, 1834, by Rev. Platt Buffett, of Stanwich	1	192
WEEKS, Aseal, [s.], of Oyster Bay, b. Oct. 14, 1703	LR1	1
Elizabeth, d. [ ], of Oyster Bay, b. [ ]	LR1	1
Martha, d.[ ], of Oyster Bay, b. Dec.[ ], 1705	LR1	1
Martha, m. Timothie KNAP[P], Feb. 13, 1713, by Sam[ue]l Hoit, J. P.	LR1	449
Martha, m. Timothie KNAP[P], Feb. 16, 1713/14, by Sam[ue]ll Hoit, J. P.	ER	123
Martha, m. Timothy MEAD, Feb. 28, 1723/4, by Rev. Richard Sackett	1	48
Martha, m. Timothie MEAD, Feb. 28, 1723/4, by Rev. Richard Sacket	ER	191-2
Phebe, d. [ ], of Oyster Bay, b. Oct. 26, [ ]	LR1	1
Stephen, [s. of], of Oyster Bay, b. Apr 26, 1701	LR1	1
WHELPLEY, David, s. Jonathan, b. June 16, 1704	CP	106
Hannah, d. Jonathan, b. Apr. 12, 1696	CP	106
Hannah, d. Jonathan, b. Nov. 3, 1707	CP	106
Hannah, m. John BURLEY, Feb. 20, 1723	1	49
Hannah, m. John BURLEY, Feb. 20, 1723	ER	190
Isaac, s. Jonathan, b. Apr. [ ], 1706	CP	106
Jonathan, s. Jonathan, b. Aug. 6, 1698	CP	106
Mary, d. Jonathan, b. July 24, 1692	CP	106
Nathan, s. Jonathan, b. [ ] 9, 1701	CP	106
WHITE, Barton Fowler, m. Anna Augusta BELCHER, b. of Greenwich, Nov. 27, 1823, by Isaac Lewis	1	170
WHITING, -----, Mr., of R. I., had d. Mary JONES, wid. of Harding, of Newburn, Carven Co., N. C.	1	92
[WHITNEY], WHITTNE, Elizabeth, m. Samuell HURLEY, May 8, 1723, by Samuell Peck, J. P.	1	49
Elizabeth, m. Samuell HURLEY, May 8, 1723, by Samuel Peck, J. P.	ER	190
WILCOX, Delia Ann, m. Hiram P. ROWEL, b. of Fairfield Co., June 30, 1825, by Rev. S. Martindale	1	172
WILLIS, Caleb, m. Rebecca RATHBURN, Dec. 28, 1758, by Rev. Abraham Todd	1	89-90
Cynthia, d. John, m. Ebenezer MERRETT, Aug. 17, 1783	1	134
Henry William, [s. Caleb & Rebecca], b. July 9, 1759	1	89-90
WILLMUTT, Rachall, d. Francis, b. Oct. 29, 1756	1	81-2
WILSON, WILLSON, Abigail, [d. Solomon], b. Feb. 26, 1757	1	126
Abigail, [d. Solomon], b. Feb. 26, 1757	ER	224
Amos, [s. Solomon], b. May 2, 1741	1	126

	Vol.	Page

WILSON, WILLSON, (cont.)

	Vol.	Page
Amos, s. [Solomon], b. May 2, 1741	ER	224
Ann, m. Caleb HUESTIS, b. of Greenwich, May 23, [1830], by E. S. Raymond	1	184
Benjamin, [s. Solomon], b. Mar. 8, 1751	1	126
Benjamin, [s. Solomon], b. Mar. 8, 1751	ER	224
David, m. Sarah BURNS, b. of Greenwich, Mar. 25, 1840, by Rev. Platt Buffett	1	207
Deborah, [d. Solomon], b. Jan. 11, 1749	1	126
Deborah, [s. Solomon], b. Jan. 11, 1749	ER	224
Hannah, m. Thomas CILLEY*, July 29, 1731, by Joshua Knapp, J. P. *(Or "CELLY")	ER	203
Hannah, [d. Solomon], b. Nov. 17, 1746	1	126
Hannah, [d. Solomon], b. Nov. 17, 1746	ER	224
Hannah, m. Thomas CILLEY, July 29, 1751, by Joshua Knapp, J. P.	1	61
James, s. Sally GREEN, Feb. 21, 1828, by Ebenezer Raymond	1	179
John B., m. Ann Eliza CARHEART, Oct. 10, 1837, by E. S. Raymond	1	198
Lavina, m. James JAMESON, Dec. 23, 1832, by E. S. Raymond	1	188
Lydea, [d. Solomon], b. Mar. 26, 1765	1	126
Lydia, d. [Solomon], b. Mar. 26, 1765	ER	224
Margaret, m. Floyd MILLS, b. of Greenwich, [ ] 16, 1843, by D. B. Butts	1	213
Mary, of Greenwich, m. Lewis HAIGHT, of New York City, Mar. 29, 1838, by E. S. Raymond	1	200
Mary Ann, m. Samuel SLAGLE, Jan. 4, 1836, by James Jarman	1	199
Nancy, m. Isaac W. KNAPP, b. of Greenwich, Sept. 15, 1841, by Thomas Payne	1	207
Nancy G., of Greenwich, m. A[a]ron C. WAKEMAN, of South Salem, Westchester Co., N. Y., May 10, 1837, by E. S. Raymond	1	198
Naomi, [d. Solmon], b. Jan. 12, 1744	1	126
Naomi, [d. Solmon], b. Jan. 12, 1744	ER	224
Nehemiah, [s. Solomon], b. Oct. 10, 1755	1	126
Nehemiah, [s. Solomon], b. Oct. 10, 1755	ER	224
Peter, [s. Solomon], b. Mar. 27, 1760	1	126
Peter, [s. Solomon], b. Mar. 27, 1760	ER	224
Sarah G., of Greenwich, m. John H. FINLEY, of New York City, Mar. 29, 1838, by E. S. Raymond	1	200
Solomon, [s. Solomon], b. Mar. 12, 1753	1	126
Solomon, [s. Solomon], b. Mar. 12, 1753	ER	224
William Henry, m. Ann Wallace BUTTS, b. of Greenwich, Jan. 3, 1847, by Rev. B. M. Yarrington	1	216

	Vol.	Page
WINENS, Joanna, m. John REYNOLD, Feb. 16, 1740	ER	223*
WINENT, Joanna, m. John REYNOLD, Feb. 16, 1740	1	119
WINTON, WINTAN, Mary, m. John JININS, Jan. 18, 1725/6, by Joshua Knapp, J. P.	1	63
Mary, m. John GININS, Feb. 18, 1731/2, by Joshua Knapp, J. P.	ER	204
WOOD, Halsey, s. Joseph, b. Jan. 14, 1737/8	1	59
Halsey, s. Joseph, b. Jan. 14, 1737/8	ER	219
Prudence, d. Joseph, b. Mar. 10, 1722, at Huntington, Nassau Island, N. Y.; m. Nathaniel MEAD, s. David, of Greenwich, Mar. 27, 1745	1	125
Prudence, d. Joseph, of Huntington, N. Y., b. Mar. 10, 1722; m. Nathaniel MEAD, s. David, of Greenwich, Mar. 27, 1745	ER	229
Silas, m. Mary Reynolds FINCH, b. of Greenwich, Nov. 30, 1825, by Platt Buffett	1	172
Sibell*, d. Jonah, of Huntingtown, Nassau Island, m. Silvanus MEAD, June 2, 1763 *(Sybil)	1	112
William, of New York, m. Sarah DAYTON, of Stanwick, Dec. 30, 1821, by Platt Buffett	1	167
WOODEMORE, George, s. Rose, b. Sept. 11, 1796	1	159
Rose, had s. George, b. Sept. 11, 1796	1	159
WOOL, William, m. Elizabeth MONROE, (colored), b. of Greenwich, Mar. 23, 1833, by Rev. Platt Buffett, of Stanwich	1	191
WORDEN, Amea, [child of Samuel], b. Dec. 23, 1747	1	93
Amos, [s. Samuel], b. Apr. 12, 1745	1	93
Amos, s. [Samuel], b. Apr. 12, 1745	1	215
Andrew, m. Mary HOLMES, d. Isaac, Nov. 28, 1759	1	95
Arnea, [child of Samuel], b. Dec. 23, 1747	ER	215
Charity, [d. Samuel], b. June 21, 1750	1	93
Charity, [d. Samuel], b. June 21, 1750	ER	215
Elizabeth, [d. Richard], b. Mar. 18, 1752, O. S.	1	119
Elizabeth, [d. Roger], b. Mar. 18, 1752 O. S.	ER	234
Gilbert, [s. Richard], b. Mar. 23, 1750 O. S.	1	119
Gilbert, [s. Roger], b. Mar. 23, 1750 O. S.	ER	234
Isaac, [s. Samuel], b. Nov. 4, 1759	1	93
Isaac, [s. Samuel], b. Nov. 4, 1759	ER	215
Mary, [d. Samuel], b. Jan. 10, 1735	1	93
Mary, d. [Samuel], b. Jan. 10, 1735	ER	215
Mercy, [d. Samuel], b. Jan. 30, 1755	1	93
Mercy, [d. Samuel], b. Jan. 30, 1755	ER	215
Nathaniel, s. Job., b. May 26, 1766	1	118
Noah, [s. Andrew & Mary], b. Aug. 22, 1760	1	95
Phebe, [d. Samuel], b. Feb. 11, 1737	1	93
Phebe, d. [Samuel], b. Feb. 11, 1737	ER	215
Rebecca, [d. Samuel], b. July 21, 1740	1	93
Rebecca, d. [Samuel], b. July 21, 1740	ER	215

	Vol.	Page
WORDEN, (cont.)		
Roger, [s. Richard], b. Feb. 8, 1748 O. S.	1	119
Roger, [s. Roger], b. Feb. 8, 1748 O. S.	ER	234
Samuel, [s. Samuel], b. Sept. 10, 17[ ]	1	69
Samuel, s. [s. Samuel], b. Sept. 30, 1742	1	93
Samuel, s. [Samuel], b. Sept. 30, 1742	ER	215
WRIGHT, RITE, Frederick, of Mass., m. Elizabeth **AUSTIN**, of Greenwich, Dec. 16, 1832, by Rev. Platt Buffett, of Stanwich	1	189
Jeames, "bisket" baker, d. Mar. 9, 1690	LR1	448
James, "bisket" baker, d. Mar. 9, 1690/1	ER	75
YOUNG, Ann Genette, m. Stephen **MARSHALL**, b. of Greenwich, Apr. 29, 1838, by Rev. Platt Buffett	1	200
Joseph, of Stamford, m. Phebe **ADAMS**, of Greenwich, Nov. 5, 1838, by Rev. William Riddle, of Stamford	1	202
Nancy Ann, of Greenwich, m. Joseph **AYRES**, of Stamford, Feb. 10, 1839, by Rev. Platt Buffett	1	203
NO SURNAME,		
Aaron, [s. [ ] & Elizabeth], b. Jan. 22, 1755; d. Apr. 19, 1755	CP	108
Abigail, m. John **SMITH**, Mar. 28, 1745	1	100
Abigail, m. John **SMITH**, [ ], Mar. 28, 1745	ER	219
Alli, had twins, Nancy Elizabeth & Augustus Jarvis, (black), b. July 25, 1824	1	148
An[n], [twin with Elizabeth, d. [ ] & Elizabeth], b. Dec. 6, 1744	CP	108
Anna Eliza, d. Alli (black), b. Mar. 6, 1821	1	148
Elizabeth, m. Timothie **RENOLDS**, [ ], by Jeames Renolds, J. P.	CP	104
Elizabeth, m. Daniel **CHAPMAN**, Aug. 25, 1744	ER	229
Elizabeth, [d. [ ] & Elizabeth], b. May 26, 1746	CP	108
Elizabeth, [twin with An[n], d. [ ] & Elizabeth], b. Dec. 6, 1744; d. Jan. 6, 1755	CP	108
Elizabeth, w. [ ], d. Apr. 29, 1759	CP	108
Elizabeth, m. Daniel **CHAPMAN**, Aug.[ ]	1	109
Hannah, [d. [ ] & Elizabeth], b. Feb. 16, 1748; d. Sept. 10, 1758	CP	108
Huldah, b. Mary 25, 1787; m. Benoni **PECK**, s. David, Dec. 2, 1812	1	131
Lilly, m. Cull **BUSH**, Feb. 21, 1832, in Harrison, Co. of Westchester, N. Y., by E. S. Raymond	1	187
Lucy, [d. [ ] & Elizabeth], b. Aug. 17, 1750; d. Sept. 16, 1752	CP	108
Lydea, d. [ ] & Lydea, b. Dec. 8, 1754	1	70
Silas, [s. [ ] & Elizabeth], b. Sept. 1, 1752	CP	108
Silva, d. Jenney (black), b. Sept. 2, 1797	1	148
Susannah, m. James **MEAD**, [ ] 25, 1719/20, by		

	Vol.	Page
NO SURNAME, (cont.)		
Rev. Richard Sackett	CP	106
William Harris, s. Alli (black), b. Apr. 9, 1819	1	148

www.ingramcontent.com/pod-product-compliance
Lightning Source LLC
Chambersburg PA
CBHW050842230426
43667CB00012B/2113